WORD
BIBLICAL
COMMENTARY

General Editors
David A. Hubbard
Glenn W. Barker †

Old Testament Editor
John D. W. Watts

New Testament Editor
Ralph P. Martin

WORD
BIBLICAL
COMMENTARY

VOLUME 11

2 Samuel

A.A. ANDERSON

WORD BOOKS, PUBLISHER • DALLAS, TEXAS

Word Biblical Commentary
2 Samuel
Copyright © 1989 by Word, Incorporated

Library of Congress Cataloging-in-Publication Data
Main entry under title:

Word biblical commentary.

Includes bibliographies.
1. Bible—Commentaries   Collected Works.
BS491.2.W67   220.7'7   81–71768
ISBN 0–8499–0210–X (vol. 11) AACR2

Printed in the United States of America

The author's own translation of the text appears in italic type under the heading "Translation."

9801239 AGF 987654321

Norman Walker Porteous

Teacher, colleague, and friend

Contents

Editorial Preface

The launching of the *Word Biblical Commentary* brings to fulfillment an enterprise of several years' planning. The publishers and the members of the editorial board met in 1977 to explore the possibility of a new commentary on the books of the Bible that would incorporate several distinctive features. Prospective readers of these volumes are entitled to know what such features were intended to be; whether the aims of the commentary have been fully achieved time alone will tell.

First, we have tried to cast a wide net to include as contributors a number of scholars from around the world who not only share our aims, but are in the main engaged in the ministry of teaching in university, college, and seminary. They represent a rich diversity of denominational allegiance. The broad stance of our contributors can rightly be called evangelical, and this term is to be understood in its positive, historic sense of a commitment to Scripture as divine revelation, and to the truth and power of the Christian gospel.

Then, the commentaries in our series are all commissioned and written for the purpose of inclusion in the *Word Biblical Commentary*. Unlike several of our distinguished counterparts in the field of commentary writing, there are no translated works, originally written in a non-English language. Also, our commentators were asked to prepare their own rendering of the original biblical text and to use those languages as the basis of their own comments and exegesis. What may be claimed as distinctive with this series is that it is based on the biblical languages, yet it seeks to make the technical and scholarly approach to a theological understanding of Scripture understandable by— and useful to—the fledgling student, the working minister, and colleagues in the guild of professional scholars and teachers as well.

Finally, a word must be said about the format of the series. The layout, in clearly defined sections, has been consciously devised to assist readers at different levels. Those wishing to learn about the textual witnesses on which the translation is offered are invited to consult the section headed *Notes*. If the readers' concern is with the state of modern scholarship on any given portion of Scripture, they should turn to the sections on *Bibliography* and *Form and Structure*. For a clear exposition of the passage's meaning and its relevance to the ongoing biblical revelation, the *Comment* and concluding *Explanation* are designed expressly to meet that need. There is therefore something for everyone who may pick up and use these volumes.

If these aims come anywhere near realization, the intention of the editors will have been met, and the labor of our team of contributors rewarded.

General Editors: *David A. Hubbard*
Glenn W. Barker †
Old Testament: *John D. W. Watts*
New Testament: *Ralph P. Martin*

Author's Preface

It has been a great honor and privilege to contribute to the Word Biblical Commentary series, and consequently I owe a great debt of gratitude to the editors of the series, in more ways than one.

It is only right that I should also acknowledge my indebtedness to the countless generations of scholars and students of the Bible who have wrestled with the problems of the Books of Samuel, and with the Old Testament as a whole. Thus they have enabled me to reap of the fruit of their labors. It would be impossible to list their numerous, valuable contributions but a special mention must be made of Professor P. Kyle McCarter's outstanding and masterly work on Second Samuel in particular. Even where I have differed from him, I have greatly benefited by his clear and scholarly arguments and comments.

My gratitude is also due to Professor John D. W. Watts for his great considerateness and for his encouragement which were very much appreciated, especially during the periods of my ill health. Likewise, I am indebted to my colleagues at Manchester University but, in particular, I wish to thank Dr. Adrian H. W. Curtis who often made helpful comments in our discussions on Samuel and the Old Testament in general, and whose practical help and friendship have been invaluable.

Last but not least, I must express special thanks to my wife Lilian whose quiet and unstinted support throughout the years has been greatly appreciated.

May, 1988   A. A. ANDERSON
University of Manchester

Abbreviations

BWANT	Beiträge zur Wissenschaft vom Alten und Neuen Testament
BZ	*Biblische Zeitschrift*
BZAW	Beihefte zur *ZAW*
CBQ	*Catholic Biblical Quarterly*
CBQMS	*CBQ* Monograph Series
CHALOT	W. L. Holladay, *Concise Hebrew and Aramaic Lexicon of the Old Testament* (Leiden: E. J. Brill, 1971)
CHM	*Cahiers d'histoire mondiale*, Paris
CJT	*Canadian Journal of Theology*
ConB	Coniectanea biblica
CTA	A. Herdner, *Corpus des tablettes en cunéiformes alphabétiques*
DOTT	*Documents from Old Testament Times*, ed. D. W. Thomas (London: T. Nelson, 1958)
EAEHL	*The Encyclopedia of Archaeological Excavations in the Holy Land*, ed. M. Avi-Yonah, 4 vols. (London: Oxford UP, 1975)
EnBib	*Encyclopaedia Biblica*, ed. T. K. Cheyne and J. Sutherland Black (London: Adam and Charles Black, 1912)
EncJud	*Encyclopedia judaica*
EstBib	*Estudios Bíblicos*
ETL	*Ephemerides theologicae lovanienses*
EvT	*Evangelische Theologie*
FRLANT	Forschungen zur Religion und Literatur des Alten und Neuen Testaments
GKC	*Gesenius' Hebrew Grammar*, ed. E. Kautzsch; tr. A. E. Cowley; 2d ed. (Oxford: Clarendon, 1910)
GTT	J. Simons, *The Geographical and Topographical Texts of the Old Testament* (Leiden: E. J. Brill, 1959)
HALAT	W. Baumgartner, *Hebräisches und aramäisches Lexikon zum Alten Testament*, rev. 3d ed. of KB (Leiden: E. J. Brill, 1967)
HAT	Handbuch zum Alten Testament
HKAT	Handkommentar zum Alten Testament
HSM	Harvard Semitic Monographs
HTR	*Harvard Theological Review*
HUCA	*Hebrew Union College Annual*
IB	*Interpreter's Bible*
IBD	*The Illustrated Bible Dictionary*, ed. J. D. Douglas et al., 3 vols. (Leicester: Inter-Varsity Press, 1980)
ICC	International Critical Commentary
IDB	*Interpreter's Dictionary of the Bible*, ed. G. A. Buttrick, 4 vols. (Nashville: Abingdon, 1962)
IDBSup	Supplementary volume to *IDB*, ed. K. Crim (Nashville:Abingdon, 1976)
IEJ	*Israel Exploration Journal*

IJH	*Israelite and Judean History*, ed. J. H. Hayes and J. M. Miller (London: SCM, 1977)
Int	*Interpretation*
IOS	*Israel Oriental Studies*
JAOS	*Journal of American Oriental Society*
JBL	*Journal of Biblical Literature*
JBLMS	*JBL* Monograph Series
JBR	*Journal of Bible and Religion*
JCS	*Journal of Cuneiform Studies*
JNES	*Journal of Near Eastern Studies*
JNSL	*Journal of Northwest Semitic Languages*
JPOS	*Journal of the Palestine Oriental Society*
JSOT	*Journal for the Study of the Old Testament*
JSOTSup	*JSOT* Supplement
JSS	*Journal of Semitic Studies*
JTS	*Journal of Theological Studies*
KAT	Kommentar zum Alten Testament
KB	L. Koehler and W. Baumgartner, *Lexicon in veteris testamenti libros* (Leiden: E. J. Brill, 1951-53)
KHC	Kurzer Hand-Commentar zum Alten Testament
KS	O. Eissfeldt, *Kleine Schriften,* 6 vols. (Tübingen: J. C. B. Mohr, 1962-79)
KSGVI	A. Alt, *Kleine Schriften zur Geschichte des Volkes Israel,* 2 vols. (Munich: C. H. Beck'sche, 1953)
NCB	New Century Bible Commentary
NedTTs	*Nederlands theologisch tijdschrift*
NICOT	New International Commentary on the Old Testament
OBO	Orbis biblicus et orientalis
OBT	*Overtures to Biblical Theology*
OLP	Orientalia lovaniensia periodica
OLZ	*Orientalische Literaturzeitung*
Or	*Orientalia*
OrAnt	*Oriens antiquus*
OTL	Old Testament Library
OTS	*Oudtestamentische Studiën*
PCB	*Peake's Commentary on the Bible,* ed. M. Black and H. H. Rowley (Edinburgh: T. Nelson and Sons, 1962)
PEQ	*Palestinian Exploration Quarterly*
PJ	*Palästina-Jahrbuch*
POTT	*People of Old Testament Times,* ed. D. J. Wiseman (London: Oxford UP, 1973)
RB	*Revue Biblique*
RivB	*Rivista biblica*
SANT	Studien zum Alten und Neuen Testament
SBLMS	Society for Biblical Literature Monograph Series
SBS	Stuttgarter Bibelstudien
SBT	Studies in Biblical Theology
ScrHier	Scripta Hierosolymitana

SEÅ	*Svensk exegetisk årsbok*
Sem	*Semitica*
SJT	*Scottish Journal of Theology*
SOTSMS	Society for Old Testament Study Monograph Series
ST	*Studia theologica*
STDJ	Studies on the Texts of the Desert of Judah
TBC	Torch Bible Commentaries
TDNT	*Theological Dictionary of the New Testament,* ed. G. Kittel and G. Friedrich; tr. G. W. Bromiley; 10 vols. (Grand Rapids: Eerdmans, 1964-74)
TGUOS	*Transactions of Glasgow University Oriental Society*
THAT	*Theologische Handwörterbuch zum Alten Testament,* ed. E. Jenni and C. Westermann, 2 vols. (Munich/Zürich, 1971)
ThB	Theologische Bücherei
TLZ	*Theologische Literaturzeitung*
TOTC	Tyndale Old Testament Commentaries
TQ	*Theologische Quartalschrift*
TRu	*Theologische Rundschau*
TS	*Theological Studies*
TWAT	*Theologisches Wörterbuch zum Alten Testament,* ed. G. J. Botterweck and H. Ringgren, 5 vols. (incomplete) (Stuttgart: Kohlhammer, 1973-)
TynB	*Tyndale Bulletin*
TZ	*Theologische Zeitschrift*
UF	*Ugaritische Forschungen*
UT	C. H. Gordon, *Ugaritic Textbook* (Rome: Pontificium Institutum Biblicum, 1965)
VD	*Verbum domini*
VT	*Vetus Testamentum*
VTSup	*VT* Supplements
WMANT	Wissenschaftliche Monographien zum Alten und Neuen Testament
WO	*Die Welt des Orients*
ZAW	*Zeitschrift für die alttestamentliche Wissenschaft*
ZBK	Züricher Bibelkommentare
ZDMG	*Zeitschrift der deutschen morgenländischen Gesellschaft*
ZDPV	*Zeitschrift der deutschen Palästina-Vereins*
ZTK	*Zeitschrift für Theologie und Kirche*

BIBLICAL AND APOCRYPHAL BOOKS

Gen	Genesis	Judg	Judges
Exod	Exodus	Ruth	Ruth
Lev	Leviticus	1-2 Sam	1-2 Samuel
Num	Numbers	1-2 Kgs	1-2 Kings
Deut	Deuteronomy	1-2 Chr	1-2 Chronicles
Josh	Joshua	Ezra	Ezra

Neh	Nehemiah
Esth	Esther
Job	Job
Ps(s)	Psalm(s)
Prov	Proverbs
Eccl	Ecclesiastes
Can	Canticles
Isa	Isaiah
Jer	Jeremiah
Lam	Lamentations
Ezek	Ezekiel
Dan	Daniel
Hos	Hosea
Joel	Joel
Amos	Amos
Obad	Obadiah
Jonah	Jonah
Mic	Micah
Nah	Nahum
Hab	Habakkuk
Zeph	Zephaniah
Hag	Haggai
Zech	Zechariah
Mal	Malachi

Sir	Ecclesiasticus or The Wisdom of Jesus son of Sirach
1-2 Macc	1-2 Maccabees
Matt	Matthew
Mark	Mark
Luke	Luke
John	John
Acts	Acts
Rom	Romans
1-2 Cor	1-2 Corinthians
Gal	Galatians
Eph	Ephesians
Phil	Philippians
Col	Colossians
1-2 Thess	1-2 Thessalonians
1-2 Tim	1-2 Timothy
Titus	Titus
Phlm	Philemon
Heb	Hebrews
James	James
1-2 Pet	1-2 Peter
1-2-3 John	1-2-3 John
Jude	Jude
Rev	Revelation

MODERN TRANSLATIONS

AV	Authorized Version
JB	Jerusalem Bible
KJV	King James Version
NAB	New American Bible
NEB	New English Bible
NIV	New International Version

RAV	Revised Authorized Version
RSV	Revised Standard Version
RV	Revised Version
TEV	Today's English Version

HEBREW GRAMMAR

abs	absolute
acc	accusative
coh	cohortative
conj	conjunction
consec	consecutive
constr	construct
dittogr	dittography
fem, f	feminine
fut	future

gen	genitive
hap. leg.	*hapax legomenon*
haplogr	haplography
hiph	hiphil
hithp	hithpael
hoph	hophal
impf	imperfect
impv	imperative
inf	infinitive

juss	jussive	prep	preposition
masc, m	masculine	pron	pronoun
niph	niphal	pronom	pronominal
pass	passive	ptcp	participle
perf	perfect	sg	singular
pers	person	subj	subject
pl	plural	suff	suffix

TEXTUAL NOTES

Aq	Aquila	G^O	LXX MSS, Hexaplaric witnesses
Aram	Aramaic		
Heb.	Hebrew	LXX	Septuagint
K	Kethibh	MT	Masoretic Text
G	Septuagint, LXX	OG	Old Greek
G^A	LXX MS, Alexandrian Codex	OL	Old Latin
		Q	Qere, to be read
G^B	LXX MS, Vatican Codex	$4QSam^{a,c}$	Samuel MSS from Qumran Cave IV
G^L	LXX MSS, Lucianic recension	Syr	Syriac
		Tg	Targum
G^M	LXX MS, Codex Coislianus	Vg	Vulgate
		Theod	Theodotion
G^N	LXX MS, Codex Basiliano-Vaticanus	Symm	Symmachus

MISCELLANEOUS

chap(s).	chapter(s)	MS(S)	manuscript(s)
col(s).	column(s)	n.	note
diss.	dissertation	NT	New Testament
ed(s).	edition; edited by; editor(s)	OT	Old Testament
		p.	page
ET	English Translation	pl.	plate
FS	Festschrift	SN	Succession Narrative
HDR	History of David's Rise	tr.	translated; translator
lit.	literally	UP	University Press
Lief.	Lieferung(en), part(s)	v(v)	verse(s)
mg	margin	vol(s).	volume(s)

Main Bibliography

COMMENTARIES

(referred to in the text by authors' names alone)

Ackroyd, P. R. *The Second Book of Samuel.* The Cambridge Bible Commentary. Cambridge: Cambridge UP, 1977. **Brockington, L. H.** "I and II Samuel." *PCB.* Rev. ed. Ed. M. Black and H. H. Rowley. London and Edinburgh; Nelson, 1962. 318–37. **Budde, K.** *Die Bücher Samuel erklärt.* KHC 8. Tübingen and Leipzig: J. C. B. Mohr, 1902. **Caird, G. B.** "The First and Second Books of Samuel." *IB* 2. New York and Nashville: Abingdon, 1953. 853–1176. **Caspari, D. W.** *Die Samuelbücher.* KAT 7. Leipzig: Deichter, 1926. **Dhorme, P. E.** *Les Livres de Samuel.* Études bibliques. Paris: Gabalda, 1910. **Driver, S. R.** *Notes on the Hebrew Text and the Topography of the Books of Samuel.* 2d ed. Oxford: Clarendon, 1913. **Ehrlich, A. B.** *Randglossen zur hebräischen Bibel* 3. Leipzig: Hinrichs, 1910. **Goldman, S.** *Samuel.* Soncino Books of the Bible. London and Bournemouth: Soncino Press, 1951. **Gordon, R. P.** *I and II Samuel: A Commentary.* Exeter: Paternoster Press, 1986. **Goslinga, C. J.** *Het Tweede Boek Samuël.* Commentaar op het Oude Testament. Kampen: J. H. Kok, 1962. **Gressmann, H.** *Die älteste Geschichtsschreibung und Prophetie Israels (von Samuel bis Amos und Hosea).* Die Schriften des Alten Testaments 2/1. Göttingen: Vandenhoeck & Ruprecht, 1921. **Gutbrod, K.** *Das Buch vom Reich: Das zweite Buch Samuel.* Die Botschaft des Alten Testaments. Stuttgart: Calwer Verlag, 1973. **Hertzberg, H. W.** *I & II Samuel: A Commentary.* OTL. Tr. J. S. Bowden. London: SCM, 1964. **Keil, C. F.** *Die Bücher Samuels: Biblischer Commentar über das Alte Testament* 3/2. 2d ed. Leipzig: Dörffling und Franke, 1975. **Kirkpatrick, A. F.** *The Second Book of Samuel.* Cambridge Bible for Schools and Colleges. Cambridge: Cambridge UP 1890. **Klostermann, A.** *Die Bücher Samuelis und der Könige: Kurzgefasster Kommentar zu den Heiligen Schriften des Alten und Neuen Testaments.* Nördlingen: Beck, 1887. **Mauchline, J.** *1 and 2 Samuel.* NCB. London: Oliphants, 1971. **McCarter, P. K.** *II Samuel: A New Translation with Introduction, Notes and Commentary.* AB 9. Garden City, N. Y.: Doubleday, 1984. **McKane, W.** *I and II Samuel: The Way to the Throne.* TBC. London: SCM, 1963. **Nowack, W.** *Richter, Ruth und Bücher Samuelis übersetzt und erklärt.* HAT 1/4. Göttingen: Vandenhoeck & Ruprecht, 1902. **Payne, D. F.** *Samuel.* Daily Study Bible. Edinburgh: Saint Andrew Press; Philadelphia: Westminster Press, 1982. **Rehm, M.** *Die Bücher Samuel.* 2d ed. Echter-Bibel 7/1. Würzburg: Echter-Verlag, 1956. **Schultz, A.** *Das zweite Buch Samuel: Exegetisches Handbuch zum Alten Testament 8/2.* Münster: Aschendorff, 1920. **Smith, H. P.** *A Critical and Exegetical Commentary on the Books of Samuel.* ICC. Edinburgh: Clark, 1899. **Snaith, N. H.** *Notes on the Hebrew Text of 2 Samuel XVI–XIX.* Study Notes on Bible Books. London: The Epworth Press, 1945. **Stoebe, H. J.** *Das erste Buch Samuelis.* KAT 8/1. Gütersloh: Gerd Mohn, 1973. **Stolz, F.** *Das erste und zweite Buch Samuel.* ZBK AT 9. Zürich: Theologischer Verlag, 1981. **Thenius, O.** *Die Bücher Samuels.* Kurzgefasstes exegetisches Handbuch zum Alten Testament 4. 2d ed. Leipzig: S. Hirzel, 1864. **Vaux, R., de** *Les Livres de Samuel.* 2d ed. La Sainte Bible. Paris: Les Éditions du Cerf, 1961. **Wellhausen, J.** *Der Text der Bücher Samuelis untersucht.* Göttingen: Vandenhoeck & Ruprecht, 1871.

GENERAL STUDIES

(referred to in the text by short titles)

Abel, F.-M. *La Géographie de la Palestine.* 2 vols. 2d ed. Paris: J. Gabalda, 1933–38.
Aharoni, Y. *The Land of the Bible: A Historical Geography.* 2d ed. Tr. A. F. Rainey.
London: Burns and Oats, 1979. **Alt, A.** *Essays on Old Testament History and Religion.*
Tr. R. A. Wilson. Oxford: Blackwell, 1966. **Beer, G.** and **Meyer, D. R.** *Hebräische
Grammatik.* 2 vols. Berlin: W. de Gruyter, 1952–55. **Blau, J.** *A Grammar of Biblical
Hebrew.* Porta Linguarum Orientalium 12. Wiesbaden: Otto Harrassowitz, 1976.
Blenkinsopp, J. "Theme and Motif in the Succession History (2 Sam. xi 2ff) and the
Yahwist Corpus." VTSup 15 (1966) 44–57. ———. *Gibeon and Israel: The Role of Gibeon
and the Gibeonites in the Political and Religious History of Early Israel.* SOTSMS 2. Cam-
bridge: Cambridge UP, 1972. **Bright, J.** *A History of Israel.* 3d ed. London: SCM,
1981. **Brockelmann, C.** *Hebräische Syntax.* Neukirchen: Verlag der Buchhandlung der
Erziehungsvereins, 1956. **Brockington, L. H.** *The Hebrew Text of the Old Testament.*
Oxford: Oxford UP; Cambridge: Cambridge UP, 1973. **Buccellati, G.** *Cities and Nations
of Ancient Syria. An Essay on Political Institutions with Special Reference to the Israelite
Kingdoms.* Rome: University of Rome, 1967. **Carlson, R. A.** *David the Chosen King. A
Traditio-Historical Approach to the Second Book of Samuel.* Uppsala: Almquist and Wiksells,
1964. **Christ, H.** *Blutvergiessen im Alten Testament. Der gewaltsame Tod des Menschen
untersucht am hebräischen Wort dām.* Basel: Friedrich Reinhardt Kommissionsverlag,
1977. **Conroy, C.** *Absalom Absalom! Narrative and Language in 2 Sam 13–20.* AnBib
81. Rome: Biblical Institute Press. 1978. **Cross, F, M.** *Canaanite Myth and Hebrew
Epic. Essays in the History of the Religion of Israel.* Cambridge, Mass.: Harvard UP, 1973.
Dahood, M. *Psalms I–III.* AB 16–17a. Garden City, N.Y.: Doubleday, 1966–1970.
Dalman, G. *Arbeit und Sitte in Palestina.* 7 vols. Gütersloh: C. Bertelsmann, 1928–42.
Driver, S. R. *A Treatise on the Use of the Tenses in Hebrew and Some Other Syntactical Ques-
tions.* Oxford: Clarendon Press, 1892. ———. *An Introduction to the Literature of the Old Testa-
ment.* 8th ed. Edinburgh: T. & T. Clark, 1909. **Eissfeldt, O.** *Die Komposition der Samuelis-
bücher.* Leipzig: J. C. Hinrichs, 1931. ———. *The Old Testament: An Introduction.* Tr.
P. R. Ackroyd. Oxford: Blackwell, 1965. **Ewald, H.** *The History of Israel.* Vol. 3. Tr.
J. E. Carpenter. London: Longmans, Green & Co, 1878. **Flanagan, J. W.** *A Study of
the Biblical Traditions Pertaining to the Foundation of the Monarchy in Israel.* University
of Notre Dame: Ph.D. Diss., 1971. **Fohrer, G.** *Introduction to the Old Testament.* Tr. D.
Green. London: SPCK, 1970. **Fokkelman, J. P.** *Narrative Art and Poetry in the Books of
Samuel.* Vol. 1: *King David (II Sam. 9–20 & I Kings 1–2).* Assen: Van Gorcum, 1981.
Gibson, J. C. L. *Canaanite Myths and Legends.* 2d ed. Edinburgh: T. & T. Clark,1978.
Giesen, G. *Die Wurzel* שבע *"schwören." Eine semasiologische Studie zum Eid im Alten
Testament.* BBB 56. Königstein/Ts.-Bonn: Peter Hanstein Verlag, 1981. **Gottwald,
N. K.** *The Tribes of Yahweh: A Sociology of the Religion of Liberated Israel, 1250–1050
B.C.E.* London: SCM, 1979. **Grønbaek, J. H.** *Die Geschichte vom Aufstieg Davids (1
Sam. 15 – 2 Sam. 5): Tradition und Komposition.* Copenhagen: Prostant Apud Munks-
gaard, 1971. **Gunn, D. M.** *The Story of King David: Genre and Interpretation.* JSOTSup
6. Sheffield: University of Sheffield, 1978. **Halpern, B.** *The Constitution of the Monarchy
in Israel.* HMS 25. Chico, CA: Scholars Press, 1981. **Herrmann, S.** *A History of Israel
in Old Testament Times.* Tr. J. Bowden. 2d ed. London: SCM, 1981. **Holladay, W. L.**
A Concise Hebrew and Aramaic Lexicon of the Old Testament. Leiden: E. J. Brill, 1971.
Ishida, T. *The Royal Dynasties in Ancient Israel: A Study on the Formation and Development
of Royal-Dynastic Ideology.* BZAW 142. Berlin: W. de Gruyter, 1977. **Jastrow, M.** *A
Dictionary of the Targumim, the Talmud Babli and Yerushalmi, and the Midrashic Literature.*
2 vols. New York: Pardes Publishing House, 1950. **Joüon, P.** *Grammaire de l'Hébreu
biblique.* 2d ed. Rome: Pontifical Biblical Institute, 1947. **Jung, K. N.** *Court Etiquette*

in the Old Testament. Drew University: Ph.D. Dissertation, 1979. **Kegler, J.** *Politisches Geschehen und theologisches Verstehen.* Calwer Theologische Monographien 8. Stuttgart: Calwer Verlag, 1977. **Kittel, R.** *Geschichte des Volkes Israel.* Vol. 2. Gotha: Friedrich Andreas Perthes, 1922. **Lambdin, T. O.** *Introduction to Biblical Hebrew.* London: Darton, Longman & Todd, 1976. **Mayes, A. D. H.** *Israel in the Period of the Judges.* SBT. 2d ser. 29. London: SCM, 1974. **Mettinger, T. N. D.** *King and Messiah: The Civil and Sacral Legitimation of the Israelite Kings.* ConB. OT ser. 8. Lund: CWK Gleerup, 1976. **Meyer, D. R.** *Hebräische Grammatik.* Vol. 3: *Satzlehre.* Berlin, New York: W. de Gruyter, 1972. **Miller, J. M.** and **Hayes, J. H.,** eds. *A History of Ancient Israel and Judah.* OTL. London: SCM, 1977. **Noth, M.** *The History of Israel.* 2d ed. Tr. P. R. Ackroyd. London: Adam and Charles Black, 1960. ———. *Die israelitischen Personennamen im Rahmen der gemeinsemitischen Namengebung.* Stuttgart: W. Kohlhammer, 1928. ———. *The Laws in the Pentateuch and Other Essays.* Tr. D. R. Ap-Thomas. Edinburgh and London: Oliver & Boyd, 1966. ———. *The Deuteronomistic History.* Tr. J. Doull et al. JSOTSup 15. Sheffield: University of Sheffield, 1981. **Ohler, A.** *Israel, Volk und Land.* Stuttgart: Verlag Katholisches Bibelwerk, 1979. **Payne, D. F.** *Kingdoms of the Lord: A History of the Hebrew Kingdoms from Saul to the Fall of Jerusalem.* Exeter: Paternoster Press, 1981. **Phillips, A.** *Ancient Israel's Criminal Law.* Oxford: Blackwell, 1970. **Pisano, S.** *Additions or Omissions in the Books of Samuel.* OBO 57. Göttingen: Vandenhoeck & Ruprecht, 1984. **Plöger, J. G.** *Literar-kritische, formgeschichtliche und stilkritische Untersuchungen zum Deuteronomium.* Bonn: Peter Hanstein Verlag, 1967. **Rad, G. von,** *Old Testament Theology.* 2 vols. Tr. D. M. G. Stalker. Edinburgh, London: Oliver & Boyd, 1962–65. ———. *The Problem of the Hexateuch and Other Essays.* Tr. E. W. Trueman Dicken. Edinburgh, London: Oliver & Boyd, 1965. **Rost, L.** *The Succession to the Throne of David.* Tr. M. D. Rutter and D. M. Gunn. Sheffield: Almond Press, 1982. **Rudolph, W.** *Chronikbücher.* HAT 21. Tübingen: J. C. B. Mohr, 1955. **Rupprecht, K.** *Der Tempel von Jerusalem: Gründung Salomos oder jebusitisches Erbe?* BZAW 144. Berlin and New York: W. de Gruyter, 1977. **Salmon, J.** *Judicial Authority in Early Israel: An Historical Investigation of Old Testament Institutions.* Princeton Theological Seminary: Th.D. Diss., 1968. **Schäfer-Lichtenberger, C.** *Stadt und Eidgenossenschaft im Alten Testament.* BZAW 156. Berlin and New York: W. de Gruyter, 1983. **Schreiner, J.** *Sion-Jerusalem: Jahwes Königssitz. Theologie der Heiligen Stadt im Alten Testament.* SANT 7. Munich: Kösel-Verlag, 1963. **Schulte, H.** *Die Entstehung der Geschichtsschreibung im Alten Israel.* BZAW 128. Berlin and New York: W. de Gruyter, 1972. **Schunck, K.-D.** *Benjamin: Untersuchungen zur Entstehung und Geschichte eines israelitischen Stammes.* BZAW 86. Berlin: Töpelmann, 1963. **Seters, J. van.** *In Search of History: Historiography in the Ancient World and the Origins of Biblical History.* New Haven and London: Yale UP, 1983. **Simons, J.** *Jerusalem in the Old Testament: Researches and Theories.* Leiden: E. J. Brill, 1952. ———. *The Geographical and Topographical Texts of the Old Testament.* Leiden: E. J. Brill, 1959. **Soggin, J. A.** *Das Königtum in Israel: Ursprünge, Spannungen, Entwicklung.* BZAW 104. Berlin: Töpelmann, 1967. **Ulrich, E. C., Jr.** *The Qumran Text of Samuel and Josephus.* HSM 19. Missoula, MT: Scholars Press, 1978. **Vaux, R. de.** *Ancient Israel: Its Life and Institutions.* Tr. J. McHugh. London: Darton, Longman & Todd, 1961. ———. *The Early History of Israel: From the Entry into Canaan to the Period of the Judges.* 2 vols. Tr. D. Smith. London: Darton, Longman & Todd, 1978. **Veijola, T.** *Die Ewige Dynastie: David und die Entstehung seiner Dynastie nach der deuteronomistischen Darstellung.* Annales Academiae Scientiarum Fennicae B193. Helsinki: Suomalainen Tiedeakatemia, 1975. ———. *Verheissung in der Krise: Studien zur Literatur und Theologie der Exilszeit anhand des 89. Psalms.* Annales Academiae Scientiarum Fennicae B220. Helsinki: Academia Scientiarum Fennica, 1982. **Watson, W. G. E.** *Classical Hebrew Poetry: A Guide to Its Techniques.* JSOTSup 26. Sheffield: University of Sheffield, 1984. **Weinfeld, M.** *Deuteronomy and the Deuteronomic School.* Oxford: Clarendon Press, 1972. **Whitelam, K. W.** *The Just King: Monarchical Judicial Authority in Ancient Israel.* JSOTSup 12. Sheffield:

University of Sheffield, 1979. **Whybray, R. N.** *The Succession Narrative: A Study of II Sam. 9–20 and I Kings 1 and 2.* SBT 2d ser. 9. London: SCM, 1968. **Williams, R. J.** *Hebrew Syntax: An Outline.* 1st ed. 1967. 2d ed. 1976. Toronto, Buffalo and London: University of Toronto Press, 1976. **Williamson, H. G. M.** *1 and 2 Chronicles.* NCB. Grand Rapids: Wm. B. Eerdmans; London: Marshall, Morgan & Scott, 1982. **Würthwein, E.** *Die Erzählung von der Thronfolge Davids—theologische oder politische Geschichtsschreibung?* Theologische Studien 115. Zürich: Theologischer Verlag, 1974. **Yadin, Y.** *The Art of Warfare in Biblical Lands in the Light of Archaeological Discovery.* Tr. M. Pearlman. London: Weidenfeld and Nicolson, 1963.

ADDITIONAL BIBLIOGRAPHY

Andersen, F. I. *The Sentence in Biblical Hebrew.* Janua Linguarum. Series Practica 231. The Hague: Monton, 1974. **Davidson, A. B.** *Hebrew Syntax.* Edinburgh: T. & T. Clark, 1942. **Day, P. L.** "Abishai the *śāṭān* in 2 Samuel 19:17–24." *CBQ* 49 (1987) 543–47. **Fontaine, C.** "The Bearing of Wisdom on the Shape of 2 Samuel 11–12 and 1 Kings 3," *JSOT* 34 (1986) 61–77. **Freedman, D. N.** "Early Israelite History in the Light of Early Israelite Poetry." In *Unity and Diversity: Essays in the History, Literature and Religion of the Ancient Near East,* ed. H. Goedicke and J. J. M. Roberts. Baltimore: Johns Hopkins, 1975. 3–35. **Hayes, J. H.,** and **Miller, J. M.** *Israelite and Judaean History.* OTL. London: SCM Press, 1977. **Ishida, T.** "Royal Succession in the Kingdoms of Israel and Judah with Special Reference to the People under Arms as a Determining Factor in the Struggle for the Throne." VTSup 40 (1988) 96–106. **Kennedy, A. R. S.** *Samuel.* The Century Bible. London: Caxton, 1905. **Mace, D. R.** *Hebrew Marriage: A Sociological Study.* London: Epworth Press, 1953. **Murphy-O'Connor, J.** *The Holy Land: An Archaeological Guide from the Earliest Times to 1700.* Oxford/New York/Toronto/Melbourne: Oxford UP, 1980.

Introduction

THE TEXT OF 2 SAMUEL

Bibliography

Barthélemy, D. "Redécouverte d'un chaînon manquant de l'histoire de la Septante." *Qumran and the History of the Biblical Text.* Ed. F. M. Cross and S. Talmon. Cambridge, MA; London, England: Harvard UP, 1975. 127–39 (= *RB* 60 [1953] 18–29). ———. "La Qualité du Texte Massorétique de Samuel." *The Hebrew and Greek Texts of Samuel.* 1980 Proceedings IOSCS, Vienna. Jerusalem: Academon, 1980. 1–44. **Cross, F. M.** "The History of the Biblical Text in the Light of Discoveries in the Judaean Desert." *Qumran and the History of the Biblical Text.* Ed. F. M. Cross and S. Talmon. Cambridge, MA; London, England: Harvard UP, 1975. 177–95 (= HTR 57 [1964] 281–99). **Driver, S. R.** *Notes on the Hebrew Text and Topography of the Books of Samuel.* 2d ed. Oxford: Clarendon Press, 1913. **Gooding, D. W.** "An Appeal for a Stricter Terminology in the Textual Criticism of the Old Testament." *JSS* 21 (1976) 15–25. **McCarter, P. K., Jr.** *1 Samuel.* AB 8. Garden City, New York: Doubleday, 1980. **Pisano, S.** *Additions or Omissions in the Books of Samuel.* OBO 57. Freiburg, Schweiz: Universitätsverlag. Göttingen: Vandenhoeck & Ruprecht, 1984. **Roberts, B. J.** *The Old Testament Text and Versions.* Cardiff: University of Wales Press, 1951. **Shenkel, J. D.** "A Comparative Study of the Synoptic Parallels in I Paraleipomena and I–II Reigns." *HTR* 62 (1969) 63–85. **Talmon, S.** "The Old Testament Text." *Qumran and the History of the Biblical Text.* Ed. F. M. Cross and S. Talmon. Cambridge, MA; London, England: Harvard UP, 1975. 1–41 (= *The Cambridge History of the Bible.* Ed. P. R. Ackroyd and C. F. Evans. Cambridge: Cambridge UP, 1970. 159–99). **Thackeray, H. St. J.** "The Greek Translators of the Four Books of Kings." *JTS* 8 (1907) 262–78. ———. *The Septuagint and Jewish Worship, a Study in Origins.* Schweich Lectures 1920. London: Milford for the British Academy, 1921. **Tov, E.** "Lucian and Proto-Lucian." *RB* 79 (1972) 101–13. ———. "The Textual Affiliations of 4QSam[a]." *JSOT* 14 (1979) 37–53. ———. *The Text-Critical Use of the Septuagint in Biblical Research.* Jerusalem: Simor Ltd., 1981. **Ulrich, E. C.** *The Qumran Text of Samuel and Josephus.* HSM 19. Missoula, MT: Scholars Press, 1978. ———. "4QSam[c]: A Fragmentary Manuscript of 2 Samuel 14–15 from the Scribe of the Serek Hay-yahad (1QS)." *BASOR* 235 (1979) 1–25. **Würthwein, E.** *The Text of the Old Testament.* Tr. E. F. Rhodes. 4th ed. London: SCM Press, 1980.

The Hebrew text (MT) of 2 Sam has not been well preserved; it is often defective in certain respects and must have suffered in the process of textual transmission, mainly due to scribal errors, such as haplographic omissions in particular (cf. *Comment* on 13:21; n. 14:30.c-c.). Consequently, the value of the versions, especially that of LXX, was recognized long ago. Otto Thenius was one of the first commentators who extensively used the LXX for the improvement of the Hebrew text of Samuel (see his commentary, published in 1842). However, it was Julius Wellhausen (*Der Text der Bücher Samuelis untersucht,* 1871) who developed and refined the earlier methods. Wellhausen and his followers assumed that the LXX was essentially based on a Hebrew text clearly divergent from, and not infrequently superior to, the MT, even allowing for the differences due to the translating techniques used. Equally valuable was the contribution made by S. R. Driver (*Notes on the Hebrew Text and the Topography of the Books of Samuel*, 1890 [2d ed. 1913]). However, other scholars (e.g., P. A. H. de Boer) have taken a more cautious, if not depreciative, attitude to the usefulness of the Greek versions and recensions. In any case, one should not undervalue the MT (see Barthélemy's comments in *The Hebrew and Greek Texts of Samuel*, 1–44).

As regards the Books of Samuel, the situation became slightly clearer in 1952 with the discovery of fragments of certain Hebrew MSS of Samuel in the Qumran Cave IV. These fragments (4QSam^{a-c}) date from the third (4QSam^b) to the first century B.C. (4QSam^{a,c}). Of these only 4QSam^{a,c} are directly relevant to 2 Sam (see Cross, *BASOR* 132 [1953] 15–26; Ulrich, *BASOR* 235 [1979] 1–25). The conclusion of a preliminary study of these fragments was that not infrequently they differed from MT but agreed with LXX, and also vice versa. Some of the Qumran readings were reflected in the biblical text used by Josephus as well as in the Lucianic tradition. The inference was that the difference between MT and LXX must have existed already in the LXX *Vorlage*, and that it is highly unlikely that all the variants could be due to the interpretative activities of the translators.

Cross (cf. *HTR* 57 [1964] 281–99) has attempted to provide an explanation for the different text traditions, advocating the theory of three local texts which, apparently, go back to an Urtext in Palestine. His proposed three text-types are:

(a) The Egyptian—represented by LXX although the real witness is the unrevised Old Greek (OG) which can be best "recovered" from LXX^B (unfortunately, for the text of 2 Sam, it is relevant only in 2 Sam 1–9).

(b) The Palestinian—represented, to a greater or lesser extent, by the Qumran fragments as well as by the citations of Samuel and Kings in Chronicles and in Josephus, and by the Proto-Lucianic recension. This text-type, as a whole, is fuller than the MT, and it is often characterized by conflation; therefore it is sometimes described as expansionistic.

(c) The Babylonian—represented by the proto-Masoretic text and the MT. Occasionally it is described as short or sober text in comparison with the other two. The Egyptian text-type is closer to the Palestinian text than to the Babylonian.

Many scholars accept this scheme of three text-traditions (see, however, the questions raised by Gooding, *JSS* 21 [1976] 15–25) but some of them, at least, may be skeptical about the proposed geographical associations with the three main centers of Jewish life and culture. In particular, there is little evidence for the Babylonian link. Similarly, Barthélemy (IDBSup, 879) has remarked that we cannot "automatically qualify as Egyptian every Hebrew *Vorlage* of a book of the LXX." Perhaps, it might be more reasonable to assume a precanonical fluidity, characterized by a plurality of redactional traditions (so Barthélemy, ibid.). Thus in this situation the MT may well have existed side by side with other texts.

Our major textual witnesses used in the *Notes* include the Old Latin (OL), alongside the Greek versions mentioned above; it was made in the second and third centuries of our era, and it often reflects the text of the Old Greek.

The Targum Jonathan (Tg) is the authoritative or official Aramaic version of our Historical books (Joshua, Judges, Samuel, and Kings) and of the Prophets (Isaiah, Jeremiah, Ezekiel, and The Twelve). It is rather close to the MT and therefore it seldom offers any helpful variants. This Targum was already established in Babylon by the fifth century A.D. but some parts of it may go back to a much earlier time.

The Syriac version (Syr) or the Peshitta has a complicated history but, on the whole, it is fairly close to the MT. It was apparently based on Old Syriac, and has affinities with the Targums (at least in parts); in the course of transmission, in particular, it was influenced also by the Greek texts.

The Vulgate (Vg) was the crowning achievement of Jerome, and its translation took place between the years 390–405 (see Würthwein, *The Text of the Old Testament*, 92). It was based on the Hebrew text but Jerome used also the existing Greek versions.

We have not assumed the automatic priority of any one particular version, and we accept McCarter's (*1 Sam*, 8) observation that "none of the ancient witnesses to the text of Samuel has a monopoly on primitive readings." Therefore each variant should be considered on its own merits.

The major texts cited in the *Notes* are the following:

(a) Masoretic Text (MT): *Liber Samuelis. Biblia Hebraica Stuttgartensia*, Boer, P. A. H. de, ed. Stuttgart: Württembergische Bibelanstalt, 1976.

(b) Septuagint (LXX): *Septuaginta I*, Rahlfs, A., ed. 9th ed. Stuttgart: Württembergische Bibelanstalt, 1935.

(c) Targum (Tg): *The Bible in Aramaic. Vol. II: The Former Prophets*, Sperber, A., ed. Leiden: E.J. Brill, 1959.

(d) Vulgate (Vg): *Biblia Sacra Iuxta Vulgatam Versionem. Vol. I: Genesis—Psalmi*, Weber, R. et al. eds. 2d ed. Stuttgart: Württembergische Bibelanstalt, 1975.

THE LITERARY HISTORY OF 2 SAMUEL

Bibliography

Ackroyd, P. R. "The Succession Narrative (so-called)." *Int* 35 (1981) 383–96. Alt, A. *Kleine Schriften zur Geschichte des Volkes Israel*, 3 vols., ed. M. Noth. Munich: C. H. Beck, 1953–59. Blenkinsopp, J. "Theme and Motif in the Succession History (2 Sam. XI 2ff.) and the Yahwist Corpus." VTSup 15 (1966) 44–57. Campbell, A. F. *The Ark Narrative (1 Sam 4–6; 2 Sam 6): A Form-critical and Traditio-historical Study*. SBLDS 16. Missoula, MT: Scholars Press, 1975. Cargil, J. "David in History: A Secular Approach." *Judaism* 35 (1986) 211–22. Carlson, R. A. *David the Chosen King: A Traditio-historical Approach to the Second Book of Samuel*. Tr. E. J. Sharpe and S. Rudman (notes). Uppsala: Almquist & Wiksells, 1964. Clements, R. E. "History and Theology in Biblical Narrative." *Horizons in Biblical Theology* 4–5 (1982–83) 45–60. Coats, G. W. "Parable, Fable, and Anecdote: Storytelling in the Succession Narrative." *Int* 35 (1981) 368–82. Cohen, M. A. "The Rebellions during the Reign of David: An Inquiry into Social Dynamics in Ancient Israel." In *Studies in Jewish Bibliography, History, and Literature in Honor of Edward Kiev*, ed. C. Berlin. New York: Ktav, 1971. 91–112. Conrad, J. "Zum geschichtlichen Hintergrund der Darstellung von Davids Aufstieg." *TLZ* 97 (1972) cols. 321–32. ———. "Der Gegenstand und die Intention der Geschichte von der Thronfolge

Davids." *TLZ* 108 (1983) cols. 161–76. **Cook, S. A.** "Notes on the Composition of 2 Samuel." *AJSL* 16 (1899/1900) 145–77. **Crüsemann, F.** *Der Widerstand gegen das Königtum.* WMANT 49. Neukirchen—Vluyn: Neukirchener Verlag, 1978. **Delekat, L.** "Tendenz und Theologie der David-Salomo-Erzählung." In *Das ferne und nahe Wort,* FS L. Rost, ed. F. Maas. BZAW 105. Berlin: Töpelmann, 1967. **Dietrich, W.** *Prophetie und Geschichte: Eine redaktionsgeschichtliche Untersuchung zum deuteronomistischen Geschichtswerk.* Göttingen: Vandenhoeck & Ruprecht, 1972. ———. "David in Überlieferung und Geschichte." *Verkündigung und Forschung* 22 (1977) 44–64. **Flanagan, J.** *A Study of the Biblical Traditions Pertaining to the Foundation of the Monarchy in Israel.* University of Notre Dame, IN: Ph.D. Diss., 1971. ———. "Court History or Succession Document? A Study of II Samuel 9–20 and I Kings 1–2." *JBL* 91 (1972) 172–81. **Garsiel, M.** *The First Book of Samuel: A Literary Study of Comparative Structures, Analogies and Parallels.* Tr. P. Hackett. Ramat-Gan, Israel: Revivim Publishing House, 1985. **Gressmann, H.** *Die älteste Geschichtsschreibung und Prophetie Israels.* Die Schriften des Alten Testament II/1. 2d ed. Göttingen: Vandenhoeck & Ruprecht, 1921. **Grønbaek, J. H.** *Die Geschichte vom Aufstieg Davids (1.Sam. 15 – 2.Sam. 5). Tradition und Komposition.* Copenhagen: Prostant apud Munksgaard, 1971. **Gros Louis, K. R. R.** "The Difficulty of Ruling Well: King David of Israel." *Semeia* 8 (1977) 15–33. **Gunn, D. M.** "David and the Gift of the Kingdom (2 Sam 2–4, 9–20, I Kgs 1–2)." *Semeia* 3 (1975) 14–45. ———. "Traditional Composition in the 'Succession Narrative.'" *VT* 26 (1976) 214–29. ———. *The Story of King David: Genre and Interpretation,* JSOTSup 6. Sheffield: University of Sheffield, 1978. **Hagan, H.** "Deception as Motif and Theme in 2 Sm 9–20; I Kgs 1–2." *Bib* 60 (1979) 301–26. **Hoffner, H. A., Jr.** "Propaganda and Political Justification in Hittite Historiography." *Unity and Diversity: Essays in the History, Literature, and Religion of the Ancient Near East.* Ed. H. Goedicke and J. J. M. Roberts. Baltimore and London: Johns Hopkins, 1975. 49–62. **Ishida, T.** *The Royal Dynasties in Ancient Israel: A Study on the Formation and Development of Royal-Dynastic Ideology.* BZAW 142. Berlin: W. de Gruyter, 1977. **Jackson, J. J.** "David's Throne: Patterns in the Succession Story." *CJT* 11 (1965) 183–95. **Jones, G. H.** *1 and 2 Kings.* Vol. 1. NCB. Grand Rapids: Wm. B. Eerdmans; London: Marshall, Morgan & Scott, 1984. **Langlamet, F.** "Pour ou contre Salomon? La rédaction prosalomonienne de I Rois, I–II." *RB* 83 (1976) 321–79; 481–529. **McCarter, P. K., Jr.** "The Apology of David." *JBL* 99 (1980) 489–504. ———. "'Plots, True or False.' The Succession Narrative as Court Apologetic." *Int* 35 (1981) 355–67. ———. "The Historical David." *Int* 40 (1986) 117–29. **Meadows, J. N.** *A Traditio-Historical Study of II Samuel 9–20, I Kings 1, 2.* Louisville, KY: Southern Baptist Theological Seminary, Ph.D. Diss., 1975. **Mowinckel, S.** "Israelite Historiography." *ASTI* 2 (1963) 4–26. **Nelson, R. D.** *The Double Redaction of the Deuteronomistic History.* JSOTSup 18. Sheffield: University of Sheffield, 1981. **Noth, M.** *The Deuteronomistic History.* Tr. J. Doull et al. JSOTSup 15. Sheffield: The University of Sheffield, 1981. **Rad, G. von.** *The Problem of the Hexateuch and Other Essays.* Tr. E. W. Trueman Dicken. Edinburgh and London: Oliver & Boyd, 1966. **Radjawane, A. N.** "Das deuteronomistische Geschichtswerk." *TRu* 38 (1974) 177–216. **Ridout, G. P.** *Prose Compositional Techniques in the Succession Narrative (2 Samuel 7, 9–20, I Kings 1–2).* Graduate Theological Union, San Francisco: Ph.D. Diss., 1971. **Rost, L.** *The Succession to the Throne of David.* Tr. M. D. Rutter and D. M. Gunn. Sheffield: The Almond Press, 1982. **Schicklberger, F.** "Die Davididen und das Nordreich: Beobachtungen zur sog. Geschichte vom Aufstieg Davids." *BZ* 18 (1974) 255–63. **Schulte, H.** *Die Entstehung der Geschichtsschreibung im alten Israel.* BZAW 128. Berlin and New York: W. de Gruyter, 1972. **Seeligmann, I. L.** "Hebräische Erzählung und biblische Geschichtsschreibung." *TZ* 18 (1962) 303–25. **Segal, M. H.** "The Composition of the Books of Samuel." *JQR* 55 (1965) 318–39; 56 (1965/66) 32–50. **Seters, J. van.** "Histories and Historians of the Ancient Near East: The Israelites." *Or* 50 (1981) 137–85. ———. *In Search of History: Historiography in the Ancient World and the Origins* *of Biblical History.* New Haven and London: Yale UP, 1983. **Thornton, T. C. G.** "Solomonic Apologetic in Samuel and Kings." *CQR* 169 (1968) 159–66. **Vanderkam, J. C.** "Davidic Complicity in the Deaths of Abner and Eshbaal: A Historical and Redactional Study." *JBL* 99 (1980) 521–39. **Veijola, T.** *Die Ewige Dynastie: David und die Entstehung seiner Dynastie nach der deuteronomistischen Darstellung.* Helsinki: Suomalainen Tiedeakatemia, 1975. ———. "Remarks of an Outsider concerning Scandinavian Tradition History with Emphasis on the Davidic Traditions." *The Productions of Time: Tradition History in Old Testament Scholarship.* K. Jeppesen and B. Otzen, eds. Sheffield: Almond Press, 1984. 29–51. **Ward, R. L.** *The Story of David's Rise: A Traditio-Historical Study of I Samuel xvi – II Samuel v.* Vanderbilt University, Nashville, TN: Ph.D. Diss., 1967. **Weiser, A.** "Die Legitimation des Königs David: Zur Eigenart und Entstehung der sogen. Geschichte von Davids Aufstieg." *VT* 16 (1966) 325–54. **Wharton, J. A.** "A Plausible Tale: Story and Theology in II Samuel 9–20, I Kings 1–2." *Int* 35 (1981) 341–54. **Whybray, R. N.** *The Succession Narrative: A Study of II Sam. 9–20 and I Kings 1 and 2.* SBT 9, 2d ser. London: SCM, 1968.

The composition of the Books of Samuel should not be seen in isolation because Joshua, Judges, Samuel, and Kings form a sort of extensive account of Israel's history from the Conquest or Settlement of Canaan to the Babylonian exile. Since the viewpoint of these books is, more or less, that of Deuteronomy, they are said to comprise the so-called Deuteronomistic history; not infrequently the Book of Deuteronomy, too, is ascribed to this extended history of the people of Israel (see Noth, *The Deuteronomistic History*). It is fairly clear that Deuteronomy, Joshua, and Judges are closely linked, and similarly the division between Judges and 1 Sam is somewhat artificial. Likewise the story of David does not finish with 2 Sam 24 but comes to an end in 1 Kgs 1–2. Traditionally, Joshua, Judges, Samuel, and Kings have formed one large group in the Hebrew canon, namely, the *Former Prophets,* and this may be a further pointer to the essential unity of the four historical books. Moreover, it is of some interest that in LXX both Samuel and Kings form a unit, and together they make up the four books of *Kingdoms* or *Reigns.*

How this Deuteronomistic History came into being is a very long and complicated process. At the present time, it is often thought that Noth's single-stage theory (ibid., 79–88) presents a view which is too simplified to account for all the data, and the same may be true also of the two-stage view of Cross (cf. *Canaanite Myth,* 274–89). Thus it is possible that we should discern several different hands in the production of the Deuteronomistic History in its final form (cf. Dietrich, *Prophetie und Geschichte,* 139–48).

However, our present concern is mainly with the Books of Samuel, especially the Second Book. The canonical division of Samuel into two books is a fairly late phenomenon and was, probably, introduced by the Greek translator/s. The Samuel scroll from Qumran suggests that the two books of Samuel must have formed one scroll in Hebrew (see Ulrich, *Qumran Texts,* 9–11). This is also supported by the Masoretic note in 1 Sam 28:24 (see *BHS*) indicating "the midpoint of the book of Samuel." Similarly, at the end of our Second Book of Samuel there is a Masoretic note giving the *total* of the verses in Samuel.

Traditionally, the authorship of the Books of Samuel has been ascribed to Samuel (so the Babylonian Talmud, *Baba Bathra* 14b–15) or to Samuel, Gad, and Nathan (cf. 1 Chr 29:29). However, there is no real justification for these assumptions although it is true that Samuel was one of the principal actors in the First Book of Samuel. The complex nature of the Books of Samuel seems to exclude any simple solution, such as the view that the whole work originally constituted a single, homogeneous literary unit. In actual fact, there are a number of pointers that suggest that the work is some sort of compilation. Thus, for instance, there seem to be a number of parallel accounts or doublets exhibiting greater or lesser divergencies, and even some apparent contradictions, especially in the First Book of Samuel. These and similar problems and observations tend to support the claim that no *single author* could have written the Books of Samuel. Consequently, several solutions have been proposed to account for the composition of Samuel but no hypothesis has commanded a general acceptance. Therefore we shall briefly note some of the main solutions offered.

One of the oldest explanations was the attempt to trace in the Books of Samuel the Pentateuchal sources 'J' and 'E.' Thus, for instance, the German commentator Karl Budde (1902) argued that Samuel was the result of joining together two *parallel* sources: 'J' and 'E.' Clearly there are some affinities between certain portions of Samuel and the Pentateuchal materials attributed to the above sources, but it is doubtful that these very limited affinities could provide strong enough foundation for such and similar hypotheses (cf. also Eissfeldt's view in his *Introduction*, 279).

An alternative to the parallel source theory was what might be called the fragmentary hypothesis, such as the one advocated by Hugo Gressmann (1921) who argued that Samuel is a collection of many individual narratives of larger or smaller size. Eventually this collection underwent a Deuteronomistic redaction at some stage in its history. A sort of variation of Gressmann's view is the so-called "successive blocks" theory which is, perhaps, the best tentative solution (in one of its many forms), and many scholars have worked along some such lines.

As regards 2 Samuel it has been customary to speak of four main blocks of material which (or parts of which) form our book:

(a) The History of David's Rise (1 Sam 16 [or 15] – 2 Sam 5).
(b) The Ark Narrative (1 Sam 4–6 + 2 Sam 6).
(c) The Succession Narrative (2 Sam 9–20 + 1 Kgs 1–2).
(d) The Appendices (2 Sam 21–24).

Since the Succession Narrative is by far the largest narrative block, we shall take it as the basis of our discussion. It may well be that this complex holds the key to one possible interpretation or reading of 2 Samuel.

The origin of the term "Succession Narrative" (SN) is usually associated with Leonhard Rost and his study, *Die Überlieferung von der Thronnachfolge Davids*, published in 1926; its English translation was produced in 1982. In this work he argued that in the Books of Samuel we do not find two parallel, continuous sources, 'J' and 'E' (or call them what you like, so Rost) but that there are two main complexes which could be called the History of the Rise of David (HDR) and the History of the Succession to David or Succession Narrative (SN) for short.

However, Rost was not the first to draw attention to the theme of succession in 2 Samuel. For instance, Karl Budde in 1906 (in his *Geschichte der althebräischen Literatur*, 35) spoke of David's family story in 2 Sam 10–19 (20) + 1 Kgs 1–2, and he pointed out that these chapters dealt mainly with the history of succession to David's throne. Similarly, Bernhard Stade (in *EnBib*, cols. 4278–79) described 2 Sam 9–20 as a continuous narrative which exhibits the same peculiarities of style throughout, "and must therefore be attributed to one and the same writer." To this narrative he added also 1 Kgs 1–2, and concluded that the purpose of their author was to "show how it was precisely that Solomon should have come to be David's successor" (cols. 4278–79). There were also other scholars who had put forward similar views prior to Rost but it was to his credit that he dealt with the problems far more systematically and in greater detail; therefore it is customary to associate Rost's name with the origin of the designation the "Succession Narrative." Clearly, there were also criticisms, as illustrated by such reviews as those of H. Gressmann (*ZAW* 44 [1926] 309–10), H. M. Wiener (*JPOS* 7 [1927] 135–41), and C. Kuhl (*TLZ* 53 [1928] 99–100).

To a greater or lesser extent, many scholars accept the basic views expounded by Rost, but opinions differ considerably when they come to define the limits and unity of the main complexes, as well as their purpose and dating. Roughly speaking, the HDR comprises 1 Sam 16 – 2 Sam 8 while the SN is often limited to 2 Sam 9–20 + 1 Kgs 1–2. Obviously, there exist numerous variations on the delimitation of the two principal narratives but the above limits may serve as a starting point. In a sense, it is reasonable to assume that the account of David's Rise (HDR) should begin with his anointing in 1 Sam 16 (cf. Weiser, *VT* 16 [1966] 325–54); however, Grønbaek (*Aufstieg*, 16, 25–27) would include also chap. 15, while McCarter (13) and many others limit the HDR to 1 Sam 16:14–2 Sam 5:10. The conclusion of the HDR raises more problems, and there is even less agreement. Occasionally it has been claimed that 2 Sam 8:15 marks the end of the HDR (cf. Alt, *Essays*, 187; Flanagan, *Foundation of the Monarchy*, 49, 123; Ackroyd, *Int* 35 [1981]385) because this verse has a certain finality when it states, "so David ruled over all Israel, and he maintained law and justice for all his people." The remaining three verses (vv 16–18) of the chapter may be a later addition, and they provide a list of the chief officials of David's administration.

However, in our discussions of the narrative blocks, we should never take it for granted that some of the original materials of this or any other complex, could not have been displaced or even omitted. There is also the possibility that not all the present sections or verses in any complex are part of the *original* narrative. For instance, even if the HDR extended from 1 Sam 16 to 2 Sam 8, it is very likely that at one time 2 Sam 6 may have formed part of an independent complex, the Ark Narrative. Similarly, 2 Sam 7 or Nathan's oracle (and David's responsive prayer) may have existed as a separate unit (cf. its poetic version in Ps 89:19–37 [20–38]). In any case, this chapter in its final form is either the work of the Deuteronomistic editor(s) or greatly influenced by them. However, Weiser (*VT* 16 [1966] 342–54), Mettinger (*King and Messiah,* 41–55) and others have contended, perhaps rightly, that Nathan's prophecy, in some form or other, may have constituted the conclusion or "the triumphant finale of the HDR" (so Mettinger, ibid., 55). Although this is plausible, other possibilities have an equally good claim, especially 2 Sam 5:10 with its, "So David grew stronger and stronger for Yahweh, the God of Hosts, was with him," could serve as a suitable conclusion (so, for instance, McCarter [*1 Samuel,* 30] and others).

The limits of the SN are notoriously difficult to delimit. Most scholars would agree that stylistically and thematically, 1 Kgs 1–2 is far closer to 2 Sam 9–20 than to the other chapters in the Books of Kings (contra Mowinckel, *ASTI* 2 [1963] 11–13). These two chapters are closely linked with the events and persons in 2 Sam (see Schulte, *Geschichtsschreibung,* 169), and it may not be a mere coincidence that Joab appears as active participant only in the narratives found between 2 Sam 2:12 and 1 Kgs 2:34 and nowhere else. The assertion (see Flanagan, *JBL* 91 [1972] 173) that 1 Kgs 1–2 may have existed as a distinct unit, separate from 2 Sam 9–20, seems doubtful for the above reasons. Even less likely is the view that these two chapters were originally part of the following narrative, as argued by Mowinckel (*ASTI* 2 [1963] 11–13). All in all, it seems that the conclusion of the SN should be sought in 1 Kgs 1–2, especially in 2:46b which states, "so the kingdom was established in the hand of Solomon." Less convincing is the suggestion that the ending is to be found in 1 Kgs 2:12, the main objection being that the following verses describe the actual implementation of David's wishes expressed in 2:5–9. Furthermore, vv 10–12 form an annalistic note, and as such it may well be a Deuteronomistic addition because it is reminiscent of the customary formulae found elsewhere in the Books of Kings.

Thus we assume that 1 Kgs 1–2 is an integral part of the SN, and that it provides clues to the extent and purpose of the SN as a whole. It is difficult to reconstruct the historical setting of the SN but 1 Kgs 1–2 may provide some information, however tendentious and limited it may be; we would suggest that at least these *two* chapters reflect the author's own time. The essential factor in this possible historical situation must have been the apparent political stalemate at the very end of David's reign. Although Adonijah is described as having staged a coup (1 Kgs 1:5–11) with the help of Joab and Abiathar, the priest, yet they were not immediately punished for what can only be described as high treason, when Solomon and his supporters carried out their successful countercoup. It is possible that at this point the question was one of co-regency and that David was able to prevent bloodshed. Even Joab may have continued as commander of the national army (excluding, of course, the mercenaries) as, perhaps, is implied by 1 Kgs 2:35. Thus although Solomon's party had the upper hand, they did not have an absolute freedom of action, and Adonijah and Joab constituted a real, continual threat to Solomon's prospects. Moreover, such a situation would create a fertile soil for intrigues and accusations. Only some three years later (see 1 Kgs 2:39) when David was dead, Solomon was able to take full control and to resort to more permanent solutions in eliminating Adonijah, Joab, and the Saulide chief(?) Shimei, and in banishing Abiathar. The charges brought against them appear to be, in essence, trumped-up charges (except, perhaps, in Abiathar's case; see 1 Kgs 2:26) to justify the pseudo-legal killings of Adonijah, Joab, and Shimei. If our reading of the situation is right, it suggests that Adonijah's party may have commanded a strong support even at this late stage; therefore their elimination required at least some sort of explanation or justification. The prolonged "house arrest" of Shimei, and his subsequent judicial killing may imply that also the Saulide claims to kingship were not, as yet, a thing of the past. Thus, on the one hand, it was necessary to exonerate Solomon for taking the drastic and questionable measures and, on the other hand, it was imperative to scotch any suggestions that David had been rejected as Yahweh's chosen king.

Thus with this hypothetical reconstruction in mind, we may turn once more to the quest for the *beginning* of the SN. Chapter 9 has often been taken as the start of the narrative; however, it opens with the words, "Is there still anyone left of the house of Saul . . .?" which provides a hardly satisfactory opening of the SN, as already realized by Rost himself (*Succession,* 67). Moreover, the question in 9:1 seems to presuppose a comparatively recent enthronement of David as king of Israel. Before this point in time David was not in control of Transjordan or of the territory of Israel as a whole, and therefore he could not very well send for Jonathan's son Mephibosheth who was residing in Lo-debar, i.e., in Transjordan. Furthermore, this concern of David for the house of Saul on account of Jonathan could hardly be placed later than the first few years of David's rule because in the Books of Samuel a considerable stress is placed upon David's covenantal obligation to Jonathan. In view of this, it would be surprising that David would be depicted as having reigned over Israel for a number of years without even being aware that Jonathan had a son who was still alive but not in possession of his grandfather's estate. Mephibosheth was, apparently, five years old when his father died in battle (4:4) and thus even David may have known of his birth, especially if the strong link between David and Jonathan is authentic.

We may also note that chap. 9 implies that it was at this point that David dealt with the ownership of Saul's estate; this, too, would point to the beginning or the early part of David's rule over Israel, when such matters as the ownership of the estate of the previous king, would be most likely settled. It could be added that politically speaking it would be wise to locate one's potential opponents as soon as possible. Therefore a note such as 5:1–3 which tells us of the enthronement of David as king over Israel would provide a reasonable, if not necessary, setting for chap. 9, even if it was originally preceded by the Gibeonite episode in 21:1–14 (see *Form/Structure/Setting* of 21:1–14). It is, however, less certain that the rest of chap. 5 belonged to the SN since the rest of this chapter contains some materials which exhibit considerable differences in style and presentation. These smaller units may have been added at some later time, as link materials, filling in gaps in the sequence of the main narrative. The same may be, more or less, true of chaps. 6–8. Most of chap. 6 may have belonged to the so-called Ark Narrative (see Campbell, *Ark Narrative,* 28–54) which, at one time, may have served its own specific purpose apart from the SN. Similarly, chap. 7 in its present form is considerably different in style and character from the rest of the SN. David Gunn (*King David,* 67) has remarked that chap. 7 "is ideologically obvious and tediously repetitive," thus providing a complete contrast to the SN which he has well described as "a subtle story told in a compelling manner." However, a simpler version of the Dynastic oracle (7:1–17) would have helped the apologetic purpose of the SN in emphasizing the election of David, especially if it was seen as unconditional (cf. 7:14–15). Chap. 8 is largely an annalistic catalogue of David's military successes, and it probably derives from some court source. It may well be a Deuteronomistic compilation in its present setting (cf. McCarter, 251), illustrating David's triumphs.

On the other hand, chaps. 2–4 offer a more or less coherent story which has clear stylistic and thematic affinities with chaps. 9–20 + 1 Kgs 1–2. Both parts make extensive use of direct speech and provide elaborate portrayal of secondary characters. There is also a common pragmatic, ostensibly nonreligious attitude if we omit 2:1–4 with its oracular consultation. One may also note a certain amount of common linguistic features, such as vocabulary and phraseology, as well as various forms of repetition, foreshadowing, use of similes, etc.

However, the most important fact is that chaps. 2–3 give a detailed account of Asahel's death which in turn brought about the killing of Abner by Joab (3:26–39). The culmination of this sequence comes at the end of David's reign when the king is said to have given strict instructions to Solomon to execute Joab for the murders of Abner and Amasa (1 Kgs 2:5–6; 28–35). Thus the end of the SN seems to presuppose chaps. 2–3, and together they form a sort of inclusion or ring composition. Moreover, without chaps. 2–3 the end of the SN would remain obscure, especially since the rights and wrongs of Joab's killing of Abner may have been far less obvious in the actual situation than they were in the *present* narrative. Similarly, the circumstances of Amasa's killing are equally ambivalent (cf. 20:4–10).

Of course, an argument based on events presupposed by later events is not conclusive because in historical narratives one thing or event usually presupposes another, and thus it is difficult to find the appropriate cut-off point. However, in our case there is some additional justification. We are told that there was a long war between the house of Saul and that of David (3:1), and yet we have only one single episode of these hostilities, namely, 2:8–32. The noteworthy point is that apart from the casualties (twenty and three hundred and sixty, respectively), this battle had no apparent military significance as far as we can judge. Thus its main purpose can only be to describe in detail the events surrounding Asahel's death, and to stress Abner's blamelessness and his great reluctance to kill Asahel, Joab's brother. The obvious implication is that Abner's choice was to kill in self-defense or be killed. This would tend to emphasize Joab's guilt, especially if some circles may have questioned the "legality"of Joab's execution.

We may also note the relative lengths of some of the military episodes. Thus the takeover of Hebron is described in some three verses (2:1–4a) and the fall of Jerusalem is depicted in a short, somewhat obscure passage (5:6–10) while *twenty-four* verses are devoted to the battle episode in which Asahel lost his life and which gave rise to the far-reaching consequences leading to Joab's elimination. Thus the quantitative aspect, too, may be an indication of the author's specific interests. Not that the capture of Jerusalem was less important (assuming that this episode was part of the SN) than the battle at Gibeon but the Gibeon-battle account must have served the particular purpose of the author of the SN, foreshadowing Abner's death and the subsequent execution of Joab. All this goes to show that the primary aim of the author was not the glorification of David or Solomon but the exoneration of the king and his successor, for putting Joab to a shameful death after his lengthy and distinguished military service devoted to David's interests. To a large extent the Joab-vignettes are intent on discrediting Joab and his cause (note in particular such statements as those in 3:39; 16:10; 19:22).

Consequently, it could be reasonably argued that the SN began at least with 2:8 or 2:12 (so already, e.g., Schulte, *Geschichtsschreibung*, 140–42; Gunn, *King David*, 67); we would be inclined to add also 2:1–4a in spite of its oracular consultation which is not typical of the SN but is characteristic of the HDR (cf. 23:2–4; 30:7–8). Perhaps, it is not improbable that the SN actually began with 1:1–16. The death of Saul was a well-known fact and therefore it may have served as a useful starting point for a new work involving his successor (cf. Josh 1:1; Judg 1:1). Moreover, also this initial section may have had an apologetic purpose, explaining as to how David came to be in the possession of the royal insignia before he was king of Israel (see Whitelam, *The Just King*, 104–5). It is not impossible that the death of the Amalekite (2 Sam 1:15–16) and the deaths of Joab and Shimei, in particular, may form another inclusion in that both involve the elimination of those who had endangered or even killed Yahweh's chosen king.

Thus the hypothetical SN may have extended from 2 Sam 1:1 to 5:10, omitting David's lament for Saul and Jonathan (1:17–27), the Jabesh-Gileadite fragment (2:4b–7), and the list of David's sons (3:2–5). These early chapters may have been followed by 21:1–14 + chaps. 9–20 + 1 Kgs 1–2. Also in this latter part of the SN there may have been some later additions such as 12:7b–12, but scholarly opinions on this question are greatly divided. The inclusion of chaps. 6–8 is equally disputed.

Naturally, there could be many objections to our proposed tentative outline of the limits of the SN. It could be demurred that the HDR had been deprived of several integral if not necessary sections. In a sense this may be true but there is a possible compromise. It is unlikely that the HDR and the SN were composed at one and the same time, and so each complex must have had its own original purpose and function. It seems that the main aim of the HDR was to present Saul as the *rejected* king of Israel and David as his legitimate, divinely chosen successor. The latter is not depicted as a usurper but as the better man for the royal office. Jonathan, too, was not deprived of the throne which he virtually abdicated in David's favor (cf. 1 Sam 20:13–16).

We would argue that the themes of Saul's rejection and of David's legitimation had their greatest, although not their only, relevance at the beginning of David's reign. We could well assume that the many subsequent victories of David and the expansion of his kingdom would have been interpreted by most, if not all, people as a clear proof that David was indeed the chosen king of Israel. Therefore we would suggest an early date for the HDR since at a later stage the polemical support would be hardly required. However, some eminent scholars have taken the opposite view. For instance, Grønbaek (*Aufstieg*, 260) has contended that the complex was directed against Jeroboam while Conrad (*TLZ* 97 [1972] cols. 329–30) has suggested Jehu as a possible candidate. Nevertheless, these and similar views appear less likely because these kings did not base their kingship on the legitimacy or permanency of the house of Saul.

Since one of the main themes of the HDR was the repudiation of Saul for certain misdeeds or disobedience, it may have provided a sort of precedent. If Yahweh can choose a king and then reject him for his subsequent disobedience then the question could be asked, at the *end* of David's reign, whether his rule and life had not provided far more reasons for rejection than Saul's reign had provided for his repudiation. Was not David called "a man of blood" (16:7) who had liquidated at least seven Saulides (21:1–14) for some offense of Saul? Was not the king himself the murderer of Uriah (by proxy), and an adulterer in the bargain? Did he not overlook for many years Joab's murder of Abner because the carrying out of justice might not have been expedient in the given circumstances (3:39)? Were there not some people who actually believed that David had had a hand in Abner's tragic death (3:36–37)? Also Ishbosheth's murder may have been laid at David's door although there is no *explicit* evidence. However, the head of the murdered Ishbosheth was brought to David in Hebron (4:8)! Above all, were not the rebellions against David's rule clear indications that he had not administered justice and equity to all his people, and that consequently Yahweh was no longer with him? It would be surprising if such and similar questions were not asked during the final years of David's reign and at the beginning of Solomon's rule. If Saul and his house could be rejected, why not David and his unsavory family? It seems that even David himself accepted Yahweh's punitive judgment implicit in Absalom's rebellion (15:25–26; 16:10–12) although he hoped that Yahweh might show him mercy.

Thus the SN may have been designed to answer the above questions, doubts, and accusations. Consequently, the principle of selectivity used by the author is not indicative of any anti-Davidic or anti-Solomonic tendencies as suggested, for instance, by Delekat (*Das ferne und nahe Wort*, 26–29) and Würthwein (*Thronfolge*, 11–32). The seemingly unfavorable episodes had to be chosen and had to be dealt with because it was exactly these events that needed explanation or refutation. They could not be simply suppressed because they were public knowledge. Hence for these reasons David's adultery with Bathsheba and the murder of Uriah were depicted as *already punished* through the death of Bathsheba's illegitimate child (12:15–18) while David's acceptance by Yahweh was made obvious through the birth of Solomon whose Yahweh-given name was Jedidiah, the beloved of Yahweh (see 12:24–25), thus foreshadowing Solomon's rule. Similarly, Absalom's rebellion had to be interpreted as David's punishment for the mismanagement of his family and the kingdom (cf. 16:10–12) while David's humble repentance and his acceptance of Yahweh's judgment were portrayed as resulting in his restoration. Thus David was indeed chastened by Yahweh but he was not permanently rejected like Saul (cf. 7:14). The "proof" of this was the victory of David's forces over Absalom's army.

For the later writers, such as the Chronicler, these problems were, apparently, of "academic" interest, and therefore the Chronicler could simply omit such passages as the Bathsheba-David-Uriah story or the rebellion of Absalom. On the other hand, most of the contemporaries of the author of the SN, if he wrote in the early part of Solomon's reign, would have been quite familiar with most of the actual events and with the existing versions of these incidents. They did not need to be specifically reminded of the Bathsheba episode and similar disagreeable events but there was a real necessity for the Davidic court to justify, in some way or other, the activities of David and his family. It was essential to show that in spite of the unpleasant events David still had divine approval and remained the chosen king, and therefore entitled to select his legitimate successor, namely, Solomon (1 Kgs 1:29–30).

Now we can return to the earlier objection that the expansion of the limits of the SN has removed relevant, if not necessary, sections from the HDR. However, this does not necessarily follow, especially if the SN was composed later than the HDR. In this way the former author may have been able to make use of the HDR and any other existing materials relevant to that period and containing accounts or information which required an apologetic treatment. In other words, the end of the HDR need not have determined the beginning of the SN; therefore episodes which originally may have belonged to the HDR could have been reworked, to a greater or lesser extent, by the author of the SN for his own purposes. This "overlapping" may account for the difficulties of delimiting the end of the HDR and the beginning of the SN; it may also take care of some of the linguistic "overlap." Furthermore, the editor (Deuteronomistic?) who used both the HDR and the SN may have exercised his own discretion in the choice and further adaptation of his sources, thus introducing a further complication in our tentative analysis of 2 Sam.

In view of our previous arguments, it seems that the SN was not written to the greater glory of Solomon (contra Mettinger, *King and Messiah*, 28; et al.) but rather it was intended to show that David was not under a curse in spite of the past events, and that Solomon was the rightful heir contrary to the popular expectations (cf. 1 Kgs 2:15) and despite his youth and parentage. So only in a limited sense can this complex be called a succession narrative. It was not written to answer the question, "Who of David's sons will be king?" (as Rost has argued) because by the time the SN was composed, the answer to this question was already an accomplished fact. It is far more likely that the question on the lips of many people was, "Is *any* of David's sons fit to sit on the throne of Israel?" This would be linked with the preliminary question, "Has David himself been rejected by Yahweh?" (cf. also Thornton, *CQR* 169 [1968] 160). Assuming the authenticity of 19:10 which mentions the anointing of Absalom, one could justifiably infer that those who had anointed Absalom as king of Israel and Judah must have believed that David was no longer fit to be their ruler, and that even Yahweh had cast him off.

The Saulides and their supporters probably went a step further in claiming that not only *some* of David's sons had disqualified themselves from the royal office but that the whole Davidic house had become unfit for the high task. So during the rebellion of Absalom, Jonathan's son is reputed to have said,

"Today the house of Israel will give me back the kingdom of my father" (16:3). Also the rebellion of Sheba, the Benjaminite, (20:2) may point in the same direction irrespective of whether Sheba envisaged the restoration of the house of Saul or not.

Although behind the SN there is a very basic chronological scheme, it was not supposed to be a comprehensive, sequential account of David's reign; the selective process seen in the choice of the episodes seems to point to its apologetic nature. Consequently, we regard the SN essentially as an apology rather than simply a political propaganda (cf. Whybray, *Succession Narrative*, 50–55) although the differences between the two are not always easy to define. H. A. Hoffner (*Unity and Diversity*, 49) has given a useful definition of apology as a literary type although he had in mind the Hittite documents; however, his definition has some relevance also for the SN. He states that an apology is "a document composed for a king who had usurped the throne, composed in order to defend or justify his assumption of kingship by force." Obviously, the SN is a more complex "document" but essentially it, too, is an "official" interpretation of significant events.

At the same time there is no need to reject those views which assert that the SN is a real work of art (so Gunn, *King David*, 37–38) although we would doubt that this was the primary purpose in the composition of the SN. There is no reason why a good, artistic apology could not be produced by a man of great literary talent, and why it could not be entertaining as well as informative.

Similarly, we could allow for certain wisdom influences that can be detected in the SN although this does not amount to saying that the SN is an example of wisdom literature. In a way, the SN is as historical as any of the OT historical books but it is obvious that the word "historical" in this context has certain limitations imposed upon it by the cultural setting (see Gunn, *King David*, 20–21). Therefore the SN can only loosely be described as a historical narrative, and it is doubtful that it was ever intended as a work of history approaching *our* sense of the word (cf. also Whybray, *Succession Narrative*, 19).

The author of the SN may have been a contemporary of at least some of the events recorded but the detailed conversations found in the complex need not be taken as illustrations of the author's first hand knowledge; they may well be part of the author's considerable artistic skill. He may not have had any more information about the private conversations than Thucydides had for his "historical speeches" or Josephus for his battle-scene orations.

The disproportionate length of the Absalom narrative is a puzzle but a possible explanation is that the author himself may have been familiar with these events and that he used his considerable literary talents. Moreover, the subject matter itself was of great importance because Absalom's rebellion was the most dangerous threat to David's kingship, resulting in the temporary rejection of David by the people in general; it also unleashed other tensions, rivalry, and even hostilities which "fed" on David's real and imaginary failures and favoritism (cf. 19:41–43). Therefore all these interrelated events may have been given a more detailed treatment than some other incidents, emphasizing above all the ceaseless scheming of Absalom, the gentleness and conciliatory nature of David (18:5), and the callousness of Joab (cf. 18:14–15; 19:5–7) but leaving to Yahweh the final decision (see 15:25; 16:11–12). The Absalom narrative may have been used not simply as a critique of Absalom and defense of David but it may have been relevant also to the policies of Solomon because Adonijah is portrayed (at least implicitly) as a second Absalom, both having the same rebellious aims and perverse character (compare, for instance, 14:25 and 1 Kgs 1:6; 15:1 and 1 Kgs 1:5b; 15:10 and 1 Kgs 1:5a, 11, 18; 16:22 and 1 Kgs 2:17). Thus the author suggests that only Solomon's timely actions forestalled Adonijah's takeover of the throne and the elimination of Yahweh's chosen ruler (cf. 12:24–25; 1 Kgs 1:12, 21).

Obviously, there are also other ways of understanding the interrelationships between the various narratives or documents. For instance, McCarter has suggested that the author or Solomonic apologist wrote only 1 Kgs 1–2 *with reference to* the already existing materials and that he "combined them with his own composition (1 Kgs 1–2)" (McCarter, 13; see also Conroy, *Absalom*, 104). McCarter sees the different materials in 2 Samuel as "a series of originally independent documents, each with its own literary unity and internal thematic integrity" (*Int* 35 [1981] 362). This would be especially true of the Absalom story (chaps. 13–20) but we are not quite convinced that 2 Sam 13–20 and 1 Kgs 1–2 must necessarily come from two *different* authors. Any decisions on this and similar points are difficult because in an apologetic work the author would usually take up the current divergent versions of the relevant events requiring an "official" interpretation. Thus the essential question is to what extent the author/editor adapted and rewrote the earlier stories or documents which must have been selected by him for his specific task. In their unchanged, original form they would hardly serve apologetic purposes. Therefore we would stress the authorial aspect more than the editorial, although the evidence seems to be inconclusive either way.

The identity of the author of the SN remains an insoluble problem. Any proposed identifications, such as Ahimaaz son of Zadok, or Nathan the prophet, or an unnamed royal tutor or scribe, are merely informed guesswork. However, we can agree with Jones (*1 and 2 Kings* 1:57) that "it can be reasonably claimed that the work originated from court circles."

The SN may have been aimed at the Israelite elite who usually exercised great political power, rather than at the population in general. The main means of communication may have been the scribal schools. It is less likely that this purpose was served by the prophetical circles since not infrequently they were critical of the monarchy and its institutions. On the other hand, there were also prophets, such as Nathan, who were supportive of the monarchy.

So far we have not dealt with the so-called appendices in chaps. 21–24. Most scholars would agree that this "block" is a later addition to the SN and that it is not fully integrated into the larger narrative. It is just possible that this composite supplement was formed out of miscellaneous materials and added to the SN at one and the same time (see also *Form/Structure/Setting* of 24:1–25). However, many scholars favor Budde's three stage theory (see *Form/Structure/Setting* of 21:1–14) or a variation of it.

Although the appendices appear to be intrusive and without a real context, nevertheless they provide a fairly fitting conclusion to David's effective reign, especially with the Psalm of Thanksgiving in 22:1–51 and the Last Words of David in 23:1–7.

THE USE OF 2 SAMUEL IN THE SCRIPTURES

Bibliography

Braun, H. "Das Alte Testament im Neuen Testament." *ZTK* 59 (1962) 16–31. **Bruce, F. F.** *This Is That: The New Testament Development of Some Old Testament Themes.* Exeter, Devon: Paternoster Press, 1968. **Childs. B. S.** "Psalm Titles and Midrashic Exegesis." *JSS* 16 (1971) 137–50. **Chisholm, R. B., Jr.** *An Exegetical and Theological Study of Psalm 18/2 Samuel 22.* Dallas Theological Seminary: D.Th. Thesis, 1983. **Duling, D. C.** "The Promises to David and Their Entrance into Christianity—Nailing Down a Likely Hypothesis." *NTS* 20 (1973/4) 55–77. **Eaton J. H.** *Kingship and the Psalms.* 2d ed. Sheffield: JSOT Press, 1986. **Ellis, E. E.** *Paul's Use of the Old Testament.* Grand Rapids, MI: Baker Book House, 1957. **Fitzmeyer, J. A.** "The Use of Explicit Old Testament Quotations in Qumran Literature and in the New Testament." *NTS* 7 (1961) 297–333. **Gese, H.** "Der Davidsbund und die Zionserwählung." *ZTK* 61 (1964) 10–26. **Goppelt, L.** *Typos: The Typological Interpretation of the Old Testament in the New.* Tr. D. H. Madvig. Grand Rapids, Michigan: William B. Eerdmans, 1982. **Hillers, D. R.** "Ritual Procession of the Ark and Psalm 132." *CBQ* 30 (1968) 48–55. **Kaiser, W. C., Jr.** *The Uses of the Old Testament in the New.* Chicago: Moody Press, 1985. **Kruse, H.** "David's Covenant." *VT* 35 (1985) 139–64. **Kuske, M.** *The Old Testament as the Book of Christ: An Appraisal of Bonhoeffer's Interpretation.* Tr. S. T. Kimbrough, Jr. Philadelphia: Westminster Press, 1976. **Lindars. B.** *New Testament Apologetic: The Doctrinal Significance of the Old Testament Quotations.* London: SCM Press, 1961. **McKenzie, S. L.** *The Chronicler's Use of the Deuteronomistic History.* HSM 33. Atlanta: Scholars Press, 1985. **Porter, J. R.** "The Interpretation of 2 Samuel 6 and Psalm 132." *JTS* 5 (1954) 161–73. **Roberts, J. J.** "The Davidic Origin of the Zion Tradition." *JBL* 92 (1973) 329–44. **Smith, D. Moody, Jr.** "The Use of the Old Testament in the New." In *The Use of the Old Testament in the New and Other Essays.* FS W. F. Stinespring, ed. J. M. Efird. Durham, NC: Duke University Press, 1972. 3–65. **Stendahl, K.** *The School of St. Matthew and Its Use of the Old Testament.* Lund: CWK Gleerup, 1967. **Turpie, D. M.** *The Old Testament in the New: A Contribution to Biblical Criticism and Interpretation.* London and Edinburgh: Williams and Norgate, 1868. **Watts, J. D. W.** *Isaiah 34–66.* WBC 25. Waco, TX: Word Books, 1987.

Even a cursory reader of the Bible would sooner or later come to the conclusion that not infrequently Scripture cites, or alludes to, Scripture. However, on closer examination it appears that the exact relationships are not easy to define. Sometimes it is far from clear who depends upon whom since the composition, history, and dating of the relevant materials are often problematic, and the results are usually hypothetical.

The interrelationship may express itself in three main ways:

(a) There are direct quotations, with or without specific citation formulas, as well as free quotations which are the result of greater or lesser modifications and adaptations. The text of the citations may depend upon the available scrolls or other written documents (including possible testimonia, florilegia or similar collections of proof texts) but sometimes they may be derived from the writer's own memory. Citations may also take the form of compound or collated quotations which come from more than one author or source (cf. Matt 21:13; Rom 11:8–10). Moreover, quotations may be taken not only from the original language but also from various existing translations, making use, if necessary, of variant readings. It is likely that occasionally quotations may "evoke the whole passage from which it has been selected" (Lindars, *New Testament Apologetic*, 14) and the same may be true also of allusions. Thus they can serve as pointers to a whole set of concepts; see for instance, Luke 1:32 which points to the Davidic covenant and its implications.

(b) Then there are allusions which often create certain problems since they lack any sort of introductory formulas, and they are essentially more or less indirect or implied references. In many cases it is impossible to be certain whether an allusion was deliberately intended by the author or not. People sharing the same cultural and religious heritage may easily produce what might be described as fortuitous "allusions" due to their common culture and linguistic usage. On the other hand, it is likely that some intended allusions may well have escaped later readers.

(c) The third form of relationship is even more general and less direct; namely, an earlier work or text may serve as a source or inspiration of later concepts or themes.

In view of all this, it is clear that any given total number of quotations and allusions (e.g., in the NT) may vary considerably from scholar to scholar (see Kaiser, *Uses of the Old Testament in the New*, 2–3). When we look more closely at the use of 2 Samuel in the Scriptures, we note that it is mainly confined to certain of the so-called Historical books (Kings and, especially, Chronicles), the Prophets, the Psalms, and the New Testament. There are a few allusions to David also in the Pentateuch, e.g., in Gen 49:10; Num 24:17 (cf. S. Mowinckel, *He That Cometh* [tr. G. W. Anderson. Oxford: Blackwell, 1956] 12–13).

The most extensive direct use of 2 Samuel is found in 1 Chronicles. There is little doubt that the Chronicler used the Books of Samuel and Kings as his main sources for the history of the Judean monarchy although his Hebrew text may not have been of the same text type as our MT even making allowances for the relatively poor state of the present text of 2 Samuel. Blocks of material from 2 Samuel have been tacitly cited by the Chronicler either verbatim or quasi-verbatim; thus the contents of 2 Samuel are covered by 1 Chr 10–22. However, the Chronicler was not a mere expositor of his earlier source or a simple compiler of materials but he used his sources selectively and creatively by means of more or less exact citations and other techniques, such as explanation, harmonization, emendation, reshaping of existing materials, up-dating, additions or omissions (especially of passages unfavorable to David), and so on (see Williamson, *1 and 2 Chronicles*, 21–23). It seems quite obvious that the Chronicler's purpose and interests must have determined the nature of his use of 2 Samuel and of his other sources. It is not far wrong to claim that to him David was the model king and his reign was the ideal period in Israel's history as a whole. Such an evaluation of David and his kingship led, no doubt, to certain major omissions of large blocks of material, such as 2 Sam 1–4; 11:2–12:25; 13:1–21:17; 22; 23:1–7 (cf. McKenzie, *The Chronicler's Use of the Deuteronomistic History,* 36). On the other hand, by incorporating additional material, the Chronicler was able to stress David's cultic interests which resulted, according to the Chronicler, in the creation and organization of the Jerusalem cult (cf. 1 Chr 15:2–24; 16:4–42; for more details, see Kirkpatrick, 22–23).

The use of 2 Samuel in the Books of Kings is less clear. It is likely that 1 Kgs 1–2 forms part of the so-called SN, and the apparent citations of, and allusions to, 2 Sam in 1 Kgs 1–2 (see for instance, 1:48; 2:4, 31–33) may be simply due to the same author or editor/s (for a contrasting view, see McCarter, 13). In any case, the possible citations from, and allusions to, 2 Sam (cf. 1 Kgs 5:17–19 [3–5]; 8:15–20) must be seen in the wider context of the Deuteronomistic history as a whole, taking into account also the subsequent editorial work. Quite prominent in the Deuteronomistic history is the promise-tradition of 2 Sam 7 (cf. for example 1 Kgs 8:25; 9:5; 11:12; 2 Kgs 8:19; 21:7).

2 Samuel and the Prophetical books (particularly Isaiah, Micah, Jeremiah, and Ezekiel) have in common certain Davidic themes and messianic motifs (cf. e.g., Isa 4:2; 9:2–7; 11:1–5, 10; 16:5; Jer 17:25; 23:5–6; 30:9; Ezek 34:23–24; 37:24–25; Hos 3:5; Mic 5:1–4). However, in the absence of direct citations it is difficult to say whether or not the prophets were familiar with the actual materials now contained in 2 Samuel. On the other hand, there is little doubt that the prophets knew of, and attached great importance to, the Davidic traditions including the divine promise (or covenant) to the house of David (see for instance, Isa 55:3–4; Ezek 34:23–24).

The two essential elements of this promise were the continuance of the Davidic royal line (cf. 2 Sam 7:13, 16; Isa 55:3; Ezek 34:23) and the father-son relationship between God and the Davidic king (see 2 Sam 7:14; Pss 2:7; 89:27–28 [26–27]). Perhaps the most obvious, but not the only, channel of this knowledge or tradition may have been Israel's cult, especially the royal psalms (such as Pss 2, 18, 72, 110, 132, etc.).

Also in the Psalter the evaluation of the interdependence is a difficult task, and a very good example of this particular problem is provided by Ps 89:4–5;20–38 (3–4;19–37). In this instance there is no agreement among scholars as to the precise nature of the obvious synoptic relationship between the Samuel pericope and the relevant section in Ps 89. Can it be claimed that 2 Sam 7:1–17 is dependent upon Ps 89 (as for instance, has been argued by G. W. Ahlström, *Psalm 89: Eine Liturgie aus dem Ritual des Leidenden Königs* [Lund: CWK Gleerup, 1959] 182–90) or is the psalm a reshaped and adapted version of Nathan's oracle in 2 Sam (as claimed by Mettinger [*King and Messiah,* 256]) or do both versions of this oracle go back to a common source or an original prophecy, even though their respective "histories" may have been considerably different (for further details, see *Form/Structure/Setting* of 7:1–17)? These possibilities show that any solution is, at its best, a tentative one. We are inclined to favor the third main suggestion (cf. also J. L. McKenzie, "The Dynastic Oracle: II Samuel 7," *TS* 8 [1947] 195, 215).

Ps 132 is also closely linked with our discussion, and vv 11–12 clearly refer to 2 Sam 7:12–16. Veijola (*Verheissung in der Krise,* 75) has well argued that this psalm probably reflects the redactional sequence and structure of 2

Sam 6–7, and therefore may be dependent (at least in this respect) upon 2 Sam (see also J. R. Porter, *JTS* 5 [1954] 161–73).

Unequivocal references to the Davidic stories are found in the so-called psalm titles or historical headings (see Pss 3, 7, 18, 30, 34, 51, 52, 54, 56, 57, 59, 60, 63, and 142). It is usually thought that these headings are not original. They reflect, most likely, the interpretation of the psalms by subsequent generations, especially since there is often little or no obvious relationship between the contents of the respective psalms and their historical notes. This process of "historization" was carried even further by the versions, such as LXX, Targum, and Peshitta (see Childs, *JSS* 16 [1971] 143). All the above historical notes, with the exception of Ps 7, have clear allusions to incidents and persons attested in the Books of Samuel although there are some minor problems with the superscriptions of Ps 34 (cf. 1 Sam 21:10) and Ps 60 (cf. 2 Sam 8:13); Ps 30 refers to the dedication of the temple. This particular understanding of the psalms in terms of the Davidic stories is not entirely unexpected or unjustified in view of the strong tradition that David was both a skillful musician and a composer of songs (see *Form/Structure/Setting* of 2 Sam 22:1–51). This information is explicitly stated in 1 Sam 16:18, 23; 2 Sam 22:1; 23:1 (cf. also 2 Chr 29:27; Neh 12:36) and, particularly, in the late Qumran composition, 11QPs[a] DavComp (see J. A. Sanders, *The Psalms Scroll of Qumran 11 [11QPs[a]]*, DJD 4 [Oxford: Clarendon Press, 1956] 92) where we read that David wrote four thousand and fifty psalms and songs for cultic use. One may also note the old traditional view that David was the author of the Book of Psalms (cf. A. Cohen, *The Psalms* [Hindhead, Surrey: Soncino Press, 1945] xi; see also Mark 12:36–37; Acts 2:25; 4:25; Rom 11:9). In this connection of special interest is 2 Sam 22:1–51 which corresponds to Ps 18. Both versions differ only on minor points, and many scholars have accepted the psalm's explicit claim (in its heading) to Davidic authorship (see *Form/Structure/Setting* to 2 Sam 22:1–51). The psalm seems to consist of two parts both of which may be early. However, it is not easy to decide whether or not they were actually composed by David. Nevertheless, the psalm has been associated with him, and therefore it came to be inserted into the so-called Samuel Appendix as a poetic summary of David's life and experiences. See also 2 Sam 23:1–7.

The Jewish expectations of the Davidic messiah were, to a large extent, associated with the Davidic covenant; the starting point of this hope may well have been the prophecy of Nathan in some form or other. Unfortunately, the history of this pericope and the tracing of its influence seem to be a problematic undertaking, unless the dynastic oracle had attained its present form already in the time of David, which seems less likely (see *Form/Structure/Setting* of 2 Sam 7:1–17).

This messianic theme had a very great importance for the NT, and it is essentially on this point that 2 Sam makes its main contribution to the NT as a whole. In the NT direct citations from 2 Sam as well as from the other historical books are very few in number. For the sake of comparison, we note the statistics provided by Ellis (*Paul's Use of the Old Testament*, 11,150–52). According to him, Paul quotes the OT ninety-three times. Thirty-three citations come from the Pentateuch, twenty-five from Isaiah, nineteen from

the Psalms while only two are derived from 2 Samuel. As regards the use of
2 Samuel in the NT as a whole, Nestle-Aland's *Novum Testamentum Graeca*
(Stuttgart: Deutsche Bibelstiftung, 1981, 749) lists forty-eight citations and
allusions. However, of these only Rom 15:9 (see 2 Sam 22:50 = Ps 18:50
[in LXX Ps 17:50]); 2 Cor 6:18 (see 2 Sam 7:14); Heb 1:5b (see 2 Sam
7:14); and Rev 21:7 (see 2 Sam 7:14) could be regarded as either citations
or free, adapted quotations. The rest are more or less plausible allusions,
and Fitzmyer (*NTS* 7 [1961] 298) has remarked that this type of usage is
occasionally reminiscent of the so-called *style anthologique* in which OT expressions and phrases have been worked "into the very fabric of the composition,
in a manner which resembles a *cento*" (298).

In general, the OT citations have served "to secure confirmation of some
NT statement by an authority respected by the Jews . . ." (K. Grobel, "Quotations," *IDB* 3 [1962] 977). Thus an essential purpose of many NT quotations
and allusions, as far as they refer to Jesus, was to provide a proof that Jesus
was indeed the expected Davidic messiah. However, the wider context shows
that only the life, death, and resurrection of Jesus do indicate the *true nature*
of his messiahship. Jesus was indeed the "Son of David" (see for instance,
Matt 1:1; 9:27; 21:9, 15; Mark 10:47) yet there is more than meets the eye
(cf. Mark 12:35–37; Acts 2:29–36; Rom 1:3–4)!

An interesting allusion to 2 Sam 5:6–8 may be Matt 21:1–14 (see Gordon,
51). The somewhat difficult Samuel pericope depicts David's capture of Jerusalem, which eventually resulted, so it has been argued, in the exclusion of
the blind and the lame from the temple (הבית; 2 Sam 5:8). On the other
hand, in the Gospel of Matthew, Jesus as the "Son of David" entered Jerusalem
not as a conquering warrior king but as a gentle and righteous ruler, riding
on a donkey (Matt 21:5, 9); he expelled the extortioners from the house of
God (Matt 21:12) but *the lame* and *the blind* came to him in the temple and
he healed them (Matt 21:14). Thus there may be a sort of typological comparison in which the characteristic escalation or heightening in the antitype has
taken the form of a contrasting reversal (cf. Goppelt, *Typos,* 18). In Gordon's
(51) view the point of this typological allusion is "to show how our Lord's
exercise of his kingly power differs from David's." Jesus has come to bless
and to set things right!

Although it is not certain that the original participants or readers were
aware of this hypothetical, implicit typology, nevertheless, the possibility remains. The collocation of the "blind" and the "lame," as such, is not unusual
(cf. Matt 11:5; 15:30).

Some scholars (e.g., Ackroyd, 162; McCarter, 389) believe that some elements in the story of Jesus' betrayal probably allude to the episode of David's
flight from Jerusalem and to his betrayal by Ahithophel, in 2 Sam 15–17,
and that thus the NT account may have been enriched by its OT counterpart
(compare, e.g., John 18:1 with 2 Sam 15:23 [the crossing of Kidron] and
Matt 27:5 with 2 Sam 17:23 in the LXX version [the suicide of Ahithophel]).

All in all, we can conclude that 2 Samuel or its component parts provided
both an impressive comprehensive picture of David and his reign and also
inspiration and support for a number of theological themes (cf. Kruse, *VT*
35 [1985] 140).

2 Samuel

Report of Saul's Death (1:1–16)

Bibliography

Boecker, H. J. *Redeformen des Rechtslebens im Alten Testament.* WMANT 14. Neukirchen-Vluyn: Neukirchener Verlag, 1964. **Grønbaek, J. H.** "Juda und Amalek." *ST* 18 (1964) 26–45. **Hauer, C. E., Jr.** "The Shape of Saulide Strategy." *CBQ* 31 (1969) 153–67. **Jastrow, M., Jr.** "Dust, Earth, and Ashes as Symbols of Mourning among the Ancient Hebrews." *JAOS* 20 (1899) 133–50. **Keel, O.** "Der Bogen als Herrschaftssymbol." *ZDPV* 93 (1977) 141–77. **Koizumi, T.** "On the Battle of Gilboa." *AJBI* 2 (1976) 61–78. **Mabee, C.** "David's Judicial Exoneration." *ZAW* 92 (1980) 89–107. **Margalit, B.** "Ugaritic Lexicography 1." *RB* 89 (1982) 418–23. **Oren, E.** "Ziklag: A Biblical City on the Edge of the Negev." *BA* 45 (1982) 155–66. **Ward, E. F. de.** "Mourning Customs in 1, 2 Samuel." *JJS* 23 (1972) 1–27; 145–66.

Translation

[1] *After the death of Saul, David returned from smiting the Amalekites.[a] He[b] had been in Ziklag two days* [2] *when on the third day there came a man from Saul's camp,[a] with his clothes rent and dust on his head. When he came to David, he fell to the ground,[b] showing his respect.[c]* [3] *David said to him, "Where have you come from?" "I have escaped from the Israelite camp," he replied.* [4] *"Tell me, what happened?" David asked him. "The[a] army fled from the battle and many[b] of them fell and died," he answered, "even Saul and his son Jonathan are dead."* [5] *"How do you know that Saul and his son Jonathan are dead?"[a] said David to the young man who[b] had brought the news.* [6] *The young man[a] explained,[b] "I happened by chance to be[c] on Mount Gilboa[d] when I saw Saul leaning upon his spear, while the chariots[e] and horsemen[f] were already close by.* [7] *Turning round, he saw me and called out to me. In reply I said, 'Here I am.'* [8] *Then he asked me, 'Who are you?' and I answered[a] 'I am an Amalekite.'* [9] *Thereupon he said to me, 'Stand beside me and kill me for the hand of death[a] has seized me although I am still alive.'[b]* [10] *So I stood beside him and killed[a] him for I knew that he would not survive after he had been severely wounded. Then I took the crown that was upon his head and the armlet[b] that was upon his arm, and I have brought them here to my lord."* [11] *David took hold of his garments[a] and tore them, and all the men with him did likewise.* [12] *So they lamented, wept, and fasted until evening for Saul and his son Jonathan, and for the people of Yahweh,[a] the house of Israel, because they had fallen by the sword.* [13] *David said to the young man who had brought him the news, "Where are you from?" "I am the son of a protected alien,[a] an Amalekite," he replied.* [14] *Then David asked him, "How is it that you were not afraid to raise[a] your hand to destroy the anointed one of Yahweh?"* [15] *David then called one of his[a] young men and said, "Come and strike[b] him down!" So he struck him down and he died.* [16] *At the same time, David said to him, "Your blood[a] be upon your own head for your mouth has testified against you when you said, 'I[b] myself killed the anointed one of Yahweh.'"*

Notes

1.a. Reading הָעֲמָלֵקִי with some MSS and Syr. MT has הָעֲמָלֵק which, unless it is a scribal error, may give the reader a choice between the proper name "Amalek" (עֲמָלֵק; so G, Vg) and the gentilic noun "Amalekite" (הָעֲמָלֵקִי) or, collectively, "Amalekites."

1.b. MT has "and *David* had been . . ."; the repetition of "David" is unnecessary, and the omission is supported by Vg.

2.a. Lit., "from the army (or "camp"), from Saul." This may be a hendiadys (see Williams, *Syntax*, § 72) and therefore we render: "from Saul's camp." G has understood מֵעַם שָׁאוּל "from Saul" as "from the people of Saul" (i.e., מֵעַם שָׁאוּל).

2.b. G^{LA} add ἐπὶ πρόσωπον ("upon [his] face" = עַל פָּנָיו). This idiom is well attested in the OT (cf. 2 Sam 9:6; 1 Kgs 18:7; Ruth 2:10), but there is no need to alter the MT.

2.c. The Heb. וַיִּשְׁתַּחוּ (often translated "and he did homage") is now regarded as the hishtaph conjugation of חוה "to bow down." (See *HALAT*, 283–84; cf. also J. A. Emerton, "The Etymology of *hištaḥᵃwāh*," *OTS* 20 [1977] 41–55; G. I. Davies, "A Note on the Etymology of *HIŠTAḤᴬWÂH*," *VT* 39 [1979] 493–95.) It is just possible that the last two verbs in v 2 form a sort of verbal hendiadys, although it is usually the first verb that qualifies the second (see Lambdin, *Biblical Hebrew*, § 173).

4.a. The direct speech is introduced by the recitative אשׁר (see Williams, *Syntax*, § 467); however, this particle could be regarded as the beginning of an object clause (see GKC, § 157c).

4.b. The Heb. הרבה "many (of them)" is taken as the subj of the verb "fell" (see *HALAT*, 245), although it appears to be a hiph inf abs from רבה "be many." Cf. also Jonah 4:11.

5.a. MT has the sg form מת "are dead," which agrees with the nearer subj (Saul).

5.b. Syr offers a different version: "David said to the young man, 'Show me how Saul and his son Jonathan died.'" However, the reply seems to support the MT.

6.a. Omitting המגיד לו "who had brought him the news," following G and Syr; the phrase may be an unnecessary repetition from v 5.

6.b. Lit., "said."

6.c. Several MSS read נקראתי "I was called" for נקריתי "I happened to be," but the latter reading is more likely in our context. The two verbs are often confused or their respective forms are not infrequently interchanged (see GKC, § 75rr). This may explain the use of נקרא instead of נקרה. Usually an inf abs before a verb emphasizes the verbal idea; hence, perhaps, "it was entirely by chance that I happened to be . . ." On the other hand, it is possible that at the beginning of a statement there may be little if any emphasis (see GKC, § 113o).

6.d. גלבע "Gilboa" is regarded by some as a comparative form of גבע "hill"; see *HALAT*, 183.

6.e. רכב is, most likely, a collective noun, hence "chariots."

6.f. MT reads בעלי הפרשׁים, which may mean either "owners of horses" or "owners of horsemen" (cf. G οἱ ἱππάρχαι "commanders of cavalry"). W. L. Holladay (*Lexicon*, 299) has pointed out that originally there were two slightly different words, denoting "horseman" and "horse," respectively, but now we have a homonym (see also Driver, 232; D. R. Ap-Thomas, "All the King's Horses," in Durham and Porter eds., *Proclamation and Presence*, 135–51).

8.a. Lit., "I said to him." G omits "to him."

9.a. The Heb. noun שׁבץ is a *hap. leg.* in the OT, and its meaning is not clear. The versions offer no certain tradition. So Tg has רתיתא "terror," G σκότος δεινόν "terrible darkness," Vg *angustiae* "distress," and so on (see Driver, 233). In view of the context, we suggest the paraphrase: "the hand of death"; NEB has "the throes of death."

9.b. The exact meaning of the final phrase is also uncertain, but the correctness of the MT seems to be assured by the close parallel in Job 27:3 כי כל עוד נשׁמתי בי "for my breath is still within me." The constr form כל is separated from the gen by the intervening עוד, and consequently it is often taken adverbially (see GKC, § 128e). However, it is possible that the constr relationship could be broken in certain cases (cf. Dahood, *Psalms III*, 381–82; Williams, *Syntax*, § 30). C. F. Whitley ("The Positive Force of the Hebrew Particle בל," *ZAW* 84 [1972] 217) emends כל into בל, rendering, "but *indeed* still my life is in me." However, this emendation is hardly necessary.

10.a. Most scholars regard the *wāw* before the verb as a *wāw* consecutive, and read ואמתתהו "and I killed him"; see also GKC, § 107b n.2.

10.b. The Heb. noun lacks the article, and therefore Caspari (404) suggests that the final *hē* in אצעדה represents the 3 m sg suff, namely, "his (armlet)" while others read והצעדה, without the prosthetic (?) *ʾāleph* but supplying the missing article (see Driver, 233).

11.a. K reads בבגדו "his garment" while Q and many MSS have the pl form בבגדיו which is supported by the pl pronom suff in ויקרעם "and he tore them."

12.a. G must have read יהודה "Judah" for יהוה "Yahweh," but 2 Kgs 9:6 may support MT.

13.a. In MT אִישׁ בֶּן "son of a man" is in apposition to גֵּר "alien," as genus and species (see Williams, *Syntax*, § 65a); cf. also Judg 4:4; 6:8.

14.a. Lit., "to put forth your hand."

15.a. So G. However, the addition of "his" may be an interpretative explanation.

15.b. In MT the two imperatives are coordinated in an asyndetous construction (see Brockelmann, *Syntax*, § 133a), without the "and." It is possible that the first imperative functions merely as a hortatory particle (so Andersen, *The Sentence*, 56).

16.a. K has the pl noun דְּמֵי "the blood shed by you"; Q suggests the sg דְּמַךְ "your (own) blood."

16.b. The Heb. pronoun אָנֹכִי "I" is probably used emphatically (see GKC, § 135a; Meyer, *Grammatik* 3 [1972] § 93 [2b]).

Form/Structure/Setting

Vv 1–16 form a fairly clear unit which opens with the words, "After the death of Saul," indicating both a continuation and a new period (see Josh 1:1; Judg 1:1). The literary unity of this section has been disputed and it has been claimed, especially in the past, that vv 1–16 are composed of fragments from two different accounts or two sources (J and E). The usual division, with minor variations, is vv 1–4, 11–12 and vv 5–10, 13–16 (see Schulte, *Geschichtsschreibung*, 131), the latter version being regarded as more recent and less plausible (so Gressmann, 124) while the former one makes a good sense on its own. However, it is doubtful that this claim can be sufficiently substantiated although theoretically it is possible. The supposed features which are thought to point to two sources (see Budde, 193) may well be stylistic variations used by the author or editor (e.g., אִישׁ "man" in v 2 and נַעַר "young man" in vv 5, 6).

Another difficult problem is the relationship between the two parallel accounts of Saul's death in 1 Sam 31:1–7 and 2 Sam 1:1–16. Essentially they agree but there is one major divergence: in the former account Saul kills himself (1 Sam 31:4) while in the latter narrative it is the Amalekite who kills Saul in compliance with the king's command (2 Sam 1:10). Both stories cannot very well be right on this point (but cf. Goldman, 187), consequently some scholars feel that it is the Amalekite's version that rings true (so Mauchline, 197). Nevertheless, at least in the present arrangement it must have been fairly clear to the readers that the Amalekite was exaggerating his own role in this particular episode and that he eventually received his due "reward." Obviously, David had to take the Amalekite's version at its face value, and act accordingly because this report was the first intimation of Saul's death and, in the circumstances, there was no reason to question it. Although the Amalekite's account turned out to be partially fictitious, it was preserved because it provided an explanation as to how David came into possession of the royal insignia (v 10). To all appearances, David was prepared to fight against Saul and the people of Israel and therefore was with the Philistine forces on that fateful campaign, although in the end he was forced to withdraw before the final battle was joined. It is quite likely that David had no option, and we do not know what he might have done had he taken part in the decisive fight. In view of the ambiguous situation it is not impossible that some of David's opponents may have blamed him for his part (real or imagined) in Israel's defeat (cf. 2 Sam 16:7–8) and may have claimed that the royal insignia had been given to him by the Philistines as a token of their favor (see Whitelam, *The Just King,* 104–5). If so, then David's Amalekite campaign (1 Sam 30:1–25) and the Amalekite's report (2 Sam 1:1–16) were important testimonies in order to demonstrate, contrary to appearances, that David was not involved in the routing of the Israelite army.

Comment

1 The ancestor of the Amalekites was, according to the OT tradition, one of the grandsons of Esau (Gen 36:12; 1 Chr 1:36), and thus they were linked with the Edomites. In the biblical stories the Amalekites appear, mainly, as a nomadic desert tribe (see G. M. Landes, *IDB* 1:101–2), usually found in southern Palestine and the Sinai peninsula.

There existed a perpetual enmity between Amalek and Israel, dating from Israel's settlement in Canaan (Exod 17:8–16; Num 14:43–45). This hostility or even blood feud between the two peoples persisted, only to be resolved by a total extermination of the Amalekites (Deut 25:17–19; 1 Sam 15). See also J. H. Grønbaek, "Juda und Amalek," *ST* 18 (1964) 26–45.

Ziklag was a royal grant given to David by Achish, his Philistine overlord of Gath, and it remained the private property of the kings of Judah (1 Sam 27:6). The location of Ziklag is uncertain but its identification with Tell-el-Khuweilfeh (some fourteen miles or twenty-three kilometers north of Beersheba) has been widely accepted (see Simons, *Texts,* § 1633). A. F. Rainey (*IDBSup,* 984–85) has argued, however, that a more likely site is Tell-el-Maliḥah, some eighteen miles (twenty-nine kilometers) east of Gaza; Oren (*BA* 45 [1982] 155–57) has suggested Tell esh-Sharia in the northwestern Negeb.

2 The Amalekite is said to have come from the army of Israel or their camp, but it is not stated whether he served as a fighting man and was, in a sense, a deserter, or whether he had been forced to join the Israelite army in some other capacity. Landes (101–2) has proposed that the Amalekite may have been a mercenary in the Philistine forces but this seems less likely because he recognized not only Saul (by the insignia?) but also Jonathan's body.

The fact that the Amalekite looked like a mourner need not be an indication of his personal grief; this could well reflect the customary mourning practices (see 2 Sam 3:31 where David orders Joab to mourn for Abner whom he had murdered).

Torn clothes and dust on one's head were the usual signs of mourning (see Gen 37:34; Josh 7:6; 1 Sam 4:12; 2 Sam 13:31). This could be accompanied also by other expressions of sorrow, such as the girding on of sackcloth (2 Sam 3:31; Lam 2:10; Joel 1:8; Amos 8:10), by lying on the ground (Josh 7:6; 2 Sam 13:31), by weeping and wailing (Gen 37:35; 2 Sam 1:12; 18:33), and fasting (1 Sam 31:13; 2 Sam 3:35). For further details, see de Ward, *JJS* 23 (1972) 1–17.

3 Whitelam (*The Just King,* 100) finds in the questions and answers "traces of formal judicial language" but it is equally possible that any interested person might pose similar questions in order to obtain the desired information.

The verb נמלט "escaped" usually implies some sort of previous danger (see *THAT* 2 [1976] 421–22) which, in this instance, could be either the victorious Philistines (attacking the Israelite camp) or the Israelites who may have forced him into their service.

4 There is a similar question and answer in 1 Sam 4:16–17, and the parallel is quite striking. McCarter (*1 Samuel*, 113) regards this as "an example of the common use of a literary motif by different writers." However, the description of similar incidents may well follow a conventional literary pattern. The Amalekite's reply is somewhat reminiscent of the short battle-reports (see *Form/Structure/Setting* of 2 Sam 5:17–25).

We have rendered the Hebrew העם as "the army" although frequently it denotes the totality of Israel or the community, i.e., "the people." But it may refer also to the militia or the people organized for war or some other function (see C. Umhau Wolf, "Terminology of Israel's Tribal Organization," *JBL* 65 [1946] 45–49; G. W. Anderson, "Israel: Amphictyony: ʿAM; ḴĀHĀL; ʿĒḎĀH," in H. T. Frank and W. L. Reed, eds., *Translating and Understanding the Old Testament*, 150).

The Amalekite did not mention the death of the other sons of Saul (see 1 Sam 31:2) but he may have been ignorant of that fact. In any case, Jonathan was the heir apparent and also David's special friend. This may imply that the Amalekite may have been familiar with Israelite personalities and politics.

5 David's question tries to ascertain whether the man is telling rumors or the truth. In this verse the Amalekite is described as "the young man who had brought him the news" but this change is not a convincing argument for a different literary source.

The Heb. נער may, in some contexts, indicate a young man of noble birth (so J. Macdonald, "The Status and Role of the NAʿAR in Israelite Society," *JNES* 35 [1976] 149) but it is unlikely that our Amalekite belonged to a higher social class; he is described as a protected alien who was usually low in the social scale (see de Vaux, *Ancient Israel*, 74–75).

6 Mount Gilboa is the modern Jebel Fuquʿah, a ridge of limestone hills at the eastern end of the valley of Jezreel, and south of the hill of Moreh. It attains the height of some 1640 feet (500 meters) and it is somewhat surprising to find chariots (see de Vaux, *Ancient Israel*, 222) in action on the slopes of Mount Gilboa, assuming that this part of the Amalekite's story is right (see also George Adam Smith, *Historical Geography*, 402–3). In 1 Sam 31:3 it was the archers who had overtaken Saul but the two episodes need not be identical in all details. On the other hand, the archers may have been part of the chariot crews; however, Yadin (*Warfare*, 250) points out that the Philistine charioteers were usually armed "with the spear and not the bow."

Furthermore, it is not clear whether Saul was standing and leaning upon his spear or whether he was wounded (see 1 Sam 31:3) and therefore lying on the ground, at the same time leaning against his spear for some support (cf. Judg 16:26).

9 Saul was, apparently, severely injured (so G in 1 Sam 31:3) and therefore he ordered his own mercy killing (cf. Judg 9:54), being afraid that the Philistines would abuse and dishonor him (cf. Judg 16:25).

10 The verb נפל usually means "to fall" but the idea of being wounded may be implicit in some cases, depending upon the context. Note such expressions as ". . . fell and died" (2 Sam 1:4; 2:23).

The crown and the armlet were symbols of royal status. The crown, in particular, seems to indicate not only the authority of its wearer but also the sacred nature of his office (see L. E. Toombs, *IDB* 1:746; cf. also Exod 39:30; 2 Kgs 11:12; Ps 21:4[3]; 89:40[39]). It is unlikely that the reference is to the heavy state crown (see 2 Sam 12:30); the battle situation seems to require a lighter object, a sort of fillet as a sign of royalty. The etymology of אצעדה ("armlet") is not clear but its meaning here is obvious from the context. Egyptian and Assyrian rulers are often depicted with ornamented armlets or bracelets on their arms (see ANEP, nos. 441, 442, 617, 626).

The Amalekite brought these objects to David hoping, no doubt, for a better reward (2 Sam 4:10) than he might gain from the house of Saul. He did not say explicitly that he regarded David as Saul's successor but this seems to be implied.

David is addressed as "my lord," but it is merely an expression of common courtesy; it also avoids the direct address "to you" (O. Eissfeldt, "אדון," *TDOT* 1 [1971] 62).

11 The tearing of one's garments is usually the immediate reaction to the news of someone's death (see Gen 37:34; 2 Sam 13:31). This response would have been more appropriate directly after the news in v 4 but it is understandable that David would wish to verify the young man's report, and hence the delay. Consequently, the position of this verse need not necessarily imply that vv 5–10 are a later insertion into the narrative.

12 Lamentation, weeping, and fasting were some of the more common expressions of mourning (see *Comment* on v 2; also de Vaux, *Ancient Israel*, 59–61). The grief was, no doubt, real, but most of these responses were the expected, customary reactions to death in the family or community.

It is often argued that "the house of Israel" is tautological, inserted here after "Yahweh" had been altered (accidentally?) to "Judah" (see Driver, 233). However, the phrase may be in apposition to "the people of Yahweh"; such a collocation is not improbable (see 2 Kgs 9:6).

13 From the previous conversation David would know that the young man was a foreigner or immigrant but it is possible that he wished to establish whether the Amalekite came under Israelite jurisdiction or not (so G. C. Macholz, "Die Stellung des Königs in der israelitischen Gerichtsverfassung," *ZAW* 84 [1972] 163–64). It is doubtful, however, that it would have made any real difference to David even if the man had not been an Amalekite immigrant. Blood had been shed and therefore there existed a bloodguilt in its wider sense, and some action had to be taken. It may well be that David acted as Saul's kinsman (גאל). It is just possible that the consequences might have been different had the killing been done by an enemy in the context of a battle (cf. 1 Kgs 2:5).

The גר or "protected alien" is often mentioned in the OT, and it is very likely that his social status as well as his legal position underwent considerable changes during the biblical period (see de Vaux, *Ancient Israel*, 74–76; D. Kellermann, "גור," *TDOT* 2 [1977] 443–48). Usually the *gēr* was relatively poor and under divine protection (cf. Deut 10:18–19; Ps 146:9). He had certain rights in Israel (Lev 25:6; Num 35:15; Deut 14:29) but he did not have all the privileges enjoyed by the Israelites. In the pre-exilic period he may not have been fully liable for breach of Israel's laws (see Deut 14:21) but this would hardly apply to bloodguilt.

The expression יהוה משיח "the anointed of Yahweh" occurs eleven times in the OT, and with the exception of Lam 4:20 all the other references are in the Books of Samuel. This phrase points to the close relationship between Yahweh and the king; the phrase "the anointed of Israel" is not attested. One of the main consequences of the anointing was the inviolability of the king (see 1 Sam 24:11[10]; 26:9, 11, 23; 2 Sam 19:22[21]).

Anointing as such was not confined to Israel (see Kutsch, *Salbung,* 33–72; Mettinger, *King and Messiah,* 185–232), but it is questionable whether the Israelite practice was an imitation of similar rites in Egypt or among the Hittites (cf. Ishida, *Royal Dynasties,* 75).

The above title is important for the evaluation of 2 Sam 1:1–16. If it is argued, as some have done, that it is "highly probable that Saul was never anointed" (Mettinger, 197) then the title, as applied to Saul, is an anachronism; but even so the essence of the story would remain unchanged. Saul had become king because it was believed that Yahweh was with him (1 Sam 10:7; 11:6, 13), and as a divinely chosen leader he was, more or less, inviolable (see Exod 22:27[28]) whether anointed or not. It is far from certain that the inviolability of Yahweh's anointed was an invention of the later Davidic court to protect the Judean kings but it would be in the king's interests to stress such a belief (cf. Thornton, "Studies in Samuel," *CQR* 168 [1967] 416).

15 It is not necessary to assume that 2 Sam 4:10 differs substantially from the present version of the Amalekite's punishment (but see Budde, 193; Kennedy, 194). It is unlikely that the former account was meant to show that David *himself* had killed the messenger simply for bringing the *news* of Saul's death (cf. Schulte, *Geschichtsschreibung,* 132).

16 The words "your blood be upon your own head" may be a formula (or a variation of such an expression) used to emphasize the guilt of the criminal and, at the same time, to protect the man who carried out the death penalty (or who ordered it) from any possible consequences (see Boecker, *Redeformen,* 139; K. Koch, "Der Spruch 'Sein Blut bleibe auf seinem Haupt' und die israelitische Auffassung vom vergossenes Blut," *VT* 12 [1962] 413; H. Christ, *Blutvergiessen im Alten Testament,* 110–11).

Explanation

The death of Saul is movingly described in 1 Sam 31:1–7 while the Amalekite's divergent version of this event (2 Sam 1:6–10) seems to contain some deliberate distortions. This would not surprise the Israelite readers because traditionally the Amalekites were their bitter enemies and savage raiders (cf. Exod 17:8; Num 14:45; Judg 10:12; 1 Sam 30). Similarly, they may have regarded also the young Amalekite sojourner as little more than a plunderer of the dead although, ironically, he was put to death for his lie, claiming that he himself had killed King Saul. Of course, there may be also other explanations for the Amalekite's story but anyone who knows the alternative account would naturally assume that the Amalekite was lying for personal gain. Even if vv 5–10 are a later insertion into the narrative, they do not claim to be a *correction* of the other story but simply the Amalekite's version of events which, among other things, provides the only explanation as to how David came to be in possession of the royal insignia.

Irrespective of whether the Amalekite told the truth or not, David acted correctly from the legal point of view; the man had "confessed" his crime and therefore no further evidence was required. The Amalekite's fate was an unmistakable warning to any potential regicide as well as an indication of the sacrosanct nature of Yahweh's anointed.

Since most, if not all, readers would be aware of the partially fictitious nature of the Amalekite's story, it seems that its primary function was to counter any possible rumors or accusations leveled against David. Had not Saul been David's bitter enemy? Had not David and his men been in the Philistine ranks shortly before the battle of Gilboa? Was not David in possession of the royal insignia? It would not require much imagination for some to argue that David had helped to bring about Saul's death and was duly rewarded by the Philistines. If such a situation existed then the present story as well as the account of David's defeat of the Amalekites (1 Sam 30), would be the best defense of David: he simply could not be in two places at the same time.

Our story may contain also an implicit symbolism: the old order is at an end and David is on the threshold of a new venture. Saul, the king of Israel, was dead and the Israelite army was scattered and demoralized. The Philistines were once more taking over Israelite cities (1 Sam 31:7), and David's land grant from the Philistines, namely, Ziklag, lay in ruins. It is at this point that the Amalekite brought the royal crown and armlet to David, little realizing that he was prostrating before the future king of Judah and all Israel. The man's actions were, most likely, motivated by a hope for reward and yet, unintentionally, he was the instrument by means of which Yahweh proleptically "crowned" the future king of Israel.

David's Lament over Saul and Jonathan (1:17–27)

Bibliography

Eissfeldt, O. "Zwei verkannte militär-technische Termini im Alten Testament." *VT* 5 (1955) 232–38. **Fenton, T. L.** "Ugaritica: Biblica." *UF* 1 (1969) 65–70. ———. "Comparative Evidence in Textual Study: M. Dahood on 2 Sam. i 21 and *CTA* 19 (1 *Aqht*), I, 44–45." *VT* 29 (1979) 162–70. **Fokkelman, J. P.** "שדי תרומות in II Sam 1:21a: A Non-existent Crux." *ZAW* 91 (1979) 290–92. **Freedman, D. N.** "The Refrain in David's Lament over Saul and Jonathan." *Ex Orbe Religionum*, ed. C. J. Bleeker, S. G. F. Brandon, M. Simon. Lugduni Batavorum: E. J. Brill, 1972. **Gevirtz, S.** *Patterns in the Early Poetry of Israel.* Studies in Ancient Civilization, 32. Chicago: The University of Chicago Press, 1963. **Holladay, W. L.** "Form and Word-play in David's Lament over Saul and Jonathan." *VT* 20 (1970) 153–89. **Jahnow, H.** *Das Hebräische Leichenlied im Rahmen der Völkerdichtung.* BZAW 36. Giessen: Alfred Töpelmann, 1923. **Keel, O.** "Der Bogen als Herrschaftssymbol." *ZDPV* 93 (1977) 141–77. **Nysse, R. W.** "An Analysis of the Greek Witnesses to the Text of the Lament of David." *The Hebrew and Greek Texts of Samuel.* Ed. E. Tov. Jerusalem: Academon, 1980. **Sekine, M.** "Lyric Literature in the Davidic-Solomonic Period in the Light of the History of Israelite Literature." *Studies in the Period of David and Solomon and Other Essays*, ed. T. Ishida. Winona Lake, IN: Eisenbrauns, 1982. **Shea, W. H.** "David's Lament." *BASOR* 221 (1976) 141–44. **Stuart, D.** *Studies in Early Hebrew Meter.* HSM 13. Missoula, MT: Scholars Press, 1976. **Watson, W. G. E.** "Verse-pattern in Ugaritic, Akkadian and Hebrew Poetry." *UF* 7 (1975) 489–91. **Woźniak, J.** "Drei verschiedene literarische Beschreibungen des Bundes zwischen Jonathan und David." *BZ* 27 (1983) 213–18.

Translation

[17] *David uttered this lament* [a] *over Saul and Jonathan his son,* [18] *saying, (For the instruction of the people of Judah.* [a] *A Lament called "Bow."* [b] *Derived from the Book of Jashar.)* [c]
[19] *"Israel, your Splendor* [a] *is slain on your heights!* [b]
How are the warriors fallen!
[20] *Tell it not in Gath,*
tell [a] *not the news of victory in the streets of Ashkelon;*
lest the daughters of the Philistines rejoice,
lest the daughters of the uncircumcised exult.
[21] *Hills of Gilboa,* [a] *let there be* [b] *no dew,*
let there be [b] *no rain on you, mountain slopes!* [c]
For there the warriors' shields were defiled,
defiled was the shield of Saul, no [d] *longer anointed* [e] *with oil.*
[22] *From the blood of the slain,*
from the fat of the warriors,
the arrows [a] *of Jonathan did not turn back,*
the sword of Saul used not to return empty.
[23] *Saul and Jonathan who were beloved and gracious,* [a]
neither in life nor in death were they parted.

They were far swifter than eagles,[b]
they were far stronger than lions.
24 *Daughters of Israel, weep for*[a] *Saul,*
  who clothed you[b] *with ornate*[c] *scarlet garments,*
  who set ornaments of gold on your dress.
25 *How are the warriors fallen in the midst of the battle!*[a]
  Jonathan is slain on your heights![b]
26 *I am heartbroken over you, my brother;*
  Jonathan, you have been exceedingly gracious to me.
  Your love to me was wonderful,[a]
  surpassing the love of women.
27 *How are the warriors fallen!*
  Lost are the weapons of war!"

Notes

17.a. "Lament" is probably a cognate acc, although it is definite in form (cf. GKC, §117q).

18.a. G^L has before "Judah": Ισραηλ καί "Israel and"; however, this seems to be an exegetical addition.

18.b. "Bow" (קשת) is lacking in G^A but is attested in other major versions. The omission may be due to the failure to understand the significance of קשת in this context.

18.c. Tg reads ספרא דאוריתא "book of instruction," which may be an interpretive rendering of MT.

19.a. G has στηλωσον "set up a pillar" (similarly also Tg); however, it presupposes the consonantal text of MT.

19.b. G contains a doublet: "for the slain" = על מתיך, which seems to be a partial dittogr of על במותיך "on your heights."

20.a. Many Heb. MSS and versions add the conj "and" (ו), but MT is preferable as the shorter reading; the asyndetous construction appears to be more effective.

21.a. MT may offer a choice between הרים בגלבע "hills in Gilboa" and הרי הגלבע "hills of Gilboa"; see Driver, 236. We have opted for the latter alternative, although it is possible that the preposition ב "in" may justifiably intervene in a constr chain or bound structure (cf. Gevirtz, *Patterns*, 85 n.40; Williams, *Syntax*, § 30).

21.b. The phrase "let there be" is supplied on the basis of the context (cf. GKC, § 147c); lit., "no dew and no rain." The versions, too, are forced to provide a suitable verb, but there is no need to emend the text (see the Ugaritic parallel in Gibson, *Canaanite Myths*, 115; cf. Fenton, *VT* 29 [1979] 164).

21.c. "Mountain slopes" is a rendering of the problematic ושדי תרומת, assuming that the text is not corrupt. The more traditional rendering used to be "fields of offerings" (KJV, RV, RSV^mg). The initial *wāw* may be either an emphasizing particle or, more likely, a *wāw* introducing the voc (see Dahood, *Psalms III*, 400–402). We retain the MT, taking the phrase as a semantic equivalent of מרומי שדה "high fields" in Judg 5:18 (see Fokkelman, *ZAW* 91 [1979] 290). Although תרומה usually means "offering" (see BDB, 929), the root is רום "be high, exalted," and therefore it is possible that its meaning here is the same as that of מרום "height." The versions, on the whole, do not offer any real help, but they seem to support the consonantal text.

21.d. Syr and Tg omit the negative particle, thus describing Saul as the anointed one. Freedman (*Ex Orbe*, 123) takes בלי "not" as an asseverative particle, hence "duly anointed with oil."

21.e. The Heb. משיח "anointed one" is usually used of persons and not of things (BDB, 603), and therefore the present text may imply that Saul had not been anointed, unless it means "*no longer* the anointed one." We follow many Heb. MSS in reading משוח, which is a pass ptcp ("anointed"); if so, it could describe Saul's shield (see Mettinger, *King and Messiah*, 200). The confusion between *wāw* and *yōd* is frequent in written MSS.

22.a. The Heb. קשת "bow" may stand for "arrows"; so already Tg, which adds גירי "arrows of (the bow of Jonathan)." It could be noted that קשת is a feminine noun while the verb is masculine; this may be a lapse of gender due to the intervening words. Some scholars emend the verb נשוג to תשוג "used to turn back," which provides a good parallel to תשוב "used to return" in v 22c, thus achieving concord with its subj.

23.a. "Beloved and gracious" may be in apposition to "Saul and Jonathan" and need not form the predicate (see Driver, 238). We regard the phrase as a relative clause (cf. Williams, *Syntax*, § 538).

23.b. The word order in Heb. may indicate additional emphasis, stressing the comparison.

24.a. Some MSS have על "over" instead of the less frequent אל which, in the present context, has probably the same meaning. No emendation is called for.

24.b. The Heb. equivalent of "you" is an obj suff on the ptcp, but it is masc in form while the antecedent is "daughters of Israel." However, no correction is required because the 2 f pl verbal suff is not attested in the OT (see Budde, 199–200). Although the ptcp is already definite, due to the suff, it has the article (cf. GKC, § 116f) which, in this case, may be equivalent to the relative pronoun (see Williams, *Syntax*, § 82).

24.c. עדנים is usually taken to mean "luxuries" or "dainties," but one would expect an article of clothing. Therefore some scholars emend it to סדינים "fine linen"; so Smith, 263. G points to עדיים "ornaments," using the same word here as for עדי "ornament" in v 24c. Perhaps no alteration is needed since it is possible that עדנים may denote "luxurious ornaments" (cf. Holladay, *Lexicon*, 266). Some versions take the word adverbially, e.g., RSV "daintily," RV "delicately." We understand עם עדנים as "together with ornaments," hence "ornate (scarlet garments)"; for this use of עם "with," see Cant 1:11; 5:1.

25.a. Gressmann (123) deletes the whole verse as a bad variant of v 19, while Nowack (154) regards בתוך המלחמה "in the midst of the battle" as a gloss. However, we are dealing with three refrains (vv 19, 25, 27), which are not identical and need not be so. The versions support MT.

25.b. This phrase, too, has caused problems, and there are some variants. G^L and Theod read εἰς θάνατον ἐτραυματίσθης "in death you have been struck down." We retain the MT because the latter part of v 25b corresponds to v 19a, and "Jonathan" balances "your Splendor" (= Saul?).

26.a. Freedman (*Ex Orbe*, 123) takes the verb נפלאתה "was wonderful" as two words: נפלא אתה "you were extraordinary." This is possible, and the second *ʾāleph* may have been lost due to haplogr; it could be a case of shared consonants (cf. W. Watson, "Shared Consonants in Northwest Semitic," *Bib* 50 [1969] 93–101; but see also A. R. Millard, "Scriptio Continua," *JSS* 15 [1970] 2–15). The versions do not support this proposal, and although the form of נפלאתה is anomalous, it is capable of reasonable explanation (see GKC, § 75oo); we prefer MT.

Form / Structure / Setting

The Hebrew קינה is a funerary lament or dirge, and as such it is different from the numerous laments found in the Psalter. Neither the noun (קינה; 19 times in OT) nor the verb (קונן; 7 times in OT) occurs in the Book of Psalms. Claus Westermann ("Struktur und Geschichte der Klage im Alten Testament," *ZAW* 66 [1954] 46) has well outlined the main differences between these two literary types. The dirge or funerary lament (*Totenklage*) deals with the actual event of death and the dead, and essentially it is backward looking. It often addresses the dead in the second person, and there is no mention of God (cf. Sekine, *The Period of David and Solomon*, 5). It depicts the mournful situation and calls the hearers to lamentation. The general or distress lament (*Notklage*) is, on the other hand, forward looking and, basically, a supplication to God (see Stählin, *TDNT* 3 [1965] 148–55).

The normal *Sitz-im-Leben* or setting of the funerary lament is the house of mourning or the funeral procession itself. David's elegy, due to the specific circumstances, was composed, at least traditionally, in honor and memory of Saul and Jonathan, on the occasion of receiving the news of their death; therefore its form and structure may deviate from that of the customary funerary lament (see Budde, 196). Elegies are often composed in the so-called *qînāh* or unbalanced meter (3+2; cf. Stuart, *Hebrew Meter*, 15) and they are frequently introduced by אֵיךְ or אֵיכָה "how"; see Lam 1:1; 2:1; 4:1; Jer 9:18[19].

The funerary dirge may have originally been part of the cult of the dead (so Fohrer, *Introduction*, 275) but in the Israelite setting there was not, apparently, such a cult, and therefore the dirge may have been a modified relic of ancient mourning customs and may have served, among other things, as a eulogy for the dead and as an expression of grief.

Apart from the personal dirge, such as David's elegy, there existed also the so-called collective or political dirge, which bewailed the fate of peoples or cities (see Lam 1 and 2), and the prophetic dirge, which portrayed the imminent disaster in realistic terms (cf. Ezek 26:17–18; Eissfeldt, *Introduction*, 95).

David's elegy comprises vv 19–27 while vv 17–18 form its introduction. The Davidic authorship is occasionally disputed but, as Budde (196) has remarked, it can neither be proved nor can it be seriously challenged. The contents of the lament clearly favor the traditional view although some have assumed that the elegy was written by an unknown poet speaking in the name of David (cf. Grønbaek, *Aufstieg*, 221; T. L. Fenton, *UF* 1 [1969] 68). However, there is a strong tradition that David was famous for his literary activities (see 11QPsᵃ DavComp in J. A. Sanders, *The Psalms Scroll of Qumran Cave 11*, DJD 4 [Oxford: Clarendon Press, 1965] 92), and therefore there is no compelling reason to question seriously the Davidic authorship. Stolz (189) assumes the possibility that an originally short dirge (vv 26–27) may have been later expanded either by David or some other poet.

It is often noted that the dirge comes rather late in the sequence of events in 2 Sam 1; a possible explanation is that originally the account did not include the elegy, and that at some later stage an editor took it from the collection of poems called the Book of Jashar, and inserted it in its present place after the narrative account. This would also explain the reference to the above anthology in v 18.

We know very little about the Book of Jashar (סֵפֶר הַיָּשָׁר) apart from the fact that it is quoted also in Josh 10:12–13 and, possibly, in 1 Kgs 8:12–13 (= 8:53a in G; cf. Eissfeldt, *Introduction*, 133) if "the Book of the Song" (so G) is an error for the Book of Jashar, i.e., ᾠδή "song" may be a translation of the Heb. שִׁיר "song," which may be a scribal error (transposition of letters?) for יָשָׁר. Both Josh 10:12–13 and 2 Sam 1:19–27 suggest that the collection may have dealt with the heroic exploits of the Israelites. This ancient anthology was, apparently, similar to the Book of the Wars of Yahweh (Num 21:14), but it is unlikely that the two collections were identical, although Yahweh could be described as יָשָׁר "just" (cf. Deut 32:4; Ps 25:8).

Whether the Book of Jashar was of Judean origin (so E. Nielsen, *Oral Tradition*, SBT 11 [London: SCM Press, 1954] 52) or of Ephraimite provenance (so J. Dus, "Gibeon: eine Kultstätte des ŠMŠ und die Stadt des benjaminitischen Schicksals," *VT* 10 [1960] 361) is difficult to decide since the two clear examples point in different directions. Furthermore, the exact translation of הַיָּשָׁר is uncertain; the more common renderings are "the Upright" (NEBᵐᵍ, RSVᵐᵍ) and "the Just" (JB); see also J. A. Soggin, *Joshua*, OTL (London: SCM Press, 1972) 122.

There is some uncertainty as to the actual beginning of the elegy. It has been argued that the introductory verb ויאמר "he said" in v 18 should be immediately followed by the opening words of the poem, as in 2 Sam 3:33; 1 Macc 9:21 (cf. Gevirtz, *Patterns*, 73–76; Holladay, *VT* 20 [1970] 162–68) and that therefore we should resort to emendation. However, since the elegy is clearly taken from another source, the Book of Jashar, it is plausible that ללמד בני יהודה קשת lit., "to teach the sons of Judah the bow" could be regarded as the superscription of the poem, similar to the headings of many biblical psalms (cf. Ps 60:1; see also 2 Sam 22:1 and Ps 18:1). If so, it could be rendered, "For the instruction of the people of Judah. (A Lament called) 'Bow'" (cf. Jer 9:19[20]). The word "Bow" (קשת) is, most likely, the title of the elegy, referring either to Jonathan's favorite weapon (v 22; cf. also 1 Sam 18:4: 20:20) or, more likely, to Jonathan himself; however, Saul or both Saul and Jonathan are possible candidates. For the latter alternative there may be a parallel in the use of "the chariots of Israel and its horsemen" (2 Kgs 2:12) as an epithet of Elijah and of Elisha (2 Kgs 13:14). Also in Zech 10:4 "the battle bow" (קשת מלחמה) seems to be a designation of the ruler in question. Similarly, it is likely that "the weapons of war" (2 Sam 1:27) refers to Saul and Jonathan, not to any military equipment. In Jer 51:20 an unnamed nation (Babylon?) or its ruler is described as Yahweh's "hammer and weapon of war" (cf. Isa 13:5; Jer 50:23; Hos 1:5; see also Keel, *ZDPV* 93 [1977] 172–75).

Thus it is plausible that v 18 contains the superscription of the poem, followed by the indication of its source. The reason why this lament should be taught to the people of Judah is not given, but it may be of some relevance that the funeral laments concerning Josiah also became traditional in Judah and "were written in Lamentations" (2 Chr 35:25). Eissfeldt (*Introduction*, 133) has suggested that this type of poem was thought to have "power to arouse courage and boldness in the young men." This is possible but other reasons cannot be excluded.

The basic structural element of the elegy seems to be the refrain, "How are the warriors fallen." Its occurrences in vv 19 and 27 mark out the major inclusion, and thus indicate the beginning and the end of the dirge. This is an additional reason for regarding v 19a as the opening line of the poetic composition. The same refrain is found also in v 25, and it divides the lament into two sections: vv 19–24 and 25–27. The first is concerned with the fate and deeds of Saul and Jonathan while the latter section laments for Jonathan, and is more like an actual funerary dirge. The unity of the first section (vv 19–24) is further emphasized by vv 20 and 24, where "the daughters of the Philistines" (v 20) balances "the daughters of Israel" (v 24).

This dirge, like funerary laments in general, is characterized by the frequent contrast of *once* and *now* or *past* and *present*. It stresses the good points and qualities of the dead, and no ill is spoken of the departed. One would not expect a distortion of truth but allowance should be made for a certain amount of poetical license which would account for some of the minor inconsistencies between this lament and other relevant sources relating to Saul and Jonathan (cf. also H. L. Strack and P. Billerbeck, *Kommentar zum Neuen Testament aus Talmud und Midrasch,* vol. 4:1 [Munich: C. H. Beck'sche Verlagsbuchhandlung, 1954] 582–607).

Comment

17 The lament expresses sorrow over Saul and Jonathan; both are mentioned four times by name in the dirge, and are thus indicated as the chief *dramatis personae* of the poem. It seems that also the fourfold repetition of גבורים "warriors" in vv 19, 21, 25, 27 may be an allusion to the king and his heir, not to the fallen Israelite warriors in general although their fate is implicit in that of their leaders; in any case, the lament is over Saul and Jonathan (v 17).

18 This verse is an exegetical crux. However, since the consonantal text is supported, more or less, by all the major versions, and because a reasonable sense can be derived from it, methodologically it seems right to refrain from any emendations of the present text. For a different attitude to the problem, see Gevirtz (*Patterns,* 76) and Holladay (*VT* 20 [1970] 162–68). In our opinion, v 18 contains the superscription of the poem, giving also the name of the ancient collection from which it was taken. Therefore the actual beginning of the dirge is v 19.

It has been suggested that "Bow" is not a suitable title for an elegy (see McKane, 176). Hebrew books are often referred to by their initial word or words (cf. בראשית which designates "Genesis") or some other significant word (cf. במדבר which stands for "Numbers"). Consequently, קשת "Bow" may, perhaps, belong to the same category. However, the structure of the present form of the dirge seems to be against this suggestion; one would have to assume that the dirge has not been quoted in full (cf. 1 Chr 16:8–22 and Ps 105; 1 Chr 16:23–34 and Ps 96:1–13). NEB takes קשת as an abbreviation for קינת שניהם הזאת "this dirge over them," which is theoretically possible but hardly convincing.

19 The Heb. צבי can stand for two different words (so BDB, 840) meaning either "beauty, honor" or "gazelle." It is not impossible that both homonyms have a common etymology (see Freedman, *Ex Orbe,* 119). Driver (234) has suggested that "The Gazelle" was Jonathan's sobriquet (but see Cross, *Hebrew Epic,* 122) by which he was known among the warriors and the people in general. It may be relevant to note that in 2 Sam 2:18 Asahel is said to have been "swift as a gazelle" (cf. also 1 Chr 12:9), while Jonathan and Saul are described as being "swifter than eagles" (2 Sam 1:23). However, a more likely alternative is "The Beauty" or "The Splendor." In ancient Israel, as elsewhere, kings were often depicted as incomparably handsome and abounding in various outstanding qualities (see Judg 8:18; 1 Sam 9:2; 10:23–24; 16:12; 17:42; 2 Sam 14:25; 1 Kgs 1:6; Ps 45:3[2]; Isa 33:17). Therefore it is plausible that הצבי refers to Saul as the Splendor of Israel par excellence. This type of description was, perhaps, part of the court style, and such language often transcended the historical realities (so von Rad, *Old Testament Theology* 1 [1962] 322).

The phrase "How are the warriors fallen" occurs three times (vv 19, 25, 27) as if a sort of refrain. The second reference is explicitly associated with Jonathan, and the third may refer to Saul and Jonathan, pictured as "weapons of war"; it is possible that the first occurrence of this refrain is to be connected with Saul (as Israel's Splendor or Glory). The refrain is, most likely, an exclamation (see GKC, § 148b) but it could be taken as a rhetorical question, "How is it possible . . ." (so JB).

The Heb. במה frequently denotes a cultic high place (see P. H. Vaughan, *The Meaning of 'bāmâ' in the Old Testament: A Study of Etymological, Textual and Archaeological Evidence.* SOTSMS 3. Cambridge: Cambridge University Press, 1974), but in our setting it need not mean a "place of worship" (cf. Gevirtz, *Patterns,* 77); it may simply denote "height" or "ridge" (see K.-D. Schunck, "במה," *TDOT* 2 [1977] 140). Nevertheless, it is conceivable that later Israelites may have seen a possible association between the illegitimate high places and the tragic sacrifice "offered" on Mount Gilboa.

There is no real reason to translate על במותיך חלל as "over thy bodies of slain" (so Gevirtz, *Patterns,* 81, 95; cf. also Holladay, *VT* 20 [1970] 164). As noted above, the "warriors" (גבורים) are, most likely, Saul and Jonathan since the dirge was composed with them in mind and no other persons are explicitly mentioned. On גבורים see H. Kosmala, *TDOT* 2 [1977] 367–82. McCarter (74–75) takes על במותיך as an idiomatic expression meaning "standing erect." For a more detailed discussion, see *Comment* on 22:34.

20   This verse consists of two bicola, both examples of synonymous parallelism. However, the first one (v 20a) lacks balance since the first colon has no corresponding synonym to בחוצות "in the streets of"; cf. Amos 5:16. Consequently some scholars read ברחבות גת "in the squares of Gath" (similarly Gevirtz, Holladay). On the other hand, such an imbalance in a bicolon may well be deliberate, and there is no evidence that the Israelites observed a *strict* meter and balance in successive lines (cf. also Mic 1:10).

Gath and Ashkelon are probably representative of the Philistine cities as a whole. Gath was the city of David's overlord (1 Sam 27:5–7), and it was situated in the north of Philistia but its exact location is still uncertain (see A. F. Rainey, "Gath," *IDBSup,* 353). Tell eṣ-Ṣâfi, at the place where Wadi Elah enters the western Shephelah, is the most likely candidate (cf. E. Stern, *EAEHL* 4 [1978] 1024–27). Another popular choice is Tell el-Manšiyyah (see H. E. Kassis, "Gath and the Structure of the 'Philistine' Society," *JBL* 84 [1965] 259–61).

Ashkelon was another member of the Philistine pentapolis, the only one directly situated on the seaboard, and well known as a seaport (cf. Y. Aharoni, *The Land,* 18). It is mentioned as early as the nineteenth century B.C. in the Egyptian Execration texts (see *EAEHL* 1 [1975] 121).

The verse as a whole may be a sort of literary device which states the impossible in order to express a fervent wish (cf. also Josh 10:13), namely, that Israel's humiliation should not be magnified in Philistia (cf. 1 Sam 18:6–7). The expression "Tell it not in Gath" probably became proverbial in Israel (see Mic 1:10). In actual fact the Philistines sent the news of their victory throughout the whole land (1 Sam 31:9).

The Philistines were, apparently, the only uncircumcised people among Israel's immediate neighbors, and the term "uncircumcised" approximates to "foreigner" (see *TDNT* 6 [1968] 75). It is a common epithet for the Philistines, and it may well have an opprobrious undertone.

21 The Heb. ושדי תרומת is a well-known *crux interpretum,* and some scholars emend the text to שרע תהומת "upsurgings of the deeps" (so RSV, similarly NAB) on the basis of the Ugaritic parallel *bl šrʿ thmtm* "without watering by the two deeps" (so Gibson, *Canaanite Myths,* 115). This proposal is well argued by Fenton (*VT* 29 [1979] 162–70) and others, and it is superior to the older emendations (see Driver, 236). However, we retain the MT because it makes a reasonable sense and is semantically possible although "heights," the suggested rendering of תרומת, is not attested in OT (see also Freedman, *Ex Orbe,* 122; Shea, *BASOR* 221 [1976] 142). Stylistically v 21a may form a pivot pattern or exhibit the "two-way middle" (see M. Dahood, "Hebrew Poetry," *IDBSup,* 670), but we regard v 21a as a bicolon with a chiastic arrangement:

> Hills of Gilboa, (let there be) no dew,
> and (let there be) no rain on you, mountain slopes.

In a sense, the author has pronounced a curse on the Hills of Gilboa and this, too, may be an emphatic expression of a heartfelt wish. The place of defeat should become a barren land, and thus the very hills would mourn for the fallen heroes (cf. Jer 4:28; 12:4; Amos 1:2).

The warriors' shields were defiled either by the blood of the slain foes or by the hands of the uncircumcised enemies (see 1 Sam 31:8–10; cf. also H. F. Fuhs, "געל," *TDOT* 3 [1978] 47). Furthermore, the shield of Saul was no longer anointed with oil to keep it in good condition (see Isa 21:5; A. R. Millard, "Saul's Shield not Anointed with Oil," *BASOR* 230 [1978] 70). It may be that there is an implicit reminder of the fact that Saul, too, is no longer the anointed king since he is dead.

The word מגן "shield" may, in some contexts, mean "chieftain," "suzerain" (see Dahood, *Psalms I,* 16–17). M. O'Connor (*Hebrew Verse Structure* [Winona Lake, Indiana: Eisenbrauns, 1980] 231) renders 21b as "There the warriors' leader was disgraced, leader Saul was anointed with oil." It is doubtful, however, that this and similar renderings are any improvement. Our interpretation is supported by גבורים "warriors" in v 21b if this word refers, as is likely, to Saul and Jonathan.

22 Here we find a short bicolon followed by a longer one, as suggested by the syntactical structure. The author praises the heroic attainments of Israel's king and his son. The sword of Saul was always victorious, and the arrows (lit., "bow") of Jonathan never missed their mark (cf. Jer 50:9b).

"Blood" (דם) and "fat" (חלב) form a fixed word pair, often associated with sacrifice (see Gevirtz, *Patterns,* 88); hence it is possible that the poet may have thought of Saul and Jonathan's victories as reminiscent of sacrifice offered to God. For war as sacrifice, see Isa 34:6; Jer 46:10; Zeph 1:7. It may seem unusual that also the enemies or their leaders(?) are designated by the same term גבורים that is used of Saul and Jonathan in vv 19, 21, 25, 27; however, the greater the stature of the defeated foe, the greater is the victory gained.

23 This verse may be either a tricolon or, more likely, a longer bicolon followed by a shorter one. The traditional reading of the MT would suggest: ". . . beloved and gracious in their life, in their death they were not parted." However, this would spoil the balance of the lines or cola; furthermore, "life" and "death" may well form a merism, denoting totality by citing the two extremes. Therefore both concepts may well belong to the same colon; consequently, Saul and Jonathan were *never* parted. We should not take the poetic eulogy as an exact statement of fact (cf. 1 Sam 20:30, 33; 22:8).

The "eagle" (נשר) is rather a general term and may include most large birds of prey; sometimes it may refer specifically to vultures (Mic 1:16). The swiftness of this monarch of birds was proverbial (cf. Deut 28:49; Prov 23:5; Lam 4:19) just as the lion was a symbol of great strength (Judg 14:18; 2 Sam 17:10).

24 Here we find a tricolon (4+4+4), and it provides an antithesis to v 20b; the joy of the daughters of the Philistines is contrasted with the grief of the daughters of Israel.

The general sense of the verse is clear but some of the details are uncertain. Scarlet was the clothing of kings and of the wealthy (cf. Prov 31:21; *TDNT* 3 [1965] 812–14), but in this context scarlet and gold refer to the rich booty which Saul may well have gained during his numerous wars (see 1 Sam 14:47). Clearly, we must reckon with some poetic exaggeration, but, in spite of this, the elegy may imply that Saul's reign may have been characterized by some material prosperity.

25 This verse re-echoes v 19 in a somewhat reverse order. Here the phrase, "How are the warriors fallen" introduces the verse while in v 19 the same expression concludes the bicolon. Here the final colon refers to Jonathan; in v 19 the reference is, most likely, to Saul.

26 It is difficult to analyze this verse poetically, but it is possible to see in it two bicola; the first one is probably arranged chiastically (יהונתן נעמת לי מאד and צר לי עליך אחי). Holladay finds in this verse a tricolon (*VT* 20 [1970] 189); so also Gevirtz (*Patterns*, 95).

The verse depicts Jonathan's love and graciousness to David, and in more recent times it has been suggested by some exegetes that Jonathan's love for David was tantamount to a homosexual relationship (see T. Horner, *Jonathan Loved David: Homosexuality in Biblical Times* [Philadelphia: Westminster Press, 1978]). The language of the poem may, perhaps, permit such an interpretation, but the general attitude of the OT as a whole (see especially Lev 18:22; 20:13) seems to contradict this exegesis (cf. also M. H. Pope, "Homosexuality," *IDBSup*, 415–17). Furthermore, one must bear in mind the poetic nature of this lament and the fact that David's heterosexual relationships are well attested.

The "love of women" (אהבת נשים) may also include mother's love for her children and that of a wife for her husband. The Heb. אהבה "love" may denote even Yahweh's love for his people (cf. Isa 63:9; Jer 31:3; Hos 3:1; 11:4; see also G. Wallis, "אהב," *TDOT* 1 [1974] 99–118).

27 The main problem of this verse is the interpretation of "the weapons of war." The reference may be either to the weapons of the fallen heroes (cf. v 21b; 1 Sam 8:12; NEB has "their armour left on the field") or, more likely, to Saul and Jonathan. Freedman (*Ex Orbe,* 123) regards the above phrase as an indirect object, rendering, "and perished with (their) weapons." However, the structure of the verse seems to be verb-subject; verb-subject, and this may be an instance of synonymous parallelism. If so, "the weapons of war" would be parallel to "warriors."

Explanation

This beautiful and artistic elegy attests the high standard of Israel's lyric poetry. It contains no explicit religious allusions of any kind, but this feature may well belong to the nature of this particular literary genre, the funerary lament. Nevertheless, this poem, just as Israelite life in general, must be ultimately seen in its religious setting. Therefore Israel's defeat was no military accident but part of the divine plan. On the other hand, there was no harm in stressing the achievements and positive qualities of the fallen heroes in one's final tribute to them. In such a situation it would be churlish, even by present-day standards, to dwell on the failures and weaknesses of the dead. Consequently, the dirge is a poetic eulogy and not an objectively detached analysis of the life and work of Saul and Jonathan, and we see only some of the positive aspects of the two tragic warriors. However, even allowing for some poetic exaggeration, the lament may reflect something of the contemporaries' experience of Saul's reign or, at least, reminiscences of it. If so, then it is not entirely impossible that the rule of the first king of Israel may have been a time of relative prosperity and limited military success. There is little doubt that Saul's kingship prepared the way for David's reign and empire.

David King in Hebron (2:1–4a)

Bibliography

Frick, F. S. *The City in Ancient Israel.* SBLDS 36. Missoula, MT: Scholars Press, 1977. **Kutsch, E.** "Wie David König wurde." *Textgemäss.* 75–93. **Levenson, J. D.** "I Samuel 25 as Literature and as History." *CBQ* 40 (1978) 11–28. ——— and **Halpern, B.** "The Political Import of David's Marriages." *JBL* 99 (1980) 507–18. **Lindblom, J.** "Lot Casting in the Old Testament." *VT* 12 (1962) 164–78. **Madl, H.** "Die Gottesbefragung mit dem Verb *šāʾal.*" *Bausteine Biblischer Theologie.* Ed. H.-J. Fabry. BBB 50. Köln and Bonn: Peter Hanstein Verlag GMBH, 1977. **Weisman, Z.** "Anointing as a Motif in the Making of the Charismatic King." *Bib* 57 (1976) 378–98. **Zobel, H.-J.** "Beiträge zur Geschichte Gross-Judas in Frü- und Vordavidischer Zeit." VTSup 28 (1975) 253–77.

Translation

[1] *After this[a] David inquired of Yahweh, saying, "Shall I go up to one of the cities of Judah?" "Go up," Yahweh replied to him. Then David inquired further, "Where shall I go up?" "To Hebron," was the reply.* [2] *So David went up there[a] with his two wives, Ahinoam of Jezreel and Abigail, the widow[b] of Nabal the Carmelite.[c]* [3] *David also brought up[a] the men[b] who were in his service, each man with his family, and they settled down in the towns[c] of Hebron.* [4a] *Then the men of Judah came and there they anointed David king[a] over the house of Judah.*

Notes

1.a. Lit., "And it came to pass after this" (KJV).
2.a. G adds the explanatory note "to Hebron."
2.b. Or "the wife of," which is the usual rendering of אשת.
2.c. A few Heb. MSS have, perhaps rightly, the fem form הכרמלית "Carmelitess"; similar variations are found also in 1 Sam 27:3; 30:5.
3.a. G omits this phrase (העלה דוד). The word order in the MT (obj-verb-subj) has no real justification and may imply the priority of the G reading.
3.b. We follow G in reading והאנשים; MT has ואנשיו "and his men," but the pronom suff seems superfluous in view of the following אשר עמו "who were with him" or ". . . in his service."
3.c. Syr^AC read simply "in Hebron" (בחברון), which may be a deliberate simplification.
4.a. The major versions (G, Syr, Tg, and Vg), apart from a few MSS, suggest a verbal form ("to reign"), which is an interpretation of the consonantal text.

Form/Structure/Setting

This pericope is reasonably self-contained and deals very concisely with the takeover of Hebron and David's swift rise to kingship over Judah. It is, perhaps, a summary of a more detailed account of the relevant events since it would be very surprising if the story of this important step in David's life had been transmitted only in this laconic form. It may well be that the HDR, of which the present pericope seems to be an integral part, was primarily intended to justify David's claim to rule Israel; therefore the Hebron episode had little relevance for the main purpose of the larger narrative (see Alt,

Kleine Schriften 2 [1953] 40). In any case, the Hebron anointing was only the first stage in David's ascent to the throne of Israel.

In v 1 we find a brief, indirect description of the use of the lot-oracle. W. Dommershausen ("גורל," *TDOT* 2 [1977] 454) has suggested that the answers quoted in the pericope are expansions of the simple "Yes" answer. It seems that the questions were phrased in such a form that they could be answered either by "Yes" or "No"; if so, then the present question "Where shall I go up?" has been rephrased.

It seems that the main function of this short report was to stress that the first thing David did after the mourning over Saul and Jonathan, was to seek Yahweh's counsel; the Philistines and their possible plans are not even alluded to. It is plausible that Yahweh's oracular reply was thought to refer, in retrospect, not only to Hebron's takeover but also to David's anointing in Hebron.

Comment

1 The Hebrew ויהי אחרי־כן (KJV "and it came to pass after this") is a recurrent transition-marker, and it is fairly characteristic of 2 Samuel (see 8:1; 10:1; 13:1; 21:18; cf. also 15:1). It may be a pre-Deuteronomic formula (for further details, see Conroy, *Absalom*, 41–42).

David inquired of Yahweh either by using the sacred lots (cf. 1 Sam 14:37–42; 23:9–11; 30:7–8; 2 Sam 5:19, 23) or by consulting a seer or prophet (cf. 1 Sam 28:6; 2 Sam 7:2–3). The lots were, apparently, associated with the problematic ephod (see 1 Sam 23:9; 30:7), and they were, most likely, manipulated by a priest (cf. Num 27:21; 1 Sam 14:19, 36; 30:7–8; see also Lindblom, *VT* 12 [1962] 164–78; W. Dommershausen, "גורל," *TDOT* 2 [1977] 450–56). Eventually the lots or the so-called Urim and Thummim became part of the high priestly dress (Exod 28:30; Lev 8:8; cf. *IDB* 4 [1962] 739–40).

Hebron was not only an ancient town (Num 13:22) but also an important royal city in Judah. Its previous name was Kiriath-arba (Judg 1:10), which probably meant "city of four (quarters)" or "Tetrapolis" (see, however, Josh 14:15; cf. E. Lipiński, "Anaq-Kiryat ʾArbaʿ-Hebron et ses Sanctuaires Tribaux," *VT* 24 [1974] 41–55). Hebron is traditionally linked with the patriarchs (Gen 13:18; 23:19; 35:27; 37:14), and the biblical accounts tell us that Sarah and Abraham were buried in the vicinity of the city (Gen 23; 25:9–10). According to Josh 15:13–14 and Judg 1:20, the city was taken by the Calebites but later it was incorporated into the territory of Greater Judah.

Hebron is situated in the Judean hill country, some nineteen miles (thirty kilometers) south-southwest of Jerusalem, and is the highest town in Palestine, some 3,000 feet (915 meters) above the sea level.

It is likely that David's move to Hebron was done with the express permission of the Philistines (so Stolz, 190) so that David's new kingdom became a vassal state and part of the Philistine system of government (so Alt, "The Formation of the Israelite State in Palestine," *Essays*, 212). This would explain, at least to some extent, the prolonged war between David's forces and those of Ishbosheth (2 Sam 3:1). Saul's defeat and death meant that the Philistines were now free to exercise their influence over most parts of Palestine, including

Judah. David's rule over Judah could be seen as an extension of the Philistine control; likewise, David's hostilities with Israel may have served the Philistine interests because this could have been one of the means whereby the Philistines kept Israel in check.

That the citizens of Hebron welcomed David's rule is possible but far from certain. The verb עלה "go up" may have a military connotation (as in Judg 1:1; 2 Sam 5:17, 19; Isa 7:6; Jer 48:18) although in this context it may simply indicate that the geographical location of Ziklag was relatively lower than that of Hebron (see also A. E. Glock, *Warfare in Mari and Early Israel* [Dissertation, The University of Michigan, 1968] 222 n.41; Soggin, *Das Königtum*, 65). It is plausible that before David's takeover of Hebron, the city may have belonged to the Calebites, and was outside the territory of the tribe of Judah. In that case it would have been ruled by its own elders or chiefs who, on the whole, may have shared Nabal's feelings when he exclaimed, "Who is this David? Who is this son of Jesse?" (1 Sam 25:10). Nabal, too, was a Calebite (1 Sam 25:3) and his attitude to David was not entirely unreasonable because the latter was demanding from Nabal protection money for not raiding his flocks (1 Sam 25:6–8).

Thus it is possible that David imposed his protection upon Hebron either by a military action (see Kegler, *Politisches Geschehen*, 45) or by a mere show of force. The takeover of Hebron was not simply a change of ruler or administration, but it involved the resettlement of some 600 men and their families. Furthermore, this may have led to a possible redistribution of the available land (cf. 1 Sam 22:7; see also Herzog and Gichon, *Battles of the Bible*, 77). The total number of David's troops and their dependents would be in the region of 2,000, and it is usually thought that most ancient cities in Palestine were comparatively small (see Frick, *The City in Ancient Israel*, 79–80); therefore few cities would be anxious to accept such a large number of settlers.

2 The mention of the two wives of David need not have been intended as a deliberate pointer to his links with the local clans (see 1 Sam 27:5) although this fact may have helped David. Jezreel was, apparently, a town in the hills of Judah, near Carmel and Juttah (cf. Josh 15:55–56), and is not to be identified with the well-known city in the plain of Jezreel in northern Israel (see Simons, *Texts*, § 709). Also Nabal's town Carmel was situated in the Judean hills, southeast of Hebron; it should not be confused with the Carmel range in the north (for the opposite view, see F. Schicklberger, "Die Davididen und das Nordreich. Beobachtungen zur sog. Geschichte vom Aufstieg Davids," *BZ* 18 [1974] 261 n.22).

Students of the OT have long been aware that the only other Ahinoam in the Hebrew Bible was the wife of Saul, the daughter of Ahimaaz (1 Sam 14:50), and the only other Abigail was the sister of David (2 Sam 17:25; 1 Chr 2:15, 16). Recently, Levenson and Halpern (*JBL* 99 [1980] 507–18) have argued that the two Ahinoams were one and the same person, and so also the two Abigails. In view of 2 Sam 12:8 it is plausible that at some later stage David may have married Ahinoam, the widow of Saul, but it is less likely that she was Ahinoam *of Jezreel*.

The identification of the two Abigails is based on an ingenious argument (Levenson and Halpern, 511–13) and is within the limits of possibility. However, in that case Abigail must have been David's half-sister (cf. Gen 20:12) although later even such marriages were forbidden (Lev 18:9, 11; 20:17; Deut 27:22).

3 The expression "towns of Hebron" is without parallel. Usually we find such phrases as "Megiddo and its villages" (lit., ". . . its daughters," Judg 1:27) or "Ashdod, its towns (lit., "its daughters") and its villages" (Josh 15:47). We see no need to emend עָרֵי "the towns of . . ." into עִיר "the town of . . ." (so Smith, 266) or to follow some Syriac MSS which simply read "in Hebron." "The towns of Hebron" may refer to the townships dependent on Hebron (or to a southern confederation?) rather than to the four quarters of the city (see Ackroyd, 30). Perhaps, the expression has been influenced by "the cities of Judah" in v 1.

4a Mettinger (*King and Messiah*, 141–42) equates "the men of Judah" with those elders who had been the recipients of David's gifts (1 Sam 30:26–31), and whose towns already formed "a political confederation of towns in Judah" (142). This is, of course, possible, but the above localities are explicitly described as "places where David and his men had roamed" (1 Sam 30:31) and not as members of any particular tribal league. Similarly, Zobel (VTSup 28 [1974] 254–56) envisages a Greater Judah with Hebron as its metropolis, which he identifies with "the house of Judah." On the other hand, the so-called Greater Judah may well be a Davidic creation (see Ishida, *Royal Dynasties*, 65–66). Originally, "Judah" may have been a geographical designation for the hill country extending roughly from Bethlehem to Hebron (cf. de Vaux, *Early Israel*, 547), but, eventually, the region gave its name to the clans that lived there. It is plausible that the tribe of Judah (not Greater Judah) had been part of Saul's kingdom (so Aharoni, *The Land*, 289; Mayes, *Israel*, 3–4); this would explain why the sons of Jesse served in Saul's army (1 Sam 17:12–18). After Israel's defeat and Abner's withdrawal to Transjordan (2 Sam 2:8) the house of Saul must have lost control over Judah.

Thus it seems that David first became the ruler of Hebron, which would have been the main partner in a confederation of cities (or clans?), primarily south of Hebron (see 1 Sam 30:26–31; cf. Zobel, VTSup 28 [1974] 256–68). At some later stage the "men of Judah" (not the elders of Hebron) made him king also over the house of Judah. It may well be that this point marked the beginning of Greater Judah even though Hebron remained the center of the new political entity for the time being.

The anointing of David is said to have been carried out by the men of Judah (2 Sam 2:4a). One could follow Martin Noth (*The Laws*, 164 n.32) who regards v 4a as "a shortened form of expression" and argues that "the anointing must certainly have been carried out by priests" (cf. 1 Kgs 1:34), perhaps in the local sanctuary (Mamre?). On the other hand, Kutsch (*Textgemäss*, 80) has pointed out that both here and in 2 Sam 5:3 the explicit subject of the verb "to anoint" is not a priest or a prophet but the *people* or their representatives (see also Judg 9:8–15). Perhaps, Mettinger (*King and Messiah*, 198–208) is right in suggesting that it is probable that "from Solomon onwards the rite was performed by a priest" (208) while previously the anointing was a secular rite carried out by the representatives of the people; only later it became a sacral act which brought about a new relationship between

God and the king, and therefore it would be performed by a priest acting in the name of Yahweh. This explanation assumes that the accounts of anointing in 1 Samuel are either later interpretations or that we are dealing with two different types of anointing, one divine and leading to the status of the anointed of Yahweh, the other secular and leading to the office of a king of a particular territory. Thus we see that although Absalom was anointed by the people (2 Sam 19:10), this did not, apparently, make him into the anointed of Yahweh. Consequently, Joab who killed Absalom, did not suffer the same fate as the unfortunate Amalekite (2 Sam 1:16) nor was he even *accused* of daring to slay the anointed of Yahweh. Similarly, the wise Ahithophel did not reckon with the sanctity of Yahweh's anointed when he counseled the killing of David (2 Sam 17:2). Nevertheless, we should not over-emphasize the possible difference between the sacral and secular in early Israel (see Halpern, *The Constitution*, 13). It is also possible that the rite of anointing underwent a process of reinterpretation in the course of time.

It may be of some interest that in 2 Sam 5:3 David made a covenant with, or gave certain assurances to, the elders of Israel, but there is no mention of any covenant in our pericope. However, in view of the brevity of this passage, one should not necessarily assume that there was no such contract (so Alt, Ishida, et al.) unless David's kinship, achievements, and military strength made a negotiated agreement superfluous in his dealings with Judah.

We are not told how David's investiture was understood in Mahanaim by Abner and Ishbosheth; it is possible that Judah's change of allegiance was regarded as a rebellion, assuming that Judah had previously been part of Saul's kingdom (cf. Kittel, *Geschichte*, 135).

Explanation

This pericope is primarily concerned to emphasize the religious setting of David's move to Hebron; it was guided by Yahweh alone. The author was not interested either to indicate David's relationship with the Philistines at this point or to describe the nature of Hebron's takeover; nor is there any indication that David was invited by the people of Hebron to settle there (cf. Judg 11:4–11). Previously, David had been a Philistine vassal (1 Sam 27:2–7), and it is very likely that he continued this advantageous relationship. In times past he had claimed to have raided the area around Hebron (1 Sam 27:10–11) in his master's service; *now* he annexed it. Furthermore, it is highly unlikely that at this stage David could have acted contrary to the wishes of the Philistines. For various reasons it would have been important to stress any change in David's subordinate status had there been any such alteration in the existing political dependence. It is just possible that this pericope implies a contrast between David's rise to kingship in Hebron, which is depicted as due to *Yahweh's* guidance, and Ishbosheth's installation as king on *Abner's* initiative (2 Sam 2:8–9).

Since the use of the sacred lots or the Urim and Thummim requires the formulation of the question before the answer is given, it may imply that David was already contemplating leaving Ziklag. The immediate reason must have been the burning down of the town by the Amalekites (1 Sam 30:2).

An added stimulus may have been the tacit or explicit approval given to David's plans by his overlord, the ruler of Gath. From the latter's point of view, the extension of David's rule would be seen as an expansion of the Philistine sphere of influence and control.

The anointing of David has raised many questions and it is difficult to avoid the conclusion that his anointing by the men of Judah and, later, by the elders of Israel established a new relationship between David and the respective groups, thus providing primarily the civil legitimation of the new king. It may well be that the sacral interpretation of anointing represents a later stage, and that David's anointing by Samuel (1 Sam 16:13) belongs to this subsequent development, especially if the HDR is later (?) than the SN. Moreover, the threefold repetition of the *sacral* anointing of David would be difficult to explain satisfactorily. In the light of the Saul narratives, it seems that one became the *Lord's* anointed once for all.

David's Message to Jabesh-Gilead (2:4b–7)

Bibliography

Fox, M. "Tôḇ as Covenant Terminology." *BASOR* 209 (1973) 41–42. **Glueck, N.** *Hesed in the Bible.* Tr. A. Gottschalk. Cincinnati: The Hebrew Union College Press, 1967. **Hillers, D.** "A Note on Some Treaty Terminology in the Old Testament." *BASOR* 176 (1964) 46–47. **Noth, M.** "Jabes-Gilead: Ein Beitrag zur Methode AT Topographie." *ZDPV* 69 (1953) 28–41. **Ottosson, M.** *Gilead: Tradition and History.* Tr. J. Gray. ConB: OT Series 3. Lund, Sweden: CWK Gleerup, 1969. **Stoebe, H. J.** "Die Bedeutung des Wortes *ḥäsäd* im AT." *VT* 2 (1952) 244–54. **Wächter, L.** *Der Tod im Alten Testament.* Arbeiten zur Theologie 8. Stuttgart: Calwer Verlag, 1967.

Translation

[4b] *When David was told:* [a] *"The men of Jabesh-Gilead have buried* [b] *Saul," * [5] *he sent messengers to the men* [a] *of Jabesh-Gilead and said to them, "May Yahweh bless you because you have done this loyal deed to* [b] *Saul your lord, in that you buried him.* [6] *Now therefore, may Yahweh show you lasting loyalty* [a] *and I, for my part, offer to you this* [b] *friendship because you have done such a deed.* [7] *From now on, let your hands be strong and be valiant; although* [a] *Saul your lord* [b] *is dead, the house of Judah has already anointed me* [c] *king over them."* [d]

Notes

4b.a. The verb וַיַּגִּדוּ "they informed" may be an impersonal 3 pl, expressing a pass, "(David) was told" (cf. Williams, *Syntax,* § 160). However, it is likely that in the present context the readers may have regarded "the men of Judah" as the obvious subj of the verb.

4b.b. Omitting the relative particle אֲשֶׁר with G-L, Syr, and Vg. MT could, perhaps, be rendered, "(It is) the men of Jabesh-Gilead who buried Saul." Possibly the particle has been accidentally misplaced and should be transferred before אַנְשֵׁי "men of," as implied by G.

5.a. G has "leaders," which may represent the Heb. בַּעֲלֵי, but this is probably a deliberate alteration in view of the context.

5.b. MT reads עִם "to," "with," while 4QSamᵃ has עַל "upon"; similarly also G (ἐπί).

6.a. Lit., "loyalty and truth" (חֶסֶד וֶאֱמֶת) but perhaps a hendiadys (cf. Williams, *Syntax,* § 72).

6.b. The demonstrative pronoun (הַזֹּאת) has no real antecedent, and therefore Wellhausen (153) has suggested תַּחַת אֲשֶׁר "because" instead of the present אֲשֶׁר הַזֹּאת "this . . . because." MT may be right, but the pericope may have been derived from a larger narrative.

7.a. Taking כִּי in a concessive sense (cf. *HALAT,* 449).

7.b. MT has the pl form of the noun (so also in v 5), which may indicate respect. For the pl of "majesty," see GKC, § 124i.

7.c. The position of the pronoun (i.e., the obj marker with the pronom suff) implies a certain emphasis.

7.d. MT has לִמְלֹךְ עֲלֵיהֶם "king over them," while 4QSamᵃ has reversed the order, reading עֲלֵהֶם לָן; similarly G.

Form / Structure / Setting

Although vv 4b–7 presuppose 1 Sam 31:12–13, there is no reason to assume that the former unit is a direct continuation of the latter. Whether our pericope is part of the preceding passage (vv 1–4a), depends largely upon the interpretation of וַיַּגִּדוּ (see *Notes* above). The impression is that vv 4b–7 presuppose a somewhat different context from that provided by vv 1–4a; consequently, the former pericope may form a separate unit and may be a later insertion (so Veijola, *Dynastie*, 53 n.49).

The pericope deals with David's message to the Jabesh-Gileadites, and at best it probably represents the gist of what was said and done. It has been thought by some scholars that the reply to David's message had been omitted by a later editor because of its negative nature (so Budde, 203), but, in that case, the whole section could have been deleted. It is not improbable that no reply was required although the communication could be regarded as a shrewd political move to win the allegiance of the men of Jabesh-Gilead. However, the latter could hardly form an effective alliance with David, being separated from the new kingdom by Ishbosheth's territory; Jabesh-Gilead could not have been far from Mahanaim, the new "capital" of Israel. Nevertheless, *friendly* relationships could be fostered irrespective of any political and other limitations, and this may well have been the intention of David. There is, of course, the possibility that an indirect answer to David's message is found in vv 8–9 (see also Grønbaek, *Aufstieg*, 226). Abner's support for Ishbosheth may have been a reflection of the attitude of the Israelites as a whole.

The actual message of David is found in vv 5b–7, and it forms a messenger speech although it lacks the characteristic messenger formula, "Thus says so-and-so" (cf. C. Westermann, *Basic Forms of Prophetic Speech* [Tr. H. C. White. Philadelphia: The Westminster Press, 1967] 100–128). V 4 gives the background information while v 5 is a report of the sending of the messengers, and it also provides the identification of the addressees.

The communication must have been sent shortly after the death of Saul and David's investiture. Whether the two events were causally linked is not clear, but the death of Israel's king and its consequences must have contributed to David's rise to kingship in Judah, especially if Judah had been an integral part of Saul's kingdom.

Comment

4b Jabesh-Gilead was an important town in Transjordan but its location is far from certain. The two main possibilities are Tell el-Maqlub (see Simons, *Texts*, § 671) and, especially, Tell Abu Kharaz (see N. Glueck, "The Explorations in Eastern Palestine, IV," *AASOR* 25–28 [1951] 268–75). According to Eusebius (*Onomastikon*, 110, lines 11–13) the town was six miles (ten kilometers) from the city of Pella, on the road to Gerasa (see further Ottosson, *Gilead*, 195–96). The approximate area is some fifteen miles (twenty-four kilometers) southeast of Bethshan (cf. 1 Sam 31:11–12).

The fuller account of the daring deed by the men of Jabesh-Gilead is given in 1 Sam 31:11–13. Their heroic action may have been inspired by Saul's rescue of their city at the beginning of his reign (see 1 Sam 11:1–11). For the people of antiquity it was a terrible fate to be left unburied, and the Hebrews, no doubt, shared the same belief (cf. Deut 28:26; 1 Kgs 14:11; Ps 79:3; Eccl 6:3; Jer 16:4). It may have been thought that those who had not received a proper burial lacked even that little comfort which could be theirs in death (cf. Isa 14:18–20); see also C. Ryder Smith, *The Bible Doctrine of the Hereafter* (London: The Epworth Press, 1958) 38–39.

5 David's message begins with a formula of blessing, "May Yahweh bless you" (cf. Ruth 2:20; 1 Sam 15:13; 23:21; see also J. Scharbert,"ברך," *TDOT* 2 [1977] 284–85). It expresses appreciation and praise for the outstanding loyalty of the Jabesh-Gileadites to their dead king.

The Heb. חסד "loyalty, loyal deed" is difficult to translate adequately. It often presupposes an existing relationship, not necessarily a covenant, within which it operates. It usually has an element of reciprocity: one good deed should give rise to a corresponding action (cf. H.-J. Zobel, "חסד," *TWAT* 3 [1978] 58; Glueck, *Hesed*, 35–55). In one sense, חסד is the means whereby a society is turned into a caring community in which relationships enrich, not degrade, both parties. It can operate in a secular as well as a sacral realm. In our context we have translated חסד by "loyalty" rather than by "kindness" (JB, NIV); "faithfulness" might be a reasonable alternative.

6 Since the Jabesh-Gileadites had dealt loyally with their lord, it was proper that David's wish should be that Yahweh might continue to show his faithfulness to them. In a way, David has taken up Saul's obligation in as far as he regards it as his duty to reciprocate the men of Jabesh-Gilead in offering them his friendship; perhaps, this is an implicit claim to be the true heir of Saul.

There is some uncertainty as to the proper rendering of הטובה (e.g., KJV has "goodness," RSV "good," NEB, NIV "favor"). In recent years it has been noted that the Heb. טוב in certain contexts may refer to covenantal relationships (see Fox, *BASOR* 209 [1973] 41; Mettinger, *King and Messiah*, 147; I. Johag, "טוב —Terminus Technicus in Vertrags- und Bündnisformularen des Alten Orients und des Alten Testaments," in H.-J. Fabry, ed., *Bausteine Biblischer Theologie* [BBB 50. Köln and Bonn: Peter Hanstein Verlag, 1977] 3–23). In this verse its probable meaning may be "friendship" (cf. Hillers, *BASOR* 176 [1964] 47) although it is not impossible that David's hope was to make a treaty or covenant with the men of Jabesh-Gilead (so Ishida, *Royal Dynasties*, 71). However, it seems doubtful whether such a political treaty would have been practicable in the existing situation.

7 Finally, David encourages Saul's faithful compatriots by pointing out that although their king is dead, there is a ray of hope because he, David, has been made king of Judah. We do not know whether at this point David was already aware of the crowning of Ishbosheth, but, in any case, the main reason for the encouragement was David's own rise to effective power.

Explanation

Although this brief passage concerns only David and the men of Jabesh-Gilead, it is likely that in the present setting it was ultimately addressed to all Israel, especially v 7. One could nearly say that the first recorded act of the new king of Judah was to offer friendship and comfort to a group of Israelites, with the implication that David may be a Judean but his heart belongs to all Israel.

Theologically, it is no accident that Saul is dead. Both success and failure are, in one way or another, the outworking of Yahweh's purposes. At a later time the Chronicler (1 Chr 10:13) pointed out that Saul died for his unfaithfulness; likewise, David's rise to power could be regarded as an indication of his loyalty to Yahweh. Therefore in the circumstances it ought to be obvious that Israel's future rests with David, and no one else.

Once more, David is presented as the man who works with Yahweh and not against him (v 6). Consequently, David does not stir up rebellion in Israel or what is left of it. He does, however, offer his hand in friendship and hopefully expects the right response at the right time, as in the case of Judah. Thus David waits till circumstances will eventually bring Israel to him.

Whether this is an accurate picture of the historical David or not, we do not know; clearly, there was also another side to him.

Ishbosheth King of Israel (2:8–11)

Bibliography

Lindars, B. "The Israelite Tribes in Judges." VTSup 30 (1979) 95–112. **Lipiński, E.** "אשבעל and אשיה and Parallel Personal Names." *OLP* 5 (1974) 5–13. **Ohler, A.** *Israel, Volk und Land.* 108–11. **Schunck, K.-D.** "Erwägungen zur Geschichte und Bedeutung von Mahanaim." *ZDMG* 113 (1963) 34–40. ———. *Benjamin: Untersuchungen zur Entstehung und Geschichte eines israelitischen Stammes.* BZAW 86. Berlin: Verlag Alfred Töpelmann, 1963. 122–30. **Soggin, A.** "The Reign of ʾEšbaʿal, Son of Saul." *Old Testament and Oriental Studies.* BibOr 29. Rome: Biblical Institute Press, 1975. 31–49. **Tsevat, M.** "Ishbosheth and Congeners: The Names and Their Study." *HUCA* 46 (1975) 71–87.

Translation

⁸ *Meanwhile Abner, the son of Ner, the commander of Saul's army* ᵃ *had taken Ishbosheth,* ᵇ *son of Saul, and brought him over to Mahanaim.* ⁹ *There he made him king over Gilead, Asher,* ᵃ *Jezreel, Ephraim, and Benjamin, that is to say, over all* ᵇ *Israel.* ¹⁰ *Ishbosheth, son of Saul, was forty years old when he became king over Israel, and he reigned two years.* ᵃ *The house of Judah, however,* ᵇ *followed David.* ¹¹ *The length of David's reign over the house of Judah, in Hebron, was seven years and six months.*

Notes

8.a. 4QSamᵃ supplies the missing article, reading הצבא (cf. also Joüon, *Grammaire,* § 137r); however, the following relative clause may make the noun (צבא) definite, and therefore the article may be omitted.

8.b. Aq, Theod, and Symm read Ειωβααλ "Ishbaal."

9.a. The MT's האשורי "the Ashurites" (so rsv) may be corrupt. Syr and Vg suggest הגשורי "Geshurites" or גשור "Geshur," while Tg has בית אשר "the house of Asher," which is often regarded as the best reading, indicating האשרי "the Asherites" or simply אשר "Asher."

9.b. MT has כלה "all of it" and has retained the original form of the 3 sg suff; a few MSS read כלו. Since כלה is in apposition and follows the noun it qualifies, it may add some emphasis (see Brockelmann, *Syntax,* § 62f; Davidson, *Syntax,* § 29 Rem. 6).

10.a. Many MSS read the sg שנה for MT שנים "years." Usually the thing enumerated is in pl (see Davidson, *Syntax,* § 36).

10.b. The Heb. אך denotes an adversative relationship (see Andersen, *The Sentence,* 174).

Form / Structure / Setting

As we have already seen, vv 1–11 have been usually divided into three sections, and the total impression is that we are dealing with very compressed and fragmentary material. However, there is a discernible sequence of events, especially if v 4b was originally the report of the men of Judah; this seems less likely although the subsequent readers may have understood the pericope in that way.

Vv 1–4a and 8–11 are associated by certain contrasts and similarities. Thus Ishbosheth's move to Mahanaim (v 8) has its parallel in David's move to

Hebron (v 3), while the crowning of the former (v 9) provides an obvious counterpart to David's anointing (v 4a); yet one set of events is apparently depicted as the outworking of Yahweh's blessing, while the other is the result of Yahweh's rejection.

It is also clear that vv 8–11 serve as a sort of prologue to the civil war episode (2:12–3:1) by introducing Abner, Ishbosheth, and their center of activities, Mahanaim (v 8).

There is a fairly general agreement that the chronological data in vv 10a and 11 are Deuteronomistic additions in the style of the "formulaic introductions to accounts of later Israelite and Judean kings" (Noth, *The Deuteronomistic History*, 125 n.8; cf. also Flanagan, *The Foundation of the Monarchy*, 45).

Comment

8   We have taken v 8 as roughly contemporaneous with the events in the preceding verses although the literary sequence need not be identical with the historical progression.

The relationship between Abner and Ishbosheth, as described in the OT tradition, is far from clear. It is more likely that Abner and Saul, father of Ishbosheth, were cousins, although 1 Sam 14:50 could be taken to mean that Abner was Saul's uncle (cf. McCarter, *1 Samuel*, 256; Soggin, *Das Königtum*, 66).

Abner was a seasoned warrior who had accompanied Saul on various campaigns (cf. 1 Sam 17:55; 20:25; 26:5) and who became the commander of Saul's forces. Now, after the death of Saul, he was the effective ruler of Israel while Ishbosheth was little more than a figurehead.

The name of Saul's son appears in the OT in two forms (but see also 1 Sam 14:49 where "Ishvi" may be yet another form of his name). In 2 Samuel we find אישבשת "Ishbosheth" or "Man of Shame," while in 1 Chronicles (8:33; 9:39) we have אשבעל "Eshbaal" or "Baal exists" (so Albright, *Archaeology*, 206 n.62); Noth (*Personennamen*, 138–39) takes it as an equivalent of אישבעל "Man of Baal." It is usually thought that the latter form is the historical name of Saul's son, and "Ishbosheth" is regarded as an intentional scribal alteration to avoid, or to defame, the name of the Canaanite deity, Baal. If this is right, it does not necessarily follow that Saul must have been a worshiper of Baal. It is more plausible that "Baal" may have been used as a title of the God of Israel, meaning "Lord" (see "בעל," *TDOT* 2 [1977] 181–200). Eventually the title became ambiguous and improper, and therefore it was replaced by the pejorative בשת "shame." It is not impossible that this supposed distortion of the name was intended also to calumniate Saul (so Hertzberg, 249). More recently, Tsevat (*HUCA* 46 [1975] 77–85) has revived and elaborated an earlier view, arguing that בשת in this context is not the usual Hebrew name for "shame" but rather a divine name or epithet. He admits that tendencies to defame pagan deities were not uncommon in post-biblical times, but he doubts their existence for the biblical period. Furthermore, he asserts that one person may be denoted, for various reasons, by more than one name, and that this was the case with "Ishbosheth" and "Eshbaal." His arguments are plausible but they will not convince everyone. His case would be stronger if both forms were used in 2 Samuel.

Mahanaim was an important town in Transjordan, associated with Jacob's wanderings (Gen 32). Its exact location is uncertain but it must have been some distance from Jordan (see 2 Sam 2:29) and probably not too far from the river Jabbok. Aharoni (*The Land,* 439) identifies it with Tell edh-Dhahab el Gharbi while de Vaux and others prefer Tell Hajjāj (for references, see *POTT,* 252 n.47). In Solomon's time Mahanaim became the center of an administrative district (1 Kgs 4:14).

The author does not explain why Abner chose Mahanaim as the provisional "capital" of the reduced kingdom. It must have been outside the Philistine reach, and there is no real evidence that the latter ever controlled Transjordan. Possibly the population of Mahanaim included some Benjaminite elements (see Schunck, *ZDMG* 113 [1963] 38) and therefore Abner and Ishbosheth could hope to find some loyal support.

The transfer of the capital from Gibeah (or Gibeon?) to Transjordan may well imply that the west bank of Jordan was, more or less, under the Philistine domination. It is unlikely that Ishbosheth became a vassal of the Philistines (so Kamphausen, "Philister und Hebräer zur Zeit Davids," *ZAW* 6 [1886] 47–48; Conroy, *Samuel, Kings,* 94) because in that case there would be no need for the Israelites to abandon their capital or center of administration. It is equally unlikely that two vassals would be engaged in prolonged mutual hostilities (2 Sam 3:1).

9 Much has been written concerning the manner in which Ishbosheth was made king. It is usually pointed out that he was neither designated by Yahweh nor acclaimed by the people, and that therefore he lacked the two basic conditions necessary for kingship (see Herrmann, *History,* 145; Kutsch, *Textgemäss,* 77). This is, of course, possible but far from certain; we simply lack explicit information. Ishbosheth is said to have been made king by Abner, and there is no doubt that the latter was the main agent in these events, but it would be surprising if other persons or groups were not involved had they been regarded as essential to the process of legitimate investiture. We may note that since Abner had to consult the elders of Israel when he planned to make alliance with David (2 Sam 3:17), it would be reasonable to assume that the same elders played also some part in Ishbosheth's elevation to kingship. It is true that later David referred to Ishbosheth as a "righteous man" אִישׁ צַדִּיק; see 2 Sam 4:11) and not as "the anointed of Yahweh" (cf. 2 Sam 1:14), but the latter designation may be implied when David stressed that the killing of Ishbosheth was more abhorrent than the slaying of Saul (2 Sam 4:10–11). Although the killers of Saul's son were not explicitly charged with sacrilegious killing, this, too, may be implicit. It is unlikely that 2 Sam 4:10 means that the Amalekite (cf. 2 Sam 1:5–10) was put to death merely for bringing the *news* of Saul's death.

It has been argued that at this time the royal anointing was not much more than a political act in a religious setting (see *Comment* on 2 Sam 2:4a), and, in any case, it would be surprising if the Benjaminites did not regard Ishbosheth as the rightful and legitimate king. Otherwise Abner's kingmaking would appear a pointless undertaking (see Ishida, *Dynasties,* 76 n.87).

A considerable difficulty is caused by the description of Ishbosheth's kingdom. At first sight, it would seem that this territory included Transjordan

(Gilead), Galilee (Asher), the Plain of Esdraelon (Jezreel), and Central Palestine
(Ephraim and Benjamin). However, there are some problems. Since the defeat
of Saul at Gilboa, the Central Highlands must have passed into Philistine
control. This would explain why Abner, Ishbosheth, and their men resided
in, and operated from, Mahanaim. Also the Plain of Esdraelon could hardly
have been dominated by the Israelites; there were, no doubt, Canaanite enclaves (cf. Judg 1:27) and, probably, a Philistine garrison in Bethshan (cf. 1
Sam 31:10). It is possible that Jezreel in this context denotes only the town
of Jezreel, at the edge of the plain, but this would not solve all our problems
(cf. Soggin, *Oriental Studies*, 42). Ohler (*Israel, Volk und Land*, 108) is of the
opinion that Jezreel may denote the tribe of Issachar (cf. Josh 19:17–18)
since the town is part of the tribal allotment.

There is also considerable uncertainty as to the right reading and meaning
of הָאֲשׁוּרִי (see *Notes* above). The two most likely possibilities are the reading
suggested by Tg אָשֵׁר "Asher" or that provided by Syr and Vg, namely,
גְּשׁוּר "Geshur." Yet Geshur must have had its own king quite early in David's
reign (cf. 2 Sam 3:3) and therefore it could hardly have been annexed by
the Israelites at this point in time. Furthermore, David's marriage with the
daughter of the king of Geshur could be seen as part of an attempt to isolate
Ishbosheth's kingdom. Unfortunately, also the other alternative, "Asher," has
its problems. It could not very well be controlled without the possession of
Zebulun, Issachar, and Naphtali. A doubtful solution is to regard the above
list of territories as giving administrative districts (cf. 1 Kgs 4:1–19) rather
than tribal possessions (see Schunck, *Benjamin*, 129); it may be questioned
whether Saul had already established such an administrative system.

The last item in the list, "all Israel," does not, apparently, add any further
territory as if "and the rest of Israel" but is "an inclusive designation of the
places already mentioned" (Lindars, VTSup 30 [1979]) 102 n.12). This "Israel"
clearly did not include Judah and Simeon. In the wider context it seems
that Ishbosheth was able to exercise his authority only over Transjordan
(contra Soggin, *Das Königtum*, 67 n.16); the Benjaminites in his service may
have followed him from their original home base. Thus the above territorial
list may represent merely Ishbosheth's *claim* to rule *all* Israel even though
in actual fact he could not even defend his own tribe Benjamin (cf. also
Bright, *History*, 196).

10–11 We are informed that Ishbosheth "was forty years old when he
became king and he reigned two years." Most scholars regard this statement
as a Deuteronomistic addition and therefore comparatively late but not necessarily wrong. However, David is said to have been thirty years of age when
he became king (2 Sam 5:4), and since Jonathan appears to have been the
eldest son of Saul (see 1 Sam 14:49; 31:2; 1 Chr 8:33), he ought to have
been some forty-five years old at the time of his death. Yet in 1 Samuel we
gain the impression that Jonathan and David were roughly of the same age
rather than belonging to two practically different generations. Furthermore,
in 2 Sam 4:4 there is an editorial note that Jonathan had a son who was
five years old when Jonathan died, and the implication is that he was the
only son. It is usually argued that most marriages in Israel took place at an
early age (see de Vaux, *Ancient Israel*, 29). If so, Jonathan could not have

been much more than twenty-five years old when he was killed in the battle.

Moreover, there is no evidence that the other sons of Saul left any children at all. Thus 2 Sam 21:8 implies that apart from the two sons of Rizpah, Saul's concubine, and the son of Jonathan, there were no other surviving sons or grandsons of Saul through the male line. The most probable explanation is that Jonathan's brothers may have been still too young to have had any children while Jonathan, the eldest son, had only one child. Therefore it is just possible that Ishbosheth was the youngest of Saul's sons and that therefore he had not taken any part in the final battle at Gilboa. If this interpretation is provisionally acceptable, then it would explain some other points in the story. It could account for the fact that Ishbosheth had not, apparently, taken Rizpah, his father's concubine, to wife. Many scholars have asserted that in early Israel and elsewhere in the ancient Near East, the successor or claimant to the throne took over the wife or the harem of the previous king; Absalom and Adonijah have been cited as the obvious examples of this practice in the OT (see 2 Sam 16:21–22; 1 Kgs 2:13–25; M. Tsevat, "Marriage and Monarchical Legitimacy in Ugarit and Israel," *JSS* 3 [1958] 237–43; Soggin, *OT and Oriental Studies*, 45). On the whole, this is plausible but, if so, then Ishbosheth ought to have claimed Rizpah at the beginning of his political career. Furthermore, Ishbosheth speaks of Rizpah as his father's concubine and not as his own, when he accuses Abner of having intercourse with her (2 Sam 3:7). Hence it is possible that either Ishbosheth had not made use of this practice or he was still too young to marry his father's concubine. Also the statement that Abner had *taken* Ishbosheth and *brought* him to Mahanaim (2 Sam 2:8) would fit better a younger boy than a man of forty years. The same inference may, perhaps, be drawn also from 2 Sam 3:8b. In view of all this, we assume that it is more likely that Ishbosheth was a minor and that the "forty years" is either a scribal error or simply a round figure in the absence of the exact figure.

There is no reason to doubt that Ishbosheth ruled for two years (v 10), but the present arrangement of our sources seems to suggest that both David and Ishbosheth began their respective reigns, more or less, at the same time. Another impression gained from our material is that soon after Ishbosheth's death David became king over Israel (cf. 2 Sam 4:12–5:4). Therefore it has been argued that David's reign in Hebron (seven and a half years) should be only slightly longer than that of Ishbosheth, yet the figures given indicate a difference of five years (2 Sam 2:10–11; 5:4–5). Consequently, if the data are correct, there are two main possibilities: either there was an interregnum of five years *before* Ishbosheth's reign actually began or a similar period *after* his reign. The former view was already proposed by H. Ewald (*History* 3 [1871] 112–13) and more recently a similar suggestion has been well presented by A. Soggin (*OT and Oriental Studies*, 34–40). He has suggested that initially Abner wished to become king himself, but when after five years his efforts came to nothing, he made Ishbosheth king over Israel. However, since the latter's main, if not the only, claim to kingship was based on the dynastic principle (see Ishida, *Dynasties*, 76), it would be more natural for him to be crowned soon after his father's death rather than five years later. If, on the other hand, the dynastic succession was not accepted by the people as a whole, then this delayed enthronement would be even less explicable, unless it was because of his age. On the whole, an interregnum before Ishbosheth's accession seems less likely, and we assume that the author did not think it relevant to give an account of the events in Israel between the death of Ishbosheth and the anointing of David as king over Israel (2 Sam 5:3). It is quite possible that the remnant of Ishbosheth's kingdom continued hostilities with David since the prolonged war mentioned in 2 Sam 3:1 may indicate a period lasting more than two years. Gutbrod (34) attempts to solve this exegetical problem by linking vv 10a and 12, regarding the intervening material as a later addition. In that case the translation should be: "When Ishbosheth had reigned two years, Abner went out. . . ."

Of course, Israel may have joined Judah immediately after the demise of Ishbosheth (so Stolz, 206), but this seems to be contradicted by 2 Sam 5:5 which states that David reigned *over Judah* seven years and six months (in Hebron), and that he ruled in Jerusalem *over all Israel and Judah* for thirty-three years. Taken at their face value the data would imply that soon after David was anointed king over Israel, he moved to Jerusalem. However, expressions of this nature need not always be regarded as precisely formulated statements (see *Comment* on 2 Sam 5:5).

The actual chronology of the two reigns is uncertain. Bright (*History*, 195 n.25) places the beginning of David's reign in ca. 1000 B.C. (cf. also D. N. Freedman, "The Chronology of Israel," *The Bible and the Ancient Near East*, ed. G. E. Wright. [New York: Routledge and Kegan Paul, 1961] 209). On this reckoning Ishbosheth's reign began in the same year or ca. 996/5 (so Soggin, *OT and Oriental Studies*, 40). We may also note that Freedman (*Unity and Diversity*, 16) places David's accession to the throne of Judah during the reign of Saul, some five years before the latter's death. However, this would require alterations in our sources.

Explanation

Ishbosheth and his rule were of little importance to our author except that the former stood between David and the throne of Israel. This insignificance is even further stressed by the fact that Abner is depicted as the real power behind Ishbosheth, who may well have been a minor. It seems that the principle of dynastic succession must have been accepted in Israel, and that therefore Abner had no other option but to make Ishbosheth king. It is unlikely that this was an arbitrary experiment on the part of Abner, and that the latter neglected the importance of established or accepted practices, such as anointing of the new king and the acclamation by the people or their representatives at the time of the investiture.

Although Ishbosheth claimed to rule a substantial territory, it appears that the new kingdom comprised mainly, if not entirely, the Israelite Transjordanian areas. Due to its limited size and resources, the practical effectiveness of the truncated kingdom was greatly limited. It would be difficult if not impossible to muster any sizable tribal levy while the economic state of the kingdom would not permit a mercenary force. Therefore Ishbosheth had to depend on a limited number of loyal supporters, primarily from his own tribe.

There is little reason to doubt that Ishbosheth's reign lasted for two years and that subsequent to this there was either an interregnum of five years or David ruled some five years *in Hebron* over Judah and Israel, having been king of Judah alone for two years.

Hostilities between Judah and Israel   (2:12–3:1)

Bibliography

Batten, L. W. "Helkath Hazzurim, 2 Samuel 2, 12–16." *ZAW* 26 (1906) 90–94. **Blenkinsopp, J.** *Gibeon and Israel.* 63–64. ———. "Did Saul Make Gibeon His Capital?" *VT* 24 (1974) 1–7. **Eissfeldt, 0.** "Ein Gescheiterter Versuch der Wiedervereinigung Israels." *La Nouvelle Clio* 3 (1951) 110–27. (= *KS* 3 [1966] 132–46). ———. "Noch Einmal: Ein Gescheiterter Versuch der Wiedervereinigung Israels." *La Nouvelle Clio* 4 (1952) 55–59. (= *KS* 3 [1966] 147–50). **Fensham, F. C.** "The Battle between the Men of Joab and Abner as a Possible Ordeal by Battle." *VT* 20 (1970) 356–57. **Gordon, C. H.** "Belt-wrestling in the Bible World." *HUCA* 23 (1950–51) 131–36. **Greenberg, M.** "The Hebrew Oath Particle Ḥay/Ḥē." *JBL* 76 (1957) 34–39. **Gunn, D. M.** "The 'Battle Report': Oral or Scribal Convention?" *JBL* 93 (1974) 513–18. ———. "Narrative Patterns and Oral Tradition in Judges and Samuel." *VT* 24 (1974) 286–317. **Hoffner, H. A.** "A Hittite Analogue to the David and Goliath Contest of Champions?" *CBQ* 30 (1968) 224. **Lehmann, M. R.** "Biblical Oaths." *ZAW* 81 (1969) 74–92. **Long, B. 0.** *The Problem of Etiological Narrative in the Old Testament.* BZAW 108. Berlin: Verlag Alfred Töpelmann, 1968. **Macdonald, J.** "The Status and Role of the NAʿAR in Israelite Society." *JNES* 35 (1976) 147–70. **Ottosson, M.** *Gilead: Tradition and History.* Tr. J. Gray. ConB. OT Series 3. Lund, Sweden: CWK Gleerup, 1969. **Pritchard, J. B.** "Gibeon's History in the Light of Excavation." VTSup 7 (1959) 1–12. **Sasson, J. M.** "Reflections on an Unusual Practice Reported in ARM X:4." *Or* 43 (1974) 404–10. **Sukenik, Y.** "Let the young men, I pray thee, arise and play before us." *JPOS* 21 (1948) 110–16. **Tidwell, N. L.** "The Philistine Incursions into the Valley of Rephaim (2 Sam. v 17ff.)." VTSup 30 (1979) 190–212. **Vaux, R. de.** "Single Combat in the Old Testament." *The Bible and the Ancient Near East.* Tr. D. McHugh. London: Darton, Longman and Todd, 1972.

Translation

[12] *Abner, son of Ner, and the servants of Ishbosheth,[a] son of Saul, went[b] out from Mahanaim to Gibeon.[c]* [13] *Also Joab, son of Zeruiah, and the servants of David went out,[a] and they met[b] at the pool of Gibeon. There they sat down, one company on one side[c] of the pool and the other on the opposite side[c] of the pool.* [14] *Then Abner said to Joab, "Let[a] certain seasoned warriors get up and engage[b] in a trial of arms before us." Joab answered, "Let them arise."* [15] *So they arose and crossed over in equal numbers,[a] twelve for Benjamin,[b] that is for Ishbosheth,[c] son of Saul, and twelve from the servants of David.* [16] *Then each man seized[a] his opponent by the head and thrust his dagger[b] into his opponent's side, falling down together. Therefore the place which is at Gibeon was called the Field of Adversaries.[c]* [17] *That day there was a fierce battle, and Abner and the men of Israel were beaten[a] by[b] David's servants.*

[18] *The three sons of Zeruiah were there,[a] Joab, Abishai, and Asahel. Now Asahel was as swift as a[b] gazelle in the open country.* [19] *So Asahel pursued Abner and turned neither to the right nor to the left in his chase after Abner.* [20] *Then Abner turned round and said, "Is that[a] you, Asahel?" "Yes," he replied.* [21] *So Abner*

said to him, "Turn aside[a] *to your right or your left and capture*[b] *one of the younger warriors and take his battle-gear*[c] *for yourself." But Asahel was unwilling to turn aside from following him.* [22] *Once again, Abner said to Asahel, "Turn aside from following me! Why*[a] *should I strike you to the ground? How could I then face Joab, your brother?"* [23] *But when he still refused to turn aside, Abner struck him in the abdomen with the butt*[a] *of his spear so that the spear protruded from his back; so he fell there and died on the spot.*[b] *All who came*[c] *to the place where Asahel had fallen and died*[d] *stood still.*

[24] *However, Joab and Abishai pursued Abner. The sun had already gone down when*[a] *they reached the hill of Ammah*[b] *which is opposite Giah,*[c] *on the way going to the pasture lands of Gibeon.*[d] [25] *In the meantime, the Benjaminites had rallied to Abner and formed themselves into a single body of men, and they made their stand on the top of another hill.* [26] *Then Abner called to Joab, "Must the sword go on devouring forever?* [a] *Do you not realize*[b] *that the end-result will be bitter? Will you never order the troops to end the pursuit of their kinsmen?"* [27] *Joab answered, "As God*[a] *lives, if you had not spoken, the troops would have given up the pursuit of their kinsmen only in the morning."* [28] *Then Joab sounded the horn, and all the troops stopped and pursued*[a] *no longer the men of Israel; neither did they renew their fighting.* [29] *Abner and his men marched through the Arabah all that night; eventually they crossed Jordan and marched on all the morning till they came to Mahanaim.* [30] *When Joab had abandoned the pursuit of Abner, he assembled all his troops; besides Asahel only nineteen of David's soldiers were missing.* [31] *In contrast, David's soldiers had inflicted a considerable defeat upon Benjamin, that is the men of Abner,*[a] *so that three hundred and sixty men had died.*[b] [32] *Then they took up Asahel and buried him in his father's tomb at Bethlehem.*[a] *After this Joab and his men*[b] *marched all night and reached Hebron by daybreak.*[c] [3:1] *The resultant war between the house of Saul and the house of David was long drawn out,*[a] *but David grew stronger and stronger*[b] *while the house of Saul became weaker and weaker.*[c]

Notes

12.a. See n. 8.b.

12.b. The verb יצא is sg and agrees with the nearer subj (see GKC, § 146f; Blau, *Grammar*, § 67.2).

12.c. Some Greek MSS seem to be confused about the name of this location, but it is not infrequent that "Gibeon" is confused with "Gibeah" (גבעה) or "Geba" (גבע) or "hill" (גבעה). There is no reason to question the authenticity of the MT.

13.a. G^AL add "from Hebron" (= מחברון). However, the shorter reading may be preferable although the length of the gap in 4QSam^a may support the addition.

13.b. Lit., "and they met them." MT has also יחדו "together" after גבעון "Gibeon," which seems to qualify the verb "met"; however, many scholars regard it superfluous and delete it although it is preserved in the versions. Nowack (157) takes it as a corruption of an adj that may have qualified "pool."

13.c. The Heb. demonstrative pronoun (זה . . . זה) in this context does not differentiate between the nearer and the more distant object (see Brockelmann, *Syntax*, § 23b).

14.a. The coh יקומו "let them arise" is strengthened by the addition of the enclitic נא (see GKC, § 108b).

14.b. The usual meaning of שחק in the piel is "to make sport, play" (so KJV, RV, RSV). Here it may have a more specific sense of "to fight."

15.a. Lit., "by number" (i.e., being counted).

15.b. 4QSamᵃ and G read "for the sons of Benjamin" (לבני בנימין).

15.c. 4QSamᵃ has [איש, which may point either to אישבשת or to אישבעל.

16.a. *BHK* adds אנשי בנימין "men of Benjamin" and ידו "his hand," thus suggesting, "Then each of the Benjaminites seized the head of his opponent with his hand." However, this is no improvement on the MT.

16.b. חרב is usually rendered by "sword," but in this given situation it would be the shorter type of sword or dagger that would be used.

16.c. *BHK* proposes הצדים "sides," while G suggests הַצָּרִים "adversaries"; this would require only slight revocalization.

17.a. The Heb. verb is singular, agreeing with the nearer subj (i.e., Abner); see GKC, § 146f.

17.b. Lit., "before" (so RSV, RV).

18.a. Some MSS omit שם "there," but it is attested in the versions.

18.b. Lit., "as one of the gazelles." For the structure, see Judg 16:7, 11; 2 Sam 13:13; Ps 82:7.

20.a. For this use of זה "this" as an enclitic, see GKC, § 136d; Joüon, *Grammaire*, § 143a.

21.a. RV "turn thee aside"; for the expression, see GKC, § 119s.

21.b. Lit., "seize for yourself"; see Joüon, *Grammaire*, § 133d.

21.c. The meaning of חלצה is uncertain, but it suggests something that is stripped off (cf. *HALAT*, 306). G has τὴν πανοπλίαν "armor"; Tg reads זרויה "his garments, equipment."

22.a. G has ἵνα μή "lest," probably an interpretive alteration (but see Brockelmann, *Syntax*, § 173). For the use of למה "why?" see GKC, § 150e.

23.a. The MT's אחרי is usually used as a conj ("after") or as prep ("behind"), but here it serves as a substantive, meaning "end" (so *HALAT*, 34). Many older commentators have followed Klostermann in reading אחרנית "backwards" (cf. Driver, 243). Ackroyd (38) assumes that באחרי may be a dittogr of מאחריו "from after him" in v 21; if so, it should be omitted.

23.b. Lit., "in his place." K has תחתו, while Q reads תחתיו. The meaning in either case is the same.

23.c. For the use of the sg form of ptcp (הבא "who came"), see Joüon, *Grammaire*, § 135c, 139i.

23.d. The verb "died" (וימת) is omitted by Syr but is found in the other versions.

24.a. For the paratactic construction, see Joüon, *Grammaire*, § 166c; Blau, *Grammar*, § 105.

24.b. The word אמה has no article and may be a proper noun, "Ammah" (see Simons, *Texts*, § 745–46); the usual meaning of אמה is "cubit." Aq and Theod read ὑδραγωγός "aqueduct"; similarly Vg (see also *HALAT*, 60). BHK suggests גבעה אחת "a hill" as in v 25.

24.c. For "Giah" (גיח) Gᴮᴬ have Γαι (= גיא "valley"); Aq, Symm, and Theod read φάραγγος "ravine." The Heb. גיח may, perhaps, mean "spring," of which Γαι (so G) may be a corruption; cf. "river Gihon" in Gen 2:13.

24.d. For גבעון "Gibeon," Gᴸ, Aq, and Theod have βουνός "hill," which presupposes גבעה "hill" or "Gibeah" but is no improvement.

26.a. G translates εἰς νῖκος "unto victory," but this reflects a late usage of נצח "lastingness"; see Driver, 128–29.

26.b. For the verbal form ידעתה "you know," see Joüon, *Grammaire*, § 42f.

27.a. The major versions have "as Yahweh lives," which is the more common form of this oath (cf. *THAT* 1 [1971] 554).

28.a. A few MSS read רדפו, the pf aspect, instead of the impf (cf. GKC, § 107e).

31.a. 4QSamᵃ has מאנשי "from the men of" instead of ובאנשי, lit., "and among the men of," apparently in apposition to מבנימן "from Benjamin." G has "of the men of Abner."

31.b. Gᴸ and Syr omit מתו "they died," while G has παρ᾽ αὐτοῦ (= מאתו "from him"), which may presuppose the MT. The verb may seem to be superfluous, but in the OT we often find נכה "to smite" conjoined to a verb of killing or dying (cf. 2 Sam 1:15; 2 Kgs 12:22[21]).

32.a. Some Heb. and Aram. MSS have the prep ב "in" before בית לחם "Bethlehem," but the MT reading may be an adv acc indicating the place of action (see Joüon, *Grammaire*, § 126h; Driver, 37 n.2).

32.b. Budde (207) regards יואב ואנשיו "Joab and his men" as a later addition, due to its position in the present sentence. This is possible but not an inevitable conclusion.

32.c. Lit., "and it became light" (see Joüon, *Grammaire*, § 152e; Brockelmann, *Syntax*, § 35a).

3:1.a. G reads ἐπὶ πολύ, which may point to הרבה "much," perhaps a misreading of the MT's ארכה "long drawn out."

3:1.b. For the Heb. idiom, see GKC, § 113u. Here the ptcp הלך from "to go" is coordinated with the adj חזק "strong."

3:1.c. Here we have the same idiom as in n. 3:1.b., except that the pl forms have replaced the sg ones; probably בית שאול "the house of Saul" is treated as a collective (see GKC, § 145c). However, 4QSamᵃ has the sg הולך (the following word being only fragmentary); also G has the sg equivalents.

Form / Structure / Setting

2 Sam 2:12–3:1 seems to form a single narrative consisting of two stages: 2:12–16 and 2:17–3:1. There is some uncertainty whether v 17 should go with the first part or not, but we regard it as the introduction to the second phase of the battle while the first part ends with the etiological statement in v 16b. We feel that there are insufficient grounds for rejecting the view that the two episodes give us successive stages of *one* military undertaking. Of course, it is not impossible that originally there may have been two military engagements and two independent stories, the Gibeon incident and the account of the battle near the hill of Ammah, joined together by the editor so that v 17 served as the connecting link (so Grønbaek, *Aufstieg*, 230). However, in such a case it is difficult to see the reason for the etiological story which, on its own, is somewhat obscure and inconclusive. It would make better sense if it were seen as the actual prelude to the main battle which, in its turn, provided the setting for the death of Asahel and its repercussions (but see Flanagan, *Foundation of the Monarchy*, 45–46).

We infer from the description of the hostilities that the main purpose of the author was not to portray the progress of the civil war as such but rather to depict a particular battle the significance of which was to be found in the ensuing enmity between Joab and Abner, and in its tragic consequences. Little if anything would have been gained by dwelling on the antagonism and tensions between Judah and Israel. Therefore the prolonged hostilities are summed up in a single verse (3:1), the main emphasis of which is the observation that the house of David became stronger while the house of Saul continued its decline.

The first section (vv 12–16) is essentially a battle account (see Gunn, *VT* 24 [1974] 286–90) although it concerns a passage at arms rather than the usual type of military engagement (see Sukenik, *JPOS* 21 [1948] 110–16).

Vv 12–13 set the scene for the eventual contest while v 14 gives very scanty information concerning the negotiations(?) preceding the combat. One would expect that both parties would have to agree on the conditions and consequences of this particular contest (cf. Yadin, *Warfare*, 265–67) unless such engagements followed a well established pattern (cf. 1 Sam 17:1–10). Vv 15–16a describe the actual combat and v 16b is an etiological statement. It does not follow, however, that the story was created for the sake of the etiology; the latter seems to be of secondary importance and need not lessen the historicity of the contest (cf. Long, *Etiological Narrative*, 1–4; J. Bright, *Early Israel in Recent History Writing* [SBT 19. London: SCM Press, 1956]

89–110). There are no further allusions in the OT to this type of combat, after the time of David.

It seems that the second section (2 Sam 2:17–3:1) could be defined as an extended battle account in which the confrontation between Abner and Asahel (vv 18–23) plays an important role. The narrative contains all the major elements of such battle accounts (see Gunn, *King David*, 51–58), e.g., the statement that the battle was joined (v 17a), a brief mention of the outcome of the conflict (v 17b), a list of casualties (vv 30–31), and a description of the death of Asahel who was a person of some importance (vv 18–23). It is of some interest that the fallen hero, Asahel, belongs to the *victorious* party (see Gunn, *VT* 24 [1974] 288). In a way this loose pattern may support the essential unity of this account; 3:1 is, most likely, a redactional comment.

Grønbaek (*Aufstieg*, 231), following Mowinckel, is of the opinion that originally vv 18–25 were not a description of a pursuit, after the enemy's defeat, but it was an independent account of a tournament (*Kampfspiel*) in the form of a race (*Wettlauf*) where the winner took the opponent's belt, the story being a local tradition associated with "Gibeat-Amma" (i.e., "the hill of Ammah"). This suggestion is within the limits of possibilities, but in that case Abner must have changed the rules of the game during the race, and killed Asahel. Furthermore, it is questionable whether we should regard vv 26–27 as a later addition (Grønbaek, 233). Abner's pursuit by Joab and Abishai should, most likely, be seen as part of the wider military operation and not as a private undertaking.

Comment

12   The Heb. יצא "to go out" in this context suggests a military campaign (cf. Gen 14:8; 1 Kgs 20:21). Unfortunately, the author has not given the reasons which led to these hostilities. The meeting of the protagonists was not a chance encounter because the destination (i.e., Gibeon) was clear from the very outset. Eissfeldt (*KS* 3 [1966] 144) and many other scholars have argued that Abner's purpose was to subdue Judah, but one would have expected that the first step ought to have been the liberation of the central highlands which were, most likely, in the Philistine control (see Ottosson, *Gilead*, 201).

Gibeon was a well-known Canaanite city (see Josh 9:17–18) and a political and religious center of considerable importance. Its identification with el-Jîb is no longer disputed (see Pritchard, VTSup 7 [1959] 1–3; W. L. Reed, "Gibeon," *AOTS*, 237–38), and it is situated some six miles (ten kilometers) north of Jerusalem. A number of scholars have suggested that Gibeon became Saul's royal capital (so, e.g., Blenkinsopp, *VT* 24 [1974] 1–7); although the hypothesis cannot be proved, it is, at least, probable.

13   Possibly Joab's troop set out from Gibeon (not from Hebron as suggested by some Greek MSS) to meet the challenge of Abner's forces. David was a Philistine vassal and the defense of Gibeon may have been one of his duties. The confrontation took place at the pool of Gibeon which has occasionally been identified with the great cylindrical cistern in Gibeon cleared during the excavations of 1956–57 (*EAEHL* 2 [1976] 446–47; see also Mauchline, 205). However, this would place the subsequent combat within the city itself, and this is less likely; would a *field* (of Adversaries) be located in the city? Jer 41:12 probably refers to our location when it mentions "the great pool in Gibeon"; this would hardly be a cistern (but see Pritchard, VTSup 7 [1959] 9).

14 The Heb. נער is usually translated by "young man" but in a military setting it may indicate a seasoned warrior, perhaps a professional soldier; only such expert fighters would normally be chosen to take part in a representative combat. See Macdonald, *JNES* 35 (1976) 157–70; Yadin, *Warfare*, 267.

The usual usage of the verb שׂחק would suggest that Abner and Joab planned some sort of game or mock battle (so most older commentators) but more recently scholars have come to regard this episode as a deadly serious representative combat involving twelve pairs of chosen warriors. Hence שׂחק probably means "to hold a contest" or "to engage in single combat, to fight" (see Eissfeldt, *KS* 3 [1966] 138–43). Such and similar trials at arms are attested elsewhere in the ancient Near East (cf. *ANET*, 240, lines 18–22; de Vaux, *The Bible and the Ancient Near East*, 127–31). Yadin (*Warfare*, 266) finds references to a similar combat also in 1 Sam 17:1–11; 2 Sam 22:18–19; and 1 Chr 11:23 (cf. also Tidwell, VTSup 30 [1979] 203).

15 In this particular instance each opposing side chose twelve warriors to take part in the contest. Eissfeldt (*KS* 3 [1966] 146) is of the opinion that the number twelve symbolizes the twelve tribes of Israel (cf. Ewald, *History* 3 [1871] 114) and that the ultimate aim of the contest was the unity of the whole Israel. However, this rests on the assumption that there was already an established twelve-tribe system before the Davidic monarchy.

The specific mention of "Benjamin" may indicate that the backbone of Ishbosheth's forces was formed by the loyal Benjaminites unless "Benjamin" stands for "Israel" (cf. v 17) as *pars pro toto*.

16 The description of the single combat in v 16a probably represents only the final stage of the fight; otherwise the death of all the participants would be a near certainty. For a pictorial representation of a similar(?) contest, see Yadin, *Warfare*, 267.

It is usually thought that this particular contest ended in a draw and that all twenty-four combatants killed each other. This is plausible but one cannot exclude the possibility that the agreed terms of the contest were not kept by the losing side. There is, however, no real justification for the view that the Benjaminites perpetrated a mean treachery (see n. 16.a) although they may have had a certain advantage (cf. Judg 3:15, 21; 20:16) which Abner may have hoped to exploit since it was he who proposed the contest (see also Batten, *ZAW* 26 [1906] 92).

Considerable uncertainty surrounds the name of the battlefield and the etiological wordplay, if any, is obscure; it may be linked with the word צד "side," but this would require an emendation in v 16b (cf. Long, *Etiological Narrative*, 5–9). Perhaps, it would be simpler to accept the G reading (see n. 16.c) since this requires only a revocalization of the MT. Thus the name of the battleground may have been "the Field of Adversaries" so that the etiology was based on the account of the hostilities as a whole and not associated with any specific word in the story.

17 Commentators have noted the different terms used to describe the opposing forces. E.g., here we have "Abner and the men of Israel," in v 25 the reference is to Abner and the Benjaminites (similarly in v 31) while in v 28 the term used is "Israel." Grønbaek (*Aufstieg*, 233) argues that this change in terminology is not accidental but is indicative of different sources of information. This may be so but we are inclined to be less confident; the variation could well be due to stylistic or other reasons.

"That day" in the present context must refer to the same day on which the representative combat took place at Gibeon (vv 12–16), unless the redactor has joined together two unconnected stories, which is less likely.

18 Zeruiah was, apparently, David's sister (1 Chr 2:16) or his half-sister (2 Sam 17:25). Her three sons are never identified by the name of their father who by this time may have been dead (see 2 Sam 2:32) but it is less certain that this was the *reason* for the above description of David's nephews.

Joab and Abishai must have been seasoned warriors (cf. 1 Sam 26:6–8) while Asahel was, most likely, the youngest of the brothers if the order of the names can be taken as an indication of their seniority (cf. also 1 Chr 2:16). Thus he would be less experienced in the arts of war but it is doubtful that he was "a mere stripling" (Kirkpatrick, 63); see 2 Sam 23:24; 1 Chr 11:26). Joab may have become the commander of David's forces after the capture of Jerusalem (cf. 1 Chr 11:6); in our narrative he was already in charge of a smaller unit.

Asahel was known for his swiftness, and Josephus (*Ant.* 7.14) adds that Asahel could even outrun a horse! In this passage he is compared to a gazelle, proverbially noted for its speed (cf. 1 Chr 12:8 [MT 9]; Prov 6:5).

19–22 The reconstructed conversation between Abner and Asahel probably took place when Abner stopped(?) and turned round. An experienced warrior like Abner would hardly keep his back turned to his opponent at close quarters. It may well be that Abner's words were in essence ironic (contra Nowack). He could gain no glory in killing Asahel, and his advice to the latter was to choose an opponent of "his own size."

It is unlikely that Abner's killing of Asahel created bloodguilt (contra Budde, Stolz, et al.) since this blood was shed in war (see 1 Kgs 2:5, 31–33; cf. also 2 Sam 3:28–30). The difference may not always be clear but it is difficult (though not impossible) to see how *all* blood shed in war could be avenged, except by another war. It is also a question how lasting and effective is a peace treaty after a war or hostilities; see vv 26–27. Does such an agreement put an end to blood-feuds? It seems that Abner's primary concern may have been his own honor rather than his hypothetical friendship with Joab (so Keil, 235) or fear of the latter.

The exact meaning of חליצה is not clear. Gordon (*HUCA* 23 [1950–51] 132) has argued that it was originally a "wrestling-belt" worn on the waist of the warrior but later it may have come to mean "a soldier's battle-gear" (133). This may well be right but it need not imply that Abner and Asahel were engaged in a belt-wrestling or in a specific race.

The structure of vv 21–22 emphasizes the seriousness of Abner's warning; there are three imperatives in v 21 (נטה לך "turn aside"; אחז לך "capture"; קח לך "take") which are balanced by the imperative סור לך "turn" and the two interrogative clauses in v 22. Similarly, Asahel's refusal in v 21 has its counterpart in v 23a. Thus Abner, having done all that was possible, had no other option but to kill Asahel or be killed himself.

23 There is some uncertainty as to how Asahel actually died. Probably Abner used the butt of his spear, thus giving a further proof of his superiority, rather than *striking backwards* with the butt-end, while running (so Kennedy, 201) or stopping suddenly and letting Asahel run on his spear (cf. Hertzberg, 252). Asahel was struck in the abdomen and not "under the fifth rib" (KJV; see *HALAT*, 318). It is of some interest that חמש, meaning "abdomen," occurs only three times elsewhere in the OT (2 Sam 3:27; 4:6; 20:10).

Some scholars regard "All who came . . ." as a later addition by one who knew 2 Sam 20:12 (see Nowack, 158), but it is not impossible that both narratives are by one and the same author and part of the so-called Succession Narrative. Hertzberg (252) does not regard this information as "a reference to a halt made by the pursuing warriors but to a custom which was in force for later generations." Such a custom is possible, but there is no reason that David's men could not have been stunned by Asahel's death.

24 Joab and Abishai continued the pursuit but hardly on their own (cf. 2 Sam 20:10). At sunset they had reached the hill of Ammah. The exact location of this place is uncertain; it is possible that the last part of v 24 is textually corrupt. Since the hill is further defined in v 24b, it may not have been a well-known location. Hence the emendation of *BHK* (see n. 24.b) is tempting. In that case Joab and his men came to *a* (חתא) particular hill while Abner and his followers gathered themselves on *another* (אחת) hill, close by. It is doubtful that the versions had any additional information on this subject.

"Giah" is likewise unknown outside this passage. Most versions regard it as a common noun ("valley"), but they presuppose, more or less, the same consonantal text. "Opposite" (על פני) may also denote "east" (so JB, NAB). It is doubtful that "Ammah" and "Giah" were associated with Gibeon's water supply (see Stolz, 196).

"The pasture lands of Gibeon" is a possible translation, but it is somewhat odd that the combatants had not got beyond the vicinity of Gibeon by nightfall. Budde (206) has suggested "Geba" (גבע) for "Gibeon"; this would be some five miles (eight kilometers) from Gibeon.

25–27 We assume that the opposing parties gathered themselves on two *different* hills (contra Wellhausen, 155), at a shouting distance (cf. Driver, 244). From here Abner appealed to Joab to stop further bloodshed, pointing to the kinship of the two groups (v 26b) and emphasizing the bitterness of war. Joab's reply began with the customary oath formula, "As God lives," although normally the divine name "Yahweh" is used in this expression. The exact translation of the oath is disputed. Following Greenberg (*JBL* 76 [1957] 34–39) one could render it as "By the life of Yahweh," taking חי "life" as a construct noun. However, such variations as חי אני "as I live" raise doubts as to whether חי is a construct form. Perhaps, we could paraphrase the oath by "As surely as God lives" (but see also Lehmann, *ZAW* 81 [1969] 83–86).

Joab in his answer states that had not Abner made his appeal, then only in the morning his soldiers would have given up the pursuit and killing.

This may have been the usual practice after a successful battle (see 1 Sam 14:36).

28 Caspari (411 n.4) thinks that the trumpet was part of the commander's equipment, and this is plausible (cf. 2 Sam 18:16; 20:1, 22). The trumpet (שופר) was usually made of ram's horn (cf. Josh 6:4, 8) and its main function was signaling (see *IDB* 3 [1962] 473). See also *Comment* on 6:15.

29 Abner and his forces returned to their home base in Mahanaim, and their route took them through part of the Arabah which, in this instance, must refer to the Jordan valley between the Sea of Galilee and the Dead Sea. It can also denote the continuation of the Jordan rift between the Dead Sea and the Gulf of Aqabah (see Aharoni, *The Land*, 35–36).

The latter part of v 29 is less clear. The problem is כל הבתרון which may be either a geographical designation, such as "ravine" (so Hertzberg), "Bithron" (so RV, NIV), or an indication of the time taken to traverse the area between the Jordan valley and Mahanaim (hence "all the morning"; similarly, RSV, JB, NAB, NEB). The latter alternative may well be right, and it would balance כל הלילה "all that night" in v 29a. Furthermore, the former alternative would make כל הבתרון the direct object of וילכו "they went, marched"; this is possible but rare (see Driver, 245).

30 Ackroyd (39) prefers a different sentence division, joining "Asahel" to the beginning of v 31 (hence "But Asahel and David's forces . . ."). However, this rendering places an undue emphasis on Asahel's achievements(?) during the final battle.

31 The Benjaminites are hardly to be distinguished from the rest of Abner's men (cf. Goldman, 199) although in the circumstances Saul's kinsmen (i.e., the Benjaminites) may have formed the nucleus of Abner's troop (see also Eissfeldt, *Komposition*, 26). The losses attributed to them may be an exaggeration unless David's soldiers were greatly superior in military skill (so Keil, Smith, et al.).

It is unlikely that the MT means that three hundred were wounded and sixty men died (so Ehrlich, quoted in Driver, 245). Driver rightly notes that in the OT such a differentiation is rare.

32 The MT seems to suggest that Asahel was buried the night after the battle, and that there was still time for Joab and his men to reach Hebron by the early morning. Some scholars (e.g., Goldman, Kirkpatrick, Thenius) regard this as a difficult feat, and they suggest, perhaps rightly, that the march to Hebron took place the following night.

3:1 This isolated verse summarizes the effect of the whole civil war: while the house of Saul continued its decline, David went from strength to strength. We are not told how long the hostilities lasted but they may well have continued longer than the two years assigned to the reign of Ishbosheth (2 Sam 2:10).

Explanation

Vv 12–16 give an extremely terse account of the military encounter at Gibeon. Why the two forces should meet at this strategic place is not stated but it could hardly have been a chance meeting. There are many possible explanations but we tentatively offer the following outline.

It is fairly clear that Ishbosheth's power-base was Mahanaim and that his effective rule extended mainly (if not only) over the Transjordanian territories. Consequently, it is plausible that he (or Abner) wished to recover, if possible, Benjamin and Ephraim. This would involve, most likely, the removal of any Philistine outposts from their strategic positions. If so, the Gibeon venture may have been intended as a probing military operation. Since there are good reasons for believing that David was *still* a Philistine vassal, the presence of his mercenaries at Gibeon was understandable. In a sense, this may have been a test of loyalty to his Philistine overlord. Hence the forces of David may have been in possession of Gibeon, or they were simply assisting a hypothetical Philistine garrison. Thus it was from here that they set out to meet Abner's challenge, unless the Greek text is right in suggesting that Joab and his men went out from Hebron. Had David's intention been to extend his kingdom at the expense of Israel, his forces would hardly return to Hebron after their successful battle with Israel. In any case, the later negotiations between Abner and David imply that the latter ruled only over Judah. Furthermore, it is highly doubtful that the Philistines would have permitted such an extension of David's kingdom while David still needed time.

The Gibeon encounter was in the nature of a representative combat between twelve chosen men from each side. As the text now stands, it seems that all twenty-four participants died, more or less simultaneously, and that the contest ended without any decisive result. This is possible but rather unusual. Whatever the actual outcome may have been, the result was a full-scale battle between the forces of Abner and Joab, in which the troops of the former were beaten.

It is noteworthy that although there was, apparently, a lengthy period of hostilities between the forces of David and those of Ishbosheth (2 Sam 3:1), this conflict is not so much depicted as a war between Judah and Israel but rather as a strife between the two royal houses. The author was not concerned to outline the successive phases or battles of the civil war; his main interest was to provide the setting and explanation for the subsequent enmity between Joab and Abner, which led to the murder of Abner and to the eventual punishment of Joab. Without this episode the *nature* of Abner's death would remain ambiguous and Solomon's execution of Joab would appear more questionable. From our point of view, it seems that Abner killed in self-defense while Joab committed a foul murder.

Of course, it is not impossible that the negative evaluation of the sons of Zeruiah, especially of Joab (see 2 Sam 3:28–29, 39; 16:10; 19:22 [MT 23]; 1 Kgs 2:5), was imposed upon the earlier stories in the light of later events and politics. Joab found himself in opposition to Solomon, and it is probably *this fact* that led to his death. Only a murderer would be taken from Yahweh's altar (Exod 21:13–14) but this is what happened to Joab. Yet if his offense was so heinous, is it not strange that he was not punished in David's reign? Was David powerless (2 Sam 3:39) or was it an acceptable(?) alternative to leave the *known* murderer to God's punishment?

David's Family in Hebron   (3:2–5)

Bibliography

Malamat, A. "Aspects of the Foreign Policies of David and Solomon." *JNES* 22 (1963) 1–17. **Mazar, B.** "Geshur and Maacah." *JBL* 80 (1961) 16–28. **Myers, J. M.** *I Chronicles.* AB 12. Garden City, NY: Doubleday, 1965. **Rudolph, W.** *Chronikbücher.* HAT 21. Tübingen: Verlag von J. C. B. Mohr (Paul Siebeck), 1955. **Sacon, K. K.** "A Study of the Literary Structure of 'The Succession Narrative.'" *Studies in the Period of David and Solomon and Other Essays.* Ed. T. Ishida. Winona Lake, IN: Eisenbrauns, 1982. **Stamm, J. J.** "Hebräische Ersatznamen." *Studies in Honor of Benno Landsberger on His Seventy-fifth Birthday, April 21, 1965.* The Oriental Institute of the University of Chicago. Assyriological Studies 16. Chicago: The University of Chicago Press, 1965. ———. "Hebräische Frauennamen." VTSup 16 (1967) 301–39.

Translation

[2] *Sons were born*[a] *to David in Hebron. His firstborn was Amnon, of*[b] *Ahinoam from Jezreel;*[c] [3] *his second Chileab,*[a] *of Abigail, the widow of Nabal*[b] *from Carmel;*[c] *the third Absalom, son of Maacah, the daughter of Talmai, king of Geshur;* [4] *the fourth Adonijah, son of Haggith; the fifth Shephatiah, son*[a] *of Abital;* [5] *the sixth Ithream, of David's wife*[a] *Eglah. These were born to David in Hebron.*

Notes

2.a. K reads וִלְדוּ (a contracted pual form?; see GKC, § 69u), while Q has וִיָּלְדוּ (niph), which is supported by 4QSamª although the latter has the sg form of the verb with pl subj.

2.b. The Heb. ל may introduce a dative of reference ("belonging to"; so Driver, 246), or it may help to express a gen by circumlocution (cf. GKC, § 129g).

2.c. Lit., "the Jezreelitess."

3.a. The name of David's second son is uncertain. G has Δαλουια "Daluiah," while in 1 Chr 3:1 and Josephus (*Ant.* 7.21) we find דָנִיאל "Daniel." Tg, Vg, and Syr (כלב) follow MT. It seems that 4QSamª supports the G reading, assuming that the reconstruction is right, but Aq, Symm, and Theod read Αβια "Abiah."

3.b. G omits אשת נבל "widow of Nabal"; so also 1 Chr 3:1 and 4QSamª. Tg, Vg, and Syr follow MT.

3.c. Lit., "the Carmelite."

4.a. 4QSamª has לאביטל "of Abital" for MT's בן אביטל "son of Abital." G with its τῆς Αβιταλ supports the former reading (so also Josephus).

5.a. 1 Chr 3:3 has אשתו "his wife" for אשת דוד "the wife of David."

Form / Structure / Setting

Vv 2–5 give a list of David's sons born in Hebron, and it may have been derived from a state archive (so Hertzberg, 253). It is far from certain that these verses are part of the list found in 2 Sam 5:13–16 (as suggested by Budde); the former gives also the names of the *sons' mothers* while the latter provides only the names of the *sons* born in Jerusalem. Both lists are placed together by the Chronicler (1 Chr 3:1–9), but this does not prove that the two lists originally formed a single document.

Many scholars do not regard vv 2–5 as part of the original narrative (see

Veijola, *Dynastie*, 11 n.48; Noth, *The Deuteronomistic History*, 55 n.11) although Eissfeldt (*Komposition*, 26) is of the opinion that these verses are not secondary even though v 6 seems to be the direct continuation of v 1. Vv 2–5 fit in well with the idea of the gradual increase of the house of David (v 1), and therefore they need not necessarily be considered as a later interpolation.

Sacon (*The Period of David and Solomon*, 45) has pointed out, perhaps rightly, that vv 1a and 6a form an inclusion, and that the list of the sons is once more bracketed by vv 2a and 5b. The later inclusion is more obvious but the former one, too, is possible. In his view, the section comprises vv 1–6a.

Comment

2 David's *firstborn* son was Amnon, and this description seems to rule out Hertzberg's suggestion (253) that David may have had sons before he settled down in Hebron (similarly, also Buccellati, *Cities and Nations*, 222). It is unlikely that an Israelite would have more than one firstborn son. For בכור "firstborn," see *TDOT* 2 (1977) 121–27.

Amnon's name (אמנון) probably means "faithful" (BDB, 54) while Noth (*Personennamen*, 228) classifies it as a non-religious name.

"Ahinoam" (אחינעם) means "my brother is delight" (BDB, 27), but the reference may be to the deity (see Noth, *Personennamen*, 166; Stamm, VTSup 16 [1967] 317).

3 The name of Abigail's son is problematic (see n. 3.a). Myers (*1 Chronicles*, 17), following Freedman, argues that the original form of כלאב "Chileab" was יכל אב "the father prevails," the present name being a shortened form. Also Rudolph (*Chronikbücher*, 27) holds the view that the name has nothing to do with כלב "Caleb" but means "*ganz der Vater*" ("entirely the father"), which he regards as a sort of nickname for Daniel, his real name. Nevertheless, it is possible that כלאב is a cognate of כלב "Caleb," since Abigail, the mother of Chileab, may have belonged to the tribe of Caleb (so Gutbrod, 39 n.4). Chileab probably died young because he did not figure in the later events associated with the succession to the throne.

Abigail (cf. Stamm, VTSup 16 [1967] 316) was the widow of Nabal (see 1 Sam 25) and they both may have come from Carmel, near Hebron (see *Comment* on 2:2).

4 The third son, Absalom, played an important role in later events (see 2 Sam 13–19). His name אבשלום is often taken to mean "(the) father is peace" (cf. BDB, 5); thus it is a theophorous name, "(the divine) father is peace" or, perhaps, "(the divine) father is (the god) Shalom" (see H. Ringgren, "אב," *TDOT* 1 [1974] 16; cf. also Stamm, *Studies in Honor of Benno Landsberger*, 416–18).

"Haggith" may mean "born during a festival" (see Stamm, VTSup 16 [1967] 322; Noth, *Personennamen*, 222).

Absalom's mother, Maacah, was the daughter of the king of Geshur which was, apparently, a small Transjordanian kingdom between Bashan and Hermon (cf. Simons, *Texts*, § 7), i.e., in the Golan (see Mazar, *JBL* 80 [1961] 17). This marriage in particular may have had a political significance, and by means of it David may have gained an ally, thus weakening the strategic position of Ishbosheth's kingdom (see Levenson and Halpern, *JBL* 99 [1980] 518; Malamat, *JNES* 22 [1963] 8).

Adonijah (אדניה, "Yahweh is lord") is the first of David's sons to have a Yahwistic theophoric name which includes the element "yah" (see Noth, *Personennamen*, 117–21). It is noteworthy that the two lists (2 Sam 3:2–5 and 5:13–16) mention seventeen sons of David but only two of them have Yahwistic names in the MT. It may be, perhaps, significant that neither David's brothers nor his father had Yahwistic names.

For "Maacah," see Stamm, VTSup 16 (1967) 332. The meaning is uncertain and the same(?) name is used both of men (cf. 1 Kgs 2:39; 1 Chr 11:43) and of women.

"Shephatiah" (שפטיה) is the other Yahwistic name, and it means "Yah(weh) has judged" (see BDB, 1049); it is classed as a thanksgiving name (*Dankname*) (cf. Noth, 169–95).

For "Abital" (אביטל), see Stamm, 317. It probably means "my (divine) father is protection" (cf. also the analogous יהוטל; see D. N. Freedman and P. O'Connor, "יהוה," *TWAT* 3 [1980] 540).

5 The name "Ithream" (יתרעם) is probably related to יתר "be left over"; so Barr, *Philology*, 183. Noth (*Personennamen,* 197) links it with תרה, and translates as "may the tribal god protect."

Ithream's mother, Eglah, is described as "David's wife" which is somewhat unusual in the given context. Wellhausen (157) has argued that one would expect the name of Eglah's former husband, as in the case of Abigail, "the wife (i.e., widow) of Nabal" (v 3). Smith (274) has suggested אחות "sister" (i.e., half-sister) for אשת "wife," but this is unlikely because David is said to have had only *two* sisters, Zeruiah and Abigail (see 1 Chr 2:16).

"Eglah" probably means "heifer" (so BDB, 722; Noth, 230). Such and similar animal names were quite frequently used as proper names in the ancient Near East (see Stamm, VTSup 16 [1967] 329).

Explanation

The original purpose of this list is no longer clear, but it may have been linked with the question of succession. In its present setting, it probably serves as an illustration of the steady growth of the house of David and as an indication of the divine blessing and approval. The list may also provide a preliminary introduction to some of the *dramatis personae* who will become significant at a later stage, e.g., Amnon, Absalom, and Adonijah. The order of the sons may shed some light on the subsequent intrigues and struggles for the succession to the throne of David.

It is unlikely, though not impossible, that each wife had only one son; therefore it seems that the list names only the firstborn son of each wife. Absalom, of course, had a sister, Tamar (2 Sam 13:1).

The many wives of David were both an indication of his status in the society and a means whereby political ties could be established and strengthened. Due to our limited information the role of David's marital politics is less clear, but its importance should not be underestimated.

David and Abner   (3:6–39)

Bibliography

Ben-Barak, Z. "The Legal Background to the Restoration of Michal to David." VTSup 30 (1979) 15–29. **Brongers, H. A.** "Fasting in Israel in Biblical and Post-biblical Times." *OTS* 20 (1977) 1–21. **Christ, H.** *Blutvergiessen*, 36–61; 94–97. **Giesen, G.** *Die Wurzel* שבע *"schwören,"* 319–21. **Glück, J. J.** "Merab or Michal." *ZAW* 77 (1965) 72–81. **Koch, K.** "Der Spruch 'Sein Blut bleibe auf seinem Haupt' und die israelitische Auffassung vom vergossenen Blut." *VT* 12 (1962) 396–416. **Lehmann, M. R.** "Biblical Oaths." *ZAW* 81 (1969) 74–91. **Lemche, N. P.** "David's Rise." *JSOT* 10 (1978) 2–25. **Neufeld, E.** *Ancient Hebrew Marriage Laws.* London/New York/Toronto: Longmans, Green and Co., 1944. **Phillips, A.** "NEBALAH: A Term for Serious Disorderly and Unruly Conduct." *VT* 25 (1975) 237–41. **Plautz, W.** "Monogamie und Polygamie im Alten Testament." *ZAW* 65 (1963) 3–27. **Schmidt, L.** *Menschlicher Erfolg*, 126–31. **Stoebe, H. J.** "David und Mikal. Überlegungen zur Jugendgeschichte Davids." *Von Ugarit nach Qumran*, 224–43. **Thomas, D. W.** "KELEB 'Dog': Its Origins and Some Usages of It in the Old Testament." *VT* 10 (1960) 410–27. **Tsevat, M.** "Marriage and Monarchical Legitimacy in Ugarit and Israel." *JSS* 3 (1958) 237–43. **Vanderkam, J. C.** "Davidic Complicity in the Deaths of Abner and Eshbaal: A Historical and Redactional Study." *JBL* 99 (1980) 521–39.

Translation

⁶*While*[a] *the hostilities*[b] *continued between the house of Saul and the house of David, Abner remained the mainstay in the house of Saul.* ⁷*Now Saul had a concubine whose name*[a] *was Rizpah, the daughter of Aiah.*[b] *One day Ishbosheth, son of Saul,*[c] *said to Abner, "Why have you slept*[d] *with my father's concubine?"* ⁸*Abner became indignant at the words of Ishbosheth and exclaimed, "Am I a worthless dog?*[a] *So far*[b] *I have been loyal to the house of your father Saul, to*[c] *his kinsmen and his friends, in that I have not delivered you*[d] *into David's power,*[e] *yet today you have charged me with an offense involving this woman.*[f] ⁹*May God do thus to Abner, and even more so,*[a] *if I do not accomplish for David what Yahweh has sworn to him;*[b] ¹⁰*namely, to transfer the kingdom from the house of Saul and to establish the house of David over Israel and over Judah, from Dan to Beersheba."* ¹¹*Ishbosheth*[a] *could not say a single word in reply to Abner because he was afraid*[b] *of him.*

¹²*Then Abner sent messengers to David, instead of going himself,*[a] *with this message, "To whom does the land really belong?*[b] *Make an agreement with me, and you will have my full support in that I will bring*[c] *the whole of Israel over to you."* ¹³*David's*[a] *reply was, "Good, I*[b] *will indeed make an agreement with you but on one condition,*[c] *that you shall not see my face unless*[d] *you bring Michal, Saul's daughter, when you come to see me."* ¹⁴*Then David sent messengers to Ishbosheth, son of Saul, saying, "Give me my wife Michal whom I betrothed to me at the price of a hundred*[a] *Philistine foreskins."* ¹⁵*So Ishbosheth sent and took her from her husband*[a] *Paltiel,*[b] *son of Laish.* ¹⁶*Her husband went with her as far as Bahurim, weeping*[a] *all the way. Then Abner said to him, "Go, return!" So he returned.* ¹⁷*In the meantime*[a] *Abner had sent a word to the elders of Israel, "Previously*

you had been seeking David for your king. [18] *Now then, take action for Yahweh has given his promise to David, saying, 'By the hand of my servant David I will save* [a] *my people* [b] *Israel from the hand of the Philistines and from the hand of all their enemies.'"* [19] *Abner also* [a] *spoke to the Benjaminites and, finally, he went to Hebron to tell David all that was acceptable to Israel and to the whole house of Benjamin.*

[20] *When Abner, accompanied by twenty men,* [a] *came to David in Hebron, David made a feast for Abner and his men.* [b] [21] *Then Abner said to David, "I will arise and go, and I will gather all Israel to my lord, the king, that they may make an agreement with you,* [a] *and that you may be king over all that your heart desires." So David sent Abner away, and he went in peace.* [22] *At the same time,* [a] *David's men and Joab were returning* [b] *from a raid, bringing much spoil with them. Abner, however, was no longer with David in Hebron for he had sent him away, and he had gone in peace.* [23] *So when Joab and the whole company that was with him arrived, Joab was told,* [a] *"Abner son of Ner, came to the king* [b] *but he has sent him away and he has gone in peace."* [24] *Then Joab went to the king and said, "What have you done? What an opportunity* [a] *when Abner came to you! Why then have you sent him away so that now he is getting out of our reach.* [b] [25] *You know* [a] *Abner, son of Ner! He came but to deceive you, to spy out all your movements,* [b] *and to find out all that you are doing."* [26] *So Joab left David and sent messengers after Abner. They brought him back from the well of Sirah, but David had no knowledge of this.* [27] *When Abner returned to Hebron,* [a] *Joab took him aside into the gateway* [b] *as if to talk with him privately. There he stabbed him in* [c] *the abdomen, and he died for the blood of Joab's* [d] *brother Asahel.* [28] *Later, when David heard of it, he said, "I and my kingdom are forever guiltless before Yahweh of the murder* [a] *of Abner, son of Ner.* [29] *May the bloodguilt descend* [a] *upon the head of Joab and upon* [b] *all his father's* [c] *house! May the house of Joab never lack one suffering from a discharge or skin disease or one who is fit to wield only a spindle or one doomed to die by the sword or one in want of bread!"* [30] *Joab and Abishai murdered* [a] *Abner* [b] *because he had killed their brother Asahel in battle at Gibeon.*

[31] *Then David commanded Joab and all the people with him, "Rend your garments, put on sackcloth, and lament before Abner." King David himself walked behind the bier.* [32] *When they had buried Abner in Hebron, the king wept aloud at the tomb of Abner; also all the people wept.* [a] [33] *Then the king lamented for* [a] *Abner:*

"Should Abner have died the death of a lawless man?
[34] *Your hands were not bound* [a] *in chains,* [b]
your feet were not put in fetters!
You have fallen as one falls before wicked men."
And all the people [c] *wept again for him.* [35] *When afterwards all the people came to persuade David to eat bread while it was still day, David took an oath, saying, "May God do thus to me and even more so if* [a] *I taste bread or anything else before the sunset."* [36] *So all the people took note of this and they approved; in fact, everything* [a] *the king did seemed good to all the people.* [37] *Consequently, all the people and all Israel realized that day that the plan to kill Abner, the son of Ner, had not come from the king.* [38] *Then the king said to his servants, "Do you not realize that a great leader* [a] *has fallen this day in Israel?* [39] *However, I am still weak as yet al-*

though anointed king; these men, the sons of Zeruiah, are too strong for me. Therefore, may Yahweh requite the evildoer according to his evil deed."

Notes

6.a. For the construction, see GKC, § 164g.

6.b. Lit., "war" (מלחמה).

7.a. G, 4QSamᵃ omit ושמה "and her name"; however, retain MT (cf. 2 Sam 13:1, 3).

7.b. Gᴸ adds "and Abner took her." This may be an explanatory note, improving the transition from v 7a to v 7b.

7.c. The verb "said" has no explicit subj in MT (and Tg). We follow the reading of G which may be supported by 4QSamᵃ; Vg adds only "Hisboseth" ("Ishbosheth").

7.d. Lit., "Why have you gone in unto . . . ," which is an idiomatic expression for cohabitation. Strictly, the reference is to the man entering a woman's quarters (so E. A. Speiser, *Genesis*, 45).

8.a. Following G and omitting אשר ליהודה "which belongs to Judah." This phrase is probably a gloss on כלב "dog," which may have been understood by some later scribe as the proper name "Caleb," the tribe or clan incorporated in Judah.

8.b. Lit., "today" (היום).

8.c. A number of MSS and versions insert the conj "and" (ו) before the preposition (אל "to"), but there is no real necessity for it.

8.d. For the orthography of המצילתך ". . . delivered you," see GKC, § 75qq. The above form belongs to the III-*Hê* verbs, but our verb is מצא (cf. Zech 11:6).

8.e. Lit., "(I have not caused you to fall) into the hand of David."

8.f. Some read אשה "a woman," omitting the article with G. However, the article here may have a demonstrative force (see GKC, § 126b).

9.a. Lit., "and thus may he add to me."

9.b. G adds, unnecessarily, "in that day"; see, however, 1 Kgs 1:30.

11.a. G and Syr add "Ishbosheth"; this is helpful although it need not be the original reading.

11.b. MT has a verbal noun (יראה "fear") governing an acc (אתו "him"); cf. GKC, § 115d.

12.a. MT has תחתיו (so Q) which, if correct, refers either to Abner (i.e., "instead of . . . himself") or, less likely, to David (i.e., "where he was"). Gᴸ adds "to Hebron" which makes good sense, but its authenticity is questionable.

12.b. The Heb. text is uncertain. The twofold repetition of לאמר "saying" is odd, and for ארץ "land" we would expect הארץ "the land." Wellhausen (158) omits למי ארץ לאמר "to whom belongs the land, saying," which he regards as a double dittogr of the immediately preceding לאמר. This is possible since the phrase is omitted in Gᴸ. The G may contain an inner corruption at this point (cf. Driver, 248). In view of the textual uncertainty and in absence of any generally accepted solution, we retain the MT even though it may not preserve the original reading.

12.c. Lit., "(and behold my hand is with you) to bring . . ."

13.a. Not in MT but in G and Syr.

13.b. The first person pronoun (אני) before the verb may add emphasis to the whole response (see Davidson, *Syntax*, § 73 R.1; Joüon, *Grammaire,* § 146a).

13.c. Lit., "but one thing I am asking of you."

13.d. MT reads כי אם לפני, and it has been argued that כי אם and לפני are mutually exclusive. Perhaps, the MT offers two alternative variants: לפני הביאך "before you bring" and כי אם הבאת "unless you bring"; so G (see Driver, 248).

14.a. Syr (following 1 Sam 18:27) has מאתין "two hundred," but this is, perhaps, a deliberate emendation for the sake of harmony.

15.a. Reading אישה "her husband" with the versions.

15.b. In 1 Sam 25:44 we find the shorter form פלטי "Palti"; so also Syr.

16.a. Lit., "going and weeping after her." For the coordination of the two inf abs (הלוך ובכה), see GKC, § 113s.

17.a. The phrase is supplied. However, the sequence of events is not clear from the context (cf. Thenius, 153).

18.a. So most MSS and versions, reading אושיע for הושיע "he has saved" (?), which may be an inf constr instead of the coh (so GKC, § 113dd n.4). However, the original reading may have had the inf abs before the impf: הושע אושיע "I will indeed save"; cf. Thenius, 153.

18.b. G omits עמי "my people."

19.a. The Heb. גם "also" refers to the verb and not to Abner; so also the second גם.

20.a. עשרים "twenty" usually takes the sg of איש "man" when the latter follows the numeral (see GKC, § 134e), but there is no real necessity to read עשרה "ten"; so Ehrlich, *Randglossen,* 280.

20.b. Lit., "(the) men who were with him." Budde (212) regards לאנשים as definite (contra *BHS*), "for the men."

21.a. G wrongly "and I will make a covenant with him."

22.a. For this use of הנה "behold," see McCarthy, *Bib* 61 (1980) 337–38.

22.b. *BHS* has the sg form בא, while we would expect either באו "they returned" or, better, the pl ptcp באם "they were returning." The pl is suggested by two MSS and all the major versions. The letter ם could have been omitted due to haplography.

23.a. Here the active theme in the 3 pl seems to be used to express the pass (cf. GKC, § 144f). G has "it was reported."

23.b. 4QSamᵃ and G have דויד "David"; Syr combines both, reading מלכא דויד "King David."

24.a. MT has הנה "behold," which probably expresses an excited perception (see McCarthy, *Bib* 61 [1980] 332–33).

24.b. Lit., "and he is going away"; for the structure in which a finite verb is followed by an inf abs, see GKC, § 113r. G adds "in peace" (= בשלום), but this may make the fourfold repetition of "in peace" somewhat cumbersome (cf. Driver, 249).

25.a. G has ἦ οὐκ "do (you) not (know)?" suggesting הלו (= הלא), which may be the correct reading, or an emendation, of הלוך at the end of v 24.

25.b. Lit., "your going out and your coming in." MT has the normal form מבואך, while Q suggests the unusual מובאך "your coming in."

27.a. 4QSamᵃ must have read חברונה "to Hebron." MT omits the directive ה or *Hê locale* (see GKC, § 90c–i).

27.b. Some scholars (e.g., Driver, 250) read אל ירך "to the side of (the gate)" for אל תוך "to the midst of. . . ." G has "by the side of the gate," while the MT may simply mean "inside the gateway" (cf. Zech 5:8).

27.c. The preposition "in" may have been accidentally omitted in MT (see 2 Sam 2:23; 4:6; 20:10, which have אל "in"); 4QSamᵃ reads עד "upon." Ulrich (*Qumran Text,* 56) regards על "upon" as the original expression (so also some Heb. MSS).

27.d. So G.

28.a. MT has the pl דמי lit., "bloods of . . . ," while 4QSamᵃ and Gᴸ have the sg (=דם); they also take the whole phrase as the beginning of v 29 (similarly NAB). However, this expression has no real parallel; on the other hand, the verb יחלו ". . . descend" is provided with an explicit subj.

29.a. 4QSamᵃ has יחול, the sg form of the verb due to the sg of דם "blood"; see above. "Bloodguilt" is supplied from the context (see v 28).

29.b. Read על "upon" with several MSS, 4QSamᵃ, Tg, and Syr for MT's אל (an equivalent of על?).

29.c. 4QSamᵃ reads יואב "Joab" for אביו "his father"; one of the readings may be an accidental transposition of letters, and the former reading may well be right (see Ulrich, *Qumran Text,* 126).

30.a. G has "they lay in wait" (= ארבו), but this may be a later attempt to reconcile v 30 with v 27.

30.b. The ל in לאבנר "Abner" is an equivalent of the obj marker את (cf. GKC, § 117n).

32.a. G has rearranged the text to read, ". . . at his tomb; and all the people wept for Abner."

33.a. Some MSS and 4QSamᵃ read על "over" for MT's אל "for." G has ἐπὶ "upon."

34.a. The ptcp אסרות "bound" is negated by לא, which is a comparatively infrequent usage and may add a certain emphasis to the whole clause (see GKC, § 152d).

34.b. Reading with 4QSamᵃ בזקים "in chains." This improves the parallelism and may well be the original variant.

34.c. 4QSamᵃ alone omits העם "the people," but this is probably a scribal error.

35.a. Some scholars suggest אם "if" for כי אם, as in 1 Sam 3:17; 25:22 (so Budde, 214). However, Driver (252) may be right in regarding כי as introducing the oath (so in 1 Sam 14:44) while אם expresses it.

36.a. Reading כל "everything" for ככל "as everything," following G. MT may be due to dittogr.

38.a. Deleting the conj ו "and" before גדול "great"; so G and Syr. The MT could be rendered "a leader and a great (man)" (cf. 2 Sam 7:9).

Form / Structure / Setting

The narrative in vv 6–39 could be roughly divided into four sections; vv 6–11 depict Abner's quarrel with Ishbosheth, while vv 12–21 deal with Abner's negotiations with David, involving the restoration of Michal (vv 13–16) and the planned covenant with Israel. Unfortunately, the finalization of the negotiations did not materialize because of Abner's tragic and untimely death (vv 22–27). The last section (vv 28–39) shows that David had no part in the murder of Abner; he curses Joab and laments for Abner.

These various elements are fairly well blended together, but certain verses are often regarded as secondary. So Veijola (*Dynastie,* 59–60) views vv 9–10 as a later Deuteronomistic addition (contra Nübel, Mildenberger); the open rebellion declared by Abner seems a very drastic step in comparison with Ishbosheth's accusation, which even Abner himself considered as based on a trifling incident.

Also vv 17–19 are seen as formulated by the Deuteronomistic editor (Veijola, 60–62), to stress that Abner was not engaged in rebellious intrigues but carried out the will of Yahweh, and that he had behind him the full support of all Israel, including Benjamin. The additions have close affinities with 1 Kgs 2:5–6, 31b–33.

Similarly, vv 28–29 and 38–39 are assigned to the same editor (Veijola, 46), while Ackroyd (48) is of the opinion that v 38 may be a continuation of the lament in vv 33–34 or an alternative dirge over Abner.

Most scholars take also v 30 as a later gloss to explain the negative attitude (v 39) to the *sons* of Zeruiah (i.e., Joab and Abishai; cf. 2 Sam 2:18; 1 Chr 2:16).

All these suggestions are plausible, but one is more hesitant to ascribe vv 28–29 and 38–39 to the Deuteronomistic editor. They may well belong to the same tradition that felt it necessary to justify the murder of Joab on Solomon's orders (1 Kgs 2:31–34). Even if Joab's killing of Abner and Amasa had been plain murders, David's legal lethargy would still have required some justification. It seems that Solomon is "vindicated" at David's expense; the latter is made into a feeble king (2 Sam 3:39) who delegated to Yahweh the execution of justice, which he himself ought to have implemented.

Comment

6 Since Abner is portrayed in our sources as a positive hero, we take the participle מתחזק "kept faithful to" (cf. *HALAT,* 291) in a good sense which is its normal usage (see Driver, 246); cf. NEB ". . . made his position gradually stronger." For the use of the participle with the perfect of היה to express an action continuing in the past, see GKC, § 116r.

7 As far as we know, Saul had only one concubine, Rizpah (cf. 2 Sam

21:8). Her name רצפה may mean "glowing stone (or coal)" (BDB, 954), and it may describe the brightness of the child's eyes (see Stamm, VTSup 16 [1967] 324). She was the daughter of Aiah (איה, meaning "falcon"). For the use of animal names as proper nouns, see Noth, *Personennamen*, 229–30.

The exact marital status of a concubine is uncertain. The Heb. פלגש "concubine" may be a foreign loanword (cf. Greek πάλλαξ "concubine" and Latin *pelex*). Neufeld (*Marriage Laws*, 123–34) regards פלגש as being "more a prostitute than an actual concubine," but it is more likely that in most cases she was a legitimate wife of second rank (see Plautz, *ZAW* 65 [1963] 9–13), perhaps mainly drawn from the lower or slave classes (so Mace, *Hebrew Marriage*, 129).

The original significance and reasons for Abner's involvement with Rizpah are no longer clear to us. Many commentators assume that "the marriage of a former king's wife bestows legitimacy on an aspirant who otherwise has no sufficient claim to the throne" (Tsevat, *JSS* 3 [1958] 241). Consequently, it has been argued that Abner wished to take over the kingship in Israel and that therefore he slept with Rizpah, Saul's concubine (see Grønbaek, *Aufstieg*, 237; Stolz, 199). This is possible but far from certain. There is no clear indication of it in the text itself; if anything, Abner's protestation of loyalty seems to exclude this interpretation. Furthermore, the kingship was, practically, Abner's for the taking; Ishbosheth's reprimand would scarcely deter Abner if the kingship over Israel were his ultimate aim (cf. v 11). Abner's military prowess and kinship with Saul might provide a far better claim to the throne than the take-over of Saul's concubine, even assuming that such a procedure was a recognized practice in Israel at that time. On the above argument Rizpah ought to have become Ishbosheth's wife if indeed the wives and concubines of the dead ruler belonged to his successor (cf. Ackroyd, 42, 155). Had she become a concubine of Ishbosheth, Abner's indiscretion would have been tantamount to adultery. It is, of course, possible that the young king was still a minor and that for this reason he had not married Rizpah (see *Comment* on 2 Sam 2:10–11).

Moreover, Abner himself (or the editor) must have viewed the affair with Rizpah as an insignificant indiscretion (v 8). His reply could even be taken as a denial of the accusation. Since the author is favorably disposed toward Abner, it may well be that Abner is depicted as the loyal benefactor of the house of Saul, who has been unjustly denounced. Hence his righteous anger and surprising volte-face.

8 The rhetorical question, "Am I a dog's head?" is a well known *crux interpretum*. We omit "which belongs to Judah" (see n. 8.a) lest the pejorative undertones of "dog's head" are associated with Judah (and David). The accusation, whatever its implications, refers to Abner's sexual relationship with Rizpah, and therefore his reply ought to take up this point. Since sexual promiscuity of dogs is nearly proverbial, Abner's exclamation is fairly apposite (cf. Deut 23:18 [MT 19]). For this reason the translation, "Am I a Calebite chief . . ." is rather unlikely (see Winckler, *Geschichte* 1 [1895] 25). In view of 2 Kgs 6:25, where a donkey's head denotes the most worthless part of the animal, we propose "worthless dog" as a paraphrase of "dog's head."

The house of Saul is further defined by "his kinsmen and his friends." The Heb. מרעהו must be a plural ("his friends"), although the letter *yōdh* is missing before the pronominal suffix (see GKC, § 91k). Since Abner was a close relative of Saul (see *Comment* on 2:8) the reference to "kinsmen" and "friends" may indicate a possible power struggle between Abner and certain other members of the house of Saul.

The twofold repetition of "this very day" serves to emphasize the contrast between Abner's loyalty and Ishbosheth's ingratitude.

9–10 Abner's oath is essentially a form of self-cursing which originally must have been accompanied by some sort of symbolic action (see 1 Sam 11:7). This form of oath is characteristic of the Books of Samuel and Kings (cf. Lehmann, *ZAW* 81 [1969] 81); it occurs elsewhere only in Ruth 1:17 (see Campbell, *Ruth*, 74). This formulary usually uses אלהים "God" instead of "Yahweh."

In his solemn affirmation Abner refers to an oath of Yahweh to David (cf. v 18), but no such explicit oath is mentioned in the preceding chapters, unless the allusion is to 1 Sam 15:28 or 22:13. It could be implicit in the anointing of David by Samuel (1 Sam 16:13) if the episode is regarded as historical. Schmidt (*Menschlicher Erfolg*, 128–31) finds the ultimate source of this oath in 2 Sam 7, but it could well be an inference from the fact that the house of David had superseded that of Saul; since it had come about, it could only have been willed and commanded by Yahweh.

The reference to Israel and Judah (v 10) indicates the dual nature of David's kingdom, the extent of which was conventionally described as "from Dan to Beersheba," the two extreme geographical points.

Dan is usually identified with Tell el-Qadi (see *EAEHL* 1 [1975] 313–21), situated at the foot of Mount Hermon, and guarding the trade route linking Tyre with Damascus. It was the old Canaanite city of Laish (Judg 18:7, 29) taken over by the tribe of Dan. Jeroboam I established here his northern sanctuary (1 Kgs 12:29).

Beersheba is identified with Tell es-Sabaʿ, some twenty-three miles (thirty-seven kilometers) southwest of Hebron, in the Judean hills, on the trade route to Egypt. It is well known from the patriarchal narratives (Gen 21, 26, 28, 46) and it must have been a religious center (Gen 21:33; 46:1). Its name probably means "well of seven" (Gen 21:30–31).

12 It seems that at this point Abner made an exploratory attempt to make a deal with David: he proposed a covenant or an agreement in return for securing Israel's allegiance to David. It is possible that the rhetorical question, "To whom does the land really belong?" is a later addition, suggesting that Abner is not committing a high treason but is simply instrumental in helping to bring about the fulfillment of Yahweh's promise to David; in other words, the land *already* belongs to David because of the above oath. However, some scholars (e.g., Kirkpatrick, 69; Kennedy, 205) have argued that the question stresses that it is *Abner* who is "the *de facto* lord of the land" (Hertzberg, 258). This is less likely because the decisive factor is Yahweh's oath (v 9) not Abner's domination.

It is not stated what privileges Abner expected to derive from this deal with David, but they may have helped to increase Joab's enmity against Abner (see Vanderkam, *JBL* 99 [1980] 531) assuming that Joab was aware of the real nature of the negotiations (see v 25). We are not entitled to infer from this verse that "David in Hebron was politically much weaker than Ishbosheth in Mahanaim" (Mauchline, 209). If anything, the general picture points in the opposite direction.

13 David's answer seems to imply that he is not engaged in a treacherous scheming but that he is determined to get what is his by right, namely, both Michal, his wife, and the kingdom.

There is no doubt that Michal became David's wife, but questions have been raised whether this happened *during* Saul's lifetime or only *after* his death (see Stoebe, *Von Ugarit nach Qumran*, 228). The latter alternative would require the rejection of the historicity of 1 Sam 18:20–27 and of the references to Michal as David's wife before 2 Sam 3:15–16. Although it is possible that the stories concerning David's early years may have been elaborated and influenced by traditional material (such as Jacob's marriage to Leah and Rachel), it seems too drastic to regard 1 Sam 18:20–27 and the related episodes as historically incorrect (so Noth, *History*, 184 n.1).

14 Occasionally it has been remarked that David's marriage or remarriage to Michal was contrary to the law in Deut 24:1–4 which forbids such a remarriage, and which is attested also in Jer 3:1. However, the situations are not alike, and there are some significant differences. First, David's case is not identical with the situation envisaged by the Deuteronomic law because he did not divorce Michal but he was forced to flee. Second, the above law may not have been in force in David's time, at least not in its present form (cf. Deut 24:4b). Third, David's case has certain parallels in the ancient Near Eastern laws (see Ben Barak, VTSup 30 [1979] 21–25) which show that a remarriage after the first husband's return from captivity or exile was the usual practice, at least in some lands, even when the wife had married another man in the meantime and had had children by him. It is likely that some such tradition may have existed also in ancient Israel because similar legal situations were bound to arise.

In view of this, it seems that David acted strictly within his legal rights; he had not divorced Michal nor had the equivalent of the bride-price (מהר) been returned to him. Therefore he was entitled to reclaim his wife. This may also account for the uncritical viewpoint of the editor and the passive attitude of Michal's second husband. The latter was obviously upset but he did not, apparently, raise any objections because legally no injustice had been done to him.

David claims to have given a hundred foreskins of the Philistines as the bride-price for Michal. However, in 1 Sam 18:27 we are told that he paid double the price demanded by Saul (1 Sam 18:25), but this does not necessarily contradict the present passage. Normally the bride-price would be some sort of payment but David was asked to perform a deed of valor by slaying a hundred Philistines (see W. Plautz, "Die Form der Eheschliessung im Alten Testament," *ZAW* 76 [1964] 299–304). The payment was made at the betrothal and from that point onwards the marriage was legally in force although its consummation was still in the future (cf. Mace, *Hebrew Marriage*, 172).

Some commentators (e.g., Ackroyd, 44) argue that vv 14–15 are part of an alternative account; in vv 13, 16 Abner is instrumental in Michal's return while in vv 14–15 David makes his demand directly to Ishbosheth. This is, of course, possible but it is equally likely that at this point Abner's negotiations with David were still secret (so Budde, 211) and therefore the request was made to Ishbosheth. Furthermore, the latter was the present head of the house of Saul, and therefore it was his duty to undo the legal injustice inflicted upon David. No doubt, Ishbosheth must have been aware of the possible political implications of David and Michal's reunion but he may have felt unable to take on both David and Abner.

15 There is some uncertainty concerning Michal's second husband. V 15 calls him Paltiel, son of Laish (so also 1 Sam 25:44), while in 2 Sam 21:8 Michal's husband is Adriel, son of Barzillai, who according to 1 Sam 18:19 was the husband of Merab, Michal's sister. There is clearly some textual confusion since two Heb. MSS and G have "Merab" in 21:8. Thus either the wife's name is wrong or that of the husband. A later, unlikely tradition (b. Sanhedrin 19b) suggests that the children mentioned in 2 Sam 21:8 were Merab's but Michal brought them up; therefore they were called by her name. Glück (*ZAW* 77 [1965] 76) has argued that the scribe simply confused the name of Michal's husband with that of Merab's because they were unimportant in his eyes; some such explanation may well be right.

The name פלטיאל "Paltiel" probably means "God is my deliverance," and to some extent it corresponds to the Aramaic name עדריאל "Adriel," which may mean "God is my help." However, the similarity is, most likely, accidental; the two persons cannot be identical because their fathers' names are different. For a more detailed discussion, see Stoebe, *Von Ugarit nach Qumran*, 232.

16 Paltiel accompanied Michal as far as Bahurim in Benjamin, on the road from Jerusalem to Jericho (see 2 Sam 16:5; 19:16–18; Simons, *Texts*, § 750). Tentatively, it is located at the modern Rās eṭ-Ṭmîm (see Abel, *Géographie* 2 [1938] 260). It was also the home of Shimei, son of Gera (1 Kgs 2:8). We are not told how Michal arrived in Hebron and what was her reception by David. Presumably Abner took her to David but it is not clear that this mission was identical with that described in v 20.

Whether Michal's return to David really strengthened his claim to Saul's throne is far from certain. This idea can hardly be linked with the inheritance rights of daughters (see Num 27:1–11; 36:1–9) but there is little doubt that marriages could establish close ties between families concerned.

17 We assume that Abner's negotiations with the elders took place *before* the return of Michal (so Thenius, 153; Keil, 239); however, the sequence of events is unclear. It is equally questionable whether the elders of Israel formed a specific college of elders (Hertzberg, 259) or a permanent institution gathered at Shechem or elsewhere (see Malamat, "Organs of Statecraft in the Israelite Monarchy," *BA* 27 [1965] 34–65). It is possible that Abner consulted the leaders of the individual tribes or localities in turn (cf. J. Conrad, "זקן," *TDOT* 4 [1980] 127). Abner's opening words may imply that, at least after Saul's death, some circles in Israel may have preferred David as Saul's successor due, no doubt, to his military achievements. The use of הייתם מבקשים "you have been seeking" probably emphasizes the continuation of the action in the past (cf. GKC, § 116r) and thus may suggest a limited dissatisfaction with Ishbosheth's rule.

18 Abner's advice is presented not so much as a political move but rather as conformity to Yahweh's plan: *only* by the hand of David will he save his people from all their enemies (cf. 1 Sam 9:16). Therefore David's monarchical claim rests on divine election but it also needs popular approval (v 17b). At Ishbosheth's enthronement (2 Sam 2:8–9) such a consultation may not have been necessary in view of the dynastic principle (assuming that it was already generally accepted) or it was simply not recorded.

19 The independent consultation of the Benjaminites is surprising because, theoretically at least, they would be part of Israel. This may, perhaps, imply that Ishbosheth's rule extended primarily over the Benjaminites (and the Transjordanian areas) while his hold over the other tribes may have been rather tenuous. On the other hand, its purpose may have been to stress that even Saul's own tribe was ready to accept David's rule (so Grønbaek, *Aufstieg*, 241).

There is some uncertainty as to the composition of the elders. Although the noun זָקֵן is the usual word for someone old, in most cases it denotes an "elder" in a more specific sense. It is doubtful that all adult males were elders in the technical sense of the word; therefore the elders may have been the leaders of clans or cities, or holders of particular offices or other qualifications. For a detailed discussion on "elders" see Conrad, "זָקֵן," *TDOT* 4 [1980] 122–31.

20 It is not clear whether Abner's twenty men were the elders of Israel (so Keil, 240) or of Benjamin (Stolz, 201) or, most likely, his bodyguard. Some have suggested that they were "the official escort to Michal" (so Goldman, 204), while Grønbaek (*Aufstieg*, 241 n.64) sees them as representatives of the ten tribes of Israel; but if so, they could have made the covenant with David then and there.

The feast was, probably, a banquet marking the end of successful negotiations and not a covenant meal unless *this* covenant was a private agreement between David and Abner, giving certain privileges to the latter. D. J. McCarthy, S.J. ("Social Compact and Sacral Kingship," *The Period of David and Solomon*, 79) regards the meal as a possible covenant rite, and he notes that שלום "peace" is a covenant word (see also Mettinger, *King and Messiah*, 138).

21 It seems that the agreed terms were satisfactory to both parties and that the final step was to be the covenant between David and the elders of Israel (cf. 2 Sam 5:3). The statement that Abner departed in peace is taken up also by vv 22 and 23; it seems that this threefold repetition is intended to stress that David was not involved in Abner's death.

22 Joab's raiding activities must have taken place outside Israel's tribal territories. Such raids would be one of the main sources of income for David. Joab's convenient absence from Hebron may have been planned by David (so Smith, 279) and this may have aroused Joab's suspicions when he was told of Abner's visit.

24–25 It seems somewhat strange that David, apparently, did not reply to Joab's complaint and that neither Joab nor his informants seemed to be fully aware of the real purpose of Abner's meeting with David. One may also note that Joab accused Abner of treachery (v 25) and that he did not charge David with the failure to avenge Asahel, unless this is implied in Joab's words. However, it is likely that Asahel's death did not give rise to a *legitimate* blood revenge (see *Comment* on 2 Sam 2:19–22). Had there existed such a blood feud, Abner would have been less trusting, unless he felt that he was under David's protection, especially if there *was* a covenant between David and Abner.

26 Unknown to David, Joab managed to effect Abner's recall on some false pretense. Abner had already reached the well of Sirah which is mentioned only here in the Old Testament. Provisionally, it is identified with *ṣirat el-ballāʿi*, a couple of miles north of Hebron (see Simons, *Texts*, § 751). Josephus (*Ant.* 7.34) calls the place "Besera" and remarks that it was "twenty stadia distant from Hebron" (i.e., some two miles).

27 When Abner arrived back in Hebron, Joab took him into the gateway, literally, "into the midst of the gate." Since Joab's pretense was to "talk privately," the most likely place would be one of the recesses of the gateway structure.

The explicit reason given for the killing of Abner was the revenge for Joab's brother Asahel but it does not follow that Abner's killing of Asahel was murder (cf. Christ, *Blutvergiessen*, 19; B. Kedar-Kopfstein,"דם," *TDOT* 3 [1978] 242–43). Pedersen (*Israel* 1–2 [1926] 388) argues that David and Abner had entered into a covenantal relationship and that therefore also Joab ought to have suspended his claims to vengeance. Whether David actually made a covenant with Abner is not certain but, in any case, Abner is not depicted in our sources as a murderer (cf. vv 33–34). Joab's deed may have been an expression of personal revenge and not a legally justifiable act. It is doubtful that killing in battle would lead to blood vengeance (see Phillips, *Criminal Law*, 85) although the question of the family's honor may have been of some relevance in this case (cf. Gen 4:23), especially when the killer was known.

28 David, on hearing of Abner's death, immediately declared his innocence and denied any complicity. It is plausible that in some Israelite circles it was believed that David was implicated in Abner's killing. However, it is difficult to see what possible gains David could have made by instigating the murder. This would make sense only if the negotiations had broken down but there is no justification for such an assumption. In a way, David may have been the loser since the unification of Judah and Israel was postponed. It has been suggested by Vanderkam (*JBL* 99 [1980] 532) that David knew full well that "Joab and Abner could not coexist in one camp, particularly if Abner were to be promoted over Joab." Hence, sooner or later Abner would be removed but Joab would bear the consequences. This is possible but in that case Abner's death may have come too soon, before David could become king of Israel, even though Ishbosheth lost his main political support. Contrary to the present form of the narrative, Vanderkam (533) concludes that "David both desired and planned the death of Abner." This is a serious indictment but not entirely beyond David's capabilities (see also Lemche, *JSOT* 10 [1978] 17–18).

All in all, we assume that in this instance David may have been innocent and, for once, was unjustly accused, unless the whole story had been drastically revised.

29 The curse on Joab and his household was a very serious undertaking. As Stanley Gevirtz ("Curse," *IDB* 1 [1962] 750) points out, West Semitic (including Hebrew) curses "were composed in a tradition which relied, primarily, not upon deity, but upon the power of the word." The essence of this curse was that the household of Joab should constantly be depleted by war, famine, and disease. The actual details are less clear. "To suffer from discharge" may well refer to some form of venereal disease (so Stolz, 201; *HALAT*, 225) while the reference to "skin disease" may denote leprosy (so most commentators).

פלך is probably a "spindle-whorl" (*CHALOT*, 292) or "spindle." If so, it would hardly serve as a crutch (so, perhaps, Tg) because it would not be long enough for this purpose. The allusion is, perhaps, to a man fit only for woman's work (cf. Prov 31:19).

At least in the present setting of this chapter, the curse must be seen against the background of Yahweh's retributive actions (see v 39b). Nevertheless, it is very surprising that in spite of this curse on Joab, David continued to rely upon his services and even entrusted to him the command of the army (see 2 Sam 8:16; 20:23; 1 Chr 18:15). Furthermore, it may be questioned whether in the practical administration of justice any judge could resort to cursing as an alternative to actual punitive measures, especially, when the criminal was known to the legal community. A possible explanation lies in v 39 which seems to say that David was simply too powerless, politically and militarily, to implement the obvious punishment on Joab (see 1 Kgs 2:31–34). In such a situation cursing might be an alternative but, on the other hand, if the actual punishment could not be enforced for fear of Joab, would cursing be an *advisable* alternative?

There is another possible explanation if one accepts the secondary nature of vv 28–29 and 38–39 (see *Form / Structure / Setting*). On this view the subsequent *political* execution of Joab on Solomon's orders (1 Kgs 2:31a) was publicly justified by presenting this judicial killing as a delayed legal punishment for Joab's previous murders (see 1 Kgs 2:5–6). Furthermore, this interpretation of the death of Joab may have been received favorably in the Northern Israel. The fact that David himself had not brought about the execution of Joab, was then accounted for by the curse on Joab's household (v 29) and by David's weakness in respect to Joab and his "party" (v 39).

30 Most exegetes regard this verse as a gloss in order to introduce Abishai as Joab's partner in crime, probably in view of vv 29 and 39. However, it is doubtful that Abishai took active part in the murder itself (see v 27). The verb הרג "killed" does not necessarily suggest a murder (see H. F. Fuhs, "הרג," *TDOT* 3 [1978] 454–55).

31 Here we find a brief description of the customary mourning rites. One of the first reactions to a report of death was to tear one's garments (Gen 37:34; 44:13; 2 Sam 1:11; 13:31). The wearing of sackcloth was an ancient mourning custom (Gen 37:34). The sackcloth was usually dark in color (cf. Isa 50:3) and was made of coarse material. It may have been shaped like a sack (cf. Josh 9:4) or it was a piece of cloth or even a loincloth (1 Kgs 20:31; Isa 20:2). Probably its shape and form varied according to circumstances (see Stählin, *TDNT* 7 [1971] 56–64). The sackcloth was often worn next to skin (1 Kgs 21:27; 2 Kgs 6:30) or, perhaps, on top of the usual garment (so Kirkpatrick, 74).

Joab and the rest of the people were commanded to lament *before* Abner, presumably preceding the bier to the burial place while David himself walked behind the bier (cf. m. Ber. 3:1). It is somewhat odd that a killer should take part in the mourning (cf. Jahnow, *Das Hebräische Leichenlied*, 54).

33–34 This brief funerary lament does not exhibit the so-called *qînāh* meter (3+2) nor does it have the characteristic אֵיךְ or אֵיכָה "how." The usual eulogy of the dead is only implicit (see *Form/Structure/Setting* on 2 Sam 1:17–27).

The first line (v 33b) is a rhetorical question directed to the mourners while the rest of the lament is addressed to the dead person. Abner was killed by treachery, a death fit only for the lawless or נָבָל. The latter term seems to denote a person who disregards law, custom, and existing relationships (see Phillips, *VT* 25 [1975] 237–41).

V 34b could, perhaps, be rendered, "yet you have fallen as the lawless before men of violence," reading כִּנְבָל "as the lawless" for the infinitive construct כִּנְפוֹל, following LXX and the possible reconstruction of 4QSam^a (see Ulrich, *Qumran Text*, 82).

35 At least in pre-exilic Israel fasting was part of the mourning rites (see Brongers, *OTS* 20 [1977] 20). Thus David and his men fasted until evening for Saul and Jonathan (2 Sam 1:12) while the men of Jabesh Gilead fasted seven days after the burial of Saul's bones (1 Sam 31:13). Similarly, David was expected to fast after the death of his child by Bathsheba (2 Sam 12:21). Hence it is natural that David should fast also for Abner.

We do not know why the people (courtiers?) urged David to eat while it was still day. This may be understood as a test of David's sincerity, and his refusal may have helped to convince the people that the king was not implicated in Abner's death.

At a later time it was customary to provide the mourners with ritually clean(?) food (cf. Jer 16:7; Ezek 24:17, 22).

36 Smith (282) has suggested that v 36b may be a gloss; it does involve a certain amount of tautology. Perhaps G is right in omitting "good" (טוֹב), cf. Syr, Vg, and also 4QSam^a. If so, v 36 could be translated, ". . . and they approved everything that the king did in the sight of all the people." The "people" may refer to the courtiers and to the inhabitants of Hebron. Schulte (*Geschichtsschreibung*, 151) speaks of "(Kriegs)volk" ("army").

37 It seems that certain doubts concerning David's motives had existed in the minds of both Judeans and Israelites. It can be questioned, however, whether the outward acts of David were able to remove all the suspicions. This would be a very cheap way to prove one's innocence.

38 In this verse Abner is praised once more, and Ackroyd (48) has well remarked that this verse "looks like a paraphrase of a further line of the poetic lament, or of an alternative form of it." Of course, the lament in vv 33–34 need not be the entire dirge.

39 Here we find a lame but not an improbable explanation why David as king and administrator of justice (cf. 2 Sam 1:15–16; 4:10–12; 14:4–20) failed to punish the murderer of Abner. There may be an implicit future aspect, namely, the day will come when David or his house will be strong enough to act (so Veijola, *Dynastie*, 31); however, v 39c looks to Yahweh as the effective judge.

The interpretation of this verse is difficult and the text may have suffered in transmission. The versions are of little help and, on the whole, they point to the present form of MT.

Thenius (156) once noted that it is very surprising that David should openly confess his own weakness and fear of Joab and Abishai, yet this may be a possible explanation as to why David as king and judge failed to punish Joab. Alternatively, one could argue that in some way or other Joab's deed had some justification: his brother's blood had been shed and the killer was known. Even at a later time a manslayer could be killed by the avenger of blood if he did not reach the city of refuge in time (see Deut 19:6). Only after David's death was Joab's deed interpreted (for political reasons?) as crime worthy of death.

Explanation

In 2 Sam 3:6–39 the conflict between the two royal houses becomes a diplomatic maneuvering, the ultimate prize being the kingship over Israel. Much of the story concerns the double-dealing of Abner, especially, if vv 9–10 and 17–19 are later additions. These verses transform what might otherwise appear as a treacherous act into a belated implementation of the divine will. Originally Abner's intentions may have had a mainly selfish and political motivation; in retrospect his dealings were seen as part of Yahweh's plan for David and Israel.

There are large gaps in our knowledge concerning the spectacular rise of David, and it is possible that he tried more than one way to win over Israel, as perhaps illustrated by his message to the men of Jabesh-Gilead, and as implied by v 17. Hence the reply of Abner to Ishbosheth (vv 8–10) may have been reconstructed by the editor in the light of later developments. If David was indeed the chosen king of Israel then the reign of Ishbosheth was, in a sense, illegitimate, and he ought to have been handed over to David, the rightful king (v 8). Here we find, perhaps, the view that a change of dynasty brings with it the elimination of the previous royal house (cf. also the fears expressed in 1 Sam 20:14–16). However, the real culprit was Abner himself who had made Ishbosheth king over Israel (2 Sam 2:9). Nevertheless, Abner may have been forgiven for the delayed carrying-out of Yahweh's purposes (vv 9–10) on the principle "Better late than never."

Another major problem is the evaluation of Abner's death. The simplest but not necessarily the right interpretation is to assume that originally Joab's killing of Abner was regarded as a justifiable homicide, belonging to a gray legal area. It raises such problematic questions as "Was Asahel killed in a battle?" "Did killing in war give rise to blood guilt?" "Did it make any difference that the killer of Asahel was known?" (Cf. Judg 8:18–21.) "How was the principle 'life for life' (Exod 21:23) understood at this time?" The fact that Joab *was not punished* during David's lifetime seems to support the above hypothesis. During Solomon's early reign Joab's killing was, apparently, conveniently reinterpreted, and Joab was put to death on this pretext. Therefore it is possible that the author or editor of our narrative may have added vv 28–29 and 38–39 to account for this punishment of Joab and to provide an apology for David's seeming legal inactivity.

The Death of Ishbosheth   (4:1–12)

Bibliography

Elliger, K. "Noch einmal Beeroth." *Mélanges bibliques.* 82–94. **Hillers, D. R.** "A Convention in Hebrew Literature: The Reaction to Bad News." *ZAW* 77 (1965) 86–89. **Lemche, N. P.** "David's Rise." *JSOT* 10 (1978) 2–25. **Mabee, Ch.** "David's Judicial Exoneration." *ZAW* 92 (1980) 89–107. **Macholz, G. Ch.** "Die Stellung des Königs in der israelitischen Gerichtsverfassung." *ZAW* 84 (1972) 157–82. **Mazar, B.** "Gath and Gittaim." *IEJ* 4 (1954) 227–35. **Mendenhall, G. E.** *The Tenth Generation.* 69–104. **Sacon, K. K.** "The Literary Structure of 'the Succession Narrative.'" *The Period of David and Solomon.* Ed. T. Ishida. 27–54. **Soggin, A.** "The Reign of ʾEšbaʿal, Son of Saul." *Old Testament and Oriental Studies.* BibOr 29. Rome: Biblical Institute Press, 1975. 31–49. **Strange, J.** "The Inheritance of Dan." *ST* 20 (1966) 120–39. **Tsevat, M.** "Ishbosheth and Congeners." *HUCA* 46 (1975) 71–87. **Vanderkam, J. C.** "Davidic Complicity in the Deaths of Abner and Eshbaal: A Historical and Redactional Study." *JBL* 99 (1980) 521–39. **Veijola, T.** "David and Meribaal." *RB* 85 (1978) 338–61.

Translation

[1] *When Ishbosheth,[a] son of Saul, heard that Abner[b] had died in Hebron, he became despondent,[c] and all Israel was terrified.* [2] *Now Ishbosheth,[a] son of Saul, had in his service two men, captains of raiding parties; the name of the one was Baanah and the name of the other Rechab, sons of Rimmon the Beerothite from the tribe of Benjamin. (Beeroth, too, was reckoned as part of Benjamin* [3] *after the original Beerothites had fled to Gittaim where they have lived as resident aliens to this day.)* (⁴*Jonathan, son of Saul, had a son whose feet were lame. He was[a] five years old when the news about Saul and Jonathan[b] came from Jezreel. So his nurse picked him up and fled, but in her panic[c] to flee, he fell and was crippled. His name was Mephibosheth.)* [5] *Rechab and Baanah, sons of Rimmon the Beerothite, came and entered the house of Ishbosheth at the hottest time of the day,[a] while he was taking his midday rest.[b]* [6] *So[a] they came inside the house pretending to fetch[b] wheat, but they stabbed him in the abdomen; subsequently both Rechab and his brother Baanah escaped.* [7] *Thus they entered the house while Ishbosheth was asleep on[a] the couch in his bedroom, and they struck him and killed him. Having cut off his head, they took it[b] and traveled all night along the Arabah.* [8] *So they brought the head of Ishbosheth to David in[a] Hebron and said to the king, "Here is the head of Ishbosheth, son of Saul, your enemy, who sought your life; Yahweh has fully avenged[b] my lord the king this day on Saul and on his offspring."* [9] *David answered Rechab and his brother Baanah, sons of Rimmon the Beerothite, saying,[a] "As surely as Yahweh lives, who has rescued me[b] from all trouble!* [10] *When one told me, 'Saul is dead,' regarding himself[a] as a messenger of good news, I seized[b] him and killed him in Ziklag in order that[c] I might give him a messenger's reward.[d]* [11] *How much more when evil men have killed an innocent man[a] on his bed in his own house! Should I not now require his blood from your hand and exterminate you from the land?"* [12] *So David commanded his men and they killed them and cut off their hands and their feet, hanging them up by the pool in Hebron, but the head of Ishbosheth[a] they took[b] and buried in the burial-place of Abner[c] in Hebron.*

Notes

1.a. MT and Tg omit the name of Saul's son (so also in v 2), while 4QSamᵃ and G provide the wrong name מפיבשת ("Mephibosheth"); Syr has the unlikely "Eshbashol" (אשבשול). The context clearly requires "Ishbosheth" (איש בשת), following the critical tradition.

1.b. G adds "son of Ner," which may be a later expansion.

1.c. Lit., "his hands became feeble" (cf. 2 Sam 2:7; 16:21; Isa 13:7; Ezek 7:17).

2.a. See n. 1.a.; we follow the G, reading היו לאיש בשת בן שאול "now Ishbosheth, son of Saul, had. . . ." 4QSamᵃ has the wrong name, "Mephibosheth."

4.a. MT has היה (supported by Tg), while 4QSamᵃ reads ויהי, lit., "and it came to pass," linking it with the following phrase ("when . . . came"). We prefer the MT since this structure is well attested elsewhere; see 2 Kgs 8:17; 14:2; 15:2, 33.

4.b. For the use of the obj gen, see GKC, § 128h.

4.c. There is no need to alter the qal inf constr into a niph form (so Ehrlich, *Randglossen*, 283).

5.a. Lit., "at the heat of the day." For the use of כ as simple particle of time, see GKC, § 118u; Brockelmann, *Syntax*, § 109b.

5.b. The Heb. משכב is a cognate acc, denoting the *activity* (i.e., "sleeping") rather than the *place* of sleeping ("bed," so G).

6.a. Following G "and, behold" and repointing MT's הֵנָּה "thither" to read הִנֵּה "behold."

6.b. The translation of the ptcp לקחי by "as though fetching" (cf. KJV) is doubtful (see Driver, 255); perhaps, we should read the qal inf constr לקחת "to fetch."

7.a. BHS has אל "not"; read על "on, upon" with BHK.

7.b. MT ". . . took his head."

8.a. The versions and some Heb. MSS add the prep ב "in."

8.b. Lit., "has wrought vengeance." For the pl form נקמות "vengeance," see Joüon, *Grammaire*, § 136j.

9.a. Lit., "and he said to them."

9.b. MT has נפשי, meaning either "me" or "my life" (KJV renders "my soul").

10.a. G probably read בעיני "before me," but this reading may be due to haplogr since in MT one *wāw* (pronom suff) immediately precedes another *wāw* (conj). Smith (285) regards G as more original, but this is less likely.

10.b. The coh אחזה is used instead of the ordinary impf (see GKC, § 108g).

10.c. The sentence is grammatically difficult but אשר probably expresses purpose (see *HALAT*, 95). Wellhausen, unnecessarily, deletes אשר. For other possibilities, see Driver, 256.

10.d. For this use of בשרה "messenger's reward," see *HALAT*, 157; O. Schilling, "בשר," *TDOT* 2 (1977) 314; cf. also 2 Sam 18:22.

11.a. MT has the obj marker את before the indefinite obj צדיק איש "an innocent man." However, it is possible that due to the context the expression is regarded as definite (see GKC, § 117d; Joüon, *Grammaire*, § 125h).

12.a. 4QSamᵃ reads wrongly מפיבשת "Mephibosheth."

12.b. 4QSamᵃ has the sg לקח "he took." NAB reads לקח ויקבר (similarly also Josephus, *Ant.* 7.52), "He took . . . and buried." However, it is unlikely that David himself would perform this task. G omits "they took."

12.c. Gᴮᴬ and 4QSamᵃ add בן נר "son of Ner."

Form/Structure/Setting

This chapter provides a parallel to 2 Sam 1:1–16. In both accounts the messengers of the tidings were personally involved in the shaping of the events, and they hoped for rewards from David. Yet the only recompense they received was death. At the same time, David is depicted as the just judge if not also as a caring kinsman of Saul and his family, and the author makes it clear that David had no part in the deaths of Saul and his sons (cf. vv 9–12). It was fortunate for David that he could benefit from these untimely deaths without actually engineering the tragic events. Nevertheless, the bearers of the news and their respective "evidence" may have caused a certain embarrassment for David and may have given rise to speculations whether David himself was in any sense involved. Therefore both narratives may serve also an apologetic purpose because the fact remains that the Amalekite and the sons of Rimmon had come to David and had fully expected some recognition. Consequently, it was imperative to stress that David was guiltless (cf. Grønbaek, *Aufstieg*, 243). David's reaction in vv 9–12 makes it clear that the sons of Rimmon had misinterpreted his attitude to the house of Saul (see P. Kyle McCarter, Jr., "The Apology of David," *JBL* 99 [1980] 489–504).

V 1 links the events of the previous chapter with those of the present narrative, without being an integral part of either chapter. It provides the setting against which the tragic events are to be seen. There is no clear indication that Abner's death was shortly followed by the murder of Ishbosheth although the impression is that the two events were close in time.

Vv 2b–4 are usually regarded as a gloss or a Deuteronomistic insertion (so Carlson, *David*, 51; Veijola, *Dynastie*, 94).

The detailed information concerning the origin of Baanah and Rechab (vv 2b–3) shows that the last claimant to the throne of Saul was not murdered by some disgruntled foreigners but by the members of Saul's own tribe (so Grønbaek, *Aufstieg*, 246).

The purpose of the data concerning Jonathan's son Mephibosheth (v 4) seems to be to make clear that because of his physical disability he could not be even considered as a fit successor to Saul or to Ishbosheth if the latter was regarded as a legitimate king by David and his supporters. Furthermore, Mephibosheth's youth (he was only five years old at the time of Saul's death) would be an additional hindrance. V 4 is not very appropriate in its present setting; it would be more fitting *after* the account of Ishbosheth's murder (see Veijola, *RB* 85 [1978] 345). Its place in the MT would be understandable if vv 2b–3 and v 4 were inserted by one and the same glossator. It is unlikely that v 4 is derived from 2 Sam 9:3b (see Budde, 216).

Veijola (*Dynastie*, 94) finds similarities between v 4 and the story of Ichabod's birth in 1 Sam 4:19–22 (cf. also Dhorme, 302), but it is doubtful that there is any dependence.

In vv 6 and 7 we have, apparently, two parallel accounts of Ishbosheth's death. V 7 was probably added to supply a more detailed version of this event.

Mabee (*ZAW* 92 [1980] 100–107) has produced a helpful, detailed analysis of the structure of vv 5–12, especially of vv 11–12, but we note only the basic subdivision: vv 5–8 which describe the Deed, and vv 9–12 which outline the Consequences. Sacon (*The Period of David and Solomon*, 46–47) argues for a concentric structure in vv 1–12; this is possible but not quite convincing.

Comment

1 Abner had been the mainstay of Ishbosheth's kingdom, and therefore the news of his death caused considerable consternation in Israel (cf. Hillers,

ZAW 77 [1965] 88). Probably, the full story and the immediate intentions of David were not, at this point, quite clear to the people of Israel, and therefore the murder of Abner could be seen as a possible renewal of hostilities against Israel.

In the light of 2 Sam 3 it is not easy to understand why Abner's death should cause dismay to Ishbosheth; perhaps, he was not fully aware of Abner's treachery.

The name of Ishbosheth may have been omitted intentionally from vv 1 and 2. So Ehrlich (*Randglossen*, 282) has argued that to call Ishbosheth simply "the son of Saul" might imply a derogatory attitude (see also 1 Sam 10:11; 20:30, 31; 22:7, 8, 9, 12, 13; Isa 7:4, 5, 6, 9; 8:6). In other words, Ishbosheth had not achieved true fame (i.e., name) in his own right. However, other examples of this usage need not be understood in a belittling sense (see D. J. A. Clines, "X, X Ben Y, Ben Y: Personal Names in Hebrew Narrative Style," *VT* 22 [1972] 266–87, especially 286).

"All Israel" in the present verse should not be taken in an absolute sense, but it denotes the Israelites under Ishbosheth's rule.

2–3   The raiding parties (גדודים) were probably made up of mercenaries and were directly responsible to the king. Their function was, no doubt, similar to that of Joab's band in Judah (cf. 2 Sam 3:22), namely, to plunder and raid in neighboring territories.

The ethnic origin of the sons of Rimmon creates certain problems. They are depicted as Beerothites from the tribe (lit., "sons") of Benjamin. Yet it is a well-known fact that Beeroth was one of the four Gibeonite cities which had entered into a covenant relationship with Israel in Joshua's time (Josh 9:17); consequently, they formed a Canaanite enclave in Benjamin. Its identification with el-Bireh, some nine miles (fourteen kilometers) north of Jerusalem, is a possibility (see Blenkinsopp, *Gibeon*, 8). Aharoni (*Land*, 212) places it tentatively at Khirbet el-Burj. In any case, it cannot have been far from Gibeon since it belonged to the so-called Gibeonite tetrapolis.

According to v 2b, Beeroth was reckoned to Benjamin, and this may imply that Saul had, apparently, annexed this Canaanite town for some unspecified reason, and that therefore its inhabitants had fled to Gittaim (v 3). This episode may be linked with the events presupposed by 2 Sam 21:1–9, which had created a blood-feud between the Gibeonites and the house of Saul (cf. Grønbaek, *Aufstieg*, 244–45).

Beeroth was, most likely, resettled by Benjaminites, and thus vv 2b–3 would explain why the Beerothites could be called Benjaminites (see Schunck, *Benjamin*, 130). Another, less likely, possibility is that the non-Israelite Beerothites became Benjaminites when their town was reckoned as part of Benjamin (so Nowack, 165; Hertzberg, 263).

There is also the view that the *Benjaminite* Beerothites went into exile *after* Ishbosheth's murder, fearing the possible consequences of this treachery (see Ackroyd, 50).

So the question is whether the sons of Rimmon were members of Saul's own tribe or whether they were the descendants of the Canaanites (so Noth, *History*, 186; Soggin, *Oriental Studies*, 47). The former alternative is more likely. We infer from 1 Sam 22:7 that, perhaps, most of Saul's servants of importance were Benjaminites, enriched by feudal grants, and thus the sons of Rimmon may have belonged to this same class of royal entourage. It is not impossible that *their* feudal grants were located in Beeroth, and that this type of expropriation of land may have been one of the reasons that the original Beerothites fled to Gittaim. It is unlikely that Ishbosheth would have entrusted the leadership of the raiding parties to men of Canaanite origin, especially if they bore a grudge against Saul (cf. Whitelam, *The Just King,* 111).

The Canaanite Beerothites settled in Gittaim which is mentioned elsewhere only in Neh 11:33. Its location is problematic but it could hardly have been a Benjaminite city (contra Smith, 283), although this might have been true in Nehemiah's time, assuming that the two locations are identical. The name "Gittaim" (גתים) may not be "the dual form of Gath, meaning 'two wine-presses'" (Kirkpatrick, 76) but a locative (so Mazar, *IEJ* 4 [1954] 230; cf. also Meyer, *Grammatik* 1 [1952] § 41.2). Strange (*ST* 20 [1966] 123) identifies Gittaim with Gath-Rimmon (Josh 19:45), but this is far from certain. "Rimmon" (= "pomegranate"?) may serve not only as a proper name designating a person but also as the name of an Aramean deity (2 Kgs 5:18) and as a place name (Josh 15:32) or a component of a place name (Josh 19:7; Judg 20:45). Consequently, Gath-Rimmon need not necessarily be linked with the sons of Rimmon, nor should the latter be regarded as worshipers of the god Rimmon (cf. Strange, *ST* 20 [1966] 123) although this is not impossible.

Mazar (*IEJ* 4 [1954] 232) identifies Gittaim with Gath, a city in the northern Shephelah, halfway between Lod and Gezer, and not with Gath of the Philistines. It should be noted that "Gath" is a fairly frequent place-name in Palestine, and often a second element in the name (see "Gath-Rimmon") serves to distinguish the different settlements called Gath.

4 In 2 Samuel we find two persons bearing the name Mephibosheth: the son of Rizpah (21:8) and the son of Jonathan (4:4; 21:7); consequently, this fact has caused some confusion. Veijola (*RB* 85 [1978] 352) asserts that all those passages which speak of Mephibosheth as *Jonathan's* son (2 Sam 4:4; 9:3, 6, 7; 21:7) are not authentic. He regards them as a product of a redactor who sought to stress David's loyalty to Jonathan. Veijola has presented a good case although his literary analysis will not convince everyone. One may also note that Veijola's view gives an undue importance to Mephibosheth, Saul's son. He and his brother Armoni were the sons of Rizpah, Saul's concubine, and they were put to death at the same time (2 Sam 21:8), but if one of them was such a potential danger to David that he had to be called to Jerusalem (Veijola, 350), why not both? The argument would be more acceptable if the reference was to Jonathan's son. Furthermore, Armoni may have been the elder brother since he is mentioned first, and therefore the greater threat to David, assuming that the sons of a concubine could inherit.

Moreover, it does not seem likely that Jonathan had *no* son, and that also the genealogy in 1 Chr 8:33–34 is wrong. Hence it is easier to assume that Jonathan's son had the same name as one of Saul's sons; for an analogy see 2 Sam 13:1; 14:27 where "Tamar" is the name of Absalom's sister as well as of his daughter.

"Mephibosheth" may be a deliberate distortion of the original name by

substituting one element of the compound proper name by "bosheth" (בשת)
meaning "shame" (see Driver, 254). However, some scholars regard "bosheth"
as a divine epithet (see *Comment* on 2:8; cf. Tsevat, *HUCA* 46 [1975] 75–83).
The former alternative is more likely because in the Books of Chronicles we
find what appears to be the original form of the proper name. There are
two variants: Meribaal (מרי בעל) in 1 Chr 9:40 and Meribbaal (מריב בעל)
in 1 Chr 8:34; 9:40. The former variant may be derived from the latter (so
Tsevat), meaning, perhaps, "Baal contends."

The news of the Israelite defeat came from Jezreel, either the city or the
plain (cf. Stoebe, *Das erste Buch Samuelis,* 503). It was here that the Israelite
army had encamped before the disastrous battle (1 Sam 29:1). Jezreel was a
border town in Issachar (Josh 19:18) which is usually identified with the
modern Zerʿin, near Mount Gilboa (see Abel, *Géographie* 2 [1938] 364–65).

The text does not tell us where Mephibosheth and his nurse were when
they heard the news; they could have been in Gibeah, Saul's hometown.

5 Noth (*Personennamen,* 40) takes Baanah as a theophoric name which
includes a shortened form of בעל "Baal"; for different possibilities, see *HALAT,*
139.

"Rechab" (רכב) probably means "charioteer," and it is, perhaps, short
for "son of a charioteer" (so Cheyne, *EnBib,* 4019).

6–7 These verses have created considerable problems for the exegetes.
It is possible that we have here not only a textual corruption (in v 6) but
also a conflation of two alternative accounts (cf. Ackroyd, 51). The words,
". . . and they escaped" in v 6 may well mark the end of one version while
v 7 may form part of another more detailed account. It is doubtful that
נמלטו "and they escaped" means "slipped in" (rsv); see also Mauchline, 213.

Many scholars follow G in v 6, rendering "And behold, the doorkeeper
of the house had been cleaning wheat, but she grew drowsy and slept; so
Rechab and Baanah his brother slipped in" (rsv). However, it is somewhat
odd that the king's residence had no guards and that a female doorkeeper
(cf. John 18:16) was the only "security officer"! Of course, it is not impossible
that the sons of Rimmon were part of the royal bodyguard. Kirkpatrick (77)
suggests that they gained entry to the house by mixing with the "wheat-
fetchers" (לקחי חטים), but this interpretation would create further exegetical
difficulties. Equally speculative is the view that v 6 refers to the killing of an
unnamed guard or porter (so Hertzberg, 264; Stolz, 203).

It is by no means certain that G has preserved the authentic reading of v
6; it may well be an ingenious attempt to make one version out of two. We
prefer the MT (with minor alterations), and we assume that vv 6 and 7 provide
a parallel account of the slaying of Ishbosheth.

For "stabbed in the abdomen," see *Comment* on 2:23.

After their murderous deed the sons of Rimmon made their way to Hebron,
David's capital, along the Arabah or Jordan valley, the Ghor (see *Comment*
on 2:29; cf. also Simons, *Texts,* § 127; Abel, *Géographie* 1 [1933] 423–29).

8 In their account to David, the sons of Rimmon depicted their killing
of Ishbosheth as done in the framework of Yahweh's just rule. It is possible
that Baanah and Rechab belonged to the same disaffected Benjaminite circles
as Abner (see 2 Sam 3:19) and that in *their* opinion they were simply bringing

about the implementation of Yahweh's promise to David (see 2 Sam 3:17–18). However, this understanding of the events is rejected by David (v 10). Lemche (*JSOT* 10 [1978] 17) is more skeptical, arguing that David obviously profited from this deed, and the killers "no sooner had they murdered their master than they hastened to Hebron to receive their reward, and of course David perforce had to execute his hired assassins if he was to maintain his innocence." This is a possibility, but David may have benefited from the crime without being involved in it.

"The enemy who sought David's life" is, most likely, Saul (contra Gutbrod, 58) rather than Ishbosheth (cf. 1 Sam 23:14). Mendenhall (*The Tenth Generation,* 85) has argued that "vengeance" in this context should be regarded as "vindication" (see also 2 Sam 22:48).

9 David's reply begins with an oath (v 9b) but its translation is uncertain. Stolz (203) renders it "By the life of . . ." (see also H. Ringgren, "חיה," *TDOT* 4 [1980] 338–40). We prefer the paraphrase, "As surely as Yahweh lives" (see *Comment* on 2:27; cf. Deut 32:40; Ruth 3:13). The same oath occurs also in 1 Kgs 1:29. The reference to Yahweh's deliverance is meant to indicate that David had no need of any human machinations.

10–11 In v 10 David refers to a less serious judicial precedent, namely, the case of the Amalekite in 2 Sam 1:2–16. However, since he had killed the Lord's anointed (1:16), his deed ought to have appeared to be more serious than the killing of an innocent man (4:11), although there were some extenuating circumstances (see 1:9). It is probable that this latter factor may have made the Amalekite's deed less heinous than the crime of the sons of Rimmon. The often noted differences between v 10 and 2 Sam 1:14–16 are probably more apparent than real; the former seems to be a greatly abbreviated and reworded version of the latter.

It is plausible that Ishbosheth, too, was anointed king (see *Comment* on 2:8–9) but that he was not regarded as Yahweh's anointed by our author since according to tradition David was already anointed by Samuel (1 Sam 16:13). Therefore Ishbosheth is described only as an "innocent man" (v 11) which may be a legal expression indicating that in the given situation he was in the right while "the wicked men" were those who had done the wrong (cf. Hertzberg, 265). Mabee (*ZAW* 92 [1980] 104) argues that even though a king had been murdered, this crime was not regicide because Ishbosheth was not anointed. However, it may well be that the question is not whether Ishbosheth was anointed but whether his anointing was recognized as valid by our author. For a possible parallel, see 2 Sam 19:10 which refers to Absalom's anointing. All in all, the killing of Ishbosheth was more offensive because he was *murdered* in his sleep whereas Saul *ordered* his own mercy killing. Thus the status of the victims may have been practically identical but the *nature* of their killing made one deed more atrocious than the other. Therefore also the punishment of the sons of Rimmon was more humiliating.

The trial of Baanah and Rechab was a simple affair although it is likely that the actual proceedings have been simplified in our account. David acted as both judge and prosecutor, and the accused must have been convicted on their own testimony which was, no doubt, more elaborate than the mere presentation of Ishbosheth's head together with the brief explanation in v

8b (see also Mabee, *ZAW* 92 [1980] 100–107). Since the crime was self-con-
fessed, there was no need of any witnesses; the judge's function was merely
to pronounce the fitting sentence. The latter appears in the form of a rhetorical
question (v 11b) although LXX, rightly, makes it into a statement of David's
intention: "Now I will require his blood . . ." The rhetorical question may
be equivalent to an emphatic affirmation. "His blood" in this context must
mean "his shed blood" (i.e., the violent death of Ishbosheth). "To require
his blood . . ." is tantamount to making one responsible for the crime (cf.
Christ, *Blutvergiessen,* 119–21). Macholz (*ZAW* 84 [1972] 164–65) is of the
opinion that David was functioning primarily as the avenger of blood (v
11b) but this is less likely.

For the use of בער "to destroy, exterminate," see *TDOT* 2 (1977) 203–4.

12 At David's command the accused were killed and mutilated, and their
dismembered bodies were hanged up by the pool of Hebron. The verb ויתלו
"and they hanged up" has no explicit object; hence some regard the cut-off
hands and feet as the accusative of the verb (cf. Smith, 284; Mauchline,
214). However, it is more likely that the bodies were displayed in public (cf.
Josh 8:29; 10:26–27). The Deuteronomic law forbidding the exposure of
dead bodies overnight (Deut 21:22–23) may not have been in existence. Also
in 2 Sam 21:9–10 there is no observance of this particular law.

Mutilation of hands and feet was not an unknown practice in the ancient
world, but its main purpose must have been the intention to disable the
person concerned (see Judg 1:6–7). In v 12 the purpose may have been to
dishonor the bodies of Baanah and Rechab.

The "pool" was probably the most public place in Hebron (so Goldman,
212), and it is often identified with Birket es-sulṭān in the southwest of the
modern Hebron (see Simons, *Texts,* § 736; but cf. also Abel, *Géographie* 1
[1933] 454).

Explanation

This chapter is a further illustration of how "the house of Saul became
weaker and weaker" (3:1), and it depicts the final stage in David's rise to
the kingship over all Israel, which culminated with his anointing by the men
of Israel (2 Sam 5:3).

The parenthetical inserts (vv 2b–3 and 4) show that even among the Benjaminites themselves there was dissatisfaction with the rule of Ishbosheth and
that the house of Saul had no other suitable claimant to the throne, since
the obvious candidate, the son of Jonathan, was a cripple and a mere stripling,
and therefore an unlikely political contestant or military leader. Consequently,
in the circumstances, David was the natural choice as shown by the following
chapter. On the other hand, certain events, such as the death of Ishbosheth,
required some explanation, and it would be surprising if David's claims met
with no opposition. Such potential opponents would, most likely, impose
their own interpretation upon certain events involving David, as done by
Shimei (2 Sam 16:7–8). Therefore some sort of apologia would be required
to eliminate or to forestall the existing or possible unfavorable interpretations
(or misinterpretations) of history. Thus our chapter may have helped to achieve

this objective by making plain that David was not a party to Ishbosheth's assassination. David dissociated himself from the cold-blooded crime by punishing the murderers in the severest possible manner. This rough justice may have brought some approval from the Northern tribes.

Thus the way to the throne of Israel was now open although we do not know whether the final step followed shortly after Ishbosheth's murder or whether a few years elapsed before Israel was ready to make David their king.

David King of Israel and Judah (5:1–5)

Bibliography

Brueggemann, W. "Of the Same Flesh and Bone (Gen 2,23a)." *CBQ* 32 (1970) 532–42. **Fohrer, G.** "Der Vertrag zwischen König und Volk in Israel." *ZAW* 71 (1959) 1–22 (= *Studien zur alttestamentlichen Theologie und Geschichte* [1949–1966]. Berlin: Alfred Töpelmann, 1969. 330–51). **Glück, J. J.** "Nagid: Shepherd." *VT* 13 (1963) 144–50. **Halpern, B.** *The Constitution of the Monarchy in Israel.* **Lipiński, E.** "NĀGĪD, der Kronprinz." *VT* 24 (1974) 497–99. **Reiser, W.** "Die Verwandtschaftsformel in Gen. 2.23." *TZ* 16 (1960) 1–4. **Richter, W.** "Die nāgîd—Formel: Ein Beitrag zur Erhellung des nāgîd—Problems." *BZ* 9 (1965) 71–84. **Thornton, T. C. G.** "Charismatic Kingship in Israel and Judah." *JTS* 14 (1963) 1–11. **Weinfeld, M.** *"Bᵉrît:* Covenant vs. Obligation." *Bib* 56 (1975) 120–28.

Translation

[1] *Then all the chiefs of Israel came to David in Hebron, saying,[a] "We are indeed[b] your own flesh and blood.* [2] *Even in the past when Saul was our king, it was you[a] who used to lead[b] Israel forth and bring[c] them home from battle. And Yahweh said to you, 'You[a] shall shepherd[d] my people Israel and you[a] shall be the chosen leader of Israel.'"* [3] *So when all the elders of Israel had come to the king in Hebron, King David made them certain promises[a] in Hebron before Yahweh, and they anointed David king over Israel.[b]* [4] *David was thirty years old when he began to reign, and[a] he reigned for forty years.* [5] *In Hebron he reigned over Judah seven years and six months, and in Jerusalem he reigned over all Israel and Judah thirty-three years.*

Notes

1.a. MT has ויאמרו לאמר (KJV "and spake, saying"), while 4QSamᵃ reads only לאמר "saying"; so also OL and 1 Chr 11:1. The latter variant is more likely since the collocation of the above verbal forms is not frequent (see Driver, 257).

1.b. Or "Here we are!" (הננו). 1 Chr 11:1 has only הנה "behold," which may be preferable (so Budde, 218).

2.a. The pronoun is emphatic (cf. GKC, § 135a).

2.b. Reading with Q and several MSS היית המוציא; the expression denotes an action continuing in the past (see GKC, § 116r).

2.c. K has המבי "who brought in," while Q, rightly, המביא. The final letter may have been omitted due to haplogr, unless it is a case of shared consonants (see Watson, *Bib* 50 [1969] 531).

2.d. Or "you shall be shepherd of . . ." (so RSV, NEB).

3.a. Lit., "covenant" (ברית), lacking in some MSS but attested by the versions and 1 Chr 11:3.

3.b. G adds "all," perhaps rightly (see v 5). However, it is not found in 1 Chr 11:3.

4.a. A number of MSS and the versions rightly add the conj ו "and," which may have been omitted due to haplogr.

Form / Structure / Setting

This brief section consists of three parts: vv 1–2 describe the reasoning of the Israelites, v 3 gives a brief account of David's investiture, while vv 4–5 provide statistical data concerning the reign of David.

The relationship between vv 1–2 and v 3 is not easy to define, and many scholars have regarded them as two doublets (cf. Dhorme, 306) or vv 1–2 are thought to be the work of a Deuteronomistic editor (cf. Caird, 1068–69; Veijola, *Dynastie*, 65). It is usually pointed out that v 1a is a verbal parallel of v 3a, and that "my people Israel" (v 2b) may presuppose a twelve-tribe unit while "Israel" in vv 1 and 3 clearly refers to the Northern tribes (see Kutsch, *Textgemäss*, 78). However, the repetition of v 1a in v 3a may well form an inclusion, and thus it may be a deliberate rhetorical device (see Gunn, *King David*, 71). It is possible that the language of v 2 is colored by the author's own time, probably during the reign of Solomon (cf. A. Weiser, "Die Legitimation des Königs David," *VT* 16 [1966] 333). Hence it is not impossible that vv 1–3 form a unity even though they themselves may be an abbreviation of a longer account. E. Kutsch ("Die Dynastie von Gottes Gnaden," *ZTK* 58 [1961] 142) sees in these verses an *expansion* of an older note. For a different analysis of these verses, see Schulte, *Geschichtsschreibung*, 165–66.

Hertzberg (267) finds in vv 1–3 two stages of one and the same transaction; first, "the active and responsible men of the tribes" approach David and, finally, we have the action of the elders forming "an official body" (see also Carlson, *David*, 55). However, this seems less likely.

There is a more general agreement on vv 4–5, and most scholars regard them as a later Deuteronomistic addition (cf. Grønbaek, *Aufstieg*, 250). This chronological note is rather appropriate in its present setting although the Chronicler has transferred it to the end of the Davidic stories (1 Chr 29:27). Noth (*Deuteronomistic History*, 55) describes vv 4–5 as a "formulaic Deuteronomistic" introduction to David's reign (cf. also 1 Sam 13:1; 2 Sam 2:10; 1 Kgs 14:21).

Comment

1 The Hebrew שבט may well stand for two apparent homonyms, one meaning "tribe, staff," the other "ruler, judge" (see Gewirtz, "On Hebrew *šēbeṭ* = 'JUDGE.'" *The Bible World: Essays in Honor of Cyrus H. Gordon*, ed. G. Rendsburg, R. Adler, M. Arfa, and N. H. Winter [New York: KTAV Publishing House, Inc. and the Institute of Hebrew Culture and Education of New York University, 1980] 61–66). It is unlikely that, literally, all tribes of Israel came to Hebron; consequently, we suggest "all the *chiefs* of Israel." Perhaps, "the elders of Israel" (v 3) was intended as an explanatory variant. Also in 2 Sam 7:7 שבט has a similar meaning (cf. its parallel in 1 Chr 17:6).

We have taken עצמך ובשרך (lit., "your bone and your flesh") as denoting kinship (so in 2 Sam 19:13, 14[12, 13]; Gen 29:14) rather than as being part of a covenantal formula, indicating abiding loyalty (as suggested by Brueggemann, *CBQ* 32 [1970] 535). This kinship may, but need not, be based on David's marriage to Michal (cf. 2 Sam 2:26; 19:42[41]). It is less likely that the implication is that the king and the people are made for each other as man and wife (cf. Gen 2:23; see Gutbrod, 66).

2 "To lead out and to bring in" belongs to the language of military affairs, and it describes the activities of the chief or leader (cf. Josh 14:11; 1 Sam

18:13, 16; 29:6; see also Plöger, *Untersuchungen,* 178–81). According to the argument of the tribal leaders, even during Saul's reign David was, in a sense, the "hidden messiah" (so Grønbaek, *Aufstieg,* 249); this was implied by David's outstanding military success.

In the ancient world the king was often designated as shepherd of his people; so also various deities (for references, see J. Jeremias, *TDNT* 6 [1968] 486–88). In the OT the title "shepherd" is rarely used of Yahweh (but see Gen 48:15; 49:24; Ps 23:1; 80:2 [1]) although he is not infrequently portrayed as a shepherd of Israel (cf. Ps 23:3; Isa 40:11; 49:10). The actual title "shepherd" is never used in our sources of any *ruling* king in Judah or Israel; on the other hand, both the political leaders (cf. Ps 78:71; Jer 2:8; Ezek 34:23) and future rulers (cf. Jer 3:15; 23:4; Ezek 34:23; 37:24) may be denoted by this term.

The word translated "chosen leader" (נָגִיד) is probably a qal passive participle of נגד, meaning "the one proclaimed" or ". . . designated" (so Mettinger, *King and Messiah,* 182), and thus a suitable term for the king-designate.

It is doubtful that originally it described the charismatic war-leader since the term is not used of any person in the pre-monarchical period (cf. Ishida, *Dynasties,* 50; Lipiński, *VT* 24 [1974] 498); for the opposite view, see Schmidt, *Menschlicher Erfolg,* 152). Lipiński (498) has argued that 1 Kgs 1:35 is the oldest occurrence of this term and so Solomon was the first historical נָגִיד or "crown prince." If so, then the secular usage provided the starting point for the theological application to express divine designation although even the so-called secular practices must have been seen in a religious context. Carlson (*David,* 54) is of the opinion that "*nāgîd* is a form of Deuteronomic definition of the national leader as the Deuteronomists felt he ought to be," but the term was not necessarily coined by the D-group.

3 David is said to have made covenant with the elders, and it is less likely that the reference is to *mutual* obligations. Therefore, he either imposed various obligations upon Israel or, more likely, made certain promises or assurances to the Israelites, sanctified by an oath (i.e., before Yahweh); for further details, see Kutsch, *Textgemäss,* 89–93; cf. also Fohrer, *Studien,* 331; Weinfeld, *Bib* 56 (1975) 122–23. This covenant or obligation did not establish a real union between Israel and Judah but what could be described as a personal union of the two states under David (see Alt, *KSGVI* 2 [1953] 43–45), each retaining its statehood (cf. 2 Sam 20:1; 1 Kgs 12:16).

However, in this transaction a certain amount of reciprocity must have been involved and implicit, if not explicit, obligations must have been undertaken by the Israelites through the act of anointing David king over all Israel. It is not clear whether the actual anointing was performed by the elders themselves or with the help of a priest (cf. 1 Kgs 1:39) or priests (see *Comment* on 2 Sam 2:4a), possibly the former alternative (cf. 2 Sam 2:4a, 7; 5:17; 19:11; see also Mettinger, *King and Messiah,* 198–203).

In the act of anointing, oil (consisting of a mixture of spices in a base of olive oil; cf. Exod 30:22–25) was poured from a container (clay flask, as in 1 Sam 10:1; 2 Kgs 9:1) or horn (see 1 Sam 16:1: 1 Kgs 1:39) on the head of the person anointed.

4 Ackroyd (53) rightly regards the chronology as idealized, but the round numbers may not be far wrong. "Thirty" often describes a man in prime of life (cf. Num 4:3). It is perhaps a coincidence that Jesus began his ministry at the age of thirty (Luke 3:23).

"Forty" is a common round figure, and "forty years" is the traditional length of a generation. Noth (*Deuteronomistic History*, 20) suggests that "forty years" in the Deuteronomistic passages usually means "the length of time in which one group of active adult men is completely replaced by the next."

5 The "seven years and six months" is usually regarded as the more accurate information while "thirty-three years" may simply make up the round number of "forty years"; G^L actually reads "thirty-two years and six months" but this seems to be a later correction.

Explanation

The present position of vv 1–3 imply, perhaps wrongly, that *soon* after Ishbosheth's assassination the elders of Israel came to Hebron and anointed David king over Israel. This is, of course, possible, but the chronological data in 2 Sam 2:10–11 and 5:4–5 suggest that there may have been an interregnum of five years.

Unfortunately, there is no simple solution, but tentatively we suggest a synthesis based on certain points. First of all, it seems that we should not take the chronological notes too literally. The essential factor in them is that David ruled seven years in Hebron and thirty-three years in Jerusalem rather than the precise length of his rule *over Judah alone.* Second, the Israel ruled by Ishbosheth may have consisted only of a few tribes or tribal elements, because we must reckon with some sort of Philistine occupation. This is implied by the fact that Ishbosheth's center of government was located in Mahanaim, in Transjordan. Third, the fact that two passages are collocated need not necessarily indicate that also the events recorded in them must be *closely* linked in time. Consequently, our provisional explanation is that only gradually David was able to establish his rule over Israel so that there may have been a sort of interregnum before he actually became king of *all* Israel. It is possible that some form of covenant (or even covenants) may have been made soon after the death of Ishbosheth with some Israelite elements but it is doubtful whether at this point all Israel could act as a political entity. Thus David's anointing may have come at the end of a lengthy process of unification rather than at the beginning. It is not improbable that some reminiscences of such a prolonged process are still found in 1 Chr 12 where various groups of Israelites joined David at different times and places. Clearly, this passage is very difficult exegetically but the proposed interpretation is a possibility.

That in our chapter as a whole we find only the bare outlines of events is suggested by the accounts of the two battles with the Philistines in vv 17–25. It is unlikely that this was the sum total of all the hostilities. More incursions and battles are described or mentioned in 2 Sam 21:15–22 and 23:8–17; consequently, it is fair to conclude that the Philistine war lasted for several years. Only after the cessation of these hostilities could one speak of an effective control of all Israel by David. Also the capture of Jerusalem must have been an important factor in consolidating David's rule.

Thus in vv 1–3 we find a simplification of a lengthy historical process, similar to that in 1 Chr 11:1 where the author omits David's rule in Hebron, as well as the reign of Ishbosheth, and David is made king over all Israel shortly after the death of Saul.

Finally, one may note that vv 1–3 suggest that David's rule over Israel rested on two main factors: Yahweh's election (v 2b) and the people's recognition of David's qualities and potential. Thus both theological and political aspects were of importance.

The Capture of Jerusalem and Its
Sequel (5:6–16)

Bibliography

Ahlström, G. W. "Was David a Jebusite Subject?" *ZAW* 92 (1980) 285–87. **Albright, W. F.** "The Ṣinnôr in the Story of David's Capture of Jerusalem." *JPOS* 2 (1922) 286–90. **Barr, J.** "The Symbolism of Names in the Old Testament." *BJRL* 52 (1969) 11–29. **Blenkinsopp, J.** "Jonathan's Sacrilege." *CBQ* 26 (1964) 423–49. **Bressan, G.** "L'espugnazione di Sion in 2 Sam 5,6–8 // 1 Chron 11,4–6 e il Problema del ṢINNOR." *Bib* 25 (1944) 346–81. **Brunet, G.** "Les Avengles et Boiteux Jébusites." VTSup 30 (1979) 65–72. ———. "David et le Ṣinnôr." VTSup 30 (1979) 73–86. **Donner, H.** "Israel und Tyrus im Zeitalter Davids und Salomos." *JNSL* 10 (1982) 43–52. **Gerleman, G.** "Die Wurzel šlm." *ZAW* 85 (1973) 1–14. **Glück, J. J.** "The Conquest of Jerusalem in the Account of II Sam 5:6–8a, with Special Reference to 'the blind and the lame' and the Phrase 'weyiggaʿ baṣṣinnôr.'" *Biblical Essays.* 98–105. **Gray, J.** *A History of Jerusalem.* London: Robert Hale, 1969. **Hauer, C. E., Jr.** "Jerusalem, the Stronghold and Rephaim." *CBQ* 32 (1970) 571–78. **Kenyon, K. M.** *Digging up Jerusalem.* London: Book Club Associates, 1974. **Krauss, S.** "Moriah—Ariel." *PEQ* 79 (1947) 45–55. **Schunck, K.-D.** "Davids 'Schlupfwinkel' in Juda." *VT* 33 (1983) 110–13. **Simons, J.** *Jerusalem in the Old Testament.* 35–194. **Stamm, J. J.** "Der Name des Königs Salomo." *TZ* 16 (1960) 285–97. **Stoebe, H.** "Die Einnahme Jerusalems und der Ṣinnôr." *ZDPV* 73 (1957) 73–99. **Sukenik, E. L.** "The Account of David's Capture of Jerusalem." *JPOS* 8 (1928) 12–16. **Veijola, T.** "Salomo—der Erstgeborene Bathsebas." VTSup 30 (1979) 230–50. **Vincent, L. H.** "Le Ṣinnôr dans la prise de Jérusalem (II Sam.V, 8)." *RB* 33 (1924) 357–70. **Watson, W. G. E.** "David Ousts the City Ruler of Jebus." *VT* 20 (1970) 501–2.

Translation

[6] *Then the king*[a] *and his men went to Jerusalem against the Jebusites,*[b] *the inhabitants of the territory, who said*[c] *to David, "You will not enter here; even the blind*[d] *and the lame could turn you away"*[e] *(meaning,*[f] *"David cannot enter here").* [7] *However, David took the stronghold of Zion, that is, the city of David.* [8] *That day David said, "Whoever would conquer the Jebusites must take possession*[a] *of the water supply . . ."*[b] *(David hates*[c] *the lame and the blind; therefore it is said, "The blind and the lame shall not enter the temple."*[d]*)* [9] *David then dwelt in the stronghold and renamed it the city of David. Moreover, David extended*[a] *the city*[b] *from the Millo towards the house.*[c] [10] *So David grew stronger and stronger*[a] *for Yahweh, the God*[b] *of hosts, was with him.* [11] *Hiram, the king of Tyre, sent messengers to David, as well as cedar wood, carpenters, and stonemasons*[a] *who built a palace for David.* [12] *And David realized that Yahweh had established him king over Israel and*[a] *that he had exalted*[b] *his kingdom for the sake of his people Israel.* [13] *After coming from Hebron, David took more concubines and wives in*[a] *Jerusalem, and more sons and daughters were born to David.* [14] *These are the names of those who were born*[a] *to him in Jerusalem: Shammua, Shobab, Nathan, Solomon,* [15] *Ibhar, Elishua, Nepheg, Japhia,* [16] *Elishama, Eliada, and Eliphelet.*

Notes

6.a. Two MSS and 1 Chr 11:4 have דוד "David"; Syr conflates both readings.

6.b. We regard היבסי "the Jebusites" as a collective noun (cf. Josh 15:63). A less likely rendering is "the Jebusite (ruler of the city)" (see Watson, *VT* 20 [1970] 502).

6.c. Syr, Tg have the pl verb (cf. also 1 Chr 11:5) but the sg is more likely because the logical subj is the collective היבסי. G reads "and it was told to . . ." which seems less plausible.

6.d. For the pointing of העורים "the blind," see GKC, § 35g.

6.e. One would expect the impf (so Wellhausen, 163) but the pf may indicate the speaker's certainty and self-confidence (cf. GKC, § 106m). For the use of the sg form, see GKC, § 145o.

6.f. Lit., "saying"; perhaps, similar to *id est*. The following phrase is probably an explanatory note.

8.a. We follow 4QSam^a in reading the juss יגע "let him reach" or "take possession" for MT's ויגע. The conjunction ו "and" is omitted also by G.

8.b. There is, probably, a lacuna in the text; the Q reading is a further indication of the textual uncertainty.

8.c. We adopt the reading of 4QSam^a שנאה "(David's soul) hates . . ." This is also suggested by Tg and Syr. On the other hand, K, Q, G, and OL make David the object of the hatred.

8.d. G has "the house of the Lord," i.e., the Temple. This may be a correct explanation.

9.a. Lit., "(David) built."

9.b. Adding העיר "the city" with 1 Chr 11:8. 4QSam^a has ויבנה עיר "and built it as a city"; this same reading is presupposed by G and Josephus; however, it may be a scribal error for the Chronicler's version (wrong division of the two words?).

9.c. Either "to the royal palace" (cf. NAB) or ". . . the Temple." Most translations, however, take ביתה as "inward."

10.a. For the collocation of inf abs and adj to express continuance, see GKC, § 113u; cf. also 2 Sam 3:1.

10.b. "God of" (אלהי) is omitted by G and 4QSam^a, as well as by 1 Chr 11:9, perhaps rightly.

11.a. Lit., "craftsmen of stone wall(s)" (?) but it seems that אבן "stone" and קיר "wall" are doublets. אבן is omitted by 4QSam^a and 1 Chr 14:1 while קיר is lacking in G. The more likely reading is חרשי אבן "craftsmen in stone" or "stonemasons" which is parallel to חרשי עץ "craftsmen in wood," i.e., "carpenters"; see also 1 Chr 22:15.

12.a. The conjunction ו "and" is omitted by 1 Chr 14:2, transforming the latter part of the verse into a causal statement ("because . . .").

12.b. There is no need to change the piel form of the verb into a niph or passive form, "was exalted" (so G, 1 Chr 14:2; *BHK*).

13.a. Reading בירושלם "in Jerusalem" with 1 Chr 14:3; MT has מירושלם "from. . . ."

14.a. The Heb. הילדים "who were born" is probably a pl ptcp from the passive qal (see Beer/Meyer, *Grammatik* 1 [1952] § 68c; GKC, § 84e).

Form / Structure / Setting

This section (vv 6–16) is composed of several originally independent fragments and two brief theological statements. Vv 6–9 provide a very short but perplexing description of the capture of the fortress of Zion, and they incorporate an etiology of an old proverb (v 8b) about the exclusion of the blind and the lame from the Temple(?). The brevity of this whole account is very puzzling, but it seems that the capture of Jerusalem did not quite serve the editor's purposes. Perhaps, the climax had been reached with David's elevation to kingship over all Israel, and in any case the status of Jerusalem was never in dispute. The editor could hardly have lacked the necessary information about the conquest of Jerusalem although it is not entirely impossible that this "capture" of Zion was not a feat of arms but was achieved by means of a peaceful surrender. Even so, one might have expected more detailed information.

Vv 10 and 12 are in the nature of short theological comments which may have been intended to tone down any undue emphasis on any human achievement, and to point to Yahweh as the real source of success. Veijola (*Dynastie,*

99) finds in vv 12a and 12b two doublets, but they may be parallel statements for the sake of emphasis.

Vv 9b and 11 give the only record of David's building projects. Such accounts are often associated with various kings of the ancient Near East, and their function is to stress the wealth, power, and greatness of the rulers concerned (see Kegler, *Politisches Geschehen*, 218–32). It is possible that v 11 is misplaced; Noth (*Deuteronomistic History*, 56) suggests that in the editor's sources v 11 "could have come next to 8:9–11." However, it could have equally well followed v 9, and it anticipates 2 Sam 7:2b (cf. Grønbaek, *Aufstieg*, 257).

Vv 13–16 may have been derived from some court document, and they give information about the sons born to David in Jerusalem; the names of daughters are not usually included in such lists. In 1 Chr this list is given twice, with some slight variants and minor additions (see 1 Chr 3:5–8 and 14:4–7; cf. Driver, 262). Grønbaek (*Aufstieg*, 254 n.117), among others, regards vv 13–16 as an addition by the Deuteronomistic editor.

The twice repeated עוֹד "more" or "again" in v 13 seems to refer back to the enumeration of the sons born in Hebron (2 Sam 3:2–5), but it is unlikely that one list is a direct continuation of the other (contra Hertzberg, 271) because there is a formal difference between them in that the earlier one gives also the names of the mothers (3:2–5).

Comment

6 "The king and his men" refers to David and his private army which he had in Hebron, not to the tribal levy. In 1 Chr 11:4 the reference is to "all Israel," but this is unlikely (cf. 1 Sam 30:1, 3; 2 Sam 2:3), especially, since the Chronicler has a tendency to stress the aspect of a united Israel (see Williamson, *Chronicles*, 98). Alt (*KSGVI* 2 [1953] 45–46) has argued that Jerusalem became David's own property and that it retained its previous status of a sovereign city-state now ruled by David, but independent of Israel and Judah. Ishida (*Dynasties*, 130) limits David's "private" property to the stronghold of Zion and asserts that "the whole territory of the ex-city-state Jerusalem was never incorporated into his property." Alt's view has been widely accepted, but it has had its critics (see Buccellatti, *Cities and Nations*, 137–93; C. Schäfer-Lichtenberger, *Stadt und Eidgenossenschaft*, 389). One may note, however, that although Judah and Jerusalem often appear as two separate entities in the OT, there is no evidence that the Davidic rulers were ever called kings of Jerusalem. Perhaps Soggin (*IJH*, 355–56) is right in denying the Davidic Jerusalem the status of a city-state but conceding some kind of limited autonomy.

According to Josh 15:63 and Judg 1:21 Jerusalem was one of the Canaanite enclaves which Israel had been unable to conquer or assimilate. Judg 1:8 must refer to some successful raid by the men of Judah but hardly to a permanent capture of Jerusalem (cf. also Judg 19:10–13; R. G. Boling, *Judges*, 55–56). Hertzberg (268) speaks of "the possession of the pasturage of Jerusalem by the men of Judah" but there is no evidence for it in Judg 1:8.

Jerusalem was an ancient and famous city already in David's time. It is

mentioned in the Ebla archives (c. 2500 B.C.), in the Egyptian Execration
Texts of the nineteenth(?) century B.C. (cf. *ANET*, 329), and in the Amarna
Letters (see *ANET*, 489) of the fourteenth century B.C. (cf. also *AOTS*, 3–15).

The name of the city is obviously pre-Israelite, and it probably meant
"the foundation of (the god) Shalem." A deity by this name is known in the
Ugaritic texts (see Gibson, *Canaanite Myths*, 126). In the Israelite period the
component "shalem" was, no doubt, associated with the Heb שלום "peace";
cf. Ps 76:3[2]; Heb 7:2.

It seems that before David's conquest of Jerusalem, Judah and Israel controlled the lands around the city to within a few miles of the city itself (so
Gottwald, *The Tribes of Yahweh*, 570) and that a state of truce must have
existed between the city and its neighbors. In Gottwald's view (ibid., 571)
David violated the status quo but "he retained the Jebusites in their former
home, even though this put them in the administrative heart of his new
Israelite kingdom."

"Jebus" (יבסי) was, apparently, the name of a Canaanite clan (cf. *IDB* 2
[1962] 807) although some other scholars, e.g., Herzog and Gichon (*Battles
of the Bible*, 77) assert that the Jebusites were "a small ethnic community,
alien to the autochthone Canaanites, who did not command any special sympathies among most of the neighboring peoples." This is clearly possible (cf.
Ezek 16:3, 45), but we know very little about the Jebusites.

Apart from the OT (see Josh 18:28; Judg 19:10; 1 Chr 11:4) there is no
other evidence that Jerusalem was ever called "Jebus." If the OT information
is historically correct, Jebus may have been an alternative name for Jerusalem
during the period of the Judges. It is possible that the Heb. היבסי simply
meant "(the city of) the Jebusites" (cf. Mazar, *The Mountain of the Lord*, 41).
Miller (*ZDPV* 90 [1974] 127) has suggested that Jebus was a village outside
Jerusalem, and that its identification with Jerusalem was a mistake. The confusion probably arose due to the fact that the Jebusites were the pre-Israelite
inhabitants of Jerusalem; hence later writers may have thought that Jebus
was the ancient name of the city (cf. Simons, *Jerusalem*, 60–61).

Watson (*VT* 20 [1970] 501–2) has proposed that היבסי יושב הארץ should
be rendered "the Jebusite ruler of the city" (502); similarly also Ahlström in
ZAW 92 (1980) 286. This is just possible, but the Chronicler understood it,
probably rightly, as "the Jebusites, the inhabitants of the city" (11:4). The
Heb. ארץ usually denotes "land" but in some contexts it may, perhaps, denote
"city" or "city state" (see M. Ottoson, "ארץ," *TDOT* 1 [1974] 401).

The reference to "the blind and the lame" provides a considerable exegetical
problem. It seems that the Jebusites regarded their city so impregnable that
even the blind and the lame could defend it and repulse David's troops.
Thus v 6b is, perhaps, the Jebusite reply to David's call for surrender (cf.
Stoebe, *ZDPV* 73 [1957] 89). Somewhat similarly, Glück (*Biblical Essays*, 99)
considers v 6b as "an epitome of the terminology used in pre-battle taunting
and reviling . . ."; in v 8 David replies in a similar vein, making "the Jebusites"
and "the blind and the lame" synonymous. Josephus (*Ant.* 7.61) has taken
the verse literally, stating that the Jebusites mocked David by placing cripples
on the wall while in Rabbinic tradition (perhaps inspired by Ps 115:5, 7)
"the blind and the lame" are taken as Canaanite idols.

The unvocalized הסיר could be understood as hiphil infinitive construct with a pronominal suffix (cf. Bressan, *Bib* 25 [1944] 357), thus making David the subject of the verb: "(except) you remove (the blind . . .)." A more recent variant of this is based on a Hittite oath-taking ceremony (*ANET*, 353–54) where a blind woman and a deaf man play an important part in the soldiers' oath-symbolism. It has been suggested that also the Jebusites paraded a number of blind and lame people on the walls as part of an oath-taking ceremony, saying, "Except thou take away the blind and the lame, thou shalt not come in hither" (Yadin, *Warfare*, 269; cf. also Brunet, VTSup 30 [1979] 69–70). The rest of the oath would have threatened with similar disabilities anyone attempting to harm the blind and the lame.

However, it is less speculative to assume that the Jebusites were simply overconfident, especially if the size of David's troops, at this point, was comparatively small. Schreiner (*Sion-Jerusalem*, 39) finds in "the blind and the lame" a Jebusite description of David's soldiers; in v 8 David takes up the insult and admonishes his troops not to be "blind and lame" (i.e., David hates such useless warriors). In Schreiner's view העורים "the blind" is a veiled allusion to עברים "Hebrews"; however, this does not account for הפסחים "the lame"; but see also Stoebe, *ZDPV* 73 (1957) 90.

7 The stronghold of Zion (its Canaanite name) was renamed "the city of David," but it is less certain that the reference is to Jerusalem as a whole. "Zion" in this context was probably the designation of the southeastern hill of Jerusalem, and the "stronghold of Zion" was the citadel guarding this same hill (see Mazar, *The Mountain of the Lord*, 41). Simons (*Jerusalem*, 243) may well be right in claiming that Zion and Jerusalem "stood in the relation of part and whole" (see also 1 Kgs 8:1). On the other hand, Ishida (*Dynasties*, 128) has argued that "'Jebus = Jerusalem' and 'the stronghold of Zion = the city of David' stood for the territory and its center, respectively."

Ohler (*Israel*, 112) suggests that David claimed for himself only the fortress which he renamed (cf. 2 Sam 12:28) while the rest of the city retained its previous name. It seems that some landed properties remained in the possession of the Jebusites (see 2 Sam 24:18, 21–24) although some of the land, at least, must have been expropriated, since Joab and Absalom are said to have possessed fields near Jerusalem (2 Sam 14:30).

There is also the question whether "the stronghold of Zion" is identical with the place of refuge (מצודה) mentioned in v 17. Schunck (*VT* 33 [1983] 112) has argued that מצודה means "refuge," "hiding place" while מצדה (with the defective spelling) denotes "fortress," "stronghold." For a different view, see Hauer, *CBQ* 32 (1970) 575 n.18. Schunck's interpretation may be correct whether or not the spelling of מצודה is an accidental error. Hence it seems that in v 17 the reference is not to the stronghold of Zion but to some other place of refuge, perhaps the cave of Adullam as implied by 2 Sam 23:13–14 which must be linked with the events of 2 Sam 5:17–25.

It is possible that the editor who placed vv 17–25 *after* the capture of Jerusalem must have assumed that the unspecified מצודה in v 17 was identical with the stronghold of Zion. However, since the two episodes may have circulated separately, the identification may be doubted.

8 This verse, especially v 8a, gives a somewhat laconic information about the capture of the stronghold of Zion, but in its present form it is either a considerably shortened account or the result of a textual corruption.

"That day" must refer to the day when the Jebusite fortress was taken by David's men. According to 1 Chr 11:4–9 David offered the office of chief and commander to the first man who would smite the Jebusites; Joab did so and became a chief (for parallels, see Josh 15:16; Judg 1:12; 1 Sam 17:25). However, the two versions should not be simply conflated; the Chronicler may have found the Samuel version too difficult and consequently may have expanded it with the help of some other source no longer extant (contra Rudolph, *Chronikbücher*, 99; Stoebe, *ZDPV* 73 [1957] 88), at the same time simplifying the account. Perhaps the takeover of Jerusalem, in whatever form, was not essential for the main themes of the document in which it was embedded, or, traditionally, the capture of the city may have been linked with Joab's heroic feat. There is no real reason why the Chronicler should have invented this detail, but it is well known that in 2 Samuel there is a noticeable anti-Joab tendency (see 2 Sam 3:29, 39; 16:10) which may account for the omission of Joab's exploit and for the abbreviated(?) form of the report (see also Bressan, *Bib* 25 [1944] 250–52).

We take the phrase "whoever would conquer the Jebusites . . ." not as a promise (see 1 Chr 11:6) but as a general statement which, at the same time, hints at the next step in the campaign: namely, the only way to victory was the capture of the stronghold's water supply (צנור). Much has been written on the possible meanings of צנור which occurs elsewhere only in Ps 42:8[7] where it probably means "waterfall" (cf. also Zech 4:12). In the course of scholarly discussions, צנור has been given the following main interpretations: (a) "weapon," such as "dagger" (G), "trident" or "pitchfork" (Sukenik), "grappling-iron" (NEB); (b) some form of mutilation (so Ginsberg, *ZAW* 10 [1933] 308); (c) one's *membrum virile* (in an oath-taking ceremony), so, e.g., Glück (*Biblical Essays*, 102); and (d) water supply system as a whole or some part of it (so most scholars); RSV, NAB, NIV have "water shaft." It seems that the best "neutral" rendering of צנור might be "water supply."

Many scholars have identified the צנור with the shaft discovered by Sir Charles Warren in 1867 (see Vincent, *RB* 33 [1924] 257–70; Simons, *Jerusalem*, 45–67). This shaft connected the Spring of the Steps or the Spring of Mary (i.e., the ancient spring of Gihon) with the settlement or stronghold on the southeastern hill. It is often thought that this tunnel may have been the proverbial Achilles' heel of Jerusalem in that David's soldiers were able either to penetrate the city through this shaft or, more likely, to cut off the water supply from the Jebusites. The former alternative would be a formidable task even if the Jebusites had neglected this weak spot in their defenses (see Mazar, *The Mountain of the Lord*, 168). However, there is no proof that this shaft was the Jebusite צנור (see J. Shiloh, "The City of David: Archaeological Project: Third Season—1980," *BA* 44 [1981] 170).

Further difficulties are created by v 8b and its connection with v 8a. We regard the latter part of the verse as a later addition, giving an etiological explanation of the proverb or saying, "The blind and the lame shall not enter the house" (cf. Gen 22:14; 1 Sam 19:24). This explanation is not found in the Chronicler's version of events, and it seems rather forced even if "house" in this context is not the Temple (so G, Vg; cf. also Mic 3:12) but David's palace. It is just possible that beggars (i.e., the blind and the lame) were forbidden to enter the Temple (cf. Acts 3:1–10); at least, such disabled people were disqualified from priestly duties (Lev 21:18). However, the Temple was not in existence in David's time, and therefore the etiology appears to be somewhat artificial (see Stoebe, *ZDPV* 73 [1957] 91); on the other hand, David was later regarded as the founder of many cultic practices and regulations (cf. 1 Chr 22–28).

If there is some textual corruption in v 8a then "the lame and the blind, the enemies of David" (so Q) may be the object of a preceding verb, accidentally omitted(?). NEB renders along similar lines, "let him use his grappling-iron to reach the lame and the blind, David's bitter enemies" (cf. also Driver, 260). This is possible but is no more convincing than some other proposals.

9 It is surprising how little we are told about the changes in Jerusalem following its takeover. The Jebusites were neither expelled (contra Josephus, 7.65) nor exterminated, and we do not know what happened to their political or religious leaders. It is possible that their social and political structures were taken over by David (so Stolz, 208) and adapted. At least in the early part of David's reign in Jerusalem, the Jebusites may have formed the more substantial element of the population. Even as late as Ezekiel (16:3), it could be said of Jerusalem, "Your father was an Amorite and your mother a Hittite."

We are better informed about the building operations undertaken by David but the details are far from clear. The MT could be rendered, "And David built round about from Millo and inward" (KJV, RV) but it seems that the object of the verb has been accidentally omitted. The Chronicler and 4QSam a supply "the city" (and this is presupposed also by Josephus) while de Vaux (165) suggests קִיר "a wall" which may have been mistakenly transposed (?) to v 11 (see n. 11.a).

The exact meaning and location of Millo (מִלּוֹא) are uncertain. Etymologically it may mean "what is full" or "what fills a gap" or both. In view of recent archaeological discoveries it seems that the Millo may refer to a system of artificial terraces supported by retaining walls with leveled filling, and by other substructures (see Mazar, *The Mountain of the Lord*, 171). According to 1 Kgs 9:15, 23; 11:27, it was Solomon who built the Millo. If this is the right interpretation then 2 Sam 5:9 uses the word מִלּוֹא proleptically, just as "the house" may refer either to the later palace or to the Temple (cf. Simons, *Jerusalem*, 132; Gray, *Jerusalem*, 32). On the other hand, it is equally possible that such a terracing existed already in the pre-Davidic period, and that Solomon rebuilt and repaired the existing structures or enlarged them. Kenyon (*Digging up Jerusalem*, 100) has argued that the uncovered complex of terracing on the eastern slope of Ophel is a Jebusite structure built to support houses on the incline of the hill. Moreover, it is obvious that this structure had been repaired on several occasions; the work done in David's time may belong to this category.

10 This verse sums up David's rise to power (cf. also Sam 3:1) and adds the theological explanation that the reason for David's success was Yahweh's presence with him. Some scholars regard this verse as the conclusion of the HDR (see Mettinger, *King and Messiah*, 41; Grønbaek, *Aufstieg*, 257).

"Yahweh, the God of hosts" (יהוה אלהי צבאות) is the longer form of the far more frequent יהוה צבאות which is usually translated as "the LORD (or Yahweh) of hosts." The latter expression cannot very well be a genitive construction (see GKC, § 125h) and therefore this shorter form may be an abbreviation of a longer phrase or a reinterpretation of such an expression as "He who creates the (heavenly) armies" (see Cross, *Canaanite Myths*, 70). It has been suggested that "Yahweh, the God of hosts" is a later interpretation of the more archaic shorter formula, whatever its origin (cf. von Rad, *OT Theology* 1 [1962] 18). Another possibility is that צבאות is in apposition, as suggested by the G rendering "the Lord, the Almighty" (κύριος παντοκράτωρ). Of course, there are also other possibilities (see *THAT* 2 [1976] 504–7; Ross, *VT* 17 [1967] 76–92).

The "hosts" may refer either to the armies of Israel (cf. 1 Sam 17:45) or, more likely, to the heavenly hosts which are always at Yahweh's service (cf. Pss 33:6; 103:21; 148:2; Isa 40:26; 45:12); however, see Eichrodt, *Theology* 2 (1967) 192.

11 According to Bright's chronology (*History*, Chart 4), David reigned c. 1000–961 B.C. while Hiram's reign is dated c. 969–936 B.C. (cf. also Josephus, *Ag. Ap.* 1.18). Other scholars may differ to a greater or lesser extent (cf. *IJH*, 351, 682) but the relevant point is that the beginning of Hiram's reign falls in the *last* decade of David's rule. This is plausible since he was also a contemporary of Solomon; however, the evidence may not be strong enough to reject v 11 as unauthentic.

The building materials and men sent by Hiram may have been part of a more extensive treaty between David and Hiram. Both Israel and Phoenicia shared common interests which must have led to friendly cooperation. Phoenicia needed food supplies from Israel (cf. 1 Kgs 5:25[11]) as well as safe trade routes through Israelite territory. In return, Israel would benefit from the resulting commerce and from the Phoenician material culture.

The present context may suggest that v 11 was intended to show that even the wealthy and influential king of Tyre was so impressed by David's achievements that his immediate reaction was to send men and materials (so Kegler, *Politisches Geschehen*, 103).

There is no real reason to doubt that "the house" built for David was his palace, not the temple (see Donner, *JNSL* 10 [1982] 50–55). V 11 may well contain reliable information about David's building activities even though there are some similarities between this verse and 1 Kgs 5:15–26 [1–12]; see however, Donner, *The Period of David and Solomon*, 212–14.

Cedar logs were well known for their durability and they were often used as pillars, as well as for roofing and paneling. They were imported from the mountains of Lebanon, and they were taken in rafts to Joppa, the nearest port to Jerusalem (see 2 Chr 2:16).

12 This verse probably followed v 10, if v 11 is regarded as misplaced or as a later insertion. In Grønbaek's opinion vv 10 and 12 are mutually exclusive but the repetitiveness may be a stylistic device for the sake of emphasis. Here, as well as in v 10, God's blessing is recognized in material success and prosperity.

From the previous events it appears that David's kingdom was what could be described as a constitutional monarchy (cf. Halpern, *Monarchy in Israel*, 241). There is also a hint of a democratic concept of kingship since the exaltation of the king was for the sake of Israel. Therefore the kingship should be for the benefit of the people and not vice versa.

13 The concubines (see *Comment* on 3:6) are mentioned before the wives but this fact may have no real significance for interpretation; G reverses the order while 1 Chr 14:3 omits "concubines." It is possible that our list includes only the sons of the wives while those of the concubines are not mentioned. This is suggested by 1 Chr 3:9 which concludes the list with the following words, "All these were the sons of David, besides the sons of the concubines. . . ." Furthermore, it is a possibility that only the firstborn sons of the various mothers are listed (so Gutbrod, 72; however, see 1 Chr 3:5). MT and the versions imply that the wives and concubines were taken *from* Jerusalem. This is plausible but 1 Chr 14:3 may be right in suggesting that David, *residing in Jerusalem*, took more wives.

14 This list mentions eleven sons in addition to the six listed in 2 Sam 3:2–5. Consequently, the later king Solomon was only tenth in the line of succession.

The names of the sons are not always transparent, at least to us, and not infrequently the exact meaning is far from clear.

"Shammua" (שמוע) is probably an abbreviated caritative form of שמעיה "Shemaiah" meaning "Yahweh has heard"; see Noth, *Personennamen*, 185.

The meaning of שובב "Shobab" is uncertain, perhaps "substitute" for a dead person (cf. KB, 954). Noth (op. cit., 258) has raised the question whether it may be an abusive name (*Schimpfname*), meaning "faithless." We prefer the former alternative; see J. J. Stamm, "Hebräische Ersatznamen," in *Studies in Honor of Benno Landsberger*, 419, 421.

"Nathan" (נתן) may be a hypocoristic name where the divine element has been omitted. It could be derived from such fuller forms as Jonathan, Elnathan, Nethanel (see also Noth, op. cit., 170).

"Solomon" (שלמה) may be a caritative form from שלום "peace," and it was the throne name of Israel's third king (see Honeyman, *JBL* 67 [1948] 23). Stamm (*TZ* 16 [1960] 296) and Gerleman (*ZAW* 85 [1973] 13) find in Solomon's name some such meaning as "substitute" (or "his substitute"), i.e., replacement for the dead child of Bathsheba. Veijola (VTSup 30 [1979] 236) sees in the "replacement" an allusion to Uriah, Bathsheba's first husband, but this view seems less likely.

"Ibhar" (יבחר) may be a name expressing a wish: "May God choose"; so Noth, op. cit., 209. "Elishua" (אלישוע) means "God is salvation" and is similar in meaning to the more frequent יהושוע "Joshua." "Japhia" (יפיע) probably means "may (God) shine"; see Noth, ibid., 204.

"Elishama" (אלישמע) or "God has heard" is a well-known name while "Eliada" (אלידע, "God knows") is of special interest because 1 Chr 14:7 may have preserved the original form of this son's name: "Beeliada" (בעלידע, "Baal knows"). This need not imply that David must have worshiped Baal because the name "Baal" may have been used as a title of Yahweh. Later even the use of the title became offensive to subsequent editors. However, F. E. Eakin ("Yahwism and Baalism before the Exile," *JBL* 84 [1965] 407–14)

is of the opinion that "David was primarily concerned to amalgamate the differing factions of his kingdom rather than to abolish any given faction" (411).

The last son born in Jerusalem was Eliphelet (אליפלט, "God is deliverance");
see also Noth, op. cit., 156.

Explanation

This composite section revolves largely around Jerusalem and David's rise
to fame, yet at the same time, the editor has clearly indicated that the triumphs
and prosperity attained were the blessing of Yahweh (vv 10 and 12). It is
evident that although God had established David's kingdom, his primary
concern was not the glorification of the king but the salvation and welfare
of his people (cf. 2 Sam 3:18).

It is also interesting that the text is silent about any political motives or
any other considerations which may have influenced David's actions. However,
vv 6 and 8 may imply that the Jebusites had insulted the king, and by implication
also Yahweh's people; consequently, such an attitude required the corresponding action (see 2 Sam 10).

The list of David's sons (vv 14–16) is a further illustration of the king as
being under divine blessing. Politically, many of the marriages may have
been diplomatic arrangements, establishing firmer relationships with various
important families and securing their support for the royal house. None of
the sons, except Solomon and Nathan (see Luke 3:31), is mentioned elsewhere.
In a sense, many sons are the strength of the family (see Ps 127:3–5) but in
David's case they eventually became also the source of great disharmony
and trouble, especially Amnon, Absalom, and Adonijah.

It may be a coincidence that none of the names in this list is a theophoric
name with an explicit Yahwistic association. On the other hand, two of the
six sons born in Hebron had Yahwistic names ("Adonijah" and "Shephatiah").
If David's wives were *from* Jerusalem (i.e., Jebusite women), then the absence
of such names would be understandable (so Stolz, 209) because more often
than not a child's name was given by its mother.

The Philistine Campaigns (5:17–25)

Bibliography

Alt, A. "Zu II Samuel 8:1." *ZAW* 54 (1936) 149–52. **Campbell, A. F.** *The Ark Narrative.* 68–72. **Gelston, A.** "The Wars of Israel." *SJT* 17 (1964) 325–31. **Gunn, D. M.** "The Battle Report: Oral or Scribal Convention?" *JBL* 93 (1974) 513–18. **Hauer, C. E., Jr.** "Jerusalem, the Stronghold and Rephaim." *CBQ* 32 (1970) 571–78. **Long, B. O.** "The Effect of Divination upon Israelite Literature." *JBL* 92 (1973) 489–97. **Plöger, J.** *Literarkritische, formgeschichtliche und stilkritische Untersuchungen zum Deuteronomium.* BBB 26. Bonn: Peter Hanstein Verlag GMBH, 1967. **Richter, W.** *Traditionsgeschichtliche Untersuchungen zum Richterbuch.* BBB 18. Bonn: Peter Hanstein Verlag GMBH, 1963. **Segal, M. H.** "The Composition of the Books of Samuel: The Conquest of Jerusalem and the War with the Philistines." *JQR* 56 (1965/66) 32–50. **Seters, J. van.** "The Conquest of Sihon's Kingdom: A Literary Examination." *JBL* 91 (1972) 181–97. **Tidwell, N. L.** "The Philistine Incursions into the Valley of Rephaim." VTSup 30 (1979) 190–212.

Translation

[17] When the Philistines heard that David had been anointed[a] king over Israel, all the Philistines went up to seek David, but David heard about it and went down to the hiding place. [18] So the Philistines came and raided[a] in the valley of Rephaim.[b] [19] Then David inquired of Yahweh, "Shall I attack[a] the Philistines? Will you deliver them into my hand?" And Yahweh said to David, "Attack,[a] for I will certainly[b] deliver the Philistines into your hand." [20] David then went to Baal-perazim where he[a] defeated them. So David said, "Yahweh has overwhelmed[b] my enemies before me like the overwhelming floodwaters." Therefore that place was called[c] Baal-perazim. [21] There the Philistines left their idols,[a] and David and his men carried[b] them off. [22] Once again the Philistines came up[a] and raided in the valley of Rephaim. [23] So David inquired of Yahweh who said, "Do not make a frontal attack,[a] but go round[b] to their rear,[c] and attack[d] them from the direction of the balsam trees.[e] [24] Then,[a] as soon as you hear the sound of marching[b] in the tops of the balsam trees, be ready to act[c] for Yahweh has gone out before you to smite the Philistine camp." [25] So David did as Yahweh had commanded him, and he smote the Philistines from Gibeon[a] as far as Gezer.

Notes

17.a. Lit., "that they had anointed." For the use of the active theme in the impersonal 3 pl to express the passive, see Williams, *Syntax,* § 160. 1 Chr 14:8 has כי נמשח דוד "that David had been anointed."

18.a. Or "spread themselves out." 1 Chr 14:9 has ויפשטו "and made a raid."

18.b. G has the interpretative τῶν τιτάνων "of the Giants"; so also Josephus (*Ant.* 7.71).

19.a. Lit., "go up" (see *Comment* on v 17).

19.b. For the emphatic use of the inf abs, see GKC, § 113n.

20.a. MT reads דוד "David."

20.b. The verb פרץ means, in general, "to make a breach, burst out" (see *HALAT*, 298).

20.c. Lit., "and he called (that place)"; for the passive meaning, see n. 17.a.

21.a. G reads "their gods" which is, no doubt, an exegetical rendering; so also 1 Chr 14:12.

21.b. The Heb. verb is singular and agrees with the nearer subject ("David"). See GKC, § 146f.

22.a. 1 Chr 14:13 omits לעלות "to go up," perhaps rightly so.

23.a. Lit., "(do not) go up"; G expands this by adding "to meet them."

23.b. MT has the causative form הסב "lead (your men)"(?), which Budde (225) regards as an appropriate military term ("make an encirclement"). G, with its ἀποστρέφου "turn away," suggests the qal (סב, "go round"); so also Driver (264) and Nowack (171). The ה of הסב may be due to dittography.

23.c. For the use of double prepositions, see Brockelmann, *Syntax,* § 119b.

23.d. Or "go against them" (cf. Jer 50:26).

23.e. Perhaps, we should supply the missing article, with 1 Chr 14:14 (and G) to read הבכאים.

24.a. Lit., "and let it be . . ." (ויהי). For the use of the jussive form to express a permissive command, see GKC, § 109k; 112z; Driver, *Tenses,* § 121.

24.b. The object marker requires a definite expression and therefore we should, perhaps, read הצעדה with 1 Chr 14:15 and many MSS. Cf. also GKC, § 117d.

24.c. NAB: "act decisively." 1 Chr 14:15 reads אז תצא במלחמה "then go out to battle" which seems to be a loose paraphrase.

25.a. MT (also Tg and Syr) reads גבע "Geba," while 1 Chr 14:16 (and G) has גבעון "Gibeon," which is usually regarded as the original reading. MT variant may be a scribal error.

Form / Structure / Setting

Many scholars are of the opinion that vv 17–25 must be placed before vv 6–10 (cf. Noth, *The Deuteronomistic History,* 56), immediately after v 3 since the Philistine invasion seems to be a direct response to David's anointing (v 17). If the Deuteronomistic editor added the chronological note (vv 4–5) then the reference to Jerusalem (v 5) may have facilitated or necessitated the placing of vv 6–10 in their present position (cf. Grønbaek, *Aufstieg,* 254). All in all, it seems likely that the capture of Jerusalem followed the defeat of the Philistines although some scholars place the Jerusalem episode between the two battle reports (see Hertzberg, 275). Obviously, certainty is impossible but it is more plausible that Jerusalem was taken *after* the Philistine threat was removed. For the opposite view, see Hauer's article in *CBQ* 32 (1970) 571–78; Aharoni, *Land,* 293.

Alt (*ZAW* 54 [1936] 150) regards 2 Sam 8 as a continuation of vv 17–25 (see also Carlson, *David,* 56–57; Veijola, *Dynastie,* 98); on the other hand, 2 Sam 8 may be an allusion to the confrontation described elsewhere. Segal (*JQR* 56 [1965/6] 33) argues that vv 17–25 are related to 2 Sam 21:15–22 and 23:9–12 and that they all may "have been derived from the same literary source" (33). Out of this material Segal reconstructs *three* separate campaigns (see ibid., 33). Whether this argument is right or not, it is quite likely that the hostilities with the Philistines involved more than two military engagements. However, it could be doubted that there was such a *single* literary source because vv 17–25 comprise two battle reports while the other information seems to be derived from hero stories (see Eissfeldt, *Komposition,* 30; Grønbaek, *Aufstieg,* 253 n.112).

One must also bear in mind Tidwell's warning (VTSup 30 [1979] 192) that there is little "justification for assuming that the present literary context of any of these fragmentary traditions is a true reflection of or a reliable guide to its original historical sequence." In his view, behind vv 22–25 there is "a battle-report of a major confrontation which either paved the way for or resulted from the capture of Jerusalem" (ibid., 211–12), while vv 18–21, in their original form, spoke of a "successful routing of a Philistine raiding party by David and his men" (ibid., 212).

V 17 is thought to be "an introductory comment setting *both* reports into a larger narrative sequence by connecting these incursions with the Philistine reaction to David's anointing" (ibid., 206).

V 22 appears to be a shortened version of vv 17 and 18; hence it may not have been the original beginning of the second battle report. Tidwell (ibid., 207) suspects also the setting in the Valley of Rephaim, but there is no obvious alternative unless the Philistine retreat from Gibeon (Geba?) to Gezer points to a more northerly starting point for the pursuit than the vale of Rephaim. The Chronicler (1 Chr 14:13) simply speaks of "the valley" but it is doubtful that he intended any other location than the Valley of Rephaim. Perhaps, he had in mind Isa 28:21 which links "the Valley of Gibeon" with "Mount Perazim" but in that case one might have expected a more explicit allusion (see, however, v 25).

In v 25a Tidwell (ibid., 211) finds "the touch of the Deuteronomistic author" while in v 25b he sees the original ending because it is formulated in the more or less conventional form ("from . . . as far as": cf. also Josh 10:41; Judg 11:33; 1 Sam 14:31).

These two, apparently abbreviated, accounts of victories over the Philistines are often described as "short battle reports" but it is doubtful whether we can speak of a literary type or *Gattung*. Furthermore, it is not clear whether such battle reports belong to oral or scribal tradition (see Gunn, *JBL* 93 [1974] 518). Van Seters (*JBL* 91 [1972] 187) describes them as "a *recording convention.*"

In these reports we find a number of recurring elements but they usually reflect the various stages in any battle. Campbell (*The Ark Narrative*, 68–69) has noted that a number of these accounts share the following structure:

(a) Confrontation of the opposing forces. This element would include the names of the participants, an outline of the preliminary stage of the encounter, the place of the battle, etc.
(b) Consultation of Yahweh. Plöger (*Untersuchungen zum Deuteronomium*, 16) prefers to speak of a formula of disclosure in which Yahweh would assure of victory.
(c) Battle account, incorporating such details as tactics (so Tidwell, VTSup 30 [1974] 194), the nature of the struggle, etc. However, the actual contest or engagement is usually not described.
(d) Consequences of battle, providing a characterization of consequences and casualty figures.

Richter (*Untersuchungen*, 262–66) has observed that in the battle reports we often find four parts which describe the different stages of the encounter and contain certain characteristic words of action:

(a) Verbs of movement (e.g., "went up").
(b) Verbs of military activity or tactics (e.g., "raided").
(c) Verbs indicating the outcome of the battle ("defeated," "smote").
(d) A concluding element describing the extent of the engagement; often

with מִן "from" and וְעַד "as far as," as in the phrase "from Gibeon as far as Gezer" (v 25).

Both battle accounts include consultation of Yahweh and in this reporting of the consultation we find two elements: (a) report of inquiry (divination), in vv 19a and 23a; and (b) oracle (vv 19b and 23b–24). For further details, see Long's article in *JBL* 92 (1973) 493 (see also Richter, *Untersuchungen*, 21–23; 182).

Comment

17 At this stage David was still a vassal of the lord of Gath, and his elevation to kingship over all Israel must have been regarded by the Philistines as rebellion (see *Comment* on 2:1). Therefore also their reaction was quite natural. It is not impossible that the Philistines first heard of David's anointing when he attempted to capture Jerusalem (cf. Caird, 1074) in order to facilitate communications between Judah and Israel. If so, David may have temporarily given up the attempt to capture Jerusalem, and he may have withdrawn to Adullam. For this use of יָרַד "to go down," see Eissfeldt, *Komposition*, 31. It is less likely, for a number of reasons, that David would have evacuated Jerusalem (but see Hauer, *CBQ* 32 [1970] 575–78) and retreated to the strong-hold of Adullam. However, the chronological relationship between the capture of Jerusalem and the Philistine campaigns remains uncertain unless the present arrangement can be taken as indicative of the original historical sequence.

The verb עָלָה "went up" is a general term but here it may have military overtones, suggesting hostile advance (cf. Hauer, *CBQ* 32 [1970] 576 n.19). The fact that the Philistines sought David may imply that they were not sure of David's whereabouts nor of his intentions. In that case the occupation of the vale of Rephaim and the consequent separation of Judah from Israel was a challenge to David. At first, David went down (from Hebron or Jerusalem?) to Adullam which had previously served (cf. 1 Sam 22:1, 4) as a hiding place (see *Comment* on 5:17). It does not necessarily follow that he was fleeing for his life and seeking refuge from the enemy; it may have been a tactical move since the מְצוּדָה "hiding place," "fortress," was the place from which he launched his counterattack. Even if the account in vv 17–21 describes only the incursion of a raiding party and not a full-scale invasion, the former exploit may have been an integral part of a more formidable Philistine military response.

18 The Heb. נָטַשׁ in a military context probably means "to plunder, gather spoils," depicting a specialized type of warlike action. The Chronicler's equivalent, פָּשַׁט, may be a synonym. If these suggestions are right, then the main aim of the Philistines on this occasion was not a decisive battle but the harassment of the opponents and the gathering of booty (see Tidwell, VTSup 30 [1979] 195–99).

The location of the Valley of Rephaim is uncertain but most scholars identify it with the modern *el Baqʿa*, southwest of Jerusalem (see Simons, *Texts*, § 211; Abel, *Géographie* 1 [1933] 402). It was famous as a corn-growing area (Isa 17:5). The word רְפָאִים "Rephaim" is of problematic origin. It could be associated with the dead (see Isa 14:9; 26:14, 19) or with a social (or mythological) group (see Gen 15:20; Deut 3:11). For a detailed discussion of this word, see Conrad E. L. Heureux, "The Ugaritic and Biblical Rephaim," *HTR* 67 (1974) 265–74; *Rank among the Canaanite Gods: El, Ba'al, and Rephaim,* HSM 21 (Missoula, MT: Scholars Press, 1979).

19 David inquired of Yahweh by using, most likely, the lots (see *Comment* on 2:1) or the ephod (see Gelston, *SJT* 17 [1964] 329). NEB takes the two separate questions as equivalent to a conditional sentence: "If I attack . . . wilt thou deliver them . . . ?" For similar double questions, see 1 Sam 14:37; 23:11; 30:8. Yahweh gave a positive answer, and this may provide an implicit contrast to Saul to whom Yahweh *did not answer* on at least two occasions (1 Sam 14:37; 28:6).

20 Baal-perazim is an otherwise unknown locality, near the Valley of Rephaim (cf. Simons, *Texts,* § 759). It is probably referred to in Isa 28:21 as "Mount Perazim." Stolz (211) has suggested that Baal-perazim was originally the name of the god venerated at this locality, and that later it became a title of Yahweh. The meaning of this name is not clear; NEB translates it "Baal of Break-through" while NAB[mg] has "the lord of scatterings." The etiology of the name seems to suggest the image of floodwaters which sweep everything before them (cf. Goslinga, 104) or of a torrential downpour (so Hertzberg, 274). Similarly, Yahweh had overwhelmed the Philistines, and therefore the battlefield was called Baal-perazim ("Lord of overwhelming floods"[?] or "the overwhelming Lord"). If the name was older than the battle itself, then it was reinterpreted in the light of later events. Driver (263) thought that at an earlier stage the name may have been that of "a fountain bursting forth out of the hill-side."

It is possible that David and his men rushed down Mount Perazim (cf. Isa 28:21) and attacked the surprised enemy in the valley (for a parallel, see Judg 4:14), sweeping them away, like raging floodwaters. The name "Baal-perazim" is an additional pointer to the primary role of Yahweh in the encounter.

21 This verse seems to be a fitting counterpart to the loss of the Ark after the defeat of the Israelite forces at Aphek (1 Sam 4–5). Now the situation is reversed and it is the Philistines who flee, abandoning their idols (or gods). These images were taken into battle in order to vouchsafe victory, just as the Israelites had used the Ark for a similar purpose (cf. 1 Sam 4:3; Num 10:35). After the fight David and his men carried off the idols as battle trophies to be displayed, perhaps, in their own sanctuary, if 1 Sam 5:2 is a valid parallel.

For v 21b the Chronicler has "and David commanded that they should be burnt with fire." Of course, the author may have had a different *Vorlage* but, in any case, the variant seems to be a later alteration to avoid any possible misunderstanding or attributing wrong motives to David (cf. 2 Chr 25:14). At the same time, David is made to conform to the Deuteronomic law (Deut 7:5, 25; 12:3).

22 This introduction to the second battle report is reminiscent of vv 17 and 18 but this may be due to the conventional nature of these reports.

23 Once more David consults Yahweh but the questions posed are not reported (cf. v 19); perhaps different means were used to find Yahweh's guidance. A priestly oracle is a possibility, and Josephus (*Ant.* 7.76) attributes the oracle to the high priest!

Whether at this point David was at Adullam or in Jerusalem (so Hertzberg, 275) or elsewhere, is not stated.

The actual details of the battle tactics remain uncertain but it is possible that David was advised not to attempt a frontal attack but to assault the Philistines from the rear, from the direction of (or "before") the balsam trees. This move probably enabled David to surprise the enemy forces which may have been far superior to those of David (cf. 1 Sam 13:5). Josephus (*Ant.* 7.75) goes as far as to claim that this enemy army was three times as large as the force defeated previously. See also Herzog and Gichon, *Battles of the Bible*, 79–80.

The exact botanical identification of בכאים is doubtful, and the translations differ considerably: "aspens" (NEB), "mastic trees" (NAB), "balsam trees" (RSV, JB, NIV), "mulberry trees" (KJV). Stolz (211) speaks of "Baca-bushes" and connects the word with בכה "to weep." In Ps 84:7[6] there is a "valley of Baca" (עמק הבכא) in the vicinity of Jerusalem, and Tidwell (VTSup 30 [1979] 207) has suggested that this location may have been the original setting of the second battle. This is plausible, but the link between the trees (בכאים) and the valley of Baca (בכא) may be only apparent. One may also note that there may have been an accidental confusion between עמק רפאים "the valley of Rephaim" and עמק בכאים "the valley of Balsam(?) trees."

24 The signal for David's attack was to be the "marching sound" in the tree tops, perhaps a rustling sound made by the leaves. See the parallels in Gen 3:8; Judg 4:14; Ps 68:8[7].

25 It was with Yahweh's help that David gained the victory and the Philistines were routed from Gibeon (so G and 1 Chr 14:16) as far as Gezer. Although the MT reads גבע "Geba," the other variant is preferable because Gibeon was closer to the main routes from Jerusalem to the coastal plain.

For Gibeon, see *Comment* on 2:12. Gezer was an ancient Canaanite city (see Murphy-O'Connor, *The Holy Land,* 185; cf. Judg 1:29), and it came into Israelite possession only when the Pharaoh gave it as dowry to his daughter (Solomon's wife; 1 Kgs 9:16). It is usually identified with Tell el-Jazar, near Abu Shusheh, some 19 miles (30 kilometers) northwest of Jerusalem.

Explanation

In the present context vv 17–25 depict two encounters between David and the Philistines, which apparently brought to an end the Philistine domination of Palestine (see also 2 Sam 8:1). In view of the book as a whole, it seems that the war with the Philistines was more prolonged, but the editor had chosen only these two select illustrations to sketch the *main* course of events. Perhaps, just as Israel had been defeated twice by the Philistines (1 Sam 4 and 31) so also the Philistines were twice routed by David.

When the Philistines heard of David's accession over all Israel, they apparently intended to separate Judah from Israel by invading the valley of Rephaim near Jerusalem, and establishing their garrison in Bethlehem (see 2 Sam 23:14) and perhaps also in other strategic locations.

The *present* form of the first battle report (vv 17–21) makes it clear that it was the full force of the enemy (i.e., "all the Philistines") that engaged David (v 17) while the latter had only "his men" (v 21; "his personal troops" [?]) at his disposal. At this point David made a tactical withdrawal to the "stronghold" which may have been Adullam rather than Jerusalem since one would hardly *go down* to it.

If we admit the possibility that the present arrangement of the events in vv 6–9 and 17–25 does not necessarily represent the original historical sequence then there is no *obvious* alternative. However, the chronological data in 2:11 and 5:5 imply that Jerusalem was taken at the beginning of David's reign over Israel although not necessarily before the initial Philistine campaigns. We could, perhaps, argue that since the war may have been a protracted affair and the second battle report (vv 22–25) may describe a major (final?) confrontation, the capture of Jerusalem may be placed *before* this decisive engagement.

David's victories are depicted as Yahweh's work, who delivers the enemy into David's power (v 19) and who goes before him to rout the foe (v 24). Of some interest is also the stress on the oracular guidance; after this episode the oracular consultation plays no explicit part. Gunn (*King David,* 75) regards this type of consultation as atypical of the so-called Succession Narrative.

With the defeat of the Philistines, the way was now open for the ancient promise of the land to be fulfilled through David. However, more obvious is the implication that what Saul had failed to achieve (cf. 1 Sam 9:16) was accomplished by David (cf. 2 Sam 3:18). Nevertheless, the real strategist and the actual victor was Yahweh himself. This may explain why in these battle reports little or no emphasis is placed upon the possible bravery and heroism of the warriors.

The Ark Brought to the City of David
(6:1–23)

Bibliography

Campbell, A. F. *The Ark Narrative*, 126–79. ——. "Yahweh and the Ark: A Case Study in Narrative." *JBL* 98 (1979) 31–43. **Clements, R. E.** *God and Temple. The Idea of the Divine Presence in Ancient Israel.* Oxford: Basil Blackwell, 1965. **Clines, D. J. A.** "X, X Ben Y, Ben Y: Personal Names in Hebrew Narrative Style." *VT* 22 (1972) 266–87. **Davies, G. H.** "The Ark of the Covenant." *ASTI* 5 (1967) 30–47. **Dus, J.** "Der Brauch der Ladewanderung im alten Israel." *TZ* 17 (1961) 1–16. **Eissfeldt, O.** "Noch Einmal: Text-, Stil- und Literarkritik in den Samuelisbüchern." *OLZ* 30 (1928) 801–12. **Fohrer, G.** "Die alttestamentliche Ladeerzählung." *JNSL* 1 (1971) 23–31. **Gerleman, G.** "Die Wurzel *šlm*." *ZAW* 85 (1973) 1–14. **Gruber, M. I.** "Ten Dance-Derived Expressions in the Hebrew Bible." *Bib* 62 (1981) 328–46. **Jeremias, J.** "Lade und Zion: Zur Entstehung der Ziontradition." In *Probleme biblischer Theologie*, ed. H. W. Wolff. Munich: Chr. Kaiser Verlag, 1971. **Maier, J.** *Das altisraelitische Ladeheiligtum.* BZAW 93. Berlin: Alfred Töpelmann, 1965. **Mettinger, T. N. D.** *The Dethronement of Sabaoth.* ConB Old Testament Series 18. Lund: CWK Gleerup, 1982. **Miller, P. D.** and **Roberts, J. J. M.** *The Hand of the Lord.* The Johns Hopkins Near Eastern Studies. Baltimore/London: Johns Hopkins University Press, 1977. **Nielsen, E.** "Some Reflections on the History of the Ark." *VTSup* 7 (1960) 61–74. **Noth, M.** "Jerusalem und die israelitische Tradition." *OTS* 8 (1950) 28–46 (= *The Laws in the Pentateuch and Other Essays.* Tr. D. R. Ap-Thomas. Edinburgh/London: Oliver & Boyd, 1966. 132–44). **Phillips, A.** "David's Linen Ephod." *VT* 19 (1969) 485–87. **Porter, J. R.** "The Interpretation of 2 Samuel VI and Psalm CXXXII." *JTS* 5 (1954) 161–73. **Ross, J. P.** "Yahweh Ṣe̱bā̱ʾôt in Samuel and Psalms." *VT* 17 (1967) 76–92. **Rost, L.** *The Succession.* 6–34. **Schicklberger, F.** *Die Ladeerzählung des ersten Samuel-Buches: Eine literaturwissenschaftliche und theologiegeschichtliche Untersuchung.* Forschung zur Bibel 7. Würzburg: Echter Verlag, 1973. **Schmitt, R.** *Zelt und Lade als Thema alttestamentlicher Wissenschaft: Eine kritische forschungsgeschichtliche Darstellung.* Gütersloh: Gerd Mohn, 1972. **Schreiner, J.** *Sion-Jerusalem.* 17–56. **Tidwell, N. L.** "The Linen Ephod: 1 SAM. II 18 and 2 SAM. VI 14." *VT* 24 (1974) 505–7. **Timm, H.** "Die Ladeerzählung (1 Sam. 4–6; 2 Sam. 6) und das Kerygma des deuteronomistischen Geschichtswerks." *EvT* 26 (1966) 509–26. **Tur-Sinai, N. H.** "The Ark of God at Beit Shemesh (1 Sam. VI) and Pereṣ ʾUzza (2 Sam. VI; 1 Chron. XIII)." *VT* 1 (1951) 275–86. **Wambacq, B. N.** *L'epithète divine Jahvé Ṣe̱baʾôt. Étude philologique, historique et éxégétique.* Bruges: Desclée, 1947. **Weisman, Z.** "The Nature and Background of Bāḥūr in the Old Testament." *VT* 31 (1981) 441–50.

Translation

[1] *Once again David gathered[a] selected warriors from [b] Israel, thirty[c] thousand in all.* [2] *Then David and all the people who were with him arose[a] and went[a] to Baalah[b] which is Kiriath-jearim belonging to Judah, to bring up from there the ark of God which is called by the name[c] of Yahweh of hosts, who is enthroned upon the cherubim.* [3] *They placed the ark of God upon[a] a new cart and brought it from the house of Abinadab, on the hill. Uzzah[b] and Ahio,[c] the sons of Abinadab, were guiding the cart;[d]* [4] *Uzzah was with the ark of God while Ahio was walking*

before the ark. [5]*David and the whole house of Israel were dancing before Yahweh with all their strength and to the sound of songs,*[a] *and of lyres, harps, tambourines, sistrums, and cymbals.*[b] [6]*When they came to the threshing floor of Nodan,*[a] *Uzzah stretched out his hand*[b] *to the ark of God, and took hold of it because the oxen*[c] *stumbled.* [7]*Then Yahweh's anger broke out against Uzzah and he*[a] *struck him down on the spot because of his presumption. Thus he died by*[b] *the ark of God.* [8]*David was distressed*[a] *because of Yahweh's outburst*[b] *against Uzzah, and so that place was called*[c] *Perez-Uzzah to this day.* [9]*David feared Yahweh that day and said, "How can the ark of Yahweh come to me?"*[a] [10]*So David was no longer willing to take the ark of Yahweh with*[a] *him to*[b] *the city of David but took it aside to the house of Obed-edom the Gittite.* [11]*The ark of Yahweh remained in the house of Obed-edom the Gittite for three months, and Yahweh blessed Obed-edom and his whole family.*[a] [12]*Then it was reported to King David, "Yahweh has blessed the family of Obed-edom and all his possessions because of the ark of God." So David went and brought up the ark of God from the house of Obed-edom to the city of David with rejoicing.* [13]*When the bearers of the ark of Yahweh had taken six steps, he sacrificed an ox and a fatted calf.* [14]*Then David, wearing*[a] *a linen loin cloth, danced before Yahweh with all his might.* [15]*So David and the whole house*[a] *of Israel were bringing up the ark*[b] *of Yahweh with joyous shouting and to the sound of the horn.* [16]*As the ark of Yahweh was*[a] *entering the city of David, Saul's daughter Michal was looking down through the window. When she saw King David leaping and whirling before Yahweh, she despised him secretly.*[b] [17]*When they had brought in the ark of Yahweh, they set it in its place inside the tent which David had pitched for it. Then David offered burnt sacrifices and peace offerings.* [18]*When David had finished offering the burnt sacrifice*[a] *and the peace offerings, he blessed the people in the name of Yahweh of hosts.* [19]*Afterwards he distributed to all the people, to the whole multitude of Israel, both men and women, to each a*[a] *round loaf of bread, a*[a] *date cake, and a*[a] *cake of raisins. Then all the people went each to his home.* [20]*When David returned to bless his own household, Saul's daughter Michal came out to meet David and said, "How dignified the king of Israel has been this day, exposing himself in the sight of the slave girls of his subjects, as any riffraff*[a] *might go on exposing himself!"* [21]*David replied to Michal, "Not before slave girls but*[a] *before Yahweh I have been dancing.*[b] *As Yahweh lives,*[b] *who has preferred me to your father and to his whole family when he appointed me the chosen leader of the people of Yahweh, I will dance before Yahweh*[c] [22]*and demean myself even more than this; I may be contemptible in your eyes*[a] *but in the judgment*[b] *of the slave girls you have mentioned, I will be honored."*[c] [23]*So Michal, Saul's daughter, had no child to the day of her death.*

Notes

1.a. The verb אסף "to gather" has dropped the א in the shortened form (see GKC, § 68h); it may be an orthographic variant rather than a scribal error.

1.b. Reading מישׂראל (so G, Vg), unless the preposition ב may mean "from" (cf. Dahood, *Psalms* 3:391–93).

1.c. G reads "seventy" but this may be an exaggeration (see G on 1 Sam 11:8).

2.a. The verbs are singular and they agree with the nearer subject (David); see GKC, § 146f.

2.b. The MT reading מבעלי יהודה could be translated as "from the citizens of Judah" (so G, Tg, Syr, Vg) or "from Baale (or Baal of) Judah" (so KJV, RV). We follow 4QSam[a] (and 1 Chr 13:6), reading בעלה היא קרי[ת] "to Baalah which is Kiria[th-jearim]."

2.c. Most scholars delete the second שם "name"; it is omitted in 1 Chr 13:6 and possibly also in 4QSamᵃ (as suggested by the spacing). The repetition of the noun may be due to dittography. RV retains both, rendering "which is called by the Name, even the name of . . ." (cf. also KJV). Many MSS read שָׁם "there" for the first שם (so G, Syr).

3.a. G, 4QSamᵃ and 1 Chr 13:7 have על "upon" for אל in MT, probably an acceptable alternative (see Williams, *Syntax*, § 306).

3.b. Some MSS have the orthographic variant עזה "Uzzah" for עזא (cf. vv 7 and 8).

3.c. G has misread אַחְיוֹ "Ahio" as אֶחָיו "his brothers."

3.d. It seems that the next six words in the MT are a dittograph: אבינדב אשר בגבעה הדשה וישאהו מבית ". . . the new. . . . And they brought it from the house of Abinadab, on the hill." These words are lacking in 1 Chr 13:7 as well as in G and 4QSamᵃ. If so, then in the process עזא "Uzzah" may have been omitted before עם ארון "with the ark of . . ."; Thenius (168) and others add ועזא הולך "and Uzzah was going. . . ."

5.a. We follow the reading of 1 Chr 13:8 בכל עז ובשירים "with all might, and with songs." MT has בכל עצי ברושים which could be paraphrased, "with all manner of instruments of cypress wood" (cf. KJV, RV, Goldman, 221).

5.b. 1 Chr has ובמצלתים ובחצצרות "and with cymbals and trumpets" for MTˢᵃᵐ ובמנענעים ובצלצלים "and with sistrums and cymbals."

6.a. ךנודן "Nodan" with 4QSamᵃ for MT נכון "Nachon"; G has "Nodar" while 1 Chr 13:8 reads כידן "Kidon."

6.b. Following the versions, 1 Chr 13:9, and 4QSamᵃ, in adding את ידו "his hand."

6.c. The Heb. בקר "oxen" is a collective noun and it is construed with a plural verb (see GKC, § 145b).

7.a. Lit., "God."

7.b. 1 Chr 13:10 (and 4QSamᵃ?) has לפני "before" for MT עם "by." G conflates both readings.

8.a. Lit., "was angry." G has "was dispirited" but it need not suggest a different verb. For the elliptical expression (i.e., the omission of אף), see Brockelmann, *Syntax*, §§ 35b, 127.

8.b. Lit., "because Yahweh had broken a breach" (so Goldman, 221). For the use of the cognate accusative פרץ "breach," see GKC, § 117p.

8.c. Or "and he called." The verb may be understood as a passive construction (so Williams, *Syntax*, § 160), following G. There is no necessity to repoint the verb as a niph form.

9.a. This rhetorical question may well have the force of an emphatic negative statement.

10.a. Or "to (him)"; so NAB.

10.b. In the MSS there seems to be a confusion between על and אל. Probably both prepositions became, more or less, interchangeable. See Brockelmann, *Syntax*, § 108c.

11.a. 1 Chr 13:14 reads ואת כל אשר לו "and all that he had" instead of ואת כל ביתו "and his whole family" in the MTˢᵃᵐ, probably following 2 Sam 6:12.

14.a. For the passive construction with an accusative, see GKC, § 121d.

15.a. "House" (בית) is lacking in a few MSS and in Syr, but see v 5.

15.b. Two MSS and Vg add ברית "covenant"; however, this "ark of the covenant of Yahweh" seems to be a deliberate expansion.

16.a. Reading ויהי with 4QSamᵃ, 1 Chr 15:29 and G for MT והיה (wrong tense?). Campbell (*The Ark Narrative*, 131) retains MT as the *lectio difficilior*.

16.b. Lit., "in her heart."

18.a. MT עולה "burnt sacrifice" is sg in form but may be used as a collective noun; v 17 has the pl עלות.

19.a. In MT אחת "one" and אחד "one" serve, in this context, as equivalents of our indefinite article (see Joüon, *Grammaire*, § 137u).

20.a. G must have read הרקדים "dancers" for הרקים "the riffraff"; the MT is more forceful.

20.b. Unless it is a scribal error, the inf abs (נגלות) is used to emphasize the preceding inf constr (see GKC, § 75y); the expression as a whole may indicate a continual action (cf. Carlson, *David*, 91). Gunn (*King David*, 74) takes the verb גלה to mean, in this context, "to show off."

21.a. The whole phrase is supplied to make explicit the intended (?) contrast.

21.b. Reading with Gᴸ ארקד חי יהוה "I have been dancing. As Yahweh lives." The shorter MT reading may be the result of a homoioteleuton (so Wellhausen, 169).

21.c. Gᴼ and Vg omit לפני יהוה "before Yahweh" but this phrase may resume the expression at the beginning of v 21.

22.a. So G; MT has "my eyes" while one MS reads עיניו "his eyes." In our view, the G provides a better contrast.

22.b. For this use of the preposition עם, see Williams, *Syntax*, § 337.

22.c. MT has the cohortative which some scholars regard as out of place, since a conviction not a wish is required by the context (so Driver, 273). However, the cohortative may, perhaps, be used here to provide a special emphasis.

Form / Structure / Setting

Chap. 6 comprises two main topics: the transfer of the ark to Jerusalem (vv 1–15, 17–19) and Michal's break with David (vv 16, 20–23). Although the latter episode is well integrated in the present context, it has been argued that the Michal story may not have been an integral part of the Ark Narrative (so Hertzberg, 277, et al.; Gunn [*King David*, 74] has suggested that this episode "may originally have belonged after 5:1–3").

For the lack of a better alternative, we accept with certain reservations and modifications, Rost's basic thesis that 1 Sam 4:1b–7:1 and 2 Sam 6 formed, at one time, a single compositional unit (see *Succession*, 33–34), the so-called Ark Narrative even though some parts of the original text may have been lost or omitted. Moreover, it is likely that the present Narrative contains certain additions and glosses. Rost himself excludes the Michal episode (2 Sam 6:16, 20–23), and regards it as a possible beginning of the Succession Narrative (ibid., 87) while Fohrer (*JNSL* 1 [1971] 30) argues that the Perez-Uzzah etiology (2 Sam 6:3–8) is a later expansion.

It is probable that this Ark Narrative originated in the Jerusalem priestly circles before the introduction of the ark into the Temple of Solomon, either late in Davidic reign or in the early part of the Solomonic period (cf. 2 Sam 6:17; see Rost, op. cit., 27; Campbell, *The Ark Narrative*, 221). The narrator of the Ark story seems to have drawn upon older material, as implied by the different genres found in the present Narrative (e.g., the battle reports in 1 Sam 4:1b–2; 10–11; the combat of the gods and the associated etiology in 1 Sam 5:2–5; the Perez-Uzzah etiology [2 Sam 6:3–8] and the Michal episode in 2 Sam 6:16, 20–23).

Of course, not all scholars accept Rost's hypothesis (see the summary of the ongoing discussion in Campbell's *The Ark Narrative*, 28–54, and in his article in *JBL* 98 [1979] 31–43); there are also some modified alternatives. So Miller and Roberts (*The Hand of the Lord*, 19) have suggested, in the light of certain Near Eastern parallels, that the beginning of the Ark Narrative is to be found in 1 Sam 2 (taking vv 12–17; 22–25; 27–36) and that the Narrative ended with 1 Sam 7:1, and did not include 2 Sam 6 (cf. also McCarter, *1 Samuel*, 23–26). The proposed beginning seems plausible because it would account, at least partly, for Israel's rejection; however, we would still retain 2 Sam 6 as the conclusion of the Narrative. Clearly, before David's victories over the Philistines, the return of the ark to Kiriath-jearim could have been regarded as a fairly satisfactory ending, and the Narrative (up to this point in time) would have been similar to the Near Eastern accounts by vanquished peoples of the capture of their gods and their subsequent return (cf. Miller and Roberts, op. cit., 9–17). However, when the Philistines were defeated and the ark was transferred to Jerusalem, some theological justification was required to account for the latter step and other changes. Furthermore, the past events were now seen in a different light and perspective because of the recent dramatic happenings. Consequently, in the new context an Ark Narrative without 2 Sam 6 would be a story without a proper ending (cf. Campbell, *JBL* 98 [1979] 42). Perhaps, the addition of 2 Sam 6 was the second stage in the redactional history. It has been noted that there is a break as one moves from 1 Sam 7:1 to 2 Sam 6:1 (see Miller and Roberts, op. cit., 23) but Campbell may be right in taking 1 Sam 7:2a as the introduction to the events in 2 Sam 6. The lapse of "many days" (1 Sam 7:2a) may well account for the difference in the personal names ("Eleazar" in 1 Sam 7:1 but "Uzzah and Ahio" in 2 Sam 6:3).

The Ark Narrative has often been described as a festal or cult legend recounting the fortunes of the ark (see Rost, *Succession*, 23–26) but it may well be more than that. In a sense, it is a theological narrative which depicts not only past events but also offers a theological interpretation of them. Campbell (*The Ark Narrative*, 165) characterizes it as "'narrated' theology, perhaps theological apologetic," while Kaiser (*Introduction*, 155), with some justification, has pointed out that the aim of the Ark Narrative was to defend "the arbitrary transfer of the ancient Israelite sanctuary to Jerusalem by David as having taken place in accordance with the will of Yahweh." If, as is very likely, the Perez-Uzzah etiology (2 Sam 6:3–8) was part of the original Narrative, then the implication is that the choice of Jerusalem as the ark's resting place must have been part of Yahweh's plan and not simply a stroke of David's political genius. Furthermore, the legitimation of Jerusalem as the chief cultic center was, at the same time, also an authentication of the Davidic rule (see Ps 78:56–72; cf. also Blenkinsopp, *JBL* 88 [1969] 148). Therefore because David was blessed by Yahweh, he could bless the people in Yahweh's name (2 Sam 6:18).

It has been suggested that "the Deuteronomist found the Ark Narrative among his sources in its entirety, and that he was responsible for dislocating it to accord with his historical presentation" (Campbell, *The Ark Narrative*, 170; cf. also Timm, *EvT* 2 [1966] 516–17). The present setting of 2 Sam 6 is very apposite; as the first part of the Ark Narrative began with two defeats of Israel by the Philistines and the loss of the ark (1 Sam 4:1b–11), so the second part of the Narrative is preceded by two humiliating defeats of the Philistines by David and the loss of their gods (2 Sam 5:17–25). The old era had ended with the departure of the glory of Israel (1 Sam 4:21–22) and the new era has dawned with the return of Yahweh's favor and blessing.

It is possible that at a later time the first entry of the ark into Jerusalem became an annual cultic event (see Mowinckel, *The Psalms in Israel's Worship* 1 [1962] 175; cf. also Pss 24 and 132) but it is less certain that its liturgy has determined the present description of the original events (however, see Rupprecht, *Der Tempel von Jerusalem*, 55–59; Mauchline, 227; Stolz, 217).

The mythological interpretations of the story, such as those by A. Bentzen ("The Cultic Use of the Story of the Ark in Samuel," *JBL* 67 [1948] 37–53) and Porter (*JTS* 5 [1954] 161–73), are imaginative and interesting but we find them somewhat unlikely.

Comment

1 The nature and function of this verse are disputed. The Hebrew עוֹד "again" links at least this verse with the preceding military campaign (5:17–25), and seems to point to a third engagement the account of which has been omitted (cf. Kennedy, 218; Blenkinsopp, *JBL* 88 [1969] 151). That there may have been a number of battles between the Philistines and David's forces is very likely, but this third (?) undertaking, as it is depicted, was only a peaceable expedition to remove the ark from its temporary resting place to Jerusalem. Campbell (*JBL* 98 [1979] 40 n.27) omits v 1 "because of its character of introduction to a military campaign and because of the partial doubling with v 2." Thus it is plausible that v 1 is a redactional link between 5:25 and the second part of the Ark Narrative (cf. Schreiner, *Sion-Jerusalem*, 40).

The "thirty thousand" chosen warriors would be more appropriate to a military campaign (see Schmitt, *Zelt und Lade*, 286) than to a cultic procession with music, singing, and dancing (see Carlson, *David*, 67), especially if בחור in this context means "chosen warriors" (see Weisman, *VT* 31 [1981] 443; H. Seebass, "בחר," *TDOT* 2 [1977] 75). G has "all the young men," which is a less suitable rendering. According to 1 Chr 13:2, 5, *all Israel* was involved in this triumphant procession.

2 Although MT's מבעלי יהודה "from the citizens of Judah" makes a reasonable sense (see Blenkinsopp, *JBL* 88 [1969] 152), it would be somewhat odd if only the men from Judah took part in the procession (or the military campaign to recover the ark?). However, Campbell (*The Ark Narrative*, 171) regards this emphasis on the citizens of Judah as "completely appropriate"; but if so, then "from there" (v 2) has no obvious antecedent unless it is found in "Gezer . . . Gibeon" (2 Sam 5:25; so Blenkinsopp, 152) or Kiriath-jearim (1 Sam 7:1). It is likely that the MT's בעלי יהודה is, or conceals, a place name (KJV: "Baale of Judah"). Segal ("The Composition of the Books of Samuel," *JQR* 56 [1965/66] 44) takes the *yōd* in בעלי as a dittograph of the initial letter of יהודה. However, if there is a scribal error, it is possible that in the old script the *hē* in the original בעלה "Baalah" has been misread as *yōd*.

It is of some interest that in Josh 15:60; 18:14 "Kiriath-baal" is glossed as "Kiriath-jearim," and so also "Baalah" in Josh 15:9. Perhaps, one could argue that "Baalah of Judah" and "Kiriath-jearim" were two neighboring localities, originally topographically distinct but identified at some later time (see Schicklberger, *Ladeerzählung*, 139). Keil (258) takes "Baale-Judah" as the Canaanite name of Kiriath-jearim (its Israelite name; see also Goslinga, 108) even though place names compounded with "Kiriath" appear to be the *older* designations; cf. Debir (previously "Kiriath-sepher"; Josh 15:15; Judg 1:11) and Hebron ("Kiriath-arba"; Josh 14:15).

Kiriath-jearim was situated halfway between Jerusalem and Gezer, and it is usually identified with Tell el-ʿAzar (see Blenkinsopp, *Gibeon and Israel*, 11). It used to be one of the chief cities of the Gibeonites (Josh 9:17).

The ark was, apparently, a box, made of acacia wood, approximately 4 by 2½ by 2½ feet (Exod 25:10–22; 37:1–9). It was built during the wilderness period (see H.-J. Zobel, "ארון," *TDOT* 1 [1974] 369; Maier, *Ladeheiligtum,*

39 n.l) and it is less likely that it was of Canaanite origin. The ark was closely associated with the presence of Yahweh (see Clements, *God and Temple*, 29) although the actual function of the ark is less clear. It seems that during the ark's history its meaning and function may have changed more than once (see W. H. Schmidt, *The Faith of the Old Testament*. 113–16). Some of the suggested functions are the following: war palladium, miniature temple, container, Yahweh's footstool, the empty throne of Yahweh, etc. (cf. Davies, *ASTI* 5 [1967] 42–45). Fohrer (*JNSL* 1 [1971] 30) calls it "the pledge of Yahweh's help." It may well be that when the ark came to be associated with the cherubim throne (cf. Schmitt, *Zelt und Lade*, 128–31; Clements, *God and Temple*, 31–39), it functioned as Yahweh's footstool (see Mettinger, *Dethronement*, 19–24) or as the stand for the throne (cf. Schmitt, op. cit., 114). The cherubim could be described as winged mythological beings or composite creatures, having both human and animal features (cf. Ezek 10:21–22; 41:18–19). They are often depicted in the iconography of Canaan as winged lions with human heads (for bibliography on this topic and further details, see D. N. Freedman and M. O'Connor, "כרוב," *TWAT* 4 [1982] 322–34). According to Mettinger (*Dethronement*, 23) the throne-seat of Yahweh was formed by the conjoined wings of the cherubim.

The statement that Yahweh's name was called over the ark does not suggest that at this point the ark was renamed as if it had belonged to another deity (so K. Galling, "Die Aufrufung des Namens als Rechtsakt in Israel," *TLZ* 81 [1956] 69; Fohrer, *JNSL* 1 [1971] 24) but rather that it belongs to Yahweh, just as the Jerusalem temple is called by Yahweh's name (see Jer 7:10–11; 32:34; 34:15; cf. also Schreiner, *Sion-Jerusalem*, 41). However, the reference may be to the ritual use of Yahweh's name (see Clements, *God and Temple*, 33). The repetition of שם "name," if it is not a scribal error, may imply that "the name of Yahweh of hosts who is enthroned upon the cherubim" may be an explanatory note (so Kirkpatrick, 90).

The original meaning of יהוה צבאות "Yahweh of hosts" is doubtful, and we assume that יהוה אלהי צבאות "Yahweh, the God of hosts" is a later interpretation of the shorter form (see H.-J. Kraus, *Theologie der Psalmen* [BKAT 15/3. Neukirchen-Vluyn: Neukirchener Verlag, 1979] 17–20). Ross (*VT* 17 [1967] 90) is of the opinion that צבאות is a title "of divine majesty taken over from Canaan" (see also *Comment* on 5:10).

3 The cart (not chariot) was simply a means of transport; being new it had a certain purity and effectiveness (cf. Judg 16:7, 11; 1 Sam 6:7) and therefore it was a fitting vehicle to transport a holy object. This was, however, contrary to the law in Num 7:9 (cf. also Num 3:29–31).

Abinadab's house was "on the hill" and Hertzberg (278) remarks that it was "perhaps the holy place" (see also Blenkinsopp, *JBL* 88 [1969] 151), but in that case it might have been called במה "high place" as in 1 Sam 9:12, 13, 14.

Uzzah is occasionally identified with Eleazar mentioned in 1 Sam 7:1 (cf. Thenius, 168) but there is no need for such an identification. It is equally doubtful that "Uzzah" is a shortened form of "Eleazar" (so Budde, 228). Uzzah could have been a grandson of Abinadab and not, necessarily, Eleazar's brother (see Hertzberg, 278; cf. also Clines, *VT* 22 [1972] 266).

"Ahio" is regarded by some scholars as an improbable proper name (so

Caird, 1077). However, in spite of G, which takes אחיו as "his brothers," it seems plausible that we are dealing with a proper name, perhaps, a variant of אחיה "Ahijah" = "Yahweh is brother" (?); see *HALAT,* 32. There is also no real justification for identifying this brother with Zadok (see Caird, 1078).

5   The exact meaning of משחקים in this verse is not clear. NAB renders it by "made merry" while NIV has "were celebrating." Possibly the people were dancing for joy to the accompaniment of songs and various music instruments (see Gruber, *Bib* 62 [1981] 345). A simpler account of a similar procession is found in v 15.

Instead of MT's בכל עצי ברושים we have followed the variant reading in 1 Chr 13:8 which is also supported by G (see *Notes*). However, if the MT is right then the reference may be to some wood percussion instruments; NEB offers a paraphrase, "to the beating of batons." This would give us in v 5b three pairs of names denoting various musical instruments (see J. A. Soggin, "'Wacholderholz' 2 Sam VI 5a gleich 'Schlaghölzer,' 'Klappern'?" *VT* 14 [1964] 374–77).

The emendation בכל עז "with all their strength" qualifies משחקים "were dancing"; for a similar usage, see v 14 and 1 Chr 13:8.

The exact translation of the various terms for the musical instruments is, in some cases at least, uncertain (see K. A. Kitchen and D. G. Stradling, "Music and Musical Instruments," *IBD* 2 [1980] 1031–40). There were three basic types of instruments: wind, string, and percussion; but our list, apparently, does not include any wind instruments unless we follow the enumeration found in 1 Chr 13:8, which mentions trumpets (see also 2 Sam 6:15).

6   MT's נכון is, most likely, a proper name "Nachon" (so KJV, RV, RSV) while NEB translates it: "a certain 'threshing-floor'" (see Ackroyd, 66; Carlson, *David,* 78). The original form of the name may have been "Nodan" (נודן; see *Notes* on 6.a).

The Heb. שמטו ". . . stumbled" is of uncertain meaning. If the verb is transitive, we should perhaps translate the whole expression by "for the oxen had nearly overturned it" (NAB ". . . were making it tip"); however, there is no explicit accusative. For a more detailed discussion, see Driver, 267; Carlson, *David,* 79).

7   MT's על השל "because of his presumption" is dubious and the derivation of של is uncertain. Carlson (*David,* 79), following KB (972), links it with the Babylonian *šullû* "treat disdainfully" while the earlier versions (KJV, RV) associated it with the Aramaic שלי "to err," hence "error" (see Driver, 267–68). NEB has "rash act" while NAB omits it. The MT may be a mutilated fragment (it is lacking in G^B) of the reading found in 1 Chr 13:10 על אשר שלח ידו על הארון "because he stretched out his hand to the ark," and this is supported by the fragmentary text of 4QSam^a. On the other hand, the Chronicler may simply be offering his own interpretation of the difficult על השל (similarly also Syr).

The Uzzah incident raises the question, "What was his error or transgression?" Hertzberg (279) notes that Uzzah had disregarded "the usual precautions taken when serving the ark" but since Uzzah acted on the spur of the moment to protect the ark, the punishment may appear rather harsh, irrespective of the possible meaning of על השל (see Mauchline, 224). A plausible

explanation is that Uzzah, like Eleazar before him (1 Sam 7:1), may have
been consecrated to have charge of the ark, and therefore he ought to have
realized that the falling of the ark was really a *sign*, namely, Yahweh's way
of stopping the procession (cf. the remote parallels in 1 Sam 5:1–5; 6:10–
15). If so, not only the sacredness of the ark was an important factor but
also the attempt (unintentional?) to frustrate or disregard the will of Yahweh;
therefore also the consequences were so severe. Thus Dus (*TZ* 17 [1961] 7)
has remarked that Uzzah sinned in that he did not grant Yahweh the freedom
to choose his own resting place. This incident could have been regarded
also as a warning to David, especially if Yahweh was not consulted at the
beginning of this undertaking.

It is difficult to believe that the Uzzah story is a mere invention. For some
reason or other, Uzzah must have died and his death was interpreted as
Yahweh's punishment and/or warning. It is also possible that "awesome objective sacrality" (so Conroy, *Samuel, Kings,* 104) was ascribed to the ark; Uzzah
touched the ark, whatever the reason, and it was the above belief that may
have been the immediate cause of his death. Whether this is what actually
happened, we do not know, but it seems that Tur-Sinai (*VT* [1951] 282) goes
too far when he regards the Uzzah story as another version of the etiological
legend in 1 Sam 6, and based on the place-name (ה)עזץ פרץ "great breach."
He remarks, "it was only in the aetiological explanation of this name that
עזא or עזה became the name of a man . . ." (284). This and similar interpretations appear too drastic (see Maier, *Ladeheiligtum,* 61); not every etiology
must be a fictitious creation (see J. Bright, *Early Israel in Recent History Writing*
[SBT 19. London: SCM Press, 1956] 91–100).

According to the Chronicler (1 Chr 15:13) the Uzzah disaster occurred
because the Levites did not participate in the transporting of the ark, while
Josephus (*Ant.* 7.81) attributes Uzzah's death to the fact that not being a
priest, he touched the holy ark.

8 It is seldom that in the OT Yahweh appears to be the object of man's
anger (cf. Gen 4:5; 1 Sam 15:11; Jonah 4:1, 4; see also D. N. Freedman
and J. Lundbom, "חרה," *TWAT* 3 [1978] 188). Keil (261) has suggested
that David was not angry with Yahweh but at the calamity (cf. Jonah 4:9).
Perhaps, ויחר should be rendered, "he was distressed" (cf. Gen 45:5).

The site of Perez-Uzzah is unknown but it must have been somewhere
along the road going from Kiriath-jearim to Jerusalem. Carlson (*David,* 80)
locates the site within the boundaries of Jerusalem but this view is mainly
based on the dubious interpretation of v 13 that the sacrifice was made "every
six paces."

The name "Perez-Uzzah" is reminiscent of "Baal-perazim" (5:20) but it is
doubtful that there is any other link.

9–10 It is of some interest that in vv 9–11 and 13–17 we find the term
"the ark of Yahweh" and not "the ark of God" which is used elsewhere in
the chapter. Some have taken this alternation as an indication of two different
sources but this is not the only explanation.

David, having experienced Yahweh's displeasure (or warning), takes no
further risks, and so the ark is taken into the house of Obed-edom which
may have been the nearest dwelling place. In view of the circumstances it is

doubtful that Obed-edom was overjoyed to receive the custody of the awesome ark (so Hertzberg, 279). Budde (230) has suggested that perhaps no Israelite was willing to take the dangerous ark and therefore it was deposited in a Philistine's house. It is true that Obed-edom is described as a Gittite or a man from Gath, and he may have been a *gēr* or a protected alien. However, since there was more than one place called Gath (see *Comment* on 4:3), it does not necessarily follow that Obed-edom must have been a Philistine. Some (e.g., Keil, 262; Goldman, 222) have suggested Gath-rimmon which was a Levitical city (Josh 21:24–26). According to 1 Chr 15:18, 24, 25, Obed-edom was a Levite (so also Josephus, *Ant.* 7.83). "Obed-edom" is most likely a theophoric name, similar to "Obadiah" (= "servant of Yahweh"), and meaning "servant [or worshiper] of Edom" (see Noth, *Personennamen*, 137–39). Thus "Edom" in this context may be a divine name (see Budde, 230; Driver, 269) rather than a reference to the *land* of Edom (so Kirkpatrick, 93).

11–12 We are not told what form Yahweh's blessings took; clearly, no further disasters had befallen Obed-edom and his household. This divine favor was interpreted by David as a sign of Yahweh's approval for his intention to bring the ark to Jerusalem. G^L adds, "and David said, 'I will turn the blessing to my house,'" but this may not be part of the original text.

13 According to 1 Chr 15:26 the bearers of the ark were Levites but many scholars consider this to be a later interpretation of the less explicit 2 Sam 6:13. The ark was no longer transported by an ox-cart but was carried (see v 3), perhaps as a result of Uzzah's death (so Budde, 230).

When the bearers of the ark had advanced six steps, a sacrifice was offered consisting of an ox and a fatted calf. In 1 Chr (15:26) this same sacrifice consists of "seven bulls and seven rams"; 4QSam[a] supports this reading which may be an elaboration to conform with later cultic practices (cf. Num 23:1; Job 42:8; Ezek 45:23). However, W. E. Lemke ("The Synoptic Problem in the Chronicler's History," *HTR* 58 [1965] 353) is of the opinion that this reading may have existed already in the Chronicler's Vorlage.

The altar must have been a temporary structure, such as erected in 1 Sam 14:33–34, and the sacrifice was performed only once, at the start of the procession (after six steps), not at every six paces, as suggested by Carlson (*David*, 88) who regards the number six as "a typical 'fertility number,'" but this is far from certain.

It is possible that David himself acted as priest (so Stolz, 216); in 1 Chr 15:26 the verb is plural ("they sacrificed") and the subject may be the Levites.

14 The linen loin cloth (אֵפוֹד; see 1 Sam 2:18) was, apparently, a priestly garment (contra Phillips, *VT* 19 [1969] 487) which would normally provide a sufficient coverage for its wearer (cf. Exod 20:26). However, David was whirling round in a wild dance (see Gruber, *Bib* 62 [1981] 339–40) and, consequently, exposed himself and caused offense to Michal (v 20). The Chronicler minimizes this unintended provocation, and states that David wore a robe of fine linen (1 Chr 15:27), perhaps, to be identified with the linen ephod (so Williamson, *Chronicles*, 126). We regard David's dancing as an expression of joy (cf. Pss 149:3; 150:4) rather than as "prelude to the sacred marriage" with Michal (so Porter, *JTS* 5 [1954] 166) or "a form of fertility rite" (Carlson,

David, 87). The bringing of the ark to Jerusalem was a unique event, not part of an established Jebusite cultic ritual. This dancing took place "before Yahweh" or before the ark. For a similar identification, see 1 Sam 4:3.

15 The horn or trumpet was usually made of a ram's horn, and was often used for signaling (see *Comment* on 2:28). For further details, see A. L. Lewis, "Shofar," *EncJud* 14 (1971) 1442–47. The Chronicler (1 Chr 15:28) elaborates and adds some other musical instruments.

16 This verse anticipates and prepares the way for vv 20–23. The coincidental (?) theme of "the Lady at the Window" need not necessarily point to an intended sacred marriage between the king and the queen (as argued by Porter [166] and Carlson [*David*, 94–96]).

Michal is called "daughter of Saul" (so also in vv 20 and 23) rather than "wife of David." Clines (*VT* 22 [1972] 272) may be right in suggesting that the threefold use of "daughter of Saul" may imply that she was not "behaving as David's wife . . . but as his opponent," like a true daughter of Saul.

17 The ark was set "in its place" which some have regarded as an allusion to an already existing shrine or sanctuary (see H. H. Rowley, "Zadok and Nehushtan," *JBL* 58 [1939] 126–27). This is only possible if we assign such passages as 2 Sam 6:17; 7:2, 6; 1 Kgs 8:4 to a later redaction. For this type of argument, see Rupprecht's *Der Tempel von Jerusalem*, 59–99, in which he says that it is possible that there was a Jebusite temple on the threshing floor of Araunah (cf. 2 Sam 24:16–25) and that the ark was housed there (similarly, Noth, *History*, 191; Stolz, 217). However, "in its place" (במקומו) may resume 1 Sam 5:11 where the Philistines send the ark away that it might return "to its place" (למקמו); this was finally achieved with the transfer of the ark to the city of David.

The tent prepared for the ark is not to be identified with the tabernacle or the tent of meeting (see 2 Chr 1:3; K. Koch, "אהל," *TDOT* 1 [1974] 127; Schmitt, *Zelt und Lade*, 242–44) although the existing tradition is not strictly consistent (cf. 1 Kgs 8:4); neither was this tent a miniature version of Solomon's temple (contra Cross).

Just as the transfer of the ark began with a sacrifice (v 13) so also it concluded with an unspecified number of offerings. In the burnt offering or holocaust the entire animal (with the exception of its skin; Lev 7:8) was consumed by fire, while in peace offerings only certain parts were burnt on the altar, a portion of the flesh being taken by the priests but the rest eaten by the worshipers (see Lev 3:1–17; 7:11–18).

The translation of שלמים is uncertain but we may note some of the more popular renderings: "communion sacrifice" (JB), "fellowship offering" (NIV, TEV), "peace offering" (NAB, RSV; cf. G), "shared-offerings" (NEB). For further discussion on sacrifices, see R. de Vaux, *Studies in Old Testament Sacrifice* (Cardiff: University of Wales Press, 1964) 27–51; H. H. Rowley, *Worship in Ancient Israel: Its Forms and Meaning* (London: SPCK, 1967) 111–43; G. Gerleman, "שלם-genug haben," *THAT* 2 (1976) 931–35.

18–19 After the offerings, David blessed the people in the name of Yahweh or "with the name of . . ." (so Kennedy, 222; see also H. A. Brongers, "Die Wendung *bešēm jhwh* im Alten Testament," *ZAW* 77 [1965] 8–9). At some later time this function became one of the duties of the Levites (see Deut 10:8; cf. Num 6:22–27).

The Ark Narrative ends with the distribution of food which was not the usual daily fare. Cakes of raisins are associated with the worship of other gods in Hos 3:1 while Jeremiah (7:18; 44:19) mentions cakes made for the queen of heaven. The implication is that David's gifts of food may have had some cultic significance.

Porter (*JTS* 5 [1954] 168) has remarked that distribution of food "has no real parallel in the Old Testament but coronation rites in the ancient Near East are commonly accompanied by a banquet and the distribution of food to all and sundry." However, there is no clear evidence that this particular installation of the ark was associated with the enthronement of Yahweh unless this aspect has been influenced by later cultic practices.

The etymology of אֶשְׁפָּר is uncertain (see Driver, 270–71) and the versions differ considerably in their renderings. This word occurs only here and in the parallel account in 1 Chr 16:3. At the present time there is a tendency to translate it as "date cake" (see *HALAT*, 93; L. Koehler, "Ashpār Dattelkuchen," *TZ* 4 [1948] 397–98). However, NAB has "cut of roast meat," and this finds some support in Syr, Tg, and Vg; Keil (265) suggests "measure of wine."

20–22 Michal greeted David with a sarcastic criticism accusing him of indecent exposure or unbecoming behavior. Stolz (217) has suggested that David may have lost his loin cloth during the ecstatic dancing (cf. also 1 Sam 19:24), and that there may be some link with Canaanite religious practices. Michal, being more conservative in her attitude, disapproved of her husband's actions. This may be so, but it is equally possible that she was not more strict in her views but rather more proud (contra Hertzberg, 281). Therefore David reminds her that he (i.e., David) is Yahweh's chosen king (see *Comment* on 5:2) while she is but the daughter of a rejected and dishonored king. Consequently, he values the praise of the so-called slave girls more than the opinion of Michal. It is doubtful that David's reply had any sexual undertones (such as suggested by Carlson, *David*, 95) and that the slave girls were sacred prostitutes (so Porter, *JTS* 5 [1954] 166).

23 The Michal episode concludes with the statement that she remained childless all her life (see *Comment* on 21:8) but there is no clear indication that her marital relationship with David ceased.

Carlson (*David*, 93) regards Michal's barrenness as "a punishment sent by Yahweh on account of her attitude to the Ark." This may be so, but the reason for Michal's punishment is not explicitly stated. It may well be that she had despised not simply her husband but also Yahweh; David's intention was not to expose himself in an unseemly manner before all and sundry but to humiliate himself before Yahweh. Thus it is ironical that Michal, the proud one, is finally disgraced by Yahweh, making complete the rejection of the house of Saul.

Explanation

The Ark Narrative as a whole shows quite clearly that a wrong attitude to Yahweh and his ark brings with it disaster. This was the fate of the sons of Eli and of the Israelite forces; likewise, calamity befell the Philistines and the citizens of Bethshemesh, as well as Uzzah. The reverse side of the coin is blessing, such as experienced by the house of Obed-edom and, later, by David. In a sense, the narrative is a movement from one opposite to the other; as in 1 Sam 7:2 all Israel lamented so in 2 Sam 6:5 all Israel rejoiced before Yahweh. A change in the attitudes of the people of Yahweh may be followed by a reversal of fortunes and abundant blessing.

In all these events Yahweh remained a free agent, not subject to any human manipulation. One could say that Yahweh is where his ark is but the blessing or curse is dependent upon Yahweh alone and cannot be controlled by others, not even David. So the beneficial presence of the ark in Jerusalem became a symbol of David's election and Yahweh's choice of Zion (see Ps 78:67–72).

Since the ark must have had some, if not considerable, religious significance for the Northern tribes, it follows that from now on Israel was bound to David and his city, at least theoretically. From now on Jerusalem was not only the administrative center of the two kingdoms but also the focal point of Israelite religion. It could be said that at this stage the rise of David had reached its climax while the Michal episode concluded the corresponding decline of the house of Saul.

In retrospect one might note that eventually Jerusalem became the gateway through which foreign influences could flow into Israelite life and religion. However, this only substantiates the generalization that everything and everyone may have a potential for good or ill.

It is very likely that in due course the transfer of the ark to the city of David became an annual event (or an integral part of such a cultic occasion), as suggested by Pss 24, 78, and 132, in particular. This need not imply that the present description of the original events was largely influenced by the existing liturgy although there could have been some interaction (e.g., in the distribution of food in v 19). This type of influence is detectable in the Chronicler's version of the ark story.

The Dynastic Oracle (7:1–17)

Bibliography

Ahlström, G. W. *Psalm 89: Eine Liturgie aus dem Ritual des leidenden Königs.* Lund: CWK Gleerup, 1959. ———. "Der Prophet Nathan und der Tempelbau." *VT* 11 (1961) 113–27. ———. *Royal Administration and National Religion in Ancient Palestine.* Leiden: E. J. Brill, 1982. **Botterweck, G. J.** "Zur Eigenart der chronistischen Davidgeschichte." *TQ* 136 (1956) 402–35. **Calderone, P. J.** *Dynastic Oracle and Suzerainty Treaty: 2 Samuel 7, 8–16.* Ateneo University Publications 1. Manila, Philippines: Loyola House of Studies, Ateneo de Manila University, 1966. ———. "Oraculum dynasticum et foedus regale, 2 Sam 7." *VD* 45 (1967) 91–96. **Caquot, A.** "Brève explication de la prophétie de Natan (2 Sam 7, 1–17)." In *Mélanges bibliques et orientaux en l'honneur de M. Henri Cazelles.* Ed. A. Caquot and M. Delcor. AOAT 212. Kevelaer: Butzon & Becker; Neukirchen-Vluyn: Neukirchener Verlag, 1981. 51–69. **Cooke, G.** "The Israelite King as Son of God." *ZAW* 73 (1961) 202–25. **Dus, J.** "Der Brauch der Ladewanderung im alten Israel." *TZ* 17 (1961) 1–16. **Fretheim, T. E.** "The Priestly Document, Anti-Temple?" *VT* 18 (1968) 313–29. **Fritz, V.** *Tempel und Zelt: Studien zum Tempelbau in Israel und zu dem Zeltheiligtum der Priesterschrift.* WMANT 47. Neukirchen-Vluyn: Neukirchener Verlag, 1977. **Gelston, A.** "A Note on II Samuel 7¹⁰." *ZAW* 84 (1972) 92–94. **Gese, H.** "Der Davidsbund und die Zionserwählung." *ZTK* 61 (1964) 10–26. **Haag, H.** "Gad und Nathan." *Archäologie und Altes Testament.* FS Kurt Galling. Ed. A. Kuschke and E. Kutsch. Tübingen: J. C. B. Mohr (Paul Siebeck), 1970. 135–43. **Herrmann, S.** "Die Königsnovelle in Ägypten und in Israel." *Wissenschaftliche Zeitschrift der Karl-Marx-Universität, Leipzig.* Gesellschafts- und sprachwissenschaftliche Reihe 3 (1953–54) 51–62. **Ishida, T.** *The Royal Dynasties in Ancient Israel.* BZAW 142. Berlin: Töpelmann, 1977. **Kruse, H.** "David's Covenant." *VT* 35 (1985) 139–64. **Kutsch, E.** "Die Dynastie von Gottes Gnaden: Probleme der Nathanweissagung in 2 Sam. 7." *ZTK* 58 (1961) 137–53. **Loewenclau, I. von.** "Der Prophet Nathan im Zwielicht von theologischer Deutung und Historie." *Werden und Wirken des Alten Testaments.* FS Claus Westermann. Göttingen: Vandenhoeck & Ruprecht; Neukirchen-Vluyn: Neukirchener Verlag, 1980. 202–15. **Loretz, O.** "The Perfectum Copulativum in 2 SM 7, 9–11." *CBQ* 23 (1961) 294–96. **Malamat, A.** "Prophetic Revelations in New Documents from Mari and the Bible." VTSup 15 (1966) 207–27. ———. "A Mari Prophecy and Nathan's Dynastic Oracle." In *Prophecy: Essays Presented to Georg Fohrer on his Sixty-fifth Birthday 6 September 1980.* BZAW 150. Berlin, New York: Walter de Gruyter, 1980. 68–82. **McCarthy, D. J.** "II Samuel 7 and the Structure of the Deuteronomic History." *JBL* 84 (1965) 131–38. ———. "An Installation Genre?" *JBL* 90 (1971) 31–41. **McKenzie, J. L.** "The Dynastic Oracle: II Samuel 7." *TS* 8 (1947) 187–218. ———. "The Four Samuels." *BR* 7 (1962) 3–18. **Mettinger, T. N. D.** *The Dethronement of Sabaoth. Studies in the Shem and Kabod Theologies.* ConB OT Series 18. Lund: CWK Gleerup, 1982. **Mowinckel, S.** "Israelite Historiography." *ASTI* 2 (1963) 4–26. **Nordheim, E. von.** "König und Tempel: Der Hintergrund des Tempelbauverbotes in 2 Samuel vii." *VT* 27 (1977) 434–53. **Noth, M.** "David and Israel in II Samuel VII." In *The Laws in the Pentateuch and Other Studies.* Tr. D. R. Ap-Thomas. Edinburgh and London: Oliver & Boyd, 1966. 250–59. **Michiko, O.** "A Note on 2 Sam 7." In *A Light unto My Path: OT Studies in Honor of Jacob M. Myers.* Ed. H. N. Bream, R. D. Heim, C. A. Moore. Gettysburg Theological Studies 4. Philadelphia: Temple University Press, 1974. 403–7. **Poulssen, N.** *König und Tempel im Glaubenszeugnis des Alten Testaments.* SBM 3. Stuttgart: Verlag Katholisches Bibelwerk, 1967. **Rabe, V. W.** "Israelite Opposition to the Temple." *CBQ* 29 (1967) 228–33. **Reid, P. V.** "*šbṭy* in 2 Samuel 7:7." *CBQ* 37 (1975) 17–20. **Sakenfeld, K. D.** *The Meaning of Hesed in the Hebrew Bible: A New*

Inquiry. HSM 17. Missoula, MT: Scholars Press, 1978. **Schmid, H.** "Der Tempelbau Salomos in religionsgeschichtlicher Sicht." In *Archäologie und Altes Testament.* FS Kurt Galling, ed. A. Kuschke and E. Kutsch. Tübingen: J. C. B. Mohr (Paul Siebeck), 1970. 241–50. **Schmitt, R.** *Zelt und Lade als Thema alttestamentlicher Wissenschaft: Eine kritische forschungsgeschichtliche Darstellung.* Gütersloh: Gerd Mohn, 1972. **Schreiner, J.** *Sion-Jerusalem, Jahwes Königssitz: Theologie der Heiligen Stadt im Alten Testament.* SANT 7. Munich: Kösel-Verlag, 1963. **Seybold, K.** *Das davidische Königtum im Zeugnis der Prophe ten.* FRLANT 107. Göttingen: Vandenhoeck & Ruprecht, 1972. **Simon, M.** "La prophétie de Nathan et le Temple: Remarques sur II Sam. 7." *RHPR* 32 (1952) 41–58. **Soggin, A.** "Der offiziel geförderte Synkretismus in Israel während des 10. Jahrhunderts." *ZAW* 78 (1966) 179–204. **Tsevat, M.** "Studies in the Book of Samuel. III: The Steadfast House: What Was David Promised in II Sam. 7:11b–16?" *HUCA* 34 (1963) 71–82. ———. "The House of David in Nathan's Prophecy." *Bib* 46 (1965) 353–56. **Ulshöfer, H. K.** *Nathan's Opposition to David's Intention to Build a Temple in the Light of Selected Ancient Near Eastern Texts.* Ph.D. Diss., Boston University Graduate School, 1977. **Van Seters, J.** *In Search of History: Historiography in the Ancient World and the Origins of Biblical History.* New Haven and London: Yale University Press, 1983. **Veijola, T.** *Verheissung in der Krise: Studien zur Literatur und Theologie der Exilszeit anhand des 89. Psalms.* Helsinki: Suomalainen Tiedeakatemia, 1982. **Vetter, D.** *Jahwes Mit-Sein—ein Ausdruck des Segens.* Stuttgart: Calver Verlag, 1971. **Weinfeld, M.** *Deuteronomy and the Deuteronomic School.* Oxford: Clarendon Press, 1972. **Weiser, A.** "Die Tempelbaukrise unter David." *ZAW* 77 (1965) 153–68. **Westphal, G.** *Jahwes Wohnstätten nach den Anschauungen der alten Hebräer.* BZAW 15. Giessen: Töpelmann, 1908. **Whybray, R. N.** *The Succession Narrative: A Study of II Sam. 9–20 and I Kings 1 and 2.* SBT. 2d Ser. 9. London: SCM, 1968.

Translation

[1] *When the king had taken up residence* [a] *in his palace, at that time Yahweh had given him peace from his enemies on all sides,* [2] *he* [a] *said to Nathan, the prophet, "Here* [b] *I am living in a palace of cedar while the ark of God is housed in a curtain-tent."* [c] [3] *"Go ahead!* [a] *Do whatever you have in mind," answered Nathan, "for Yahweh is with you."*

[4] *However, that very night the word of Yahweh came to Nathan.* [a] [5] *"Go,* [a] *say to my servant David,* [b] *'Thus has Yahweh said, "Are you going to build* [c] *me a house to dwell in?* [6] *I have not dwelt in a house from the day I brought the Israelites up from Egypt* [a] *until this day, but I have been going from place to place* [b] *in a tent (that is, a tabernacle)* [b] [7] *wherever I have wandered among the Israelites.* [a] *Did I ever ask* [b] *any of the tribal leaders* [c] *whom I commanded to shepherd my people Israel, saying, 'Why have you not built me a house of cedar?'"'*

[8] *"And now, thus you shall say to my servant David.* [a] *Thus has Yahweh of hosts said: 'It was I who took you from the pasture,* [b] *from tending the sheep* [b] *to be a chosen leader over my people Israel.* [9] *I have been with you wherever you went, destroying all your enemies before you. I have made* [a] *your fame as great* [b] *as that of the greatest in the land.* [10] *I have established a place for my people Israel and I have planted them so that they might dwell where they are, disturbed no more. Wicked men will no longer oppress them as they did previously,* [11] *ever since the time* [a] *that I appointed tribal leaders over my people Israel. Thus I have given you* [b] *peace from all your* [b] *enemies.'"* Now Yahweh is announcing* [c] *to you that he* [d] *will build* [e] *you a royal house.*

[12] *"When your days are fulfilled*
    and you rest with your fathers,
  I shall raise up your progeny after you,
    your own offspring.
  I shall establish his kingdom,
  ([13] It is he who will build a house for my name[a])
    and I shall set up firmly his throne[b] forever.
[14] *I shall be his father,*
    and he shall be my son.
  If he does wrong,[a] I shall discipline him with a rod wielded by man,
    and with blows inflicted by men.
[15] *However, I shall not withdraw[a] my good-will from him*
    as I withdrew it from Saul whom I removed out of your sight.
[16] *Thus your house and your kingdom will continue forever before me,[a]*
    and[a] your throne will be secure forever."

[17] *So Nathan gave to David a true account of all these words and of this vision.*

Notes

1.a. Following Ehrlich (*Randglossen*, 288) who gives the verb an inchoative meaning.

2.a. Lit., "and the king. . . ."

2.b. The Heb. ראה נא "see now" (so KJV) is probably used as an interjectional impv (see Williams, *Syntax*, § 191). 1 Chr 17:1 has הנה "behold."

2.c. For this use of the Heb. definite article, see GKC, § 126q.

3.a. Lit., "Go, do. . . ." (RSV). The Heb. impv לך "go" in this and similar contexts may have the force of an interjection (see Joüon, *Grammaire*, § 177f). לך is lacking in 1 Chr 17:1 and in Syr.

4.a. Some MSS (also G[L] and Syr) add הנביא "the prophet."

5.a. See n. 3.a. This formula of sending is probably a rhetorical device (cf. 2 Sam 24:12) rather than a double commission (see McCarter, 197).

5.b. Following many MSS and most versions; lit., "to my servant, to David." 1 Chr 17:4 has "to David, my servant." This doubling technique seems to be intentional; it occurs also in vv 7, 8, and 10.

5.c. 1 Chr 17:4 has לא אתה תבנה "you shall not build"; so also G, Syr. This is a correct interpretation of the Hebrew idiom.

6.a. It is lacking in 1 Chr 17:5, and its position in the MSS of G is not firmly fixed; hence it may be a later addition (but see 1 Sam 8:8).

6.b-b. Lit., "in a tent and in a tabernacle" (so RV) but the expression may be a hendiadys: "in a tent-dwelling" (see Ishida, *Royal Dynasties*, 96) or an instance of the doubling technique found in vv 5, 8a, 8b and 10. We have taken the conjunction *wāw* "and" as an explicative *wāw* (cf. Schreiner, *Sion-Jerusalem*, 91). McCarter (192) regards משכן "tabernacle" as a gloss or variant on אהל "tent."

7.a. Lit., "with all the people of Israel" (RSV). Some omit בני "the people of . . ." with 1 Chr 17:6 and G.

7.b. Following G, we regard הדבר as a piel inf abs (cf. GKC, § 113n), with the interrogative particle.

7.c. KJV: "the tribes of. . . ." 1 Chr 17:6 reads שפטי "the judges of" influenced, perhaps, by 7:11. If this is right then the MT reading is a scribal error. There is no evidence that any tribe was ever commissioned to govern Israel (so Driver, 274) but it is possible that שבט may mean not only "tribe" but also "tribal leader" (see *Comment* on 5:1). McCarter (192) following Reid (*CBQ* 37 [1975] 17–20), takes שבטי as a pl participial form: "the staff bearers of."

8.a-a. Lit., "to my servant, to David"; see n. 5.b.

8.b-b. McCarter (192), following G[B] (cf. also G[L], OL), reads מנוה הצאן "from the sheep pasture." In view of the doubling technique in vv 5, 7, and 10, we prefer MT.

9.a. G has ἐποίησα which suggests ואעש "and I made." MT reads ועשתי which is a perfect with either a *wāw* consecutive or a simple *wāw* (as in our translation).

9.b. 1 Chr 17:8 (similarly most Greek MSS) omit גדול "great." However, a wordplay may be intended between "great" and "the great ones" (גדלים).

11.a. 1 Chr 17:10 has ולמימים ". . . days"; so also G with its τῶν ἡμερῶν. MT has the singular: ולמן היום; the conjunction may be an explicative *wāw* (see Williams, *Syntax,* § 434).

11.b. Some commentators (see Driver, 275) emend the second pers suffixes to the third pers (לו and איכיו) but there is no textual evidence for this.

11.c. For the use of the Heb. perfect to express an instantaneous action or one in the process of completion, see GKC §106i. 1 Chr 17:10 has ואגד "I declare" but this change of person may be a deliberate alteration to conform to the preceding verbs in the first person.

11.d. We follow G in reading והיה "and it shall be" = "when" for יהוה "Yahweh," the final word in the verse, which seems to be a textual corruption of והיה, the real beginning of v 12.

11.e. MT has יעשה "he will make" while 1 Chr 17:10 reads יבנה "he will build" which is supported by G and 4QFlor 174, col. i, line 10. See also the corresponding expression in v 27. However, MT may be an intentional variation.

13.a. 1 Chr 17:12 reads לי "for me" instead of לשמי "for my name." G, apparently, conflates both readings.

13.b. Following 1 Chr 17:12 in reading כסאו "his throne" and omitting ממלכתו "his kingdom"; so also G^BL.

14.a. The Heb. אשר, if authentic, may introduce a conditional clause (cf. Williams, *Syntax,* § 469) although this usage is rare. McCarter (194) omits it, and simply reads ובהעותו "If he does wrong," as implied by G and Syr (cf. also Brockelmann, *Syntax,* § 123g).

15.a. MT has לא יסור ("[but my mercy] shall not depart. . . ."); however, most recent translators follow 1 Chr 17:13, G, Syr, Vg in reading לא אסיר "I shall not withdraw" which is to be expected in view of the following הסרתי "I withdrew."

16.a-a. Reading לפני ו "before me, and" with G, Syr and some Heb. MSS. MT has לפניך "before you"; the letter *kaph* may be a misreading of the expected conjunction *wāw* "and" before the following word (so G, Syr, Vg) or simply a case of dittography.

Form/Structure/Setting

2 Sam 7 is, without doubt, the theological highlight of the Books of Samuel (so Stolz, 220) if not of the Deuteronomistic History as a whole. The chapter is fairly complete in itself but it consists of two distinct parts: the dynastic oracle (vv 1–17) and David's prayer (vv 18–29) which is presented as David's response to the dynastic promise. Whether or not this dynastic oracle marked the end of the History of David's Rise, it does represent the culmination of David's ascent to political power. At this point he has been granted rest from his enemies (vv 1, 11) and Yahweh's people have been given their own land (v 10). Chap. 8 is not really a sequel but essentially a summary of David's past victories, and therefore they need not follow 2 Sam 7 chronologically.

The literary structure of the dynastic promise is reasonably simple. Vv 1–3 provide the setting and introduction for the following oracle in vv 4–16, which in its present form is composed of three main parts: (i) A negative oracle rejecting David's proposal to build a temple for Yahweh (vv 5–7) introduced by the prophetic word formula in v 4. (ii) A short survey of David's rise to fame and power (vv 8–11a), characterized by Deuteronomistic style and expressions. It has its own oracular introduction in v 8a, as if it were a separate oracle. (iii) The dynastic promise itself, comprising vv 11b–16. This section may be the oldest part of our pericope, and it exhibits certain poetic features (e.g., a sort of parallelism). Perhaps, in its present form it may not be strictly poetry but it has a poetic quality. Of special interest is the fact that Ps 89:19–37 [MT 20–38] has preserved what appears to be an expanded poetic version of the dynastic promise, which may well owe its origin to the possible cultic transmission of the divine promise. Finally, v 17 is the editorial conclusion to the whole pericope.

Nathan's oracle has its close parallel version in 1 Chr 17:1–15 as well as the previously mentioned poetic recension in Ps 89:19–37 [MT 20–38]. Consequently, the question as to their interrelationship is bound to arise. Thus some scholars have regarded Ps 89 as antedating 2 Sam 7 and the Chronicler's version (so, e.g., R. H. Pfeiffer, *Introduction to the Old Testament* [London: Adam and Charles Black, 1948] 371–73; Ahlström, *Psalm 89*, 182–84) but it is far more likely that the poetic version is a later interpretation of 2 Sam 7 (see Ishida, *Dynasties*, 82). H. van den Bussche ("Le texte de la prophetie de Nathan sur la dynastie davidique," *ETL* 24 [1948] 355–94), on the other hand, has contended for the priority of the Chronicler's account but most scholars would regard 2 Sam 7 as the *Vorlage* of 1 Chr 17:1–15 and as the basis of the poetic interpretation in Ps 89 (see N. M. Sarna, "Psalm 89: A Study in Inner Biblical Exegesis," *Biblical and Other Studies*, ed. A. Altmann [Cambridge, MA: Harvard University Press, 1963] 29–46). However, the relationship between 2 Sam 7 and Ps 89 may be more complicated. It is possible that ultimately both may go back to a common original (cf. McKenzie, *TS* 8 [1947] 216–17) but that they have undergone different changes in the course of their transmission, due to the varied purposes which they may have served.

Traditionally, Nathan's oracle (vv 4–16) has been taken as the authentic message of the prophet (cf. Ewald, *History*, 3 [1878] 132; Keil, 266) but in more recent years the apparent unity of the pericope and its nature have been explained in other ways. We can only deal with a limited number of representative views while more comprehensive surveys are to be found in the works quoted. Thus, we begin with Sigmund Mowinckel who has claimed that 2 Sam 7 is an etiological legend meant to show why Solomon and not the pious David became the builder of the temple. "The legend is a literary unit and does not admit of any literary criticism" (Mowinckel, *ASTI* 2 [1963] 10). In his opinion, the oracle is "a prose 'historicization' of the cultic usage" (10), and therefore it is dependent upon the cultic traditions (such as in Pss 89 and 132) and not vice versa. Consequently, the oracle cannot be regarded as an independent historical tradition although Mowinckel does not rule out "the possibility that Nathan actually did convey such promises to David" (*He That Cometh*, tr. G. W. Anderson [Oxford: Basil Blackwell, 1956] 101, n. 3). It is more likely, however, that the dependence is on the part of the Psalms or that both "recensions" go back to a common tradition. Furthermore, the thematic tension in the oracle (e.g., the rejection of the temple in vv 5–7, and its permission in v 13a) and certain linguistic features seem to point to a more complex literary history than that envisaged by Mowinckel.

The unity of Nathan's oracle has been explained also in terms of the so-called *Königsnovelle* hypothesis which has been well presented by Herrmann (*Wissenschaftliche Zeitschrift der Karl-Marx-Universität*, 3 [1953–54] 51–62) in his form-critical interpretation of 2 Sam 7. He has produced a detailed comparison between the Egyptian literary genre of *Königsnovelle* ("royal novelette" or "royal narrative") and Nathan's oracle, and he has come to the conclusion that also in the latter work we find the essential features of the Egyptian *Königsnovelle*. He has drawn attention to the following: the king sitting in his palace (v 1), his plan to build a temple (v 2), his conversation with the officials (in this case, Nathan; vv 2–3), a dream oracle (vv 5–16), adoption by the god (v 14). Obviously, Herrmann himself is forced to admit that in 2 Sam 7 the genre has undergone certain changes and adaptations; at least in the present form, the *immediate* recipient of the oracle is Nathan not David. Furthermore, only one official, the prophet Nathan, is involved, and above all, David does not implement his intended plan. Moreover, it is very doubtful that 2 Sam 7 or even the oracle itself is a literary unity. For these and other reasons (see Kutsch, *ZTK* 58 [1961] 151–53) it is unlikely that the *Königsnovelle* could have served as a deliberate model for 2 Sam 7; the essence of the former is to praise the king for some specific achievement while in our chapter the king's plans are temporarily postponed.

Nevertheless, Herrmann's views have been adopted in varying degrees by certain other scholars, such as Noth (cf. "David and Israel," *The Laws*, 256–59), Weiser (*ZAW* 77 [1965] 153–68) and Whybray (*The Succession Narrative*, 96–116).

Not infrequently, the literary unity of the oracle or even that of the chapter as a whole, has been maintained on the basis of editorial work. Most recent scholars would, of course, grant that there had been certain additions, but some exegetes assign a far greater role to the Deuteronomistic editor. Cross (*Canaanite Myth*, 252–58) has suggested that although the editor has made use of older oracles in poetic form (underlying vv 1–7 and 11b–16), he has recast them to produce the unity which, in its present form, is a "Deuteronomistic composition" (254). Vv 8–11a form a Deuteronomistic linkage although it, too, may reflect older material.

Similarly, Van Seters (*In Search*, 272) regards 2 Sam 7 as a Deuteronomistic text and a unified prose narration in which vv 4–17 form "the report of a prophetic oracle" reminiscent of the salvation oracles of the prose of Jeremiah. In vv 18–29 he finds a response to the salvation oracle, in the form of a prayer of thanksgiving, and he concludes that "from the point of view of form criticism there is no reason why the whole chapter cannot be considered the work of one author" (273), i.e., the Deuteronomist (280).

One may also pay special attention to Mettinger's view (*King and Messiah*, 48–63) that the pre-Deuteronomistic material of vv 1–17 consisted of two layers: the Solomonic prophecy of Nathan (vv 1a, 2–7, 12–14a, 16 [as in G], 17) and the Davidic-dynasty layer (vv 8–9, 11b, 14b–15, 16 [as in MT]) which is a redaction of the former. Mettinger finds Deuteronomistic additions only in vv 1b and 10–11a. He assigns the older layer to Solomon's reign, and he points out that at this stage it concerned only Solomon (not the dynasty). He also admits the probability that an independent oracle from the reign of David may underlie vv 1–7, which rejected David's plans to erect a temple.

This was eventually incorporated in the Solomonic document (ibid., 61). The Davidic-dynastic redaction is supposed to be the work of the author of HDR "which is taken to have been composed in the decades immediately after Solomon's death" (55).

In our view, the original oracle to David must have been positive in character (cf. 1 Kgs 8:18), on account of the close links between temple projects and dynastic promises in the ancient Near East in general (see Ishida, *Royal Dynasties*, 86–92; cf also Ulshöfer, *Nathan's Opposition*, 21–41). Thus it seems that David expressed his wish to build a *house* (temple) for the ark, and that in reply Nathan, in Yahweh's name, approved of the proposal, as implied by the phrase, "for Yahweh is with you" (v 3b). This in turn must have been followed by Yahweh's promise to build a *house* (dynasty) for David. The underlying principle may well be that expressed in 1 Sam 2:30: "those who honor me, I will honor!" Therefore it is plausible that some sort of dynastic promise was the natural sequel to vv 1–3. This is, perhaps, supported by the assumption that v 11b may be the original continuation of v 3, since both speak of Yahweh in the third person. Thus the promise itself may have been contained in, or may underlie, vv 12, 13b–16.

Unfortunately, the later years of David's reign were marred by internal troubles and civil wars (e.g., the rebellions of Absalom and Sheba), and the result was that David was not able to carry out the proposed building of the temple, as suggested by 1 Kgs 5:3 [MT 17]. However, he may have made some preparations for this task if the testimony provided by 1 Chr 22:2–5 and 28:2 is authentic. Be that as it may, the fact that David did not manage to erect a temple may have raised doubts also about the closely associated divine promises. Therefore at the *beginning* of Solomon's reign the dynastic oracle had to be presented as a spontaneous expression of Yahweh's favor, not as a response to David's well-intentioned plans. Therefore in the circumstances it was important to shift the emphasis away from David's proposal and to stress *only* the dynastic oracle. Perhaps, at this stage it formed part of the introduction to the SN or it was an important component of this document (see Mettinger, *King and Messiah*, 60).

We assign the temple rejection in vv 4–7 to an early exilic date (see *Comment on vv 5–7*) when the temple lay in ruins. This refusal may have served as an explanation of the destruction of the temple: it perished because it had not been required by Yahweh in the first place. It may have been also a partial reflection of a reaction against the Deuteronomic reform in general (cf. the attitudes reflected in 2 Kgs 18:22; Jer 44:15–19), as well as an illustration of a negative view toward the temple (cf. Jer 7:4; Isa 66:1). Eventually, this negative critique was taken up by the final Deuteronomistic redactor for *apologetical* purposes, just as Rabshakeh's speech was utilized in 2 Kgs 18–19 (cf. also Jer 44:16–19), and he transformed it into a *temporary* prohibition by the addition of v 13a. At the same time, he expressed indirectly the hopes of some sections of the exilic community, that the temple will be rebuilt and that the house of David will yet be exalted. This same view is expressed by the practically contemporaneous prophet Zechariah (6:13) who prophesied concerning Zerubbabel: "It is he who shall build the temple of the LORD, and shall bear royal honor . . ." (RSV). Also vv 1b and 8–11a could well be Deuteronomistic in origin.

Finally, we shall note McCarter's well-argued reconstruction of the literary history of 2 Sam 7:1–17, which is presented in three phases. "The earliest form of Nathan's oracle was a promise of dynasty to David made in connection with his declared intention to build a temple for Yahweh" (223). This seems to us right because the complementary nature of the temple and dynasty is hardly a Deuteronomistic invention. Moreover, it would be very surprising if David had not realized the significance of the temple for his own kingship and that of his successors (cf. 1 Kgs 12:26–29; see also K. Whitelam, "The Symbols of Power: Aspects of Royal Propaganda in the United Monarchy," *BA* 49 [1986] 170–71). McCarter's second phase involves the expansion of the primitive document (including vv 1a, 2–3, 11b–12, and 13b–15a) by a writer who probably belonged to certain prophetical circles "with a less favorable view towards the temple and towards David himself" (223). This prophetic editing is found in vv 4–9a and 15b, and its purpose was to show that a temple was neither needed nor wanted (228) and that David's success was entirely due to Yahweh.

The third and last phase is the Deuteronomistic redaction to which McCarter attributes vv 1b, 9b–11a, 13a, 16 and possible editorial touches here and there. The main effect of this redaction was the transformation of the negative attitude to the temple (vv 5b–7) into a positive support for the Solomonic temple. David did not build it because *the time* was not right during his reign (231).

This is a plausible hypothesis although we differ on a number of points. We could add numerous variations to the views noted so far but it is hoped that the few representative selections will provide a reasonable cross section.

Comment

1 It is possible that David became fully aware of the incongruity between his magnificent royal palace (see 5:11) and the humble curtain-tent for the Ark of Yahweh (cf. 6:17) soon after he had settled in his new palatial dwelling (cf. Ps 132:1–5; for a contrast, see Hag 1:4).

The concept of rest or peace from enemies is a Deuteronomistic idea (cf. Deut 12:10; 25:19; Josh 22:4; 23:1; 1 Kgs 5:18 [4]; 8:56; see also G. von Rad, "Rest for the People of God," *The Problem of Hexateuch*, 94–102). In this context "rest" is security from enemies and peace from wars. V 1b is, however, regarded by many scholars as a later Deuteronomistic insertion, and therefore it is omitted by some (so e.g., McCarter, 190); it is also lacking in the Chronicler's version (1 Chr 17:1), who may have had in mind the wars of David described in the subsequent chapters. However, the sequence of the pericopes in 2 Samuel is not always a reliable guide as to their chronological order. If authentic, our episode may well have belonged to the latter part of David's reign. Hertzberg (284) sees 2 Sam 7 as "the climax of the whole Davidic tradition," but this does not suggest the final part of David's rule.

The building of a palace (5:11) would often be linked with that of a temple (see Ahlström, *Royal Administration*, 3–4; cf. also Ps 132:1–5), and such costly activities would normally take place during periods of prolonged peace and political stability.

2 This is the first mention of Nathan, who is simply described as "the prophet" (הנביא); any further information is lacking. In the light of existing data, he was not associated with David during the pre-Jerusalem period, but this does not necessarily imply that he must have been a Jebusite prophet (so Haag, "Gad und Nathan," 140–41; Loewenclau, "Der Prophet Nathan," 206; Stolz, 222). On the other hand, it may be significant that he comes on the scene in Jerusalem and that later he was an influential member of the so-called Jerusalemite party (see 1 Kgs 1); subsequently two of his (?) sons became important royal officials (1 Kgs 4:5). He has been described also as a court prophet while R. R. Wilson (*Prophecy and Society in Ancient Israel,* [Philadelphia: Fortress Press, 1980] 264) has suggested that Nathan, at least in retrospect, "was seen as a typical northern prophet."

David's "palace of cedar" may well have been a stone structure with cedar ceilings and paneling (cf. 1 Kgs 6:9, 15). built by Phoenician craftsmen (5:11; cf. Schreiner, *Sion-Jerusalem,* 79). The same expression occurs elsewhere only in 7:7 and 1 Chr 17:1, 6.

The word for "tent" is not the usual אהל (see 6:17) but the collective (?) יריעה "curtain"; 1 Chr 17:1 has the pl יריעות. Both אהל and יריעה are used synonymously in Cant 1:5; Jer 4:20; 10:20; Hab 3:7. According to Exod 26:1 and 36:8 the tabernacle was made with ten curtains (יריעות); it is possible that most tents were constructed of goatskin curtains (see K. Koch, "אהל," *TDOT* 1 [1974] 118–30). The contrast between David's house of cedar and the curtain-tent makes it unlikely that in David's time the ark was housed in some sort of Canaanite temple (but see Rupprecht, *Der Tempel,* 102; Stolz, 221; cf. also 12:20). Thus v 2 expresses David's wish to build a worthy permanent dwelling for the ark of God, and it may be an allusion to 6:17. The expression "ark of God" is frequent in 2 Sam 6 (vv 2, 3, 4, 6, etc.), and it may be an indication of a possible link between the Ark Narrative and Nathan's oracle.

3 In view of the sentiments both expressed and implied in v 2, there is little doubt that v 3 contains Nathan's approval of David's plan. However, vv 5–7 seem to suggest an unqualified rejection of the proposal to build a temple, and therefore some scholars (e.g., McCarter, 196) have thought that vv 3 and 5–7 cannot come from one and the same author. Consequently, either v 3 expresses Nathan's initial response or his own personal opinion (so Goslinga, 129) or vv 5–7 represent a later, negative attitude to the building of the temple. In the present form of Nathan's oracle, this negativity must have been understood as only of temporary duration in view of v 13a ("He [i.e., Solomon] will build a house for my name"). Noth (*The Laws,* 257) regards Nathan's response as "a polite formality customary before the king"; similarly also Cross (*Canaanite Myth,* 242). However, in our context the phrase seems to be more than mere court language (see also K. N. Jung, *Court Etiquette in the Old Testament* [Diss., Drew University, 1979] 24–31). This thematic inconsistency, if such it is, may have been made less obvious by the possible abbreviation of the original conversation; Nathan's concise reply to David (in v 3) seems to presuppose more than is actually expressed in v 2. The prophet concludes his reply with the words, "for Yahweh is with you," which form a well-known key phrase in the David stories, pointing to the open secret of his good fortune (cf. 1 Sam 18:12, 14, 28; 2 Sam 5:10). This divine presence brought with it both blessing and success; it was by no means limited to a single act of help or deliverance but rather denoted a continuous divine activity (so Vetter, *Jahwes Mit-Sein,* 24).

4 The oracle is introduced by the well-known prophetic word formula: "the word of Yahweh came to . . ." which occurs some 200 times in the Old Testament, especially in the Books of Jeremiah and Ezekiel (see W. Zimmerli, *Ezekiel* 1, tr. R. E. Clements [Philadelphia: Fortress Press, 1979] 144–45). The reference to "that very night" (cf. Judg 6:25; 7:9) may suggest that the divine communication was thought to have come by means of a dream (so Smith, 298) or night vision (cf. v 17; Job 4:13; Ps 89:20 [19]; see also Haag, "Gad und Nathan," 140).

5 Formally, "Go, say" belongs to the so-called commissioning of the messenger whether he is a prophet (cf. Isa 6:9; 38:5; Jer 2:2; 3:12) or an ordinary bearer of news (cf. 18:21; 1 Kgs 18:8).

"My servant David" is reminiscent of Deuteronomic phraseology (see Weinfeld, *Deuteronomy*, 354) but, on the other hand, the servant terminology itself may be of ancient origin since the Oriental kings were often described as "servants" of their gods (see R. de Vaux, "The King of Israel, Vassal of Yahweh," *The Bible and the Ancient Near East* [Tr. D. McHugh. London: Darton, Longman & Todd, 1972] 155). The same, rather exclusive, expression (i.e., "Moses, my servant") is used also in Josh 1:2, 7. Van Seters (*In Search*, 276) suggests that "my servant David" means "both the recipient of the promise and the model of obedience to the Mosaic covenant."

"Thus has Yahweh said" is the familiar messenger formula which serves to authorize, at least theoretically, the contents of the following messenger speech (see C. Westermann, *Basic Forms of Prophetic Speech* [Tr. H. C. White. Philadelphia: Westminster Press, 1967] 100–102). The oracle itself begins with a rhetorical question: "Are you going to build . . . ?" being tantamount to a negative assertion (see Brockelmann, *Syntax*, § 32b), and it was so understood by 1 Chr 17:4 as well as by G and Syr. The pronoun "you" is, most likely, emphatic and in its present setting it may indicate that the negation concerns, primarily, the person (i.e., David) rather than the action itself (i.e., the building of the temple). This seems to be the intention of the final form of Nathan's oracle because the equally emphatic "he" (הוא) in v 13a provides the positive counterpart to v 5b, thus transforming what appears to be a permanent negativity (in vv 5–7) into a temporary negation (so already Caspari, 482).

However, the crux is whether v 13a should be regarded as a later addition or not. If, as it seems, it is redactional then originally vv 5–7 must have stated that Yahweh had never required a temple in the past and that he has no desire for such a house of cedar at the present, perhaps even implying that neither would he need such a building in the future.

The further question is whether vv 5–7 are part of the original words of Nathan or whether they should be taken as a subsequent insertion into the dynastic oracle. Since this prophetic utterance is rightly described as "the foundation document of David's dynasty" (Whybray, *The Succession Narrative*, 100), it is difficult to see how Yahweh's unqualified rejection of the temple could have been harmonized with his "building" of the Davidic dynasty. Therefore it seems that such an anti-temple sentiment is somewhat out of place during the monarchical period. This may find some support in the Prayer of David (vv 18–29) and Ps 89:20–38 [19–37]; in neither of these passages is there any allusion or reference to the temple. We suggest, tentatively, that the best setting for the origin of vv 5–7 is the early exilic period when the temple was reduced to rubble. These verses then would have served as an implicit explanation of the destruction of the house of Yahweh and as its evaluation: it had never been required by Yahweh and therefore it perished in the course of the people's punishment, like the temple of Shiloh (cf. Jer 7:12). Consequently, the disastrous fate of the temple need not be taken as an indication of the destiny of the house of David which still survived, and which was the recipient of Yahweh's promises. Moreover, Yahweh was free to move about among his people wherever they might be (cf. Fretheim, *VT* 18 [1968] 328). Such an explanation may well have circulated in certain circles (prophetic?) which were skeptical of the temple and its cult (cf. Isa 66:1). It is not entirely impossible that it may have voiced an implicit polemic against the Deuteronomic reform (cf. G. Westphal, *Jahwes Wohnstätten*, 160). Thus the purpose of this *vaticinium post eventum* was to serve as a literary device in order to provide a theological interpretation of a tragic event, i.e., the destruction of Yahweh's house. If so, this interpretative oracle was eventually taken up by a Deuteronomistic redactor who incorporated it into his history for apologetical reasons adding, at the same time, v 13a (and perhaps also vv 8–11b) thus rendering innocuous the anti-temple sentiment of vv 5–7. The same redactor may well have effected the necessary changes also in 1 Kgs 5:3–5 [MT 17–19] and 8:17–20.

If, on the other hand, vv 5–7 formed an integral part of Nathan's original oracle, then a number of difficult questions are bound to arise: e.g., did Yahweh object to David's initiative (so Noth, *The Laws*, 251; Gese, *ZTK* 61 [1964] 21) or did Nathan's protest against the temple reflect "a religious preference for a tent-shrine" (von Rad, *The Problem of the Hexateuch*, 119) or do these verses point to a conflict between the Jebusite party represented by Nathan and the Judahite-Yahwist group headed by Abiathar (so Ahlström, *VT* 11 [1961] 113–15)? On the whole, it seems that this assumption creates more problems than the previous suggestion.

"A house to dwell in" (v 5b) may be a deliberate contrast to "a house for my name" (v 13a), introduced by the Deuteronomistic editor. Yahweh is available to his worshipers through his name which dwells in the temple (see Deut 12:11; 14:23; 16:2; 26:2).

6 This verse appears to ignore the existence of the temple of Shiloh (Judg 18:31; 1 Sam 1, 7, 9, 24; 3:15) where the ark of God was housed in Samuel's time (see 1 Sam 3:3). Its ruins could, apparently, be seen even in Jeremiah's time (Jer 7:12, 14); however, so far there is no archaeological confirmation for this building (see S. Holm-Nielsen, "Shiloh," *IDBSup*, 823). Hertzberg (285) has argued that the temple of Shiloh was regarded only as a temporary stopping place; this would be similar to the stay of the ark in the house of Obed-edom (2 Sam 6:10). It is just possible that in retrospect Shiloh was not considered a legitimate sanctuary (see Rabe, *CBQ* 29 [1967] 230) or that the reference to the Shiloh temple is anachronistic (cf. Cross, *Canaanite Myth*, 73, n. 114). On the other hand, there is no real reason to think that the temple at Shiloh was any different from that of Solomon (so Ishida, *Royal Dynasties*, 96) although one could argue that it was not built for Yahweh and that its destruction was interpreted as a sign that Yahweh was not in it. It is also likely that a *fixed* cultic building tended to be associated with the localization of divine presence (cf. 1 Kgs 8:12–13) while the tent symbolized Yahweh's sovereign freedom.

"From the day . . . until this day" is, most likely, a Deuteronomistic expression (see 1 Sam 8:8; 2 Kgs 21:15; cf. also Weinfeld, *Deuteronomy*, 341).

Vv 6–7 stress the motif of the unlimited divine freedom, and this is depicted by the very obvious contrast between the movable tent-dwelling or shrine and the sumptuous localized temple. The story of the Ark (1 Sam 4–6; 2 Sam 6) shows that any attempt to manipulate the ark, and hence also Yahweh, must end in disaster. Perhaps some circles (whose views are expressed in vv 5–7) saw a contemporary example of this same pattern in the destruction of the Jerusalem temple in 587 B.C.

8–9   These verses provide a brief résumé of David's rise to power; however, all the initiative is with Yahweh of Hosts (see *Comment* on 5:10; 6:2), and David's success is due to God alone. He has made the lowly shepherd (cf. 1 Sam 16:1–13; Ps 78:70) into a chosen leader (see *Comment* on 5:2) of his people Israel. Ulshöfer (*Nathan's Opposition*, 121) prefers "military leader" as the translation of נגיד "chosen leader." G. F. Hasel ("נגיד," *TWAT* 5 [1984–] 209–10) stresses the religious-sacral aspect of נגיד which he regards as an honorary title (*Hoheitstitel*).

Vv 8–9a survey Yahweh's dealings with David in retrospect but it is less clear whether vv 9b–10 continue the same review of past events or whether they offer a preview of future developments. It is often argued that although the former alternative is possible, the syntactical considerations seem to support the latter suggestion (see McCarter, 202–3; Veijola, *Verheissung*, 63) because ועשתי "and I shall make" or "I have made" begins a sequence of perfects with *wāw* consecutives (?) which would be usually translated by the future tense ("I shall make . . . I shall assign . . . etc."). They are followed by two ordinary imperfects, both preceded by the negative ולא "and not"; see also Gelston's more detailed argument (*ZAW* 84 [1972] 93). However, we are inclined to follow the minority view (see Rost, *The Succession*, 44–45; Loretz, *CBQ* 23 [1961] 296), and to regard vv 9b–10 as continuing the historical review of David's reign. This interpretation is not impossible from a syntactical point of view (see Williams, *Syntax*, § 182) while the context seems to demand it. Thus vv 9b–10 may well describe in more detail the blessings of Yahweh's presence (v 9a). The victories which Yahweh had given to David (v 9a) made the latter famous (v 9b) and, at the same time, secured the land for God's people (v 10a). Thus what Joshua had partly accomplished was finally completed by David. Moreover, the phrase "Thus I have given you peace . . ." (v 11a) may form an inclusion with v 1b ("Yahweh had given him peace . . ."), and both statements appear to refer to the past events.

"I have been with you" is a recurring motif in the HDR (cf. 1 Sam 16:18; 17:37; 18:14, 28; 2 Sam 5:10; 7:3). Cross (*Canaanite Myth*, 252) takes this and similar expressions as Deuteronomistic idioms.

"All you enemies" may include internal foes (such as Saul and Ishbosheth) as well as external ones, especially the Philistines. The phrase "I have made you famous" may have political significance (so Weinfeld, *Deuteronomy*, 80; cf. also Calderone, *Dynastic Oracle*, 45–46). Ps 89:27b [MT 28b] may well express the essence of this expression by stating that Yahweh will make David "the *highest* of the kings of the earth" (cf. also 1 Kgs 1:47). McCarter, however, thinks of "the erection of a monument of some kind" (203) which may be a veiled allusion either to the Solomonic temple (cf. Gen 11:4) or to David's descendants (cf. 2 Sam 18:18).

10 "A place for my people" (מקום לעמי) is yet another *crux interpretum*, since it can denote either the land of Canaan (so most interpreters) or the temple as a (cult-)place (so e.g., Caspari, Gelston, Langlamet, McCarter). It has been argued that Israel already possessed all their land in David's reign if not before, but this would be a problem only when the perfects in vv 9b–10 are given a futuristic sense. In our opinion, v 10 does not describe the future welfare of Israel but the blessings already bestowed upon David as a result of Yahweh's active help (v 9a). The people will dwell securely and unmolested in contrast with the earlier oppressions during the period of the Judges.

Although מקום as a "place (of worship)" is attested in the OT (cf. Deut 12:5; 1 Chr 16:27; Jer 7:12, 14), this connotation seems less suitable in the present context. However, McCarter (190) and Gelston (*ZAW* 84 [1972] 93) go even further, and make מקום either the subject or the object of all the verbs in v 10. Unfortunately, most of these verbs, e.g., נטע "to plant," שכן "to dwell," רגז "to tremble," would be more appropriate to "the people" than "the temple," and therefore we follow the usual interpretation of מקום.

The metaphor of planting is frequent in Jeremiah (see 2:21; 11:17; 24:6; 31:28; 32:41; 42:10), and it may have originated in cultic language (cf. Pss 44:2 [MT 3]; 80:8 [MT 9]). McCarter (204), due to his interpretation of the verse as a whole, takes "wicked men" to be those who abused the cult, probably Hophni and Phinehas (see 1 Sam 2:12–17), but it seems more likely that the reference is to Israel's enemies in general. This is, perhaps, supported by Ps 89:22b [MT 23b] which may be an allusion to this verse; here the wicked will not harm David.

The promise of peace is implicitly conditional for the oppressions during the period of the Judges were, at least largely, due to Israel's waywardness (see Judg 3:7–8; 10:6–7; 13:1). This same cause-and-effect principle would be relevant also to the Davidic kings (cf. v 14b) even though Yahweh has promised not to withdraw his favor permanently (v 15). Another exegetical problem is the relationship between "previously" (בראשונה) and "ever since the time" (ולמן היום) (v 11a). Because the preceding verses (vv 5–10) show a certain fondness for the technique of doubling (see *Note* on 5.b.), we take the two expressions as synonymous (so also most exegetes). For "peace from all your enemies," see *Comment* on v 1. It is plausible that vv 1b and 11a form some sort of inclusion, and come from the hand of the Deuteronomistic editor.

11 "Yahweh is announcing" is taken by Mettinger (*King and Messiah*, 59 n.29) as a solemn, declarative perfect ("and hereby the LORD declares . . ."). Some scholars have regarded v 11b as a continuation of v 3 or its original, longer version because of the transition from the first person (in vv 8–11a) to the third person (as in v 3). This suggestion may well be right.

12–13 Many scholars assume that v 13a is a later addition (see *Comment* on v 5), and that thereby the original collective understanding of vv 12–15 has been narrowed down to an individualistic interpretation. One might expect a dynastic oracle to have a collective or general character. In the present form of vv 12–15, the reference is primarily to Solomon, and only by implication to the dynasty as a whole (cf. 1 Kgs 5:5 [MT 19]; 8:19).

"House for my name" is a Deuteronomistic expression (cf. 1 Kgs 3:2; 5:3, 5 [MT 17, 19]; 8:18), and it may denote a more abstract concept of God's presence. His dwelling is, of course, in heaven (Deut 4:36; 26:15; Isa 63:15; Ps 33:13–14) but he may be symbolically present through his name. Thus this "Name theology presents us with a transcendent God who is invulnerable to any catastrophe which might conceivably affect his Temple" (Mettinger, *The Dethronement*, 50). At the same time, this symbolic presence may imply also ownership (see Weinfeld, *Deuteronomy*, 193–94).

V 13b is occasionally taken as a doublet of "I shall establish his kingdom" (end of v 12) but it is more likely that both expressions are parallel, if not the two cola of a bicolon. However, in the present textual form of v 13 there is now a contrast between David's heir who will build a house for Yahweh, and Yahweh, who for his part, will established a house for David, i.e., the Davidic throne. The main feature of this kingship will be its permanent stability: it will last forever (vv 13b, 16). The same theme is also echoed in the Prayer of David (vv 24, 25, 26, and 29).

14 The Davidic king was believed to be the son of Yahweh (see Pss 2:7–8; 89:26–27 [MT 27–28]). However, this sonship was not based on a physical descent (as in Egypt) but it was, apparently, linked with three overlapping concepts: adoption, covenant, and royal grant. The father-son terminology could be used in respect of the partners of all three legal transactions. Although the word "covenant" does not occur in Nathan's oracle, it is presupposed if not alluded to, in v 15 since חסד "good-will," "covenant loyalty," etc., may well denote the essence of a covenant (see P. Kalluweettil, *Declaration and Covenant* [AnBib 88. Rome: Biblical Institute Press, 1982] 48). Extra-family adoption does not seem to be attested in the OT (except, perhaps, for Gen 15:3); nevertheless, "I shall be his father, and he shall be my son" (v 14a) may be an adoption formula but not exclusively linked with adoption as such, since sonship could be established also by covenant (cf. 2 Kgs 16:7) and royal grants (see M. Weinfeld, "Covenant, Davidic," IDBSup, 188–92). Moreover, our passage is dealing with "divine adoption" and not with an ordinary legal procedure (cf. also Mettinger, *King and Messiah*, 259–67). 4QFlor (1–2, i. 11) associates this passage with the Messiah, "the Shoot of David"; so also Heb 1:5.

V 14b continues the father-son metaphor, and the chastening of the disobedient son will be part of the parental discipline (cf. Jer 46:28); however, any punishment will be transitory (cf. 1 Kgs 11:39; 2 Chr 21:7) not like that of Saul and his house. This half-verse is omitted by the Chronicler who tends to see Nathan's oracle in the light of the ideal king.

15 The Heb. חסד "good-will" presupposes an existing relationship and denotes, in this context, the content and implementation of Yahweh's covenant to David (cf. Ps 89:33–34 [MT 34–35]). It is "the continuing divine favor" (McCarter, 208) which will uphold the Davidic house and kingdom, in contrast to its removal from Saul.

V 15b may be an expansion (so Smith, 302), and the repetition of הסררתי "I withdrew," "I removed," is awkward. The shorter form of 1 Chr 17:13 (". . . as I took it from him who was before you," so rsv) may be nearer to the original form. However, Sakenfeld (*The Meaning of Hesed*, 139) regards the shorter versions as due to haplographies, but this is less convincing.

16 "Your house and your kingdom" may be a case of hendiadys (i.e., "your royal house," so McCarter, 208; cf. Williams, *Syntax*, § 72) since the parallel term is "your throne" (v 16b). The Davidic dynasty will be a lasting royal house whether we take עד עולם as "forever" or "for a long time." Mettinger (*King and Messiah*, 56–58) accepts the G^B version of this verse as the authentic one; in that case the emended MT could be rendered as "His house and his kingdom shall endure for ever before me and his throne will be secure for ever." Thus this reading would conform to the preceding verses and therefore it may be a deliberate alteration by the translator. The MT appears to be a concluding summary: it is through his son (and the latter's descendants, by implication) that David's royal house will be established.

Explanation

The numerous scholarly studies and articles dealing with this passage bear a clear testimony both to its importance and its problematic nature. It has been rightly called the ideological summit of the Deuteronomistic history and the matrix of later messianic expectations (cf. Heb 1:5). Moreover, the dynastic oracle was in a real sense the title deed of the house of David: it legitimized both the dynastic principle and the rule of the Davidic kings.

Its composite character suggests that the resultant pericope is a sort of patchwork, yet at each successive stage the combined elements present a harmonious picture, sufficiently adequate to deal with the changing cultural, historical and religious settings and their respective demands. Originally it may have been aimed at those circles which may have questioned the dynastic succession as well as the legitimacy of the house of David. This undertaking was so successful that even when the house of David had lost its political power, Nathan's oracle still retained its relevance for future generations. They were confident that Yahweh would fulfill his promises if not in a contemporary figure, such as Zerubbabel, then at least in a future messianic figure. For the Christian community this fulfillment came about in Jesus Christ, the true son of David (see Matt 1:1; Acts 13:22–23; Heb 1:5), to whom God had given the throne of David (Luke 1:32). The oracle of Nathan had also a direct relevance for the believers in general (see 2 Cor 6:16–18).

The Prayer of David (7:18–29)

Bibliography

Brueggemann, W. *David's Truth: In Israel's Imagination and Memory.* Philadelphia: Fortress Press, 1985. **Clements, R. E.** *In Spirit and in Truth: Insights from Biblical Prayers.* Atlanta, GA: John Knox, 1985. **Coats, G. W.** "Self-abasement and Insult Formulas." *JBL* 89 (1970) 14–26. **Coppens, J.** "La Prophétie de Nathan: Sa portée dynastique." *Von Kanaan bis Kerala.* FS Prof. Mag. Dr. J. P. M. van der Ploeg O.P., ed. W. C. Delsman, J. T. Nelis, J. R. T. M. Peters, W. H. Ph. Romer and A. S. van der Woude. Neukirchen-Vluyn: Neukirchener Verlag, 1982. 91–100. **Kutsch, E.** "Die Dynastie von Gottes Gnaden." *ZTK* 58 (1961) 137–53.

Translation

   [18] *Then King David went in and sat before Yahweh. "Who am I, Lord Yahweh, and what is my house," he said, "that you have brought me thus far?* [19] *Moreover,[a] in your sight this has been a small thing, Lord Yahweh, so you have even[b] spoken of [c]the future of your servant's dynastic line;[c] [d]this is truly a divine revelation to mankind,[d] Lord Yahweh.* [20] *What more can David ask of you?[a] You yourself have singled[b] your servant out, Lord Yahweh.* [21] *For the sake of your servant[a] and according to your will, you have done this whole great thing in apprising[b] your servant.[c]* [22] *Thereby you, [a]Lord Yahweh,[a] have shown yourself as great. Truly,[b] there is none like you nor is there a god besides you, in view of[c] all that we have heard with our own ears.* [23] *And who is like your people Israel,[a] the one[b] nation on earth whom God went[c] to redeem as his own people, thus gaining fame for himself and doing great and awesome deeds[d] in driving out[e] [f]a nation and its gods[f] from before your[g] people whom you redeemed as your own from Egypt?"*

   [24] *"You have appointed your people Israel to be your own people forever, and so you, Yahweh, have become their God.* [25] *And now, Lord Yahweh,[a] carry out[b] forever the promise you have made concerning your servant and his house. Do as you have promised,* [26] *that your fame may be great forever,[a] that men may say,[a] 'Yahweh of hosts is God over Israel' and 'The house of your servant David is[b] firmly established before you.'* [27] *Because you, Yahweh of hosts, God of Israel, have announced to your servant, 'I will build a house for you,' therefore your servant has found courage[a] to offer this prayer to you.* [28] *And now, Lord Yahweh,[a] truly you[b] are God and your words are trustworthy; moreover, you have made this gracious promise to your servant.* [29] *Therefore, be pleased to bless[a] the house of your servant so that it may continue forever before you because you, Lord Yahweh,[b] have promised. So by your blessing the house of your servant shall be blessed forever."*

Notes

   19.a. 1 Chr 17:17 omits עוד "moreover"; so also G, OL and Syr.
   19.b. Heb. גם "even" is lacking in 1 Chr 17:17; similarly in G and Syr.
   19.c-c. Lit., "of the house of your servant at a distance."
   19.d-d. Most scholars regard the text as corrupt. McCarter (233) follows a slightly emended version of 1 Chr 17:17 and reads: ותראני תור האדם המעלה ". . . and shown me the generation to come." This gives a reasonable sense but it may not be the original text.

20.a. 1 Chr 17:18 adds לכבוד את עבדך "for honoring your servant" but this may be a later addition or expansion (contra Rudolph, McCarter, et al.). MT is supported by G, Syr and Vg.

20.b. For this use of ידע "to know," see G. J. Botterweck, "ידע," *TDOT* 5 (1986) 468.

21.a. So 1 Chr 17:19, reading עבדך "your servant"; this is supported by G^B. MT (followed by Tg, Syr and Vg) has דברך "your word," while G^L conflates both readings.

21.b. For this use of the inf constr, see GKC, § 114o.

21.c. 1 Chr 17:19 introduces an unnecessary repetition by reading כל הגדלות "all these great things" for MT עבדך "your servant."

22.a-a. Many MSS read יהוה אלהים "Yahweh, God," and similarly Syr, Tg and Vg. However, David's Prayer is characterized by the use of "Lord Yahweh."

22.b. For this use of כי "truly," see Williams, *Syntax*, § 449.

22.c. Many MSS and Tg have ככל "according to all" instead of בכל "in view of . . ."; both variants may well mean the same thing (see Rudolph, *Chronikbücher*, 132).

23.a. Lit., "like your people, like Israel." The second כ "like" is lacking in 1 Chr 17:21 as well as in G, Syr and Tg. However, MT may preserve an idiomatic usage (cf. Joüon, *Grammaire*, § 131i).

23.b. G must have misread (?) the Heb. אחד "one" as אחר "another."

23.c. The Heb. verb is pl (הלכו) while 1 Chr 17:21 has the expected sg form (הלך). Perhaps the *wāw* in הלכו is a misreading of the missing definite article before אלהים "God." McCarter (234) reads הלכו as *hōlīkô* "led him along," following G^BAMN; however, the Chronicler's variant may well be right.

23.d. Omitting לכם "for you," as suggested by 4QSam^a. Some MSS and Tg read להם "for them."

23.e. MT has לארצך "for your land"; 1 Chr 17:21 reads לגרש "to drive out," and this makes better sense of this context; similarly G with its τοῦ ἐκβαλεῖν "to cast out."

23.f-f. Reading גוי ואלהיו "a nation and its gods" as suggested by G (ἔθνη = גוי) and the 3 sg suff in אלהיו (so MT).

23.g. The change to the 2 sg may have been due to the rhetorical nature of the question.

25.a. Following some MSS and G^LM. MT has יהוה אלהים "Yahweh, God."

25.b. 1 Chr 17:23 reads יאמן "let it be confirmed," and this is followed by G^L.

26.a-a. This is a sort of paraphrase; MT simply reads לאמר "to say." Cf. also S. Wagner, "אמר," *TDOT* 1 (1974) 333–35.

26.b. Omitting יהיה "shall be," with 1 Chr 17:24.

27.a. Lit., ". . . found his heart."

28.a. Some Heb. MSS read יהוה אלהים "Yahweh, God"; we prefer the more common designation of our pericope.

28.b. The pronoun "you" (אתה) is emphatic, being strengthened by הוא (see GKC, § 141h).

29.a. For the coordination of the two verbs, see GKC, § 120d.

29.b. See n. 28.a.

Form / Structure / Setting

In the canonical setting vv 18–29 are presented as David's response to Nathan's oracle contained in vv 1–17. The Chronicler's version of this prayer (1 Chr 17:16–27) contains no significant changes. The prayer does not exhibit any clear structure but it could be divided into two main sections: indirect thanksgiving (vv 18–24) and the petition (vv 25–29). A more detailed outline of the contents may be presented as follows:

v 18a	Introduction
v 18b	David's self-abasement before Yahweh
vv 19–21	Yahweh's amazing graciousness
vv 22–24	The uniqueness of Yahweh and his people. Brueggemann (*David's Truth*, 78) defines these verses as doxology.
vv 25–29	David's petition for the fulfillment of Yahweh's promises.

The prayer is very much God-centered as indicated by the numerous vocatives which address Yahweh (usually "Lord Yahweh" which occurs seven times) and by the self-designation "your servant" (ten times). The central theme is the house (seven times) of David which had been promised lasting continuance.

At the present, there are two main views concerning the nature of this prayer. Some scholars (e.g., Carlson, Cross, Veijola) regard it as Deuteronomistic in its entirety. Cross (*Canaanite Myth*, 254, n. 154) has claimed that "it is a free Deuteronomistic composition presuming the Dtr oracle in vv 1–17, without clear evidence of the use of earlier sources." On the other hand, a number of exegetes find the Deuteronomistic character exhibited mainly in certain verses, especially in vv 22–25. Thus Mettinger (*King and Messiah*, 51) regards only vv 22b–26 as a Deuteronomistic interpolation since, in his view, v 27 is a continuation of v 22a. His conclusion is that vv 18–22a, 27–29 "belong to a pre-Dtr stratum of the prophecy of Nathan" and that "in its pre-Dtr form David's prayer forms a literary unity."

Also McCarter (237) acknowledges the Deuteronomistic nature of vv 22b–26 but he goes on to argue that the prayer of David "in its primitive form was associated with the ark ceremony in chap. 6 rather than the dynastic promise in chap. 7" (240). This is an interesting possibility but there seem to be more contacts between David's prayer and Nathan's oracle than between the prayer and the Ark Narrative in 2 Sam 6 (cf. vv 27a and 11b).

Our impression is that the fervent appeals to Yahweh to fulfill his promises to David may imply that the actual circumstances of the author have called in question, in some way or other, this very fulfillment. Consequently, the exilic period would provide a good historical setting for this prayer (cf. also Ps 89:46–51 [MT 47–52]). Another factor that may point in the same direction is the frequent use of "Lord Yahweh"; this is reminiscent of Ezekiel's characteristic usage of the same expanded form of the divine name (some 217 times; see W. Zimmerli, *Ezekiel 2*, tr. J. D. Martin [Philadelphia: Fortress Press, 1983] 556).

Comment

18 David, apparently, entered the curtain-tent, housing the ark, and sat back on his heels (?) in a kneeling position (see Caird, 1086). This posture in prayer is not attested elsewhere in the OT. Perhaps, the verb יָשַׁב "to sit, dwell" simply means "tarried" in this context (cf. Gen 24:55).

"Who am I . . ." is a formula of polite self-depreciation before a person of higher rank (see 1 Sam 18:18; 1 Chr 29:14) and it contains an element of truth (cf. 1 Sam 16:6–13; see also Coats, *JBL* 89 [1970] 15, 26). In this setting the formula also heightens the graciousness of God and the wonder of his guidance. "Thus far" probably refers to David's God-given success up to this point.

The compound divine name "Lord Yahweh" (or, perhaps, "my Lord . . .") is found seven times in David's prayer but nowhere else in Samuel (cf. 1 Kgs 2:26); the title is common in Ezekiel.

19 As Yahweh has been with David in the past, so he will also be with the Davidic house in the future. This stability of the royal line is the will

(תורה) of God, and it has implications for the whole mankind. W. C. Kaiser ("The Blessing of David, The Charter for Humanity," in *The Law and the Prophets*, ed. J. H. Skilton [Nutley, NJ: Presbyterian and Reformed, 1974] 311) paraphrases v 19b "This is the charter by which humanity will be directed."

20 Since it is Yahweh who has chosen or singled him out (cf. Jer 1:5; Amos 3:2), there is nothing more that David could wish for in addition. If we follow the usual rendering of v 20b ("you know . . ."), then the reference may be to God's omniscience (cf. Pss 38:9 [MT 10]; 139:1–4).

21 "For the sake of your servant" seems preferable (see Driver, 277) to ". . . your word" (i.e., promise) since the latter is concerned with future events.

The Heb. גלבך "according to your will" is occasionally repointed and translated as "this dog of yours" (so JB). If correct, this would be part of the deferential address "[who is but] a dog of yours"); cf. 1 Sam 24:14 [MT 15]; 2 Sam 9:8; Rudolph, *Chronikbücher*, 132).

The verse as a whole seems to refer to the revelation of the divine promise in v 19 (so also McCarter, 236), enabling David to see the secrets of the distant future (cf. Gen 18:17).

22–24 Verse 22 (especially v 22b) begins a hymnic praise of Yahweh, stressing his incomparability. The themes are reminiscent of other parts of the OT (see Deut 3:24; 4:35; Pss 86:8; 89:6 [MT 7]; 113:5). The text of v 23 is rather clumsy and may have undergone a textual corruption although its essence is fairly clear. The counterpart of Yahweh's incomparableness is Israel's uniqueness: no other nation has such an awe-inspiring and mighty God (see also Deut 4:7, 32–38).

V 24 reflects covenantal language and is a variation of the well-known formulation "I will be their God, and they shall be my people" (see Exod 6:7; Lev 26:12; Ezek 11:20; 37:27) which is the quintessence of the covenant concept. It also emphasizes the unbreakable togetherness of the eternal triangle: Yahweh-Israel-House of David. Note the fivefold emphatic repetition of the phrase "forever" (לעולם and עד עולם) in the prayer of David.

26 There are some interpretative problems concerning the nature and relationship of the different clauses. Perhaps לאמר "saying" should be deleted (see *Note* on 26.a.–a) to read: "That your name, O Yahweh of Hosts, God over Israel, may be great forever, and that the house of your servant David may be established before you" (cf. also McCarter, 232).

For "Yahweh of Hosts" see *Comment* on 5:10. Mettinger ("YHWH SABAOTH The Heavenly King on the Cherubim Throne," in *Studies in the Period of David and Solomon and Other Essays*, ed. T. Ishida [Winona Lake, IN: Eisenbrauns, 1982] 126) thinks it probable that "hosts" may refer to the heavenly council. In his view, "a construct relation is the least problematic" (128) explanation of the syntactic relationship between the two nouns, "Yahweh" and "Hosts." It is plausible that at some point "Yahweh" was substituted for "El" in an original אל צבאות "God of hosts" designation.

Brueggemann (*David's Truth*, 80) calls v 26 "a shrewd piece of dynastic self-service" in that "Yahweh cannot be magnified unless David is magnified as well." However, theoretically at least, this service was provided by Yahweh himself (see v 19).

27 Yahweh announced to David (lit., "uncovered his ear") that he will establish his house (or "dynasty"), and this takes up the previous dynastic oracle, especially v 11b. It is in the light of this divine promise that David uttered his prayer to Yahweh, which otherwise might have appeared rather presumptuous (see Kirkpatrick, 104).

28 The Heb. טובה "gracious promise" (rsv, "good thing") is, most likely, a synonym for covenant (so P. Kalluveettil, *Declaration and Covenant* [AnBib 88; Rome: Biblical Institute Press, 1982] 44). Therefore "to say this good thing" (or "to make this gracious promise") is synonymous with entering into a covenantal relationship with a vassal. See also the *Comment* on 2:6.

Explanation

Superficially at least, David's prayer may appear unnecessary because the petition concerns the continuation of the Davidic dynasty which had already been promised. However, if this prayer, in its indirect way, voices the hopes and the fears of the exilic community, then its importance and relevance become obvious. What the prayer in its original form (if there was such a pre-Deuteronomistic version) might have said is difficult to surmise. We agree with Brueggemann (*David's Truth*, 81) that Nathan's oracle is "Yahweh's incredible commitment to a particular historical institution" and that "the prayer is the verification of that commitment," especially if the prayer in its present form is the expression of the exilic community's experience and traditions. The four hundred years rule of the house of David was a sufficient testimony to the effective shaping of history by Yahweh's word, and so was also the punishment of individual kings during that period (see 7:14). Yahweh's promises are absolutely reliable but the nature of their fulfillment depends on many factors.

The Wars of David   (8:1–14)

Bibliography

Alt, A. "Zu II Sam. 8.1." *ZAW* 54 (1936) 149–52. Borger, R. "Die Waffenträger des Königs Darius." *VT* 22 (1972) 385–98. Eissfeldt, O. "Israelitisch philistäische Grenzverschiebungen von David bis auf die Assyrerzeit." *ZDPV* 66 (1943) 115–28. Kassis, H. E. "Gath and the Structure of the 'Philistine' Society." *JBL* 84 (1965) 259–71. Malamat, A. "Aspects of Foreign Policies of David and Solomon." *JNES* 22 (1963) 1–17. ———. "A Political Look at the Kingdom of David and Solomon and Its Relations with Egypt." In *Studies in the Period of David and Solomon and Other Essays*, ed. T. Ishida. Winona Lake, IN: Eisenbrauns, 1982. 189–204. Mazar, B. "The Aramean Empire and Its Relations with Israel." BAR 2. Ed. E. F. Campbell and D. N. Freedman. Missoula, MT: Scholars Press, 1977. 127–51.

Translation

[1] *After this David defeated the Philistines and subdued them, wresting[a] supremacy[b] from the hand of the Philistines.* [2] *Then he defeated Moab and, making[a] them lie down on the ground, he measured them off by the line: he measured[b] off two lengths to be put to death, and one full length to be kept alive. Thus the Moabites became servants to David, bearing tribute.* [3] *Next David defeated Hadadezer, son of Rehob, king of Zobah, as he went to restore his authority along[a] the River Euphrates.[b]* [4] *David also captured [a]from him[a] one thousand chariots, seven thousand[b] charioteers and twenty thousand foot soldiers, and he[c] wrecked all but one hundred chariots which he spared.* [5] *When the Arameans of Damascus came to help Hadadezer, the king of Zobah, David slew twenty-two thousand of them.* [6] *Then David placed garrisons in Aram of Damascus, and the Arameans became David's servants,[a] bearing tribute. And Yahweh made David victorious wherever he went.* [7] *David took the golden quivers carried[a] by the servants of Hadadezer, and he brought them to Jerusalem.* [8] *From Tebah[a] and Berothai, cities of Hadadezer, King David took a very large quantity of bronze.*
[9] *When Toi, king of Hamath, heard that David had defeated the whole army of Hadadezer,* [10] *he[a] sent Joram,[b] his son, to King David to greet him and to congratulate him for having fought against Hadadezer and having defeated him, because Hadadezer had been Toi's constant military opponent. And Joram[c] had with him vessels of silver, gold, and bronze.* [11] *These, too, King David dedicated to Yahweh together with the silver and gold which he had dedicated from all the nations[a] which he had subdued,* [12] *namely, from Aram,[a] from Moab, from the Ammonites, from the Philistines and from the Amalekites, as well as from the spoil of Hadadezer, son of Rehob, king of Zobah.* [13] *When David returned, he became famous on account of his[a] slaughter of the Edomites[b] in the Valley of Salt, some[c] eighteen thousand of them.* [14] *He also placed garrisons in Edom,[a] and all the Edomites became David's servants. And Yahweh made David victorious wherever he went.*

Notes

1.a. Omitting דוד "David" with 1 Chr 18:1.
1.b. Lit., "the reins of the forearm" (so Hertzberg, 288).
2.a. For this use of inf abs, see GKC, §113h.

2.b. G avoids the repetition of מדד "to measure" and suggests ויהיו, which would give us: "(two lengths) were (to be put to death)."

3.a. Or "in (the territory bordering on) the River Euphrates."

3.b. Adding פרת "Euphrates"; so Q, 1 Chr 18:3, G. Budde (240), perhaps rightly, calls this an unnecessary expansion.

4.a-a. Lacking in G, perhaps also in 4QSamª.

4.b-b. Following 1 Chr 18:4 and G, in reading אלף רכב ושבעת אלפים "a thousand chariots and seven thousand . . ." for MT אלף ושבע מאות "one thousand and seven hundred. . . ." The adopted reading seems to be required by the latter part of the verse, and is implied by 4QSamª (see Ulrich, *Qumran Text*, 56).

4.c. MT: דוד "David."

6.a. 4QSamª omits ל before עבדים "servants," as in v 14 and 1 Chr 18:2, 6, 13.

7.a. Lit., "(that were) on (the servants . . .)" but we follow some MSS in reading על "upon" instead of אל "unto"; see also Driver, 281.

8.a. MT has "Betah" while 1 Chr 18:8 reads "Tibhath." "Tebah" (cf. Gen 22:24) is attested in ancient Near Eastern texts (cf. *ANET*, 477a) and was located in the Anti-lebanon region.

10.a. MT: תעי "Toi."

10.b. 1 Chr 18:10 reads הדורם "Hadoram" for MT יורם "Joram."

10.c. An interpretative addition; not in MT.

11.a. G reads πόλεων ("cities" = ערים) for MT הגוים "the nations."

12.a. So MT, while some MSS and 1 Chr 18:11 read מאדם "from Edom"; so also G and Syr. "Edom" is probably right in view of v 14; there must have been some booty from Edom. Moreover, the plunder from Aram appears as the spoil of Hadadezer, at the end of v 12.

13.a. Some MSS have מהכות "on account of the slaughter."

13.b. MT reads ארם "Aram, Arameans"; we follow some MSS, 1 Chr 18:12, G in reading אדם "Edomites."

13.c. G adds εἰς (= עד "unto, as much as").

14.a-a. The present MT is, most likely, a conflation of two variant readings: "And he put garrisons in Edom; throughout all Edom put he garrisons" (so KJV). We follow 1 Chr 18:13, omitting נצבים בכל אדום שם "he placed garrisons in all Edom."

Form / Structure / Setting

This pericope (vv 1–14) gives a short summary of David's military achievements, and is reminiscent of the brief résumé of Saul's victories in 1 Sam 14:47–48. It is doubtful that the events in our pericope are arranged in any chronological order; essentially they are intended to illustrate David's God-given triumphs (see vv 6 and 14).

The presentation of the material is done in an annalistic fashion, and there is neither plot nor dialogue. Nor is there any clear structure although the following outline sums up the contents:

vv 1–2	Victory over the Philistines and Moabites
vv 3–8	The Aramean wars
vv 9–10	King of Hamath congratulates David
vv 11–12	The dedication of the spoils
vv 13–14a	The defeat of the Edomites
v 14b	Conclusion

One gains the impression that the Edomite episode (vv 13–14a) is a later addition (see Stolz, 226) since it comes after the dedication of the booty from various defeated peoples, including Edom (so 1 Chr 19:11). If so, the original conclusion would have been: "So David became famous (v 13a) since Yahweh made David victorious wherever he went" (v 14b).

There is some uncertainty also concerning the relationship between vv 3–8 and the Aramean wars described in 10:6–19. Miller and Hayes (*History*, 184) consider 8:3–6 as a "somewhat garbled version of the scene described in II Sam. 10:6–10." However, the exact sequence and relationship of the four (?) Aramean battles depicted in chaps. 8 and 10 are no longer clear. If anything, David's defeat of Hadadezer and its sequel in vv 3–12 may have been the final episode in a more prolonged hostilities, and therefore after the events narrated in 10:6–19. See further *Form/Structure/Setting* of 10:1–19.

McCarter (251) regards this catalog of victories as a probable "Deuteronomistic compilation of ancient fragments," and this may well be right. This résumé is only loosely linked with the wider context in that it may provide an elaboration of 7:1b and 11b, showing the manner in which Yahweh had given peace to David and his people (cf. Ackroyd, *Int* 35 [1981] 385). On the other hand, the consecration of the spoils may look forward to the time when all this gold, silver and bronze will be used for the benefit of the temple (see 1 Chr 18:8b).

Comment

1 The present setting of "after this" (see *Comment* on 2:1) may imply that David's victories were seen as the fulfillment of Yahweh's promise that wicked men will no longer oppress Israel (7:11). This was accomplished by eliminating the sources of potential danger.

The crux of this verse is מתג האמה which we have reluctantly taken as a metaphorical expression. A possible literal rendering might be "the reins of the forearm," hence perhaps "control" or "supremacy." 1 Chr 18:1 reads גת ובנתיה "Gath and its dependent villages" or ". . . its daughters." Historically this may be true (see Kassis, *JBL* 84 [1965] 269) but the Chronicler's reading is usually regarded as secondary. The versions do not offer any real help and most modern translations take מתג האמה as a place-name, "Metheg Ammah"; unfortunately, no such location is attested even though it ought to have been sufficiently important to be singled out for mention in this passage. McCarter (243) offers another suggestion; he follows G and reads המגרש "the common land"; however, this, too, is doubtful. Why only common land?

It is unlikely that v 1 was intended as a summary of the events described in 5:17–25 (see Alt, *ZAW* 54 [1936] 150); clearly, there must have been also other battles with the Philistines (see 23:9–17). It is also uncertain to what extent did David subdue the Philistines. It is doubtful that he occupied the entire territory which may have been theoretically under Egyptian control but he may have annexed certain areas. However, he definitely broke the Philistine domination over Palestine once for all.

2 Two out of every three Moabite prisoners of war were put to death, chosen by an unusual method of selection, not attested elsewhere. It does not follow that *all* David's prisoners of war were treated in the same fashion although David's handling of the Edomites was even more ruthless (see 1 Kgs 11:15–16). 1 Chr 18:2 omits the gruesome mass execution of the Moabite captives, while G and Vg change the ratio: half were put to death and half were spared. All this may imply that the Israelite economy was not able to absorb large numbers of slaves unless the measures taken had a deterrent value. David's harsh treatment of the Moabites is rather unexpected since his own great grandmother is said to have been a Moabitess (cf. Ruth 4:21–22); moreover, the Moabites had been helpful to David's parents during their enforced exile (1 Sam 23:3–4). Moab became David's vassal state and its tribute may have consisted of sheep and wool (as in 2 Kgs 3:4).

3 Hadadezer, son of Rehob, probably came from Beth-rehob, at the southern foot of Mount Hermon. In Malamat's view (*Studies in the Period of David and Solomon,* 196) Hadadezer was the leader of a powerful political bloc in Syria. By vanquishing Hadadezer, its overlord, all "these territories passed to David *en bloc* . . . it was this legacy which facilitated David's acquisition of empire" (ibid.). Thus David "took over Hadadezer's realm not only territorially, but also structurally" (*JNES* 22 [1963] 2). Zobah itself was situated east of the Anti-Lebanon range, between Damascus (in the south) and Hamath (in the north).

The latter part of the verse is somewhat ambiguous. It is not clear whether it was David or Hadadezer who was on his way to the River which would be either the Euphrates (so many MSS, Q, 1 Chr 18:3) or, perhaps, the river (Jordan) or even Yarmuk. Many scholars assume that while Hadadezer was on his way to recover territories lost along the Euphrates in the north, David used this opportunity and invaded Zobah from the south, and eventually defeated Hadadezer. However, it is equally plausible, as McCarter (247) has argued, that it was *David* who marched to the River "to leave a monument to himself" (cf. also *ANET,* 239b). On the whole, the former alternative is, perhaps, the more likely one, especially in view of the doubts expressed concerning the extent of the Davidic kingdom (see Miller and Hayes, *History,* 179).

There is also some uncertainty as to the exact meaning of להשיב ידו "to restore his authority," lit., ". . . his hand." The Heb. יד "hand" can indeed denote "stele" or "victory monument" (see 18:18) but in this context even "stele" would be symbolic of the king's authority.

4 Both the text of this verse and its interpretation are somewhat dubious. The Heb. אלף "thousand" may also denote a military unit or a clan, the actual size of which might vary from time to time. However, in our passage the word must mean "thousand" although the given figures, if the text is right, may have been exaggerated in transmission; e.g., the seven thousand charioteers seem to be too many for the thousand chariots.

Equally uncertain is the sense of רכב; it can denote a chariot or, collectively, chariotry as well as, metonymically, chariot horses. The verb עקר "to hamstring, disable" seems to point to "chariot horses" (cf. Josh 11:6, 9) but it is possible that the present reference is to the wrecking of the chariots (see *HALAT* 3:828); this would avoid different meanings for רכב in the same context. We would regard the hamstringing of horses as an extreme cruelty to animals but in the ancient world this was, apparently, an accepted military practice.

However, whether the reference is to horses or to chariots, the implication is that David could not make full use of them all. The hundred horses or chariots spared would make up only a small chariot force, if this were David's intention. There is no explicit evidence that David ever used chariotry in his military campaigns although Malamat (*Studies in the Period of David and Solomon,* 195) suggests that David must have taken over the Philistine chariotry to cope with the "mechanized" Aramean forces.

5 At this point, Damascus may have been one of Hadadezer's vassal states or part of an Aramean federation (see Mazar, *BAR* 2:131) and therefore they were obliged to assist Hadadezer. Malamat (*JNES* 22 [1963] 5) has argued that it must have been "a conquered territory" ruled by Hadadezer since there is no mention of the king of Damascus.

6 The Heb. נציב in this context may denote either a garrison (so most translators) or a prefect (so Hertzberg, McCarter) or governor (so JB). We prefer "garrison" since it would include a military commander responsible for a particular area (see also Reindl, "נצב / יצב," *TWAT* 5/5–6 [1986] 561–63).

"And Yahweh gave . . ." is identical with v 14b, and McCarter (249) rightly regards v 6b as premature at this point and due to a textual accident.

7 Most translators used to take שלט to mean "shield" but Borger (*VT* 22 [1979] 397–98) has convincingly shown that its meaning is "quiver" (cf. also Josephus, *Ant.* 7.104), either a combined container for both arrows and bow or a single one for arrows only (cf. Yadin, *Warfare,* 198, 296). The reference is, most likely, to military equipment rather than to ceremonial armor (cf. 2 Kgs 11:10).

At the end of v 7 there is a lengthy addition found in G, OL, and 4QSam[a] (cf. also 1 Kgs 14:26 in G) but the shorter reading of the MT is preferable.

8 Berothai (not to be confused with modern Beirut) is usually located in the western foothills of Anti-Lebanon. 1 Chr 18:8 reads "Cun" for "Berothai," but the two were not identical (see Aharoni, *The Land* 73, 296) although roughly in the same area.

Metals, including bronze (an alloy of copper and tin) were valuable spoils of war (cf. 2 Kgs 25:13–17). The Chronicler (1 Chr 18:8) expands our verse by adding that Solomon used this booty to make the bronze sea as well as the pillars and various temple vessels.

9–10 The Neo-Hittite Hamath (so Aharoni, *The Land,* 297) was the capital of an important kingdom, situated on the river Orontes, some 120 miles (or 190 kilometers) north of Damascus.

The Chronicler's "Hadoram" (for MT "Joram") is probably a shortened form of "Hadadram" (meaning "Hadad is exalted") while "Joram" is an abbreviated form of "Jehoram" (i.e., "Yahweh is exalted"). It is very likely that the Chronicler's version has preserved the original name of Toi's son but we do not know the reasons for this subsequent change. Hadad was a well-known ancient Near Eastern storm-god, and the substitution of his name is somewhat reminiscent of the scribal alteration of Eshbaal's name into Ishbosheth (see *Comment* on 2:8). Malamat (*JNES* 22 [1963] 7) argues that "Joram" was Hadadram's second name which the prince adopted, most likely, when Hamath became "a satellite of David." In a similar (?) manner the name of Eliakim was changed into Jehoiakim (2 Kgs 23:34) and that of Mattaniah into Zedekiah (2 Kgs 24:17) by their respective overlords.

12 It has been noted that only one Amalekite campaign (see 1 Sam 30) is attributed to David (see McCarter, 251) but this need not have been his only conflict with them.

13   McCarter (243) renders וַיַּעַשׂ דָוִד שֵׁם as "David built a monument" (our translation: ". . . became famous") but this is less likely in view of similar expressions elsewhere (cf. Gen 11:4; Isa 63:12; Jer 32:20; see also C. Westermann, *Genesis 1–11: A Commentary*, tr. J. J. Scullion, S.J. [London: SPCK, 1984] 548). If the present text of v 13 is correct (except for "Aram"), then it suggests that David gained renown due to his campaign against Edom which must have been a memorable one (cf. 1 Kgs 11:15–16). Although MT places the victory in Aram (but see n. 13.b.), Edom is the more likely location. Also the Valley of Salt (even though its identification is uncertain) points to an area south of the Dead Sea (so also the superscription to Ps 60, which attributes this or a similar victory to Joab; cf. also 2 Kgs 14:7). 1 Chr 18:12 ascribes the Edomite defeat to Abishai, son of Zeruiah (cf. Josephus, *Ant.* 7.109), and McCarter (246) combines both readings on the assumption that the original text had suffered from scribal omission. This is plausible but the unexpected introduction of Abishai seems odd because it is David who is extolled in this pericope. Nevertheless, it seems likely that the Chronicler may have known another, more detailed tradition of Edom's conquest. In any case, it is highly questionable whether all the victories attributed to David were actually achieved by him personally (see 12:27–30).

Explanation

If chap. 7 is the climax of the Davidic story, then chap. 8 is, in a sense, its conclusion. Vv 1–14 sum up the gradual expansion of the Davidic kingdom until it reached its utmost limits: "from Euphrates to the land of the Philistines and to the border of Egypt" (1 Kgs 4:21; RSV).

Although we do not know all the factors which gave rise to the hostilities described in vv 1–14, it is far from certain that *all* the Davidic wars were of a defensive nature. Most likely there were a number of contributory factors in various combinations, such as political aims, economic considerations (e.g., the control of important trade routes and access to the Red Sea), self-defense (against the Philistines), national pride and intrigues (such as brought about the Ammonite war); the so-called "domino theory" (i.e., one event giving rise to another event, etc.).

These wars must be judged in their own cultural setting in spite of such practices as unnecessary cruelty to animals, inhumane treatment of prisoners of war, and what appears to be a form of colonialism or empire building. The Israelites did not invent wars and military "techniques;" they were people of their own times but, nevertheless, they left a rich heritage to future generations. Therefore the Deuteronomistic editor could conclude in retrospect that "Yahweh made David victorious (or ". . . delivered David") wherever he went" (v 14b).

David's High Officials of State   (8:15–18)

Bibliography

Armerding, C. E. "Were David's Sons Really Priests?" *Current Issues in Biblical and Patristic Interpretation: Studies in Honor of Merrill C. Tenney,* ed. G. F. Hawthorne. Grand Rapids, MI: Eerdmans, 1975. 75–86. **Begrich, J.** "Sōfēr und Mazkîr." *ZAW* 58 (1940/41) 1–29. **Hauer, C. E., Jr.** "Who Was Zadok?" *JBL* 82 (1963) 89–94. **Heaton, E. W.** *Solomon's New Men: The Emergence of Ancient Israel as a National State.* London: Thames and Hudson, 1974. **Mettinger, T. N. D.** *Solomonic State Officials.* ConB OT Ser. 5. Lund: CWK Gleerup, 1971. **Reventlow, H. G.** "Das Amt des Mazkir." *TZ* 15 (1959) 161–75. **Rowley, H. H.** "Zadok and Nehushtan." *JBL* 58 (1939) 113–41. **Rüterswörden, U.** *Die Beamten der israelitischen Königszeit.* BWANT 117. Stuttgart, Berlin, Cologne, Mainz: W. Kohlhammer, 1985. **Soggin, J. A.** "The Davidic-Solomonic Kingdom." In *Israelite and Judaean History,* ed. J. H. Hayes and J. M. Miller. OTL. London: SCM, 1977. 332–80.

Translation

[15] So David ruled over all[a] Israel and he[b] maintained law and justice for all his people. [16] Joab, son of Zeruiah, was in command of the army. Jehoshaphat, son of Ahilud, was royal herald. [17] Zadok, son of Ahitub, and Ahimelek, son of Abiathar, were priests. Seraiah[a] was royal scribe. [18] Benaiah, son of Jehoiada, was in command[a] of the Cherethites and the Pelethites. The sons of David were[b] priests.

Notes

15.a. Lacking in some MSS and G[B.]
15.b. MT: "David."
17.a. So MT. 1 Chr 18:16 reads שׁוֹשָׁא "Shausha" while Q in 2 Sam 20:25 has שְׁוָא "Shewa"; K reads שֵׁיָא. The spelling of the name is equally uncertain in the versions (see Driver, 283–84).
18.a. Reading with 1 Chr 18:17 עַל הַכְּרֵתִי "was in command of the Cherethites." MT lacks the preposition עַל; cf. v 16a.
18.b. MT reads כֹּהֲנִים הָיוּ "were priests"; so also Aq, Vg; however, the position of the verb הָיוּ at the end of the phrase is odd (cf. the order of words in 20:26); the verb may be superfluous.

Form/Structure/Setting

V 15 provides an introduction to the list of David's chief officers and officials, as well as a setting for it. In some ways, v 15 belongs to the preceding account (see Nowack, 184) because the ideal king not only does what is just and right but he also delivers his people from their oppressors and enemies (see Jer 22:3; 23:5–6; 33:15–16). Hence vv 1–14 and v 15 may present two aspects of the functions of the model king.

On the other hand, v 15 may equally well supply the link between the account of David's military activities (vv 1–14) and the administrative list. The latter is not necessarily the official register itself but, most likely, derived from such a document found in the royal archives. It seems that only the more important state officials are enumerated.

Unless it is a mere coincidence, the list contains three pairs of officials: two military commanders (Joab and Benaiah), two "top civil servants" (Jehoshaphat and Seraiah) and two chief priests (Zadok and Ahimelek or Abiathar); cf. also Begrich, *ZAW* 58 (1940–41) 5–8. If this dual structure is intentional, its purpose may have been to lessen the accumulation of power in one pair of hands!

The order of the officials appears to be haphazard and may not reflect their relative importance. There is a parallel list in 20:23–26 which seems to be more structural, dealing with army, civil administration and cultic officials, in that order. It is possible that both lists were derived from one and the same source, and they need not reflect two different periods in David's reign (see Ackroyd, 89). However, Mettinger (*Solomonic State Officials*, 7) regards 8:15–18 as the earlier list since 20:24 adds a new office, i.e., that of Adoram who was in charge of the forced labor service. The latter list also omits David's sons as priests but adds "Ira, David's priest."

Neither the administration of the old tribal system nor the reign of Saul does provide a satisfactory explanation of the eventual complex administration required by the expanding kingdom of David. The most likely model might be that provided either by the Canaanite city states (especially Jerusalem) or by the Egyptian royal court, perhaps through the mediation of the Canaanite centers of administration (cf. Mettinger, *Solomonic State Officials*, 4). A less likely source of David's model may have been the Aramean kingdoms as well as Ammon, Edom, and Moab. Unfortunately, there is little information concerning their administrative systems.

Comment

15 David is presented as the ideal king (cf. Isa 9:7 [MT 6]; Jer 22:3; 23:5) whose reign reflects the characteristics of Yahweh's rule (see Ps 89:14 [MT 15]), and who maintains the well-being of his people. Hertzberg (293) is of the opinion that David "took over the supreme office of judge." It is, no doubt, true that the king exercised judicial functions but this does not imply that he replaced the existing legal administration. The changes provided an additional tier which functioned within the previous judicial framework.

16 Joab (see *Comment* on 2:18) was in charge of the Israelite tribal levies (הצבא) were separate from the mercenaries of Benaiah (see v 18). As commander of the militia (שר הצבא) Joab was directly responsible to the king (cf. 19:13 [MT 14]).

The actual functions of some of the officials are not defined and therefore it is difficult to find the appropriate equivalents, especially to מזכיר and ספר. The former may have been the recorder (so, e.g., JB, NIV, RAV) in charge of various state records and documents while Heaton (*Solomon's New Men*, 48–49) accepts the conventional rendering "royal herald" whose functions would be reminiscent of those of the Egyptian *whm.w*, i.e., "speaker" or Pharaoh's herald (see Begrich, *ZAW* 58 [1940–41] 11; Mettinger, *Solomonic State Officials*, 52–62). NEB prefers "secretary of state" as the rendering of מזכיר, but it is clear that the exact definition of his office must remain a guesswork (cf. Rütersworden, *Die Beamten der israelitischen Königszeit*, 91).

17 Seraiah (or Shausha?) was not an ordinary scribe but a scribe par excellence. He was one of the two chief secretaries of state or one of the most senior "civil servants" of the king. The title of "royal secretary or scribe" might be a reasonably suitable rendering of סֹפֵר (see Mettinger, *Solomonic State Officials,* 48–51).

"Seraiah" is an Israelite name with a possible meaning "Yahweh is prince" or "Yahweh persisteth" (so BDB 976; cf. also Noth, *Personennamen,* 208) while "Shausha" and its variants appear to be non-Semitic (see McCarter, 256), perhaps corruptions of an Egyptian title or office (see Soggin, *History* [ed. Hayes and Miller] 357). It is possible that the many variants of the scribe's name or title may indicate its foreign origin (Egyptian?), and that "Seraiah" is only one of the attempts to transliterate the non-Israelite name or designation.

According to the present text, Zadok and Ahimelek were priests; however, the second list of high officials in 20:23–26 states that Zadok and Abiathar were priests (v 25; so also 1 Kgs 4:4; cf. 2 Sam 15:24, 35; 19:11 [MT 12]). Hence it has been argued that the correct reading is "Abiathar, son of Ahimelek," who escaped the slaughter of the priests of Nob and joined David (1 Sam 22: 20–23). Wellhausen (177) proposed a more substantial change, reading, "Abiathar son of Ahimelek son of Ahitub, and Zadok;" thus leaving Zadok without a genealogy. Hence some scholars (e.g., Rowley, Hauer) have argued that Zadok was originally a Jebusite priest in the pre-Davidic Jerusalem, who for some reason or other gained David's favor. However, there is no compelling reason why Zadok's father could not have been called Ahitub and why another Ahitub could not have been the grandfather of Abiathar (1 Sam 22:20).

18 Benaiah was captain of David's bodyguard (23:23) or mercenary force which is described as "the Cherethites and the Pelethites." This description may well be a stereotyped expression (see de Vaux, *Early History,* 2:505) and its interpretation is problematic.

The Cherethites are often identified with the Cretans while the Pelethites are not infrequently regarded as Philistines, and the name itself as a possible dialectical variant of "Philistines." Whether or not this is correct, it seems that they are to be sought among the so-called Peoples of the Sea. In 15:18 we find another mercenary contingent, this time from the Philistine Gath, described as "Gittites." R. W. Klein (*1 Samuel,* 282–83) has remarked that the Cherethites were probably Cretan mercenaries in the service of the Philistines; but, if so, would the Negeb of the Cherethites (1 Sam 30:14) have been named after them? It is slightly more likely that they were more permanent inhabitants of this region, some distance from Ziklag.

The statement that David's sons were priests is often altered or toned down in the versions (cf. G, Syr, Tg). Already 1 Chr 18:17 calls them "chief officials" (הָרִאשֹׁנִים) next to the king or, perhaps, ". . . the elder sons of David . . . were next to the king" (cf. McCarter, 254). The reason for these and other changes may have been the wish to avoid the implication that there could have been *legitimate* non-levitical priests. No indication is given as to whether or not the priestly function of David's sons was different from that of Zadok and Ahimelek (or Abiathar). In any case, this office of the sons of David was, apparently, a temporary arrangement (cf. 20:26; 1 Kgs 4:1–6).

Explanation

David was king over all Israel and he exercised his just rule with the help of the state officials. The army was there to protect the land, the "civil service" was important for the day-to-day welfare of the people, while the cultic officials were necessary for the maintaining of the right relationships with Yahweh.

Thus, what the people had longed for at the very beginning of the monarchy (1 Sam 8:20) was now fully attained in David's reign.

David and Mephibosheth   (9:1–13)

Bibliography

Ben-Barak, Z. "Meribaal and the System of Land Grants in Ancient Israel." *Bib* 62 (1981) 73–91. Curtis, J. B. "East Is East. . . ." *JBL* 80 (1961) 355–63. Jung, K. N. *Court Etiquette in the Old Testament.* Ph.D. Drew University, 1979. Ann Arbor, MI: University Microfilms International, 1983. Langlamet, F., O.P. "David et la Maison de Saül." *RB* 86 (1979) 194–213. Mettinger, T. N. D. *Solomonic State Officials.* ConB OT Ser. 5. Lund: CWK Gleerup, 1971. Thomas, D. W. "A Consideration of Some Unusual Ways of Expressing the Superlative in Hebrew." *VT* 3 (1953) 209–24. ———. "Kelebh 'Dog': Its Origin and Some Usages of It in the Old Testament." *VT* 10 (1960) 410–27. Veijola, T. "David und Meribaal." *RB* 85 (1978) 338–61.

Translation

[1] *David asked, "Is there anyone[a] left of Saul's house to whom I may show consideration for Jonathan's sake?"* [2] *Now the house of Saul had a servant named Ziba, and he was summoned[a] to David. The king asked him, "Are you Ziba?" "Your servant," he replied.* [3] *Then the king inquired, "Is there none left of Saul's house to whom I may show my [a]utmost consideration?"[a] "There is still Jonathan's son, lame in both feet," Ziba answered the king.* [4] *"Where is he?" the king said to him, and Ziba answered the king, "He is in the house of Machir, son of Ammiel, in Lo-debar."* [5] *So the king sent and brought him from Lo-debar, from the house of Machir, son of Ammiel.* [6] *When Mephibosheth, son of Jonathan, son of Saul, came to David, he fell on his face and did homage.*

Then David asked, "Mephibosheth?" And he replied, "Yes, sir; your servant." [7] *"Do not fear," David said to him, "for I will truly show you consideration for the sake of Jonathan, your father: I will restore to you all the land of Saul, your grandfather[a] but you yourself shall continually eat food at my table."* [8] *Bowing down, he replied, "What is your servant that you should look graciously upon a dead dog such as I?"* [9] *Then the king called Ziba, [a]Saul's steward,[a] and said to him, "I have given[b] to your master's grandson[c] all that belonged to Saul and to his family.* [10] *You shall work the land for him—you and your sons and your servants— and you shall bring in the produce[a] that it may provide food for your master's household[b] and that [c]they may eat.[c] However, Mephibosheth, your master's grandson, shall continually eat food at my table."* [d]*Ziba had fifteen sons and twenty servants.*[d] [11] *Then Ziba said to the king, "Your servant will do whatever[a] my lord the king commands his servant." So Mephibosheth ate[b] at the [c]king's table[c] like one of the king's sons.* [12] *Moreover, Mephibosheth had a young son named Micah. All who dwelt in Ziba's house were servants of Mephibosheth.* [13] *However, Mephibosheth himself resided in Jerusalem because he always ate at the king's table. He was lame in both feet.*

Notes

1.a. Ehrlich (292) reads איש "anyone" for אשר, following the similar expression in v 3.

2.a. Lit., "they summoned him." For this use of the active theme in the impersonal 3 pl to express the passive theme, see Williams, *Syntax,* §160.

3.a-a. Lit., "the kindness of God" but we take אלהים "God" as having a superlative force (see Winton Thomas, *VT* 3 [1953] 210); NEB has a paraphrase: "the kindness that God requires."

7.a. Reading אבי אביך "the father of your father" with G^BM for MT אביך "your father," and assuming a loss by haplogr in the MT. Ehrlich (292) regards the G reading as an interpretative translation (cf. also BDB, 3a) while Wellhausen points out that אבי אבי "the father of the father of" does not occur (178) although the expression is not in itself impossible.

9.a-a. Lacking in Syr.

9.b. For this use of the perfect, see GKC, § 106m.

9.c. MT: "your master's son," but we follow the rendering suggested by the context.

10.a. The object "the produce" seems to be implied (cf. Hag 1:6).

10.b. So G^L which points to לבית "for the house" instead of MT לבן "for the son (or grandson) of . . . ." The former reading is preferable since a separate provision had already been made for Mephibosheth in v 7, and it is repeated in v 10b.

10.c-c. MT: "that he (Mephibosheth or the household?) may eat it." We have repointed ואכלו as 3rd masc pl:"that they may eat" (so G^LMN).

10.d-d. This sentence seems to be an informative addition.

11.a. Reading כל "whatever" (so some MSS, Syr) for MT ככל "according to all"; so RSV.

11.b. Repointing MT אכל as 3rd msg perfect (so also G). Equally suitable would be יאכל (so 2 MSS, Vg), meaning "used to eat."

11.c-c. MT wrongly "my table." We follow v 13 in reading שלחן המלך "the king's table"; G has "David's. . . ."

Form / Structure / Setting

This pericope introduces two new characters which will play some part in the subsequent chapters (see 16:1–4; 19:24–31), namely, Mephibosheth and Ziba. The chapter as a whole is intended to stress David's loyalty to his covenant with Jonathan (1 Sam 18:3–4; 20:42). Now that Yahweh had cut off all the enemies of David, the latter is able to implement his obligations to Jonathan and his house.

The pericope has a fairly simple structure. In the present form v 1 serves as an introduction which is followed by three scenes, consisting of lively dialogues: vv 2–4 (David and Ziba), vv 5–8 (David and Mephibosheth) and vv 9–11 (David and Ziba). The pericope ends with a concluding summary (vv 12–13). The three dialogues exhibit the A-B-A technique (see Carlson, 133). Most scholars are of the opinion that our chapter was originally preceded by 21:1–14 which dealt with the execution of seven members of the house of Saul, thus providing a suitable setting for chap. 9. This is plausible enough since David's question in 9:1, 3a seems to presuppose either the events of 21:1–14 as some such similar situation. Therefore it is argued that 21:1–14 and 9:1–13 "once stood in continuous narrative sequence" (McCarter, 263); Carlson (131) even speaks of "a sort of Mephibosheth cycle." Furthermore, it has been suggested that we should transfer here also the editorial note in 4:4 which explains the lameness of Jonathan's son.

Gunn (*King David*, 68) links chap. 9 with the narrative in chaps. 2–4. This seems to us more likely than the previous suggestions, especially if the consideration shown by David was associated with the inevitable royal take-over of Saul's estate in the absence of any Saulides who must have fled to avoid any possible repercussions. The treatment of the members of an overthrown royal house was usually rather severe if not "final" (see 1 Kgs 15:29; 16:11; 2 Kgs 10:6–7). It is plausible that this sort of situation was already envisaged by Jonathan's words in 1 Sam 20:15–16. Such a takeover or confiscation (?) of Saul's estate would have taken place most likely soon after David had become king of Israel (but see also Ben-Barak, *Bib* 62 [1981] 79–82). Therefore at some later stage, David was able to return the property to Mephibosheth, perhaps as a land grant.

One should also mention Veijola's argument (*RB* 85 [1978] 338–61) that in the original story Mephibosheth was a son of Saul, and that therefore all the places where Mephibosheth is described as Jonathan's son, are to be regarded as the work of a later editor who wished to stress David's loyalty to Jonathan (352). However, in view of the list of Jonathan's descendants in 1 Chr 8:35–40; 9:41–44), he must have had a son, and there is no great difficulty in accepting the canonical version that Jonathan's son had the same (or similar ?) name as Saul's son by Rizpah (see *Comment* on 4:4).

Comment

1 Smith (310) thought that "the opening of the verse is lost, or misplaced" but v 1 may well be a variant of v 3a or an editorial addition (so Veijola, *RB* 85 [1978] 347).

"To show consideration" belongs to covenant terminology and it refers to loyal fulfillment of one's obligations previously undertaken (cf. 1 Sam 20:14–16; see also *Comment* on 2:5).

2 Ziba must have been in charge of Saul's estate although it is not made clear to whom the patrimony now belonged. It is likely that it had become crown property (see Mettinger, *Solomonic State Officials*, 85); David apparently had the *right* to restore it to Mephibosheth (see also Ben-Barak, *Bib* 62 [1981] 79). If so, Mephibosheth had no more claim upon it because the paternal estate had become part of the crown lands (see also 1 Sam 8:14; 22:7).

3–6 It has been suggested that the editorial note in 4:4 may have originally belonged to our pericope, and that it should be placed after v 3 (so Budde, 245).

"Machir" is a well known name in the OT. According to Josh 17:1, etc. Machir was son of Manasseh, and the father of Gilead. Therefore it is not surprising to find Machir, son of Ammiel, in Transjordan. Judging from 17:27–29, Machir must have been a wealthy man.

The location of Lo-debar is not certain but it was a Transjordanian city in the neighborhood of Mahanaim (see *Comment* on 2:8; cf. also 17:27) where the uncle of Mephibosheth once had his temporary capital. See M. Metzger, "Lodebar und der tell el-mghannije," *ZDPV* 76 [1960] 97–102.

Machir, son of Ammiel, must have been a supporter of Saul and his house, and it is noteworthy that Mephibosheth resided with him, not on his father's or grandfather's estate. This may be due to the fact that the property no longer belonged to the house of Saul; he may also have been afraid of David (see v 7a). For a discussion of Mephibosheth's name, see *Comment* on 4:4.

7 The anxiety of Mephibosheth was quite understandable, especially if the tragic events of 21:1–14 preceded his interview with David. In any case, the customary treatment of the members of overthrown royal houses did not inspire confidence in Mephibosheth. The eventual restoration of the property was, apparently, tantamount to a royal grant; the king could give it and take away (cf. 16:4).

It was a mark of special honor to eat at the king's table (cf. 1 Sam 2:8) but it is less certain whether this royal patronage meant that Mephibosheth shared the king's personal table (see 1 Sam 20:5, 18, 27; 1 Kgs 4:27 [MT 5:7]) or whether he had his own establishment in Jerusalem (cf. 2 Sam 16:3). It may well be that the two alternatives are really complementary although if our reading of v 10 is right, then the former alternative is more likely.

8 The word "dog" (cf 2 Kgs 8:13) or the stronger expression, "dead dog" (cf. 1 Sam 24:15 [MT14]; 2 Sam 16:9), may be used as a term of either contempt or self-abasement when addressing a superior. This later usage is well attested in the ancient Near East (see Jung, *Court Etiquette,* 32–38; J. C. L. Gibson, *Textbook of Syrian Semitic Inscriptions* [vol. 1; Oxford: Clarendon Press, 1973] 37). In the OT dogs are not depicted as pets or man's best friends.

9 It is difficult to define the exact shade of meaning of the Heb. נער in specific contexts. It could mean "young man," "servant" or even "squire" (see J. Macdonald, "The Status and Role of the NAʿAR in Israelite Society," *JNES* 35 [1976] 147–70). In our pericope Ziba was no longer a youth (see v 10b), and he had been in charge of Saul's estate; hence he could well be called "Saul's steward" (or "overseer") (see H. F. Fuhs, "נער," *TWAT 5/3–4* [1985] 507–18; cf. also Gibson, *Syrian Semitic Inscriptions,* 65–66).

Both in v 9 and in v 10, we have the problem of how to translate בן אדניך. Usually it would be rendered "your master's son" but the reference could be also a grandson (see Gen 31:28; Ruth 4:17). The canonical text of 2 Samuel makes it clear that there were two persons bearing the name of Mephibosheth, namely, the son of Jonathan (4:4; 9:6, 7; 21:7) and the son of Saul by Rizpah (21:8). Therefore we translate בן אדניך (when referring to Mephibosheth) as "your master's grandson." If Veijola is right in claiming that there was only one Mephibosheth who was Saul's son, then obviously the pre-canonical narrative spoke of "your master's son" in its narrower sense. However, we are not convinced that Veijola's suggestion is right in spite of his persuasive argument (*RB* 85 [1975] 338–53).

10 The gloss at the end of the verse indicates that Ziba had the necessary manpower to carry out David's order at the beginning of the verse.

12–13 Some scholars (cf. Mauchline, 244) consider the mention of Micah at this point as premature, particularly if the events of 21:1–14 preceded those in our pericope. It seems that this reference to Mephibosheth's son may have been intended to emphasize the unending loyalty of David to Jonathan. According to 1 Chr 8:35–40; 9:41–44, Micah, Jonathan's grandson, had a fairly impressive line of descendants.

Vv 12–13 repeat, more or less, what has already been described, and they may serve as a summing-up of the present situation, and they prepare the way for the later developments in chaps. 16 and 19.

Explanation

The essence of this chapter is David's loyalty to Jonathan, and this is indicated by the threefold repetition of David's intention to show consideration or loyalty to any surviving Saulide (cf. vv 1, 3, 7). At the same time, the author may well be attempting to placate the sympathizers of the house of Saul.

It is impossible to say whether or not David was guided by any ulterior motives. More than one exegete has argued that David did not summon Mephibosheth to Jerusalem for humanitarian reasons (see Hertzberg, 299) but that the latter was politely interned, somewhat like Shimei in 1 Kgs 2:36. It is not impossible that the final editor was anticipating some such skepticism by pointing out twice (in vv 3, 13) that Mephibosheth was not politically dangerous (but see 16:3) because of his lameness which, most likely, disqualified him from the royal office (cf. 1 Sam 9:2; 16:6–7, 12; 2 Sam 14:25). Therefore David had nothing to fear from Mephibosheth even though he could be regarded as a potential enemy, especially when Micah grew older.

On the whole it seems very likely that in this instance David's actions benefited not only Mephibosheth but served also the king's own interests. The chapter must be seen in its historical setting where little or no mercy was shown to dethroned royal houses, and therefore David's attitude to Mephibosheth was clearly an act of kindness and conciliation since the latter had no bargaining power. At least formally, Mephibosheth was made like one of the king's sons (v 11), and instead of being a homeless refugee he became a fairly wealthy man (see v 10b) as long as he remained loyal to David.

David's Ammonite-Aramean Wars (10:1–19)

Bibliography

Giveon, R. "The Cities of Our God" (II Sam 10:12). *JBL* 83 (1964) 415–16. **Kegler, J.** *Politisches Geschehen und theologisches Verstehen.* Calwer Theologische Monographien 8. Stuttgart, Calwer Verlag, 1977. **Malamat, A.** "Aspects of the Foreign Policies of David and Solomon." *JNES* 22 (1963) 1–17. **Mazar, B.** "Geshur and Maacah." *JBL* 80 (1961) 16–28. ———. "The Aramean Empire and Its Relations with Israel." *BAR* 2 (1977) 127–51. **Stoebe, H. J.** "David und der Ammoniterkrieg." *ZDPV* 93 (1977) 236–46. **Yadin, Y.** "Some Aspects of the Strategy of Ahab and David." *Bib* 36 (1955) 332–51.

Translation

[1] *Some time later the king of the Ammonites died and Hanun, his son, reigned in his stead.* [2] *Then David said, "I will show some consideration to Hanun, son of Nahash, just as his father showed consideration to me." So through his servants David sent his condolences to him on account of his father. But when the servants of David entered the country of the Ammonites,* [3] *the Ammonite princes said to Hanun, their lord, "Do you really think that David is honoring your father because he has sent to you messengers with condolences?* [a]*Quite the opposite!*[a] *David has sent his servants to you to reconnoiter the country in order to spy it out and to overthrow*[c] *it."* [4] *So Hanun took the servants of David and shaved off their beards*[a] *and cut their garments in half, up to the buttocks, and sent them away.* [5] *When it was reported*[a] *to David,*[b] *he sent to meet them for the men were deeply humiliated, and he suggested, "Remain in Jericho until your beards have grown, and then return."*

[6] *When the Ammonites realized that they had become odious to David, they*[a] *sent and hired the Arameans*[b] *of Beth-rehob and the Arameans*[b] *of Zobah, twenty thousand foot soldiers, as well as the king of Maacah*[c] *and* [d]*the men of Tob,*[d] *twelve thousand.* [7] *When David heard of this, he sent Joab and* [a]*all the elite troops.*[a] [8] *Then the Ammonites marched out and drew up in battle formation at the gate of the city*[a] *while the Arameans of Zobah and Rehob, and the men*[b] *of Tob and Maacah made their own tactical arrangements in the open country.* [9] *When Joab saw that he had*[a] *a fight on his hands both in front and in the rear, he selected some troops*[b] *from all* [c]*the elite Israelite warriors*[c] *and drew up a battle formation to meet the Arameans.* [10] *The rest of the troops*[a] *he placed under the command of Abishai, his brother, who made preparations to meet the Ammonites.* [a11]*At the same time, Joab*[a] *said, "If the Arameans happen to be too strong for me, you shall give me aid but if the Ammonites happen to be too strong for you, I shall come to aid you.* [12] *Have courage! We are bound to prevail*[a] *for the sake of our people and for the cities*[b] *of our God. However, may Yahweh do what pleases him!"* [13] *So Joab and the troops with him advanced for battle against the Arameans and they fled from him.* [14] *When the Ammonites saw that the Arameans had fled, they too*[a] *fled before Abishai, and entered the city. Then Joab* [b]*ceased his campaign against*[b] *the Ammonites, and came to Jerusalem.*

¹⁵ *When the Arameans saw that they had been beaten by the Israelites, they reassembled together,* ¹⁶ *and Hadadezer sent and summoned the Arameans who were beyond the River. So they came to Helam with Shobach, the commander of Hadadezer's army, at their head.* ¹⁷ *When David was informed of it, he called up all Israel, crossed the Jordan and came to Helam while the Arameans made preparations for battle to meet David, and eventually they fought with him.* ¹⁸ *Then the Arameans fled before Israel, and David slew among the Arameans seven hundred* ᵃ *charioteers and forty thousand foot soldiers;* ᵇ *he also struck down Shobach, the commander of their army, who died there.* ¹⁹ *When all the kings who were Hadadezer's vassals, saw that they had been beaten by Israel, they made peace with Israel and became subject to it; moreover, the Arameans were afraid to help the Ammonites again.*

Notes

3.a-a. The rhetorical question in MT ("Has not David sent . . .") is equivalent to a forceful assertion (see GKC, § 148c).

3.b. Tg and 1 Chr 19:3 have "the land" (= הארץ) but the MT ("the city") is more likely (cf. v 8).

3.c. Ehrlich (294) regards הפך "to overthrow" as a synonym of the two preceding verbs. This is possible, especially in the light of the changed verbal sequence in 1 Chr 19:3.

4.a. Omitting חצי "half of" with G. This may be implied also in 1 Chr 19:4.

5.a. For this use of the active theme in the impersonal 3rd pers plur., see Williams, *Syntax* §160.

5.b. 1 Chr 19:5, G, 4QSamᵃ add על האנשים "concerning the men," which may well be the correct reading. However, Nowack (187) calls it an explanatory addition.

6.a. Lit., "the Ammonites."

6.b. We take ארם "Aram" as a collective noun "Arameans."

6.c. Omitting איש אלף "a thousand men"; cf. Ulrich, *Qumran Text*, 155.

6.d. G, Syr, Vg, 4QSamᵃ have taken איש טוב as a proper noun, "Ishtob" (Josephus: "Istobon"). In view of v 8 איש טוב may well mean "men of Tob" (or, perhaps, "the ruler [i.e., man] of Tob").

7.a-a. MT has "all the army, the elite troops," as if in apposition. McCarter (268) sees in MT a conflated reading, and retains only הגבורים "the soldiers," perhaps rightly.

8.a. Reading העיר "the city" instead of MT השער "the gate," with 1 Chr 19:9 and some Greek MSS. The word פתח "entrance" is, no doubt, a synonym of שער "gate"; cf. also 1 Kgs 17:10.

8.b. For this use of איש, see n. 6.a.

9.a. For the use of the 3 f sg verb (היתה) with the pl subject, see GKC, § 145k.

9.b. For the partitive use of מן "from," see Williams, *Syntax*, § 324; GKC, § 119w.

9.c. So with many MSS and Q.

10.a. Lit., "people."

11.a-a. This is our interpretative addition.

12.a. For this use of the hithp, see F. Hesse, "חזק," *TDOT* 4 (1980) 303.

12.b. This reading is well attested and any emendations seem to be unnecessary.

14.a. Reading גם הם "they too," with 1 Chr 19:15.

14.b-b. Lit., "returned from against" (cf. 2:30; 2 Kgs 3:27).

18.a. 1 Chr 19:18 reads אלפים "thousands" for MT מאות "hundreds."

18.b. Read איש רגלי "foot soldiers" with 1 Chr 19:18 instead of MT פרשים "horsemen."

Form / Structure / Setting

It seems that chaps. 10–12 comprise a more or less unitary account of three consecutive events during David's Ammonite-Aramean wars, namely, the defeat of Ammonite-Aramean coalition (10:6–14), the defeat of the reinforced Aramean alliance (10:15–19), and, finally, the siege and capture of Rabbah, the Ammonite capital (11:1 + 12:26–31). It is very likely that 8:3–8 is not a parallel account of 10:6–10 but that it represents the final episode in David's Aramean wars. The initial fight with the coalition forces had ended with Joab's victory but it was not, or could not be, fully exploited. This then was followed by the unsuccessful Aramean attempt to halt or preempt any possible retaliation by David. If 10:19 is a later addition, then also this victory by David was not followed up immediately. The third major event was the punitive action taken against the Ammonites, ending with the capture of Rabbah and the complete subjugation of Ammon.

Thus one would expect that the victorious Israel would now try to subdue or neutralize, once for all, Hadadezer and his vassals and allies. Consequently, 8:3–8 may well sum up these conclusive military and political developments in Syria.

The account of the Ammonite-Syrian wars was probably derived from court annalistic sources, and reworked. In the present context it provided the setting and background for the David-Bathsheba-Uriah story.

Chap. 10 consists of three main sections: vv 1–5 serve as an introduction and they provide the historical setting and the *casus belli*; vv 6–14 depict Joab's successful battle against the combined Ammonite-Aramean forces; vv 15–18 give an account of David's confrontation with the reinforced Aramean army, and its outcome, while v 19 can be regarded as a later addition but, in any case, it functions as a conclusion to the whole chapter.

Comment

1–2 The Ammonite king Nahash had been Saul's adversary (1 Sam 11) and a cruel enemy of Israel (see 1 Sam 10:27b as restored on the basis of 4QSam[a], in McCarter's *1 Samuel*, 199; cf. also Ulrich, *Qumran Text*, 166). David's friendship with him may go back to the time when David was fleeing from Saul or when he was engaged in hostilities with Ishbosheth's forces. In any case, friendly relationships (covenant ?) must have been established between the two at some stage. After the death of Nahash, David apparently sought to renew the treaty which must have existed between him and Nahash (see P. Kalluveettil, *Declaration and Covenant* [AnBib 88; Rome: Biblical Institute, 1982] 49–50).

3–4 The Ammonite princes or military leaders, aware of David's rise to political power, misunderstood or, perhaps, chose to put a false construction on David's motives. Therefore Hanun reacted and treated David's messengers with utter contempt, disregarding the respect and immunity normally given to royal envoys. The insult was aimed not only at the messengers but, above all, at David himself (cf. A. R. Johnson, *The One and the Many in the Israelite Conception of God* [Cardiff: University of Wales Press, 1961] 4–6). In a sense, it was a declaration of war (see Kegler, *Politisches Geschehen*, 290). Mauchline (245) places the event in the early part of David's reign before he had reached the peak of his power.

The exact details of the humiliation are not clear. Adult Israelites wore a

full beard, and it was a mark of one's manhood. Driver (287) follows MT
(see n. 4.a.) and assumes that shaving off half the beard refers not to the
length of the beard but to "one entire side" (287). However, the G may well
be right; the envoys had come to express their condolences, now their beards
were shorn and they were made into real mourners (cf. Isa 15:2; Jer 41:5;
48:37). The cutting of the garments may well have had a similar significance,
plus the additional humiliation: enforced indecent exposure!

5 Jericho (i.e., Tell-es-Sulṭân) is some 845 feet (258 meters) below the
sea level and it is, perhaps, one of the oldest cities in the world. It is situated
near Jordan, and David's messengers would have to pass it on their way to
Jerusalem.

6 The Ammonites had become odious to David, and this implied a complete break in their relationships (see Gen 34:30; 2 Sam 16:21). In anticipation
of the inevitable conflict, the Ammonites enlisted the help of the Arameans
(for Beth-rehob and Zobah, see *Comment* on 8:3). It is likely that the Aramean
forces were not hired as mercenaries in the strict sense (cf. Stoebe, *ZDPV*
93 [1977] 242); rather they were "bribed" to help the Ammonites and, at
the same time, they could further their own interests in weakening Israel.

In McCarter's view (271) the twenty "thousands" (אלף) may have amounted
to hardly more than about two hundred since the Heb. אלף may denote a
military unit of varying size. However, at least later generations must have
understood these figures in their literal sense.

Maacah was a small Aramean kingdom (cf. 1 Chr 19:6) situated between
Gilead in the south, and Mount Hermon in the north (see B. Mazar, "Geshur
and Maacah," *JBL* 80 [1961] 16–28). Maacah's contingent in MT is given as
"one thousand men" which seems rather small; we have taken it as a later
addition so that the "twelve thousand" may represent the combined forces
of Maacah and Tob.

Tob was, apparently, a minor city state, usually located at eṭ-Ṭayîbeh (see
de Vaux, *Early History*, 820), some twelve miles (twenty kilometers) southeast
of the Sea of Galilee. It may have been allied with, or subject to, the king of
Maacah.

1 Chr 19:6–7 gives us an expanded version of our verse by exaggerating
(?) the strength of the enemy forces and also stating the price of the hire: a
thousand talents of silver (which could buy some hundred thousand slaves!).
The Chronicler also adds that the Arameans encamped before Medeba (1
Chr 19:7). However, this seems unlikely because Medeba was too far south,
some twenty miles (thirty-two kilometers) southwest of Rabbah (but see Mazar,
BAR 2 [1977] 132).

7 In this context צבא "army" may refer to the Israelite militia as over
against the standing army of professional soldiers, here called גבורים "the
mighty men," unless we should read צבא הגבורים "the army of the professional soldiers," following G, Syr, Vg. See also M. C. Lind, *Yahweh Is a Warrior*
(Scottdale, PA/Kitchener, Ont.: Herald Press, 1980) 118, 203.

9–10 Joab may have committed a tactical error by allowing his troops to
be caught between two enemy forces. Equally well one could argue that he
showed a great tactical skill being able to deal with a military emergency (cf.
also Stoebe, *ZDPV* 93 [1977] 243).

11 Joab's instructions to Abishai, his brother, are somewhat questionable. They assume that *both* Israelite forces kept sufficient reserves so that one group could help the other when it was in danger of being overwhelmed by the enemy. The reference to Yahweh is also unexpected in our context.

12 The unique expression "cities of our God," may refer to the Israelite cities in general or, more likely, to those of southern Transjordan (see also Giveon, *JBL* 83 [1964] 416) which would be in more immediate danger. Some scholars (e.g., Klostermann, Budde, Smith) suggest "the ark (אֲרוֹן) of our God" in view of 11:11. The ark would symbolize Yahweh's presence (cf. 1 Sam 4:3, 6–7). Furthermore, the cities of Israel were not really threatened, at least at this point, since the Israelites were the attackers and the theater of war was the Ammonite territory. However, if an emendation was required, one could read "city of. . . ." (עִיר) for "cities of. . . ." (עָרֵי) or delete עָרֵי as a partial dittograph of the preceding word (נְעַד; cf. Kegler, *Politisches Geschehen*, 379 n.803).

"For our people and for the cities of our God" reminds of the battle-cry in Judg 7:18 ("For Yahweh and for Gideon").

14 It appears that for some reason or other Joab did not exploit his victory. Perhaps it was too late in the season (cf. 11:1) or Joab did not have sufficient troops for this purpose, especially if on this campaign only the standing army was at his disposal (cf. vv 7 and 17).

16 The "River" in question must be the Euphrates (see Malamat, *BAR* 2 [1977] 95). The location of Helam (חֵילָם) is uncertain but it may well be a region, rather than a city, in northern Transjordan. In view of v 17 it is unlikely that חֵילָם should be rendered as "their army" (so Thenius, 191).

18 The casualty figures seem rather excessive and they vary considerably; thus 1 Chr 19:18 and Josephus (*Ant.* 7.128) refer to seven thousand horsemen and forty thousand infantry, while Syr mentions one thousand and seven hundred charioteers and four thousand horsemen, plus many soldiers. MT and G^B have seven hundred charioteers and forty thousand horsemen. It is highly doubtful that the Arameans would use such a large number of cavalrymen, therefore "foot soldiers" may be the more plausible reading since the infantry would usually form the backbone of any army.

19 Malamat (*JNES* 22 [1963] 2) believes that "David took over Hadadezer's realm not only territorially, but also structurally." However, other scholars (e.g., Miller and Hays, *History*, 183) are more skeptical of such a total incorporation. Clearly, the Aramean political power was considerably reduced and they may well have paid tribute to David but it is less certain that "all of southern and central Syria was embraced in the empire, apparently under provincial administration" (J. Bright, *A History of Israel*, 204–5).

Explanation

The present chapter offers a tragic picture of the way in which suspicion and misunderstanding may lead to war and humiliation; even other nations may be entangled and drawn into this whirlpool of destruction.

The initial events must have been influenced by the changing political situations and attitudes. David as Saul's opponent would have been a useful ally to Nahash, the Ammonite king, while David as an increasingly powerful ruler of Israel was a potential threat to the Ammonites and other neighboring states. No doubt, the Arameans shared the Ammonite point of view.

Thus the dishonoring of David's envoys may have arisen out of understandable fear but it provided the spark that lit the ready fuse. The subsequent events transformed the international scene of this part of the ancient Near East for some decades to come.

The Ammonite-Aramean wars were, more or less, political wars although Joab could still speak of fighting for "our people and God" (or ". . . cities of God"). One may also note that there is at least no explicit consultation of Yahweh, such as described in 2:1 and 5:19, 23.

David, Bathsheba, and Uriah   (11:1–27a)

Bibliography

Augustin, M. "Die Inbesitznahme der schönen Frau aus der unterschiedlichen Sicht der Schwachen und der Mächtigen." *BZ* 27 (1983) 145–54. **Muraoka, T.** "The Greek Text of 2 Samuel 11 in the Lucianic Manuscripts." *AbrN* 20 (1981–82) 37–59. **Simon, U.** "The Poor Man's Ewe-Lamb: An Example of a Juridical Parable." *Bib* 48 (1967) 207–42. **Stoebe, H. J.** "David und Uria: Überlegungen zur Überlieferung von 2 Sam 11." *Bib* 67 (1986) 388–96. **Veijola, T.** "Salomo—der erstgeborene Bathsebas." VTSup 30 (1979) 230–50.

Translation

[1] *In the following spring[a] of the year, when the kings[b] march out[c] to battle, David sent Joab with his servants and all Israel, [d]and they devastated the Ammonites[d] and laid siege to Rabbah. David, however, remained in Jerusalem.* [2] *Then one particular evening David got up from his couch and, as he walked about on the roof of the royal palace, he saw from the roof[a] a woman bathing. And the woman was very beautiful.* [3] *So David sent someone and made inquiries about the woman, and he reported, "She is Bathsheba, daughter of Eliam, the wife of Uriah the Hittite."[a]* [4] *Then David sent messengers and took her.* [a]*When she came to him,[a] he slept with her (she had just purified herself from her uncleanness). Then she returned to her house.* [5] *When the woman realized that she was pregnant,[a] she sent a message[a] to David, saying, "I am pregnant."*

[6] *Then David dispatched a messenger to Joab, saying, "Send me Uriah the Hittite." So Joab sent Uriah to David.* [7] *When Uriah had come to him, David asked about the well-being[a]of Joab and the army, and about the progress[a] of the war.[b]* [8] *Then David said to Uriah, "Go down to your house and wash your feet!" So Uriah left the royal palace [a]and a present from the king was sent after him.[a]* [9] *However Uriah slept at the entrance of the royal palace with[a] the servants of his lord, and did not go down to his own house.* [10] *When it was reported[a] to David that Uriah had not gone down to his house, David said to Uriah, "Have you not come from a journey? Why[b] did you not go down to your house?"* [11] *Then Uriah answered David, "The ark as well as Israel and Judah are dwelling in temporary shelters while my lord Joab and my lord's servants are camping in the open field. How[a] can I go to my house to eat and to drink and to lie with my wife? As surely as Yahweh lives[b] and as you yourself live, I will not do such a thing!"* [12] *Then David said to Uriah, "Stay here another day and tomorrow I will send you back." So Uriah stayed in Jerusalem that day. But the next day[a]* [13] *David invited him to eat and drink in his presence, and made him drunk. However, in the evening he went out to sleep on his couch with the servants of his lord and he did not go down to his own house.* [14] *In the morning David wrote a letter to Joab, and sent it by Uriah.* [15] *He wrote in the letter: "Send[a] Uriah into the forefront of the fiercest battle, and then withdraw from him that he may be struck down and die."* [16] *So Joab, having watched[a] the city, placed Uriah in a sector where he knew there would be redoubtable warriors.* [17] *When the men of the city marched out to fight with Joab, there were some casualties among David's professional soldiers, and also Uriah the Hittite died.* [18] *Then Joab*

sent a messenger to report to David all the details of the battle. [19]*He also instructed
the messenger as follows: "When you have finished reporting all the details of the
battle to the king,* [20]*it is possible that the king may become angry and may say to
you, 'Why did you go so near to the city to fight? Did you not realize that they
would shoot from the wall?* [21]*Who killed Abimelech, son of Jerubbesheth?*[a] *Did
not a woman drop an upper millstone on him from the wall so that he died at
Thebez? Why did you go so near to the wall?'" Then you shall say, "Your servant
Uriah the Hittite is also dead."*

[22]*So the messenger set out, and when he arrived, he reported to David all that
Joab had sent him to say.* [23]*The messenger said to David, "The enemy had a
military advantage over us and they marched out against us in the open field.
However, we forced them back to the very entrance of the gate,* [24]*but the* [a]*archers
shot*[a] *at your servants from above the wall, and some of the king's servants died,*[b]
also your servant Uriah the Hittite is dead." [25]*Then David said to the messenger,
"Thus you shall say to Joab, 'Do not be upset about this matter*[a] *for the sword
devours indiscriminately. Intensify your attack on the city and destroy it.' So, encour-
age him!"*[b]

[26]*When Uriah's wife heard that Uriah, her husband, was dead, she mourned
over her lord.* [27]*Once the period of mourning was over, David sent and brought
her to his house. So she became his wife and bore him a son.*

Notes

1.a. Lit., "At the turn of. . . ."

1.b. Reading המלכים "the kings" with many MSS, G, Tg and Vg. MT has המלאכים "the
messengers"; cf. also GKC, § 23g.

1.c. For the elliptical expression, see Williams, *Syntax*, § 589.

1.d. This phrase is lacking in Syr while 1 Chr 20:1 has "the land of the Ammonites" as the
object of the verb.

2.a. Most textual witnesses, including MT, have read מעל הגג "from the roof" but in different
positions. McCarter (279) regards this as an indication of its secondary nature, and therefore
he omits it, perhaps rightly.

3.a. 4QSam[a] (also Josephus, *Ant.* 7.131) adds נושא כלי יואב "the armor bearer of Joab"
but this seems to be an explanatory gloss.

4.a-a. G suggests ויבא אליה "when he went in to her"; this is what we would expect in
normal circumstances and therefore the G reading is less likely.

5.a-a. MT: "she sent and told."

7.a. The same word, שלום "peace, welfare, etc." is used in both cases as well as before "the
army" (העם).

7.b. G[L] (similarly Josephus, *Ant.* 7.132), perhaps rightly, supplies Uriah's reply: "'All is well,'
he said;" this may reflect ויאמר לשלום which may have been omitted by homoioarchton. The
testimony of 4QSam[a] is ambiguous (see Ulrich, *Qumran Text*, 186–87).

8.a-a. McCarter (280) reconstructs a plausible alternative reading, based mainly on some
Greek MSS, "he marched out with the weapon-bearers" (ויצא אחרי נשאי הכלים).

9.a. Omitting כל "all," with G[L].

10.a. For the expression, see n. 10:5.a. 4QSam[a] reads ויגד "it was reported," which may be
a hoph form.

10.b. Some MSS add the conjunction, and read ומדוע "and why"; so also G[L].

11.a. Concerning the lack of the interrogative particle, see GKC, § 150a.

11.b. MT has חיך "by your life," which we regard as a corrupt abbreviation of חי יהוה "by
the life of Yahweh" or "as surely as Yahweh lives"; see also GKC, § 149a,c. The MT reading
appears to be tautological.

12.a. Following G[L] and Syr in taking וממחרת "but the next day" with what follows, and reading קרא "he invited" for ויקרא in v 13. Perhaps, the latter emendation is not necessary (cf. 1 Sam 4:20; Isa 6:1; for further references, see Fokkelman, *King David*, 450).

15.a. We read the hiph impv הבא "send" with G^L (εἰσάγαγε), of which MT's הבו "give" may be a corruption.

16.a. McCarter (281) reads בשור "as he kept watch" with 4QSam^a, the reconstruction of which is somewhat uncertain. MT has the more common verb, בשמור "when he had watched" or "having watched."

21.a. Some G MSS suggest "Jerubbaal" (ירבעל) which was the original form of Gideon's other name (see Judg 7:1). Cf. also *Comment* on 2:8.

24.a. For the irregular forms in MT, see GKC, § 75rr.

24.b. G^L gives the number of the dead as about eighteen men, but this is, most likely, an explanatory addition.

25.a. For the unusual use of the object marker (את), see GKC, § 117l.

25.b. McCarter (284) omits this phrase (וחזקהו) with G^LMN, perhaps rightly so.

Form/Structure/Setting

Chap. 11 deals with four main episodes which provide the basic structure of the narrative (see Augustin, *BZ* 27 [1983] 150). In the present form of the narrative, v 1 serves as an introduction and provides the historical setting. The first main event is David's affair with Bathsheba (vv 2–5), followed by David's efforts to tackle the unpleasant consequences created by his adultery. So vv 6–13 narrate in a lively and moving manner how the king's attempts to deceive the cuckolded husband foundered on the unsuspecting Uriah's loyalty and uprightness. Ackroyd (102) has well remarked that "Uriah drunk is more pious than David sober!" The third episode (vv 14–25) depicts both David's scheme to murder Uriah and its eventual implementation. Essentially, it was a murder dressed up as a hero's death; this method must have been chosen because it provided a convenient final solution. The last episode (vv 26–27a) concludes this series of events, both tragic and unsavory. The culprits receive their immediate "reward" and they get each other: Bathsheba becomes David's wife.

From the literary point of view vv 1–27a are fairly self-contained and form a single narrative unit but theologically they require chap. 12 for their completion because the story ends with an unrepentant David and without any divine judgment or critique on his behavior.

McCarter (290) is convinced that chaps. 11–12 are yet another contribution from the same prophetic author who produced 1 Sam 8:11–17 and similar passages. In his view, 11:1–27 may have been "received intact in the prophetic writer's source" while his own contribution may well be confined to 11:27b–12:26 or 11:27b–12:15a (McCarter, 291).

Gunn (*King David*, 38–49) has stressed the importance of traditional motifs in the David stories, and his general conclusion is equally valid for our particular chapter: "It is reasonable, therefore, to argue at the same time both for there to be genuine historical antecedents to the story and for it to have acquired non-historical characteristics through its transmission in tradition" (49). However, for us the practical differentiation is far from easy.

Comment

1 "The turn (or "return") of the year" is usually thought to refer to the spring but some exegetes take it to denote "the time of year at which the

Aramean kings marched to the aid of the Ammonites" (McCarter, 285). However, we regard it as a general reference indicating the period between the heavy winter rains and the harvest, i.e., the spring. This would be an appropriate time for military exploits (cf. 1 Kgs 20:22, 26).

We should not make too much of the variant readings "kings/messengers" since they may be no more than orthographic variants (cf. חלאמה in 10:17; a secondary linear vocalization?). The comment that David remained in Jerusalem, for reasons unknown, is not necessarily a condemnation of him; it may simply set the scene for the following story (see Simon, *Bib* 48 [1967] 209; Stoebe, *Bib* 67 [1986] 388–89).

The exact status of Joab's "servants" is not further defined but a number of more specific descriptions have been proposed, e.g., "his own guards" (JB), "his officers" (NAB), "the king's men" (NIV); however, all these suggestions belong to the realm of informed speculation.

Rabbah (meaning "the great one") was the capital city of the Ammonites, located in the area of the present day Amman, the capital of the kingdom of Jordan.

2 David may have had his bed on the roof (see 1 Sam 9:25), and from this relatively high position he would have had a good view of the neighboring houses and courtyards. There is no real reason to assume that Bathsheba actually intended to be seen by the king (but cf. Augustin, *BZ* 27 [1983] 154).

3 "Bathsheba" probably means "daughter of Sheba" or ". . . of oath(?)" but the second element (שׁבע) is ambiguous. It could also be associated with the Hebrew word for "seven" (שׁבע), hence perhaps "the daughter born on the seventh day" (cf. *HALAT*, 160).

It is unusual that Bathsheba should be identified not only by her husband's name but also by that of her father, as if the latter had a special significance for our story. If indeed her father, Eliam, was the son of Ahithophel of Gilo (23:34), then she would be the latter's granddaughter (so *Sanhedrin* 69b, 10la, followed by many recent exegetes, e.g., Hertzberg, Mauchline). However, this identification is rather tenuous. The "wife of Uriah" is mentioned also in the genealogy of Jesus (Matt 1:6).

Uriah the Hittite was a member of the elite Thirty (23:39), and in the view of Stolz (236), he probably belonged to Jerusalem's nobility which may have had Hittite associations (cf. Ezek 16:3). By the time of David, the great Hittite empire in Asia Minor was no more but its remnants survived in the form of the Neo-Hittite states in Syria, governed by a Hittite ruling class (cf. 1 Kgs 10:29). Uriah's own name, אוריה, is a good Yahwistic name, meaning "Yahweh is my light." This may imply that he was born in Israel unless he had changed his original name at some later stage.

4 Bathsheba's purification has created certain exegetical problems. Thus the NEB rendering, "though she was still being purified after her period" (cf. GKC §141e) implies that David had disregarded also the ritual law (see Lev 15:24) since in the ancient Near East menstruation usually entailed cultic uncleanness. However, it seems more likely that this parenthetic note was intended to stress that it was a favorable time for conception, and, especially, that Uriah could not have been the father of the child that was eventually born (for more details, see Simon, *Bib* 48 [1967] 213).

After this affair Bathsheba returned to her house, and as far as David was concerned, the relationship was, apparently, at an end. However, very soon there arose far-reaching consequences which influenced many lives and, perhaps, altered the course of Israelite history.

7–8 It seems that the ostensible reason for Uriah's recall to Jerusalem was to bring firsthand information about the progress of the Ammonite campaign, while the real motive was to deceive Uriah so that he might appear to be the father of the child.

"To wash one's feet" may simply refer to a necessary refreshment after a long journey (see Gen 18:4; 43:24) but it could be also a euphemistic expression for sexual intercourse, as implied by v 11 (see also Simon, *Bib* 48 [1967] 214). If soldiers on active duty were expected to observe sexual abstinence (see Deut 23:10 [MT 11]; 1 Sam 21:5 [EV 4]) then Uriah in obeying David's suggestion would have committed a serious breach of the ritual law. This is partly supported by Uriah's determined resistance to David's efforts. Although we do not know the legal consequences of such an infringement of "war regulations" it is possible that this, too, may have been at attempt to eliminate Uriah by legal means, at the same time, attributing the paternity of the child to him. The fact that the ark accompanied the army (v 11; but see also McKane, 229) suggests that this military activity was still regarded as a sort of "holy" (?) war, governed by its own strict rules, in spite of the changes brought about by the monarchy (cf. G. H. Jones, "'Holy War' or 'Yahweh War'?" *VT* 25 [1975] 656).

9 There is no indication that Uriah had become suspicious of David's motives due to court gossip (contra Hertzberg, 310), and that his own claim in v 11 should not be taken at its face value. It seems that he spent the night in the guardroom of the palace (see 1 Kgs 14:27–28).

11 The military situation depicted is not clear but it appears that while Joab and the mercenary units ("my lord's servants") were actually besieging Rabbah, the militia or national army ("Israel and Judah") were kept in reserve, perhaps to avoid a trap similar to that set in 10:8–9, unless both statements are simply parallel (so Gordon, 254).

Also the reference to "the dwelling in tents" is ambiguous. McCarter (278) and others take בסכות "in temporary shelters" as a proper noun plus a preposition, namely, "in Succoth" (so Yadin, *Bib* 36 [1955] 344–47). This is plausible because סכות is not normally used of tents (but, perhaps, see 1 Kgs 20:12, 16). On the other hand, Succoth, if it is to be identified with Tell Deir ʿAllā, would be some twenty-five miles (forty kilometers) northwest of Rabbah, and thus rather distant from the battlefield even as a strategic base, especially, if immediate support would be required by the assault troops. McKane (229) has argued that the civilians (i.e., "Israel and Judah") were celebrating the Feast of Tabernacles, and that therefore they lived in booths (סכות) and were in "a state of sanctity." Consequently, Uriah could not enjoy the comforts of his house. However, even if it were so, it is a question whether the Feast of Tabernacles was characterized by such a state of sanctity (see Judg 9:27; 21:19–21; 1 Sam 1:14).

The MT has an unusual, tautological oath: "As you live and as your soul lives" (RSV). We have emended it for reasons explained in *Note* 11.a-a., to conform to the attested oath formula in 1 Sam 20:3; 25:26; see also 2 Sam 15:21.

12 David persuaded Uriah to spend another day in Jerusalem, and in itself is was not unusual (cf. Judg 19:3–5); it might be expected from a perfect host! Clearly, David's real motive was to get the intoxicated Uriah into Bathsheba's bed; paradoxically it might have saved Uriah's life.

14–15 We are not told whether or not the letter was sealed, and whether or not Uriah could read. The essential point is that ironically Uriah was the bearer of his own death warrant. Similar motifs are attested in stories elsewhere (see Gunn, *King David*, 46) but it does not necessarily follow that therefore there could not be an underlying historical episode. This is the only occurrence of this motif in the OT.

Joab was given a difficult task: he had to engineer Uriah's death in a battle and had to make sure that any other losses should be minimal (cf. vv 20–21). It is unlikely that Joab, at this stage, knew the reason for Uriah's liquidation.

16–17 Joab, having received his instructions, inspected the defenses of the city, and assigned Uriah to a sector which was manned by Ammonite "crack troops." This movement of men (?) may have provoked an Ammonite counterattack during which Uriah and some of his comrades were killed.

19–24 MT as well as the versions contain some textual confusion which may be solved, at least partly, with the help of some Greek MSS. In vv 20–21 Joab anticipates David's anger and even what he might say, yet in vv 22–24 there is no reference to either. However, G has an expanded version of v 22 (see Pisano, *Additions or Omissions*, 49–54) which does report David's response and repeats, more or less, verbatim David's angry outburst anticipated by Joab (in vv 20b–21a). The correctness of this reading may be further supported by the Heb. כִּי (*recitativum?*) which precedes the direct speech in v 23, and could be translated as "because," thus presupposing the G version of v 22 and also introducing the messenger's explanation of the tragic events at the walls of Rabbah. The repetition of the "speech" may not appear very elegant but it may be a useful stylistic device as well as the authentic reading (contra Simon, *Bib* 48 [1967] 220). Thus v 22 may have been followed by a version of vv 20–21a.

26 The period of mourning probably lasted seven days (Gen 50:10; Judith 16:24) while Moses and Aaron were mourned for thirty days (Deut 34:8 and Num 20:29, respectively). See also E. F. de Ward, "Mourning Customs in 1, 2 Samuel," *JJS* 23 (1972) 1–27; cf. *Comment* on 3:31.

Explanation

The interpretation of this chapter is rather complicated by the fact that we do not know the real motives which prompted the *dramatis personae* to act in the way they did, nor do we have adequate information concerning the legal and social background of our narrative. Thus although adultery was a serious offense (see Lev 20:10; Deut 22:22) it is very likely that wives who committed adultery were divorced (and perhaps humiliated) but they were not put to death, during the pre-exilic period (cf. Hos 2; Jer 3:6–14).

Moreover, it would make a great deal of difference if Bathsheba were a victim rather than an accomplice. Even if death penalty were mandatory for men who were caught in *flagrante delicto,* it is highly doubtful that there was any court in Israel which could try and convict a king. Hence Uriah could hardly have been a real threat to David, unless the legal implications were more serious than those described above, and if *only the husband* (not the community) was entitled to bring the charges (cf. Num 5:11–15).

Consequently, it is far from clear why David felt it necessary to liquidate Uriah, especially since this murderous act could not remove the divine judgment. So it is possible that the only obvious gain was the outward protection of Bathsheba's and David's honor. However, in spite of Uriah's death, it is still a question whether the child could be *claimed* to be David's. It would largely depend upon the lapse of time between the adultery and David's marriage with Bathsheba, which must have been at least two months if not more.

Thus the death of Uriah appears nearly pointless while the callous scheme itself becomes exceedingly despicable. It is ironic in the extreme that the one who ought to be the guardian of the people's rights and justice should murder his loyal servant and cause the deaths of other faithful soldiers in order to protect the facade of his honor which he himself had already disgraced. Of course, it is unlikely that David intended the other casualties but the implementation of his deadly plan necessarily involved the death of innocent Israelites (v 24). Moreover, after the tragic event we have David's cynical comment when he comforted Joab by saying that this loss of men was an inevitable part of the fortunes of war!

Perhaps, the most serious charge against David was this that he was more concerned with the protection of his badly dented honor than with the caring for the divine law. One could nearly say, that as far as David was concerned, the deterrent value of the divine sanctions was zero, at least in this situation. Consequently, he was not afraid to commit a murder by proxy to cover his adultery.

Nathan's Parable and Its Sequel (11:27b–12:25)

Bibliography

Altpeter, G. "II Sam 12,1–15a: Eine strukturalistische Analyse." *TZ* 38 (1982) 46–52. **Boer, P. A. H. de.** "2 Samuel 12:25." In *Studia Biblica et Semitica Theodoro Christiano Vriezen Dedicata,* ed. W. C. Van Unnik and A. S. Van der Woude. Wageningen: Veenman, 1966. 25–29. **Brueggemann, W.** "The Trusted Creature." *CBQ* 31 (1969) 484–98. **Coats, G. W.** "Parable, Fable, and Anecdote: Storytelling in the Succession Narrative." *Int* 35 (1981) 368–82. ———. "II Samuel 12:1–7a." *Int* 40 (1986) 170–75. **Coxon, P. W.** "A Note on 'Bathsheba' in 2 Samuel 12, 1–6." *Bib* 62 (1981) 247–50. **Hagan, H.** "Deception as Motif and Theme in 2 Sm 9–20; 1 Kgs 1–2." *Bib* 60 (1979) 301–26. **Honeyman, A. M.** "The Evidence for Regnal Names among the Hebrews." *JBL* 67 (1948) 13–25. **Phillips, A.** "The Interpretation of 2 Sam. xii 5–6." *VT* 16 (1966) 242–44. **Rofé, A.** "Classes in the Prophetical Stories: Didactic Legenda and Parable." VTSup 26 (1974) 143–64. **Roth, W. M. W.** "You Are the Man! Structural Interaction in 2 Samuel 10–12." *Semeia* 8 (1977) 1–13. **Schill, S.** "Zu 2 Sam. 12, 6." *ZAW* 11 (1891) 318. **Schwally, F.** "Zur Quellenkritik der historischen Bücher." *ZAW* 12 (1892) 153–61. **Seebass, H.** "Nathan und David in II Sam 12." *ZAW* 86 (1974) 203–11. **Simon, U.** "The Poor Man's Ewe-Lamb: An Example of a Juridical Parable." *Bib* 48 (1967) 207–42. **Stamm, J. J.** "Der Name des Königs Salomo." *TZ* 16 (1960) 285–97. ———. "Hebräische Ersatznamen." *Studies in Honor of Benno Landsberger on His Seventy-fifth Birthday, April 21, 1965.* The Oriental Institute of the University of Chicago. Assyriological Studies, 16. Chicago: UC Press, 1965. 413–24. **Veijola, T.** "Salomo—der Erstgeborene Bathsebas." VTSup 30 (1979) 230–50. **Vorster, W. S.** "Reader-Response, Redescription, and Reference: 'You Are The Man' (2 Sam 12:7)." *Text and Reality. Aspects of Reference in Biblical Texts,* ed. B. C. Lategan and W. S. Vorster. Atlanta, Georgia: Scholars Press, 1985. 95–112. **Wyatt, N.** "'Jedidiah' and Cognate Forms as a Title of Royal Legitimation." *Bib* 66 (1985) 112–25. **Yaron, R.** "The Coptos Decree and 2 Sam XII 14." *VT* 9 (1959) 89–91.

Translation

27b *The thing which David had done displeased Yahweh* [1] *and he* [a] *sent Nathan* [b] *to David. When he came to him, he said to him,* [c] *"There were two men in the same city, one rich and the other poor.* 2 *The rich man* [a] *had very many sheep and cattle* 3 *while the poor* [a] *man had nothing but one little ewe lamb which he had bought.* [b] *He reared it and it grew up* [b] *together with him and with his children. It would share* [c] *his morsel of bread and would drink from his cup; it slept in his lap and was like his own daughter.*

4 *One day a traveler came to the rich man* [a] *but he was reluctant to take from his own sheep and cattle to provide for the wayfarer who had come to him. So he took the poor man's* [b] *ewe lamb and prepared it for the man who had come to him."* 5 *Then David became very indignant at the man, and he said to Nathan, "As Yahweh lives, the man who has done this deserves to die.* 6 *He shall repay the ewe lamb fourfold* [a]*, because he has done this thing and because he had no* [b] *compassion."* 7a *"You are the man!" Nathan said to David.*

7b *Thus has Yahweh, the God of Israel, said, "It was I who anointed you king*

over Israel, likewise it was I who delivered you from the hand of Saul. [8]*I gave
you your master's house,*[a] *and your master's wives in your lap. I even gave you the
house*[b] *of Israel and Judah, and had this not been enough I would have added to
you accordingly.*[c] [9]*Why then have you despised Yahweh,*[a] *doing what is evil in
his*[b] *sight? You have murdered Uriah the Hittite with the sword and have taken
his wife to be your wife. Yes, you have killed him with the sword of the Ammonites.*
[10]*Therefore the sword shall never*[a] *be far from your family because you have despised
me and have taken the wife of Uriah the Hittite to be your wife."* [11]*Thus has
Yahweh said, "I am going to raise up trouble against you out of your own family;
I will take your wives and give them to another*[a] *before your very eyes, and he will
lie with your wives in view of this sun.* [12]*Although*[a] *you did this deed in secret, I
will do it in front of all Israel and in front of the sun."* [13]*Then David said to
Nathan, "I have sinned against Yahweh!" Nathan replied to David, "Yahweh on
his part has forgiven your sin; you shall not die.* [14]*However, because you have
shown utter contempt for Yahweh*[a] *by this deed, the child who will be born*[b] *to you
shall surely die."*[c] [15a]*Then Nathan returned to his house.*

[15b]*So Yahweh*[a] *struck the child that Uriah's wife had born to David, and it
became ill.* [16]*Then David implored God*[a] *on behalf of the boy and he*[b] *fasted; he
even used to go and spend the night lying*[c] *on the ground.* [17]*When the elders of
his house stood*[a] *beside*[b] *him to raise him up from the ground, he refused and
would not eat*[c] *any food with them.* [18]*On the seventh day the child died, but the
servants of David were afraid to tell him that the child was dead because they
argued,*[a] *"When we spoke to him while the child was alive, he did not take any
notice of us; how then can we tell him that the child is dead? He might do some
harm!"* [19]*However, David became aware that his servants were whispering among
themselves and he*[a] *realized that the child was dead. Therefore David asked his
servants, "Is the child dead?" They replied, "He is dead."* [20]*Then David arose
from the ground, washed himself, and anointed himself. When he had changed his
clothes*[a] *he went to the house of Yahweh and prostrated himself in worship. Later
he went to his own house, and* [b]*at his request*[b] *they set food before him, and he
ate.* [21]*Then his servants said to him, "What is the meaning of this thing that you
have done? While*[a] *the child was alive you fasted and wept,*[b] *now that the child is
dead you get up and eat food!"* [22]*David replied, "While the child was alive, I
fasted and wept because I thought, 'Who knows? Yahweh* [a]*may be gracious to me*[a]
and the child may yet live.' [23]*But now he is dead! Why should I fast? Have I the
power to bring him back?* [a] *I shall go to him, but he will not return to me."* [24]*Then
David comforted Bathsheba, his wife: he went in to her and slept with her. Eventually,
she bore a son, and she called*[a] *his name Solomon. Yahweh loved him* [25]*and sent
a message by Nathan, the prophet, that his name should be called Jedidiah, on
account*[a] *of Yahweh.*

Notes

1.a. MT: "Yahweh."

1.b. Some MSS add the explanatory הנביא "the prophet."

1.c. Some scholars add here, on the basis of G[L], הגד נא לי את המשפט הזה "Pass judgment
on this case for me." However, we regard it as an explicative addition.

2.a. Repointing the MT to make the expression definite (so GKC §126d), and to balance
לרש "the poor man" in v 3.

3.a. For the lack of *'aleph* in רש "poor man," see GKC, § 72p.

3.b-b. Syr has only the first verb. We retain the MT since it provides a better quantitative balance to ועם בניו יחדו "and with his children together."

3.c. Lit., "eat (from)." For the frequentative use of imperfect, see GKC, § 107e; Williams, *Syntax*, § 168.

4.a. Adding the article to איש "man"; cf. GKC, § 126x.

4.b. Syr omits האיש "the man" but the fuller reading of MT balances (ה)איש העשיר "the rich man" at the beginning of the verse.

6.a. So MT. G^L has "sevenfold" (= שבעתים) which is often regarded as the original reading (cf. Driver, 291). For this use of the dual, see GKC, § 97h.

6.b. Many scholars follow Schill (*ZAW* 11 [1891] 318) in reading לו "to him" for MT לא "not," i.e., David "was reluctant to take from what belonged to him."

8.a. Syr suggests בת "daughter" but this variant may be an inner corruption in the Syr text (see Carlson, 152).

8.b. Many exegetes read בנות "daughters" with Syr instead of בית "house" in the MT.

8.c. Lit., "as they and as they;" cf. 24:3.

9.a. Omitting דבר "word of" before "Yahweh" with G^L and Theod, which may be a euphemistic gloss to avoid making Yahweh into the direct object of the verb "to despise." Cf. v 10.

9.b. So K while Q (similarly Tg, Vg) reads בעיני "in my eyes." Both variants are possible but the former fits the context better.

10.a. The Heb. עד עולם "for ever" may mean in this context: "as long as David lives" (cf. 7:14).

11.a. רעיך (lit., "your neighbor") is singular not plural (see Driver, 292) since the noun is רעה.

12.a. For the concessive use of כי, see Williams, *Syntax*, § 448.

14.a. We read יהוה "Yahweh" with one Greek MS. MT has איבי יהוה "enemies of Yahweh" which must be a euphemistic expression.

14.b. ילוד is probably a pass qal ptcp (see *HALAT*, 394 b).

14.c. The reading in 4QSam^a reflects the usual formula of capital punishment; it reads יומת "he shall be put to death" for MT ימות "he shall die."

15.a. 4QSam^a has אלהים "God," so also G^L.

16.a. Tg and Vg read "Yahweh."

16.b. Lit., "David."

16.c. 4QSam^a (as well as G^{LMN}) adds the explanatory בשק "in sackcloth"; cf. 1 Kgs 21:27. It is possible that ולן "used to spend the night" and ושכב "and used to lie" are two alternative readings.

17.a. McCarter (297) reads ויקרבו "they approached," following G^L and 4QSam^a (if the reading of the fragmentary text is right). MT has ויקמו "they stood," which is, perhaps, more problematic.

17.b. 4QSam^a reads אליו "to him."

17.c. MT has ברא for the normal ברה (so 4QSam^a and many Heb. MSS); cf. GKC, § 75rr.

18.a. Lit., "said."

19.a. MT: "David."

20.a. K has the sg שמלתו "garment," while Q reads the pl שמלתיו.

20.b-b. MT: "he asked"; perhaps the object should be supplied (i.e., לחם "bread, food") with G which has "he asked for food."

21.a. Reading בעוד "while," following G^L, Syr, Tg. MT has בעבור "for the sake of"; see also v 22.

21.b. NAB, McCarter (298) follow G and OL, and add ותשקד "and kept a vigil." However, this may be an explanatory gloss; see David's reply in v 22.

22.a-a. So K while Q reads, unnecessarily, וחנני (cf. GKC, § 120c).

23.a. Deleting עוד "again," with G^L.

24.a. So Q (ותקרא) while K reads ויקרא "he called."

25.a. G^{LMN} suggest בדבר "at the command of. . . ." MT is usually preferred as the *lectio difficilior* (but see Smith, 326).

Form / Structure / Setting

Nathan's parable and its sequel must be seen in their wider context. McCarter, e.g., has argued that chaps. 10–12 were affixed to the account of Absalom's rebellion (chaps. 13–20) "as a kind of theological preface" (276) to provide an explanation for the subsequent tragic events. This description of the function of chaps. 10–12 seems to be right in the canonical form of chaps. 10–20 but it is a question whether the original SN contained 11:27b–12:15a.

The story of the Ammonite-Aramean wars (10:1–19 + 11:1 + 12:26–31 + 8:3–8) may well have served as the historical setting and vehicle for the David-Bathsheba-Uriah story (11:2–12:25; cf. also *Form / Structure / Setting* of 10:1–19). According to McCarter (306) this latter narrative may have come from a prophetic group, and it probably incorporates an older story which is contained in 11:2–27 + 12:15b–25; this older narrative lacks any explicit ethical and theological evaluation of David's behavior. One gets the impression that this is the way kings act and therefore no further comment is needed (see also 1 Sam 8:11–17). Already Schwally (*ZAW* 12 [1892] 155–56) had argued that v 15 is a continuation of 11:27. The remainder (11:27b–12:15a) is reminiscent of later prophetic materials, such as 1 Kgs 20:35–42; Isa 5:1–7; Jer 3:1; Hag 2:10–14, but it, too, may not be homogeneous. All these observations and suggestions do not, however, preclude the possibility that the SN in its original form was produced in the early part of Solomon's reign (so Mettinger, *King and Messiah*, 32) and that its main purpose may have been to provide legitimation for the dynastic claims of the house of David as well as for Solomon's accession to the throne. Therefore chaps. 11–12, as far as they were part of the SN, served the same end: David's adultery with Bathsheba and Uriah's murder could not be denied but they could be shown in a different light. Above all, it could be stressed that David had already been punished and that therefore the dynasty as such was free from David's sin and its consequences. Furthermore, even before the succession becomes an important issue in the SN, the later successful claimant is hinted at by means of his name: Jedidiah.

The so-called prophetic section (11:27b–12:15a) consists of three main parts: the parable itself (11:27b–12:7a) which has a certain poetic quality; the oracular threat (vv 7b–12) and David's repentance (vv 13–15a).

Nathan's parable has been often defined as a "juridical parable" (see Simon, *Bib* 48 [1967] 208) which, apparently, disguises a real-life violation of the law as a parable told to the guilty person in order to lead him to pass a judgment on himself. This then means that the parable and its presentation must be as realistic as possible (cf. 1 Kgs 20:35–43) until the "camouflage" is suddenly dropped, and the unsuspecting hearer is trapped in his own self-condemnation by some such phrase as "You are the man!"

There are similar judgment-eliciting parables in 2 Sam 14:1–20; 1 Kgs 20:35–43; Isa 5:1–7, and they all share a similar basic structure, well illustrated by Nathan's parable. There is the introduction (11:27b–12:1a) which is followed by the supposed legal case (vv 1b–4) and the judgment elicited (vv 5–6); finally, the judgment is reapplied to the actual culprit himself (v 7a). In Isa 5:3–4 there is an explicit appeal for judgment but in the other parables this is only implied by the setting (but cf. the Lucianic addition in 2 Sam 12:1 "Pass judgment on this case for me").

It has been often assumed that the judgment eliciting parables in 2 Samuel depict authentic legal cases which were actually brought to David but, on

the other hand, it is more likely that they were literary devices (as in Isa
5:1–7) or constructions to provide an interpretation of events in retrospect.
It is very doubtful that any real-life legal case would be presented in such
vague terms: the parties concerned remain nameless and their location is
unspecified (cf. 15:2), there are no witnesses and many relevant questions
are not raised at all. Thus it seems that the "decision" elicited would be
applied for the sake of dramatic effect; it was part of the storyteller's art,
not a binding legal precedent (cf. also Gunn, *King David*, 41). However precious
a pet lamb may be to a poor man, its thief could hardly be put to death,
while adultery and murder had their appropriate punishments in the Israelite
law (see Exod 21:12; Lev 20:19; Deut 22:22). There is also a gulf between
the essential details of the parable and the actual crimes committed; hence
H. Gunkel (*Das Märchen im Alten Testament*, [Tübingen: Mohr, 1921] 35–37)
once suggested that the parable may have belonged to the stock of folktales
and that originally it had nothing to do with David's offenses. If so, it was
reapplied and used as a very effective literary device to stress the appalling
nature of David's transgression. Had David suddenly heard the parable without
the benefit of chap. 11 or a similar introduction, it is questionable whether
he would have guessed the specific accusation leveled against him by the
prophet's use of the parable. However, the lack of correspondence between
the parable and David's crimes need not create a problem because what is
stressed is not identity but comparison (see Vorster, *Text and Reality*, 111):
David is *like* the rich man in the parable.

The oracular threat (vv 7b–12) is reminiscent of the prophetic admonitions
(see Simon, *Bib* 48 [1967] 234). Vv 7b–8 outline Yahweh's previous acts of
kindness and deliverance, and this is followed by the accusation (v 9) and
the concluding judgment (vv 10–12). Mettinger (*King and Messiah*, 30) regards
vv 7b–10a (or 7b–12) as of Deuteronomistic origin. It is indeed possible that
these verses are a later addition since David's repentance in vv 13–15a forms
an appropriate response to the parable and provides a fitting conclusion.
Moreover, it is difficult to harmonize the threat in vv 7b–12 with the essential
data of the parable although this is not imperative.

The final episode (vv 15b–25) may well be a continuation of 11:27a, and
it consists of two main parts: David's vigil and the death of the ill-fated child
(vv 15b–23) and the birth of Solomon (vv 24–25). The relative length of
these two sections suggest that neither the final episode (vv 15b–25) nor
chaps. 10–12 as a whole, should be described as the birth story of Solomon
(cf. McCarter, 307) even though vv 24–25 are significant as pointers to the
future developments and form a sort of muted climax of chaps. 10–12. Perhaps,
this was all that was necessary at this point and appropriate in the given
circumstances.

Comment

27b It is possible that this sentence was intended to provide a deliberate
contrast to David's words addressed to Joab (v 25). Gordon (256) prefers a
more literal rendering which brings out, perhaps, the correspondence of
both verses: "Do not let this matter *be evil in your eyes* . . . ," (v 25a) and

". . . *was evil in the eyes of the Lord*" (v 27b). However, it is less certain that the meaning of "be evil. . . ." is the same in both contexts.

1–4 Here we have a parable, not an allegory or fable (but see Coats, *Int* 40 [1986] 170–75). It clearly stresses the enormity of the nature of the offense by means of a contrast of opposites: rich—poor; many flocks and herds—single pet lamb like one's own child. In the end the one who has practically everything takes away the only treasured possession of the one who has next to nothing. Thus it is not simply the act that is so monstrous, in the given circumstances, but rather the very nature of the offender as it is revealed by his actions. This is further emphasized by yet another contrast; the rich man acts as an outwardly generous and considerate host yet he is entertaining his visitor with fare obtained by the most despicable means. It is such a person who is practically worthy of death; how much more a similar man who is involved not only in stealing but also in adultery and murder.

5 The Hebrew בן מות (lit., "son of death") has given rise to much discussion. Its usual rendering has been "deserves to die" (so RSV, NEB, NIV) but McCarter (299) has argued that the above expression "is characterizing the man's behavior, not condemning him to death." Therefore he translates it by "fiend of hell." However, we follow the traditional interpretation in view of 1 Sam 20:31–32. Here Saul describes David as בן מות and Jonathan's response is, "Why should he be put to death?" Also in 1 Sam 26:16 we find a similar usage (see also Phillips, *VT* 16 [1966] 243). Perhaps, we should also note that בן מות refers essentially to a subjective judgment or evaluation, not to a legal decision (cf. the popular expression, "He ought to be shot!").

6 It is possible that v 6a, or the whole verse, is a later explanatory insertion by a scribe (cf. Seebass, *ZAW* 86 [1974] 204) who was aware that the law required only a fourfold restitution (see Exod 22:1 [MT 21:37]; cf. also Luke 19:8). The G reading ("sevenfold") may reflect a proverbial compensation (see Prov 6:31). It is also somewhat doubtful that שבעתים "sevenfold," if original, was intended to call to mind "Bathsheba" (בת שבע); but see Coxon, *Bib* 62 (1981) 250. The reader might be prepared for it but hardly the unsuspecting David! The judgment elicited by the parable must be limited to vv 5 and 6b. If v 6a were authentic, it would provide an anti-climax and, short of allegorical interpretation, it would have little or no relevance to the real-life situation underlying the disguise of the parable.

7b For the messenger formula, see *Comment* on 7:5. The anointing mentioned may refer to 1 Sam 16:13 rather than to 2 Sam 2:4 or 5:3 or both.

8 NEB (following Syr) takes the whole verse as referring to the wives which David had been given or might have had (so also McCarter, 292). This is possible but the textual evidence for this is rather slender. Unfortunately, the alternative interpretation has its own problems. Hertzberg (313) has suggested that the giving of "the house of Saul" in our context means "the possession of the female members of the house." Yet this seems tautological in view of the following "master's wives." Perhaps, "the house" is here an inclusive term, comprising both the family and its estates; this may be implied by G^L with its "everything belonging to Saul" (cf. Caspari, 542).

The "house of Israel and Judah" may refer to political supremacy rather than to the unmarried daughters of Israel and Judah. There is no evidence in the OT that David ever married Saul's wives (see *Comment* on 2:2) although such a practice is attested in the ancient Near East as a whole and, perhaps, also in Israel (see Tsevat, *JSS* 3 [1958] 237–43). It seems that Saul had only one wife, Ahinoam (see 1 Sam 14:50) and one concubine, Rizpah (see 2 Sam 3:7; 21:8); however, this evidence may not be exhaustive.

9–12 According to 11:24 Uriah was shot by an archer, therefore "the sword" in 12:9 is not to be taken in its literal sense, and consequently, there is no contradiction (see also 11:25). Some scholars regard the last sentence of v 9 as a later explanatory addition because of the double mention of the same murder.

Since David's crime involved bloodshed, so also his retributive punishment will bring with it a similar violence. V 11, in particular, looks very much like a prophecy after the event in order to provide a theological interpretation of Absalom's rebellion and, especially, of his appropriation of David's concubines (16:21–22).

13 In the MT there is a space after v 13a, which may suggest a cross-reference, in this case, perhaps, to Ps 51 which is often regarded as an early "commentary" on our text. This may also be implied by the historical note in the heading of Ps 51.

For "has forgiven your sin" the NEB offers the following paraphrase: "has laid on another the consequence of your sin." Similarly, McCarter (301) notes that "sin cannot simply be forgiven: It must be atoned for." Thus in our passage the sin is "transferred" to the child who dies instead of David. However, this must be understood in the light of the existing concept of the unitary nature of the family or its corporate responsibility (cf. also J. W. Rogerson, *JTS* 21 [1970] 5).

It may well be that this and similar ideas were essentially deductions from real-life experiences. Thus, e.g., David had clearly sinned and the child died, while David himself lived on. Consequently, in the existing religious setting, it would be quite reasonable to argue that the sin had been "transferred" to the child, and that therefore the sinner could be regarded as forgiven. If vv 7b–12 are a Deuteronomistic addition, then they would imply that at a later time it was seen in retrospect that the child's death was not the sum total of David's punishment (as suggested by v 14) but that the whole unseemly succession struggle was part of the divine judgment.

14 MT and most versions read "the enemies of Yahweh" (אֹיְבֵי יהוה) but it is very likely that אֹיְבֵי "enemies" is a euphemistic gloss, just as "the enemies of David" (1 Sam 25:22) is a substitute for "David" (so G). 4QSam[a] offers an alternative euphemism in reading דְּבַר יהוה "the word of Yahweh" (cf. Ulrich, *Qumran Text*, 138). Therefore we assume that the original reading must have been "Yahweh" and this is further supported by the usage of נִאֵץ "to show contempt," which does not appear to have a causative meaning in the OT (see *HALAT*, 622a).

15b–17 During the unspecified illness of the child, David behaved as if he were a mourner: he fasted and did not anoint himself with oil. However, all this may be linked with the fact that he besought Yahweh for the child's recovery (cf. also Isa 38:1–2).

18 The "seventh day" is to be reckoned from the time when the child

became ill, not from the day of his birth, as suggested by Kimḥi (so also
Veijola, VTSup 30 [1979] 242). Therefore the actual age of the child at the
time of its death, is unknown.

20–23 David's conduct after the death of the child appeared incomprehen-
sible to the courtiers. Instead of mourning, David now dispensed of all outward
signs of grief (cf. v 20). According to the explanation given (vv 22–23), there
was no longer any point in fasting and weeping; the child was dead and
could not be brought back to life.

To us his attitude is equally unfathomable; he had mourned previously
over Saul (1:11–12) and Abner (3:31–35), and he also mourned later over
Amnon (13:36–37) and Absalom (18:33–19:4). Therefore one can hardly
speak about David's new revolutionary attitude (so Pedersen) or to regard
the child as a sacrifice (so Hertzberg, 316). It is equally unlikely that David
mourned for the child proleptically (cf. Fokkelman, *King David*, 90); as v 22
explains, this was essentially a self-humiliation before Yahweh, as well as
supplication in the hope that God might save the child. However, it is surprising
that he did not mourn after the death of the child. V 23 does not necessarily
imply that mourning as such is pointless (as argued by Würthwein, *Thronfolge*,
26; Stolz, 242); it only states that at this stage fasting and intercession for
the child's restoration (cf. v 16) have served their useful purpose because
Sheol is a place of no return (v 23b; cf. Job 7:9; 10:21). Thus intercession
and self-humiliation should not be confused with the expression of grief
and mourning, even though we are not informed as to why David did not
mourn.

Very tentatively we would argue that temporarily Uriah's death lent respect-
ability to Bathsheba and to David, and the people in general may have thought
that the child born to Bathsheba was Uriah's. Hence David could intercede
for the babe but would not necessarily mourn for him. When eventually the
real parentage of the child became known, the behavior of David became
inexplicable and had to be reinterpreted.

Equally problematic is David's visit of the "house of Yahweh." In view of
what we have been told previously (see *Comment* on 7:2), the reference must
be to the tent which sheltered the ark, even though "house" would normally
denote a more permanent structure, such as temple. It is, of course, possible
to regard this use of "house" as an anachronism (so McCarter, 302). Less
likely is the argument by Ruprecht (*Der Tempel*, 102) that David had made
use of a Jebusite cultic building situated on Araunah's threshing floor. In
his view, this temple was renovated and enlarged by Solomon. Ruprecht
also draws attention to other Canaanite sanctuaries which had been taken
over by the Israelites; thus his suggestion is not impossible.

24 Bathsheba named her second son Solomon. In the OT the naming
of a child was usually performed by the mother (cf. Gen 29:32; 1 Sam 1:20;
4:21) but it could be done also by the father (cf. Gen 16:15; Exod 2:22).
Traditionally the name "Solomon" has been associated with שלום "peace";
cf. 1 Chr 22:9, 18; Keil, 306; Goldman, 254). More recently it has been taken
as a replacement name ("Ersatzname"; see *Comment* on 5:14), meaning, "his
replacement" and referring either to the first child who had died or, less
likely, to Uriah, Bathsheba's husband. However, Veijola (VTSup 30 [1979]

248) supports the latter alternative and argues that Solomon was really Bathsheba's firstborn, and that 11:27a ("and she bore him a son") should be followed by 12:24b ("and she called his name Solomon"). Thus the story about the "first" child (12:15b–24a) would be a legend, the intention of which was to remove from Solomon the slur that he was the offspring of adultery (Veijola, 241). All in all, it seems more likely that the death of the illegitimate child was a real event which was interpreted as a divine punishment for David's illicit union with Bathsheba. Only the birth of Solomon could be taken as a sign of divine forgiveness.

25 "Jedidiah" may well mean "beloved of Yahweh" (cf. Deut 33:12; see also Ugaritic *ydd il* "beloved of El," for which see Gibson, *Canaanite Myths*, 65, 68). A number of people in the OT, especially kings, had two names, so that in Solomon's case one name might have been a private name while the other a throne name (cf. also Honeyman, *JBL* 67 [1948] 22–23). Yet it is surprising that in spite of the significance of "Jedidiah" it does not appear anywhere else in the OT.

However, whatever may have been the function of this name, it may have been intended to foreshadow future events (cf. Fokkelman, *King David*, 92). Wyatt (*Bib* 66 [1985] 112) takes Jedidiah as a cognomen and sees in it an "affirmation of Solomon's status as heir, thus confirming the succession."

Explanation

The interpretation of Nathan's parable and the related events is closely linked with the tradition history of the material, and at its various stages it may have had different significance. It is possible that the original David-Bathsheba-Uriah narrative consisted only of 11:2–27a + 12:15b–25. Although it passes no explicit judgment on David, it is hardly complimentary to him. Therefore, we would suggest that this narrative represents the essence of the story as told by the Adonijah party, and as retold by the Solomonic faction. The former group would naturally wish to undermine the reputation and status of Bathsheba and Solomon, and perhaps also that of David himself; thus the original version may well have contributed to that end. Its polemical nature may also be implied by the possibility that the contents of David's letter to Joab may have been "leaked" by the latter when he found himself in opposition to the Solomonic party. On the other hand, the present text passes no comment whatsoever on Bathsheba; she appears as a passive figure in these events. Even David's actions are described in a fairly objective (?) manner, without any ethical or theological comments or explicit criticism.

The supposedly later (prophetical or Deuteronomistic?) material in 11:27b–12:15a offers a severe theological judgment of the above events, and sees in the struggle for succession the outworking of Yahweh's punishment, in addition to that already meted out to David through the death of Bathsheba's first child. Thus, among other things, this interpretation stresses that sin must inevitably bring retribution in its train, even David could not escape the consequences.

It seems that the later redactors took an increasingly serious view of David's transgressions, especially if vv 7b–12 were a still further elaboration of 11:27b–

12:7a + 13–15a. So in the final form chap. 12 shows evil for that it is and what it will breed. Yet there is also an element of surprise: in spite of all, Yahweh is willing to show mercy—with Jedidiah (or Solomon) there can be a new beginning. This may have been a hopeful message to the exilic community.

It is possible that the narrative contained in chaps. 11–12 was part of the Solomonic apologia or propaganda. To be successful it did not have to tell lies or distort facts; rather it had to appeal to what was already known or believed. At the same time, it had to reshape and supplement the shared information, beliefs and hopes. Thus the inherently detrimental David-Bathsheba-Uriah story could not be disregarded for it would not go away. However, it could be retold in less critical manner and it could be rendered innocuous by the addition of David's repentance, Yahweh's forgiveness and the punishment imposed. Thus the way was open for a future reversal of fortunes. Vv 24–25, in particular, contain an implicit promise of better things to come: Yahweh loved Solomon!

The Subjugation of Ammon   (12:26–31)

Bibliography

Galling, K. "Die Ausrufung des Namens als Rechtsakt in Israel." *TLZ* 81 (1956) 65–70. **Heider, G. C.** *The Cult of Molek.* JSOTSup 43. Sheffield: JSOT Press, 1985. **Keel, O.** *The Symbolism of the Biblical World.* Tr. T. J. Hallett. London: SPCK, 1978. **O'Ceallaigh, G. C.** "And *so* David did to *all the cities* of Ammon." *VT* 12 (1962) 179–89. **Sawyer, J. F. A.** "David's Treatment of the Ammonites (2 Samuel 12:31). A Study in the History of Interpretation." *TGUOS* 26 (1975–76 [1979]) 96–107. **Shea, W. H.** "Milcom as the Architect of Rabbath-Ammon's Natural Defenses in the Amman Citadel Inscription." *PEQ* 111 (1979) 17–25. **Stoebe, H. J.** "David und der Ammoniterkrieg." *ZDPV* 93 (1977) 236–46.

Translation

26 *Joab fought against Rabbah of the Ammonites and captured the royal* [a] *citadel.* 27 *Then Joab sent messengers to David* [a-a] *with the following message:* [a] *"I have fought against Rabbah and* [b] *I have captured* [c-c] *the citadel guarding the water supply.* [c] 28 *Now therefore, assemble the rest of the militia, encamp against the city and capture it yourself* [a] *lest I* [b] *capture the city* [c-c] *and my name be associated with it."* [c] 29 *So David gathered the entire militia and went to Rabbah. He fought against it and captured it.* 30 *Then he took the crown of* [a] *their king* [a] *from his head. Its weight was a talent of gold and in it* [b] *was a precious stone; from now on it was on David's head. He also brought out exceedingly great booty from the city.* 31 *Likewise, he brought out the people who were in her, and put them* [a] [b-b] *at tearing her down* [b] *with iron picks and iron axes; later he employed* [c] *them at brickworks.* [d] *He did the same to all the cities of the Ammonites and, finally, David and the entire army returned to Jerusalem.*

Notes

26.a. Wellhausen (185) alters המלוכה "royal" into המים "waters" as in v 27 (so also Driver, 293, and many others) but there is no textual support for this change.

27.a-a. Lit., "and he said."

27.b. Reading וגם "and also" with many MSS. MT omits the conjunction *wāw.*

27.c-c. MT has עיר המים (lit., "city of waters") which is probably the "royal citadel" (עיר המלוכה) mentioned in v 26. Syr and Tg read עיר המלוכה also in v 27 but this may be a deliberate emendation.

28.a. Adding with G[L] the emphatic "you" (אתה).

28.b. The pronoun אני "I" is emphatic.

28.c-c. Lit., "and my name be called over it."

30.a-a. So MT, Syr, Tg as well as G[L] and Josephus (*Ant.* 7.161) while some Greek MSS have "Milcom, their king." Many scholars simply repoint the consonantal text and read "Milcom."

30.b. Reading with 1 Chr 20:2 ובה "and in it"; so also Syr and Tg.

31.a. Assuming that the object of וישם is "them" (i.e., the people; so OL). 1 Chr 20:3 has וישר "and he sawed (them)" for MT וישם "and he put . . . ," but the former reading may be a later reinterpretation of David's punitive measures.

31.b-b. Repointing the MT מגרה as a piel (from מגר ["to drag down"]) inf constr with the 3 f sg pronom suff (so O'Ceallaigh, *VT* 12 [1962] 183), and translating it as "at tearing her (i.e., the city) down."

31.c. MT has והעביר "he made (them) pass through"; many exegetes emend it to והעביד "and he set (them) to work" or ". . . employed them."

31.d. Reading בְּמַלְבֵּן "at brickworks" or "brickmold" with Q for the rather odd בְּמַלְכֵּן (so K) which O'Ceallaigh (*VT* 12 [1962] 189) translates as "(he made them desecrate) the Molechs," and he regards it as an Aramaic plural form.

Form / Structure / Setting

This episode is a continuation of 11:1, and it belongs to the account of the Ammonite-Aramean wars (see *Form / Structure / Setting* of 10:1–19) but it need not represent the final stage of these hostilities. In the present sequence, it is a sort of flashback (see Fokkelman, *King David*, 94) but it serves as a fitting conclusion to the Ammonite war. Its logical place would be after 11:25 since it is reasonable to assume that we are dealing with one and the same war. The present displacement allows the thematically more important events to unfold without any interruption.

D. F. Payne (212) has actually suggested that "Ammon was probably the first territory outside Israel to be annexed to the Israelite throne." It is quite plausible that David would have dealt first with the smaller neighboring states before venturing against the powerful Aramean cities in the more distant north, as outlined in 8:3–8. This episode, as well as the other parts of the war report, may have been derived from the state archives which provided the raw material for the later author.

Comment

26–27 We have tentatively assumed that the "royal citadel" is the same place as "the citadel guarding the water supply" (lit., "city of waters:" so KJV, RSV). Driver (293) has drawn attention to a parallel in Polybius' account (*Histories*, 571) of the capture of Rabbah in 218 B.C. by Antiochus III. He, too, captured the city's water supply first.

28 The exact meaning of "and my name be associated with it" is not clear. It may well be a formulaic expression suggesting possession or ownership (cf. Deut 28:10; 2 Sam 6:2; 1 Kgs 8:43; see also Galling, *TLZ* 81 [1956] 67). However, it is unlikely that Joab would have become the owner of Rabbah. In our context the reference is probably to one's fame as the conqueror of a particular city (cf. Ishida, *Royal Dynasties*, 126). Joab may have been less concerned with the reputation of David as such than with the customary military practice, allowing the king to gain the victor's crown.

30 It is difficult to decide whether in this verse the reference is to "their king" or to the god "Milcom." The latter was either the name or title of the patron deity of the Ammonites (see 1 Kgs 11:33; Jer 49:1, 3; Zeph 1:5; cf. also Heider, *The Cult of Molek*, 169–70). The consonantal reading מלכם has been a frequent source of confusion. In this case, the decisive factor may be the weight of the crown which was a talent or some sixty-six pounds (= thirty kilograms), if not more. If this is not an exaggeration, the crown would rest more easily upon the head of the cultic statue than upon the head of the Ammonite king or of David. However, it is possible that the crown (or the stone?) was placed on David's head as a symbolic act (contra Deut 7:25–26). The "precious stone" could be taken in a collective sense, hence, "precious stones" (so Syr).

31 Traditionally it was thought that this verse described the gruesome tortures inflicted by David on the inhabitants of the captured Ammonite cities (so e.g., 1 Chr 20:3 as wall as G, Syr, Josephus, *Ant.* 7.161, KJV, RV).

In more recent years scholars have argued for some form of forced labor service which was imposed upon the vanquished Ammonites; however, this must involve some emendation. Although the former alternative is possible (cf. David's treatment of the Moabite prisoners of war in 8:2 as well as the Ammonite handling of captives in Amos 1:13), we regard the latter alternative as being nearer to the original text. We follow O'Ceallaigh's interpretation (*VT* 12 [1962] 184) that the Ammonites were set to raze down their own city with iron picks and mattocks (see also Keel, *The Symbolism of the Biblical World*, Plate V, which depicts a similar destructive situation). It may be of some relevance to note that in 17:27–29 we find Shobi, the son of Nahash, from Rabbah helping David during his flight from Absalom. This may suggest that David's treatment of the Ammonites was not so severe as to alienate for ever the defeated neighbors.

Sawyer (*TGUOS* 26 [1975–76 (1979)] 102–5) has argued that the original text may have read only וישם במגרה ובמלבן "and he set them to work with stone-saws and brick-molds" and that the present emotive middle section of the sentence was interpolated by the Deuteronomist during the Babylonian exile when the anti-Ammonite feeling was running high.

Explanation

The Ammonite hostilities began with the Ammonite humiliation of David's envoys, and they ended with David's defeat of the Ammonites and their dishonoring. They were not only put to forced labor but they were also set to demolish the defenses of Rabbah, their capital, and those of their other cities. At the same time, this marks the end of the Ammonite independence for some decades to come. The fate of the Ammonite king remains unknown but Ammon itself must have been incorporated into David's kingdom.

Amnon and Tamar   (13:1–22)

Bibliography

Clark, W. M. "A Legal Background to the Yahwist's Use of 'God and Evil' in Genesis 2–3." *JBL* 88 (1969) 266–78. **Delekat, L.** "Tendenz und Theologie der David-Salomo-Erzählung." In *Das Ferne und Nahe Wort*, FS L. Rost, ed. F. Maas. BZAW 105. Berlin: Töpelmann, 1967. 26–36. **Driver, G. R.** "Problems of the Hebrew Text and Language." In *Alttestamentliche Studien*, FS Friedrich Nötscher, ed. H. Junker und J. Botterweck. BBB 1. Bonn: Hanstein, 1950. 46–61. **Hoftijzer, J.** "Absalom and Tamar: A Case of Fratriarchy?" In *Schrift en Uitleg: Studiën aangeboden aan Prof. Dr. W. H. Gispen.* Kampen: Kok, 1970. 54–61. **Long, B. O.** "Wounded Beginnings: David and Two Sons." *Images of Man and God. Old Testament Short Stories in Literary Focus*, ed. B. O. Long. Sheffield: Almond Press, 1981. 26–34. **Mettinger, T. N. D.** *Solomonic State Officials.* ConB OT Series 5. Lund: CWK Gleerup, 1971. **Phillips, A.** "NEBALAH—a Term for Serious Disorderly and Unruly Conduct." *VT* 25 (1975) 237–41. **Ridout, G. P.** "The Rape of Tamar (2 Sam 13:1–22)." In *Rhetorical Criticism: Essays in Honor of James Muilenburg*, ed. J. J. Jackson and M Kessler. Pittsburgh: Pickwick, 1974. 75–84. **Roth, W. M. W.** "NBL." *VT* 10 (1960) 394–409. **Stamm, J. J.** "Hebräische Frauennamen." VTSup 16 (1967) 301–39. **Wenham, G. J.** "Bᵉtûlāh 'a Girl of Marriageable Age.'" *VT* 22 (1972) 326–48. **Wright, G. R. H.** "Dumuzi at the Court of David." *Numen* 28 (1981) 54–61.

Translation

[1] [a]*Another incident took place some time later.*[a] *Absalom, son of David, had a beautiful sister whose name was Tamar, and Amnon, son of David, desired*[b] *her.* [2] *However, Amnon felt frustrated to such an extent that he made himself sick on account of Tamar, his sister, for she was a girl of marriageable age and it seemed impossible to Amnon to do anything to her.* [3] *But Amnon had a friend whose name was Jonadab,*[a] *the son of Shimeah,*[b] *David's brother. Jonadab was very clever,* [4] *and he said to Amnon, "O son of the king, why are you so dejected morning after morning? Will you not tell me?" So Amnon told him, "It is Tamar, my brother Absalom's sister, that I desire."* [5] *Then Jonadab advised him, "Lie down on your bed and pretend to be sick. When your father comes to see you, say to him, 'Please let my sister Tamar come and* [a]*tempt me with some food;*[a] *let her prepare something tasty*[b] *in my sight*[c] *that I may watch and eat it from her hand.'"* [6] *So Amnon lay down and pretended to be sick. When the king came to see him, Amnon said to the king, "Please let my sister Tamar come and make a few*[a] *dumplings in my sight, that I may eat from her hand."*

[7] *Then David sent a message to the palace, to Tamar, saying, "Go to your brother Amnon's house and prepare some food for him."* [8] *So Tamar went to her brother Amnon's house while he was lying down. Then she took dough, kneaded it and made it into dumplings in his sight; finally, she boiled the dumplings.* [9] *Then she took the pan and set*[a] *its contents before him, but he refused to eat and ordered his servants, "Get out of my presence, every one (of you)!" So they went out of his presence, every one (of them).* [10] *Amnon then said to Tamar, "Bring the food into the bedchamber*[a] *that I may eat from your hand." So Tamar took the dumplings which she had made and brought them to her brother Amnon into the bedchamber.* [11] *But when she handed them to him to eat, he seized her, saying to her, "Come,*

lie with me, my sister!" [12] "No, my brother," she said to him, "Do not humiliate me, for such a thing is not done in Israel. Do not perpetrate this outrage. [13] As for me, where could I hide[a] my shame? But you would be like one of the social outcasts in Israel. Better speak to the king, he will not withhold me from you!" [14] However he was unwilling to listen to her; being stronger than she, he dishonored her and lay [a]with her.[a] [15] At the same time, he hated her greatly; indeed, his hatred for her was greater than the desire with which he had desired her. So Amnon said to her, "Get up and be off!" [16] She protested,[a] "Nay, this great wrong in sending me away is more grievous[b] than the other one you did to me!" But he refused to listen to her. [17] Then he called [a]his personal attendant[a] and said, "Send[b] this so-and-so away from me, and bar the door after her." [18] (She had on a long tunic for that is how the marriageable daughters of the king used to dress since their adolescence.)[a] So his servant ejected her and barred the door after her.

[19] Then Tamar put[a] ashes on her head and tore the long tunic which she had on; she also put her hands[b] on her head and went away, [c]crying as she went.[c] [20] Her brother Absalom said to her, "Has Amnon your brother been with you? Keep silent for now, my sister; he is your brother! Do not take this matter too much to heart." So Tamar dwelt as a desolate[a] woman in the house of her brother Absalom. [21] When King David heard of these events, he was angry. [22] However, Absalom did not speak to Amnon either bad or good, even though[a] he[b] hated Amnon for having humiliated his sister Tamar.

Notes

1.a-a. MT: "It happened after this."

1.b. Lit., "loved (her)" but the context itself makes obvious the nature of Amnon's love.

3.a. 4QSam[a] has יהונתן "Jonathan"; so also G[L].

3.b. 4QSam[a] reads שמעיה "Shemaiah" = "Yahweh has heard."

5.a-a. Lit., "cause me to eat food."

5.b. The Heb. הבריה simply means "food."

5.c-c. Lacking in Vg; Syr reads לי "for me."

6.a. Lit., "two."

9.a. Lit., "poured out."

10.a. Two MSS add the directive ה.

13.a. Lit., "take."

14.a-a. We take אתה as a preposition ("with") plus the 3 pers pronom suff ("her"); some MSS read עמה "with her." The MT is pointed as the accusative marker plus the above suffix but the verb שכב "to lie" is intransitive. It is possible that שכב has replaced an original transitive verb which had come to be regarded as obscene by the later scribes (see McCarter, 317); thus the accusative would be a remnant of this original expression.

16.a. Lit., "said."

16.b. Most scholars assume some textual corruption (due to graphic confusion?). We follow G. R. Driver's (*Alttestamentliche Studien*, 48–49) suggestion to read אדה (from אוד "to be grievous") for MT אודת.

17.a-a. Lit., "his servant who attended him."

17.b. MT has the pl verb (a mistake for the sg?) as if Tamar needed to be forcibly ejected.

18.a. Reading מעלומים "from adolescence" instead of MT מעילים "garments," which is slightly tautological.

19.a. Regarding ותקח "and she took" as a pregnant construction (i.e., "she took and she put"); so Conroy, *Absalom*, 34 n.66.

19.b. Reading ידיה "her hands" with G, Syr, Vg while MT has ("her hand").

19.c-c. For the structure, see GKC §113t.

20.a. Taking the *wāw* before שממה "desolate woman" as an explicative *wāw* (see GKC, § 154a n.1b).

22.a. Regarding the conjunction כִּי as having a concessive force (see Williams, *Syntax*, §448).
22.a. MT: "Absalom."

Form / Structure / Setting

It has been argued (cf. Long, *Images of Man and God*, 27) that although chaps. 13–14 are part of a larger complex, they form an episode complete in itself but not an independent story (see Conroy, *Absalom*, 92). These chapters have been regarded as a prologue to the account of Absalom's rebellion (chaps. 15–20), giving a better understanding of the major *dramatis personae* and of the events which contributed to the lengthy process of Absalom's estrangement from his father, culminating in his rebellion and eventual death. Our pericope begins this chain of events but it seems that the opposing parties had already taken their respective positions and had made their intentions clear.

It seems to us that even the Amnon-Tamar story must be seen in the wider context of the struggle for succession and not simply as a matter of private concern: Amnon's infatuation for his beautiful half-sister (so von Rad, *Problems of the Hexateuch*, 181). Amnon and Absalom were, apparently, the two obvious candidates for the throne of Israel. At this stage it was Amnon who was the front runner because he was the eldest of David's sons (see 3:2–5) while Absalom must have been the next in line since Chileab (3:3) may have died earlier. Absalom was, apparently, the most handsome of David's sons (see 14:25) as well as the son of a king's daughter (3:3) and a man of some charm. Hence it is plausible that Amnon's love for Tamar was, largely, part of his plan to put Absalom and his family in their place! In the light of Gen 20:12, we see no reason to doubt the words of Tamar (13:13b) that a marriage between Amnon and her was legally possible. Therefore Lev 18:9, 11; 20:17; Deut 27:22 may be either later than the Davidic reign or these laws were not implemented, at least in Jerusalem or in the royal family. Perhaps, the main problem was not the fact that Tamar was Amnon's half-sister but that she was Absalom's sister. Therefore it seems that although Amnon was attracted by Tamar's beauty he hoped, even more so, both to gratify his sexual desires and to humiliate Absalom through Tamar, at the same time. Consequently, it is understandable why it is noted in v 15 that Amnon's hatred for Tamar was greater than his physical attraction for her. We assume that this was not the result of a sudden change in Amnon's feelings but that it reflects the previously existing attitudes. Likewise it may be of some significance that Absalom's very first words to the distressed Tamar were the euphemistic question, "Has Amnon, your brother, been with you?" (v 20), as if he had foreseen such a possibility. Also his comment, "He is your brother!" (v 20) is, to some extent, colored by sarcasm: as a brother Amnon ought to have known better while Tamar as a sister had no satisfactory legal redress. Thus the overemphasis on the brother-sister relationship in vv 1–22 gives an ironical tone to the whole pericope, especially in retrospect.

The succession dimension may also be implied by the G addition in v 21: Amnon was David's firstborn and therefore his obvious heir; it was, perhaps, for this reason that David took no steps to remedy Amnon's outrage. In any case, the options were limited; if Exod 22:16 is relevant to our episode, then Amnon might have been expected to marry Tamar and to give a marriage present but it is questionable whether this would have suited the plans of Absalom. Moreover, Absalom's family honor was at stake, and this could hardly be satisfied by Tamar's marriage to Amnon and the marriage payment (cf. Gen 34:31). Thus the background of the Tamar-Amnon story was the tension between Amnon and Absalom, and the bone of contention was ultimately the throne of Israel.

According to Ridout ("The Rape of Tamar," *Rhetorical Criticism,* 81) our pericope has a chiastic structure; however, it is somewhat doubtful whether the component parts of the story can be arranged in a neat pattern, without some arbitrary choice. We have adapted Ridout's schema as follows:

A. Amnon's desire for Tamar (vv 1–2)
  B. Amnon's predicament and Jonadab's advice (vv 3–7)
    C. Tamar at Amnon's house (vv 8–10)
      D. Amnon's advances and Tamar's pleading (vv 11–13)
        E. Tamar's humiliation (v 14)
      D'. Amnon's rejection of Tamar and her pleading (vv 15–16)
    C'. Tamar's expulsion from Amnon's house (vv 17–18)
  B'. Tamar's predicament and Absalom's advice (vv 19–20)
A'. Absalom's hatred of Amnon (vv 21–22).

It is possible that verses 1 and 22 form an inclusion (so Conroy, *Absalom,* 17) since both verses mention the chief characters: Absalom, Amnon and Tamar.

Conroy (*Absalom,* 20) defines the function of our pericope "in terms of complication, retardation, and resolution" which have their correlatives in the reader's "expectancy, growth of tension or suspense, and relief." However, v 22 introduces a new complication (Absalom's hatred for Amnon) and gives rise to a new expectancy, thus preparing the way for the further developments in the next pericope (vv 23–39).

Comment

1 The Heb. ויהי אחרי כן is a transition-marker, and it introduces a new episode (see Conroy, *Absalom,* 41–42).

McCarter (101) and others rightly regard "Absalom" as a traditional mispronunciation of the defective spelling of the name (אבשלום). The correct vocalization is *ʾăbîšālôm,* further attested by the Greek Αβεσσαλωμ (cf. also *HALAT,* 6b). However, in translation we have retained the familiar, traditional pronunciation (i.e., Absalom), especially since it is used in the MT. See also *Comment* on 3:4.

We regard Amnon, not Aminon (contra McCarter, 319), as the right pronunciation of the name since it seems to be derived from אמן "to be faithful"; see *HALAT,* 63a; Noth, *Personennamen,* 228. "Aminon" (v 20) may be a diminutive form expressing Absalom's contempt for Amnon (so Driver, 300) unless it is simply the result of a scribal error (so already Wellhausen, 187).

The name "Tamar" probably means "date-palm" (see Stamm, VTSup 16 [1967] 328–29). She is also described as Absalom's sister rather than as David's daughter, thus preparing the reader for further developments.

2 Amnon's plans were thwarted because Tamar, being an unmarried girl or virgin (see Wenham, *VT* 22 [1972] 342–43), may have been confined to women's quarters and carefully guarded (see Ackroyd, 121). He was hardly suffering from genuine love-sickness but rather from frustration that he could not do what he wanted with Tamar (cf. Gen 22:12).

3–5 Jonadab is called Amnon's friend which seems to denote an intimate acquaintance. It is less likely that the reference is to "the best man" usually active at weddings, or to a specific office such as "the friend of the king" who may have been an official counselor (see Mettinger, *Solomonic State Officials,* 63–69).

Jonadab was David's nephew but 4QSamᵃ and Gᴸ call him Jonathan who according to 21:21 was also a son of Shimei (= Shimeah). It is plausible that Jonadab and Jonathan were brothers, hence the confusion.

Jonadab is described as חכם מאד (lit., "very clever" or ". . . wise") but in view of his unethical advise, he appears as a crafty character. So Whybray (*The Succession Narrative,* 58) has well described חכם as "a purely intellectual and morally neutral quality." Von Rad (*Wisdom in Israel,* tr. J. D. Martin [London: SCM, 1972] 20) emphasizes the aspect of being competent or skilled in some particular sphere or way, and that it may be "dissociated from a scale of values," as in Jonadab's case.

Jonadab's advice to Amnon was to feign illness in order to persuade his father, David, to send Tamar that she might take care of him. This then would provide the opportunity which Amnon had been seeking.

6 The significance of Tamar's services is not clear but it may have been believed that food prepared by a virgin in the presence of the sick man might have a special curative quality; Ackroyd (121) suggests a possible "transference of vitality."

The Heb. לבבות has been usually translated as "cakes" of some sort or other (cf. Conroy, *Absalom,* 29, n. 4) but McCarter (322) has well argued that they were "some kind of dumplings or puddings" since they were, apparently, boiled (בשל). "Heart-shaped cakes" (Hertzberg, 323) may sound more romantic but "dumplings" seem to fit the culinary process described; hence tentatively, we follow McCarter's suggestion. Wright (*Numen* 28 [1981] 61, n.5) points out that the food (in his view "cakes") "were intended to be of magical import, whether therapeutic or aphrodisiac." A belief in the former quality is plausible while the latter alternative would make Amnon's scheme too transparent. The cognate verb (לבב) which we have rendered "make" may involve a polysemantic pun. It probably had two meanings: "to make לבבות 'dumplings'" as well as "to arouse" (cf. Cant 4:9) which may have been hinted at in v 8, thus preparing a way for the ensuing events.

9–10 Amnon's imperious command to his attendants may reflect "a courtly formula of dismissal" (so Conroy, *Absalom,* 30, n. 45). It is found also in Gen 45:1. However, its translation is less easy; rsv has "send out every one from me!" but the verb is a hiphil form. We have taken it as inwardly transitive (cf. GKC, § 53d) since the command is addressed to the servants themselves. Absalom's bedchamber was, apparently, a partitioned area of a larger room (so Gordon, 263) since he could see what went on in the "kitchen"!

12–14 The "outrage" (נבלה) denotes a serious breach of customary law, which may have certain implications for Israel as a whole. The usual translation of נבלה used to be "folly" (so e.g., KJV, RSV); however, this has been shown to be inadequate (cf. Phillips, *VT* 25 [1975] 237–41). McCarter and some other scholars render it by "sacrilege" but this may take too much for granted in our passage.

Amnon's rape of Tamar was not incest (see *Form / Structure / Setting*, above) since marriage between Amnon and Tamar was possible (v 13) and there is no indication in our sources that Amnon's offense was regarded as a crime or capital offense. However, McCarter (324) has argued that Amnon was "guilty of both rape and incest." Clearly, this is not impossible because we do not know for certain what marriage prohibitions were in existence in David's time and to what extent they were recognized in Jerusalem and in the royal family.

The frequent use of sibling terms in our pericope does not necessarily point to incest but rather to the lack of fraternal feelings, on the part of Amnon. Therefore we feel that our suggestion provides a plausible alternative. Hence we would argue that in view of Exod 22:16–17, Amnon's misdeed was a rape of an unbetrothed virgin, and theoretically he would be expected to pay the so-called marriage payment and to marry the girl (see also Deut 22:28–29). Legally, the rapist had no choice although the father could refuse to give the girl to him (so Exod 22:17). Therefore by throwing Tamar out into the street Amnon added insult to injury, and revealed his unmistakable intention to humiliate both Tamar and Absalom, more or less implying that she was not fit to be married even by a rapist. Consequently, we can understand Tamar's complaint that her undeserved dismissal is a greater wrong than her previous humiliation. The latter deed could be partly compensated by marriage while her rejection was a final dishonor.

Although Tamar had warned Amnon (v 13) that his misdeed would make him like a social outcast, in the actual situation this was not strictly true. He must have remained the heir apparent, and although David was angry (v 21), he did nothing about Amnon's deceitful offense and Tamar's humiliation. Hence it is very doubtful that Amnon was socially ostracized (contra Conroy, *Absalom*, 33).

15 It has been often suggested that this verse illustrates a psychological transformation of love into hatred (Hertzberg [324]: "sexual hatred") since this so-called love was hardly more than lust while Amnon's hatred of Tamar and her family may well have been part of his mental attitude (if our interpretation of the pericope is right).

18 It seems that v 18a is a later explanatory addition (contra Conroy, *Absalom*, 34), and it would be better if it were placed after 18b.

The Heb. כתנת הפסים "the long tunic" is of uncertain meaning. In Gen 37 it is used of Joseph's coat (vv 3, 23, 32), and it has been often rendered as "multi-colored coat" or "long robe with sleeves" (RSV) or "richly ornamented robe" (NIV). We follow the interpretation provided by G^L and Josephus (*Ant.* 7.171), namely, "long tunic" (i.e., one reaching down to the ankles).

Equally problematic is מעילים "garments"; Wellhausen et al. read מעולם "of old" (so RSV) or "in olden days" (so NAB). We prefer to read מעלומים which we translate as "from adolescence;" deriving it from the same root as עלמה "girl of marriageable age."

19 Tamar behaved like a mourner as if she were a widow (cf. 20:3).

"Hands (or "hand") on her head" is an expression of grief (cf. Jer 2:37; *ANEP*, nos. 634, 640). De Vaux (*Ancient Israel*, 59) points out that this is "the pose of weeping women in certain Egyptian bas-reliefs and on the sarcophagus of Ahiram, king of Biblos."

20 The rhetorical question involves a euphemism (see Gen 39:10); Absalom, apparently, had no difficulty in guessing the nature and cause of Tamar's distress. This may well point to an existing hostility between the two half-brothers. Absalom's advice to Tamar seems rather inadequate; there may be a "tone of tenderness" (so Conroy, *Absalom*, 35) but in view of Tamar's experience the consolation sounds somewhat shallow. However, Absalom's words would appear in a different light if Tamar had rightly guessed that her brother intended revenge in due course (see v 32). It seems that Absalom had evaluated the situation quite realistically; Amnon was Tamar's half-brother, and therefore the whole incident was the concern of the "family" (i.e., David, as its head). Consequently, he may have been fully aware that little could be done to Amnon (see Exod 22:16–17) even if David were prepared to act. The existing law and custom did not take into consideration the injured family pride and honor. So Absalom must have come to the conclusion that he had no real option but to take the law into his own hands, following the example of Simeon and Levi (Gen. 34:30–31).

21 Although the MT makes a reasonable sense, most commentators follow G (and 4QSam ª, as much as survives of it) in adding the following sentence: ולא עצב את רוח אמנון בנו כי אהבו כי בכורו הוא (so *BHK*) which we render: "but he did not curb the excesses (lit., "spirit") of his son Amnon; he favored him because he was his firstborn." It may well be that this sentence is original but was omitted due to a scribal error, when the eye of the scribe skipped from the initial ולא to the following one at the beginning of v 22.

From now on Tamar lived in Absalom's house. Ehrlich (303) takes "desolate" in the sense of "unmarried."

22 This verse sums up the previous events and gives Absalom's reaction to them. It also hints to the tragedy to come.

The reference to "bad or good" may indicate that Absalom did not speak at all to Amnon. Clark (*JBL* 88 [1969] 269) argues that the above phrase implies that Absalom took no legal action but this seems less likely since the offense belonged to the sphere of family law and would not be dealt with in the court. It is also doubtful whether in the given situation Absalom would have wished to force Amnon into a marriage with Tamar. Fokkelman (*King David*, 112) suggests that Absalom did not treat Amnon "in a hostile way;" this may be a reasonable method to conceal one's hatred and planned revenge but it is less certain that it conveys the correct meaning of "bad or good."

Explanation

The meaning of this pericope can be explained adequately only when it is seen as part of chaps. 13–20 which form a self-contained literary unit. It seems that Absalom's rebellion created the most serious political crisis during David's reign, and as such it could have been seen as God's judgment of David (cf. 12:10–13). It could have even been regarded by some as a rejection of the Davidic dynasty as a whole (cf. 16:3). In view of all this, the Absalom stories in their present setting could be interpreted as an attempt to show that the fateful events were brought about not so much by David as by certain able but unworthy sons of David, and to point out how these men disqualified themselves from the high offices of kingship. It may well be that this unfitness had a bearing also upon the possible future claims of their descendants if they had any. Thus the stage would be set for the final struggle between Adonijah and Solomon.

At the same time, this narrative complex seeks to exonerate David; he did not intentionally collaborate with Amnon (13:5–7) or later with Absalom (13:26–27), nor did he have a hand in Absalom's death. In the latter instance, once again, Joab is the chief culprit! Since Absalom had an impressive following among the tribes of Israel, it is likely that chaps. 13–20 were aimed, among other things, at the mollification of Absalom's sympathizers.

The Amnon-Tamar story is one of the most sordid accounts in the OT but it contains no explicit editorial comment; however, the pleading of Tamar (vv 12–13, 16) is a more effective judgment on Amnon's actions than any editorial remarks or moralizing could have been. The fact that the narrator had refrained from passing any explicit moral judgments on the characters involved, may have been part of his technique. Nevertheless, it is fairly clear where his sympathies lie, and the very choice and presentation of the material provide an implicit evaluation. Perhaps, the apparent objectivity was a necessary element in any reasonable apologia or propaganda.

In our opinion, Amnon's offense was a rape of an unbetrothed virgin rather than incest. The outrage was made more serious by Amnon's refusal to marry Tamar. It seems that ultimately the whole incident was part of Amnon's self-assertion over against Absalom and his family. In the given circumstances Absalom could only swallow his pride or follow the example of Simeon and Levi's self-help (Gen 34:25–31). In the end, he chose the latter alternative since it increased, at the same time, his chances of succession, especially if the elimination of Amnon was a justifiable homicide rather than murder.

Absalom's Revenge and Flight   (13:23–37)

Bibliography

Blenkinsopp, J. *Gibeon and Israel*, SOTS Monograph Series 2. Cambridge: CUP, 1972. **Joüon, P.** "Notes Philologiques sur le Texte Hébreu de 2 Samuel." *Bib* 9 (1928) 302–15. **Long, B. O.** "Wounded Beginnings: David and Two Sons." *Images of Man and God. Old Testament Short Stories in Literary Focus*, ed. B. O. Long. Sheffield: Almond Press, 1981. 26–34. **Mazar, B.** "Geshur and Maacah." *JBL* 80 (1961) 16–28. **Sacon, K. K.** "A Study of the Literary Structure of the 'Succession Narrative.'" *Studies in the Period of David and Solomon and Other Essays*, ed. T. Ishida. Winona Lake, IN: Eisenbrauns, 1982. 27–54. **Schunck, K.-D.** "Ophra, Ephron und Ephraim." *VT* 11 (1961) 188–200. **Seebass, H.** "Ephraim in 2 Sam. XIII 23." *VT* 14 (1964) 497–500.

Translation

[23] *Two full years later* [a] *Absalom had sheepshearers at Baal-hazor, near Ephraim, and he* [b] *invited all the king's sons.* [24] *So Absalom went to the king and said, "Since your servant has sheepshearers, let the king and his servants* [a] *go with* [b] *your servant!"* [25] *But the king said to Absalom, "No, my son, we must not all go and be a burden on you." Although Absalom* [a] *urged* [b] *him, he was unwilling to go but gave him his blessing.* [26] *However, Absalom persisted,* [a] *"If not,* [b] *at least let my brother Amnon go* [c] *with us!"* [c] *"Why should he go with you?" the king queried him.* [27] *But when Absalom urged* [a] *him again, he sent Amnon and all the king's sons with him.* [b] *Then Absalom prepared a banquet like the banquet of a king.* [c] [28] *and he* [a] *instructed his servants, "Watch carefully! When Amnon's heart is merry with wine, I shall say to you: 'Strike Amnon!' then kill* [b] *him! Do not be afraid for* [c] *I myself have commanded you!* [c] *Be strong and courageous!" So the servants of Absalom did to Amnon as Absalom had commanded,* [a] *whereupon all the king's sons got up and each man mounted his mule and fled.*

[30] *While they were still on the way, a hearsay reached David to the effect that Absalom had killed all the king's sons and that not one* [a] *of them was left.* [31] *Then the king arose, tore his garments and lay down on the ground; also all his servants* [a] *who were standing about him tore their garments.* [a] [32] *However, Jonadab, the son of Shimeah,* [a] *responded saying, "Let not my lord presume* [c] *that* [d] *all the young squires,* [d] *the king's sons, have been killed for Amnon alone must be dead;* [e] *surely, this must have been intended by Absalom* [e] *since the day that Amnon humiliated his sister Tamar.* [33] *Therefore,* [a] *let not my lord, the king, take this matter too much to heart in presuming that all the king's sons are dead; only Amnon alone must be dead,* [34a] *while Absalom must have fled."* [a] *The servant who kept the watch, looked up and saw many people coming* [b] *along the Horonaim road by the side of the mountain.* [b] [35] *Then Jonadab said to the king, "There now, the king's sons have come! It has happened according to your servant's prediction."* [a] [36] *When he had finished speaking, the king's sons came in and wept aloud; the king also and all his servants wept very bitterly.* [37] *Absalom, however, fled and went to Talmai, son of Ammihud,* [a] *the king of Geshur, while King David mourned for his son for many days.*

Notes

23.a. Lit., "And it came to pass at (the end) of two years, days." For the idiom, see GKC §131d; Driver, 301; cf. also 14:28.

23.b. MT: "Absalom."

24.a. Some emend ועבדיו "and his servants" to וכל בניו "and all his sons"; see Joüon, *Bib*
9 (1928) 308.

24.b. 4QSamª (as well as G^L, OL, and Vg) has אל "to."

25.a. Lacking in MT.

25.b. Reading ויפצר "and he urged" with 4QSamª; MT has ויפרץ "and he pressed."

26.a. Lit., "said"

26.b. The MT ולא forms an abridged conditional clause; see GKC §159dd; cf. also 2 Kgs
5:17.

26.c-c. Omitted by McCarter (330), following 4QSamª.

27.a. See n. 25.b.

27.b-b. Reading with G and OL (so perhaps also 4QSamª, as suggested by the spacing; see
Ulrich, *Qumran Text,* 85) ויעש אבשלום משתה כמשתה המלך. The omission was probably due to
homoioteleuton (המלך . . . המלך).

28.a. MT: "Absalom."

28.b. For the form of המתם, see GKC, § 72w.

28.c-c. MT uses a rhetorical question: "Is it not that I myself. . . ?"

29.a. G, Syr, Vg add "to them" (להם).

30.a. Some Heb. MSS add additional emphasis by reading עד אחד "even one" for MT אחד
"one."

31.a-a. MT: "were standing by with garments torn." We follow G, reading הנצבים עליו
קרעו בגדיהם. The fragmentary 4QSamª (see Ulrich, *Qumran Text,* 129) offers no real help but
it may have read [קרעו איש] בגדיו ("[they tore each man] his garment").

32.a. MT reads "Shimah" (see *Comment* on 13:3–5).

32.b. G and Syr add "the king" (המלך) which may be superfluous (so e.g., Budde, 263) but
see v 33.

32.c. Lit., "say."

32.d-d. McCarter takes הנערים "the servants" as the subject of המיתו "(the servants) killed."
We regard the verb as a passive ("have been killed"); cf. Williams, *Syntax,* § 160.

32.e-e. The text may be in some disorder, as perhaps indicated by the versions. McCarter
(331), following G^{LM}, OL, reads כי על אף אבשלום היתה "This happened because of Absalom's
anger." This is partly supported by 4QSamª which omits שומה "intended." Many scholars take
שומה (Q: שימה) as a noun ("scowl;" cf. Wellhausen, 188; Driver, 303). However, this would
contradict Absalom's intention to hide his real feelings (see v 22).

33.a. MT: "And now."

34.a-a. In spite of the textual evidence, many scholars omit this phrase (ויברח אבשלום),
regarding it as a misplaced variant of the beginning of vv 37 or 38 (ואבשלום ברח "and Absalom
fled"). This threefold use of this phrase is rather repetitive but not impossible.

34.b-b. MT has a shorter reading, and we have substituted ("Horonaim") for אחריו "behind
him"(?). Perhaps, the right text has been preserved in the Greek MSS, and we follow Wellhausen's
(189) reconstruction: בדרך חרנים במורד ויבא הצפה ויגד למלך ויאמר אנשים ראיתי מדרך
חרנים מצד ההר "along the Horonaim road on the slope. Then the watchman went and told
the king saying, 'I have seen men on the Horonaim road by the mountainside.'" This omission
may have been due to homoioteleuton.

35.a. MT: "word."

37.a. So many MSS and Q; K reads עמיחור "Ammihur."

Form / Structure / Setting

This pericope is a vivid and lively episode which is an integral part of the
introduction to Absalom's rebellion (see *Form / Structure / Setting* of 13:1–22).
Nearly half of it is taken by the utterances of different characters. Although
the death of Amnon is the focal point, it is dismissed in half a line (v 29a)
because the real interest is now centered on Absalom.

The pericope consists of two main sections: vv 23–29 depict Absalom's
plot which culminates in Amnon's death, while vv 30–37 are largely concerned

with David's grief and Absalom's flight to Geshur. The place of vv 38–39 is less clear; we regard them as belonging to the following pericope since v 37 provides a reasonable and fitting conclusion (so also McCarter, 335). Fokkelman (*King David*, 114) takes v 38 as part of our pericope; so also Sacon ("The Literary Structure of 'the Succession Narrative'." *The Period of David and Solomon*, 41) who finds a concentric structure in vv 23–38b even though it may appear slightly arbitrary and forced.

Comment

23 Sheepshearing was not only an occasion of special work but also a time for feasting and rejoicing (see 1 Sam 25:2–8). Absalom had, apparently, more than one estate (cf. also 14:28–30), but this particular festive occasion took place in Baal-hazor (not to be confused with Hazor in Galilee). It is usually identified with Jebel ʿAṣûr, some five miles (eight kilometers) northeast of Bethel.

According to MT it was near Ephraim which must denote a particular settlement or town, not the tribal territory. This "Ephraim" is often identified with "Ephron" (so NEB; cf. Seebass, *VT* 14 [1964] 497–500), some four miles (six kilometers) northeast of Bethel. McCarter (330) reads "Ophrah," following G^L, equating it with "Ephron" while "Ephraim" may be an even later name of the same location (cf. John 11:54).

24–27 It seems unlikely that at this stage Absalom planned to kill David as well, and that it was for this reason that he was invited to the feast. It is more plausible to assume that Absalom's invitation to David and his servants may have been part of Absalom's clever scheme to get Amnon away from Jerusalem without arousing too many suspicions. He also had to choose a location for his vengeful act, which would provide him with an escape route.

Absalom's direct request that Amnon should attend the feast may seem rather risky and David was bound to have some misgivings. However, we should perhaps differentiate between what may have been actually said in a wider context and the story-teller's condensed presentation of such a conversation. The two need not be identical.

28 The killing of Absalom may not have been a simple murder of a drunken prince. There were, of course, a number of king's sons who may have provided at least a nominal protection for Amnon. Moreover, it is quite possible that Amnon had his own personal bodyguard. When Absalom (15:1) became the heir apparent he had a chariot as well as fifty men to run before him; so had also Adonijah (1 Kgs 1:5). It would be surprising if Amnon had not taken similar measures, and in that case it is understandable why Absalom had to wait two years to carry out his revenge.

29 Since crossbreeding was forbidden in Israel, at least at a later time (see Lev 19:19), it is likely that the mules were imported or bought from non-Israelite neighbors. Mules were often used as royal mounts (see 18:9; 1 Kgs 1:33, 38, 44; 10:25; 18:5).

30–32 The hearsay or rumor may have originated in Jerusalem among people who had some inkling of Absalom's hatred and plans, and in itself it was plausible enough (see Judg 9:5; 2 Kgs 10:1–7). However, there is no reason to assume that Absalom had actually planned a *coup d'état*; at least David's immediate reaction was grief not fear.

It is somewhat surprising that David did not check the correctness of the report or rumor (as he did in 1:5) but, after all, he may have known Absalom better than we think. David expressed his grief in the usual manner by tearing his garments (cf. 1:11; 3:31) and lying on the ground (cf. 12:16). Jonadab's counsel to David must have been based on assumption unless he had become a confidant also of Absalom.

34 The latter part of the verse seems to be defective (see n. 34.b-b.), and the Greek MSS may have preserved the original text (but see Pisano, *Additions or Omissions*, 226–32).

"Horonaim" or "the two Horons" (since the name has a dual form); there were Upper and Lower Beth-horon, some ten miles (or sixteen kilometers) northwest of Jerusalem. The king's sons may not have taken the shortest route to Jerusalem.

Hertzberg (328) et al. read "Bahurim" (בחורים) for "Horonaim" (so G) or for MT אחריו "behind him"(?), since the Horonaim road cannot be seen from the southeast hill of Jerusalem. However, we do not know for certain where the watchman was actually stationed.

37 Absalom fled to his maternal grandfather, the king of Geshur. For the location of Geshur, see *Comment* on 3:3; Mazar, *JBL* 80 (1961) 23.

The meaning of "Talmai" (תלמי) is not quite clear but it is reminiscent of the Hurrian *tal(a)mi* ("great"); see Blenkinsopp, *Gibeon and Israel*, 125, n. 35. It was also the name of one of the sons of Anak (Num 13:22; Josh 15:14; Judg 1:10). "Ammihud" (BDB: "my kinsman is majesty") is also attested as an Israelite personal name (see Num 1:10; 34:20, 28; 1 Chr 9:4).

Explanation

In a sense this pericope forms the logical conclusion to the Amnon-Tamar story by depicting the final scene in which the two-year-masquerade comes to an abrupt end with Absalom's command, "Strike Amnon!" (v 28). So at last Tamar's dishonor is avenged and Amnon is killed. Unfortunately, this does not bring us to a happy ending; most of the problems remain unsolved and the harmony is not restored. In fact, this ending is only the beginning of a new complication and it prepares the reader for even more tragic events to come: the eventual rebellion of Absalom and his death.

It is difficult to allocate the blame because we have little knowledge of the tensions and intrigues which must have existed at David's court, nor do we have any direct information about the influences that may have molded the characters of his sons. There are also many questions to which we have no satisfactory answers. Would Amnon have been a better man had his father not committed adultery? Would Absalom's revenge have been less drastic but for the example of David's murder of Uriah? Was Amnon's death a justifiable homicide or was it a premeditated murder? Could David have punished Amnon and prevented his death?

In conclusion we can only say that violence and injustice appear like festering wounds which not only weaken the whole body, person or society but may even destroy it.

The Tekoite Woman's Story and Absalom's Return (13:38–14:7, 15–17, 8–14, 18–33)

Bibliography

Bellefontaine, E. "Customary Law and Chieftainship: Judicial Aspects of 2 Samuel 14.4–21." *JSOT* 38 (1987) 47–72. **Bickert, R.** "Die List Joabs und der Sinneswandeln Davids." VTSup 30 (1979) 30–51. **Camp, C. V.** "The Wise Women of 2 Samuel: A Role Model for Women in Early Israel?" *CBQ* 43 (1981) 14–29. **Clark, W. M.** "A Legal Background to the Yahwist's Use of 'Good and Evil' in Genesis 2–3." *JBL* 88 (1969) 266–78. **Hagan, H.** "Deception as Motif and Theme in 2 Sm 9–20; 1 Kgs 1–2." *Bib* 60 (1979) 301–26. **Hoftijzer, J.** "David and the Tekoite Woman." *VT* 20 (1970) 419–44. **Jackson, J. J.** "David's Throne: Patterns in the Succession Story." *CJT* 11 (1965) 183–95. **Jepsen, A.** "Amah und Schiphchah." *VT* 8 (1958) 293–97. **Leggett, D. A.** *The Levirate and Goel Institutions in the Old Testament: With Special Attention to the Book of Ruth.* Cherry Hill, NJ: Mack Publishing Company, 1974. **Long, B. O.** "Wounded Beginnings: David and Two Sons." *Images of Man and God. Old Testament Short Stories in Literary Focus,* ed. B. O. Long. Sheffield: Almond Press, 1981. 26–34. **McKeating, H.** "The Development of the Law on Homicide in Ancient Israel." *VT* 25 (1975) 46–68. **Nicol, G. G.** "The Wisdom of Joab and the Wise Woman of Tekoa." *ST* 36 (1982) 97–104. **Phillips, A.** "Another Look at Murder." *JJS* 28 (1977) 105–26. **Schökel, L. A.** "David y la mujer de Tecua: 2 Sm 14 como modelo hermenéutico." *Bib* 57 (1976) 192–205. **Simon, U.** "The Poor Man's Ewe-Lamb. An Example of a Juridical Parable." *Bib* 48 (1967) 207–42.

Translation

[38] *By the time Absalom, having fled to Geshur, had been there three years,* [39] *the king's anger[a] ceased to be actively directed[b] against Absalom for he had become reconciled to the fact that Amnon was dead.*

[14:1] *When Joab, son of Zeruiah, perceived that the king's heart was still set against Absalom,* [2] *Joab sent to Tekoa and brought from there a wise woman, and said to her, "Pretend that you are in mourning and put on mourning clothes; do not anoint yourself with oil but act like a woman who has been mourning the dead for many days.* [3] *Then go to the king and speak to him [a]according to these your instructions."[a] So Joab put the words in her mouth.* [4] *When the Tekoite woman came[a] to the king, [b]she threw herself down,[b] her face to the ground, and did homage. "Help,[c] O king!"[d] she cried.* [5] *"What is your problem?" the king asked her. "Alas, I am a widow,"[a] she answered, "and my husband is dead.* [6] *Your maidservant has two sons, and one day the two of them got into a fight with each other in the open field, and there was no one to part them. So one struck[a] the other[b] and killed him.* [7] *Now the whole clan has risen against your maidservant, demanding, 'Give up the one who killed his brother so that we may put him to death for the life of his brother whom he killed, [a]and so we will also exterminate[a] the heir.' Thus they will extinguish my ember which is left,[b] leaving my husband neither name nor remnant on the earth.[c]* [15] *Now I have come[a] to speak to the king, my lord, of this matter because the kinsmen[b] have intimidated me. Your maidservant thought, 'I will speak to the king, it may well be that the king will deal with the plight of his handmaid,*

[16]*with the result that the king may take care to deliver his handmaid from the hand of the man* [a]*who is seeking*[a] *to destroy both*[b] *me and my son from the* [c]*God-given inheritance.'*[c] [17]*So your handmaid said, 'Let the decision*[a] *of my lord, the king, bring*[b] *peace!*[c] *Truly, my lord, the king, is like a divine messenger,*[d] *able to discern good and evil. May Yahweh, your God, be*[e] *with you!'"*

[8]*The king then said to the woman, "Go home. I myself*[a] *shall give orders concerning your case."* [9]*Thereupon the Tekoite woman said to the king, "My lord, the king, let any consequences be upon me and my father's house, but let the king and his throne be guiltless."* [10]*The king replied, "If anyone says anything to you,* [a]*bring him*[a] *to me and he will trouble you*[b] *no more."* [11]*She said, "Let the king*[a] *mention* [b]*the name of*[b] *Yahweh his*[c] *God that the avenger of blood does not multiply*[d] *the destruction so that my son is not exterminated." "As surely as Yahweh lives," he affirmed, "not a hair of* [e]*your son's head*[e] *shall fall to the ground."* [12]*Then the woman said, "Let your maidservant speak* [a]*about another matter*[a] *to my lord, the king." "Speak," he replied.* [13]*So she said, "Why then have you plotted a similar thing against the people of God? That is to say, the king has now become like one who is guilty* [a]*on account of having given*[a] *this ruling, in that the king has not restored his own banished one.* [14a]*We must indeed die (sooner or later)*[a] *and be like water spilled on the ground, which cannot be gathered up again; however, God will not (untimely) take away the life of* [b]*him who devises*[b] *plans not to keep on banished from him one who has been driven away."* [18]*Then the king answered and said to the woman, "Do not conceal from me anything I am about to ask you." "Let my lord, the king, speak," answered the woman.* [19]*Then the king said, "Is the hand of Joab with you in all this?" The woman replied and said, "As surely as you live, my lord, the king, there is*[a] *no turning to the right or to the left from anything my lord, the king, has spoken! Indeed, your servant Joab was the one who instructed me, he was the one who put all these words in the mouth of your maidservant.*[b] [20]*Your servant Joab produced this scheme in order to change*[a] *the course of events,*[a] *but my lord is as wise as a messenger of God* [b]*in that he knows everything that happens on earth."*[b] [21]*So the king said to Joab, "Now then, I have made the following decision.*[a] *Go, bring back the young man Absalom!"* [22]*So Joab threw himself down, his face to the ground, and doing homage, he blessed the king. Then Joab said, "Today your servant knows that I have found favor in your sight, my lord, the king, in that the king has granted the request of your servant."*[a] [23]*Thereupon Joab arose, went to Geshur and brought Absalom to Jerusalem.* [24]*However, the king said, "Let him depart to his own house, he shall not see my face!" So Absalom departed to his own house and he did not see the face of the king.*

[25]*In all Israel there was no one so much praised as Absalom for his* [a]*physical perfection;*[a] *from the sole of his foot to the crown of his head there was no blemish in him.* [26]*When he shaved his head—this he used to do at the end of every year when he shaved it; because it was heavy on him, he used to shave it—he would weigh the hair of his head at* [a]*two hundred*[a] *shekels by the royal standard of weights.* [27]*To Absalom were born three sons and one daughter whose name was Tamar; she grew into a beautiful woman.*

[28]*So Absalom lived in Jerusalem two years*[a] *but he did not see the face of the king.* [29]*Eventually Absalom sent for Joab in order to send him to the king but Joab would not come to him. So he sent again*[a] *the second time, yet he would not*

come. ³⁰ *Then he said to his servants, "See, Joab's field is* ᵃ*next to mine*ᵃ *and he has barley there. Go and* ᵇ*set it on fire!"*ᵇ *So Absalom's servants set the field on fire. Thereupon Joab's young men came to him with torn garments, and reported, "The servants of Absalom have set the field on fire!"* ³¹ *Now Joab arose and came to Absalom in his house, and said to him, "Why have your servants*ᵃ *set my field on fire?"* ³² *"Look here," Absalom answered Joab, "I sent for you, saying, 'Come here that I may send you to the king* ᵃ*with the following message,*ᵃ *"Why did I have to come from Geshur? It would have been better for me if I were still there. Now, therefore, let me see the king's face! If indeed there is any guilt in me, put me to death!"'"* ³³ *When Joab went to the king and told him, he summoned Absalom who came to the king* ᵃ*and did homage to him, his face to the ground before the king.*ᵃ *Then the king kissed Absalom.*

Notes

39.a. Reading רוח "anger," "spirit" with some G MSS. This is partly confirmed by 4QSamᵃ (see Ulrich, *Qumran Text*, 106). MT has דוד "David" but the verb ותכל "ceased" is 3 fem sg. We regard the verb as qal while MT takes it as piel.

39.b. Lit., "to go out."

14:3.a. Lit., "according to this word." Some scholars assume that Joab's actual words have been omitted.

4.a. Reading ותבא "and she came"; so many Heb. MSS as well as G, Syr, Vg, Tg. MT has ותאמר "and she said."

4.b-b. Lit., "she fell down."

4.c. G has "Help, O king, help!" which is more emphatic but not necessarily right.

4.d. For the use of the article with the voc, see GKC §126e.

5.a. Lit., "widow woman"; the Heb. אלמנה "widow" may have had an adjectival force (see H. A. Hoffner, "אלמנה," *TDOT* 1 [1974] 287). However, the two words may stand in apposition.

6.a. Reading with G, Vg ויך "and he struck" for MT ויכו "and he struck him".

6.b. No need to read אחיו "his brother," contra Driver (306).

7.a-a. *BHK* (following Syr) has והשמידו "and they will eliminate."

7.b. 4QSamᶜ seems to suggest either השארתי "I have remaining" or נשארתי "which is my remaining one"; so Ulrich (*BASOR* 235 [1979] 10–11).

7.c. Lit., "on the face of the earth."

8.a. The position of the pronoun אני "I" is emphatic; hence, perhaps, "I myself."

10.a-a. The Heb. והבאתו "bring him" is pointed as 2 masc sg. Most scholars repoint it as 2 fem sg.

10.b. G presupposes בו "him," referring, perhaps, to the surviving son.

11.a. Some MSS read אדני המלך "my lord, the king," as in v 9.

11.b-b. This is our interpretative addition.

11.c. MT reads "your God."

11.d. The MT מהרבית is probably an error for מהרבות, the normal hiph inf constr (plus the prep מן) of which the Q may be a defective spelling (מהרבת).

11.e-e. Lit., "of your son."

12.a-a. Lit., "a word."

13.a-a. We regard מדבר as a piel inf constr plus the prep מן "from"; so, for instance, Hoftijzer, *VT* 20 (1970) 431 n.1. Some exegetes, perhaps also the Masoretes, take it as a hithp ptcp masc sg (see Driver, 307).

14.a-a. McCarter (340) follows Gᴸ and Theod. in reading כי מת בנך "for your son is dead." This makes reasonable sense but MT has כי מות נמות "we must indeed die," which is supported by 4QSamᶜ.

14.b-b. Following the emendation suggested by Ewald (*History*, 3:174) and reading חושב "him who devises" for וחשב "but he [i.e. God] devises," Hagan (*Bib* 60 [1979] 313) translates v 14b as "God does not take away life, and he schemes. . . ."

15.a. Omitting the relative particle אשר, with some textual witnesses (see *BHS*).

15.b. The Heb. הַעָם usually means "the people" but in our context it probably denotes "clan" (see *HALAT*, 792a).

16.a-a. Adding הַמְבַקֵּשׁ "who is seeking" on the basis of G τοῦ ζητοῦντος .

16.b. Lit., "together."

16.c-c. Lit., "God's inheritance" (so NAB). G^L, Tg, Theod. suggest "Yahweh's inheritance" (נחלת יהוה).

17.a. Lit., "word."

17.b. Reading the juss יְהִי "let . . . bring" with some Heb. MSS (similarly G, OL, Vg).

17.c. Some versions have wrongly understood מְנוּחָה "resting-place, resting" as denoting, in this context, a gift or sacrifice. McCarter (346) finds here a reference to the king's final decision. We take it to mean "rest (from enemies)" or "peace".

17.d. Or "angel of God." G^L and Tg have "angel of Yahweh."

17.e. Some Heb. MSS and versions read יהיה "will be" for MT יהי "may . . . be."

19.a. The MT אֵשׁ "there is" is a variant of יֵשׁ (so 4QSam^c): cf. GKC, § 47b n.1.

19.b. 4QSam^a reads אֲמָתֶךָ "your handmaid" for שִׁפְחָתֶךָ "your maidservant."

20.a-a. Lit., "the face of the matter"(RV).

20.b-b. 4QSam^c has אֲשֶׁר בָּאָרֶץ [לָדַעַת] "to know what is on earth"; similarly G^L.

21.a. Lit., "(I have done) this thing," while Syr suggests כִּדְבָרְךָ "according to your advice"; similarly G, for MT אֶת הַדָּבָר הַזֶּה "this thing."

22.a. So Q (also 4QSam^c), reading עַבְדְּךָ "your servant" while K has עַבְדִּי "his servant."

25.a-a. Lit., "beauty."

26.a-a. G has ἑκατόν "hundred"; MT reads מָאתַיִם "two hundred" which is attested also by 4QSam^c.

28.a. Lit., "days."

29.a. "Again" (עוֹד) is omitted by some Greek MSS but it is found in 4QSam^c.

30.a-a. Lit., "at my hand."

30.b-b. K (וְהוֹצֵאתִיהָ "and I shall bring it out") is probably a scribal error (so Smith, 339); Q and 4QSam^c read וְהַצִּיתוּהָ "and set it on fire." See also GKC § 71.

30.c-c. MT has a lengthy omission (due to a homoioteleuton) which can be restored on the basis of 4QSam^c, G and OL: וַיָּבֹאוּ יַלְדֵי יוֹאָב אֵלָיו קְרוּעֵי בִגְדֵיהֶם וַיֹּאמְרוּ הִצִּיתוּ עַבְדֵי אַבְשָׁלוֹם אֶת הַחֶלְקָה בָּאֵשׁ "and Joab's young men came to him with torn garments, and said, 'The servants of Absalom have set the field on fire.'"

31.a. Reading עֲבָדֶיךָ "your servants," with many MSS; MT has עַבְדְּךָ "your servant," so also 4QSam^c.

32.a-a. Lit., "to say."

33.a-a. MT is somewhat repetitive and may have preserved two conflated (?) readings. The spacing in 4QSam^c indicates a shorter reading than that in MT. Ulrich (*BASOR* 235 [1979] 7) suggests only וַיִּשְׁתָּחוּ "and did homage."

Form / Structure / Setting

This pericope (13:38–14:33) is part of the prologue (chaps. 13–14) to the story of Absalom's rebellion and its sequel (chaps. 15–20) but there is some uncertainty about its exact beginning (cf. also *Form / Structure / Setting* of 13:1–22). We assume that 13:38 forms the opening to the account of Absalom's return, and that therefore 13:38–14:5a can be regarded as providing the setting and introduction to the Tekoite woman's story. This is then followed by the fictitious legal case presented to David by the wise woman (vv 5b–7 + 15–17) while vv 8–11 describe the judgment elicited (cf. A. Graffy, "The Literary Genre of Isaiah 5:1–7," *Bib* 60 [1979] 404–7). In vv 12–14 the so-called verdict is applied to David's treatment of Absalom and, finally, vv 18–24 provide the conclusion. The transposition of vv 15–17 after v 7 improves the logical sequence of the narrative (contra Hoftijzer), and avoids certain exegetical problems.

The structure of 13:38–14:24 is practically identical with that of the so-called judiciary parables (see Simon, *Bib* 48 [1967] 208) or the judgment eliciting parables (cf. Gunn, *King David*, 40–41; H. Niehr, "Zur Gattung von Jes 5:1–7," *BZ* 30 [1986] 99–104).

The legal case presented is, clearly, fictitious (14:3) and it is highly unlikely that the judgment elicited could have served as a real legal precedent (cf. Bellefontaine, *JSOT* 38 [1987] 48), especially since the two cases were dissimilar on several important points. Absalom had committed a well-planned and premeditated murder (13:22–29) and there were many witnesses to that effect (cf. also Deut 19:15). Moreover, he was not the single remaining heir who alone could continue his father's name; nor was his mother a destitute widow. Strictly speaking, Absalom was in no immediate danger, if at all. Thus it may be asked whether we are dealing with a literary device or with a fictitious legal case *actually presented* to David in order to establish a valid legal precedent which could be applied to Absalom's predicament. We are inclined to argue for the former alternative since the disparity between the supposed parallel cases makes any precedent-theory questionable. It is possible that the present Tekoite woman's story and its application belong to a literary construction the purpose of which was to shift the blame for the fateful restoration of Absalom on Joab, and to acquit David, the just king, from the charge of having deliberately disregarded Yahweh's law concerning murder (cf. Num 35:31; Deut 19:11–13), in the interests of his own son. Hence it is possible that this story in its *present* form is an adaptation of the judiciary parable genre which seems to have been a literary device used by the prophets to make the hearers more involved and more exposed to the message or indictment of Yahweh which usually followed the judiciary parable or its equivalent (i.e., the judgment eliciting question, such as Jer 3:1 and Hag 2:10–14). In this prophetic usage (cf. 2 Sam 12:1–15a; 1 Kgs 20:35–42; Isa 5:1–7), the legal case presented was never intended to be a real legal precedent, rather the verdict thus obtained was turned into a direct or indirect indictment. However, in 2 Sam 14 the implicit indictment amounts to an approval of David, if the Tekoite woman's story was *intended* as an apologia for the king. The implication of the story is that David had intended to keep Absalom in banishment (as Cain in Gen 4) but he was tricked by Joab. Thus David remains the law-abiding king.

It is likely that in David's time murder or, at least, fratricide was not strictly a sacral crime; therefore in *that* legal setting David's treatment of Absalom was quite understandable. However, it seems that at a later stage his actions required some justification, and this was achieved by means of the Tekoite woman's story and its application. Bickert (VTSup 30 [1979] 48–51) has argued for a pre-Deuteronomistic wisdom anecdote which was inserted between vv 1 and 23, and subsequently expanded by two later revisions. However, his source-critical analysis will not convince everyone.

Vv 25–27 form a sort of descriptive parenthesis depicting Absalom's physical perfection (vv 25–26) and the birth of his children (v 27). These verses are usually considered as secondary but, no doubt, derived from older traditions.

Vv 28–33 appear to be the natural continuation of v 24 but it is equally possible that they provide the introduction to the events described in chap.

15. In a sense these verses serve as a bridge between the two episodes, and at the same time they reveal disturbing aspects of Absalom's personality: his arrogance and high-handedness.

Comment

13:39 McCarter has suggested that it was David's "enthusiasm for marching out against" Absalom that was spent, and that he was "no longer openly hostile to Absalom" (335). At least the latter inference seems likely in view of the king's subsequent attitude to his son (see vv 24 and 28), and we have followed this line of interpretation. The RSV renders v 39a by "and the spirit of the king longed to go forth to Absalom." However, this and similar translations seem less convincing because Joab had to resort to cunning and deceit in order to "trap" David, and to secure Absalom's return. Even then there was no immediate reconciliation; for a contrary view, see Hoftijzer, *VT* 20 (1970) 419; Hertzberg, 331.

14:1 The Hebrew על may well mean "against," and therefore it seems that David was *still* hostile to his son. Consequently, Joab had to use his elaborate deception to bring about Absalom's recall (similarly also Fokkelman, *King David*, 126–27; McCarter, 344). The reasons for Joab's intervention are not obvious. He may have acted out of pure self-interest or he may have been motivated by his loyalty to David or to the kingdom (see Gunn, *King David*, 100). The author has left the readers to draw their own conclusions.

2 Tekoa was a village situated some ten miles (sixteen kilometers) south of Jerusalem, in the Judean hills. Contrary to various suggestions, it is far from certain that Tekoa must have been famous for its wisdom traditions; our story tells, primarily, about Joab's scheming rather than about the woman's wisdom. It is true that the Tekoite woman is described as wise but her status, if any, in the community is not defined. Claudia Camp (*CBQ* 43 [1981] 24) has argued that the wise women from Tekoa and Abel had *considerable* authority and responsibility in their respective local settings. This is plausible in the case of the woman from Abel (2 Sam 20:16–19) while the Tekoite woman mainly followed Joab's instructions (cf. v 19b; see also Nicol, *ST* 36 [1982] 97) even though she may have had certain "diplomatic" and other skills. In order to present her fictitious story successfully, she had to come from a more outlying district, otherwise she might have been recognized by the courtiers or even by David himself.

3 Joab instructed the Tekoite woman as a superior would give instructions to an inferior (cf. Exod 4:15; Num 22:38). If the whole incident is authentic and not merely a literary device to blame Joab for Absalom's ill-fated restoration, then we must allow for some ingenuity and quick-wittedness on the part of the woman (see Camp, *CBQ* 43 [1981] 17 n.8).

5 The seemingly redundant "my husband is dead" (v 5b) serves to stress the tragic situation in which the woman "finds" herself.

6–7 Since the woman's account is imaginary, it is not impossible that the Cain and Abel story (Gen 4:1–16) may have been in the mind of the author (see Bienkinsopp, VTSup 15 [1966] 51). However, one should not overexaggerate the parallels.

The woman stresses certain more or less relevant extenuating circumstances, such as her widowhood; the surviving son is now her only support, and his punitive death would rob her dead husband of his sole remaining heir. V 6b may also imply that there were no witnesses, hence the case could well be considered, at least theoretically, as a manslaughter. However, the clan demanded the execution of the surviving son (cf. Exod 21:12).

9 The function of this verse in its present setting is unclear. It seems that the woman is trying to assure David that *she* would be willing to bear the possible consequences if the king's decision came to be regarded (by God?) as a miscarriage of justice. On the other hand, this and similar expressions (cf. 1 Sam 25:24; see also Exod 4:10; Judg 6:15) may reflect a courtly language (cf. K. N. Jung, *Court Etiquette in the Old Testament.* Drew University: Ph.D. dissertation, 1979, 42–52). Hoftijzer (*VT* 20 [1970] 427) is of the opinion that the confession of guilt in v 9 is meant to give a further support to the woman's plea; it is a cry for forgiveness. McCarter (348) regards v 9 as a "Deuteronomistic expansion." This is plausible, especially if later hearers or readers came to understand the episode as providing a binding legal precedent.

McKeating (*VT* 25 [1975] 52) has suggested that the king is depicted as a "public *gōʾēl*." However, in this particular case he may have been "interfering with the due processes of vengeance" (59). Consequently, the bloodguilt may attach itself to the one who has prevented or neglected or interfered with the carrying out of vengeance, as perhaps also in 1 Kgs 2:5–6, 31. Hence the Tekoite woman affirms her willingness to bear the guilt, if any, to secure protection for her fictitious son.

11 The mention or remembering of Yahweh's name is, apparently, tantamount to uttering an oath in the deity's name (so Hoftijzer, *VT* 20 [1970] 428 n.1).

Phillips (*Criminal Law*, 104–5) regards the avenger of blood (גאל הדם) as an officer appointed by the community, whose task was to find and execute the murderer. On the other hand, it is equally possible that the avenger of blood was a near, or the nearest, kinsman who had the responsibility to enforce blood-vengeance (see de Vaux, *Ancient Israel,* 11). In our story he is depicted as somewhat overzealous and, perhaps, influenced by material gain (see v 7: "and so we will also eliminate the heir"). It has often been argued that blood-vengeance did not operate *within* the clan (so Phillips, *JJS* 28 [1977] 112) but even so, there may have been some possible variations in the treatment of the killer or fratricide depending upon the circumstances (cf. Gen 27:41–45; D. A. Leggett, *The Levirate and Goel Institutions,* 75–76).

13–14 These verses are very problematic both textually and exegetically. We understand the Tekoite woman's accusation as suggesting that since the king has given protection to her son, he has now become unfair or even guilty himself in not providing the same or similar protection for his own son. It is possible that in the past few years the king had acted somewhat like the avenger of blood (v 11) in respect of Absalom, while the people of God or Israel in general had been seeking Absalom's restoration. Thus Joab would represent, according to our story, the popular attitude, especially if that suited his own personal interests. There is little doubt that Absalom was a favorite of the people (see v 25) and this favoritism may have been manifest even before Amnon's death. If so, then both the rape of Tamar and the death of Amnon may have been part of the ongoing struggle (?) for succession. Since Absalom did not hesitate to scheme against his own father, he would have had even less scruples to plot against his brother, if possible.

15 In view of v 7 we have taken הָעָם to mean "kinsmen" (see Hoftijzer, *VT* 20 [1970] 439) rather than "the people." Also the verb יְרֵאֻנִי is pointed as a pl, hence "they have intimidated me." However, McCarter (339) points it as a sg since, he argues, the reference is to a *particular* kinsman who had been terrorizing the widow: if so, he might have been the avenger of blood (v 11).

The change from שִׁפְחָתְךָ "your maidservant" to אֲמָתוֹ "his handmaid" is, most likely, for stylistic reasons. For the terminology, see Jepsen, *VT* 8 (1958) 293–97.

16 It seems that this verse is meant to describe the possible consequences or result of the wish expressed in v 15b.

"The God-given inheritance" is, most likely, the family's landed property or its share in Yahweh's land (see J. L. Dybdahl, *Israelite Village Land Tenure: Settlement to Exile.* Fuller Theological Seminary: Ph.D. thesis, 1981, 54–65). Other possible meanings of the expression are "the people of Israel" and "the land of Israel" (see Hoftijzer, *VT* 20 [1970] 439).

17 The woman now uses some flattery and compares the king to a supernatural or divine being, to an angel of God. It is not certain that this particular concept was part of the royal ideology but similar ideas were in existence in Israel (cf. 1 Kgs 3:9, 12; Isa 11:2).

"Good and evil" may form a merismus, a way of expressing totality, in this case: "all, everything" (cf. also Hoftijzer, *VT* 20 [1970] 441). However, in the context of administering justice it may denote the king's ability to discern between good and evil, distinguishing right from wrong (cf. 1 Kgs 3:9; see also I. Höver-Johag, "טוֹב," *TDOT* 5 [1986] 309–11; Clark, *JBL* 88 [1969] 269). Thus it is thought that the king has absolute competence to deal with *all* legal cases since he is Yahweh's earthly representative (see Whitelam, *The Just King,* 135).

19 David may have been aware of Joab's association with the "popular movement" (?) to restore Absalom, hence the king's question to the woman. There is no indication that David suspected the woman's story; however, her application of the king's decision also to Absalom's case must have pointed to the involvement of a third party. It is difficult to say whether or not the following confession was anticipated by Joab.

"As surely as you live" or "by your life" is a variation of the well-known oath formula, "As surely as Yahweh lives." See *Comment* on 2 Sam 2:27 (cf. also 1 Sam 1:26; 17:55).

24 "Let him depart" (יָסֹב) may be an allusion to סָבַב "to change" in v 20. Thus the last word would belong to the king. Also the repetition of v 24a in v 24b emphasizes the same point.

25–26 Absalom's physical perfection and his praise in Israel may explain, at least partly, why he was so popular among the people. All this may have increased also his vanity.

The exaggerated (?) weight of Absalom's hair was some four pounds (= two hundred shekels) or some two pounds if we follow the reading of G^L.

This verse may have been intended to fill out, to some extent, the background of Absalom's unusual death, assuming that his hair actually became entangled in the branches (so Josephus, *Ant.* 7.239).

A rabbinic tradition (Nazir 4b) makes Absalom into a Nazirite but there is no justification for this assertion in our text.

The reference to the "royal standard of weights" need not be an indication of its post-exilic date (contra Wellhausen, 194). The above expression (אבן המלך) is found only here but there is no reason to doubt that such standards were in existence in Israel. Thus Gen 23:16 speaks of "weights current among the merchants" while Exod 30:13, 24 mentions "the shekel of the sanctuary." See also O. R. Sellers, "Weights and Measures," *IDB* 4 (1962) 830–33.

27 The statement that Absalom had three sons seems to be at variance with 18:18 where he is said to have had *no* sons. However, it is likely that they may have died young (so Hertzberg, 335) or could they have been put to death for Absalom's murder of Amnon (cf. Gen 42:37; Ezek 18:19–20)? However, all this is pure speculation. Fokkelman (*King David*, 150 n.35) has tried to solve the difficulty by regarding 18:18 as a later addition but even so there must have been some reason for the divergent statement.

It is unlikely that the mere occurrence of the name "Tamar" points to a tradition according to which Amnon raped Absalom's *daughter* rather than his *sister* (cf. Ackroyd, 135).

28 Although Absalom had some considerable property at Baal-hazor (see 2 Sam 13:23), he is said to have spent two years in Jerusalem as if he was under some sort of house arrest, similar to that imposed on Shimei in 1 Kgs 2:36. The fact that Absalom was excluded from the court may indicate the strength of David's anger (so Fokkelman, *King David*, 147), especially since the former needed an influential intercessor to change the king's attitude.

29–32 Joab's subsequent lack of interest in Absalom's welfare is rather surprising after his considerable efforts to obtain Absalom's recall from Geshur. It is possible that Joab came to realize that, for various reasons, Absalom was no longer useful to his own plans and therefore he became reluctant to offer any further assistance to the young prince. On the other hand, Joab's attitude may be a true reflection of his real sentiments preserved (?) in the *hypothetical older version* of Absalom's restoration.

The burning of Joab's barley crop indicates that Absalom was capable of using any means to get his own way.

Absalom's exclamation, "If indeed there is any guilt in me, put me to death" (cf. 1 Sam 20:8) need not be considered a "daring game" but rather an exaggeration for the sake of emphasis. It is difficult to see how he could have been guiltless unless the punishment was, in some way or other, already inflicted (by the deaths of his sons [??] or by his exile). Or was the fratricide regarded as a justifiable homicide brought about by Amnon's dishonorable treatment of Tamar (cf. Gen 34:25–31)?

It is unlikely that the kiss of reconciliation was thought to mark out Absalom as the future king (contra Schultz). In the OT kiss is usually a gesture of affection or greeting (cf. Gen 33:4; 50:1; Exod 18:7; 2 Sam 15:2). Although at this point Absalom may have been the eldest of David's sons, it is not impossible that during his exile it was *Adonijah* who had become or came to be regarded as the heir apparent. This may well be one of the reasons for Absalom's later rebellion. If his position had been so secure as some assume, the rebellion would have been an overhasty and totally pointless undertaking, especially in view of the popular support for Absalom. In our judgment, the revolt may suggest that Absalom simply had no other option to gain the throne but this drastic and dangerous step.

Explanation

It seems that the main function of chap. 14 was to show that the ill-advised recall of Absalom was entirely due to Joab's initiative and scheming, and that David was, in a sense, deceived by a cunning trick and trapped by his own oath, given in good faith. Even after these events, the king is represented as reluctant to overlook Absalom's crime. Thus only some five years after Amnon's death was Absalom eventually admitted into the king's presence following a special pleading (v 33) which is not further elaborated.

The story also implies that David's lenient treatment of Absalom's fratricide in the end was not a *deliberate* breach of the divine law. The king's verdict in the hypothetical case had been, most likely, justified in view of the extenuating circumstances, and by his oath the decision became, so to say, irreversible. Thus David was bound by his own oath, at least according to our narrative.

On the other hand, Joab is depicted as governed by personal considerations or self-interest. When Absalom's "friendship" became an embarrassment, Joab ignored his former protégé. Finally, a crop of barley was worth to Joab more than any question of justice or right and wrong; thus the way was now open for Absalom's subversive activities and rebellion.

Absalom's Subversive Activities   (15:1–12)

Bibliography

Bardtke, H. "Erwägungen zur Rolle Judas im Aufstand des Absaloms." *Wort und Geschichte.* FS K. Elliger, ed. H. Gese and H. P. Rüger. AOAT 18. Kevelaer: Butzon und Bercker; Neukirchen-Vluyn: Neukirchener Verlag des Erziehungsvereins, 1973. 1–8. **Boecker, H. J.** *Law and the Administration of Justice in the Old Testament and Ancient East.* Tr. J. Moiser. London: SPCK, 1980. **Cohen, M. A.** "The Rebellions During the Reign of David: An Inquiry into Social Dynamics in Ancient Israel." *Studies in Jewish Bibliography, History, and Literature in Honor of Edward Kiev,* ed. C. Berlin. New York: Ktav, 1971. 91–112. **Conrad, J.** "Der Gegenstand und die Intention der Geschichte von der Thronfolge Davids." *TLZ* 108 (1983) 161–76. **Crüsemann, F.** *Der Widerstand gegen das Königtum.* WMANT 49. Neukirchen-Vluyn: Neukirchener Verlag, 1978. **Donner, H.** "Der 'Freund des Königs.'" *ZAW* 73 (1961) 269–77. **Emerton, J. A.** "New Light on Israelite Religion: The Implications of the Inscriptions from Kuntillet ʿAjrud." *ZAW* 94 (1982) 2–20. **Hermisson, H.-J.** "Weisheit und Geschichte." *Probleme biblischer Theologie.* FS Gerhard von Rad, ed. H. W. Wolff. Munich: Kaiser Verlag, 1971. 136–54. **Hoftijzer, J.** "A Peculiar Question: A Note on 2 Sam XV 27." *VT* 21 (1971) 606–9. **Macholz, G. C.** "Die Stellung des Königs in der israelitischen Gerichtsverfassung." *ZAW* 84 (1972) 157–82. ———. "Zur Geschichte der Justizorganisation in Juda." *ZAW* 84 (1972) 314–40. **Mazar, B.** "The Military Élite of King David." *VT* 13 (1963) 310–20. **Rost, L.** "Die Stadt im Alten Testament." *ZDPV* 97 (1981) 129–38. **Rozenberg, M. S.** "The šōfᵉṭîm in the Bible." *Eretz-Israel* 12 (1975) 77–86. **Tadmore, H.** "'The People' and Kingship in Ancient Israel: The Role of Political Institutions in the Biblical Period." *CHM* 11 (1968) 46–68. **Weinfeld, M.** "Judge and Officer in Ancient Israel and in the Ancient Near East." *IOS* 7 (1977) 65–88. **Weingreen, J.** "The Rebellion of Absalom." *VT* 19 (1969) 263–66.

Translation

¹ *Sometime later* ᵃ *Absalom acquired* ᵇ *for himself a chariot and horses, as well as fifty men to run ahead of him.* ² *Moreover Absalom* ᵃ *used to rise early* ᵃ *and stand beside the way to the gate;* ᵇ ᶜ *whenever there was any man* ᶜ *who had a lawsuit to come before the king for a decision, Absalom would call* ᵈ *to him and say, "From what city are you?" When he said, "Your servant is* ᵉ *from such and such tribe* ᵉ *of Israel,"* ³ *Absalom would say to him, "Look, your claims* ᵃ *are proper and just but there is no one to hear you on the king's behalf."* ⁴ *Then Absalom would add,* ᵃ ᵇ *"Would that one would appoint me* ᵇ *to be judge in the land, then any man with* ᶜ *a suit or case* ᶜ *could come to me* ᵈ ᵉ *and I would help him to obtain justice."* ᵉ ⁵ *Whenever anyone approached to do obeisance to him, he would reach out his hand, take hold of him and kiss him.* ⁶ *This was the manner according to which Absalom treated all Israelites* ᵃ *who came to the king for judgment; so he stole the loyalty* ᵇ *of the men of Israel.*

⁷ *At the end of four* ᵃ *years, Absalom said to the king, "Let me go to fulfill the vow which I vowed to Yahweh-in-Hebron,* ⁸ *for your servant, while living in Geshur in Aram, made a vow: 'If Yahweh* ᵃ *will indeed* ᵃ *bring me back to Jerusalem, then I shall serve Yahweh.'"* ⁹ *"Go in peace!" the king said to him. So* ᵃ *he set off* ᵃ *and went to Hebron.* ¹⁰ *Then Absalom sent* ᵃ *secret agents* ᵃ *throughout all the tribes of*

Israel ^bwith the following message,^b "As soon as you hear the sound of the ram's horn, say, 'Absalom ^chas become king^c in Hebron!'" ¹¹With Absalom there went two hundred men from Jerusalem; they were invited and they went unsuspectingly, knowing nothing of the scheme. ¹²Then Absalom sent (messengers) and summoned^a Ahithophel the Gilonite, David's counsellor, from his city, from Gilo. When Absalom had offered the sacrifices, the conspiracy gained strength and the people (siding) with Absalom went on increasing.

Notes

1.a. Lit., "And it came to pass after this." 4QSam^c reads אחרי "after" for the less common מאחרי "after" in the MT.

1.b. McCarter (354) prefers the 4QSam^c reading [יעשׂ[ה "began to make use of" for MT ויעשׂ "he made" or ". . . acquired."

2.a-a. For the frequentative or iterative use of the verb, see GKC §112dd.

2.b. 4QSam^a omits השׁער "the gate." MT may have preserved a conflated reading (so McCarter, 354).

2.c-c. Reading with 4QSam^a והיה כל אישׁ for MT ויהי כל האישׁ "and it was so, that when any man" (RV).

2.d. We follow 4QSam^a (ויקרא); MT reads ויקרא "and he called." We assume the same tense for the three following verbs (ויאמר), on the basis of the partial evidence of 4QSam^a.

2.e-e. Lit., "from one of the tribes. . . ."

3.a. MT דבר ך "your word"; many MSS have the pl דבריך "your claims, arguments" which is suggested by the following pl adjectives.

4.a. Lit., "say."

4.b-b. For the syntax, see GKC, § 151a.

4.c-c. This may be an instance of legal pleonasm (so Conroy, *Absalom*, 148) or hendiadys ("just cause;" see McCarter, 354) or it could be simply a conflated reading.

4.d. The Heb. עלי "to me" is in an emphatic position.

4.e-e. Lit., "and I would do him justice" (so KJV, RV).

6.a. Lit., "Israel."

6.b. Lit., "hearts" (לב is used collectively). Driver (311) has suggested that to steal "hearts" or "understanding" means that Absalom duped the Israelites. However, v 13 may imply that the people had willingly transferred their loyalties to Absalom.

7.a. Reading ארבע "four" with G^L, Syr, Vg, and Josephus (*Ant.* 7.196); MT has ארבעים "forty." Two MSS read ארבעים יום "forty days" but this would hardly give enough time for planning the rebellion in Israel and Judah.

8.a-a. Reading the hiph inf abs השׁב (see GKC §113n) for MT ישׁיב (so K; ". . . will bring back"; Q has ישׁוב). The proposed reading may be reflected by G, Tg, and Syr (cf. Thenius, 217).

9.a-a. Lit., "he arose." G^L reads "Absalom. . . ."

10.a-a. 4QSam^c has מירושׁלים "from Jerusalem" for MT מרגלים "secret agents, spies." The former is probably a misreading of the latter variant.

10.b-b. Lit., "saying."

10.c-c. Lit., "or "is king"; RAV: "reigns."

12.a. Adding ויקרא ("and he summoned") as suggested by 4QSam^c; so also G^L (καὶ ἐκάλεσεν). See also Driver, 312.

Form / Structure / Setting

The extent of this unit (15:1–12) is largely determined by its context; it is also a component element of a larger complex (see *Form / Structure / Setting* of 15:13–16:14) which deals with Absalom's rebellion and its subsequent collapse. Our unit consists essentially of two main scenes: (a) Absalom's plot against his father (vv 1–6), and (b) Absalom's rebellion in Hebron (vv 7–12).

Already v 1 gives some indication of the direction of the forthcoming events: Absalom is aiming at nothing less than kingship itself (see also 1 Sam 8:11; 1 Kgs 1:5). The verse may be an editorial comment since it raises a puzzling problem: if Absalom was the heir apparent—why did he have to plot against David; if he was not—would not the king have been alerted to his son's dangerous ambitions? It is, perhaps, easier to explain the latter alternative than the former.

The account of Absalom's political subversion must have been greatly abbreviated and simplified. The extensive scale of the revolt seems to suggest that it must have been preceded by, at least, some negotiations and careful planning on the part of Absalom and his advisers. The pattern of subversion outlined in vv 2–5 was, most likely, only one of the ways in which Absalom gained support among the Israelites and built up his public image and following.

It is also likely that some time elapsed between Absalom's coronation in Hebron (v 10) and his march on Jerusalem. This seems to be implied by v 12 which laconically comments that "the conspiracy gained strength and the people with Absalom went on increasing." It would be rather naive to assume that David had no knowledge of this prolonged (?) political maneuvering, and that Absalom's march on Jerusalem came as a complete surprise to David and to his supporters. Consequently, v 13 can hardly be the first intimation of the rebellion.

Comment

1 Absalom provided himself with a chariot and horses, and an escort of fifty men. This may have been a case of ostentatious display (see Conroy, *Absalom*, 103) or a "tendency to megalomania" (so Fokkelman, *King David*, 166) but, at the same time, it may have concealed within it an implicit claim to royal status (cf. 1 Sam 8:11; see also Conrad, *TLZ* 108 [1983] 165). Adonijah, at a later stage, is explicitly said to have declared his intentions ("I will be king" in 1 Kgs 1:5b) and to have acquired for himself "chariots (or "chariot") and horsemen, and fifty men to run ahead of him" (1 Kgs 1:5). Thus it is plausible that the display may have served not only as an outward show (cf. Gen 41:43) but it also provided a potential military nucleus. The "fifty" was usually a standard military unit (cf. Exod 18:21; Deut 1:15; Yadin, *Warfare*, 284–86). Whitelam (*The Just King*, 141) has suggested that the upkeep of such an entourage "was probably financed by the king himself." This is possible but the question remains whether Absalom or Adonijah was the heir apparent at this point in time; the latter alternative seems more likely.

2–6 The interpretation of these verses is problematic but it is obvious that Absalom was able to exploit certain existing grievances among the people as well as specific administrative defects, in order to win over the people of Israel to his cause. The cases brought to the king were probably those which concerned "the *king's* matters" (cf. 2 Chr 19:11) and not "every kind of legal case indiscriminately" (see Boecker, *Law and the Administration of Justice*, 46). Thus the complaints may have included such concerns as military duties, taxation, forced labor service (cf. Alt, *Essays*, 101 n.46) or royal encroachment in general, since in other legal situations it would have been difficult for Absalom to give plausible opinions or judgments, day after day, in the absence of the opposing legal parties and witnesses.

Our text stresses that the main weakness of the legal administration was the lack of an official or king's representative to hear such cases (so, for instance, Weinfeld, *IOS* 7 [1977] 86 n.134). McCarter (353) translates v 3b as "but you will get no hearing from the king" (so also NEB; cf. Budde, 270) which may well describe the actual situation in David's time. We may note that no such hearer of legal cases (שמע) is mentioned in the lists of David's chief officials (see 2 Sam 8:15–18; 20:23–26). However, this "hearer of cases" may not have been sufficiently important to be included. Whitelam (*The Just King*, 140–41) has argued that Absalom's remark may have contained an *innovative* proposal while in David's view royal authority was far too important to be delegated to some other person. If so, then apparently for practical reasons it was difficult to gain access to the king in order to obtain hearing, and to penetrate the "defenses" of bureaucracy. Cohen (in *FS Edward Kiev*, 107) thinks that "David suspended his court" because the usual tribal complaint was directed against David's royal policy. However, in that case the streams of litigants would soon cease.

Thus it appears that the discontentment must have been fairly widespread in Israel as a whole to give rise to, perhaps, the most serious revolt in Israel's history. According to Weingreen (*VT* 19 [1969] 266) the main factors which brought about the rebellion were "David's ruthlessness in war and the affair of Bathsheba." Clearly, these factors may have contributed towards the stirring up of the revolt but it is doubtful that they were the only determining factors. Cohen (in *FS Edward Kiev*, 93) sees behind this and the other rebellions a different theme, namely, "the struggle between premonarchical elements in Israel-Judah and the bureaucracy created by David," while Gordon (270) mentions inter-tribal rivalry as an additional factor, which was effectively exploited by Absalom. All in all, Absalom may have temporarily combined several different, even conflicting, interests in an attempt to break and to displace David's rule. So in a way, Absalom may have served as a figurehead of several factions which hoped to find in him a useful tool to sweep away David's reign. Thus we note that Mephibosheth is reported to have said, rightly or wrongly, "Today the house of Israel will restore to me the kingdom of my father" (16:3); even David took the report of this statement seriously (16:4). On the other hand, it is unlikely that such a course of action had any place in *Absalom's* plans. Cohen (in *FS Edward Kiev*, 107) has drawn attention to Absalom's wish to be "judge" (שפט) not "king" (מלך); in his view, this implies that Absalom's regime hoped to fulfil the ideal *initial* expectations of the monarchy.

During his conspiratorial activities Absalom presented himself as the ideal judge or ruler. In this way he gained the loyalty of most people in Israel, and this latter entity must have included also Judah. This is implied by Absalom's coronation in Hebron (15:7–10) and the subsequent developments. However, it is questionable whether Absalom's real object was justice for all people; the latter may have been only a means to an end, namely, royal power for Absalom. However, it may be equally true that the various factions may have hoped to use Absalom as a cat's-paw, but it is pointless to speculate on the hypothetical nature of Absalom's political intentions.

For a Ugaritic parallel to Absalom's criticism of his father's rule, see *Keret* 16, col. vi.25–53 (Gibson, *Canaanite Myths*, 101–2).

7–8 The "four years" are often reckoned from the time of Absalom's reconciliation with his father (14:33) but it is surprising that he would have waited or delayed the fulfillment of his vow for some six years (cf. 14:28), and that consequently David's suspicions were not aroused by such a belated proposal. The king could have hardly forgotten an earlier proposal which had disastrous consequences (13:24–27)!

Hebron was a fitting rallying point for the rebellion. It was an ancient Yahweh sanctuary (cf. Gen 13:18) and it was here that David was crowned king over Judah (2:4) and eventually king over all Israel (5:1). Absalom was born here (3:2–3) and he may have retained some links with the city. Moreover, the people of Hebron may not have been too happy when *Jerusalem* was made into David's new capital with all its advantages and privileges.

"Yahweh-in-Hebron" may well be parallel with such expressions as "Yahweh of Samaria" and "Yahweh of Teman" attested in the inscriptions Kuntillet ʿAjrud (see Emerton, *ZAW* 94 [1982] 3; cf. also "Dagon-in-Ashdod" mentioned in 1 Sam 5:5). However, this does not mean that the unity of Yahweh was thereby denied (cf. Deut 6:3); it may point to local manifestations of one and the same Yahweh, as well as to different cultic traditions. On the other hand, confusions may have arisen in popular religion (cf. Ackroyd, 138–39). Some translators, however, take "Hebron" with the preceding verb: "Let me go to Hebron and pay . . ." (RAV; similarly JB, NAB).

10 The blowing of the ram's horn was part of the enthronement ritual (see 1 Kgs 1:34; 2 Kgs 9:13; de Vaux, *Ancient Israel*, 106) but in this particular setting the reference may be to the signals sent through the whole land of Israel.

"Absalom has become king" (or ". . . is now king") is a well-known formula of proclamation or accession (see 2 Kgs 9:13). A similar formula is used also in the so-called enthronement psalms (cf. Pss 93:1; 96:10; 97:1; 99:1). The possible inchoative meaning of מלך ("has become king") seems to be due to the context (cf. A. R. Johnson, *Sacral Kingship in Ancient Israel*, 2nd ed. [Cardiff: University of Wales Press, 1967] 65 n.1).

12 The name "Ahithophel" raises certain questions since it may mean "my brother is folly" (cf. BDB, 27). In view of such names as Ishbosheth and Mephibosheth (see *Comment* on 2:8; 4:4), it is probable that "Ahithophel" is a deliberate distortion of some such name as "Ahibaal" (so Mazar, *VT* 13 [1963] 317 n.1) which may mean "My divine brother is Baal." Hertzberg (338) prefers "Eliphelet" as the original name. *HALAT* (33) mentions "Quisling" as a possible paraphrase of "Ahithophel." The frequent suggestion that Ahithophel was Bathsheba's grandfather is rather tenuous (see *Comment* on 11:3). Ahithophel is the only fellow-conspirator of Absalom who is mentioned by name in the story. Perhaps, due to his outstanding wisdom he came to be regarded by David as his archenemy.

The location of Gilo is unknown but according to Josh 15:48–51 it was one of the towns in the Judean hill country, perhaps in the region of Hebron (cf. Abel, *Géographie*, 2:338; K. Elliger, "Die Heimat des propheten Micha," *ZDPV* [1934] 130).

From our text it is not clear whether it was Absalom who was offering the sacrifice or Ahithophel. The former alternative may well be more likely since the sacrifices probably marked Absalom's accession (cf. 1 Kgs 1:9, 19, 25; Nowack, 209). Thus they would indicate a complete break with David (cf. also Fokkelman, *King David*, 172).

Explanation

We do not know when Absalom began his preparations for the coup d'etat but the work must have taken several months if not years. The exploitation of legal and administrative grievances was one of Absalom's methods to gain the support of the people.

It is possible that Absalom's alienation could be traced back to the question of succession. This in its turn led to the conflict between Amnon and Absalom, and eventually between Absalom and David. In the first instance the tension was resolved by Amnon's death, while in the second the immediate solution was rebellion. Thus in a way, Absalom used the existing disaffection, grievances, and jealousies for his own purposes but, on the other hand, he himself may have served as an unwitting tool of other dissatisfied factions, such as the Saulides, some more conservative elements, and certain tribal sections, who hoped to benefit by the overthrow of David and his administration.

The subsequent developments seem to indicate that Absalom was supported not only by the northern tribes but also, if not more so, by Judah while David's power base was essentially his mercenary troops, court officials and friends.

Absalom's Revolt and David's Flight   (15:13–16:14)

Bibliography

Brueggemann, W. "On Trust and Freedom: A Study of Faith in the Succession Narrative." *Int* 26 (1972) 3–19. ———. "On Coping with Curse: A Study of 2 Sam 16:5–14." *CBQ* 36 (1974) 175–92. **Delcor, M.** "Les Kéréthim et les Crétois." *VT* 28 (1978) 409–22. **Donner, H.** "Der 'Freund des Königs.'" *ZAW* 73 (1961) 269–77. **Hoftijzer, J.** "A Peculiar Question: A Note on 2 Sam. XV 27." *VT* 21 (1971) 606–9. **Joüon, P.** "Notes Philologiques sur le texte hébreu de 2 Samuel." *Bib* 9 (1928) 302–15. **Langlamet, F.** "Pour ou contre Salomon? La rédaction prosalomonienne de 1 Rois, I-II." *RB* 83 (1976) 321–79. ———. "Absalom et les concubines de son père. Recherches sur II Sam., XVI, 21–22." *RB* 84 (1977) 161–209. **Maag, V.** "Belijaᶜal im Alten Testament." *TZ* 21 (1965) 287–99. **McCarter, P. K.** "The Apology of David." *JBL* 99 (1980) 489–504. **McCarthy, D. J.** "The Uses of wᵉhinnēh in Biblical Hebrew." *Bib* 61 (1980) 330–42. **Malamat, A.** "The Danite Migration and the Pan-Israelite Exodus-Conquest: A Biblical Narrative Pattern." *Bib* 51 (1970) 1–16. **Mettinger, T. N. D.** *Solomonic State Officials.* Coniectanea Biblica Old Testament Series 5. Lund: CWK Gleerup, 1971. **Rütersworden, U.** *Die Beamten der israelitischen Königszeit.* BWANT 117. Stuttgart, Berlin, Köln, Mainz: Verlag W. Kohlhammer, 1985. **Selms, A. van.** "The Origin of the Title 'The King's Friend.'" *JNES* 16 (1957) 118–23. **Tsevat, M.** "Marriage and Monarchical Legitimacy in Ugarit and Israel." *JSS* 3 (1958) 237–43. **Uchelen, N. A. van.** "אנשי דמים in the Psalms." *OTS* 15 (1969) 205–12.

Translation

[13]A[a] *messenger came to David, saying,* [b]*"The allegiance of the men of Israel now belongs to Absalom."*[b] [14]*At this, David said to all his servants who were with him in Jerusalem, "Arise, let us flee,* [a]*otherwise there will be no escape for us*[a] *from Absalom. Make haste to depart lest he quickly overtake us,* [b]*and bring disaster*[b] *upon us and put the city to the sword."* [15]*The king's servants then said to the king, "Whatever the king*[a] *chooses, we remain your servants."* [16]*Then the king set out with all his household following him, but he*[a] *left ten concubines*[b] *to keep the house.* [17]*So the king set out with all his household*[a] *following him, and they halted at the last house,* [18]*while all his professional soldiers passed by, all the Cherethites and Pelethites, and all the six hundred Gittites who had followed him from Gath. As they passed before the king,* [19]*he*[a] *said to Ittai the Gittite, "Why should you*[b] *go with us? Go back and stay with* [c]*King Absalom.*[c] *You are a foreigner as well as an exile* [d]*from your native place.*[d] [20]*You came but yesterday;* [a]*shall I make you wander about*[a] *with us today* [b]*wherever I might go?*[b] *Go,*[c] *return and take your kinsmen with you!* [d]*May Yahweh show you*[d] *true loyalty."* [21]*But Ittai answered the king and said, "As surely as Yahweh lives, and as my lord, the king, lives! Truly,*[a] *wherever my lord, the king, may be, there your servant will be also, regardless of death or life."* [22]*Then David said to Ittai, "Go, pass on by!" So Ittai the Gittite passed by with all his men and all the dependents that were with him.* [23]*And all the land wept aloud as the whole army*[a] *passed by. However, the king* [b]*remained standing*[b] *in the Kidron valley, while the entire army passed on* [c]*before him*[c] *along* [d]*the way of the wild olive tree.*[d]

^{24}*Zadok also was there, and all the Levites with him bearing the ark of the covenant of God, and they set down*^{a} *the ark of God*^{b} *until the whole army had crossed over from the city.* ^{25}*Then the king said to Zadok, "Take the ark of God back to the city! If I find favor in the eyes of Yahweh, he will bring me back and show me both it and its dwelling-place,* ^{26}*but if he says, 'I am not pleased with you,' well then, here I am! Let him do to me as he sees fit!"* ^{27}*So the king said to Zadok the priest,* ^{a}*"Are you not an observant person?* ^{a} *Return to the city in peace* ^{b}*both you and Abiathar*^{b} *together with your two sons, Ahimaaz, your son, and Jonathan, son of Abiathar.* ^{28}*Remember,*^{a} *I will be waiting at the fords*^{b} *of the wilderness until word comes from you to inform me."* ^{29}*Then Zadok and Abiathar brought the ark of God back to Jerusalem and they remained*^{a} *there.* ^{30}*David, on the other hand, went up the Slope of the Olives,* ^{a}*weeping as he went;*^{a} *his head was uncovered and he walked along barefooted. Also all the warriors*^{b} *that were with him were weeping as they went, and each man's head was uncovered.* ^{31}*When it was told*^{a} *to David*^{b} *that Ahithophel was among the conspirators with Absalom, David said, "O Yahweh, make nonsense of Ahithophel's plan!"* ^{32}*As David came to the summit where it was the custom to worship*^{a} *God, Hushai the Archite*^{b} *was there to meet him, with his garments torn and dust upon his head.* ^{33}*Then David said to him, "If you come with me, you will be a burden to me,* ^{34}*but if you return to the city and say to Absalom,*^{a} *'I will be your servant, O king; in the past* ^{b}*I was indeed*^{b} *your father's servant but now* ^{c}*I will truly*^{c} *be your servant!' then you will be able to frustrate for me Ahithophel's plan.* ^{35}*Remember,*^{a} *Zadok and Abiathar, the priests, are with you there; report to them*^{b} *any (useful) information* ^{c}*from the king's palace.*^{c} ^{36}*Moreover they have there with them their two sons, Zadok's son, Ahimaaz, and Abiathar's son, Jonathan; by means of them you shall pass on to me whatever you hear (of importance)."* ^{37}*So Hushai, the friend of David, came to the city just as Absalom was about to enter Jerusalem.*

$^{16:1}$*When David had passed a little beyond the summit,* ^{a}*there came to meet him*^{a} *Ziba, the steward of Mephibosheth, with a couple of saddled asses laden with two hundred loaves of bread, one hundred clusters of raisins, one hundred summer fruit, and a skin of wine.* ^{2}*So the king said to Ziba, "What do you plan to do with these things?" "The asses are for the king's family to ride on," said Ziba, "the bread*^{a} *and the summer fruit are for the soldiers*^{b} *to eat, and the wine is for drinking, meant for those who may become exhausted in the wilderness."* ^{3}*Then the king asked, "Where is your master's grandson?" "Oh, he is staying on in Jerusalem," Ziba answered the king, "for he said, 'Today the house of Israel is going to restore to me the kingdom of my grandfather.'"* ^{4}*So the king said to Ziba,* ^{a}*"From now on*^{a} *all that Mephibosheth has belongs to you!" "I pay you my homage," exclaimed Ziba, "may I find favor in your eyes, my lord, the king!"*

^{5}*As the king approached*^{a} *Bahurim, a man from the clan of Saul's family, Shimei, son of Gera, by name came out of the place,* ^{b}*cursing nonstop*^{b} *as he came.* ^{6}*Moreover, he pelted David and all the servants of King David with stones although the army and the elite troops were on (the king's) right and on his left.* ^{7}*This is what Shimei said as he cursed him, "Get out, get out, you murderer*^{a} *and* ^{b}*monster!*^{b} ^{8}*Yahweh has brought upon you all the shed blood of the house of Saul, in whose place you have reigned as king. Now Yahweh has given the kingship to your son Absalom; and here you are in your calamity because you are a murderer!"* ^{9}*Then Abishai, son of Zeruiah, said to the king, "Why should this dead dog curse my lord, the king? Let me cross over and cut off his head!"* [10] *But the king said, "What do I and you, sons of Zeruiah, have in common? Thus* [a] *he is cursing because Yahweh has told him, 'Curse David!' Therefore, who can say, 'Why have you done so?'"* [11] *David then said to Abishai and to all his servants, "See, even my son,* [a] *my own offspring,* [a] *is seeking my life. How much more this Benjaminite now? Let him alone and let him curse, for Yahweh has ordered him.* [b] [12] *But, perhaps, Yahweh will look on my affliction;* [a] *(perhaps) Yahweh will requite me with good for (Shimei's)* [b] *curse* [c] *this day."* [13] *So David and his men went along the road while Shimei continued along the side of the mountain, parallel with him,* [a] *cursing as he went* [a] *and he threw stones* [b] [c] *and was repeatedly kicking up* [c] *dust.* [14] *Eventually, the king and all the soldiers with him arrived weary* [a] *at the fords of wilderness,* [a] *and they refreshed themselves there.*

Notes

13.a. For the use of the definite article in Hebrew, see GKC, § 126q.

13.b-b. Lit., "The hearts of the men of Israel are after Absalom" (so RSV).

14.a-a. McCarter (363) reads with 4QSam[c] לנו [חתי "Then we shall have [an escape]" for MT כי לא תהיה לנו "otherwise there will be no [escape] for us." However, the MT makes reasonable sense.

14.b-b. McCarter (363) follows G[L] and reads ודחה עלינו את העיר "push down the city on top of us." This is plausible but the Lucianic reading may be an emendation of the MT: והדיח עלינו את הרעה "and bring disaster upon us." See also T. Kronholm, "נדח," *TWAT* 5 (Lief. 3/4; 1985) 259.

15.a. MT reads אדני המלך "my lord, the king" but perhaps we should delete אדני with G[L] or read אדנינו "our lord," so many Greek MSS, Vg, and Syr.

16.a. MT has המלך "the king."

16.b. The term is indefinite in MT although it is preceded by the obj marker את (cf. GKC §117d).

17.a. Reading with two Heb. MSS ביתו "his household"; MT has העם "the people" or "army" while G suggests עבדיו "his servants."

19.a. MT: "the king."

19.b. The pronoun is emphatic in Hebrew.

19.c-c. "Absalom" is our interpretative addition.

19.d-d. Following G, Syr, Vg in reading ממקומך "from your place" for MT למקומך "to your place." However, Carlson (170) takes ל to mean "from."

20.a-a. Reading אניעך (so Q) instead of אנועך (so K), since we would expect the causative form. Mauchline (272) takes the verb in a permissive sense, "Let you wander."

20.b-b. Lit., "I am going where I am going." Cf. 1 Sam 23:13.

20.c. Restoring לך "go" with G[LMN], which may have been lost due to haplogr (note the preceding הולך).

20.d-d. We follow G, inserting after עמך "with you": ויהוה יעשה עמך "and may Yahweh deal with you"; the omission may be due to haplogr (so Wellhausen, 197).

21.a. We follow Q in deleting אם "if "; K could be rendered "(I can do no other) except. . . ." See also GKC, § 163d.

23.a. Or "people" (so RSV, NIV, RAV).

23.b. We accept Wellhausen's (197) suggestion to read עמד "standing" for MT עבר "crossing." It is only later that David makes his way up the slope of the Olives.

23.c-c. Following G[L] πρὸ προσώπου αὐτοῦ we read על פניו "before him."

23.d-d. We assume that the unnecessary obj marker (את) is a corruption of an original זית "olive," as suggested by G[L] (so, for instance, Budde, 273). McCarter (365) and others follow the G[L] more closely and read במדבר (אשר) זית דרך "on the Olive Way in the wilderness."

24.a. MT has ויצק which usually means "and they poured out" but the MT may be a dialectical variation of the expected ויצגו "and they set down"; so McCarter (371). Cf. also Fokkelman, *King David*, 451–52.

24.b. Omitting with G^L the following phrase: ויעל אביתר "and Abiathar [too] went up" or
". . . offered [sacrifices]."

27.a-a. MT הרואה אתה could be rendered "Are you not a seer" (so NIV, RAV). Wellhausen
reads הכהן הראש "the chief priest" while G^L suggests the impv ראה "look!" which is followed
by McCarter (361).

27.b-b. We have added the explanatory "both you and Abiathar" to take into account "your
(pl) two sons . . ." and ראו (pl: "see!") in v 28a.

28.a. Lit., "See" (pl).

28.b. So K, reading בעברות while Q suggests בערבות "in the steppes of." We follow K
because it gives a more specific location for the purpose of passing on the information.

29.a. McCarter (366) repoints וישבו "and they remained" as a hiph form "and deposited
it," following G^B. However, the MT gives a better sense.

30.a-a. For the construction, see GKC §113s; Williams, *Syntax,* § 222.

30.b. Lit., "the people."

31.a. Either הגיד is a pass construction "was told," using the active theme in the impersonal
3 sg (see Williams, *Syntax,* § 159) or we should change the verb into a hoph (הוגד); so already
Wellhausen, 198.

31.b. Reading לדוד "to David" as suggested by 4QSam^a, some Heb. MSS and the versions.
MT omits the prep ל "to."

32.a. For this use of the impf, see GKC, § 107g.

32.b. Many scholars add רוח דוד "friend of David" after הארכי "the Archite" as suggested
by G; see v 37.

34.a. After אבשלום "Absalom" there is a lengthy addition in the G but it is far from certain
that it preserves the original reading (contra McCarter, 367).

34.b-b. We regard the *wāw* before אני "I" as an emphatic particle (so Pissano, *Additions and
Omissions,* 141).

34.c-c. See 34.b-b.

35.a. In MT the initial sentence is expressed in the form of a rhetorical question: "Are not
Zadok and Abiathar. . . ?" This may be tantamount to an affirmative statement.

35.b. Stylistic change; MT reads לצדוק ולאביתר הכהנים "to Zadok and Abiathar, the
priests."

35.c-c. G^L suggests "from the king" but this may be an interpretative rendering.

16:1.a-a. For the structure, see McCarthy, *Bib* 61 (1980) 339.

2.a. Reading with Q והלחם; K has ולהלחם "and as for the bread."

2.b. נערים can also mean "young men" (so RAV) or "servants" (so NEB, NAB). See *Comment*
on 9:9.

4.a-a. MT: הנה "behold"; cf. McCarthy, *Bib* 61 (1980) 337–39.

5.a. G with its καὶ ἦλθεν suggests ויבא "and he came." The MT ובא may be a participle but
in that case the subj would usually precede. We follow G.

5.b-b. For the use of the inf abs after the verb, see GKC §113r and t; cf. also Driver, 318.

7.a. Lit., "man of blood."

7.b-b. Lit., "man of Belial."

10.a. Reading כה "thus" with Q; K has כי "if" (?).

11.a-a. Lit., "who came forth from my loins" (so NAB).

11.b. Syr adds "curse David" (קלל את דוד) but this seems to be an interpretative repetition
of the same phrase in v 10.

12.a. Reading בעניי "my affliction," with some Heb. MSS, G, Syr, Vg. K has בעוני "my
iniquity, guilt" which may suggest "the iniquity done to me." Q reads בעיני "on my eye" (?);
KJV mg: "my tears."

12.b. Our interpretative addition.

12.c. Some MSS have קללתי "my curse," i.e., the curse uttered against me.

13.a-a. The inf abs (הלוך) is followed by an impf with waw consecutive (ויקלל "cursing");
for this irregular usage, see GKC §113t.

13.b. Omitting (contra Langlamet) the following לעמתו "parallel with him" (?), with BHK.
It would be somewhat odd if the same word (or phrase) were used twice in the same verse
with two different meanings.

13.c-c. For this use of the pf consecutive, see GKC, § 112t. Budde (276) repoints the verb
עפר "kicked up dust" as an inf abs.

14.a-a. The location seems to have been omitted; we read, tentatively, עד עברות המדבר "at the fords of the wilderness."

Form/Structure/Setting

Our pericope (15:13–16:14) is, of course, part of a more extensive narrative which could be called "Absalom's Rebellion and its Outcome," comprising 15:1–20:22. The extent of this complex story seems to be indicated by the narrative pattern, such as outlined by Conroy (Absalom, 89). We follow, with some modifications, his suggested scheme:

A. The beginning of the revolt 15:1–12
  B. David's flight (meeting scenes) 15:13–16:14
    C. Confrontation of counsellors 16:15–17:23
    C'. Confrontation of armies 17:24–19:9a [19:8a]
  B'. David's return (meeting scenes) 19:9b–41 [19:8b–40]
A'. The end of the rebellion and its aftermath 19:42 [19:41]–20:22

For a more detailed analysis, see K. K. Sacon, "A Study of the Literary Structure of 'The Succession Narrative'." *Studies in the Period of David and Solomon and Other Essays,* ed. T. Ishida (Winona Lake, Indiana: Eisenbrauns, 1982) 31–38.

In our pericope vv 13–18 provide a brief account of the near-panic in Jerusalem and David's hasty departure from the city. This is followed by five encounter scenes with Ittai (15:19–22), Zadok and Abiathar (15:24–29). Hushai (15:32–36), Ziba (16:1–4), and Shimei (16:5–13). These brief episodes illustrate either loyalty to King David or treason but no obvious significance is apparent in the actual sequence of these encounters. These five episodes correspond, to some extent, to the three meeting scenes in chap. 19, in which David meets Shimei, Mephibosheth, and Barzillai.

The additional comments in 15:23, 30–31, 37, and 16:14 give us some further information about the course of David's flight and its progress. V 31 is probably a later addition (see *Form/Structure/Setting* of 16:15–17:23). Würthwein (*Thronfolge,* 44) questions the authenticity of the Shimei scene, and he suggests that his real offense was of a political nature; being the political leader of Benjamin, he apparently gave military support to the rebels.

This account of David's withdrawal from Jerusalem and his flight to the wilderness has no clearly developed plot but it presents us with a series of successive incidents which will have some bearing upon the subsequent events and their understanding. There is a great deal of movement in this pericope; there is coming and going, there is marching, crossing, and ascending. Some of the decisions en route appear to have been taken on the spur of the moment, without any previous planning (see 15:25–29, 32–37).

Comment

13 The messenger may have been sent by David himself to ascertain the situation. The origin and status of the participants at Absalom's coronation may have provided the information needed. It is equally possible that the bearer of the distressing news may have been a man loyal to David, who accidentally had witnessed the approach of Absalom's army (see Fokkelman, *King David*, 177).

14 The hasty evacuation of Jerusalem may have been intended to forestall a possible encirclement as well as to avoid the ruin of the city (cf. v 14b); it may also hint at the great military strength and potential of the rebel forces. Although Transjordan (or at least some of its cities) had been sympathetic to the *Saulide* cause (cf. 2:1–9), yet David sought refuge there rather than trust the defenses of Jerusalem. It is possible that David hoped to increase his army by possible reinforcements from this area, especially if Joab and his troops were stationed in this region.

16 The reference to the concubines prepares the way for 16:21–22. The actual status of the concubines (פלגשים) is not clear (see *Comment* on 3:7) but they need not have been slave wives. Some scholars (for instance, Langlamet, *RB* 83 [1976] 352) regard the concubine episode as a later addition providing the fulfilment of the predictive judgment in 12:11–12; see Würthwein, *Thronfolge*, 40. Moreover, if Tsevat (*JSS* 3 [1958] 241) is right that "the marriage of a former king's wife bestows legitimacy on an aspirant," then David would have been very unwise to leave behind any concubine.

17 Unless v 17a is a later addition, it resumes v 16a. The king and his servants stopped at the last house in the outskirts of Jerusalem. NEB, apparently, suggests a well-known landmark, "the Far House" (so also RV mg). It is likely that David wished to review his remaining troops, and to evaluate their military potential.

18 This verse is textually uncertain, as indicated by the variations in G and other versions. We regard the Cherethites and Pelethites (see *Comment* on 8:18; Delcor, *VT* 28 [1978] 409–22) and the Gittites as being in apposition to the "professional soldiers" (עבדים); see also Rüterswörden, *Die Beamten der israelitischen Königszeit*, 12).

McCarter (364) follows a different textual reconstruction, and in his view the "six hundred" were "David's personal army, raised before he went to Gath." This is plausible since we find references to the "six hundred" in 1 Sam 23:13; 27:2; 30:9. However, the "six hundred" may be a designation of any large military unit; Malamat (*Bib* 51 [1970] 9) suggests "a 'brigade' in force."

The Gittites were probably formed into a military unit during David's service with Achish, the overlord of Gath (cf. 1 Sam 27:1–12) although v 20a may imply that they had arrived on the scene comparatively recently. Ackroyd (144) has suggested that the Gittites may have been "a special bodyguard, perhaps, connected with religious duties."

19 The name "Ittai" (אתי) may be of Semitic origin; see Delcor, *VT* 28 (1978) 411–13. Could Ittai and his Gittites be associated with the Beerothites who had fled to Gittaim (2 Sam 4:2–3)?

It is not clear why David tested the fidelity of Ittai; perhaps, the present episode was intended to contrast the loyalty of a foreign mercenary with the disloyalty of Absalom and David's former friends and supporters.

20 "Yesterday" is not to be taken literally; it simply suggests that the Gittites had joined David not long ago.

"True loyalty" (lit. "loyalty and truth") describes the constancy of Yahweh in maintaining his promises. See also K. D. Sakenfeld, *Faithfulness in Action: Loyalty in Biblical Perspective.* OBT 16. Philadelphia: Fortress Press, 1985, 31–32.

22–23 The Heb. טף usually denotes "children" but in this context it may include also women and the elderly (so *HALAT* 362). "All the land" means, most likely, "the whole city" or "all the inhabitants of the city." In Conroy's view (*Absalom*, 126) this may be an instance of the personification of the *land*.

"The wild olive tree" may have been yet another familiar landmark (see v 17); such trees could last for many years.

24 This verse is problematic both textually and exegetically. Most scholars tend to regard the reference to the Levites as a later gloss which may have replaced an original reference to Abiathar, and of which ויעל אביתר ("and Abiathar went up") may be a surviving fragment. It is less likely that Abiathar offered a sacrifice (but see Fokkelman, *King David*, 185).

25 In David's words and actions there is an apparent contradiction. On the one hand, he sees in the present events the hand of Yahweh, and throws himself on Yahweh's mercy (v 25; 16:12) while, on the other hand, he takes various practical steps, such as to create a "spy network" (vv 27–28, 35–36) in order to weaken his opposition and to frustrate their plans.

27 The latter part of the verse (i.e., "Your [pl] two sons with you [pl]"), suggests that originally two persons (Zadok and Abiathar) were addressed, and that, once more, Abiathar has been eliminated from the text (so Nowack, 212).

There is considerable uncertainty as to the exact meaning of הרואה אתה which we have rendered "are you not an observant man" thus indicating Zadok's (and Abiathar's ?) new "undercover" task. MT could be translated, "Are you a seer?" (i.e., "you are *not* a seer!"), but this would be stating the obvious. For a more detailed discussion of this phrase, see Hoftijzer, *VT* 21 (1971) 606–9, who translates it: "mark ye" or "listen attentively" (609).

The name "Ahimaaz" (אחימעץ) may mean "my brother is wrath" (so BDB, 27) or ". . . is counselor" (*IDB* 1 [1962] 69).

Brueggemann (*Int* 26 [1972] 14) sees the ark as "a guarantee and security for David." However, the king orders the ark back to Jerusalem for, in a sense, it could be a double-edged sword. Yahweh may well be where his ark is but this in itself is no guarantee of success, as experienced by the Israelites (1 Sam 4). All in all, the nearness of Yahweh can be a potentially dangerous factor, as well illustrated by the Uzzah incident (2 Sam 6:6–11). However, in the present passage the ark functions somewhat like the Trojan horse, and its return serves essentially as a "cover-story" for Zadok and Abiathar's intelligence activities.

30 "The Slope of Olives" may be an earlier designation of the Mount of Olives, on the east side of the Wadi Kidron.

There is some uncertainty whether David and his soldiers went bareheaded (so McCarter, 361) or whether they *covered* their heads in mourning. The custom implied by Ezek 24:17, 23 seems to point to the former alternative. It would also make a better sense of the practice of putting dust or ashes on one's head (see 2 Sam 13:19; Neh 9:1; Job 2:12). For the use of חפה

"to cover" or "to uncover" (?), see R. Gordis, "Hebrew Roots of Contrasted Meanings," *JQR* 27 (1936–37) 41–43.

32–36 It is possible that during the early monarchical period there was a holy place or sanctuary on top of the middle summit of the Mount of Olives. There David was met by Hushai the Archite as if in answer to his prayer.

The derivation of חושי "Hushai" is uncertain. McCarter (371–72) is of the opinion that it may indicate an ethnic origin (Aramean or Edomite or Arabian). According to Josh 16:2 the Archite clan was part of Benjamin. It seems that originally David's plan was to use also Hushai as a spy since the king could not foresee that Hushai might be asked by Absalom to give counsel.

37 "The Friend of David" is not simply an honorary title (contra de Vaux, *Ancient Israel*, 129) but it could also denote a royal official of high standing. In 1 Kgs 4:5 he is listed among the high officials of Solomon; the office of the king's friend may be of foreign origin. His actual functions are not defined but he may have acted as the king's intimate counsellor (cf. Rüterswörden, *Die Beamten der israelitischen Königszeit*, 73). It seems less likely that his main responsibility involved only royal weddings (as argued by van Selms, *JNES* 16 [1957] 119–21). Fokkelman (*King David*, 191 n.40) takes "friend" in this context in its ordinary sense; see 16:17 which speaks of David as Hushai's friend (רע). However, it would make better sense if Hushai was a high-ranking royal official rather than merely a personal friend. An official could serve *any* king, as suggested by 16:18.

16:1 If this episode is authentic, Ziba must have sympathized with David, since he could not predict the possible outcome of the rebellion; if anything, David's prospects at this point were rather bad.

For the use of נער "steward," see *Comment* on 9:9; מפי־בשת for "Mephibosheth," see *Comment* on 4:4.

The provisions brought by Ziba are reminiscent of those provided by Abigail in 1 Sam 25:18. Somewhat uncertain is the nature of the "hundred summer fruit" which may have included figs and pomegranates. Not infrequently the weight or measure is omitted after the numeral (see GKC §134n); hence McCarter (362) speaks of "one hundred baskets of summer fruit." However, "one hundred baskets" might make a very cumbersome load for *two* asses.

3 It is difficult to judge whether Ziba's accusation of Mephibosheth was justified or not. David, clearly, regarded it as true, at least at this stage. Later, of course, Mephibosheth claimed that Ziba had slandered him (19:27). Nevertheless, it seems that David was not quite convinced by this protestation. Although "the chances of a lame man gaining the kingship at this point were very remote" (so Ackroyd, 151), it must be noted that Mephibosheth had a son who by this time may have been nearly twenty years old (cf. 4:4; 9:12). Therefore the house of Saul had at least one fit potential candidate for the kingship.

4 This verse illustrates the use of the royal prerogative to confiscate land or property from an enemy or opponent, and to give it to another person as a land-grant (cf. also 9:7).

5 Bahurim, east of Jerusalem, was the home-town of Shimei (see *Comment* on 3:16), and he may well have been accompanied by his kinsmen (as in

19:17[16]). This may partly explain David's reluctance to punish him on this particular occasion.

According to 1 Sam 10:21 Saul's family belonged to the Matrite clan. Although "Gera" (גרא) is known as a Benjaminite clan (cf. Gen 46:21), "Shimei, son of Gera" need not necessarily suggest that Shimei belonged to the *clan* of Gera. The name "Gera" may be a shortened form of a compound name consisting of גר "sojourner, client," plus a personal name. Cf. also גרשם in Exod 2:22, which may mean "stranger there."

Shimei is probably a shortened name (Noth, *Personennamen*, 185), probably from "Yahweh has heard" (so T. M. Mauch, "Shimei," *IDB* 4 [1962] 331).

6 The exact interpretation of this verse is not clear. We have taken v 6b as a circumstantial clause indicating an unusual situation (see GKC §141e). On the other hand, the "army" and the "elite" may also be objects of Shimei's wrath (so McCarter, 362). However, the absence of the obj markers in v 6b may lend some support to the former alternative.

The "army" in this context must have consisted of the mercenary soldiers (the Cherethites, Pelethites, and the Gittites) while the elite troops (גבורים) probably formed David's personal bodyguard.

7 The exact meaning and etymology of בליעל "monster, devilish fellow" are uncertain (see B. Otzen, "בליעל," *TDOT* 2 [1977] 131–36). In 22:5–6 the above word is associated with Sheol and death while in some other contexts (cf. Judg 19:22; 20:13; 1 Sam 2:12) it describes people who are either antisocial or criminal. Such translations as "worthless fellow" (RSV) or "rogue" (RAV) may not be strong enough; McCarter (373) suggests "hellfiend."

Shimei describes David also as איש הדמים which may well mean "murderer." Van Uchelen (*OTS* 15 [1969] 212) would prefer the rendering "bloodthirsty man" because, in his opinion, "there is no hint at any criminal offence" (208). However, even though a Saulide would not say that David had actually killed any member of the house of Saul, he could be held *responsible* for their deaths. Hence he could not very well be described as רצח "killer, murderer" but rather as איש הדמים "a man responsible for bloodshed"—and *therefore* a murderer.

8 Many scholars have argued that Shimei's accusation of David refers to the elimination of the seven descendants of Saul at Gibeon (see 21:1–14), assuming that this event preceded the rebellion of Absalom. Otherwise the charge might concern the death of Abner (3:31–39) and Ishbosheth (4:5–12), since the Saulides may have blamed David for both these murders. It is not impossible that even the death of Saul and Jonathan were, to some extent, blamed on David since, at that time, he had been a Philistine ally (see McCarter, *JBL* 99 [1980] 500).

9 According to Exod 22:28 it was a crime to curse the ruler of one's people; so Abishai, David's nephew and Joab's brother (see *Comment* on 2:18), was ready with a final solution but it was rejected by David.

"The dead dog" in reference to another person is a formula of insult. For this derogatory expression, see *Comment* on 9:8; cf. also Jung, *Court Etiquette*, 35.

10–11 In David's view, Shimei was cursing him because Yahweh had told him to do so (v 11), and this is supported by David's interpretation of the dramatic events (v 11). If Shimei was referring to the deaths of the Saulides described in 21:1–9, then David was, in a way, responsible for the punishment meted out. Therefore he submitted himself to Shimei's cursing realizing, no doubt, that it was Yahweh who had, in some way or other, instigated the punitive action against the house of Saul (see 21.1). Consequently, David could only trust Yahweh's *ultimate* purpose even though he did not understand the meaning of the present affliction (cf. v 12). Thus Shimei was no more than a mouthpiece of Yahweh, and therefore it would serve no purpose to kill Shimei, especially if he was accompanied by his kinsmen (see 19:16–17)!

The exact meaning of the idiomatic rhetorical question, "What do I and you . . . have in common?" is not quite clear. It could be rendered literally as "What to me and to you?" See also Judg 11:12; 2 Sam 19:23; 1 Kgs 17:18; 2 Kgs 3:13.

12 David is hoping for a reversal of fortunes through God's forgiveness (cf. Ps 25:18). Yahweh may yet balance the curse of Shimei with a blessing.

13 Ackroyd (152) notes that there is a space in the text after בדרך " . . . the road," and it has been suggested that this points to a cross reference (in this case, perhaps, to Ps 3 which has in its title the note: "When he fled from Absalom his son").

14 The context clearly requires a place name or location, which has been either accidentally omitted or corrupted into עיפים "weary." Since "the fords of the wilderness" were the first stage in David's flight (see 15:28; 17:16), we assume that עד עברות המדבר "at the fords of the wilderness" has dropped out due to a scribal error. However, alternative suggestions are equally possible, such as עד המים "to the water"; so Joüon, *Bib* 9 [1928] 312), על הירדן "beside the Jordan," following GL.

Explanation

This episode dealing with David's flight before the advancing army of Absalom draws attention to two important aspects: it shows that the present calamity is regarded as Yahweh's work (15:26; 16:10–11), and it affirms that any change of fortunes can come about only through Yahweh's favor and intervention (15:25; 16:12). Therefore David is prepared to leave his future in the hands of God. Furthermore, it is likely that such acts as weeping, going barefooted, and uncovering one's head, were expressions of penitence, and thus the right response to Yahweh's displeasure. It is less certain that we should see in these actions a "ceremonial acted out by David and the people" (Ackroyd, 147).

David does not speculate as to the nature of his transgressions but he unquestioningly accepts that Yahweh's judgment is just. McCarter (376) is right when he sums up David's attitude by saying, "He acknowledges the curse, humbles himself, and hopes for 'something good' to come of it in the end." Indeed in the latter part of the larger narrative we see that in spite of David's failures and sins, Yahweh has forgiven him, and therefore the kingdom has been once more given to David. This would then answer the possible current question whether or not the house of David was *still* the chosen dynasty. The outworking of the events show that he had not been *permanently* rejected (like Saul and his house) but only temporarily punished (on the basis of the principle stated in 7:14–15).

The narrator does not think it inappropriate that, at the same time, David should take various practical steps to frustrate the schemes of Absalom and his collaborators. The author sees human actions in the wider framework of the divine will (see 17:14b), and therefore it is not a question of either/or. David as a military leader was expected to do his best in the circumstances but ultimate success depended upon Yahweh.

Absalom and His Counsellors
(16:15–17:23)

Bibliography

Cook, S. A. "Notes on the Composition of 2 Samuel." *AJSL* 16 (1899–1900) 145–77. **Flanagan, J. W.** "Judah in All Israel." In *No Famine in the Land: Studies in Honor of John L. McKenzie,* ed. J.W. Flanagan and A. W. Robinson. Missoula, MT: Scholars Press for the Institute of Antiquity and Christianity—Claremont, 1975. 101–16. **Fohrer, G.** "Der Vertrag zwischen König und Volk in Israel." *Studien zur alttestamentlichen Theologie und Geschichte 1949–1966.* BZAW 115. Berlin: Töpelmann, 1969. 330–51 = *ZAW* 71 (1959) 1–22. **Glueck, N.** *Ḥesed in the Bible.* Tr. A. Gottschalk. Cincinnati: The Hebrew Union College Press, 1967. **Langlamet, F.** "Pour ou contre Salomon? La rédaction prosalomonienne de 1 Rois, I–II." *RB* 83 (1976) 321–79; 481–529.

Translation

[15] *Meanwhile, Absalom and all the army,[a] the men of Israel, entered Jerusalem, and Ahithophel was with him.* [16] *When the Friend of David, Hushai the Archite, came to Absalom, he[a] said to Absalom,* [b]*"Long live the king! Long live the king!"*[b] [17] *But Absalom said to Hushai, "Is[a] this your loyalty to your friend? Why did you not go with your friend?"* [18] *"It is not so,"[a] said Hushai to Absalom, "rather I am* [b]*for him*[b] *whom Yahweh and his people* [c]*(that is, all the Israelites)*[c] *have chosen;* [d]*with him I shall stay.* [19] *Furthermore,[a] whom should I serve? Shall I not* [b]*serve the king's son?*[b] *As I have served[c] your father, [d]so I shall be at your service."[d]*

[20] *Then Absalom said to Ahithophel, "Give counsel as to what we should do."* [21] *So Ahithophel said to Absalom, "Have intercourse with your father's concubines whom he has left behind to keep the house. Then all Israel will realize that [a]you have made a complete break with your father,[a] and so the determination[b] of all those who are with you will be strengthened."* [22] *Therefore they pitched a tent for Absalom on the roof, and Absalom went in to his father's concubines in the view of all Israel.*

[23] *In those days the counsel given by Ahithophel was highly regarded, as if one[a] had consulted the oracle of God. To such an extent was all the counsel of Ahithophel esteemed both by David and Absalom!* [17:1] *Then Ahithophel said to Absalom, "Let me select[a] twelve thousand men and let me set out that I may pursue David this very night.* [2] *Thus I will come upon him while he is weary and weak,[a] and I will cause him to panic. And when all the army that is with him flee, I shall kill only the king.* [3] *Then I will bring back to you all the people, [a]as a bride returns to her husband. It is only one man's life[a] that you are seeking—the people as a whole shall remain intact."* [4] *And the plan seemed just right to Absalom and all the elders of Israel.*

[5] *Then Absalom said, "Now call[a] Hushai the Archite also,[b] and let us hear what it is that he[c] has to say."* [6] *When Hushai came to him,[a] Absalom said to him, "This is the plan Ahithophel has suggested. Shall we[b] follow his plan? If[c] not, you better speak!"* [7] *Hushai then answered Absalom, "This time the advice Ahithophel has given is not sound.[a]* [8] *You know yourself," Hushai said, "that your father and*

*his men are formidable warriors and (at the moment) they are furious, like a bear
who has lost her cubs in the wild.*[a] *Moreover, your father is a seasoned warrior; he
will not camp with the troops.* [9][a]*Even now*[a] *he may be hiding in one of the gorges
or some such place. And supposing that some of them*[b] *fall in the initial attack,
anyone hearing will say, 'There has been slaughter among the army that follows
Absalom.'* [10]*Even if he is a brave man whose heart is like that of a lion—he, too,
will lose courage, for all Israel knows that your father is a formidable warrior and
that those who are with him are brave men.* [11][a]*I, for my part, offer the following
advice:*[a] *'Let all Israel, from Dan to Beersheba, be gathered to you, as numerous
as the sand that is by the sea,*[b] *with yourself*[c] *marching in* [d]*their midst.*[d] [12]*So we
shall come upon*[a] *him in whatever*[b] *place he may be found, and we shall descend
on him as dew falls on the ground; not even one will be left, neither he nor anyone
of the men with him.* [13]*However, if he retreats into a city, then all Israel will
bring ropes to that city, and we shall drag it*[a] *into the wadi until not even a
pebble remains there.'"* [14]*Then Absalom and all the men of Israel said, "The advice
of Hushai the Archite is better than the advice of Ahithophel." So Yahweh had
decreed in order to frustrate the good counsel of Ahithophel so that he*[a] *might bring
ruin upon Absalom.*

[15]*Then Hushai said to Zadok and Abiathar, the priests, "This is how Ahithophel
counselled Absalom and the elders of Israel, and this is how I myself counselled.*
[16]*Send quickly, now, a warning*[a] *and inform David as follows: 'Do not spend the
night at the fords*[b] *of wilderness,* [c]*but be sure to cross over*[c] *lest the king and all
the army that is with him be annihilated.'"*[d] [17]*Now Jonathan and Ahimaaz were
staying at En-Rogel, and a maidservant*[a] *went from time to time and brought
information to them; then they would go and pass the information to King David,
since they dared not to be seen entering*[b] *the city.* [18]*However, a youth saw them
and informed Absalom while the two of them left quickly and went to the house of
a man in Bahurim, who had a well in his courtyard. Then they climbed down
into it,* [19]*and* [a]*the man's wife*[a] *took and spread a cover over the mouth*[b] *of the
well, scattering upon it sand*[c] *so that nothing (of it) could be noticed.* [20]*When the
servants of Absalom came to the woman in the house, they asked, "Where are
Ahimaaz and Jonathan?" "They passed by hurriedly*[a] *to the water," the woman
said to them. Now although they searched, they found nothing, so they returned to
Jerusalem.* [21]*After they had gone,* [a]*Jonathan and Ahimaaz*[a] *climbed out of the
well and went to inform King David. They said to David, "Arise and cross the
water at once, for so and so has Ahithophel counselled against you."* [22]*So David
and the army that was with him, set out and crossed the Jordan, and by the morning
light there was not one left who had not crossed the Jordan.*

[23]*When Ahithophel saw that his plan was not implemented, he saddled his ass*[a]
*and set out and went to his house in his own city. Then, having given final instructions
concerning his family, he hanged himself. So he died and was buried in his father's
tomb.*

Notes

15.a. The "army" (העם) is lacking in G. Perhaps, it should be omitted as an alternative
reading to "the men of Israel." Driver (319) notes that כל העם "all the army" is usually with
David while כל איש ישראל "all the Israelites" are with Absalom.

16.a. MT has "Hushai."

16.b-b. This formula is written only once in G and two Heb. MSS. Its omission may be due to haplogr.

17.a. In MT the question is expressed without the help of any interrogative particle (see GKC §150a).

18.a. MT has only לא "No."

18.b. So Q reading לו; K has לא "no."

18.c-c. We regard וכל איש ישראל "and all the men of Israel" as an explanatory note.

18.d. The verb בחר is sg, thus agreeing with the nearer subj (see Williams, *Syntax*, §230).

19.a. Lit., "and the second (point is)." This usage is rather uncommon (see Conroy, *Absalom*, 133 n.75).

19.b-b. In MT there is no verb, and "the king's son" is a paraphrase of בנו "his son."

19.c. The verb עבד "to serve" is followed by לפני "before," which is unusual. Some Heb. MSS have instead the obj marker את.

19.d-d. A possible literal rendering: "so I will be in your presence" (RAV).

21.a-a. Lit., "you have become odious to your father."

21.b. Lit., "the hands."

23.a. Q adds איש "man, one" but this is already implied by the verb. Most scholars follow K.

17:1.a. G and Vg suggest after the verb the reflexive לי "for myself" which is more idiomatic (see GKC §119s).

2.a. Lit., "weak of hands." For the circumstantial clause, see GKC §141e.

3.a-a. G may have preserved the original text, so we read: כשוב הכלה אל אישה רק נפש איש אחד "as a bride returns to her husband. It is only one man's life. . . ." MT could be rendered "as the return of all is the man whom you seek."

5.a. Most versions presuppose the pl קראו "call."

5.b. Lacking in two Heb. MSS; not really required.

5.c. The pronom suff in בפיו (lit. "in his mouth") is stressed by גם הוא (see GKC §135f).

6.a. MT has "Absalom."

6.b. Probably not a plural of majesty (see GKC §124g) but referring both to Absalom and his staff.

6.c. Many MSS read, rightly, ואם "but if not."

7.a. Lit., "good."

8.a. G^B reads καὶ ὡς ὗς τραχεῖα ἐν τῇ πεδίῳ "or a sow snared in the wild." However, its originality is doubted by many scholars (contra McCarter, 382).

9.a-a. Lacking in OL and in one MS of G^L.

9.b. G^L must have read העם "the army" for MT בהם "among them." Retain MT.

11.a-a. G^B reads ὅτι οὕτως συμβουλεύων ἐγὼ συγεβούλευσα which suggests כי כה יעץ אנכי יעצתי "for thus I strongly suggest." However, opinions differ as to the authenticity of this variant reading.

11.b. Some MSS and Tg have the usual expression על שפת הים "on the sea-shore."

11.c. MT's ופניך "and your presence" may be an alternative expression for "you" (or "you yourself").

11.d-d. MT reads בקרב "in battle" but this may be an Aramaism and comparatively late. We follow the versions, reading בקרבם "in their midst."

12.a. So most versions. MT's אל may be equivalent to "upon" since אל and על are often used interchangeably in Samuel.

12.b. Q rightly reads אחד "one" which is the masc form; K has the feminine אחת "one." מקום "place" is masc.

13.a. MT has אתו "it" for the expected אתה (i.e. the obj marker plus the 3rd fem sg suff), since עיר "city" is fem. Fokkelman (*King David*, 457) suggests that אתו refers to David and that David and the city are seen as one.

14.a. Stylistic change; MT has "Yahweh."

16.a. Our stylistic addition.

16.b. Reading with many MSS בעברות "at the fords of" instead of בערבות "in the steppes of."

16.c-c. For the use of the inf abs with the finite verb, see GKC §113l.

16.d. Lit., "swallowed up." This is clearly a metaphorical usage (see Conroy, *Absalom*, 126 n.51) and we take the ל before מלך "king" as a dative of reference (so Snaith, 35).

17.a. For the use of the article to denote a person as yet unknown, see GKC §126r.
17.b. One Heb. MS reads ולבוא "or entering (the city)"; similarly G^L, Syr, Vg.
19.a-a. MT reads only האשה "the woman"; Fokkelman (*King David*, 224) translates it as "the women."
19.b. Some MSS (and also most versions) read פי "the mouth of" for MT פני "the surface of." We follow the former alternative.
19.c. Reading חריפות "grains of sand" for MT הרפות (BDB: "grain or fruit") which McCarter (389) renders "groats." However, the meaning remains doubtful (see also Driver, 324).
20.a. Reading, tentatively, מהרה "hurriedly" with Budde (280), for MT מיכל (BDB: "brook, stream" [?]) the meaning of which is uncertain. The G^L may offer some support to the proposed reading, with its σπεύδοντες "hurrying." McCarter (383) suggests מיבל המים "in the direction of the watercourse."
21.a-a. An interpretative addition.
23.a. MT: "the ass."

Form / Structure / Setting

This episode (16:15–17:23) is mainly concerned with the confrontation between the two counsellors, Ahithophel and Hushai, and with the consequences of their respective advice.

A possible outline of the narrative is as follows:

A. Absalom and Ahithophel arrive in Jerusalem   16:15
B. Hushai insinuates himself into Absalom's confidence 16:16–19
C. Ahithophel's plan   16:20–17:4
D. Hushai's alternative scheme   17:5–14
E. The success of Hushai as informer   17:15–22
F. The suicide of Ahithophel   17:23

In this episode as a whole, Absalom is to some extent in the background while the chief actors are Ahithophel and Hushai. The counsel of the former is, under the circumstances, rather restrained but practically sound; it promises quick success with the minimum loss of life. According to 12:11–12, Absalom's cohabitation with his father's concubines was seen as part of the divine punishment on David.

Hushai's advice (17:7–13) consists of two main parts: (a) the rebuttal of Ahithophel's plan (vv 8–10) and (b) his counter-proposal (vv 11–13). His scheme is characterized by rhetorical exaggerations and double meanings rather than by any clear military strategy. However, its acceptance is explained in theological terms—it was achieved through Yahweh's intervention (17:14).

The literary unity of this episode has been disputed by a number of scholars who find in it later additions. Thus, already Cook (*AJSL* 16 [1899–1900] 163) had contended that Ahithophel's advice concerning the concubines (16:21–23) was not part of the oldest form of the narrative.

Würthwein (*Thronfolge*, 33–42) has produced a more detailed argument to the effect that 15:31; 16:21–23; 17:5–14, 15b, 23 are to be regarded as redactorial (as well as the related 15:16b and 20:3). In his opinion the *erroneous* advice of Ahithophel was his suggestion regarding the treatment of David's concubines (37–40), being the counterpart to the prayer of David in 15:31. He has also pointed out that Ahithophel's second and wise counsel (17:1–4) which is balanced by the sending of Hushai (15:34–36) to defeat Ahithophel's plan, would have lost its essential advantage of surprise, had the advice of the first one been carried out. Moreover, 17:24 may be taken to imply that Absalom must have pursued David without much delay; it was only fortunate for David that he was forewarned in time by his spies (17:16–22). Therefore Würthwein suspects the authenticity of the concubine scene as well as Hushai's counsel (41). See also Langlamet, *RB* 83 (1976) 353–54. Mettinger (*King and Messiah*, 29) assigns 17:5–14 to a Deuteronomistic redaction.

We have followed a somewhat similar interpretation of the narrative (cf. also Gunn, *King David*, 115–16), and it seems that Ahithophel's counsel was the one actually followed without undue loss of time (cf. 17:24); unfortunately it was frustrated because David had set up an efficient spy network (17:15–22). Thus Hushai's counsel may well be a redactional addition since 17:15a looks like a continuation of 17:4. Hence it is plausible that Ahithophel eventually hanged himself not because of hurt pride (in that Absalom and the elders of Israel had rejected his plan), but rather that his suicide took place *after* the final defeat of Absalom or, perhaps, after his military scheme had misfired due to Hushai's treachery.

The concubine scene, too, may be a later addition in order to provide the fulfilment of Nathan's prophecy (see 12:11–12). On the other hand, it is not entirely impossible that Ahithophel's offer that he should lead the pursuit after David, may actually presuppose the concubine incident, and it does not imply any disrespect for Absalom's military abilities (as suggested by Payne, 238).

Even if Hushai's plan was part of the original narrative, it was *not* accepted by Absalom, and therefore Hushai advised David to cross Jordan as soon as possible. One could perhaps argue that Hushai wanted to play safe and therefore he sent the above instructions to David. However, 17:24 seems to imply that it was Ahithophel's plan that was implemented although for obvious reasons it did not achieve the desired results.

Comment

15 The reference to the Israelites need not suggest that Absalom's support came only (or mainly) from the northern tribes. The term "Israelites" must include also Judeans (contra Alt, *Essays*, 229). See also 17:11.

16 The exclamation, "Long live the king" is usually linked with the royal investiture (see Mettinger, *King and Messiah*, 131). In our particular setting it is not simply an acclamation but, perhaps, it is equivalent to an elliptic oath whereby a person "places himself under the jurisdiction of the one to whom he refers in his oath" (134). Of course, Hushai was either thinking of David (so McCarter, 384) or, more likely, simply deceiving Absalom.

At least theoretically, kingship rested both on divine designation and popular choice (see Alt, *Essays*, 195; Mettinger, *King and Messiah*, 129–30, 182–84). In Absalom's case the popular acclamation was already obvious and the divine choice was implicit in his anointing (19:11[10]).

The repetition of "Long live the king" may serve to emphasize Hushai's feigned enthusiasm. Perhaps it is not accidental that Hushai avoids saying, "Long live King *Absalom*" (cf. 1 Kgs 1:25, 31, 34, 39).

17   Absalom's sarcastic question alludes to Hushai's title, "Friend of David" (see *Comment* on 15:37). There may be a play on the two meanings of "friend."

The loyalty (חֶסֶד) in question may well be allegiance to the king (cf. Glueck, *Ḥesed,* 50; see also *Comment* on 2:5). Hushai appears to Absalom as a disloyal individual, yet Hushai *is* loyal, but only to David.

18–19   Absalom, no doubt, regarded Hushai's words as a form of flattery, but in essence they may have been a restatement of Hushai's loyalty to Yahweh and, by implication, to David. Hushai offers his services to Absalom, being a good "civil servant," and he pretends that he is true to the dynasty as represented by Absalom.

21–22   Würthwein (*Thronfolge,* 39) seems right in arguing that it is unlikely that the take-over of the harem of the previous king legitimated the new king's claim to the throne. Thus the cohabitation with the concubines of David may not have given Absalom any special legal claim to the kingship (contra Tsevat, "Marriage and Monarchical Legitimacy in Ugarit and Israel," *JSS* [1958] 241); it is doubtful that this act could add anything to what was already given by the divine choice and popular acclamation. This cohabitation in our context may have served as an indication that as far as Absalom was concerned—David was dead. Was it a deliberate deception to give the impression to the people in general that David was *actually* dead (cf. Budde, 278)? According to Lev 18:8; 20:11; Deut 22:30 [MT 23:1]; 27:20 it was forbidden for a son to take his father's wife, at least while the father was alive (cf. also Gen 35:22; 49:3–4). If so, the deception (?) may have strengthened the resolve of Absalom's supporters since this final humiliation of David was a deliberately public act, at least according to the narrator.

Gunn (*King David,* 116) has pointed out that Absalom's take-over of David's concubines may have been a *formal* act, while von Rad (*The Problem of the Hexateuch,* 184) calls it "a symbolic action intended to gain the confidence of the people for Absalom."

The verb בָּאַשׁ "to become odious, stink," probably suggests that Absalom had become odious to his father or that he had acted disgracefully, and that therefore a complete and irreversible break had taken place. In such a situation there was only one course of action, as is well illustrated by 1 Sam 27:12; see also Gen 34:30; 1 Sam 13:4; 2 Sam 10:6. Tsevat (242) proposes the following rendering: "You have challenged your father."

The tent was, most likely, the bridal tent (cf. Ps 19:5[4]; Joel 2:16), and the whole proceedings were, more or less, equivalent to a royal wedding (so Stolz, 262) but with wider implications. Fokkelman (*King David,* 210) assumes that this tent was erected on the same roof from which David had seen and desired Bathsheba. This association may have existed, at least, in the mind of the narrator.

23   At this time "the oracle of God" (lit., "the word . . .") may have been obtained by means of the Urim and Thummim (see *Comment* on 2:1).

17:1–3   Ahithophel's plan was strategically sound, as indicated by David's hasty retreat from the fords (17:22). The "twelve thousand" may refer to the *twelve* tribes but this is less certain.

Since Ahithophel regarded Absalom as the rightful king, the simile of the home-coming of the young wife is not inappropriate. However, some scholars have argued that the verb שוב "to return" is not quite fitting (so Smith, 352). Perhaps, one should not press the "return" aspect; NEB translates the verb by "is brought."

The "people" in this context may refer to David's army (so McCarter, 379) but it may also include David's supporters in general. The majority of the people of Israel and Judah had already sided with Absalom (see 15:13; 17:4b).

5–10 Hushai's criticism of Ahithophel's scheme appeals to the well-known fact that David was a seasoned warrior who would not take undue risks, and that his smaller army was largely made up of crack troops. Therefore even if the tribal militia had some initial success in a night attack, they might easily panic during the battle. Some scholars follow the G^L reading and assume that the losses mentioned are those inflicted upon *Absalom's followers* (see Fokkelman, *King David*, 222).

11–12 "From Dan to Beersheba" is a sort of merismus which expresses a totality in a shortened form (see Watson, *Classical Hebrew Poetry*, 321). Unless the expression is an exaggeration, it is a further indication that Absalom's support was derived both from Israel and Judah. See also *Comment* on 3:10.

Hushai proposes that Absalom should personally lead the militia of all Israel, and assures that as a result the destruction of David and his forces would be a certainty. Ahithophel's plan, on the other hand, was concerned mainly with the elimination of one person, David (17:2–3).

The dew simile probably points to the all-enveloping nature of the attack which will be entirely beyond the enemy's ability to resist or control (see Mic 5:6[7]). However, Ehrlich (316) regards this simile as inappropriate in a military context.

Budde (279) takes נותר as a first person plural hiphil imperfect; so also JB: "(we shall) not leave. . . ." Most exegetes, however, explain the verb as a niphal perfect (cf. Smith, 353).

17 "En-Rogel" or "Rogel Spring" was near the confluence of the Kidron and Hinnom valleys, and it is usually identified with the present-day *Bîr Ayyūb* or "Job's Well."

The relaying of the information must have been done more than once, as suggested by the verbs (see GKC §112k) although not necessarily *before* Hushai's message.

18–19 Jonathan and Ahimaaz sought refuge in Bahurim, Shimei's village (see *Comment* on 16:5), with some sympathizers of David's cause. The well in which they hid themselves was, apparently, covered and camouflaged with sand (?) so that no trace could be seen. Although the Hebrew word for sand (חריפות or חרפות) is uncertain, the purpose of the exercise favors "sand" as the more likely material. For a similar incident, see Josh 2:6.

21 Ahithophel's counsel must have been reported in detail but our narrator takes the information for granted.

23 Ahithophel retired to his own town Gilo (see *Comment* on 15:12) and gave what might be described as his death-bed instructions. This may imply that he made arrangements about the distribution of the property and provisions for the family (see 2 Kgs 20:1 = Isa 38:1; cf. also Deut 21:16).

Since he was buried in his father's tomb, it implies that no stigma was attached to an act of suicide at this time. See also Judg 9:54; 1 Sam 31:4–5;

1 Kgs 16:18. Although some later Jewish traditions condemn suicide, the earlier writers make no explicit negative comment. 2 Macc 14:41–46 seems to imply that a righteous suicide may have a share in the future resurrection (see J. A. Goldstein, *II Maccabees* [AB 41a; Garden City, NY: Doubleday, 1983] 492–93).

Explanation

This section of the larger narrative complex deals with the confrontation of the two counsellors of Absalom. In its *present* form, this encounter is seen as a real event in which the strategically inferior plan of Hushai was eventually preferred to the militarily sound scheme of Ahithophel. However, in the light of the subsequent events (see especially 17:24) it seems that this present shape of the story is a later literary construction. It seems that in actual fact it was Ahithophel's advice that was followed although it was frustrated by Hushai's betrayal and with the assistance of his collaborators.

On the other hand, if Hushai's counsel is taken as authentic, then he himself may not have been sure whether or not he had convinced Absalom's war-council (see 17:15). Therefore to be safe—he advised David and his army to cross the river Jordan immediately. If 17:24 refers to this same event, then the implication is that Hushai's advice was not in the end adopted by Absalom and the elders of Israel.

The present story seems to stress that the frustration of Absalom's plans and David's deliverance were, in the first place, the work of Yahweh as an answer to David's prayer (15:31).

Ahithophel's suicide was attributed to the *rejection* of his counsel but the essential question is, "Was it rejected?" It seems more plausible to assume that he took his life at some later stage, perhaps after the battle in the Forest of Ephraim. As one of the chief supporters of Absalom, he was a marked man, especially since he had advocated the elimination of David himself (cf. 17:2; see also 1:14 which affirms the inviolability of Yahweh's anointed).

Some scholars find a parallel between Ahithophel and Judas (cf. Matt 27:5), as well as between the betrayal of David and that of Jesus; some of the locations mentioned occur in both accounts but this may be inevitable. Ackroyd (162) is right in commenting that "the narrative of Jesus' passion is deeply enriched with such Old Testament allusion and analogy."

The Decisive Battle and Absalom's Death   (17:24–19:9a[8a])

Bibliography

Bartlett, J. R. "Sihon and Og, Kings of the Amorites." *VT* 20 (1970) 257–77. **Gunn, D. M.** "David and the Gift of the Kingdom. (2 SAM 2–4, 9–20; 1 KGS 1–2)." *Semeia* 3 (1975) 14–45. **Haupt, P.** "Deal gently with the young man." *JBL* 45 (1926) 357. **Langlamet, F.** "Pour ou contre Salomon? La rédaction prosalomonienne de 1 Rois, I–II." *RB* 84 (1976) 321–79. **Levenson, J. D.** and **Halpern, B.** "The Political Import of David's Marriages." *JBL* 99 (1980) 507–18. **Mendenhall, G. E.** "The Census Lists of Numbers 1 and 26." *JBL* 77 (1958) 52–66. **Moran, W. L.** "The Ancient Near Eastern Background of the Love of God in Deuteronomy." *CBQ* 25 (1963) 77–87. **Schunck, K.-D.** "Erwägungen zur Geschichte und Bedeutung von Mahanaim." *ZDMG* 113 (1963) 34–40. **Ward, E. F. de.** "Mourning Customs in 1, 2 Samuel." *JJS* 23 (1972) 1–27, 144–66.

Translation

[24] *David had already reached Mahanaim when (some time later) Absalom crossed the Jordan, both he and all the men of Israel with him.* [25] *Absalom had set Amasa over the army in place of Joab. Amasa was the son of a man named Ithra[a] the Ishmaelite,[b] who had married[c] Abigail,[d] the daughter of Nahash, the sister of Zeruiah, Joab's mother.* [26] *So Israel and Absalom encamped in the land of Gilead.*

[27] *When David came to Mahanaim, Shobi, son of Nahash, from Rabbah of the Ammonites, Machir, son of Ammiel, from Lo-debar, and Barzillai the Gileadite from Rogelim* [28] [a] *brought couches for sleeping and blankets,[a] as well as bowls and pottery jars. They also brought wheat, barley, flour, roasted corn, beans, lentils,[b]* [29] *honey, [a]curds, sheep,[a] and [b]cheese from the herd[b] for David and the troops with him to eat, for they assumed[c] that the army would be hungry, exhausted, and thirsty in the wilderness.*

[18:1] *David then mustered the troops[a] that were with him, and appointed over them commanders of thousands and commanders of hundreds.* [2] *Next, David [a]sent out[a] the army: a third under the command of Joab, a third under the command of Abishai, son of Zeruiah, Joab's brother, and a third under the command of Ittai the Gittite. Furthermore, the king said to the soldiers, [b]"I am determined to march out[b] with you myself."* [3] *But the soldiers protested,[a] "You shall not march out; for if we should flee,[b] they will not pay any attention to us.[b] Even if half of us should die, they will not pay any attention to us; but you[c] are worth ten[d] thousand of such as us. Now, therefore, it is better that you should be ready to help[e] us [f]from the city."[f]* [4] *Then the king said to them, "I will do what seems best to you." So the king stood by the gate while the entire army marched out by hundreds and by thousands.* [5] *The king instructed Joab, Abishai, and Ittai, "Deal kindly[a] for my sake with the young man Absalom!" Thus all the army heard when the king instructed all the commanders concerning Absalom.* [6] *So the army marched out into the field (of battle) to meet Israel, and the battle took place in the Forest of Ephraim.[a]* [7] *There the army of Israel was defeated by the mercenaries[a] of David, and there* were ᵇmany casualtiesᵇ that day—twenty thousand men. ⁸The fighting spreadᵃ over the whole area, and the forest swallowed up more men that day than the sword devoured.

⁹Absalom was riding on a mule, when he found himself confronted by David's men. So the mule boltedᵃ under ᵇthe tangled branchesᵇ of a large tree,ᶜ and Absalom'sᵈ head was caught fast in the tree; thus he became suspendedᵉ midairᶠ while the mule under him ran off. ¹⁰When a certain man saw this, he reported to Joab, saying, "I have just seen Absalom hanging in a tree." ¹¹"What, you actually saw him?"ᵃ said Joab to the man who had made the report to him, "Why then did you not strike him to the ground on the spot? I would indeed have given you tenᵇ pieces of silver and a belt." ¹²But the man said to Joab, "Even if I ᵃwere weighingᵃ a thousand ᵇshekels of silverᵇ upon my hands, I would not lay a hand on the king's son; for in our own hearing the king instructed you and Abishai and Ittai, saying, 'Protect ᶜfor my sakeᶜ the young man Absalom.' ¹³Supposing I had dealt treacherously against hisᵃ life—nothing can be hidden from the king—then you yourself would have stood aloof." ¹⁴Then Joab said, ᵃ"I will not keep on waiting like this before you."ᵃ So he took three dartsᵇ in his hand and thrust them into the heart of Absalom while he was still alive in the midstᶜ of the tree. ¹⁵Finally the young men, Joab's weapon-bearers, surrounded Absalom and killed him. ¹⁶Joab then sounded the horn, and the army returned from pursuing Israel for Joab restrained the troops.ᵃ ¹⁷And they took Absalom and flung him into ᵃa certain large pitᵃ in the forest, and ᵇpiled upᵇ over him a very large heap of stones. Meanwhile, all the Israelites fled, each man to his home.ᶜ

¹⁸During his lifetime Absalom had taken and erected a pillarᵃ which is in the king's valley, for he said, "I have no son to cause people to remember my name." So he called the pillar by his own name; thus to this day it is called Absalom's monument.

¹⁹Then Ahimaaz, son of Zadok, said, "Let me run and bring the news to the king that Yahweh has deliveredᵃ him from the grasp of his enemies." ²⁰But Joab answered him, "You are not to be a bearer of news this day, you can bear the news another day. Today you shall not bear news becauseᵃ the king's son is dead." ²¹Then Joab said to ᵃa certain Cushite,ᵃ "Go, report to the king what you have seen." So the Cushiteᵇ bowed low before Joab and set off running. ²²But Ahimaaz, son of Zadok, said again to Joab, "Come what may, I will run also, after the Cushite!" ᵃ"Why on earthᵃ should you run, my son?" said Joab. "There will be no reward forthcoming for you."ᵇ ²³However, ᵃAhimaaz said,ᵃ "Come what may, I will run!" So he said to him, "Run!" Then Ahimaaz set off running by ᵇway of the Jordan plain,ᵇ and he by-passed the Cushite.

²⁴David was sitting between the two gates when the watchman went up to the roof of the gateway by the wall; as he looked out, he saw a man running alone.ᵃ ²⁵So the watchman shouted out and reported to the king. "If he is alone," said the king, "he must have news." As he came nearer and nearer, ²⁶the watchman saw another man running; so heᵃ called ᵇto the gate-keeper,ᵇ saying, "There is anotherᶜ man running alone." The king remarked, "This one, too, is a messenger." ²⁷Then the watchman said, ᵃ"It seems to me,ᵃ that the running of the first one is like the running of Ahimaaz, son of Zadok." The king replied, "He is a good man and he comes on accountᵇ of good news." ²⁸As Ahimaaz came nearᵃ he greetedᵇ the king and did homage to him,ᶜ his face to the ground, and he said, "Blessed be Yahweh,

your God, who has handed over the men who raised their hands against my lord, the king." [29] *Then the king asked, "Is the young man Absalom safe?"*[a] *"I saw a great commotion," replied Ahimaaz,* [b] *"when Joab sent your servant*[b] *but I do not know what it was about."* [30] *"Turn aside and stand here," said the king. So he turned aside and stood.* [31] [a] *At that point,*[a] *the Cushite came and said,*[b] *"Let my lord, the king, receive the tidings that Yahweh has delivered you*[c] *this day from the power of all those who rose up against you."*[c] [32] *But the king said to the Cushite, "Is the young man Absalom safe?" "May the enemies of my lord, the king, and all those who rise up against you* [a] *with evil intent*[a] *be like that young man!"* [19:1 [18:33]] *Then the king was very upset; he went up to the roof-chamber of the gate and wept.* [a] *As he went,*[a] *he spoke thus, "O, my son Absalom. O, my son Absalom. I wish*[b] *that I myself*[c] *had died in your place. O, Absalom, my son, my son!"*

[19:2 [1]] *It was reported to Joab, "The king is weeping and mourning,*[a] *over Absalom."* [3] [2] *Thus the victory that day was turned into mourning for the whole army when they*[a] *heard that day that the king was broken-hearted over his son.*[b] [4] [3] *So the army came*[a] *stealthily into the city that day, stealing in like an*[b] *army that had disgraced itself by fleeing in battle.* [5] [4] *But the king covered his face and cried*[a] *out in a loud voice, "My son Absalom. Absalom,*[b] *my son, my son."* [6] [5] *Then Joab went to the king into the house*[a] *and said, "Today you have put to shame*[b] *all your servants who have saved your life as well as the lives of your sons and daughters, the lives of your wives and* [c] *your concubines,*[c] [7] [6] *by loving those who hate you and hating those who love you. Indeed, you have made it very plain today that officers and men*[a] *are nothing to you. Now I know for certain that if Absalom were alive today and all of us were dead, then that would be pleasing to you!* [8] [7] *Now then, go out at once, and mollify your servants! I swear*[a] *by Yahweh that if*[b] *you do not go out, not a single man will remain with you this night. This will be more disastrous for you than any other disaster that has come upon you from your youth until now."* [9] [8] *So the king got up and sat in the gate. When the troops were told,*[a] *"The king is sitting in the gate," they all came before the king.*

Notes

25.a. Some Greek MSS and OL suggest יתר "Jether"; so also 1 Kgs 2:5, 32 and 1 Chr 2:17.

25.b. MT has הישראלי "the Israelite" but this seems odd. Most scholars follow 1 Chr 2:17 and G^A in reading הישמעאלי "the Ishmaelite."

25.c. Lit., "had gone to," and may suggest a ṣadiqa type of marriage in which the wife was visited by her husband at various times. The wife and the children remained in the maternal home (see de Vaux, *Ancient Israel*, 29).

25.d. Reading אביגיל "Abigail" with 1 Chr 2:17; MT has אביגל "Abigal."

28.a-a. There is no verb in MT but G^B may have preserved the original text: ἤνεγκαν δέκα κοίτας καὶ ἀμφιτάπους "they brought ten beds and rugs" which suggest הביאו עשרת משכב ומרבדים. Many scholars follow Klostermann and read, perhaps rightly, ערשת "couches" for עשרת "ten"; we have adopted this reading.

28.b. We have omitted קלי "roasted corn" after עדשים "lentils" since it had already been mentioned.

29.a-a. Perhaps we should read וחמאת צאן "and curds from the flock" for MT וחמאה וצאן "and curds and sheep." This would provide a parallel for the following "cheese from the herd," if this latter translation is correct.

29.b-b. The translation of שפות בקר is problematic, since it שפות a *hapax legomenon* and its etymology is uncertain. NEB has "fat cattle," as if from "the 'cream' of the herd"; cf. BDB 1045–46. See also Conroy, *Absalom,* 153.

29.c. Lit., "said."

18:1.a. Lit., "the people."

2.a-a. G^L suggests וישלש "and he divided . . . into three parts"; this is read by many commentators. However, MT is plausible and goes well with David's declaration (cf. Conroy, *Absalom,* 153).

2.b-b. MT is emphatic. For this use of the inf abs, see GKC §113n.

3.a. Lit., "said."

3.b-b. 4QSam^a suggests לא ישים לנו לב "no one will pay attention to us"; cf. Ulrich, *Qumran Text,* 107–8.

3.c. So G^{BAN}, reading כי אתה "but you" for MT כי ותה "for now [there are ten thousand . . .]."

3.d. For עשרה "ten," see GKC §97g. Ehrlich (318), in view of the unusual form, suggests "ten regiments" (not "ten thousand").

3.e. K has לעזיר (defective for the hiph inf constr להעזיר "to bring help"); we follow Q which reads לעזור "to help."

3.f-f. MT מעיר "from (the) city" needs the article (so Driver, 328); hence some prefer the G reading בעיר "in the city" or "from the city"; cf. Conroy, *Absalom,* 154.

5.a. McCarter (405) follows Haupt (JBL 45 [1926] 357) in deriving MT לאט "deal kindly" (as if from אט) from לוט "to cover, veil"; hence "Protect . . . for me."

6.a. Some Greek MSS have read מ חנים "Mahanaim" but this may be an interpretative emendation.

7.a. Lit., "servants."

7.b-b. Or "great slaughter" (RAV).

8.a. K has the unusual form נפצות (*BHS:* נפצית) while Q reads the niph fem ptcp נפוצת (from פוץ "be dispersed").

9.a. Lit., "went."

9.b-b. The exact meaning of שובך is not clear. BDB (959) proposes "network of boughs" while *CHALOT* (349) suggests "tangle of branches."

9.c. The אלה may be an undefined mighty tree, such as an oak (so NEB, JB) or a terebinth (so NAB, RAV). For the use of the article, see GKC §126qr.

9.d. Not in MT; supplied.

9.e. Following the versions and 4QSam^a in reading ויתל "was left hanging" (so McCarter) for the problematic MT ויתן "and he was put."

9.f. Lit., "between heaven and earth."

11.a. "Him" is our explanatory addition. Budde (283) reads ראיתו ". . . saw him," assuming a wrong division of words.

11.b. G^{LMN}, Josephus (*Ant.* 7.240), and 4QSam^a have read חמשים "fifty" for MT עשרה "ten."

12.a-a. A literal rendering. Hertzberg (354) et al.:"felt . . . the weight of." See also Driver, 329.

12.b-b. Lit., "silver," i.e., silver pieces such as used in trade, the weight of which would be a shekel (some 11.5 grams or 0.4 ounce).

12.c-c. Reading with the versions לי "for my sake"; MT has the problematic מי which Driver (329) paraphrases as "whosoever ye be." McCarter (401) regards מי as an enclitic *mem* which requires no translation. This is plausible as long as לי is a possible vocalization of this enclitic.

13.a. So K; Q reads בנפשי "with my life" or "against . . ." G^B links wrongly v 13a with v 12 ("so as to do no harm to his life"); similarly Wellhausen (201) who also emends the text.

14.a-a. G^L has διὰ τοῦτο ἐγὼ ἄρξομαι (= לכן אחלה לפניך "therefore I will begin before you") which is preferred by many commentators. We follow the MT since the informer has no intention of killing Absalom.

14.b. So with G^B (βέλη = שלחים). MT שבטים may mean "sticks" (so McCarter) or rods.

14.c. Lit., "heart"; cf. Exod 15:8.

16.a. Lit., "the people," i.e., David's army. Thenius (235) quite plausibly finds here a reference to the remnant of Absalom's army (i.e., "for Joab wished to spare the people of Israel"); so also Fokkelman (*King David,* 247). However, in that case העם "the people" would be used in two different senses in one and the same verse.

17.a-a. For this use of the definite article, see GKC §126qr.

17.b-b. Some exegetes (for instance, Budde, 284) regard MT ויצבו "they erected, set up," as not very appropriate; therefore Budde reads ויקימו "and raised up" (see also Josh 7:26; 8:29) while McCarter (402) prefers ויצברו "and heaped up." However, the change may not be really necessary.

17.c. Lit., ". . . tent." K reads לאהלו "to his tent," while Q has the pl לאהליו "to their own tents" (so NAB) as in 1 Sam 4:10.

18.a. MT מצבת "pillar" has no article although it is preceded by the obj marker; see GKC, §117d. Some scholars add the article (so Driver, 330).

19.a. Lit., "judged" (or "vindicated").

20.a. Reading with Q על כן "because"; K omits כן due to a scribal error (?).

21.a-a. The versions take כושי as a personal name, "Cushi" (so also KJV). However, since the word has the article in vv 21–30 (except in v 21b), we translate it "Cushite"; see also GKC, §126qr.

21.b. MT lacks the article; probably a scribal error. Read הכושי ("the Cushite").

22.a-a. For the enclitic use of MT זה "this," see GKC, §136d.

22.b. McCarter (402) reads מצאת "from going forth." Wellhausen (203) regards מצאת as a hoph ptcp; i.e., "(no reward) will be given (to you)." However, MT gives a reasonable sense. See also GKC, § 74i.

23.a-a. Supplying "Ahimaaz" (so G^L), and reading with G ויאמר "and he said."

23.b-b. Lit., "the way of the Oval" (cf. Driver, 331).

24.a. G seems to have read לפניו "toward him" (so McCarter, 403) after לבדו "alone," but this may be an explanatory addition.

26.a. Lit., "the watchman."

26.b-b. G^L suggests על השער (i.e., "the watchman *upon the gate* called"). This reading is accepted by many exegetes, and it may well be right.

26.c. אחר "another" is probably implied; it is supplied by most versions (see *BHS*).

27.a-a. "I see."

27.b. MT אל seems to be equivalent to על "upon, on account of"; but see Snaith (52): "*to* a good reward he will come."

28.a. Reading ויקרב "and he came near" for MT ויקרא "and he called out"; so already Wellhausen (203). G^L has καὶ προσῆλθεν "and approached."

28.b. Lit., "he said (to the king), 'All is well!'"

28.c. MT "the king."

29.a. Adding the interrogative particle ה with some MSS, and reading השלום "is . . . safe?" However, the question could have been implied by the tone of voice (see Conroy, *Absalom*, 73, n. 120).

29.b-b. Omitting את עבד המלך "the servant of the king," being a misplaced duplicate of את עבדך "your servant"; so Wellhausen (204). For the use of ל in לשלח "when . . . sent," see GKC §114f.

31.a-a. MT has the attention-calling הנה "behold."

31.b. Omitting the superfluous הכושי "the Cushite" after ויאמר "and he said," with Syr and Vg.

31.c. Syr has "him" but this may be a stylistic alteration.

32.a-a. Ehrlich (322) links לרעה "with evil intent" with כנער "like the young man" as a *tertium comparationis,* but the distance between the two words is rather great.

19:1[18:33].a-a. G^LMN suggest בבכתו "as he wept," and this is preferred by many exegetes. We follow MT בלכתו "as he went."

1[33].b. For the use of מי יתן "I wish," see GKC, §135f.

1[33].c. MT אני is used to emphasize the preceding pronom suff; see GKC, §151c.

2[1].a. We follow some Heb. MSS, supported by Syr and Tg, which read the ptcp (מתאבל) instead of ויתאבל "and he mourned."

3[2].a. Lit., "the army."

3[2].b. Some MSS add אבשלום "Absalom" after בנו "his son."

4[3].a. For the use of לבוא "to come back," see GKC, §114o.

4[3].b. MT has the generic article, see GKC, §126qr.

5[4].a. MT reads "*the king* cried. . . ."

5[4].b. Lacking in some Heb. MSS.

6[5].a. Few MSS add the directive ה to הבית "the house."
6[5].b. Ehrlich (323) regards הבשת as intransitive: "you have behaved shamefully (before your servants)."
6[5].c-c. MT: "the lives of your. . . ."
7[6].a. Lit., "servants."
8[7].a. G^L reads "they have sworn" but this seems less likely.
8[7].b. Adding אם "if" with G and 4QSam^a.
9[8].a. McCarter suggests the hoph ויגד "and it was told" for MT הגידו "they told" which may be an alternative way of expressing the pass voice; see GKC §144f.

Form / Structure / Setting

This section of the Absalom-Narrative comprises 17:24–19:9a[8a] and contains four main episodes:

A. David in Mahanaim	17:24–29
B. The battle and Absalom's death	18:1–18
C. The reports of victory and Absalom's death	18:19–32
D. David's grief over Absalom	19:1[18:33]–9a[8a]

It is likely that our present text contains some later glosses and additions but there is no general agreement on this point. Würthwein (*Thronfolge*, 46 n.80) regards the information about Amasa in 17:25 as an addition which interrupts the sequence of vv 24 and 26. Other scholars (for instance, Langlamet, *RB* 84 [1976] 355) have argued that 17:27–29 is secondary and that its function was to prepare the reader for 19:32–40[31–39]. Also 18:18 appears to be a parenthesis.

The decisive battle receives surprisingly little attention (see 18:6–8, 16) probably because the central theme of this section is the tragic end of Absalom. In this connection, the narrator is at pains to stress, on the one hand, the great concern of David for the safety of his rebellious son (18:5, 29, 32) and, on the other hand, Joab's total disregard for the king's wishes and feelings, which led to the demise of Absalom. From the narrative it is obvious that David did everything that was in his power to protect Absalom while it is equally clear that Joab bears full responsibility for the young man's cruel and unnecessary death. Rightly or wrongly, the reader gets the impression that the narrator is trying to convince those who still sympathized with Absalom's aims, that David was utterly blameless as regards the humiliation of Absalom while Joab is presented as the evil genius. The situation envisaged may have arisen out of the fact that the rebellion ended in an uneasy compromise: David once more became the king while Amasa, Absalom's commander-in-chief, became commander of David's army (militia?) instead of Joab. It is possible that a new covenant was renegotiated since the return of David did not appear to be automatic. Moreover, the existing tensions must have continued, as implied by Sheba's revolt (20:1–2). Clearly, Amasa's murder by Joab (20:8–10) must have created some further problems. Thus it is understandable that stories of an apologetic nature must have served an important purpose.

Comment

24 Since we do not know the actual sequence of events, it is not clear whether the two verbs in v 24 describe more or less simultaneous actions or whether some time had elapsed *before* Absalom was able to undertake the pursuit (see Conroy, *Absalom,* 53). If indeed Ahithophel's death (v 23) preceded the events in v 24 then one could, perhaps, argue that his attempt to surprise David failed (because *he* was not aware of the betrayal) and that therefore he took his life. In any case, the crossing of Jordan by Absalom and his forces must belong to a somewhat later stage, thus giving David and his followers ample time to cross the river and to reach Mahanaim which may have been some thirty miles (or fifty kilometers) from the Jordan fords.

For the location of Mahanaim, see *Comment* on 2:8; cf. also Bartlett, *VT* 20 (1970) 264, n. 1. Mahanaim had been the headquarters of Ishbosheth if not the capital of his truncated kingdom, and therefore it had close links with the Saulides and Benjamin (see Schunck, *ZDMG* 113 [1963] 38). Consequently, it may seem surprising that David sought refuge there; on the other hand, he had little choice. Moreover, his sizeable mercenary force would effectively inspire a hospitable reception for him and his men.

25 According to 1 Chr 2:9–17 Amasa was David's nephew and Joab's cousin. However, in his genealogy there are several problems. Firstly, Amasa's father is described in the MT as an Israelite but this gentilic in our context seems to be out of place (cf. Uriah the Hittite or Ittai the Gittite). Therefore the variant reading "the Ishmaelite" may well be right (see n. 17:25.b.). However, Levenson and Halpern (JBL 99 [1980] 512) favor the reading suggested by Gᴹ: "the Jezreelite" (היזרעלי). Secondly, Amasa's mother Abigail, David's sister, is said to have been the daughter of Nahash. Wellhausen (201) may be right in pointing out that "Nahash" is not a feminine proper noun, and that in this context it may be a duplicate of נחש בן "son of Nahash" in v 27, since one would expect Abigail to be the daughter of Jesse (ישי) which is actually read by some Greek MSS; however, this may be a deliberate correction. Hertzberg (357) suggests that Abigail may have been David's half-sister, since she is called sister of Zeruiah, Joab's mother (see also the *Comment* on 2:2), rather than sister of David.

26 The word order: Israel—Absalom is regarded by some commentators as anomalous but its significance, if any, is not obvious. Conroy (*Absalom,* 54) suggests that this foreshadows Absalom's "dishonourable end," while McCarter (394) has argued that "and Absalom" may be an explanatory addition since the term "Israel" is somewhat ambiguous in our setting. This may be right.

Gilead was a Transjordanian highland region, north of the Dead Sea, extending northwards nearly as far as Wadi Yarmuk; see also Simons, *Texts* § 93.

27–29 David made Mahanaim his temporary base. There he was met by a group of men of importance from the Transjordanian area, who may have been representatives of their particular localities (so Budde, 281).

First to be mentioned is Shobi, son of Nahash. It is probable that he was the brother of Hanun (see 10:1) and thus of the old Ammonite royal house. It is unlikely, however, that at this time Ammon would have had its own king (see 12:30) although Shobi must have been a man of some wealth and importance or even a regent of Ammon (so Stolz, 266).

Machir had been a staunch supporter of the house of Saul as well as the apparent guardian of Mephibosheth (see *Comment* on 9:3–6); it is not certain that he supported David with genuine enthusiasm. He and others may have been swayed by the presence of David's troops. On the other hand, the narrator seems to stress the *loyal* spontaneity of Machir and Barzillai (so McCarter, 395).

Barzillai was an influential Gileadite, from Rogelim the location of which is uncertain (see Simons, *Texts*, §784). His identification with Barzillai, the father of Adriel the Meholathite (see 21:8), is questionable although not impossible since both come from roughly the same area. Budde (281) regards ברזלי "Barzillai" as an Aramaic name (cf. also *HALAT*, 149); it is usually associated with ברזל "iron."

Conroy (*Absalom*, 54, n. 27) suggests that the list of supplies of food and equipment may have been derived from some army quartermaster but there may be simpler explanations.

18:1 "Thousands" and "hundreds" were military units, not necessarily indicative of their numerical strength. Traditionally, this organization goes back to Mosaic times (see Exod 18:21; Deut 1:15).

2–4 The threefold division of the army was part of the customary military organization (see Judg 7:16; 9:43; 1 Sam 11:11; 13:17). One may also note that the importance of Joab, Abishai, and Amasa as military commanders may point to some sort of nepotism, but this was partly inevitable.

The verbal exchange between David and the troops (vv 2b–4a) was probably intended to explain why David was absent from the battlefield; it need not be an addition by a pro-Davidic redactor (as suggested by Würthwein, *Thronfolge*, 44–45). Although it was one of the main tasks of the king to lead his people into battle (see 1 Sam 8:20), yet the officers persuaded David to remain behind. In any case, the fact was that David had been absent from the battle and therefore the narrator has provided an explanation. It was not due to to fear or weakness on David's part (cf. also 11:1 and its regrettable sequel) but due to the wish of the troops. The king was believed to be the life of the people (see 21:17) and the source of their wellbeing; therefore the above request is plausible.

However, Gunn (*Semeia* 3 [1975] 23–24) is more critical of the possible underlying reasons, and he has suggested that David may have been regarded as a risk to his own troops. This is not impossible, seeing that David's outlook during this campaign was, to some extent, distorted by his feelings for Absalom. There is also the question of David's age at this point in time. The impression one gains is that he may have been fairly advanced in years.

6 The battle was fought in the Forest of Ephraim which must be located somewhere in Transjordan, perhaps in the vicinity of Mahanaim. "Ephraim" is, of course, the name of one of the Israelite tribes west of Jordan but it does not follow that the battle took place outside Transjordan. Hertzberg (358) thinks that the Forest of Ephraim was part of an area east of Jordan, settled by the west-Jordanian tribe, thus reminiscent of the settlements by Manasseh (cf. Josh 17:5–6).

7 The Israelite losses amounted to some twenty thousand men. McCarter (405) follows Mendenhall's argument (*JBL* 77 [1958] 63), and estimates the losses as between one hundred and two hundred and eighty men. This means that the size of the "thousand"-unit would be some ten to fourteen soldiers. If so, it is difficult to see what the numerical strength of the "hundred"-unit may have been (cf. 18:1).

9 Traditionally, Absalom was thought to have been caught by his hair (so already Josephus, *Ant.* 7.239) but the text speaks only of Absalom's head being caught in the branches or "wedged in the fork of a tree" (so Mauchline, 285). That Absalom's pride and glory, namely, his hair, brought about his humiliation and death may be part of a moralizing exposition, as attested by the Talmud (Sotah 9b).

11 The translation of this verse is problematic. Some exegetes (e.g. McCarter, 396) take והנה ראית as a conditional sentence ("If you saw him . . . ," contra GKC, § 159w n.1. Joab's words והנה ראית seem to resume the informer's הנה ראיתי "I have just seen."

Mauchline (285) is of the opinion that Joab may have offered a reward for killing Absalom but this depends upon the translation of עלי לתת "I would have given . . . " as "then I would have been *obliged* to give you . . ." (cf. also GKC, § 114l and 119aa; Brockelman, *Syntax,* § 110b). We assume that Joab is *tempting* the soldier with a bribe to go back and kill Absalom (similarly also Gordon, 285) rather than referring to a previously promised reward.

Alongside the ten pieces of silver, Joab also offered a belt, probably a sword-belt or warrior's belt which must have had some specific value or significance (cf. 1 Sam 18:4; 2 Kgs 3:21; see also *Comment* on 2:19–22).

12–13 These verses give a negative picture of Joab: he is dealing perfidiously with David, and he would, most likely, leave his obedient servant in a tight spot had he killed Absalom (cf. Ps 38:12[11]). McCarter (398) removes the latter accusation by rendering v 13b as "and you were stationed some distance away."

It is slightly odd that after Absalom's death David, apparently, asked no questions as to the manner of his son's tragic end; however, we should not assume too much. It is not entirely impossible that Amasa's promotion was Joab's demotion (see 19:14[13]) and that it was part of David's punishment (?) of Joab.

14–15 These two verses need not be seen as contradictory (as suggested by Langlamet, *RB* 84 [1976] 355). Joab may have severely wounded Absalom while his weapon-bearers simply made sure that the rebel prince was really dead. This is reminiscent of the work of Jonathan's weapon-bearer in 1 Sam 14:13. Hertzberg (359) sees Joab's action as symbolic (so also Mauchline, 286) but this seems less likely.

17 Absalom was not buried in the usual family grave (cf. 2:32) but was given "the burial of an accursed man" (McCarter, 407), reminiscent of Achan (Josh 7:26) and of the fate of the defeated kings in Josh 8:29; 10:27. Stolz (267) thinks of a mass grave in view of the Hebrew definite article (i.e., "*the* great pit"). Whether this really was the *final* resting place of Absalom is not certain; cf. also 21:12–14 where David "sanctions" the re-burial of the remains of Saul and Jonathan.

18 This redactional note owes its present place to the association of the pillar with Absalom's burial cairn. The former was set up in the King's valley, also known as the Valley of Shaveh (see Gen 14:17), but its precise location is unknown. Occasionally, it is tentatively identified with the Kidron valley (so Ackroyd, 169) or located at the confluence of Kidron and Hinnom valleys (so McCarter, 408; see also Simons, *Texts* §364). The pillar of Absalom is not to be confused with the late Hellenistic Absalom's Tomb.

Absalom's statement that he has no son to continue his name, is at odds with 14:27 but it does not follow that he had never had any sons; see *Comment* on 14:27.

The pillar seems to have been an inferior alternative to the maintaining of one's name by means of male descendants (cf. 1 Sam 15:12; Isa 56:5). Stolz (267–68) sees in the pillar a possible phallic significance.

19–23 It is not clear as to why Joab was so unwilling to let Ahimaaz carry the news. Verse 22 suggests that it was merely a matter of reward but Gordon (286) points to David's unpredictable attitude towards messengers of bad tidings (cf. 1:15–16; 4:8–12); however, in the cases cited the messengers themselves were implicated in the unfortunate events.

In spite of Joab's arguments, Ahimaaz was determined to carry the news, and eventually Joab gave in. It is possible that the young man was indeed very eager for reward. It is usually thought that the Cushite took the direct but more difficult route to Mahanaim while Ahimaaz, aware of this, chose the longer but easier road along the valley of lower Jordan (see Simons, *Texts* §137, 407). The text does not make it clear whether or not both runners took the same route.

Cush was, roughly, speaking, the region south of Egypt, i.e. Sudan (cf. also Simons, *Texts* § 58; R. J. Williams, "The Egyptians," *Peoples of the Old Testament*, ed. D. J. Wiseman [Oxford: The Clarendon Press, 1973] 79). Thus the Cushite was a foreigner although his status is not described.

27 McCarter (409) suggests that "a good man" may imply political loyalty and that therefore David assumes that the news must be good (see also Conroy, *Absalom,* 72, n.114). However, this seems less likely because the messengers would come from David's own army, and their loyalty would not be in question. If indeed the messengers of good news often received rewards then there might be a tendency to use the less important members of one's staff for evil tidings.

28 The *greeting* of Ahimaaz (i.e., שלום) may also denote, at the same time, the essence of his message (so Budde, 287). The formula,"Blessed be Yahweh" introduces Ahimaaz's report as if it were a thanksgiving (see Conroy, *Absalom,* 72 n.116). Yet Ahimaaz avoids the telling of the whole truth (v 29) and this may point to his *greed* for a possible reward.

The verb סגר "handed over" is usually followed by ביד "into the power of . . ."; cf. 1 Sam 17:46; 24:18; 26:8. It is lacking in our verse.

19:1[18:33] The threefold repetition of "Absalom" and the fivefold repetition of "my son" in this verse accentuates the depth of David's grief and anguish. Such a stylistic feature may be part of the usual language of funeral lamentation.

6[5] The exact meaning of הבית "the house" in this context is not certain. The king may have been still in the roof-chamber or, by now, he could have gone to his own "palace" (NAB: "his residence").

Joab's scathing rebuke of David contains a number of exaggerations. It is questionable (although not impossible) whether Absalom would have really exterminated the house of David in its entirety, including his wives, concubines, and daughters (see 1 Kgs 16:11; 2 Kgs 10:6–8).

7[6]–9a[8a] It seems that Joab has arbitrarily extended David's love for Absalom to all the rebels, and that he has interpreted the king's grief as hate for his own men and officers.

One may also question the reality of Joab's ultimatum (v 8[7]) which, taken at its face value, would be practically tantamount to another rebellion. Stolz (269) even assumes that in such a case Joab would have have taken over the kingship himself. However, this is rather hypothetical.

It is possible that the negative representation of Joab is part of the fairly clear anti-Joab bias which characterizes the so-called SN, at least in its present form.

Explanation

David's choice of Mahanaim as his temporary capital must have been dictated by practical considerations, and his reception was, to some extent, influenced by diplomatic factors (as perhaps in the case of Shobi) as well as by common sense and by the presence of David's troops.

It is impossible to say how much time had elapsed between Absalom's entry into Jerusalem and the fateful battle in the Forest of Ephraim (in the vicinity of Mahanaim), but it is obvious that the whole rebellion was quelled by this one decisive battle. The numerical strength of the opposing armies is unknown but the losses of Absalom's forces are said to have been in the region of twenty thousand men (18:7). However, much depends upon the interpretation of אלף "thousand." It is reasonable to infer that David's army was considerably smaller than that of Absalom but it was mainly composed of experienced and better equipped soldiers. Absalom's forces, on the other hand, consisted mainly of volunteers from all the tribes of Israel rather than of conscripts.

It seems that the unusual wooded battleground must have favored the professional soldiers of David, and it may well be that the battlefield was deliberately chosen by the defenders (i.e., David's commanders). The account of the battle itself is very short (18:6–8), and it seems that the narrator's main intention was to stress the nature of Absalom's death and the different reactions to it by David and his followers. He also notes that even Nature (i.e., the forest) fought on David's behalf (cf. Josh 10:11; Judg 5.20–21).

The traditional account of Absalom's death may have to be slightly modified. It is not certain that he was caught by his *hair* in the branches of a large tree; possibly he was stunned by the impact and trapped by the tangled branches. It is rather ironic that Joab, who according to the present form of the narrative was largely responsible for Absalom's recall from Geshur, was now the cause of his death. It is doubtful that Joab acted solely in the interests of the state; it is more likely that he seized this opportunity to settle a personal grudge against his cousin Absalom who may have spoiled some of Joab's cherished schemes.

David as king and father found himself in a difficult predicament. Strictly speaking, Absalom was a traitor but he was also David's son. It seems that initially the father's grief over the death of his son was far greater than the king's gratitude to the troops for their victory. In a sense it was also ingratitude to Yahweh who was the real author of the military success. Following Joab's brutal ultimatum (19:8[7]), David rather submissively fulfilled his royal duties and reviewed the troops.

This final "gate scene" may call to mind the initial "gate scene" in 15:2–6 which paved the way for the subsequent rebellion; thus they may form an inclusion.

David's Return to Jerusalem and Sheba's Revolt (19:9b[8b]–20:22)

Bibliography

Boecker, H. J. *Redeformen des Rechtslebens im Alten Testament.* WMANT 14. Neukirchen-Vluyn: Neukirchener Verlag, 1964. **Brichto, H. C.** *The Problem of "Curse" in the Hebrew Bible.* JBLMS 13. Philadelphia: Society of Biblical Literature, 1968. **Cohen, M. A.** "The Rebellions During the Reign of David: An Inquiry into Social Dynamics in Ancient Israel." *Studies in Jewish Bibliography, History, and Literature in Honor of Edward Kiev,* ed. C. Berlin. New York: Ktav, 1971. 91–112. **Crüsemann, F.** *Der Widerstand gegen das Königtum.* WMANT 49. Neukirchen-Vluyn: Neukirchener Verlag, 1978. **DeVries, S. J.** *Yesterday, Today, and Tomorrow: Time and History in the Old Testament.* London: SPCK, 1975. **Emerton, J. A.** "Sheol and the Sons of Belial." *VT* 37 (1987) 214–17. **Kallai, Z.** "Judah and Israel—A Study in Israelite Historiography." *IEJ* 28.(1978) 251–61. **Kaplan, J.** "The Identification of Abel-Beth-Maachah and Janoah." *IEJ* 28 (1978) 157–59. **MacLaurin, E. C. B.** "QRT-ɔABLM." *PEQ* 110 (1978) 113–14. **Malamat, A.** "UMMATUM in Old Babylonian Texts and Its Ugaritic and Biblical Counterparts." *UF* 11 (1979) 527–36. **Pritchard, J. B.** "Gibeon's History in the Light of Excavation." VTSup 7 (1959) 1–12. **Sasson, J. M.** "Reflections on an Unusual Practice Reported in ARM X:4." *Or* 43 (1974) 404–10. **Tadmor, H.** "'The People' and Kingship in Ancient Israel: The Role of Political Institutions in the Biblical Period." *CHM* 11 (1968) 46–68.

Translation

9b[8b]*Israel had now fled, each man to his own home;* [a] 10[9]*nevertheless, all the people throughout the tribes of Israel kept on arguing, saying, "It was the king who delivered us from the grasp* [a] *of our enemies, it was he who rescued us from the grasp* [a] *of the Philistines; but now he has fled from the land* [b]*because of Absalom.*[b] 11[10]*Yet Absalom whom we anointed over us, has died in battle—why then are we* [a] *inactive about restoring the king?"* [b]*When the talk of all Israel reached the king,*[b] 12[11]*King David sent (a message) to* [a]*Zadok and Abiathar, the priests,*[a] *saying, "Speak to the elders of Judah as follows, 'Why should you be the last in bringing the king back to his house?* [b] 13[12]*You are my brothers, you are my bone and my flesh! Why then should you be the last to bring back the king?'* 14[13]*Say to Amasa (in particular), 'Are you not my bone and my flesh? May God do thus to me and even more so if you are not commander of my army for life, in place of Joab.'"* 15[14]*So* [a]*he won over* [a] *the hearts of all the men of Judah like (the heart of) one man, and they sent a message to the king, "Return, you and all your servants!"* 16[15]*Consequently, the king* [a]*set out to return* [a] *and came to the Jordan while* [b]*the men of Judah* [b] *came to Gilgal, having come* [c] *to meet the king to bring him* [d] *across the Jordan.* 17[16]*Also Shimei, son of Gera, the Benjaminite from Bahurim, came down hastily* [a] *together with the men of Judah, to meet King David,* 18[17]*and with him there were a thousand men from Benjamin, while Ziba, the steward of Saul's estate, with fifteen sons and twenty servants who were with him, rushed* [a] *into the Jordan before the king,* 19[18]*and crossed* [a] *the ford again and again, to bring across the king's household and to do whatever seemed good to him.*[b]

When Shimei, son of Gera, had crossed the Jordan, he prostrated before the king, [20][19]*and said to the king, "Let not my lord charge me with (my) wrongdoing! Do not call to mind the wrong your servant committed on the day when my lord, the king, left Jerusalem, in order that the king might take action.* [21][20]*For your servant knows that he*[a] *has sinned. So today, as you see,*[b] *I have come first of*[c] *all the house of Joseph to come down to meet my lord, the king."* [22][21]*Then Abishai, son of Zeruiah, replied and said, "Should not Shimei* [a]*be put to death*[a] *for this because he has cursed the anointed one of Yahweh?"* [23][22]*But David said, "What do we have in common, you sons of Zeruiah, that you should act this day as my prosecuting counsel?* [a]*Shall anyone be put to death in Israel this day?*[a] *For* [b]*do you not know*[b] *that today I am king (once more) over Israel?"* [24][23]*Then the king said to Shimei, "You shall not die," and the king swore an oath to him.*

[25][24]*Also Mephibosheth, grandson*[a] *of Saul, had come down to meet the king. He had neither cared for his feet nor cared for his moustache, nor even washed his clothes, from the day the king departed until the day he came back in peace.* [26][25]*So when he came from*[a] *Jerusalem to meet the king, the king said to him, "Why did you not go with me, Mephibosheth?"* [27][26]*"My lord, the king," he said, "My servant deceived me, for your servant,* [a]*being lame,*[a] *said to him,*[b] *'Saddle*[c] *me an ass*[d] *that I may ride on it and go with*[e] *the king.'* [28][27]*Instead, he has slandered your servant to my lord, the king. But my lord, the king, is like an angel of God.* [a]*Do as you think right!*[a] [29][28]*For the entire family of my grandfather*[a] *were nothing but men worthy of death, as far as my lord, the king, was concerned, yet you set your servant among those who eat at your table. What right do I have left* [b]*to complain any more to the king?"*[b] [30][29]*Then the king said to him, "Why do you go on talking*[a] *about your affairs? I have decided:*[b] *"You and Ziba shall divide the estate.'"* [31][30]*"Let him have it all," said Mephibosheth to the king, "now that my lord, the king, has come home in peace."*

[32][31]*Barzillai the Gileadite had also come down from Rogelim, and he went along with the king* [a]*to the Jordan*[a] *in order to see him off at Jordan.*[b] [33][32]*Now Barzillai was very old, eighty years of age; it was he who had provided for the king during his stay*[a] *in Mahanaim, for he was a very prominent man.* [34][33]*So the king said to Barzillai, "You must come along with me and I will provide for* [a]*your old age*[a] *in Jerusalem with me."* [35][34]*But Barzillai said to the king, "How many are* [a]*the remaining days of*[a] *my life that I should go up with the king to Jerusalem?* [36][35]*I am already*[a] *eighty years old, can I discern between good and bad? Can your servant taste what he*[b] *eats and what he*[b] *drinks? Can he*[b] *still appreciate the voice of singing men and women? Why then should your servant continue to be a burden to my lord, the king?* [37][36]*Your servant* [a]*has come along*[a] *but a short distance with the king; why should the king reward me with such a reward?* [38][37]*Please, let your servant go back that I may eventually die in my own city, close to the tomb of my father and mother. However, there is your servant Chimham*[a]—*let him go along with my lord, the king. Do for him whatever you think best!"* [39][38]*Then the king said, "(So be it.) Let Chimham come along with me, and I shall do for him whatever you*[a] *think best. Moreover, I will do for you whatever you may ask of me."* [40][39]*Then the entire army crossed the Jordan but the king* [a]*remained behind.*[a] *When the king had kissed Barzillai and blessed him, (the latter) returned to his own place* [41][40]*while the king crossed over to Gilgal, and Chimham*[a] *crossed over with him.*

Now all the warriors of Judah and some of^b the warriors of Israel escorted^c the king. ^{42 [41]}Meanwhile all the men of Israel kept coming to the king and saying to him,^a "Why have our brothers, the men of Judah, carried you off and brought the king and his family across the Jordan together with all of David's men?" ^{43 [42]}Then all the men of Judah answered the men of Israel, "(We did so)^a because the king is closely related to us!^b Why then are you angry about this matter? Have we ever eaten at the king's expense or have gifts^c been given to us?" ^{44 [43]}But the men of Israel retorted to the men of Judah, saying, "We have ten shares in the king, ^aand so also we have more claim on David than you!^a Why then have you treated us contemptuously? ^bAnd why^c should not our proposal to bring back the king have been implemented first, by us?"^b (In the end) the arguments of the men of Judah became more fierce than those of the men of Israel.

^{20:1} There happened to be a troublemaker^a named Sheba, son of Bichri, the Benjaminite, and he sounded the trumpet and declared:

"We have no share in David,
we have no portion in the son of Jesse.
Every man off to his home, O Israel!"

² So all the men of Israel deserted David to follow Sheba, son of Bichri, but the men of Judah stood by their king from Jordan to Jerusalem. ³ When David came to his house in Jerusalem, he took the ten concubines whom he had left behind to keep the house, and he placed them ^aunder guard;^a he maintained them but ^bhe did not have marital relationships with them.^b So they remained confined until the day of their dying, ^cbeing in a permanent widowhood.^c

⁴ The king said to Amasa, "Call up for me the men of Judah. ^aThen within three days^a present yourself here." ⁵ So Amasa went to call up Judah ^abut he delayed^a beyond the appointed time which David had set him. ⁶David said to Joab^a "Now Sheba, son of Bichri, ^bwill give us more trouble^b than Absalom. ^cNow then,^c take your lord's servants and pursue him, lest he find^d for himself some fortified cities, and lest ^ehe pluck out our eyes."^e ⁷ So the men of Joab sent out after him^a as well as the Cherethites and Pelethites, and all the elite warriors. They went out from Jerusalem to pursue Sheba, son of Bichri. ⁸As they were near the great stone that is in Gibeon, Amasa came towards them. ^aNow Joab was dressed in his tunic^a and over it he was girded^b with a dagger fastened in its sheath at his thigh. Then, as he went forward, it fell out. ⁹ "How are you, my brother?" said Joab to Amasa. Then Joab grasped^a Amasa's beard with his right hand to kiss him. ¹⁰ Thus Amasa was not on his guard against the dagger that was in Joab's (left) hand. So he struck him with it in the belly and spilled^a his entrails on the ground. Thus he died without a second stroke.

Then Joab and Abishai, his brother, pursued^b Sheba, son of Bichri, ¹¹while one of Joab's own men stood by Amasa^a and said, "Whoever favors Joab and whoever is for David, (let him) follow Joab!" ¹²Amasa was still weltering in blood, in the middle of the road. When the man saw that all the soldiers stopped, he removed Amasa from the road into the field and threw a garment over him, because he realized^a that anyone who came by the body^b would stop. ¹³ When it was removed^a from the road, everyone went on after Joab to pursue Sheba, son of Bichri. ¹⁴ The latter passed through all the tribes of Israel to Abel of^a Beth-Maacah while all the Bichrites^b assembled^c and they, too, went in after him. ¹⁵ Then (Joab's troops)^a came and besieged him in Abel of Beth-Maacah. They heaped^b up a ramp towards the city, and it stood already by the outer wall. And all the troops that were with Joab ᶜwere bent on destructionᶜ to bring down the wall. ¹⁶ Thenᵃ a wise woman called out from the city, "Listen! Listen! Please, tell Joab, 'Come here that I may speak to you!'" ¹⁷ So Joab drew near and the woman said, "Are you Joab?" He answered, "I am." "Listen to the suggestionᵃ of your handmaid!" "I am listening," said Joab. ¹⁸ Then she said, "In times past there used to be a saying,ᵃ namely, 'Let them but inquire at Abel!' ᵇ And thus they restored complete harmony,'ᵇ ¹⁹ I (represent) the peace-loving, loyal Israelites but you are seeking to destroy a city that is a mother in Israel. Why should you swallow up Yahweh's heritage?" ²⁰ Then Joab answered and said, ᵃ"Far from it!ᵃ Far be it from me that I should seek to swallow up or destroy the heritage of Yahweh! ²¹ The matter is not quite so because a man from the hill country of Ephraim, called Sheba, son of Bichri, has raised his hand against the king, againstᵃ David. Hand over him alone, and I will depart from the city." Then the woman said to Joab, "Right,ᵇ his head shall be thrown to you over the wall!" ²² So the woman wentᵃ to all the people, with her wise counsel, and they cut off the head of Sheba, son of Bichri, and threw it to Joab. He then sounded the horn and they dispersed from the city, each man to his home, while Joab himself returned to Jerusalem, to the king.

Notes

9b[8b].a. In this set expression MT usually has the pl form לאהליו "to his tents." One MS has the sg form.

10[9].a. Budde (288) et al. read מכל "from all" with some Greek MSS, for MT מכף "from the grasp," or "from the hand," since the latter anticipates "from the grasp of the Philistines." However, this repetition may serve the purpose of emphasis.

10[9].b-b. McCarter (415) and some older commentators suggest ומעל ממלכתו "and from control of his kingdom," following some Greek MSS. MT makes reasonable sense even though מעל "because of" may be slightly unusual (see Budde, 289).

11[10].a. This is a stylistic adaptation; MT: "you."

11[10].b-b. Transferring ודבר כל ישראל בא אל המלך "When the talk of all Israel reached the king" from v 12b to the end of v 11[10]. This sentence must have been accidentally misplaced (see G, OL).

12[11].a-a. 4QSamᵃ must have read only אל צדוק הכוהן "to Zadok the priest" but this reading seems less likely in view of the previous partnership of Zadok and Abiathar (cf. 15:24, 35; 17:15).

12[11].b. We omit the second אל ביתו "to his house" at the end of the verse, as an addition to the previous clause after it had been wrongly inserted at the end of v 12[11].

15[14].a-a. Some Heb. MSS point ויט as qal "was inclined," but in that case the obj marker (את) before לבב "heart" is superfluous. MT points it as hiph.

16[15].a-a. Lit., "he returned."

16[15].b-b. So G; MT: "Judah."

16[15].c. Some Heb. MSS read לרדת ". . . come down" (so also Gᴸ); cf. v 21.

16[15].d. MT: "the king."

17[16].a. The verb וימהר "made haste" seems to have an adverbial force (so BDB, 555).

18[17].a. Perhaps we should omit the wāw before צלחו "they rushed."

19[18].a. Reading with Tg ועברו "and they crossed . . . again and again," which can be taken in a frequentative sense (see Driver, 335). MT has ועברה.

19[18].b. Lit., "in his eyes" (so Q בעיניו); K has the sg בעינו.

21[20].a. Stylistic alteration. Lit., "I."

21[20].b. A paraphrase of והנה "and behold."

21[20].c. For the use of ל to express a genitive by circumlocution, see GKC, §129a.

22[21].a-a. Some Heb. MSS read ימות "die" for MT יומת "be put to death."

23[22].a-a. We regard the sentence as a question, adding the interrogative particle to היום

"today" and reading הַהַיּוֹם. However, the question may have been expressed by intonation (cf. Williams, *Syntax*, §542).

23[22].b-b. Reading יָדַעְתָּם "you know" as suggested by G^L; so already Budde, 291. MT has יָדַעְתִּי "I know."

25[24].a. Lit., "son." Syr adds בֶּן יוֹנָתָן "son of Jonathan," which may be an explanatory gloss (similarly some Greek MSS).

26[25].a. The prep is not expressed in MT. Perhaps we should read מִירוּשָׁלַם "from Jerusalem"; so already Thenius, 241.

27[26].a-a. In MT this expression ("for your servant is lame") is at the end of the verse.

27[26].b. Adding לוֹ "to him" with G.

27[26].c. Reading the emphatic impv חִבְשָׁה "saddle" for MT אֶחְבְּשָׁה "I will saddle"; so RAV.

27[26].d. חֲמוֹר is a male ass but the suff in עָלֶיהָ "on it" is feminine. The lapse of gender is probably due to the intervening word.

27[26].e. Many Heb. MSS read אֶל "to" instead of MT אֶת "with."

28[27].a-a. Lit., "do what is good in your eyes."

29[28].a. Lit., "father."

29[28].a. McCarter (417) follows G^L and reads וַיִּזְעַק "but when he cried out . . ." for MT וַלְזַעֵק "to complain." However, this seems less likely in view of the preceding sentence.

30[29].a. Instead of תְּדַבֵּר "go on talking" G^L suggests תַּרְבֶּה "go on multiplying (your words)"; so already Budde (292).

30[29].b. Lit., "said." For this usage of the pf, see GKC, §106i.

32[31].a-a. Some scholars (for instance, Smith, McCarter) omit הַיַּרְדֵּן "the Jordan" as a gloss, perhaps rightly so in view of the following יָרַד.

32[31].b-b. MT אֶת בַּיַּרְדֵּן (so K) probably offers a mixed reading: אֶת הַיַּרְדֵּן "the Jordan" (so Q) and בַּיַּרְדֵּן "at the Jordan." McCarter (418) follows G^L in reading מֵיַּרְדֵּן "from the Jordan."

33[32].a. MT has בְּשִׁבְתּוֹ which may mean "during his stay." However, the form of שִׁיבָה "stay" (?) is problematic. Therefore most exegetes follow the G reading ἐν τῷ οἰκεῖν αὐτὸν which suggests בְּשַׁבְתּוֹ "while he was staying." Cf. also Driver (337) who regards the MT reading as an obvious error.

34[33].a-a. We follow G τὸ γῆράς σου "your old age," which suggests אֶת שִׂיבָתֶךָ "your old age"; so already Josephus (*Ant.* 7.272). MT has אִתָּךְ "(for) you."

35[34].a-a. Lit., "the days of the years of." G^L suggests כַּמֶּה יָמִים יִהְיוּ שָׁם "How many days would I have there," and this is followed by McCarter (418).

36[35].a. Lit., "today." See De Vries, *Yesterday, Today, and Tomorrow*, 222–23.

36[35].b. MT uses the first pers verbs.

37[36].a-a. Omitting אֶת הַיַּרְדֵּן "the Jordan." MT and most textual witnesses suggest that Barzillai *crossed the Jordan* but this seems less likely. אֶת הַיַּרְדֵּן may be a scribal addition when עָבַר was understood to mean "cross over."

38[37].a. G^L adds "my son" (= בְּנִי); so also Syr.

39[38].a. G^LMN, Syr may be right in suggesting the first pers sg pronoun.

40[39].a-a. We accept the reading by G^L which points to עָמַד "stood, remained" for MT עָבַר "crossed over"; see also Driver, 338.

41[40].a. MT has כִּמְהָן "Chimhan" for the usual כִּמְהָם "Chimham"; perhaps a scribal error.

41[40].b. "Some" is our paraphrase; MT: "half."

41[40].c. So Q (הֶעֱבִירוּ); K reads וַיַּעַבְרוּ "they passed along" while G suggests the ptcp עֹבְרִים "were passing along."

42[41].a. MT: "the king."

43[42].a. An explanatory addition.

43[42].b. MT: "to me" (collectively).

43[42].c. Reading מַשְׂאֵת "gifts" for the problematic נִשָּׂאת which Thenius (245) and others have taken as a niph inf abs from נשא "to take, carry away." G reads ἢ δόμα ἔδωκεν "or has he given us a gift," which is followed by, what may be, a doublet ἢ ἄρσιν ἦρεν ἡμῖν "or has he brought us a portion." McCarter (419) regards the MT as secondary and prefers the G reading.

44[43].a-a. McCarter et al. follow G, OL, and read בְּכוֹר "firstborn" for MT בְּדָוִד "on David." NEB offers a paraphrase: "What is more, we are senior to you."

44[43].b-b. This is a paraphrase.

44[43].c. The force of the preceding מַדּוּעַ "why" may extend also to this following sentence.

20:1.a. Lit., "son of Belial."

3.a. Lit., "in a house of guard."

3.b-b. Lit., "he did not go in to them." Some MSS read אליהן "to them" (with the third fem pl suff) for MT אליהם, with the third masc pl suff. Note also ויתנם "and he placed them (masc pl)"; see GKC, §135o.

3.c-c. MT אלמנות חיות is difficult. Perhaps it could be taken to mean "widowhood of lifetime"— hence permanent widowhood. McCarter et al. follow G χῆραι ζῶσαι, which suggests אַלְמָנוֹת חִיּוֹת "widows while alive." Tg could be rendered "widows of their living husband" but this is less likely since the concubines were now, most likely, widows of Absalom.

4.a-a. For the construction, see Driver, 341.

5.a-a. The verb is, apparently, from אחר "to delay"; Q suggests the hiph form ויוחר "he came too late;" so HALAT, 10. See also GKC, § 68i.

6.a. MT has "Abishai," while Syr has "Joab." We follow Syr because Joab was already in charge of some mercenary troops (see 18:2); it also makes a better sense of the following verses.

6.b-b. Taking ירע as a hiph ("to cause trouble") of רעע.

6.c-c. Reading ועתה "now then" instead of MT אתה "you," with some Heb. MSS. G conflates both: καὶ νῦν σὺ "and now, you."

6.d. So two Heb. MSS (ימצא for מצא); cf also GKC, §107 n.3.

6.e-e. This is a difficult phrase. We have taken it as a metaphor for permanent injury; McCarter (426) follows GB which reads καὶ σκιάσει (= והצל), meaning "and cast a shadow over." Nowack (232) reads ממנו "from us" for עיננו "our eye," hence "lest he take them (i.e., the cities) from us." These and other variants may point to an unusual idiom rather than to a corrupt text.

7.a. I.e., after Joab. Driver (342) suggests אחרי אבישי יואב "Joab . . . after Abishai" for אחריו אנשי יואב "the men of Joab . . . after him." McCarter (427), influenced by GL, reads ויצעק אחריו אבישי (את) יואב "So Abishai called out after him Joab."

8.a-a. Reading ויואב מדו לבוש "now Joab was dressed in his tunic"; so already Löhr, Nowack, et al.

8.b. Read the pass ptcp חגור "was girded," following G.

9.a. Many Heb. MSS have the fuller form ותאחז for ותחז "and he grasped"; cf. GKC, §68h.

10.a. McCarter (428) prefers the pass form וישפכו "they were spilled," as suggested by G.

10.b. MT has the sg רדף "pursued"; 4QSama reads the pl רדפו.

11.a. GL and OL supply the name "Amasa."

12.a. Lit., "saw."

12.b. "The body" is paraphrastic; MT: "him."

13.a. MT's הגה may be a third masc sg hoph pf from יגה "to remove"; cf. HALAT, 369. Fokkelman (King David, 460) takes it as a hiph ("after he had removed him").

14.a. MT has "and" (= GL) but, if correct, it may be an explicative conj ("that is to say"); cf. Williams, Syntax, §434; Fokkelman, King David, 460.

14.b. MT has הברים "the Berites," which is not attested elsewhere. It may be an error for הבכרים "the Bichrites," which is implied by G: see also Driver, 345.

14.c. Q reads ויקהלו "they gathered together" while K has ויקלהו "they treated him with contempt." We follow McCarter who suggests (428) נקהלו "assembled" which is implied in the G reading ἐξεκκλησιάσθησαν "were assembled").

15.a. The subj of the verb is not expressed explicitly in MT.

15.b. Lit., "poured."

15.c-c. Lit., "were destroying."

16.a. Some scholars (cf. Driver, 346) transfer ותעמד בחל "and it/she stood by the wall" from v 15 to the beginning of v 16. These words may have been accidentally misplaced (so Ackroyd, 190) but the change is not absolutely necessary.

17.a. Lit., "words of."

18.a. Reading with G דבר "words, saying"; MT points the consonantal reading as an inf abs. The change was already suggested by Budde (303).

18.b-b. G has καὶ ἐν Δαν = ובדן "and in Dan."

20.a-a. Some Heb. MSS omit the second חלילה "far be it"; the repetition in MT may be due to dittography.

21.a. Some Heb. MSS omit the prep ב "against"; similarly G, Syr, Vg.
21.b. Lit., "behold."
22.a. Budde (303) follows G (which has a doublet at this point) and reads ותדבר "and she spoke . . . (in her wisdom)." However, MT is sufficiently clear (so Ehrlich, 329).

Form / Structure / Setting

This section (19:9b[8b]–20:22) forms the conclusion of the Absalom story which began in chap. 13. Our section consists of two main parts:

(a) David's problems and return to Jerusalem   19:9b[8b]–44[43]
(b) Sheba's rebellion   20:1–22.

In the first part, verses 9b[8b]–16[15] depict the immediate aftermath of Absalom's defeat and death, and the subsequent deliberations by the Israelites. David attempted to facilitate this process by appealing to the Judeans (vv 12[11]–15[14]) but by this means he also sowed the seeds of future conflict. This is followed by three meeting scenes, with Shimei (19:17[16]–24[23], Mephibosheth (19:25[24]–31[30]), and Barzillai (19:32[31]–41[40]). These episodes recall those in chaps. 15–16, and they show very clearly David's conciliatory and generous attitude (to mark his second coronation??). Finally, vv 42[41]–44[43] describe the resultant friction between Judah and Israel, which culminated in Sheba's revolt or "secession" (so Gordon, 293).

This brings us to the second part which deals essentially with Sheba's defiance. Here we have several successive scenes which mark the progress of the story. First, Sheba raises his rebel cry (20:1–2) and is joined, apparently, by all Israel. Next, the king enters Jerusalem and deals with his unfortunate concubines (v 3). Then, vv 4–13 relate Amasa's first and last commission by the king as well as his violent death, while vv 14–22 recount what seems only the final stage of Sheba's revolt. Since Joab had at his disposal all the Cherethites, Pelethites, the elite troops as well as the Judean militia, one can only conclude that, at least, at the beginning Sheba must have posed a real threat to David's rule. The very end (v 22) comes as an anti-climax or non-event but it would be wrong to assume that the whole of David's army was required to chase Sheba and a handful of his supporters throughout the borders of Israel (v 14).

We are equally uncertain as to Sheba's motives. Thus, for instance, Budde (296) regarded Sheba's revolt as the final attempt by the tribe of Benjamin to win back the lost kingdom of Saul and that Sheba hoped to usurp the throne for himself. Others would argue that his aim was to gain the crown for the Saulides (cf. Tadmor, *CHM* 11 [1968] 56).

A further complication is created by Amasa's activities. Thus Mauchline (295) believes that Amasa disobeyed David's orders, and that he was actually "organizing a force in Israel" (295). However, this can hardly be deduced from the fact that Amasa met Joab at Gibeon (v 8) or from the challenge in v 11. He may have been *sent* to Gibeon by David (cf. 20:4) to follow the mercenary contingents. Likewise, Ackroyd (189) argues that Amasa was engaged in "rebellious activity on his own." All this is possible but in that case Amasa's death would have been regarded as a deserved punishment for treachery rather than a foul murder. Consequently, it would have been far more difficult to frame Joab for Amasa's murder (see 1 Kgs 2:5, 32). It is not improbable that the detailed account of Joab's treacherous atrocity was an indirect attempt to show that *David* had no hand in this crime; this brings to mind Abner's murder and its consequences in 3:22–39.

Comment

9b[8b] This verse resumes the statement about Israel's flight in 18:17, and adds its sequel. The well-known expression, "each man fled to his own house (or "tent")" may imply not only defeat but also a collapse of the military organization as such (see Alt, *Kleine Schriften*, 3 [1959] 239–42); cf. 1 Sam 4:10; 2 Sam 18:17; 2 Kgs 14:12; 2 Chr 25:22.

10[9] The niph (see GKC, § 51d) of the verb דין "to judge" is found only here but there is no real necessity to emend נִדּוֹן ". . . quarreling" to נִלּוֹן ". . . complaining," following G^{LM}.

In McCarter's (420) view it was the army (הָעָם) which urged the "staff-bearers (שִׁבְטֵי) of Israel" (i.e., the elders of Israel) to restore David's rule. This is possible but we take שִׁבְטֵי as "tribes of" (see *Comment* on 5:1; cf. P. V. Reid, "*šbṭy* in 2 Samuel 7:7," *CBQ* 37 [1975] 17–20). It seems that the Israelite army or militia had disbanded itself by fleeing, each man to his home, and therefore in this context "the people" may well be a more suitable rendering of הָעָם.

11[10] This is the only explicit mention of Absalom's anointing but there is no valid reason to suspect it (cf. Mettinger, *King and Messiah*, 118–23). This may imply that David had ceased to be king of Judah and Israel, and therefore a specific action had to be taken to restore David's kingship. It is not improbable that he was anointed at Gilgal (cf. 19:16[15], 41[40]).

12[11] At this point David was apparently exploiting the north-south jealousy in order to force the hand of the men of Judah to take the lead in restoring him to his throne. This in turn provoked a heated response by Israel, i.e., the northern tribes (see vv 41–43[40–42]).

13[12] David makes good use of his priestly functionaries, and appeals to the men of Judah on the basis of his kinship with them; at the same time, he may have been hinting at possible privileged relationships (cf. the somewhat similar situation in 1 Sam 22:7). For the formula of relationship, "my bone and my flesh," see *Comment* on 5:1; cf. also Gen 2:23; Judg 9:2; W. Reiser, "Die Verwandtschaftsformel in Genesis 2:23," *TZ* 16 (1960) 1–4.

14[13] David's treatment of Amasa is of special interest. He not only forgave him for his part in the abortive revolt but he also made him commander of the militia in the place of Joab (cf. 20:4–5). It is unlikely that this command extended also over the mercenaries and the elite troops. Thus it seems that Amasa must have been a man of considerable influence, perhaps even a potential candidate for the kingship (so Payne, 249). This may have been part of the price which David had to pay for the cooperation of Judah and their goodwill.

David's oath is in the form of a self-cursing, common in the OT (cf. 1 Sam 3:17; 2 Sam 3:35; 1 Kgs 2:23; 2 Kgs 6:31). Perhaps it was intended as a counterpart to Joab's oath in v 8[7].

15[14] "He won over" may refer either to David or Amasa (so Gᴸ); the latter alternative may well be right.

17[16]–19[18] These verses create certain problems since it is not clear whether both Shimei and Ziba, together with their men, crossed the Jordan or only Ziba with his sons and servants. We understand that at first it was Ziba who made the crossing, and that only at a later stage Shimei crossed the river to petition the king on the other side. Of course, syntactically בעברו "when he crossed" may refer to the king (so McCarter, 413) but *that* crossing is mentioned only later in v 41[40]. Gordon (290) assumes that although Shimei's story is told at this point, it took place *after* the events in v 39[38].

The meaning of צלח "rushed" is doubtful. Ehrlich (324) and McCarter (420) take it to mean "waded through" (cf. the Aramaic צלח).

21[20]–22[21] Strictly, the "house of Joseph" refers to the Joseph tribes: Ephraim and Manasseh, but in our context it describes the northern tribes in general.

The offense of Shimei was that he had cursed the king (see 16:5–8). To curse, or to show disrespect for, the ruler of one's people was a very serious crime (cf. Exod 22:27[28]; 1 Kgs 21:10; Brichto, *The Problem of "Curse,"* 138–41). Therefore Abishai's angry outburst had, no doubt, some legal foundation and it was not merely a subjective indignation.

23[22] For the expression, "what do we have in common?" see *Comment* on 16:10. McCarter (413) renders it: "What do you . . . have against me?"

We take שטן in this context not as "adversary" but as "accuser" (see Zech 3:1). Abishai acts as if he were a prosecuting counsel; however, David is prepared to overlook Shimei's crime, at least temporarily (cf. 1 Kgs 2:8–10). DeVries (*Yesterday, Today, and Tomorrow,* 221) has pointed out that the reconciliation was based on two main considerations: (a) David wished to secure the goodwill of the house of Joseph; (b) Shimei was supported by a thousand Benjaminites (cf. v 17[16]). No doubt, these were important relevant factors but the narrator himself seems to suggest that the amnesty was linked, at least primarily, with David's resumption of his kingship (v 23[22]). This is reminiscent of the events recorded in 1 Sam 11:12–15. Fokkelman (*King David,* 302) assumes, perhaps wrongly, that David continued a practice which was instituted by Saul.

Mettinger (*King and Messiah,* 119) may be right in speaking of a "second coronation" at Gilgal (?), and this may account for David's leniency. David's return to the throne does not appear to have been an automatic process (see Whitelam, *The Just King,* 145) since he had to wait for the people's specific invitation (see vv 10–16 [9–15]). Whitelam suggests that David "now had to negotiate for the throne." If so, one can understand the background of David's conciliatory moves.

24[23] David gave Shimei his oath that he will not be put to death but it seems that the inherent danger of Shimei's curse remained and could harm the house of David (so J. Gray, *I and II Kings*² [OTL; London: SCM, 1970] 103). This dilemma was overcome by Solomon who contrived to bring about

Shimei's death, thus removing the potential threat of the curse (see 1 Kgs 2:36–46) and, at the same time, also a potential enemy.

25[24]–31[30] Also Mephibosheth (see *Comment* on 4:4) had come to greet the king but it is not quite clear where their meeting took place. Verse 25[24] implies that Mephibosheth came down to Jordan while v 26[25] may be taken to suggest that he met the king in Jerusalem (so MT). The simplest solution may be to follow some Greek minuscules in reading מירושלם "from Jerusalem" in v 26[25]; so also rsv, nab, niv. Conroy (*Absalom*, 98, n. 11) argues that ירושלם on its own may mean "*from* Jerusalem."

It is possible that Mephibosheth had an uneasy conscience (see 16:3) and that his self-justification (vv 27[26]–29[28]) was economical on truth. Since Ziba could hardly have foreseen the outcome of Absalom's revolt, his material assistance to David (16:1–2) might well be taken as a genuine decision to side with David. Moreover, the promised reward could not be implemented during *Absalom's* reign. Thus, if anything, Ziba had risked his welfare, if not life. However, in the end we are unable to decide with any certainty as to who told the truth (see De Vries, *Yesterday, Today, Tomorrow*, 218, n. 257). Also David's half-measures (v 30[29]) show a reluctance to deal with this thorny question, unless the king believed Mephibosheth but, at the same time, wished to reward Ziba's helpful service in time of need (so McCarter, 422). However, in either case, Mephibosheth was the loser. Conroy (*1–2 Samuel, 1–2 Kings*, 127) comments that *both* men are depicted in a bad light and that "the house of Saul is thus discredited."

According to the narrative, Mephibosheth's outward appearance suggested that he had been in mourning although some of the details are not clear. "To care (or "do") one's feet" may, perhaps, mean "to cut one's toenails" (so McCarter, 421) while others see here an allusion to washing one's feet.

Furthermore, it is not obvious why the neglect of Mephibosheth's *moustache* received this particular mention; probably, the reference is to his beard in general (cf. neb); see also Ezek 24:17, 22.

On the whole, it seems that the narrator's aim was to stress Mephibosheth's grief at David's departure, and there is no hint in the story that this sorrow was nothing more than good acting. Unfortunately, we are not told as to how Mephibosheth was deceived or left in the lurch by Ziba.

In v 28[27] David is described as an angel of God (cf. also 14:17, 20). This is primarily a courtly flattery rather than a doctrine of royal super-intelligence (but cf. 1 Kgs 3:28).

It is not stated why the whole house of Saul was thought to be worthy of death; for אנשי מות (lit. "men of death"), see Emerton, *VT* 37 (1987) 216. It is possible that the reason may have been Saul's hostilities against David and his family or simply the customary practice of exterminating the deposed king's family (see 2 Kgs 10:6–11).

32[31]–38[37] There is some doubt whether Barzillai crossed the Jordan or not (see vv 37[36] and 40[39]). We assume that he went only *as far as* the Jordan which would be the obvious point to bid farewell to the king (cf. Gen 18:16).

Barzillai was, apparently, David's host, and therefore the king wished to repay Barzillai's kindness. However, the aged Gileadite declined the kind offer and gave his reasons. He had already reached a good old age (see Ps 90:10) and therefore he would have been unable to enjoy the pleasures of court-life (cf. Josephus, *Ant.* 7.273). He also pointed out that he was no longer able to tell the difference between good and bad. We take it as a rhetorical exaggeration, referring to what is pleasant and unpleasant rather than to ethical values (see I. Höver-Johag, "טוב," *TDOT* 5 [1986] 309). The court singers (v 36[35]) were, most likely, entertainers rather than part of the cultic personnel (so Budde, 293).

Barzillai has only one wish for himself, namely, to die in his own city and to be buried in the family tomb (cf. also 2:32; 17:23). He speaks of the tomb of his "father and mother"; the addition of "mother" in this context is unusual (cf. Nowack, 230–31) but not improbable.

Chimham must have been Barzillai's son (so G^L Josephus, *Ant.* 7.274). According to 1 Kgs 2:7 David's consideration must have been extended, at least eventually, to several sons of Barzillai. The derivation of the name כמהם "Chimham" is not clear (cf. Noth, *Personennamen,* 225 and n.5) but it may mean "pale of complexion" (McCarter [422]: "Paleface").

39[38] David responds by inviting Chimham to accompany him. The phrase "whatever you think best" may take up the same stock expression in v 38[37], and must be understood in the context of courtly language (see Jung, *Court Etiquette,* 24–30).

41[40] Caird (1149) regards "and half the warriors of Israel" as "a foolish interpolation" since up to this point only the men of Judah had been on the scene. In view of v 44[43] it seems that the men of Benjamin (v18[17]) may have been reckoned with Judah. However, Kallai (*IEJ* 28 [1978] 257) argues that "Greater Judah" included Judah and Simeon. The acceptance of Caird's view would make a better sense of the following verse, and the complaint of the men of Israel would have more force; however, there is no textual support. Perhaps "half" may mean here "a fraction" or simply "some."

42[41]–44[43] The actual issue involved in this dispute was not very serious in itself (see Gordon, 292) but it may have been the proverbial last straw. There is little doubt that friction had existed already previously between Judah and Israel, and the later revolts of Sheba and Jeroboam were the consequences of such internal tensions. Similar problems had plagued the tribes of Israel even during the period of the Judges (cf. Judg 8:1; 12:1).

As regards the variant readings "David/firstborn" (see n. 19:44[43].a-a. above), we follow the former variant. It is not obvious why Israel as a whole should be regarded as the firstborn unless the Joseph tribes are taken to represent Israel in its entirety (cf. also 1 Chr 5:1–2). On the other hand, since Israel formed the major part of the united kingdom, they could be justified in claiming a greater share in David.

Fokkelman (*King David,* 316) has noted that *David* is addressed by the Israelites but the answer is provided by the men of Judah. He understands the final sentence in v 44[43] as suggesting that the arguments of the Judeans seemed more weighty to David than those of the Israelites. However, his comment that David "is a born quitter" seems hardly justified, at least by this particular context.

20:1 The name שֶׁבַע "Sheba" may be linked either with the word for "seven" or with "oath" (see Noth, *Personennamen*, 146–47), and it may be a shorter form of a compound, theophoric name (cf. Exod 6:23; 2 Kgs 11:2).

Sheba may have been a kinsman of Saul (so Bright, *History*[3], 210) if "Bichri" is to be identified with "Becorath" (1 Sam 9:1); at least, he was of the same tribe as Saul.

Sheba's defiant slogan was later taken up in 1 Kgs 12:16. Driver (340) regards it as a call to resume the old tribal independence but the nature of the supposed organization, if any, is a matter of speculation. According to Jewish tradition the expression לְאֹהָלָיו "to his tents" is a scribal correction of לֵאלֹהָיו "to his gods," but this seems unlikely in our context.

2 The exact meaning and implications of this verse are not clear. Taken literally, it suggests that once more all Israelites revolted against David and joined Sheba's forces. If so, we have no information as to how Sheba's rebellion came to its inglorious end without a single blow being struck. Perhaps we should differentiate between sympathizing with the aims of the rebellion and actively taking part in it.

Verse 2 seems to suggest a situation where David ruled Judah while all Israel followed Sheba's lead. If indeed there were no battles between the opposing parties, then one is tempted to assume that Israel was eventually torn apart by factional interests (as in its later history) until Sheba was even deserted (?) by his own kinsmen in Abel of Beth-Maacah.

4–5 From the story it appears that David's mercenary forces were not strong enough to tackle the military emergency on their own. Therefore Amasa, David's new commander of the tribal militia, was ordered to call up the men of Judah for military service against Israel or the elements involved. It is quite possible that at this stage David was not fully aware of the potential military strength of his opponents, and that therefore he was taking no chances.

The time allotted to Amasa to carry out the "mobilization" was extremely short (three days) and consequently he was delayed. Was this unrealistic time limit a deliberate trap for Amasa? We cannot tell.

6–7 There is also some uncertainty as to whether David gave his orders to Abishai (so MT) or to Joab (so Syr). In the light of subsequent events, it is possible that Joab was still the commander of some troops at least.

8 This verse contains some textual problems and certain emendations seem to be required (see *Notes* above). We do not follow the so-called two-sword theory but we find the explanation provided by Stolz (277) quite reasonable. In his view, Joab's tunic was girded up to facilitate marching, and therefore the sword or dagger did not fall to the ground but rather into the folds of the soldier's garment. Consequently, there was no need for *two* swords nor did the dagger need to be retrieved from the ground. However, it does not follow that the murder was a spontaneous act, without any premeditation.

The great stone may have been a well-known landmark, possibly an altar (so Ackroyd, 189), such as mentioned in 1 Sam 14:33. Pritchard (VTSup 7 [1959] 6) suggests the "big high place" at Gibeon (see 1 Kgs 3:4).

11 Joab left one of his trusted men to deal with the dying Amasa and the bystanders. The word נער in this setting may denote a reliable and experienced soldier rather than a "young man" (see *Comment* on 2:14: cf. also H. F. Fuhs, "נער" *TWAT* 5 [1984–86] 515).

12 The gruesome picture of Amasa's agony does not contradict the statement in v 10 that he died without receiving a second dagger stroke. Joab may have wished to prolong his suffering, and therefore deliberately he did not administer the *coup de grâce*.

The soldiers addressed must have been the Judean militia who had followed Amasa (so McKane, 279) rather than the troops of Joab and Abishai (as suggested by Gordon, 295). Clearly, they would be confused and hesitant, seeing the slain body of their commander.

14 Abel is identified with *Abil el-Qamh* (see Simons, Texts §788) some twelve miles (or twenty kilometers) north of Lake Huleh, and a few miles from Tell Dan. Abel may have been associated with the small Aramean kingdom of Maacah (see *Comment* on 10:6).

The text of this verse is in some disorder. One could tentatively assume that וכל הברים has been misplaced and ought to be read after ויבא, translating: "He (i.e., Sheba) passed through all the tribes of Israel to Abel of Beth-Maacah, and they (i.e., the tribes) treated him with contempt; but the Bichrites (MT: "Berites") went in after him." We have deleted אף "also," following some Heb. MSS, G, and Syr.

16 The wise woman acted as the spokesperson of the people of the beleaguered city. Fokkelman (*King David,* 331) regards the initial speech of the woman (v 16b) as poetry but it might be better to claim that it has a sort of poetic quality.

18–19 The text of the G diverges from that of the MT but it is far from certain that the former is textually superior (cf. D Barthélemy, "La qualité du Texte Massorétique de Samuel," *The Hebrew and Greek Texts of Samuel,* ed. E. Tov [Vienna/Jerusalem: Academon, 1980] 31–33). The addition of "Dan" in G remains unexplained (so also Pisano, *Additions or Omissions,* 148).

The essence of the woman's argument seems to be that the inhabitants of Abel are not rebels but people of good sense. Therefore there is no need to destroy the venerable metropolis in Israel, thereby swallowing up Yahweh's inheritance. The people of Abel are quite willing to cooperate. It is not explained why the citizens did not start the negotiations at the beginning of the siege!

20–22 Joab then makes clear that his aim is not to devastate the city but to punish Sheba who had rebelled against the king. In the end the woman persuades the inhabitants of Abel to agree to Joab's demands. So Sheba is beheaded and Joab and his army withdraw. The implication is that either Sheba had only comparatively few supporters with him or he had lost their support; perhaps both. Stolz (278) draws our attention to Sheba's rights to asylum (cf. Gen 19:1–11; Judg 19:22–30) but his "rights" may be questioned since legally he was now a criminal, having lifted up his hand against the king, and therefore it is unlikely that he had any legal claim. Moreover, it is doubtful that in a military situation such claims would receive any attention. Cf. Judg 4:17–22.

Explanation

The tide had at last turned for David. The military threat has been eliminated, at least temporarily, and David now awaited the people's response to his overtures.

It seems that Absalom's anointing meant that David was now deposed, not simply by a usurper (Absalom) but also rejected by the people who had previously chosen him. Even Yahweh's attitude had been negative for a while.

All this would explain, at least partly, why David's victorious troops simply did not march on to Jerusalem, and why David himself had to use the services of Zadok and Abiathar to negotiate with Judah and Amasa to persuade them to recall their previous king (cf. 19:12[11]–15[14]). Moreover, Amasa's appointment over David's militia must have been a considerable concession on the part of David. The recent victory may have been seen as indicative of Yahweh's favor, but David still needed the people's "acclamation" or invitation to be king once more.

It seems that the narrator has skipped over many important developments and has picked out only certain aspects which were relevant to his immediate purpose. There was clearly a reluctance to restore David, for reasons which are not stated. There were also tensions between Judah and Israel, and perhaps also between other sectional interests, culminating in Sheba's revolt (cf. 1 Kgs 12:16), of which we have only a very scanty information. The conclusion of the Sheba episode might suggest that the whole affair was but a damp squib (20:22), yet David assumed, rightly or wrongly, that Sheba's defiance might become even more dangerous than Absalom's revolt (cf. 20:6; see also 20:2a). Was this merely a rhetorical exaggeration or did the narrator simply omit the more prolonged (?) hostilities since his aim was to advocate the unity of the kingdom, not its instability.

The chapter closes with the ignominious death of Sheba and the return of Joab to the king in Jerusalem. Although Absalom and Sheba are now dead, the whole Absalom story points beyond itself. In the background of the narrative there is the growing confrontation between the aging king and the overbearing Joab, and the solution can only be a new king. However, the real question is who?

David's Inner Cabinet   (20:23–26)

Bibliography

Bright, J. "The Organization and Administration of the Israelite Empire." *Magnalia Dei: The Mighty Acts of God.* Ed. F. M. Cross, W. Lemke, P. D. Miller, Jr. Garden City, NY: Doubleday, 1975. 193–208. **DeVries, S. J.** *1 Kings.* WBC 12. Waco, TX: Word Books, 1985. **Mazar, B.** "King David's Scribe and the High Officialdom of the United Monarchy of Israel." *The Early Biblical Period: Historical Studies.* Ed. S. Ahituv and B. A. Levine. Jerusalem: Israel Exploration Society, 1986. **Mettinger, T. N. D.** *Solomonic State Officials: A Study of the Civil Government Officials of the Israelite Monarchy.* ConB, OT Ser. 5. Lund: Gleerup, 1971. **Rainey, A. F.** "Compulsory Labour Gangs in Ancient Israel." *IEJ* 20 (1970) 191–202. **Rüterswörden, U.** *Die Beamten der israelitischen Königszeit.* BWANT 117. Stuttgart, Berlin, Cologne, Mainz: W. Kohlhammer, 1985. **Strange, J.** *Caphtor/Keftiu: A New Investigation.* Leiden: E. J. Brill, 1980. **Vaux, R. de.** "Titres et fonctionnaires égyptiens à la cour de David et de Salomon." *RB* 48 (1939) 394–405.

Translation

[23] *Joab [a]was in command of[a] the entire army.[b] Benaiah, son of Jehoiada, was in command of the Cherethites[c] and the Pelethites.* [24] *Adoram[a] was in charge of the corvée. Jehoshaphat, son of Ahilud, was royal herald.* [25] *Sheva[a] was royal scribe. Zadok and Abiathar were priests.* [26] *Ira the Jairite was David's priest.*

Notes

23.a-a. Lit., "over" (reading על "over" instead of אל, which may well have the same meaning [see *HALAT*, 49]).

23.b. Omitting ישראל "Israel" with G[MN] (see 8:16). One could, perhaps, omit the article before צבא and regard the latter as a constr ("army of [Israel]").

23.c. Reading with Q הכרתי "the Cherethites"; K has הכרי "Carians" (?); see Driver, 348.

24.a. G and Syr suggest אדונירם "Adoniram," as in 1 Kgs 4:6.

25.a. So Q; K has שיא "Sheya," while in 8:17 the name appears as שריא "Seraiah."

Form/Structure/Setting

Verses 23–26 form a roster of David's chief officials, which may have been derived from the royal archives in Jerusalem (cf. also the Neo-Babylonian register of officials in *ANET*, 307–8). It seems that our list includes only those officials who were important enough to belong to the "inner cabinet" of David's administration (see also *Form/Structure/Setting* of 8:15–18). McCarter (435) is of the opinion that the two lists of David's chief officials in 8:15–18 and 20:23–26 are simply variants and that they derive from a single source.

Other scholars have argued that the two administrative lists reflect an earlier and a later stage of David's reign (so Mettinger, *Solomonic State Officials,* 7). It is pointed out that this may be implied by the respective positions in the text and by the fact that the second list includes a new office, that of the chief of enforced labor, which became especially important in Solomon's reign.

Moreover, Adoram who was in charge of the corvée (v 24) was probably the same person as Adoniram, son of Abda, in 1 Kgs 4:6; they both occupied the same office. The same (?) Adoram appears again at the beginning of Rehoboam's reign, as the officer in charge of forced labor (see 1 Kgs 12:18). However, in that case he must have been an old man by Rehoboam's time. This is possible but doubtful.

A good case can be made for the view that our administrative list is an editorial insertion while 8:16–18 fits more naturally in its canonical setting. Consequently, it has been suggested that 20:23–26 owes its present position to the hypothetical transference of 21:1–14 from its supposed original place (before 9:1–13) to its present position (before 21:15–22). In this process the preceding verses (8:16–18), too, were reduplicated (cf. McCarter, 435). Thus 8:16–18 was left in its original place while a duplicate version was transferred with 21:1–14. If so, the duplicate version was brought up to date to reflect the situation after Absalom's rebellion, nearer the end of David's reign.

Comment

23 Joab was, probably, the most important officer, and therefore he may have been mentioned first. He was in charge of the tribal militia and perhaps of some other troops, otherwise his peacetime army might be very small! Benaiah, on the other hand, commanded the professional soldiers, the Cherethites and the Pelethites (see *Comment* on 8:18) and therefore had at his disposal a fairly formidable force. Hence, in practical terms Benaiah may have had more real power than Joab (cf. 1 Kgs 1).

The Cherethites and Pelethites are, most likely, ethnic designations (cf. 1 Sam 30:14) rather than two names of special *classes* of soldiers.

24–25 Adoram was in charge of the forced levy or corvée (מס) which may have been composed of non-Israelite elements (see 1 Kgs 9:21 = 2 Chr 8:8). However, it is not impossible that later in Solomon's time also Israelites may have been involved in forced labor service (cf. 1 Kgs 5:27[13] but see Mettinger, *Solomonic State Officials,* 134), since it was only a temporary conscription. The main purpose of this institution was to provide sufficient labor for the royal building projects.

"Adoram" may be an alternative form of "Adoniram" ("the Lord is exalted"). However, (Mettinger, 133) regards the longer form as a later correction to avoid the offensive pagan element of the name (i.e., הד/אד); also Wellhausen (208) takes it as a non-Israelite name. If so, Adoniram may have been a foreigner. Mazar (*The Early Biblical Period,* 130) considers "Adoram" ("Hadoram") as a Canaanite proper name of which "Adoniram" is a Hebraized form. Hence Adoniram may have been a member of the Canaanite nobility.

For מזכיר "royal herald" and סופר "royal scribe" or "secretary of state," see *Comment* on 8:16, 17.

26 There is practically no further information about Ira the Jairite. He may have come from Havvoth-Jair in Gilead (cf. 1 Kgs 4:13; cf. also Driver, 349) although Blenkinsopp ("Kiriath-Jearim and the Ark," *JBL* 88 [1969] 156) links Ira with Kiriath-Jearim.

Also the exact function of Ira is disputed. Wellhausen (208) has suggested that the introductory וְגַם "and also" shows that he was a priest like Zadok and Abiathar. On the other hand, Hertzberg (375) is of the opinion that Ira had taken over the priestly functions of David's sons (cf. 8:18); unfortunately, the priestly functions of David's sons are equally uncertain. Goldman (236) proposes that כֹּהֵן "priest" may refer to "a civil, not an ecclesiastical minister" yet Zadok and Abiathar were "real" *priests*.

Explanation

This list of David's high officials gives us an insight into the administration of the early monarchy, and it names the officials in pairs: two military (Joab and Benaiah), two civil (Jehoshaphat and Sheva), and two cultic officials (Zadok and Abiathar); the function of Ira remains questionable. It is not improbable that this pairing was a deliberate safeguard lest too much power is concentrated in a single officer.

Adoram who was in charge of the corvée may have had closer links with the military than with the other two "departments" of David's government, especially since the forced labor levy may have been formed essentially by prisoners of war and elements from conquered peoples.

The Famine and the Gibeonite Revenge (21:1–14)

Bibliography

Blenkinsopp, J. *Gibeon and Israel. The Role of Gibeon and the Gibeonites in the Political and Religious History of Early Israel.* SOTSMS 2. Cambridge: Cambridge University Press, 1972. **Brock, S. P.** "An Unrecognised Occurrence of the Month Name ZIW (2 SAM XXI 9)." *VT* 23 (1973) 100–103. **Cazelles, H.** "David's Monarchy and the Gibeonite Claim (II Sam. xxi, 1–14)." *PEQ* 87 (1955) 165–75. **Dus, J.** "Gibeon—eine Kultstätte des ŠMŠ und die Stadt des benjaminitischen Schicksals." *VT* 10 (1960) 353–74. **Fensham, F. C.** "The Treaty Between Israel and the Gibeonites." *BA* 27 (1964) 96–100. **Glück, J. J.** "Merab or Michal." *ZAW* 77 (1965) 72–81. **Miller, J. M.** "Saul's Rise to Power: Some Observations concerning 1 SAM 9:1–10:16; 10:26–11:15 and 13:2–14:46." *CBQ* 36 (1974) 157–74. **Polzin, R.** "HWQYᶜ and Covenantal Institutions in Early Israel." *HTR* 62 (1969) 227–40. **Poulssen, N.** "An Hour with Rispah: Some Reflections on II Sam. 21:10." *Von Kanaan bis Kerala.* Ed. J. P. M. Delman, J. T. Nelis, J. R. T. M. Peters, W. H. Ph. Römer and A. S. van der Woude. Neukirchen-Vluyn: Neukirchener Verlag, 1982. **Sheppard, G. T.** *Wisdom as a Hermeneutical Construct.* BZAW 151. Berlin/New York: Gruyter, 1980. **Schunck, K.-D.** *Benjamin: Untersuchungen zur Entstehung und Geschichte eines israelitischen Stammes.* BZAW 86. Berlin: Töpelmann, 1963. **Veijola, T.** "David und Meribaal." *RB* 85 (1978) 338–61.

Translation

[1] *In the time of David there was a famine,[a] year after year, for three years. So David sought [b]Yahweh's guidance[b] and Yahweh said, "There is blood-guilt on Saul and on his[c] house because he put the Gibeonites to death."* [2] *Then David summoned the Gibeonites and spoke to them, [a](now the Gibeonites were not of Israelite origin; they were of the remnant of the Amorites. Although the Israelites had made a treaty with them by an oath, Saul had sought to slay them, being zealous[b] for the people of Israel and Judah).[a]* [3] *So David said to the Gibeonites, "By what means shall I make expiation [a]that you may bless[a] the heritage of Yahweh?"* [4] *The Gibeonites answered him, "Our[a] case against Saul and his house is not a matter of silver or gold but neither is it for us to put anyone to death in Israel." Then he said, "Whatever you have in mind—I will do it for you!"* [5] *So they said to the king, "As for the man who [a](nearly) annihilated us,[a] who intended [b]to destroy us[b] so that we should have no foothold anywhere within the borders of Israel,* [6] *let seven men of his descendants [a]be given[a] to us so that we may execute them before Yahweh [b]in Gibeon, on the mountain of Yahweh."[b] Then the king replied, [c]"So be it, I will give them up."[c]*

[7] *However, the king spared Mephibosheth, the son of Jonathan, the son of Saul, because of their mutual oath sworn by Yahweh, that existed between David and Jonathan, the son of Saul.* [8] *But the king took the two sons of Rizpah, the daughter of Aiah, whom she bore to Saul, namely, Armoni and Mephibosheth, as well as the five sons of Merab,[a] the daughter of Saul, whom she bore to Adriel, the son of Barzillai, the Meholathite,* [9] *and handed them over to the Gibeonites who executed them on the mountain before Yahweh; [a]the seven of them[a] died[b] together. So they were put to death [c]in the first days of the harvest,[c] at the beginning of the barley*

harvest. ¹⁰ *Then Rizpah, the daughter of Aiah, took sackcloth and spread it out for herself on the rock, from the beginning of the harvest until the rains poured down on them from the heavens. She did not allow the birds of the air to alight upon them by day nor the beasts of the field by night.* ¹¹ *When David was told*ᵃ *what Rizpah, the daughter of Aiah, Saul's concubine, had done,* ¹² *he*ᵃ *went and took the bones of Saul and the bones of his son Jonathan from the citizens*ᵇ *of Jabesh Gilead, who had secretly taken them from the open square of Beth Shan, where the Philistines had hung them on the day they*ᶜ *had killed Saul on Gilboa.* ¹³ *So he brought up from there the bones of Saul and the bones of his son Jonathan; also the bones of those who had been executed* ᵃ*were gathered up,*ᵃ ¹⁴ *They buried*ᵃ *the bones of Saul and Jonathan, his son, in Zelah, in the land of Benjamin, in the tomb of his father Kish, and they did all that the king had commanded.*

After that God was moved by the entreaties for the land.

Notes

1.a. Gᴸ adds the explanatory, "in the land."

1.b-b. Lit., "the face of Yahweh."

1.c. The pronom suff is lacking in MT but it may be preserved in the superfluous article of הדמים "blood-guilt" so that the original reading may have been ביתה דמים "blood-guilt . . . his house" (so already Wellhausen, 208).

2.a-a. This is an obvious parenthesis.

2.b. For the form of the inf construction, see GKC §74h.

3.a-a. Budde (307) et al. read וברכתם "that you may bless," following G εὐλογήσετε which may be an interpretative translation. GKC §110i remarks the impv in MT (וברכו) as expressing intention; hence no emendation may be required.

4.a. Reading לנו "to us," with Q (K has לי "to me"; probably *collective*).

5.a-a. Lit., "he annihilated us"; but this may be a rhetorical exaggeration.

5.b-b. Following Wellhausen in reading להשמידנו "to destroy us" for MT לנו נשמדנו "(devised) against us; we have been destroyed" (?).

6.a-a. Following Tg in reading יתנו "let them be given"; Q has the sg יתן which may be a passive qal (so *HALAT*, 694), meaning "let it be given." 4QSamᵃ reads the pl ונתתם "and give. . . ."

6.b-b. We accept Wellhausen's proposal (331) to read as follows: בגבעון בהר יהוה "in Gibeon, on the mountain of Yahweh." MT has בגבעת שאול בחיר יהוה "in Gibeah of Saul, the chosen one of Yahweh." Also G reads "Gibeon."

6.c-c. Lit., "I will give."

8.a. Reading מרב "Merab" for מיכל "Michal." The former is supported by Gᴸ and some Heb. MSS.

9.a-a. Following Q in reading שבעתם "the seven of them"; MT has שבעתים "seven times" which does not give a good sense.

9.b. Lit., "fell."

9.c-c. Brock (*VT* 23 [1973] 103) has suggested that Gᴸ reading ζειῶν hides the Heb. זו (i.e., the old name for the second month); hence the original reading may have been בימי זו "in the days of Ziv"; so also McCarter (436).

11.a. For the structure, see GKC §121a.

12.a. Lit., "David."

12.b. MT has בעלי which may mean "the lords of" (thus McCarter, 440).

12.c. MT has "Philistines."

13.a-a. Lit., "they gathered up" (ויאספו); we take the active theme in the impersonal 3 pl as a pass construction. See Williams, *Syntax,* §160.

14.a. Gᴸ has the sg, "he buried."

Form/Structure/Setting

2 Sam 21:1–14 is a fairly self-contained composition, and it (or only the events described in it) may have originally preceded chap. 9 (see *Form/Structure/*

Setting of 9:1–13), since David's question in 9:1 and Shimei's accusation in 16:7–8 seem to presuppose some such situation as envisaged by 21:1–14. In such a case 21:7 must be a later addition for it takes for granted the events of 9:1–5.

Our episode is part of the so-called Appendices to the Book of Samuel, which comprise chaps. 21–24. In a way also 20:23–26 is linked with the Appendices. The material in 20:23–24:25 is of a varied nature and McCarter (16) has rightly noted that, as a whole, this section "is neither part of the Deuteronomistic history nor related to the earlier literature it embraced." This complex contains miscellaneous materials (both in prose and verse), relevant to the reign of David but they have not been integrated into the so-called SN; in fact, they disrupt the sequence of events.

These appendices have, what appears to be, a symmetrical or chiastic arrangement but it may not have been intended originally. Possibly, it emerged during the editorial process and could be represented in the following way:

A. Offense of Saul and its expiation (21:1–14)
  B. Lists of heroes and their exploits (21:15–22)
    C. David's praise of Yahweh (22:1–51)
    C'. Yahweh's oracle to David (23:1–7)
  B'. Lists of heroes and their exploits (23:8–39)
A'. Offense of David and its expiation (24:1–25)

Most scholars accept Budde's (304) explanation of the redactorial process, with greater or lesser modifications. He argued that 21:1–14 (preceded by 20:23–26) and 24:1–25 were inserted first. Then came the addition of the lists in 21:15–22 and 23:8–39, between the two above stories. Finally, there was the insertion of the poems (22:1–51 and 23:1–7). Verses comprising 20:23–21:14 were probably transferred before the insertion of the other materials, and thus provided a suitable anchorage for the later additions. This would be understandable if 21:1–14 was a rebuttal of Shimei's accusation in 16:7–8. There is no literary connection between 21:15–22 and 23:8–39; the latter has its own beginning, and thus facilitated the insertion of the poetical sections. Both hero lists may come from a common archival source. See also *Form/Structure/Setting* of 24:1–25.

Comment

1 The immediate cause of the famine is not specified but ultimately it was believed to have been brought about by Saul's blood-guilt. At the same time, it was an indication of divine displeasure or anger (see Ezek 14:21; cf. also the Plague Prayers of the Hittite King Mursilis in *ANET*, 394–96). The author does not elaborate on the details of Saul's offense but the allusion seems to be to some sort of oppression (?) rather than a military operation. Obviously, not all the Gibeonites were exterminated but it is not certain that only *seven* Gibeonites perished (cf. v 6).

So David looked for Yahweh's counsel or "sought an audience with Yahweh" (so McCarter, 436). Literally, David "sought the face of Yahweh," which may suggest a cultic act in the sanctuary (see S. Wagner, "בקשׁ," *TDOT* 1

[1977] 237). The cultic place in question may have been Gibeon (cf. 1 Kgs 3:4). According to a rabbinic tradition (*Yebamoth*, 78b), David consulted Yahweh by means of lots; this is possible but other means are equally likely.

2 The Gibeonites are described as Amorites who are usually regarded as pre-Israelite inhabitants of Canaan but no longer an ethno-political entity (see M. Liverani, "The Amorites," *Peoples of Old Testament Times* [ed. D. J. Wiseman, Oxford: Clarendon Press, 1973] 126). The incorporation of the Gibeonites into Israel may go back to the time of Joshua (see Josh 9:3–27) but they must have remained ethnically distinct. In some way or other, Saul must have violated the sworn treaty between Israel and the Gibeonites, thus incurring blood-guilt.

It is unlikely that this slaughter of the Gibeonites is to be associated with the massacre of the priests of Nob (contra Hertzberg, 382). According to v 2 this incident had been occasioned by Saul's zeal for the people of Israel and Judah but its exact nature is not described. Schunck (*Benjamin*, 131–38) has well argued that Saul wished to annex Gibeon to make it into his new capital since his native Gibeah was not really suitable for this purpose.

3–4 David allows the Gibeonites to suggest the means of expiation, and they mention two alternatives: compensation and blood-vengeance. The former is, in their view, inadequate in the circumstances while the latter is beyond their legal rights. However, David is prepared to make special concessions in this case.

6 The exact meaning of the hiph form of the verb יקע is uncertain, and this problem is reflected by the differing translations both ancient and modern. G may suggest crucifixion in the sun (similarly Tg and Vg) while Syr thinks of a sacrifice. The same variety is also attested by the modern versions: "hang them" (RSV, RAV), "hurl them down" (NEB), "dismember them" (NAB), etc.

In view of this uncertainty we have translated הוקיע by the blanket term "execute," leaving the exact method of punishment unspecified. It may be that the meaning is, in this setting, "to dismember." This has been well argued by Polzin (*HTR* 62 [1969] 236) who is of the opinion that this possible dismemberment was the implementation of the acted-out conditional curse, uttered at the treaty-making.

Apart from Near Eastern parallels, there are also two OT analogies in Gen 15:10–18 and Jer 34:18 (cf. also Judg 19:11–20:48; 1 Sam 11:1–11; 15:33). Thus we read in Jer 34:18 that Yahweh will punish the covenant-breakers by making them "like the calf which they cut in two and passed between its parts" when they made their covenant. So "the hacked animal becomes an analogue of their fate" (R. P. Carroll, *The Book of Jeremiah: A Commentary* [London: SCM Press, 1986] 650).

It is less clear that this procedure was influenced by the Canaanite myth about the killing of Mot (see Cazelles, *PEQ* 87 [1955] 168–70) or that the story depicts a royal sacrifice to restore the fertility of the land. From the context it is obvious that the bodies were exposed to the elements, and this, too, may have been an aspect of the fate of those who had violated their treaty oath (see Fensham, *BA* 27 [1964] 100), as elsewhere in the ancient world.

The Gibeonite request for *seven* men of Saul's family need not necessarily indicate that only seven Gibeonites had been killed by Saul; as Cazelles (*PEQ* 87 [1955] 172) points out, the figure "seven" may be "symbolic of the total figure of the slain Gibeonites." If this episode preceded chap. 9, then the implication is that David knew of no more members of Saul's family.

"The mountain of Yahweh" is probably the Gibeonite high place mentioned in 1 Kgs 3:4, and usually identified with Nebi Samwil, a mile south of Gibeon (see Blenkinsopp, *Gibeon and Israel*, 7).

7 This verse may well be a later addition if 21:1–14 stood originally before 9:1–13, because in 9:1 David is not aware of Mephibosheth's whereabouts. The oath mentioned in v 7 refers to the covenant which Jonathan made with David (cf. 1 Sam 18:3; see also 1 Sam 20:17, 42; 23:18).

It seems that both Jonathan's son and one of the sons of Rizpah bore the same name, Mephibosheth. Veijola (*RB* 85 [1978] 352) has contended that all those passages which speak of Mephibosheth (or Meribaal) as *Jonathan's* son are *not* authentic. However, it could be argued that the names were not identical (at least originally) but rather similar, and that therefore there arose some confusion, apart from the deliberate scribal alterations (i.e., substituting בשׁת "shame" for בעל "Baal"; see *Comment* on 4:4). Thus McCarter uses "Meribaal" for Jonathan's son but "Mippibaal" of Rizpah's offspring.

8 Rizpah was Saul's concubine (see *Comment* on 3:7) or wife of second rank. It seems that Saul had only one wife, Ahinoam (1 Sam 14:50), and one concubine.

It is usually thought that "Michal" (so MT) is a scribal error for "Merab" who was the wife of Adriel from Meholah (see 1 Sam 18:19) while Michal's second husband was Paltiel (2 Sam 3:15). Moreover, Michal apparently had no children at all (contra Glück, *ZAW* 77 [1965] 72).

Stolz (281) regards it as susprising that Merab's sons should be killed because they did not belong to Saul's family but to the important family of Barzillai. It is equally unexpected that the same (?) Barzillai the Gileadite should support David during Absalom's rebellion (19:31–32), assuming that the two men are one and the same person. Hertzberg (384) rejects this identification. Adriel (see *Comment* on 3:15) was a native of Meholah or Abel-meholah, often identified with Tell Abû Sûs. It is also later associated with Elisha (1 Kgs 19:16).

9 The execution took place during the first days of the barley harvest in April (i.e., in the month of Ziv). It is less likely that this event was a form of sacrifice although it may have been part of some ritual act since it was performed before Yahweh.

10 Rizpah's intention must have been to protect the dead bodies so that they could be eventually properly buried. For a corpse to be left exposed to the birds and beasts (see 1 Sam 17:44, 46; Ps 79:2; Jer 16:4) was a great dishonor and punishment. Whether such a treatment affected one's form or quality of afterlife remains uncertain (see L. Wächter, *Der Tod im Alten Testament* [Stuttgart: Calver Verlag, 1967] 175–76).

12–14 Rizpah's devotion to the dead may have influenced David, inspiring him to give Saul and Jonathan a proper burial in their family tomb (v 14). Also the remains of the executed Saulides may have been buried at the same time and the same place. This is clearly stated by the addition in G, which

suggests ואת עצמות המוקעים "and the bones of those who had been executed."
By this means David would publicly indicate that he had no personal grudge
or enmity against the Saulides, just as he dissociated himself from the murders
of Abner (3:31–37) and Ishbosheth (4:9–11). However, it is easy to be generous
to dead enemies.

The reference to the bones of Saul and Jonathan may mean no more
than their ashes since it is clearly stated in 1 Sam 31:12 that their corpses
were burnt by the Jabesh Gileadites. This is somewhat odd since cremation
was not normally practiced in Israel (cf. Amos 2:1), except as a special form
of punishment (cf. Lev 20:14; Josh 7:25). Perhaps, the intention was to protect
the bodies of Saul and Jonathan from any further dishonor on the part of
the Philistines.

"Zelah" is usually understood as one of the towns of Benjamin (Josh 18:28)
but whose location is unknown. Miller (*CBQ* 36 [1974] 159) has suggested
that "Saul's home village was not Gibeah but ṣēlā." On the other hand, McCarter (437) takes it to mean a "chamber" of the tomb (similarly already Budde,
309); this seems a reasonable possibility.

Explanation

The prolonged famine in question may have occurred before Absalom's
revolt, perhaps even before the Bathsheba/Uriah episode. It would be customary to regard the disaster as sent by Yahweh, being an expression of his
anger.

We do not know how reliable were the methods of consulting Yahweh,
especially if the Urim and Thummim were used. However, David arrived at
the conclusion that the calamity was entirely due to Saul's offense against
the Gibeonites. So *David* took the initiative in consulting the Gibeonites, and
as a result seven members of the house of Saul were executed by the Gibeonites.
Their argument was not based on collective responsibility but on the desire
to destroy the house of Saul in its totality. However, this was not fully accomplished; Mephibosheth, the son of Jonathan, was spared because of the covenantal relationship between David and Jonathan.

Thus the story represents David as being both just to the Gibeonites and
loyal to Jonathan. It is possible that the narrative was intended as a rebuttal of Shimei's charge in 16:7, namely, that David had wrongly shed the
blood of the house of Saul. No doubt, there were also others in Israel who
shared the same sentiments. This possibility then may explain the present
position of our pericope *after* Absalom's and Sheba's revolts. Shimei had interpreted Absalom's rebellion as Yahweh's punishment for the harm which David
had done to the family of Saul. Now, after David's victories it was fairly
clear that Yahweh was favorably disposed to David. Thus the story was
an attempt to provide the *Davidic* interpretation of the death of the seven
Saulides.

Many scholars have seen in the events of our pericope a clever political
act whereby David got rid of his political rivals from the house of Saul, and
at the same time he appeared as the zealous doer of Yahweh's will. David
needed a pretext to eliminate Saul's family, and he found it in the famine.

In this way he also turned away any possible scrutiny of his own past deeds.

This line of argument receives some support from v 2 which points out that *Saul* had acted in the interests of his people, and not for any personal reasons or gains. Also the appeal to the treaty oath (v 2) is not very convincing because such oaths and treaties must have been broken fairly frequently (especially in the sphere of politics), often for quite good reasons. However, in retrospect a "good reason" may become a crime when interpreted in light of some recent disaster.

Encounters with the Philistines (21:15–22)

Bibliography

Gordon, R. P. "The *Gladius Hispaniensis* and Aramaic ʾispānîqê," *VT* 35 (1985) 496–500. **Hoffmann, A.** *David: Namensdeutung zur Wesensdeutung.* BWANT 100. Stuttgart: W. Kohlhammer, 1973. **Horwitz, W. J.** "The Significance of the Rephaim." *JNSL* 7 (1979) 37–43. **L'Heureux, C. E.** "The yᵉlîdê hārāpaʾ—A Cultic Association of Warriors." *BASOR* 221 (1976) 83–85. **Moor, J. D. de.** "Rāpiʾūma-Rephaim." *ZAW* 88 (1976) 323–45. **Pakozdy, L. M. M. von.** "Elḥānān—der frühere Name Davids?" *ZAW* 68 (1956) 257–59. **Willesen, F.** "The Yālid in Hebrew Society." *ST* 12 (1958) 192–210. **Yadin, Y.** "Goliath's Javelin and the ארגים מנור." *PEQ* 86 (1955) 58–69.

Translation

[15] *Once again the Philistines were at war with Israel. So David, together with his servants, went down and they fought with the Philistines. When David became exhausted,* [16] *Ishbi-benob[a] who was one of the descendants of Haraphah thought to kill David;* [b]*his bronze spearhead (alone)[c] weighed three hundred shekels[b] and he was girded with a new* [d]*warrior's belt.[d]* [17] *However Abishai, son of Zeruiah, came to David's assistance; he struck down the Philistine and killed him. Then David's men* [a]*swore to him,[a] saying, "You shall not go out with us to battle again, lest you extinguish the lamp of Israel."* [18] *After this, there was another fight with the Philistines at Gob.[a] At that time Sibbecai the Hushathite killed Saph who was one of the descendants of Haraphah.* [19] *Then there was yet another battle at Gob with the Philistines, and Elhanan, son of Jair[a] the Bethlehemite, killed Goliath the Gittite, whose spearshaft was like a weavers' rod.* [20] *A further battle took place at Gath. There was a gigantic[a] man who had six fingers on each hand and six toes on each foot, twenty-four in all; he, too, was a descendant of Haraphah.[b]* [21] *So when he taunted Israel, Jonathan, son of Shimeah,[a] David's brother, killed him.* [22] *These[a] four were descendants of Haraphah in Gath, and they fell by the hand of David and by the hand of his servants.*

Notes

16.a. Reading with many MSS and Q: וישבי "and Ishbi." McCarter (448) takes וישבו (so K) to mean "and he captured him" (from שבה "to capture").

16.b-b. Lit., "the weight of whose spearhead was three hundred bronze shekels" (reading שקל "shekel" for MT משקל "weight").

16.c. Our explanatory addition.

16.d-d. Our explicative addition. Syr and Vg suggest חרב חדשה "new sword."

17.a-a. Omitted by G and Vg.

18.a. McCarter reads גזר "Gezer," as in 1 Chr 20:4; G must have read גת "Gath."

19.a. So 1 Chr 20:5, and following the Q reading יעיר "Jair." MT has יערי ארגים "Jaare-Oregim," which seems doubtful. The word ארגים is omitted by Gᴸ. In 2 Sam 23:24 we find an "Elhanan, son of Dodo of Bethlehem," who may have been the same Elhanan as mentioned in 21:19.

20.a. Reading מדה "stature" with 1 Chr 20:6 (cf. Isa 45:14). MT (K) has מדין "Midian" (?) while Q reads מדון "quarrel," hence "quarrelsome man" (?).

20.b. We regard הרפה as a proper noun since the initial ה is retained after the prep ל (cf. GKC §35n).

21.a. So Q (שמעה) while K has שמעי "Shimei." There is another variant in 1 Sam 16:9 (שמה).

22.a. In MT the sentence begins with the obj marker את. For the construction, see Brockelmann, *Syntax*, §35c.

Form / Structure / Setting

Although our pericope (21:15–22) is part of the Appendices to 2 Samuel (see *Form / Structure / Setting* of 21:1–14), in its present form and place it has no real context, but its contents suggest that the events depicted in it must belong to the account of David's Philistine wars. However, there is no proof that they were contemporary with the battles described in 5:17–25 or that they must be derived from the same source. This unit contains four brief, stereotyped episodes (for a contrasting style, see 1 Sam 17) which may have come from some ancient archive. It is doubtful that the original source was the Book of the Wars of Yahweh (Num 21:14) or the like (but see Hertzberg, 386), since the above episodes merely describe the exploits of *human* heroes.

Verses 15–17 give an account of David's narrow escape from death (or capture?) with Abishai's help. So David's men made a solemn oath that he should not go out in battle lest he endanger his life. A similar oath is mentioned in 18:3.

The next two episodes are depicted in vv 18 and 19 respectively, while the fourth one is portrayed in vv 20–21. V 22 sums up the previous events which involve Philistine champions from the same family (or cultic or military association ?) and it provides the conclusion to this pericope. The latter forms, incidentally, a sort of prologue to the following song of thanksgiving.

Comment

16 The text at the beginning of the verse may be corrupt but the versions offer little reliable help (see Pisano, *Additions or Omissions*, 152–53). McCarter (448), on the basis of G^L and of the misplaced note after v 11 in G^{BA}, reads וישבו דדו בן יואש "and Dodo son of Joash . . . captured him." However, it is far from certain that this reading represents the original text.

We assume that during the battle David grew weary and that Ishbi-benob attempted to kill him. The form of this Philistine's name is odd (so Nowack, 239) but it is hardly worse than "Dodo, son of Joash."

The Philistine is described as "one of the descendants of Haraphah or Raphah" (בילידי הרפה). However, Willesen (*ST* 12 [1958] 192–210) and L'Heureux (*BASOR* 221 [1976] 83–85) have argued that ילידי הרפה does not mean "the children/descendants of Rapha" (L'Heureux, 83) but rather "the votaries of Rapha" (84) who "were fighting men initiated into an elite group whose patron was *(h)rp*" (84–85). McCarter regards this "cultic association of warriors" (450) as devoted to the god "Rapha-in-Gath." Many exegetes find in רפה "Raphah" an allusion to the mysterious Rephaim, the legendary pre-Israelite inhabitants of Canaan (cf. Gen 15:20; Deut 2:11; 3:11; Josh 17:15). In such a case רפה may be a collective noun (so Mauchline, 305).

It is possible that the ה before רפה is not the article but an integral part of the name. Willesen (*ST* 12 [1958] 200) may be right in linking הרפה with the Greek ἅρπη "scimitar."

Also the description of the Philistine's equipment is rather problematic. The Heb. קַיִן is found only here; G suggests "spear" but "spearhead" might be more plausible (cf. 1 Sam 17:7). Its weight was three hundred shekels or some seven and a half pounds (or three and a half kilograms).

McCarter (448) follows Klostermann et al. in reading קוֹבָעוֹ "his helmet," as in 1 Sam 17:38.

The Heb. חֲדָשָׁה means "new" and it is possible that a noun has been accidentally omitted. Syr and Vg suggest "a (new) sword"; similarly Tg (see also Gordon, *VT* 35 [1985] 496–500). Ehrlich (332) has argued that חֲדָשָׁה was used adverbially, and that the Philistine was girded for the first time with a warrior's belt. This may have been a mark of special distinction (cf. NEB "a belt of honor"; see also 18:11).

17 Although one of the main functions of the king was to fight the wars of his people (1 Sam 9:16; 2 Sam 18:3; cf. also Veijola, *Dynastie*, 119), nevertheless, his life was of an even greater importance. In a sense, the king *was* the very life of the people (cf. Lam 4:20). The lamp-metaphor may be based on the continually burning lamp in the temple (Exod 27:20). In figurative usage, lamp may be a symbol of life (cf. Job 21:17; Prov 20:20; 24:20).

18 Hushah (cf. 1 Chr 4:4) was some four miles southwest of Bethlehem (see Simons, *Texts*, § 322). For "Sibbecai," see n. 23:27a.

"Gob" is mentioned only in this verse and v 19; its location is unknown although Stolz (283) identifies it with Gibbethon (Josh 19:44), west of Gezer (?). However, the authenticity of the reading itself is questionable.

19 According to 1 Chr 20:5, Elhanan, son of Jair, killed Lahmi, brother of Goliath the Gittite, while in 1 Sam 17 it was David who slew Goliath the Gittite. It is often thought that the Chronicler has attempted a harmonization between 1 Sam 17 and 2 Sam 21:19, by creating a brother to Goliath.

The problem as to who killed Goliath is sometimes resolved by identifying David with Elhanan (so already in Jewish tradition). Thus Honeyman ("The Evidence for Regnal Names among the Hebrews," *JBL* 67 [1948] 23–24) has argued that "David" was the king's throne name while "Elhanan" was his personal name (see also Pakozdy, *ZAW* 68 [1956] 257–59). He also suggests the emendation of יַעְרֵי "Jaare" into יִשַׁי "Jesse," on the assumption that שׁ had been misread as עַר.

McCarter (449) retains יַעְרֵי but translates it "the Jearite (from Bethlehem)," hence a native from Kiriath-jearim but living in Bethlehem.

Hertzberg (387) is of the opinion that the name "Goliath" may have come to designate a *type*; this is somewhat reminiscent of Kirkpatrick's view (197) that there may have been two giants who were called by the same name "Goliath."

Occasionally it has been argued that Elhanan's victory over Goliath has been simply transferred to David (so, for instance, Stolz, 283) to magnify the king's achievements.

The spear of Goliath is likened to a weaver's rod, and the point of the comparison is, most likely, not the *size* of the spear but rather its *construction*. It has been suggested that it may have had loops attached to it to improve its effectiveness (see Yadin, *PEQ* 86 [1955] 68).

20 The giant killed at Gath was noted for his physical abnormalities, not unknown in the ancient world. For Gath, see *Comment* on 1:20.

Explanation

21:15–21 and 23:8–39 give an account of the successes and bravery of David and his warriors while 22:1–51 balances this description with a theological explanation of David's life and experiences.

There is, perhaps, truth in Payne's (263) suggestion that the later readers of these events would take pride that *their* ancestors had had a share in establishing and maintaining the Davidic kingdom. This would be at least one function of the hero-exploits.

David's Psalm of Thanksgiving (22:1–51)

Bibliography

Anderson, A. A. *Psalms (1–72)*. The New Century Bible. London: Oliphants, 1972. **Chisholm, R. B.** *An Exegetical and Theological Study of Psalm 18/2 Samuel 22*. Diss., Dallas Theological Seminary, 1983. **Craigie, P. C.** *Psalms 1–50*. WBC 19. Waco, TX: Word Books, 1983. **Cross, F. M.** and **Freedman, D. N.** "A Royal Song of Thanksgiving: II Samuel 22 = Psalm 18." *JBL* 72 (1953) 15–34. **Dahood, M.** *Psalms I: 1–50*. AB 16. Garden City, NY: Doubleday, 1966. **Kraus, H.-J.** *Psalmen 1*. BKAT 15. 5th ed. Neukirchen-Vluyn: Neukirchener Verlag, 1978. **Macintosh, A. A.** "A Consideration of Hebrew גער." *VT* 19 (1969) 471–79. **Schmuttermayr, G.** *Psalm 18 und 2 Samuel 22: Studien zu einem Doppeltext*. SANT 25. Munich: Kösel Verlag, 1971. **Stadelmann, L. I. J.** *The Hebrew Conception of the World*. AnBib 39. Rome: Biblical Institute Press, 1970. **Tromp, N. J.** *Primitive Conceptions of Death and the Nether World in the Old Testament*. BibOr 21. Rome: Pontifical Biblical Institute, 1969.

Translation

¹ *David uttered the words of this song to Yahweh on the day when Yahweh delivered him from the grasp* [a] *of all his enemies and of the grasp* [a] *of Saul.*
² *He said:*

"Yahweh is my cliff,
    my fortress and my deliverer;
³ *(He is)* [a] *my God,* [a] *my rock,*
    in whom I seek refuge.
(He is) my shield and the horn of my salvation,
    my stronghold and my refuge;
(He is) my savior
    [b] *who will save me* [b] *from violent men.* [c]
⁴ [a] *On account of the boastful,* [a] *I cried, 'Yahweh!'*
    on account of the enemies [b] *I called out for help.* [b]
⁵ *For the waves of death engulfed me,*
    the torrents of [a] *deadly trouble* [a] *terrified me.*
⁶ *The cords of Sheol enmeshed me,*
    the snares of death confronted me.
⁷ *So in my troubles I cried, 'Yahweh!'*
    to my God I cried.
From his temple he heard my voice,
    and my cry for help (reached) his ears.
⁸ *Then the earth shook and quaked,*
    even the foundations of the heavens [a] *trembled;*
    they shook violently because he was angry.
⁹ *Smoke went up from* [a] *his nostrils,*
    and devouring fire from his mouth;
    glowing coals spread fire away from him.
¹⁰ *He parted the heavens as he descended,*

     a storm-cloud (was) beneath his feet.
[11] *He mounted a cherub[a] and flew,*
     he soared[b] on the wings of the wind.
[12] *He set darkness around him,*
     [a]*his canopy[a] was the sieve of waters.[b]*
[13] *On account of the brightness before him,[a]*
     glowing coals were set alight.
[14] *Yahweh thundered from the heavens,*
     the Most High gave forth his voice.
[15] *He sent forth (his) arrows, and scattered them,*
     (his) lightnings,[a] and threw them into confusion.
[16] *The channels of the sea[a] were seen,*
     the foundations of the world were laid bare,
     at Yahweh's shout,
     by the (mere) breath of wind from his nostrils.
[17] *Reaching[a] down from on high, he took me,*
     he drew me out of [b]deep waters.[b]
[18] *He delivered me from my mighty enemies,[a]*
     from those who hated me, because they were too strong for me.
[19] *They confronted me on the day of my calamity,*
     but Yahweh became my support.
[20] *He brought me out into a broad place,*
     he saved me because he delighted in me.
[21] *Yahweh rewarded me according to my righteousness,*
     according to the cleanness of my hands;
[22] *because I have kept the ways of Yahweh,*
     and [a]I have not acted wickedly (by turning aside) from my God;[a]
[23] *because all his laws[a] were before me,*
     [b]*and from his statutes I did not turn away.[b]*
[24] *I have been blameless before him,*
     and I was on my guard against [a]any sin on my part.[a]
[25] *So Yahweh requited me according to my righteousness,*
     according to my cleanness in his sight.
[26] *With the loyal you show yourself loyal,*
     with the blameless[a] you show yourself blameless.
[27] *With the pure you show yourself pure,*
     but with the crooked you show yourself tortuous.[a]
[28] *Indeed, you[a] save humble folk,*
     [b]*but your eyes are upon the proud to bring (them) low.[b]*
[29] *You (alone) are my lamp, O Yahweh.*
     (You alone are) my God[a] who lightens my darkness.
[30] *With you I can charge any (enemy) troop,*
     with my God I can jump any wall.
[31] *As for God[a]—his way[b] is perfect,*
     the word of Yahweh is (well) refined;
     he is a shield to all who seek refuge in him.
[32] *Indeed, who is God but Yahweh?*
     who is a rock but our God?

³³*He is the God ^awho girded me^a with strength,*
   he set me free, the one whose way^b is perfect.
³⁴*(He is the one) who makes my feet^a like those of deer,*
   he enables me to stand on any heights.^b
³⁵*(He is the one) who trains my hands for battle,*
   so that my arms could even bend^a a bow of bronze.
³⁶*You have given me your shield^a of victory,^b*
   and your help^c has made me great.
³⁷*You have lengthened my stride beneath me,*
   so that my feet^a did not slip.
³⁸*So, when I pursued my enemies, I destroyed them,*
   I did not turn back until they were exterminated.
³⁹*When^a I smote them, they did not rise,*
   they fell under my feet.
⁴⁰*You have girded^a me with strength for battle,*
   you have made my adversaries kneel ^bat my feet.^b
⁴¹*You have given^a me the necks of my enemies,*
   my adversaries I destroyed for sure.^b
⁴²*They^a cried for help^a but there was no deliverer,*
   even to Yahweh, but he did not answer them.
⁴³*I ground them like the dust of the earth,^a*
   like the mud of the streets I trampled^b them.
⁴⁴*You delivered me from the strife of my^a people,*
   you kept^b me at the head of nations.
People whom I did not know served me,
   ⁴⁵*they^a became obedient at the mere report (of me).*
⁴⁶*Foreigners shriveled up,*
   ^athey came trembling from their strongholds.^a
⁴⁷*Yahweh is eternal! Blessed be my rock!*
   Let God of my salvation^a be exalted.
⁴⁸*(He is) the God who gave me vengeance,*
   ^awho brings peoples down^a under me;
   ⁴⁹*who rescued me from my enemies.*
You have lifted me above those who rise up against me,
   you have delivered me from violent men.^a
⁵⁰*Therefore I will praise you, O Yahweh, among the nations,*
   I will sing praises to your name;
⁵¹*(to the one) who magnifies^a the victories of his king,*
   who keeps his promises to his anointed one,
   to David and to his descendants forever."

Notes

1.a. Lit., "psalm."
3.a-a. Taking אלהי as "the God of" (so RAV).
3.b-b. Reading ישעני "he will save me," with G^L: MT has תשעני "you will save me."
3.c. We take חמס "violence" as a collective noun ("violent men") while McCarter (455) reads the pl חמסים "violent men." Many modern versions render "violence" (so, for instance, NEB, NAB).

4.a-a. We take מהלל as a qal ptcp plus the prep מן used collectively, and parallel to מאיבי "on account of my enemies."

4.b-b. Reading with McCarter (456): אשוע "I cried for help"; cf. Ps 18:7a. MT has אושע "I was saved."

5.a-a. This is our paraphrase of "Belial" (בליעל); see *Comment* on 16:7.

8.a. In Ps 18:8[7] we have הרים "mountains" instead of השמים "the heavens."

9.a. For this use of ב (usually "in"), see Brekelmans, "Some Considerations on the Translation of the Psalms by M. Dahood: The Preposition *b*=*from* in the Psalms According to M. Dahood," *UF* 1 (1969) 8.

11.a. Or "cherubim" (if כרוב is here a collective noun); so also G.

11.b. MT has וירא "and he appeared," which seems to be an orthographic error for וידא "and he soared," as in Ps 18:11[10].

12.a-a. Reading סכתו "his canopy," as in Ps 18:12[11]; similarly G and Syr. We take סכתו with the second colon.

12.b. We omit the last two words of the verse: עבי שחקים "thick clouds"; they may well be a gloss on חשרת מים "sieve of waters," which is a *hapax legomenon* in OT.

13.a. Some translators add ברד "hail" after נגדו "before him"; similarly Gᴸ and Ps 18:13[12]. Our tentative translation does not require this addition.

15.a. The word ברק "lightning" is probably collective in meaning. Ps 18:15 has the pl ברקים.

16.a. One MS and Ps 18:16 has מים "waters" but also here the first *mem* may be an enclitic *mem* belonging to the preceding word (so Cross and Freedman, *JBL* 72 [1953] 26).

17.a. The Heb. ישלח "he stretched out" is probably elliptical, and ידו "his hand" (cf. Ps 144:7) may be implied.

17.b-b. Lit., "many waters" (or "mighty . . .").

18.a. The parallelism with "those who hated me" may suggest that איבי "my enemy" is collective, hence "my enemies."

22.a-a. This sentence is problematic and its pregnant construction has no close parallels; however, see GKC §119xy for somewhat similar structures. Gᴸ must have read רשעתי בעיני ". . . acted wickedly in the sight of," while Dahood (*Psalms 1–50*, 111) suggests רשעתים אלהי "I have (not) been guilty, O my God," regarding the *mem* as an enclitic.

23.a. Reading משפטיו "his laws" with Q. K has the sg משפטו "his law."

23.b-b. Ps 18:23 reads וחקתיו לא אסיר מני "I have not removed his statutes from me." This is also supported by Gᴸ and may, perhaps, be the right reading.

24.a-a. Lit., "my sin."

26.a. The structure of vv 26–27 suggests that גבור "warrior" may be a later addition. MT has גבור תמים "blameless warrior" but גבר "man," as in Ps 18:26, seems more likely than גבור. McCarter (458) argues that the original text of the second colon was עם נקי תנקה "with the guiltless you are guiltless," which has suffered due to haplogr and in the process of correction. He finds textual support for this in Gᴸ.

27.a. MT has תתפל which may mean "shew thyself unsavoury" (ᴋᴊᴠ). Ps 18:27 reads תתפתל "show yourself tortuous," and we have followed this reading.

28.a. We take the obj marker את as an archaic form of אתה "you"; so also Ps 18:28. Moreover, the accusative (עם עני "a humble people") has no article.

28.b-b. Gᴸ and Ps 18:28 may point to the more original reading: ועיני רמים תשפיל "but the eyes of the proud you will bring low"; see Cross and Freedman, *JBL* 72 (1953) 28.

29.a. MT has ויהוה "and Yahweh"; we follow Ps 18:29 which reads אלהי "my God."

31.a. האל "God" is a nominative absolute, and as such it may add emphasis (so Chisholm, *Psalm 18/2 Samuel 22*, 235).

31.b. Dahood (*Psalms 1:1–50*, 114) takes דרך "way" as "dominion" (similar to the Ugaritic *drkt*) but the traditional rendering may be right (contra McCarter, 469).

33.a-a. Reading with 4QSamᵃ מאזרני "who girded me"; similarly Ps 18:33. MT has מעוזי "my refuge."

33.b. Reading with K דרכו "his way"; Q has דרכי "my way."

34.a. So Q as well as Ps 18:34, reading רגלי "my feet"; K has רגליו "his feet."

34.b. Reading במות "heights" for MT במותי "my heights." The *yodh* may be due to dittography. Dahood (*Psalms I:1–50*, 115) takes the suff as 3 sg.

35.a. The subj of the verb (נחת) seems to be זרעתי "my arms" although there is a lack of agreement in gender (see GKC §145o).

36.a. McCarter (471) links מגן which usually means "shield," with the Ugaritic *mgn* ("gift"). Hence he proposes (454): "the gift (of your victory)." This seems a plausible alternative.

36.b. Or "salvation."

36.c. Reading ועזרתך "your help" with 4QSamᵃ, MT has ענתך which could mean "your answer." Ps 18:36 reads ענותך which is rendered "your triumph" by Dahood (*Psalms I:1–50*, 116).

37.a. Lit., "ankles;" קרסל is a *hapax legomenon*.

39.a. We have omitted the first word ואכלם "I destroyed them," which seems to be a variant reading of the preceding verb, as perhaps suggested by Gᴸ.

40.a. 4QSamᵃ reads ותאזרני "you have girded me," while MT has the defective form ותזרני.

40.b-b. Lit., "beneath me."

41.a. Reading נתתה "you have given" for the defective MT תתה see GKC, § 66k.

41.b. This is a paraphrase of the emphatic *wāw;* cf. Williams, *Syntax*, § 438.

42.a-a. So one Heb. MS, G as well as Ps 18:42[41], reading ישועו "they cried for help"; MT has ישעו "they looked"; so NEB, NAB).

43.a. 4QSamᵃ reads על פני ארח "upon the surface of the road"; this may have been the original reading (see also Ps 18:43a). MT has only ארץ "the earth."

43.b. Omitting the preceding verb אדקם "I crushed them," with 4QSamᵃ; it may have been an alternative reading.

44.a. Ps 18:44 omits the pronom suff (i.e., "my").

44.b. Gᴸ and Syr suggest תשימני "you set me."

45.a. We omit the MT בני נכר יתכחשו לי "foreigners will shrink before me" (for this meaning of כחש see Eaton, *JTS* 19 [1968] 603) which may well be a misplaced alternative reading of בני נכר יבלו "foreigners will fade away" in v 46. Also 4QSamᵃ seems to have had a shorter reading at this point (see Ulrich, *Qumran Text*, 109–10).

46.a-a. Both the text and its translation are doubtful. Ps 18:46 has ויחרגו "they came trembling" (?) for ויחגרו "they were girded" (?). McCarter (455) renders v 46b "they came fettered by their collars." Linguistically this is possible but it is questionable whether any of our tentative suggestions is right. We render v 46b as "They (i.e., the foreigners) came trembling (ויחרגו) from their strongholds" (cf. Schmuttermayr, *Psalm 18 und 2 Samuel 22*, 180).

47.a. MT reads אלהי צור ישעי "the God of the rock of my salvation" (so KJV) but we omit צור "rock," which is lacking in Ps 18:47. It would be a repetition of the practically identical צורי "my rock" in the preceding colon.

48.a-a. Ps 18:48 has וידבר "he subdued . . ." while 4QSamᵃ reads ומרדד "and who subdued."

49.a. The Heb. איש "man" is used collectively.

51.a. We have followed K and Ps 18:51, which read מגדיל "who magnifies." Q has מגדול "Migdol" (?), the meaning of which is not clear.

Form / Structure / Setting

According to the heading (v 1), this psalm was uttered on the day when Yahweh had delivered David from all his enemies, including Saul. However, it seems that this verse is an interpretative addition, reminiscent of the "historical" notes in the headings of certain Psalms (see Pss 3; 7; 34; 51; 52; 54; 56; 57; 59; 60; 63; 142; cf. also B. S. Childs, "Psalm Titles and Midrashic Exegesis," *JSS* 16 [1971] 137–50). No such single day of victory is known to us, and it is more likely that this "historical" note looks back at David's victories in general. If David were the author of this psalm, we might have expected some more specific allusions or references to David's past experiences. As it is, the descriptions are very general and would suit very well a recurrent cultic setting at one of the annual festivals (perhaps Tabernacles). Thus, apart from the editorial notes (vv 1 and 51c), there is no obvious internal support for the Davidic authorship of this poem (contra Delitzsch, Kirkpatrick, Chisholm, et al.). On the other hand, the psalm does exhibit certain archaic linguistic features (see Cross and Freedman, *JBL* 72 [1953] 15–20), and it resembles such examples of archaic poetry as Exod 15; Deut 32–33; Judg 5; Hab 3; etc. (see Schmuttermayr, *Psalm 18 und 2 Samuel 22*, 24). Consequently, McCarter (475), Schmuttermayr (*ibid.*), et al. are of the opinion that it is unlikely that the main parts of the psalm were later than the ninth century B.C.

This brings us to the related question of the psalm's literary integrity. Many exegetes, especially in the more distant past, have contended for the unity of the poem (see, for example, Weiser, Chisholm, Craigie) while others find two or more originally independent units in our psalm (so, for instance, H. Schmidt, *Die Psalmen*, HAT 1.15. [Tübingen: J. C. B. Mohr, 1934] 26–30; E. Baumann,"Struktur-Untersuchungen im Psalter 1," *ZAW* 61 [1945–48] 131–36; McCarter, 473–75; et al.). We are inclined to accept the view that our present psalm was composed of two older poems: an individual song of thanksgiving for deliverance (vv 2–20) and a royal thanksgiving for victory (vv 29–51ab). The two parts were eventually combined by means of the connecting material (vv 21–28) which may come from the hand of a Deuteronomistic editor who probably used some other older materials, such as the wisdom motifs in vv 26–28. Thus the psalm in its present form cannot be earlier than the seventh century B.C. However, some scholars are less certain about the Deuteronomistic language in vv 21–25 (see Kraus, *Psalmen*[1], 140).

The structure of the psalm could be, tentatively, represented in the following way:

v 1	Editorial heading to the psalm as a whole
A. Psalm of Deliverance (vv 2–20)	
vv 2–4	Introduction: Praise and expression of confidence
vv 5–7a	Psalmist's plea to God
vv 7b–17	Yahweh's theophany
vv 18–20	The deliverance of the psalmist
B. Connecting Material (vv 21–28)	
vv 21–25	The integrity of the psalmist
vv 26–28	Wisdom motifs
C. Royal Psalm of Victory (vv 29–51ab)	
vv 29–31	Expressions of confidence
v 32	Yahweh's incomparability
vv 33–37	Yahweh equips his servant for war
vv 38–46	God-given victory
vv 47–51ab	Conclusion: Praise of God
D. v 51c	Interpretative addition

Comment

1 Dahood (*Psalms I:1–50*, 104) translates שאול as "Sheol." This is plausible since Saul is, in a sense, already included among the enemies while the deliverance from Sheol is implied by v 6.

However, the usual rendering "Saul" is equally plausible. Since v 1 is an editorial comment and since it was meant to link the psalm with David, the reference to "Saul" might be expected. In that case the *wāw* before מכף

"from the grasp of" may indicate a certain emphasis: "especially . . ." (see GKC, §154a, n. 1b).

2–3   The divine epithets used in these verses depict Yahweh as a place of refuge and safety, as well as a protector and deliverer. McCarter (464) pairs some of the epithets and treats each pair as a hendiadys, e.g., "my cliffside stronghold" for "my cliff and my fortress." This is plausible but we have preferred the more traditional rendering.

The epithet "shield" (מגן) may, perhaps, mean "sovereign" in our context (so McCarter, 465). In Ps 84:10[9] "shield" is parallel to "the anointed one" (i.e., king); cf also Ps 89:20[19].

"Horn of my salvation" (v 3) may suggest that Yahweh is the effective means of the psalmist's deliverance. In the OT the horn is often used as a symbol of strength (cf. 1 Kgs 22:11; Ps 92:10).

4   The translation of this verse is rather problematic. We assume that v 4 forms a sort of inclusion with v 7a whose equivalent in Ps 18:7a[6a] has both אקרא "I cried" and אשוע "I called for help." Consequently, there is some justification for our emendation. For the translation of the impf by a past tense, see Williams, *Syntax*, §177.

5–6   The mortal danger is represented by the picture of death and Sheol as all-engulfing waters, and as an inescapable hunter whose traps and nets are ever ready.

8   The Heb. ארץ may sometimes denote the underworld (see Dahood, *Psalms I:1–50*, 106) but it is less likely in this particular context (contra Dahood); it is more plausible in Ps 18:8 where the foundations of the *mountains* reach into the underworld (see Tromp, *Primitive Conceptions*, 45).

9–11   Here Yahweh is depicted as if he were the fire-breathing Leviathan (see Job 41:18–21). Smoke and fire usually accompany Yahweh's theophanies (cf. Exod 24:17; Deut 4:24; Isa 30:27).

We take נטה as "to spread apart" or "spread open," following Cross and Freedman (*JBL* 72 [1953] 24). For a parallel, see Ps 144:5; Isa 63:19[64:1]. Sometimes the heavens are depicted as a tent or spread-out curtain (see Ps 104:2; Isa 40:22; Stadelmann, *The Hebrew Conception of the World*, 49–53).

The cherubim were thought to be winged creatures (cf. Exod 25:20; 1 Kgs 6:24; Ezek 10:8), and they are sometimes envisaged as composite figures, having a human face and animal body, or any other variations (see Ezek 10:20; 41:18–19). They could serve as Yahweh's throne or as bearers of it (cf. Pss 80:2[1]; 99:1) and also as a means of "transport" (see also *ANEP*, p. 221, pl. 689).

12   The verse is textually and exegetically difficult (cf. Ps 18:12[11]). The MT could be translated, "He set darkness around him as a canopy, the thick clouds (were) a sieve of waters." The picture of clouds as sieve may have been suggested by the falling of rain drops.

14   "The Most High" (עליון) may have been originally associated with the cult of El in the pre-Israelite Jerusalem (see Gen 14:18–24). Later this divine epithet was applied to Yahweh (see H.-J. Zobel, "עליון," *TWAT* 6 [1 / 2; 1987] 131–51).

Thundering was the most common theophanic motif in the OT (cf. Exod 19:16; Pss 77:18–19[17–18]; 144:6). Thus Yahweh appears as if he were a storm god.

15 The main problem in this verse is the antecedent of the pronom suffixes (i.e., *them*). We have assumed that the reference is to the enemies mentioned in v 4. Horeover, the verbs פוץ and המם are often part of the Holy War accounts (see Chisholm, *Psalm 18/2 Samuel 22*, 189); therefore the allusion to the adversaries is likely. On the other hand, some scholars (for instance, Dahood, Johnson, McCarter) argue that the above suffixes refer to the arrows and lightnings (see also the parallel in Ps 144:6).

16 At Yahweh's shout the very springs of the sea were uncovered (for Ugaritic parallels, see Stadelmann, *The Hebrew Conception of the World*, 158–60). The verse may be also a reminder of the deliverance at the Red Sea (see Ps 106:9).

The phrase "breath of wind from his nostrils" may be an emphatic expression in which "wind" (רוח) is an appositional genitive (see Chisholm, *Psalm 18/2 Samuel 22*, 196, n. 3), perhaps, "the blast from his nostrils."

17 The purpose of the actions in the preceding verses was to prepare the way for the psalmist's deliverance from the destructive forces. It is just possible that the rare verb משה "to draw out" may have been intended as a pointer to the Mosaic story (cf. Exod 2:10). However, it is doubtful that the psalmist meant to present himself as a second Moses (cf. Ridderbos, *Die Psalmen: Stylistische Verfahren und Aufbau mit besonderer Berücksichtigung von Ps 1–41*. BZAW 117 [Berlin, New York: W. de Gruyter, 1972] 170) since Exod 2 stresses divine providence while our psalm speaks of direct divine intervention.

18–20 The deliverance was entirely due to Yahweh who became the psalmist's firm support (cf. Isa 10:20). It was like being brought into a broad place where one can breathe freely, without being hemmed in by enemies and choked by affliction.

21–25 The chiastic arrangement of v 21, and the contents of the following verses, may emphasize that Yahweh's gracious intervention is also *fair* in that it takes into consideration one's loyalty, obedience, and integrity.

26–28 These verses illustrate Yahweh's talionic justice (so Chisholm, *Psalm 18/2 Samuel 22*, 216) which is applied both to the righteous and the wicked. He is just to all—on their own terms.

It is less likely that in v 27b (see תתפל) there is a deliberate word play on Ahithophel's name, as argued by Carlson (*David*, 151–52).

29 Yahweh is David's lamp or source of life and prosperity (cf. Job 18:6; Prov 20:20; 24:20); he dispels his servant's darkness and brings him back to life (cf. vv 6, 16–17).

30 The translation and interpretation of this verse is problematic. The verse might be paraphrased, "With your help I can charge a whole troop of foes single-handed, with the help of my God I can scale the enemy's walls."

The verb ארוץ "I can run" is, perhaps, used elliptically and therefore the prep (such as על "against") may be implied.

McCarter (469) reads אדוץ גדוד "I can leap a gully," which would provide a parallel to the next colon. Nowack (247) follows Kimchi's suggestion and derives ארוץ from רצץ "to crush," and reads גדר "wall" for גדוד "troop"; however, רצץ is hardly ever used in military contexts.

Thus it seems that the verse depicts in hyperbolic language two warlike scenes where the psalmist, having derived his strength and courage from Yahweh, can therefore face any odds.

31 This verse forms a tricolon, and it is possible that an original bicolon has been expanded in the course of transmission. McCarter (469) regards the second colon as intrusive.

32 The two rhetorical questions express Yahweh's incomparability (cf. also 1 Sam 2:2; 2 Sam 7:22; Isa 43:11; 44:7–8). The Psalmist does not deny the existence of other gods but simply asserts Yahweh's uniqueness. McCarter (469) calls it a "monotheistic formula" but, at the same time, he doubts whether it was part of the original text.

33 The second colon is problematic. We follow Ps 18:33[32] which has ויתן חמים דרכי "he made my way perfect." McCarter (459) regards MT ויתר "he set free" as the defective spelling of ויתאר "he mapped out (a complete dominion for me)." This means taking דרך "way" as "dominion" (see n. 32.b.).

34–35 McCarter (470) sees in vv 34–35 "the divine manufacture of the psalmist"; he is made to stand upright (על במותי "upon my haunches") with legs like tree trunks (אילות). Yahweh also shapes the elbows (i.e., the "bows of my arms") of the psalmist. This is a possible interpretation of a difficult verse but we have followed the more traditional exegesis which gives a reasonable sense.

37 The word picture is not quite clear: either the psalmist's stride has been lengthened so that he could move swiftly and surely or his path has been widened for unimpaired movement (so NAB, NIV, RAV).

41 The scene depicted is either that of retreat (cf. Exod 23:27) or of total defeat of the enemies (i.e., the victor places his foot on the neck of the enemy, as in Josh 10:24). V 41b seems to suggest the latter alternative.

42 The fact that the enemies appealed to Yahweh may suggest that they may have been internal enemies. Whether foes such as Absalom, Sheba and their supporters were intended is doubtful, although this may well have been so in the later interpretation of the psalm.

47 We would suggest that חי in reference to God may sometimes mean not only "alive," "living" but also "everlasting," "eternal," especially if חיים "life" in certain contexts may denote "eternal life" (cf. Ps 21:5[4]; see also E. Jenni, "עולם" *THAT* 2 [1976] cols. 237–38).

51 Some scholars regard either the whole verse or only v 51c as a later addition because of its explicit reference to David (cf. Schmuttermayr, *Psalm 18 und 2 Samuel 22,* 199–200).

Explanation

The canonical form of our psalm could be regarded as a re-presentation of David's varied experiences and deliverance, in which successive kings, their people, and even the common individual could share here and now. The same God who delivered David is also the God of all for "who is God but Yahweh" (see v 32). He is loyal to those who are loyal (v 26a); he is the one who saves not only the king but also the humble folk (v 28).

Even if the psalm was part of the cultic drama, the above suggestion is still valid.

The Oracle of Yahweh to David (23:1–7)

Bibliography

Boer, P. A. H. de. "Texte et traduction des paroles attribuées à David en II Samuel xxiii 1–7." VTSup 4 (1957) 47–56. **Cooper, A. M.** "The Life and Times of King David according to the Book of Psalms." *The Poet and the Historian: Essays in Literary and Historical Biblical Criticism.* Ed. R. E. Friedman. Harvard Semitic Studies 26. Chico, California: Scholars Press, 1983. 117–31. **Gerleman, G.** "Die sperrende Grenze: Die Wurzel ʿlm im Hebräischen." ZAW 91 (1979) 338–49. **Mettinger, T. N. D.** "'The Last Words of David': A Study of Structure and Meaning in II Samuel 23:1–7." SEÅ 41–42 (1976–77) 147–56. **Mowinckel, S.** "'Die lezten Worte Davids,' II Sam 23:1–7." ZAW 45 (1927) 30–58. **Nyberg, H. S.** "Studien zum Religionskampf im Alten Testament." ARW 35 (1938) 329–87. **Olmo Lete, G. Del.** "David's Farewell Oracle (2 Samuel xxiii 1–7): A Literary Analysis." VT 34 (1984) 414–37. **Richardson, H. N.** "The Last Words of David: Some Notes on II Sam. 23, 1–7." JBL 90 (1971) 257–66. **Sanders, J. A.** *The Psalms Scroll of Qumrân 11 (11QPsª).* DJD 4. Oxford: Clarendon Press, 1965. **Sheppard, G. T.** *Wisdom as a Hermeneutical Construct.* BZAW 151. Berlin/New York: Walter de Gruyter, 1980.

Translation

¹ *These are the words of David.*
   The utterance of David, son of Jesse,
      the utterance of the man ᵃ*whom God raised up,*ᵃ
   the anointed of the God of Israel,
      the favorite of Israel's protector.
² *The spirit of Yahweh has spoken through me,*
      his word is upon my tongue.
³ *The God of Israel spoke,*
      to me the rock of Israel said:
   *"He who rules justly*ᵃ *among men,*
      *he who rules in*ᵇ *the fear of God,*
⁴ *is* ᵃ*surely like*ᵃ *the morning light (when) the sun rises,*
      ᵇ*(even like the light of)*ᵇ *a cloudless morning.*
   *(He is) like*ᶜ *brightness after rain,*
      (producing) fresh grass from the earth."
⁵ *Truly*ᵃ *my house is right*ᵇ *with God,*
      for he has given me an everlasting covenant
      set forth in every respect and guaranteed.
   *For surely*ᶜ *he will make my welfare*
      and (my) desires prosper.
⁶ *"But as for the evil men—*
      *they all are like*ᵃ *thorns* ᵇ*thrust away,*ᵇ
      *they cannot be taken*ᶜ *by hand,*
⁷ *nor will any man touch them,*
      *except*ᵃ *(with) an* ᵇ*iron-tipped spear shaft.*ᵇ
   *They shall be totally consumed by fire."*ᶜ

Notes

1.a-a. Reading הקים אל ". . . God raised up," with 4QSamᵃ and Gᴸ. MT has הקם על "was raised up on high" [RSV] or, as suggested by Richardson (*JBL* 90 [1971] 259): "the Most High raised up."

3.a. Taking צדיק "righteous" as an adverbial accusative ("justly"); cf. GKC, § 118q.

3.b. The prep ב "in" may have dropped out; it is found in many MSS and versions. However, באדם may be presupposed in the following colon, hence "he who rules (among men) fearing God" (cf. Sheppard, *Wisdom*, 151, n. 74).

4.a-a. Some omit the *wāw* "and" before כאור "like the light," with most versions, but it may be an emphatic *wāw*.

4.b-b. This seems to be implied by the context.

4.c. Reading כנגה "like brightness" instead of MT מנגה "from brightness" (?).

5.a. We have taken כי לא as having an asseverative force (see Richardson, *JBL* 90 [1971] 263; Cross, *Canaanite Myth*, 235 n.74). Some translators treat the expression as introducing a negative rhetorical question ("Is not [my house right . . .]," so NIV; RSV has "Yea, does not my house . . .").

5.b. Taking כן to mean "right" (see *HALAT*, 159; Cross, *Canaanite Myth*, 235 nn. 74 and 75).

5.c. See n. 5.a.

6.a. Perhaps we should read כקוץ "like thorns" for MT בקוץ "in . . ." (?); the mistake (?) may be due to a confusion of *beth* and *kaph*.

6.b. MT מנד is probably a hoph ptcp of נדד "to move" or "wander around," hence "banished," "thrust away."

6.c. Taking MT יקחו as a pass qal (so Richardson, *JBL* 90 [1971] 265).

7.a. We follow McCarter (479) who reads אם לא "except," following Gᴸ, for MT ימלא "he will be filled."

7.b-b. Lit., "iron and the shaft of a spear" (so NAB).

7.c. We omit the final word (בשבת) of the verse, the meaning of which is obscure, and which most scholars regard as superfluous. It may be a misplaced dittograph of the same consonantal group in the following verse.

G has taken it as "their shame" (= בשתם); MT may, perhaps, be paraphrased as "on the spot" (so McCarter, 479).

Form / Structure / Setting

2 Sam 23:1–7 is part of the "Appendices" (see *Form / Structure / Setting* of 21:1–14), namely, chaps. 21–24. Our particular unit (vv 1–7) is described in the heading (v 1a) as "The last words of David" but in the light of its contents it seems more appropriate to designate it as "Yahweh's oracle to David," reminiscent of the oracle of Balaam (see Num 24).

In this unit, v 1a may be defined as the superscription while vv 1b–2 form the actual introduction (see the parallel in Num 24:3–4). Here David is portrayed as a prophet as well as the anointed one of Israel. In vv 3–4 there is another brief introduction (v 3a) to the divine oracle (vv 3b–4) which is expressed in the form of a wisdom saying (see Sheppard, *Wisdom*, 151–52), extolling the reign of the just king. This is followed by David's assertion (v 5) that his house (or "dynasty") is right with God (cf. 7:16).

We assume that also vv 6–7 are part of the divine word through David, reminiscent of wisdom utterances. They depict the destiny of evil rulers (or evil men in general ?), alluding, perhaps, to the fate of the northern kings.

The dating of this material is rather difficult. As McCarter (486) et al. have pointed out, there are no traces of the Deuteronomistic language, and the divine epithets may well belong to the early monarchic period; hence they conclude that the Davidic date and authorship is not impossible. On the other hand, the contents of v 5 may suggest some distance in time between the dramatic and sometimes unsavory events of David's reign and the present poem. Nevertheless, it presupposes the monarchical period, perhaps after the fall of Samaria in 722 B.C.

In a sense this unit forms a fitting conclusion of the effective reign of David since 1 Kgs 1–2 depicts only a "shadow" of the former king. In a few words the author has given his readers a very brief theological evaluation of David's reign in general. Stolz (293) has defined the *Gattung* or literary type of this poem as "Königsspiegel" or "royal ideal." If so, vv 6–7 may have in mind the opposite, namely, evil rulers such as those in the northern kingdom who indeed perished. Consequently, the poem may come from the reign of Hezekiah or Josiah, both of whom had considerable interest in the fortunes of the northern territories of Israel.

Comment

1 The introductory formula is virtually the same as the opening formula of Balaam's oracles (see Num 24:3, 15; cf. also Prov 30:1; 31:1).

The Heb. נאם "oracle," "utterance," is usually associated with prophetic utterances, and Ackroyd (217) infers from this that "David is here understood as a prophetic figure, not unlike Balaam."

The phrase הקם על is ambiguous. It is possible that על is tantamount to a divine name. Nyberg (*ARW* 35 [1938] 329) regards על as an old synonym of עליון "Most High," and the 4QSamᵃ reading אל "God" may lend some support to this argument. See n. 1a–a.

In recent decades זמרות ישראל has been often taken as a divine epithet "the protector of Israel" (McCarter [476]: "the stronghold of . . ."). It is likely that זמרות is a plural of majesty (cf. GKC §124g–i) and that זמרה may denote "strength" (cf. *HALAT*, 263) or "protection"; for other possible occurrences, see Exod 15:2; Isa 12:2; Ps 118:14; cf. also Richardson (*JBL* 90 [1971] 261). Thus David would be described as the darling or favorite of Yahweh, i.e., Israel's protector (parallel to "the God of Israel").

However, the traditional rendering "the sweet psalmist of Israel" (so, e.g., RSV, RAV) is not impossible. David came to be known as a skilled composer of psalms and as a man inspired by the prophetic spirit (see Sanders, *Psalms Scroll*, 91–93).

2 The verb is masculine in Hebrew while the subj רוח "spirit" is usually feminine. Perhaps the lapse of gender is due to the intervening word ("Yahweh"); Olmo Lete (*VT* 34 [1984] 416) revocalizes the verb as feminine.

The "spirit" in this context is not the source of ecstatic behavior or experience (cf. 1 Sam 11:6) but of prophetic inspiration (as in Prov 16:10; cf. also 1 Kgs 22:24; 1 Chr 12:18).

3 Justice can be implemented only by people living in right relationship to God (i.e., living in the fear of God or in awe of him).

The by-product of this is divine blessing, picturesquely described in v 4. Verse 3b is often regarded as a wisdom saying or part of it.

4 The text and its translation are very problematic but the tentative rendering and arrangement may, perhaps, provide the gist of the intended meaning.

The description of the king in terms of the sun and its light is fairly frequent in the ancient Near East, especially in Egypt (cf. I. Engnell, *Studies in Divine Kingship in the Ancient Near East* [Oxford: Blackwell, 1967] 6). McCarter (484) has remarked that "sun" was "also a royal title in Israel" but the evidence is somewhat limited (see also S. Mowinckel, *He That Cometh* [tr. G. W. Anderson; Oxford: Blackwell, 1965] 227, n. 3).

For a parallel to v 4a, see Sanders, *Psalms Scroll*, 92, xxvii.11.2–4; for v 4b, cf. Ps 72:6.

5 The initial colon of the verse can be understood in more than one way, as attested by the versions, both ancient and modern (cf. n. 5.a.). We take it as a positive statement while Mettinger (*King and Messiah,* 280), for instance, regards the whole verse as a rhetorical question. KJV translates it: "Although my house be not so with God . . ." but this seems to be a less satisfactory rendering.

It is just possible that the whole verse is a sort of parenthesis since it seems to separate the royal ideal (vv 3b–4) from its negative counterpart (vv 6–7).

"The everlasting covenant" exists in perpetuity and is binding forever (see P. Kalluveettil, *Declaration and Covenant* [AnBib 88. Rome: Biblical Institute Press, 1982] 186). The implications of this covenant are well depicted in Ps 89:4–5[3–4], 20–38[19–37]. Nonetheless, even such a covenant does not give a blank cheque to individual rulers (see 7:14; Ps 89:31–33[30–32]). However, Mettinger (*King and Messiah,* 282) has argued that the term "covenant" (ברית) "is not attested as a term for the Davidic covenant until the exilic period" and that from this time onwards the normative form of the Davidic covenant was "unconditional formulation."

6–7 For בליעל "the evil men," see *Comment* on 16:7. The word in this context is used collectively, and Richardson (*JBL* 90 [1971] 264) has suggested that it is probably an ellipsis for בני בליעל (or) בן "son (or "sons") of Belial."

It is possible that vv 6–7 provide the negative counterpart to the righteous king and his rule (vv 3b–4), and thus it may allude to the unrighteous kings of Northern Israel who perished. However, it is equally possible that the godless (or "evil men") were the enemies of the Davidic dynasty (so Gordon, 311) or simply godless men in general. In any case, their fate is destruction (cf. Mal 3:19–21[4:1–3]); they are like thorns (cf. Isa 33:12b) that are only fit for the fire.

Explanation

In 23:1–7 the prophetic literary type is used as a retrospective theological explanation or commentary on David and his house or dynasty. Thus it provides a very brief but fitting conclusion to the narrative of the preceding chapters and to the psalm in chap. 22.

In a sense, it offers not only a royal ideal (or *Königsspiegel*) by which all future kings should be judged but it also depicts an ideal for all human beings, both great and small. Those who do justice and act in the fear of God, will be blessed and they will be a blessing to others, while those who love chaos and destruction (i.e., "men of Belial") will *receive* their hearts' desire.

David's Heroes and Some of Their Exploits (23:8–39)

Bibliography

Bartlett, J. R. "The Use of the Word ראש as a Title in the Old Testament." *VT* 19 (1969) 1–10. **Braun, R.** *1 Chronicles.* WBC 14. Waco, TX: Word Books, 1986. **Elliger, K.** "Die dreissig Helden Davids." *PJ* 31 (1935) 29–75. **Galling, K.** "Goliath und seine Rüstung." VTSup 15. Leiden: E. J. Brill, 1966. 150–69. **Gottwald, N. K.** *The Hebrew Tribes: A Sociology of the Religion of Liberated Israel, 1250–1050 B.C.E.* London: SCM Press. 1979. **Mastin, B. A.** "Was the ŠĀLÎŠ the Third Man in the Chariot?" VTSup 30 (1979) 125–54. **Mazar, B.** "The Military Élite of King David." *The Early Biblical Period: Historical Studies*, ed. S. Ahtuv and B. A. Levine. Tr. Ruth and Elisheva Rigbi. Jerusalem: Israel Exploration Society, 1986. **Miller, P. D., Jr.** "Animal Names as Designations in Ugaritic and Hebrew." *UF* 2 (1971) 177–86. **Stoebe, H. J.** "Gedanken zur Heldensage in den Samuelbüchern." In *Das Ferne und nahe Wort*, FS Leonard Rost, ed. F. Maass. BZAW 105. Berlin: Töpelmann, 1967. 208–18. **Tidwell, N. L.** "The Philistine Incursions into the Valley of Rephaim (2 Sam. v 17 ff.)." VTSup 30 (1979) 190–212. **Vaux, R. de.** *The Bible and the Ancient Near East.* Tr. D. McHugh. London: Darton, Longman, and Todd, 1972. 122–35. **Vogt. E.** "*El haš^elōšā lō'-bā*" *Bib* 40 (1959) 1062–63. **Willesen, F.** "The Philistine Corps of the Scimitar from Gath." *JSS* 3 (1958) 327–35. **Zeron, A.** "Der Platz Benajahus in der Heldenliste Davids (II Sam 23:20–23)." *ZAW* 90 (1978) 20–27.

Translation

[8] *These are the names of David's mighty men. Ishbaal,[a] [b]son of Hachmon,[b] the chief of the Three;[c] [d]he wielded his spear[d] against eight hundred (men), (all) slain on a single occasion.* [9] *Next to him, among the three mighty men,[a] was Eleazar, son of Dodo, the Ahohite;[b] [c]he was[c] with David at Pas-dammim[d] when the Philistines assembled there for battle. (On that occasion) the Israelites retreated* [10] *but he[a] stood his ground and smote the Philistines until his hand grew weary and stuck fast to the sword. So Yahweh brought about a great victory that day; (only) then the soldiers began to return to him—to strip (the dead)![b]* [11] *Next to him was Shamma, son of Agee the Hararite.[a] (Once) the Philistines had assembled at Lehi where there was a plot of land [b]with a crop of[b] lentils,[c] and the troops fled from the Philistines* [12] *but he took his stand in the middle of the plot and defended it and defeated the Philistines. Thus Yahweh brought about a great victory.* [13] *One harvest time, the three[a] from the Thirty went down and came[b] to David, to the cave of Adullam while a detachment of Philistines was encamped in the Valley of Rephaim.* [14] *At that time David was in (his) mountain stronghold while the Philistines had a military outpost in Bethlehem.* [15] *Then, (one day,) David had a hankering, and he said, "Oh, that someone would give[a] me a drink of water from the well[b] which is by the gate of Bethlehem."* [16] *So three of the elite soldiers broke through the Philistine camp and drew water from the well[a] which is by the gate of Bethlehem. When they brought it to David, he refused to drink it but poured it out to Yahweh,* [17] *saying, "Far be it from me, O Yahweh, that I should do this! [a]I shall not drink the blood of these men who went[a] [b]at the risk of[b] their lives!" So he refused to drink it.*
These are the deeds the three mighty men performed.

¹⁸ *Abishai, Joab's brother,* ^a*son of Zeruiah,*^a *was chief of the Thirty;*^b *he wielded his spear over three hundred (men), slain (on a single occasion),*^c *and he became famous among the Thirty.*^d ¹⁹^a*He was more honored than (the rest of) the Thirty,*^a *and he became their commander; however, he did not attain to the Three.* ²⁰ *Benaiah, son of Jehoiada, was* ^a*a brave man*^a *from Kabzeel, mighty in deeds. He killed* ^b*the two distinguished warriors*^b *of Moab. Once he went into a pit and killed a lion on a snowy day.* ²¹ *He also killed an Egyptian,* ^a*a man of unusual size.*^a *The Egyptian had a spear in his hand while Benaiah*^b *went down against him with a club. He snatched the spear from the Egyptian's hand, and killed him with his own spear.* ²² *These were the deeds that Benaiah, son of Jehoiada, performed. Thus he became famous among the Thirty*^a *elite warriors.* ²³ *He was more honored than (the rest of) the Thirty but he did not attain to the Three. David set him over*^a *his bodyguard.*

²⁴ *Asahel, brother of Joab, was among the Thirty. (So also) Elhanan, son of Dodo from*^a *Bethlehem,*
²⁵ *Shammah the Harodite,*
   Elika the Harodite,
²⁶ *Helez the Paltite,*
   Ira, son of Ikkesh of Tekoah,
²⁷ *Abiezer the Anathothite,*
   Mebunnai^a *the Hushathite,*
²⁸ *Zalmon the Ahohite,*
   Mahrai the Netophathite,
²⁹ *Heleb,*^a *son of Baanah the Netophathite,*
   Ittai, son of Ribai, of Gibeah of the Benjaminites,
³⁰ *Benaiah the Pirathonite,*
   Hiddai from the brooks of Gaash,
³¹ *Abi-albon*^a *the Arbathite,*
   Azmaveth the Bahurimite,^b
³² *Eliahba the Shaalbonite,*
   ^a*Jashen the Gimzonite,*^a
   Jonathan, son of^b ³³ *Shamma the Hararite,*
   Ahiam, son of Sharar^a *the Hararite,*
³⁴ *Eliphelet, son of Ahasbai the Maacathite,*
   Eliam, son of Ahithophel the Gilonite,
³⁵ *Hezrai the Carmelite,*
   Paarai the Arbite,
³⁶ *Igal, son of Nathan from Zobah,*
   Bani the Gadite,
³⁷ *Zelek the Ammonite,*
   Nahrai the Beerothite, the weapon-bearer^a *of Joab, son of Zeruiah,*
³⁸ *Ira the Ithrite,*
   Gareb the Ithrite,
³⁹ *Uriah the Hittite.*
   Thirty-seven in all.

Notes

8.a. Reading יֹשְׁבְעָל; MT has ישׁב בשׁבת ("Josheb-Bassheveth," so RSV, RAV). G^L seems to have preserved the original form of the name Ιεσβααλ (= יֹשְׁבְעָל "Baal exists"). At a later stage this was deliberately altered to ישבשת (cf. G Ιεβοοθε) which must have become ישב בשבת (see Mazar, *The Early Biblical Period*, 91, n. 20; cf. also *Comment* on 2:8).

8.b-b. Reading, on the basis of 1 Chr 11:11, בן חכמון "son of Hachmon."

8.c. Reading השלשה "the Three" with G^L: so already Wellhausen (213). MT has השלשי (probably "the third part [of the army]"). 1 Chr 11:11 (K) reads השלושים "the Thirty."

8.d-d. So 1 Chr 11:11 (הוא עורר את חניתו). MT seems unintelligible at this point although some exegetes find here a proper name: "Adino the Eznite" (so RAV).

9.a. Q has הגבורים "the mighty men"; K omits the article.

9.b. Omitting בן "son of," and reading האחוחי "the Ahohite," with 1 Chr 11:12.

9.c-c. Adding הוא היה "he was," with 1 Chr 11:13.

9.d. So 1 Chr 11:13. McCarter (490) assumes a longer omission in MT, and reads בחרפם הפלשתי בפס דמים והפלשתים "when the Philistine defied them at Pas-dammim, When the Philistines . . . ," However, we prefer the *shorter* reading.

10.a. Reading והוא "but he", so G^L.

10.b. An explanatory addition as also in Syr, Tg, and Vg.

11.a. Mazar (*The Early Biblical Period*, 91, n. 25) suggests החרדי "the Harodite"; i.e., from Harod, near Bethlehem.

11.b-b. Lit., "filled with."

11.c. 1 Chr 11:13 has שעורים "barley" for MT עדשים "lentils." Budde (320) regards the latter as the original reading since this crop is less frequent.

13.a. Reading with Q שלשה "three" for MT (K) שלשים "thirty"; so 1 Chr 11:15 as well as the major versions.

13.b. Omitting the preceding ראש "chief" (?) with G^B and Syr; some take it with השלשים, rendering "the thirty chief men" (so RAV) but this would require a minor emendation (i.e., הראשים).

15.a. Here a wish is expressed in the form of a question; see GKC, §151a.

15.b. So K; Q reads בר "cistern."

16.a. See n. 15.b.

17.a-a. Reading הדם האנשים האלה אשתה ההלכים "shall I drink the blood of these men who went"; cf. G and 1 Chr 11:19. MT has הדם האנשים ההלכים "is it the blood of the men who went." The rhetorical question seems to be equivalent to a strong negative assertion.

17.b-b. Or "at the price of"; for this use of the prep ב, see GKC, § 119p.

18.a-a. Lacking in G^L and 1 Chr 11:20.

18.b. Reading השלשים "thirty" with Syr; MT (K) has השלשי "third" (?) while Q reads השלשה "the three."

18.c. Our explanatory addition; see v 8b.

18.d. We read בשלשים "among the Thirty"; MT has בשלשה "among the Three." 1 Chr 11:20 (K) reads ולא שם בשלושה "he did not have a place [lit., "name"] amongst the Three."

19.a-a. MT has מן השלשה הכי נכבד "was he not the most honored of three?" (so RAV). We follow Syr in reading מן השלשים הוא נכבד "he was more honored than the Thirty."

20.a-a. Omitting בן "son of" with G and reading with Q איש חיל "a brave man."

20.b-b. G suggests שני בני אראל "the two sons of Ariel." See *Comment* on 23:20.

21.a-a. Reading איש מדה "man of size" with 1 Chr 11:23; MT (Q) has איש מראה "a man of appearance" (RSV: "a handsome man").

21.b. Lit., "he."

22.a. Reading בשלשים "among the Thirty"; MT has "among the Three."

23.a. Taking אל "to" in the sense of על "over"; these two preps seem to be used interchangeably, at least at times.

24.a. So 1 Chr 11:26, reading מבית לחם "from Bethlehem"; MT omits the prep.

27.a. 1 Chr 11:29 reads סבכי "Sibbecai" for מבני "Mebunnai"; perhaps the same person as Sibbecai in 2 Sam 21:18.

29.a. Many MSS read חלד "Heled"; so also 1 Chr 11:30. In 1 Chr 27:15 we find "Heldai" (חלדי) the Netophathite.

31.a. 1 Chr 11:32 has אביאל "Abiel."

31.b. MT reads הברחמי "Barhumite" but perhaps we should change it to הבחרמי "Bahurim-ite," i.e., a Benjaminite from Bahurim (see *Comment* on 3:16).

32.a-a. Reading ישן הגמזני "Jashen the Gimzonite" for MT בני ישן יהונתן "sons of Jashen, Jonathan"; see RSV. We regard בני as a partial dittograph of the previous word, and יהונתן

"Jonathan" as the son of Shamma (v 33), as implied by 1 Chr 11:34. The place of Jashen's origin must have been accidentally omitted. 1 Chr 11:34 has הגזוני "the Gizonite" but since "Gizon" is not attested elsewhere, Elliger has suggested הגמזוני "the Gimzonite."

32.b. Adding בן "son of," with G.

33.a. 1 Chr 11:35 reads שכר "Sachar" for MT שרר "Sharar"; similarly G^L.

37.a. MT (K) has the pl form; we follow Q in reading the sg נשא "bearer."

Form / Structure / Setting

The present unit (23:8–39) is introduced by v 8a which would be more appropriate to vv 24–39. The unit consists of four main sections:

    A   vv 8b–12 + 17b
    B   vv 13–17a
    C   vv 18–23
    D   vv 24–39a
         v 39b forms the editorial conclusion to the list.

Section A is a brief summary of the heroic exploits of the Three: Ishbaal, Eleazar, and Shamma. They may have been acknowledged as champions of single combat (cf. Stolz, 296).

Section B describes the foolhardy act of devotion by the three nameless warriors from among the Thirty, although the editor may well have identified them with the Three in vv 8b–12. However, this is hardly justified because the Three were not, apparently, part of the Thirty (cf. vv 19, 23). Consequently, vv 13–17a may be a later addition (so Wellhausen, 214).

Section C (vv 18–23) deals with the deeds of Abishai and Benaiah. It is surprising that neither Joab nor his exploits (cf. for instance, 1 Chr 11:6) are mentioned in any of the four sections, apart from the reference "brother of Joab."

Section D (vv 24–39a) provides us with a list of the Thirty, which according to our interpretation gives thirty-one names plus the Three as well as Abishai and Benaiah, making a total of thirty-six. However, the textual evidence is not very clear in places; a more expanded form of this list appears in 1 Chr 11:11–47, unless the Chronicler has combined two or more versions of such lists or sources (cf. Braun, *1 Chronicles*, 159). McCarter (500) may be right in assuming that our list of the Thirty begins with Asahel (v 24) and that it represents the "membership as it stood when the list was made"; thus it was not retrospective, including both past and present members. If so, the death of Asahel, brother of Joab (2:18–23), would provide a *terminus ad quem*. The retrospective aspect might be more appropriate to the Chronicler's expanded list (1 Chr 11:11–47).

Elliger (*PJ* 31 [1935] 47–60) et al. have noted that more than half of the warriors listed are from Judah or from territories close by. However, the significance of this geographical arrangement (if intentional) and the fact that nearly all of them are listed in the first part of the roster, is less clear. On this problem see also Mazar, *The Early Biblical Period*, 99–103.

In the present setting our hero-stories appear to be somewhat marginal to the main narratives about the house of David and its fortunes, and thus they are incorporated in the Appendices (chaps. 21–24).

The date of this list of the Thirty need not be identical with the recounted military exploits against the Philistines. The essential question is "When did David make his break with his Philistine overlord of Gath?" It is possible that during the early part of David's reign in Hebron, he was still a Philistine vassal. It is not entirely impossible that some of the incidents may belong to the pre-Ziklag period. Moreover, the military encounters described may have been, at least primarily, local skirmishes with the Philistines whose main aim, at this stage, may have been looting and plunder rather than conquest (cf. also Tidwell, VTSup 30 [1979] 199–200).

Comment

8 Ishbaal was the chief or head (see Bartlett, *VT* 19 [1969] 10) of the Three. It is less clear how the Three were related to the Thirty. Hertzberg (404) has suggested that the Three probably belonged to the Thirty but formed a special group within it. In Mazar's view (*The Early Biblical Period*, 90) the Three formed the supreme command, and one of them was "head of the three;" see also Bartlett, *VT* 19 (1969) 10. De Vaux (*Ancient Israel*, 220) has argued that the Thirty was "a special company of picked men" while Yadin (*Warfare*, 277) speaks of "a kind of supreme army council which was largely responsible for framing the internal army regulations . . ." whose members "served as the permanent commanders of the militia army." All in all, the Thirty may have been a designation of a military unit (cf. 1 Chr 11:42b) which usually included picked warriors.

The MT *šālîš* may denote a military officer, and Mastin (VTSup 30 [1979] 154) conjectures that "the king's adjutant was given this designation because he was 'of the third rank.'"

Ishbaal is depicted as having slain eight hundred men ("three hundred" in 1 Chr 11:11) single handed (?); it is more plausible that this was achieved with the help of the troop under his command.

10 The sentence, "So Yahweh brought about a great victory that day" is a later theological comment by the editor (Deuteronomistic ?). See also the similar comment in v 12 (cf. Veijola, *Dynastie*, 119).

11–12 Shamma's heroic deed took place at Lehi which is associated with Samson in Judg 15:9–20. In Budde's view (320) he defended the *people* rather than the *field*, hence he reads ויצילם "defended them." However, the MT may be more likely since the purpose of the raid may well have been plundering or destruction of the crops.

13 This incident may have happened during David's days as outlaw (cf. 1 Sam 22:1); so Ackroyd, 224. However, some scholars follow Wellhausen (214) in reading מצדת "stronghold" for מערת "cave." Hertzberg (405) sets the event shortly before David's attack in 5:17–21. Unfortunately, all these attempts at dating remain hypothetical.

Adullam was some sixteen miles (or twenty-five kilometers) southwest of Jerusalem but it is less certain that "the cave of Adullam" is to be equated with the town itself (see also Simons, *Texts* §697–98). Mazar (*The Early Biblical Period*, 92, n. 29) identifies it with David's fortified camp (at the village of el-Khadr) near Bethlehem.

For the Valley of Rephaim, see *Comment* on 5:18. The Heb. חיה which
we have rendered "detachment" may have been originally a designation of
a social unit (clan ?) but came to be restricted to military organization (see
N. K. Gottwald, *The Hebrew Tribes*, 261).

15 There is no need to assume that David and his soldiers were short
of water supplies (cf. Ackroyd, 224); it was, most likely, a sentimental longing
for a drink of cool water from one's native place.

Some exegetes note that since there is no such a well known at Bethlehem
at a later time, therefore the Q reading (בור "cistern") is more likely (see
Gordon, 313). On the other hand, wells are not necessarily eternal.

16–17 This verse portrays the great devotion and loyalty of the soldiers
to their king; they were quite prepared to indulge even his whims. David is
fully appreciative of the well-intentioned but foolhardy heroism. By pouring
out the water as libation to Yahweh (cf. Gen 35:14), he emphasizes that
only Yahweh is fit to receive such a costly offering.

18 It is usually pointed out (see, for instance, Driver, 367) that it is unlikely
that there was a *second triad* (cf. MT) of heroes.

The institution of the Three and Thirty belonged to the early part of
David's reign or military service. At a later stage, this military organization
must have come to an end. It is plausible that the *composition* and *command*
of these military units (?) may have changed in the course of time due to
casualties and replacements.

Mazar (*The Early Biblical Period*, 93, n. 33) perhaps rightly regards the
following description of Abishai's heroic deed, "he wielded his spear . . ."
as a gloss derived from v 8; the verbal similarity is great.

20 Stolz (295) retains MT (Q) בן איש חיל rendering it "son of a wealthy
man."

Kabzeel was situated in the extreme south of Judah, towards the borders
of Edom (Josh 15:21) but its exact location remains uncertain (see Simons,
Texts, § 803). Some scholars have suggested the site of Tell ʾIra (see R. G.
Boling and G. E. Wright, *Joshua* [AB 6; Garden City, NY: Doubleday, 1982]
381).

We have taken רב פעלים as "mighty in deeds," while Zeron (ZAW 90
[1978] 22) follows N. H. Tur-Sinai, and argues that Benaiah or his father
may have been "the chief of the workers" or chief over the forced labor.
However, this is less likely because in these summaries the emphasis is usually
on the *deeds* performed.

An even greater problem is the word אראל which we have rendered "distinguished warriors." It seems that in our context the word could denote either
a proper name, "Ariel" (cf. Ezra 8:16) or "warrior" (*HALAT*, 80). However,
other interpretations are not impossible; so NAB speaks of "two lions" while
RAV refers to "two lion-like heroes of Moab." We have assumed that אראל
is a term for a distinguished warrior even though the more obvious literal
rendering might be "lion of God" or "very great lion" (see Miller, *UF* 2
[1970] 185–86). Braun (*1 Chronicles*, 158) regards it as a "technical term applied
to military leaders."

21 Benaiah's fight against the Egyptian looks like a single combat between
two champions (see R. Bartelmus, *Heroentum in Israel und seiner Umwelt*
[ATANT 65. Zürich: Theologischer Verlag, 1979] 129; de Vaux, *The Bible*

and the Ancient Near East, 124–27). It is likely that also some of the other incidents belong to this same category (cf. 21:15–22).

23 The body-guard of David was, most likely, formed by the Cherethites and Pelethites (see *Comment* on 8:18 and 20:23) since later Benaiah was in charge of these foreign mercenaries.

At the end of this verse G adds "And these are the names of the mighty men of David, the king." This sentence serves as an introduction to the following list but may be an imitation of the similar introductory statement in v 8.

24 NAB assumes that a more detailed account of Asahel's exploits must have been omitted or lost at this point, and so it starts the list with "Among the Thirty were: Elhanan. . . ."

Elhanan may have been the slayer of Goliath in 21:19, which see.

25 Both Shammah and Elika were from Harod which is probably not to be identified with the Spring of Harod (see Judg 7:1), but with a location near Bethlehem (see n. 11.a.).

Elika's name is missing from the Chronicler's list (11:27), probably due to a scribal omission.

26 Helez the Paltite may have been a Calebite since Pelet was a clan of Caleb (cf. 1 Chr 2:47). However, it is equally possible that the reference is to Beth-pelet in the extreme Judean south (see Josh 15:27).

27 Anathoth was the later home of Jeremiah (Jer 1:1) and it was located some three miles (five kilometers) northeast of Jerusalem (see Simons, *Texts,* § 337).

28 Netophah was in the vicinity of Bethlehem (cf. Neh 7:26) and McCarter (498) accepts its identification with Khirbet Bedd Fālûṣ, near the Spring of en-Nāṭûf. See also Simons, *Texts,* §807.

30 Benaiah the Pirathonite was an Ephraimite from Pirathon (see Judg 12:15). If it is to be identified with the present day Farʿāta, it would be some six miles (ten kilometers) southwest of Nablus.

31 "Azmaweth" means "Death is strong," and it may contain an allusion to the god of Death (so McCarter, 498). However, Noth (*Personennamen,* 231) regards it as the name of an unknown plant, and he repoints it and reads ʿazmôt.

32 The location of Shaalbin ("Shaalbim" in Judg 1:35) may be Selbît some eight miles (twelve kilometers) north of Beth-shemesh.

Gimzon, too, is located in southern Judah (see 2 Chr 28:18); 1 Chr 11:34 reads "Gizon" which is not attested in the OT.

35 The "Carmel" mentioned here must be Khirbet el-Karmil, some nine miles (fourteen kilometers) south of Hebron, rather than the Carmel in Northern Israel (cf. Simons, *Texts,* § 685).

36 Zobah may be the Aramean kingdom which was defeated by David; see *Comment* on 8:3. However, McCarter (493) reads רב צבא בני חגרי "the commander of the army of the Hagrites" for MT מצבה בני הגדי "from Zobah, Bani the Gadite." The Hagrites were nomadic people who dwelt in the region of Gilead (see 1 Chr 5:10).

39 According to our interpretation of the text there are only thirty-six names in vv 8–39. Mazar (*The Early Biblical Period,* 99, n. 64) has suggested that "Zabad son of Ahlai" in 1 Chr 11:41 may be the missing name.

Explanation

Verses 8–23 are very similar in nature and style to 21:15–21, and therefore both sections may serve the same purpose: to honor the heroes of the past and to stress their loyalty and devotion to King David. The same may be true of the list of the Thirty (vv 24–39); these mighty men had served and supported their king in all the changing circumstances. To have the devotion of such men is also an indirect tribute to David himself. The roster ends with Uriah the Hittite, and this may be either a mere accidental occurrence or a veiled reminder that even David was human.

The exploits of the heroes may shed some light also on the archaic practice of single combat which must belong to the early part of David's reign. Whether the Three were David's select champions and experts in single combat (so Stolz, 296) is uncertain. It is plausible, however, that this method of military engagement provided some of the word-pictures which portray Yahweh as a warrior (cf. Isa 42:13).

David's Census and the Plague (24:1–25)

Bibliography

Ackroyd, P. R. "The Old Testament in the Making." *The Cambridge History of the Bible*, vol. 1. Ed. P. R. Ackroyd and C. F. Evans. Cambridge: Cambridge UP, 1970. 67–113. **Ahlström, G. W.** "Der Prophet Nathan und der Tempelbau." *VT* 11 (1961) 113–27. **Bickert, R.** "Die Geschichte und das Handeln Jahwes. Zur Eigenart einer deuteronomistischen Offenbarungsauffassung in den Samuelbüchern." In *Textgemäss: Aufsätze und Beiträge zur Hermeneutik des Alten Testaments*, FS E. Würthwein, ed. A. H. J. Gunneweg and O. Kaiser. Göttingen: Vandenhoeck & Ruprecht, 1979. 9–27. **Clements, R. E.** *God and Temple: The Idea of the Divine Presence in Ancient Israel.* Oxford: Blackwell, 1965. **Dietrich. W.** *David, Saul und die Propheten: Das Verhältnis von Religion und Politik nach den prophetischen Überlieferungen von frühesten Königtum in Israel.* WMANT 122. Stuttgart, Berlin, Köln, Mainz: Verlag W. Kohlhammer, 1987. **Fuss, W.** "II Samuel 24." *ZAW* 74 (1962) 145–64. **Gibson, J. C. L.** "Life and Society at Mari and in Old Israel." *TGUOS* 18 (1959–60 [1961]) 15–29. **Haag, H.** "Gad und Nathan." In *Archäologie und Altes Testament*, FS Kurt Galling, ed. A. Kuschke and E. Kutsch. Tübingen: J. C. B. Mohr, 1970. 135–43. **Hoffner, H. A.** "The Hittites and Hurrians." *Peoples of Old Testament Times.* Ed. D. J. Wiseman. Oxford: Clarendon Press, 1973. 197–228. **Lemke, W. E.** "The Synoptic Problem in the Chronicler's History." *HTR* 58 (1965) 349–63. **Mendenhall, G. E.** "The Census Lists of Numbers 1 and 26." *JBL* 77 (1958) 52–66. **Rosén, H. B.** "Arawna—nom hittite?" *VT* 5 (1955) 318–20. **Rupprecht, K.** *Der Tempel von Jerusalem: Gründung Salomos oder jebusitisches Erbe?* BZAW 144. Berlin/New York: Walter de Gruyter, 1977. **Saggs, H. W. F.** *The Encounter with the Divine in Mesopotamia and Israel.* London: Athlone Press, 1978. **Sanders, J. A.** "Census." *IDB* 1 (1962) 547. **Schenker, A.** *Der Mächtige im Schmelzofen des Mitleids: Eine Interpretation von 2 Sam 24.* Orbis Biblicus et Orientalis 42. Freiburg: Universitätsverlag; Göttingen: Vandenhoeck & Ruprecht, 1982. **Schmid, H.** "Der Tempelbau Salomos in religionsgeschichtlicher Sicht." In *Archäologie und Altes Testament*, FS Kurt Galling, ed. A. Kuschke und E. Kutsch. Tübingen: J. C. B. Mohr, 1970. 241–50. **Schmidt, L.** *Menschlicher Erfolg und Jahwes Initiative: Studien zu Tradition, Interpretation und Historie in Überlieferungen von Gideon, Saul und David.* WMANT 38. Neukirchen-Vluyn: Neukirchener Verlag, 1970. **Speiser, E. A.** "Census and Ritual Expiation in Mari and Israel." *BASOR* 149 (1958) 17–25. **Wyatt, N.** "'Araunah the Jebusite' and the Throne of David." *ST* 39 (1985) 39–53.

Translation

[1] *Once again, the anger of Yahweh was kindled against Israel, and he incited David against them, saying,* [a]*"Go, count*[a] *Israel and Judah."* [2] *So the king said to Joab* [a]*and to the military commanders*[a] *who were with him, "Go around all the tribes of Israel from Dan to Beersheba and count the people that I may know the number of the people."* [3] *But Joab said to the king, "May Yahweh your God multiply*[a] *the people a hundred times over, even while the eyes of my lord, the king, see it. But why does my lord, the king, take pleasure in such a scheme?"* [4] *The king's word, however, prevailed against Joab and against the military commanders. So Joab and the military commanders went out from*[a] *the presence of the king to count* [b]*the people of Israel*[b] [5] *Then they crossed the Jordan and began*[a] *from Aroer* [b]*and*

from[b] *the city that is in the middle of the valley (then they continued in the direction of) Gad and toward Jazer.* [6] *So they came to Gilead and to the land below Hermon,*[a] *and went to Dan,*[b] *by-passing*[c] *Sidon.* [7] *Then they came (up to) the fortress of Tyre and all the towns of the Hivites and the Canaanites. Finally, they finished*[a] *at Beersheba, in the Negeb of Judah.* [8] *Having ranged through all the land, they returned to Jerusalem at the end of nine months and twenty days.* [9] *Then Joab gave the figures of the census of the people to the king; there were in Israel 800,000*[a] *able-bodied men* [b]*fit for military service;*[b] *in Judah (there were) 500,000*[c] *men.*

[10] *After David had counted the people, his conscience*[a] *smote him, and he said to Yahweh, "I have sinned greatly in what I have done. But now, O Yahweh, forgive the guilt of your servant for I have acted foolishly."* [11] *When David arose (next) morning, the word of Yahweh came to* [a]*the prophet Gad, David's seer,*[a] *saying,* [12] *"Go and speak to David, 'Thus has Yahweh said: "I offer you three (punishments); choose one of them and* [a]*I will bring it upon you."'"*[a] [13] *So when Gad came to David to report to him, he said to him, "Shall seven*[a] *years of famine come*[b] *upon your land? Or will you flee before your enemy*[c] *for three months while he pursues you? Or shall there be three days' pestilence in your land? Now then, consider carefully what answer I shall take back to the one who sent me."* [14] *Then David said to Gad, "I am in a serious predicament. (However,) let us*[a] *fall into the hand of Yahweh for his mercy is great, but let me not fall into the hand of man."* [15] *So Yahweh sent a pestilence in Israel from morning until the appointed time, and there died from the people, from Dan to Beersheba, seventy thousand men.* [16] *When the angel of Yahweh stretched out his hand towards Jerusalem to destroy it, Yahweh relented of the disaster and said to the angel who was causing the destruction among*[a] *the people, "Enough now! Stay your hand!" (At that point) the angel of Yahweh was standing*[b] *by the threshing floor of Araunah*[c] *the Jebusite.* [17] *When he saw the angel smiting the people, David said to Yahweh, "I myself have sinned; I,* [a]*the shepherd, have committed evil.*[a] *But these sheep, what have they done? Let your hand be upon me and upon my father's house."* [18] *That same day Gad came to David and said to him, "Go up,*[a] *erect an altar to Yahweh on the threshing floor of Araunah*[b] *the Jebusite."* [19] *So David went up according to the instructions*[a] *of Gad, as Yahweh had commanded.* [20] *When Araunah looked down and saw the king and his servants coming towards him, he*[a] *went forth and did homage to the king, with his face to the ground.* [21] *Then Araunah said, "Why has my lord, the king, come to his servant?" "To buy the threshing floor from you," said David, "To build an altar to Yahweh in order that the plague may be checked among the people."* [22] *At this, Araunah said to David, "Let my lord, the king, take and offer up whatever seems right to him.* [a]*Here you have*[a] *the oxen*[b] *for burnt offering as well as the threshing sledges and the yokes of the oxen*[b] *for the wood."* [23] *All these Araunah*[a] *gave to the king. Then Araunah said to the king, "May Yahweh your God accept you favorably."* [24] *But the king said to Araunah, "No,* [a]*it is imperative that I buy (it)*[a] [b]*from you*[b] *for a price; I cannot offer to Yahweh my God burnt offerings that cost me nothing." So David bought the threshing floor and the oxen for fifty shekels of silver.* [25] *Then David built there an altar to Yahweh, and offered burnt offerings and peace offerings. Thus Yahweh was moved by entreaties for the land, and the plague* [a]*was checked in Israel.*[a]

Notes

1.a-a. For the asyndetous construction of the two imperatives, see n. 1:15.b.

2.a-a. Following G^L, and reading ואל שרי "and to the commanders of"; so also v 4. Similarly 1 Chr 21:1 which has העם "the people," or "army," for MT חיל "army." MT could be rendered ". . . to Joab, the commander of the army, who was with him."

3.a. Deleting the *wāw* with 1 Chr 21:3; so also G^L and Syr. See, however, GKC, § 154b.

4.a. MT has לפני "before" while most versions point to מפני "from the presence of."

4.b-b. Lit., "the people, Israel" (i.e., in apposition).

5.a. G^L has καὶ ἤρξαντο "and they began," which suggests ויחלו. MT has ויחנו "and they encamped," which seems a less likely beginning of the undertaking.

5.b-b. MT reads ימין "south of"; we follow G^L which suggests ומן "and from."

6.a. Reading תחת חרמון ("below Hermon") with Grätz, for MT תחתים חדשי "Tahtim Hodshi (so NIV, RAV) which, if correct, is not otherwise attested in the OT. NEB has read החתים קדשה "(the land of) the Hittites, to Kadesh," with G^L. However, the Kadesh on the Orontes may be too far north while the Kadesh of Naphtali (Tell Qades) may be too far south.

6.b. Omitting the following Hebrew word (i.e., יען). NEB takes it as a proper noun "Iyyon" (see 1 Kgs 15:20).

6.c. MT has וסביב "and around"; G and Syr suggest a verb, such as ויסבבו "they went around."

7.a. Lit., "they came out."

9.a. G^L has "900,000" while 1 Chr 21:5 reads "1,100,000."

9.b-b. Lit., "who drew the sword."

9.c. G^L has "400,000" while 1 Chr 21:5 gives "470,000."

10.a. Lit., "his heart"; cf. 1 Sam 24:5.

11.a-a. 1 Chr 21:9 omits הנביא "the prophet"; Syr has only "Gad the prophet."

12.a-a. Lit., "I will do it to you."

13.a. So MT: 1 Chr 21:12 has שלוש "three": so also G^L. This may well be the right reading, producing a triad of three years, three months, and three days.

13.b. Omitting לך "to you."

13.c. Reading the sg צרך "your enemy" in view of the following והוא "while he."

14.a. G has the sg "me," perhaps rightly.

16.a. For this partitive use of the prep ב "among," see GKC, § 119i.

16.b. Reading עומד "was standing" with 4 QSama and 1 Chr 21:15; MT has היה "was" which may be a partial dittography of the preceding יהוה "Yahweh."

16.c. Omitting the article before the proper noun; so also 4QSam^a. 1 Chr 21:15 reads ארנן "Ornan."

17.a-a. Reading with 4QSam^a הרעה הרעתי ". . . the shepherd, I have committed evil"; so also G^L and OL (cf. Ulrich, *Qumran Text*, 86). MT has only העויתי "I have done wrong."

18.a. For the asyndetous construction, see n. 1:15.b.

18.b. Reading with Q ארונה "Araunah"; K has the variant (?) ארניה.

19.a. Lit., "the word of"; so RAV.

20.a. MT has ארונה "Araunah."

22.a-a. Lit., "Behold."

22.b. The Heb. בקר "ox" is probably used collectively: "oxen."

23.a. Omitting המלך "the king" after "Araunah" so also G, OL, Syr, Tg, and Vg.

24.a-a. Lit., "I must buy (it)."

24.b-b. Reading מאתך "from you" with many MSS. MT has מאותך (as if it were an accusative).

25.a-a. Lit., "was held back from Israel."

Form/Structure/Setting

The final chapter of the Supplement to the Books of Samuel is, at least editorially, linked with 21:1–14 which is often thought to have preceded chap. 9 (but see Fuss, *ZAW* 74 [1962] 146–49). Eissfeldt (*Introduction*, 278) has suggested that at one time chap. 24 probably followed chap. 9. He assumes that the reason for the removal of these two units may have been the editor's desire to show that the famine and the plague were to be viewed as part of Yahweh's punishment "for David's sin against Bathsheba and Uriah"; see also v 17. However, it is equally possible that 21:1–14 was transferred to its present ·place in order to make Shimei's accusation in 16:7–8 appear entirely groundless. Chap. 24 was placed after 21:1–14, probably, on account of their common "punishment theme," irrespective of the chapter's original place in the sequence of events during David's reign.

The insertion of the two separate lists (21:15–22 and 23:8–39) is slightly more difficult to explain. Either the whole Supplement was formed at one and the same time from existing materials or it came into being in three stages, as argued, for instance, by Budde (304). Both alternatives would provide a fairly reasonable tentative explanation but the former seems simpler for practical reasons (see also Fuss, *ZAW* 74 [1962] 148–49). Clearly, other possibilities cannot be excluded. Since chap. 24 looks forward to the building of the temple, at least by implication, the lists are not inappropriate in their present midway position. Similarly, the psalm in 22:1–51 fits reasonably well into its canonical setting because it is preceded by two highly dangerous but eventually unsuccessful revolts against David (chaps. 15–20), as well as by the four-giant episode (21:15–22) in which David nearly lost his life. Hence the thanksgiving is a fitting conclusion to this progression of dramatic events and to the checkered career of David as a whole.

Also the Last Words of David (23:1–7) follow quite naturally the previous psalm of thanksgiving, and they could hardly be fitted into 1 Kgs 1–2 which is not much more than a *postscript* to David's active life. Moreover, both poems look retrospectively at David's experiences and therefore they form a thematic unity for all practical purposes.

Our chapter 24 can be divided into three sections:

> A. The Census (vv 1–9)
> 1. David orders the census (vv 1–4a)
> 2. The itinerary (vv 4b–7)
> 3. The statistics of the census (vv 8–9)
> B. The Plague (vv 10–17)
> 1. Connecting verse (v 10)
> 2. The alternative punishments offered to David (vv 11–14)
> 3. The Plague (vv 15–17)
> C. The Purchase of the Threshing Floor (vv 18–25)
> 1. Yahweh's message through Gad (vv 18–19)
> 2. The purchase of the threshing floor (vv 20–24)
> 3. David offers a sacrifice to Yahweh (v 25a)
> 4. Conclusion (v 25b)

V 1 is usually regarded as a redactorial link between 21:1–14 and chap. 24. Similarly v 10 may be a connecting link between the census episode (vv 1–9) and the Gad-narrative (vv 11–15 ?). Rupprecht (*Der Tempel von Jerusalem*, 7–8), for instance, has argued that v 15 forms the natural conclusion to the

Gad-story while the altar etiology begins with v 16 which speaks of a premature halting of the *plague* (מגפה "plague" in vv 21 and 25) while in v 15 the *pestilence* (דבר "pestilence"; also in v 13) rages until its *appointed time*. However, the meaning of the "appointed time" is far from certain (see *Comment* on v 15). V 17 is occasionally regarded as secondary (cf. also v 10), and so also the references to Gad in vv 18 and 19.

Nevertheless, it does not necessarily follow that originally there must have been three independent stories (as suggested, e.g., by Schmid [*Archäologie und Altes Testament*, 245–48]), namely, a story about David's census, another story in which Gad offered to David the choice of three punishments, and a Jebusite etiological story (see Dietrich, *David, Saul und die Propheten*, 42–48; Rupprecht, *Der Tempel von Jerusalem*, 6–9). At least in the present context the above three sections form one narrative depicting three main stages in the sequence of events involving momentous consequences. It is not impossible that an original story or even stories may have been subsequently elaborated but it is questionable whether we can reconstruct, with any reasonable certainty, the contents of this hypothetical original. Differences will inevitably arise; thus, e.g., Fuss (*ZAW* 74 [1962] 160) finds the original form contained in vv 2, 4b, 8–9, 15aαb, 17, 18, 19 while McCarter (518) suggests vv 1–9, 15, 16b, 20–25 as the original nucleus.

Not infrequently attention is drawn to the symmetrical arrangement of chaps. 21–24 (see also *Form / Structure / Setting* of 21:1–14). However, this seemingly artistic structure may well be accidental, arising out of the redactional process.

Von Rad (*Old Testament Theology*, 1:318) describes chap. 24 as a Jerusalemite *hieros logos* which explained the existence of "an altar of Yahweh in the previous Canaanite city of the Jebusites" or as the *hieros logos* of the Jerusalem temple (so Rudolph, *Chronikbücher*, 141) which explained the foundation of the particular holy place. It seems that at an earlier stage the site of this altar was not, as yet, identified with the temple hill, unless this equation is implicit in the narrative and was obvious to any reader. Likewise, 1 Kgs 6–9 gives no indication of this identification although the author may have had his own reasons. However, the question may be raised whether the two sites were in fact identical.

It has been argued that the גרן ארונה "threshing floor of Araunah" was not simply an agricultural *workplace* but rather a cultic place (see Ahlström, *VT* 11 [1961] 115–17). Thus David is thought to have erected an altar on a Jebusite holy site, adapting it to Yahweh worship, following Gad's instructions (v 18). Some scholars would go even further and suggest that David took over a Jebusite *temple* which eventually housed the ark of the covenant (see Rupprecht, *Der Tempel von Jerusalem*, 13–17). However, the available evidence for such a view is very tenuous (cf. e.g., 12:20 which is a possible reference to a temple [?] in Jerusalem during David's reign). On the other hand, there is some explicit contrary evidence (such as 7:1–7, 13) which would have to be explained away.

According to 2 Chr 3:1 the temple site is further identified with Mount Moriah (see Gen 22:2, 14), the place where Abraham was ordered to sacrifice his son Isaac (see Williamson, *1 and 2 Chronicles*, 203–5). However, this equation is usually regarded as doubtful; it may have been intended "to magnify the sacredness of this spot" (so H. H. Rowley, *Worship in Ancient Israel* [London: SPCK, 1967] 77).

One may also add that the punishments proposed by Gad (vv 12–13) remind one of the punitive triad of sword, famine, and pestilence which is often mentioned in the later prophetic books (see, e.g., Jer 14:12; 15:2; 21:7, 9; 24:10; 27:8; Ezek 5:12; 6:12).

Comment

1 The expression "once again" may be a redactional pointer to the events described in 21:1–14.

The present form of the narrative suggests that Yahweh's wrath may have been due to some unspecified sin on the part of Israel (cf. 1 Sam 2:25; 2 Sam 16:10–12). Therefore he instigated (cf. 1 Sam 26:19) David to carry out the census to bring about the deserved punishment. This would be reminiscent of 1 Kgs 22:19–23 where Yahweh is said to have misled the prophets of Ahab (?) in order to bring the Israelite king to his doom. However, in our pericope vv 10 and 17 emphasize that the sin was David's alone. Moreover, it would also suggest that Yahweh had to instigate a second offense to punish the first. Stolz (301) finds in our narrative an element of divine unpredictability.

It is possible, of course, that some natural disaster (i.e., plague) came to be interpreted as Yahweh's judgment in retrospect.

In 1 Chr 21:1 it is Satan (שטן; without the article) or the Accuser who incited David to take the census of his people. This does not lessen David's personal responsibility but, at least, Yahweh no longer appears as the instigator of evil (see Saggs, *The Encounter with the Divine*, 113). This alteration may be part of the gradual process in which evil came to be associated with the demons or Satan in particular (cf. R. S. Kluger, *Satan in the Old Testament* [Evanston: Northwestern University Press, 1967] 151–62).

2 As stated in v 9, the census concerned only men of military age, so that its purpose may have been the organization of the tribal militia. At the same time, it may have been also linked with taxation or forced labor service.

The military nature of the census may, perhaps, imply that the reason for Yahweh's anger was David's lack of trust. The king and the people should not rely on their own strength but they should depend upon Yahweh (cf. 1 Sam 14:6; Isa 31:1). Yahweh can deliver his people and give them victory "by many or by few" (1 Sam 14:6).

The expression "from Dan to Beersheba" (see *Comment* on 3:10) describes the traditional extreme points of the land of Israel (see also 1 Sam 3:20; 2 Sam 17:11).

3 For once Joab is presented as the voice of good sense but it is not explained why the census was thought to be a dangerous and even improper undertaking. Such a potential danger in numbering the people, is also mentioned in Exod 30:12 (see J. I Durham, *Exodus*, WBC 3 [Waco, TX: Word Books, 1987] 401). These reservations concerning this head count may go back to earlier times; none of the explanations provided by exegetes is convincing.

5 It seems that Aroer and the unnamed city (cf. Deut 2:36; Josh 13:9, 16) were the starting points of the census count. From here they proceeded north, to Gad, towards Jazer. McCarter (504) reads, following G^L, הנחל הגדי אל יעזר ("the wady of the Gadites near Jazer") but it seems more likely that the unnamed city was near Aroer rather than some forty miles (sixty-four kilometers) north of Aroer. The latter was probably located by the village of ʿAraʿîr, near Dibon, while Jazer may be identified with Khirbet es-Sar, some eight miles (twelve kilometers) west of present day Amman.

6–7 The exact route taken by Joab and his team is not clear. It seems that having reached the northern boundary, at the foot of Mt. Hermon, they began their return journey, by-passing Sidon and Tyre and the other non-Israelite cities which were not under Israelite control. S. Herrmann (*History*, 156) infers that they must have gone "primarily through the territory occupied by the pre-Israelite population, and not through the territory of the states of Israel and Judah." However, it seems more likely that the biblical author is mainly sketching the outer boundaries of the Davidic kingdom, and that all the towns *within those boundaries* were subject to the census. Fuss (*ZAW* 74 [1962] 156), on the other hand, regards this description as both ideal and secondary. The itinerary is missing in 1 Chr 21.

Little is known of the Hivites; they appear only in the OT (see Gen 10:17; 34:2; Josh 9:7; Judg 3:3) and they are often confused with the Horites. Hoffner (*Peoples of Old Testament Times*, 225) regards "Hivite" and "Horite" as ethnic terms "which at times identify Hurrians." What is certain is that they belonged to the pre-Israelite inhabitants of Canaan.

Negeb (lit., "south") was the Judean desert in the south, and Beersheba was the last major southernmost settlement of Judah.

9 Ackroyd (231) et al. infer, probably rightly, from the separate enumeration of Israel and Judah that they must have had "separate administrative and military organization." See also Alt, *Essays*, 215–19.

The numbers of the men fit for military service are rather high, and they would point to a total population of some five million. The figures would be more reasonable if the "thousand" (אלף) designated a unit of fighting men composed of a much smaller number of men than one thousand (cf. Gottwald, *Tribes*, 270–76).

10 McCarter (511) rightly notes that guilt cannot be simply taken away but it is questionable whether the solution was to request Yahweh to *transfer* the guilt "to someone or something else." We understand the prayer for forgiveness as an appeal to God to deal graciously in the administration of his *justice*, leaving the means and the methods to God alone. See also *Comment* on 12:13.

13 Yahweh gave David three options or choice of three punishments, most likely equal in their severity even though they are presented on a decreasing scale: years—months—days. The reason for the options is not given; ultimately they all come from Yahweh.

14 It is not explicitly stated what David's choice was; however, G expands at this point, adding that David actually chose the plague option, and that this incident occurred during the time of the wheat harvest (cf. also 21:9).

Occasionally it has been argued that this choice points to a degree of selfishness in David since he chose a punishment which affected the *people*.

However, it is doubtful that this aspect was in the mind of the narrator; his emphasis is to be found in v 14: "Let us fall in (or "by") the hand of *God.* . . ."

15 The "appointed time" cannot very well refer to the *end* of the three day period because Yahweh intervened *before* this point was reached (cf. v 16). It seems that the plague lasted hardly a day (if our interpretation is right), but its severity was very great.

Thus the reference may be to some fixed point of the day, perhaps, some cultic occasion (cf. Tg which suggests the time of the burnt offering). McCarter (506) follows G and reads עת סעד ("dinnertime"); NEB has "the hour of dinner." On the whole, none of the suggested explanations is quite convincing (see also Driver, 377).

Dietrich (*David, Saul und die Propheten,* 44) regards the plague mentioned in v 15 as originally different from the disaster brought about by the destroying angel in v 16.

According to 1 Chr 21:14 only seventy thousand people died on account of the plague. MT reads "seventy-seven thousand"; however, most exegetes follow the reading of G and the Chronicler.

16 The name "Araunah" has given rise to a great deal of discussion. Most scholars regard the name as non-Semitic, perhaps of Hurrian or Hittite origin (cf. F. Gröndahl, *Die Personennamen der Texte aus Ugarit* [Studia Pohl 1; Rome: Pontifical Biblical Institute, 1967] 224–25; Rosén, *VT* 5 [1955] 318–20). McCarter (512) rightly notes that Araunah was "a pre-Israelite citizen of Jerusalem, a Jebusite of Hurrian or Hittite ancestry."

Other scholars (e.g., Ahlström, *VT* 11 [1961] 117–18) argue that Araunah was the last Jebusite king. This is largely based on the MT text of v 23 but this textual support is rather dubious (see v 23). A variation of this view is the assumption that Araunah was not David's contemporary but that he figured in some old Jebusite *hieros logos* which came to be incorporated in the story of David (so already Gressmann; cf. Fuss, *ZAW* 74 [1962] 162–63).

Occasionally it has been argued that "Araunah" is not a proper name but rather a title, "lord" (see Hoffner, *Peoples of Old Testament Times,* 225). However, in the present context it appears to have been taken as a proper name, even though in v 16 it has the article (a scribal error?).

At this point the Chronicler's version (1 Chr 21:16) has an expansion which gives a more detailed description of the angel of Yahweh and of David's reaction. The Chronicler's reading is supported by 4QSam^a (see Ulrich, *Qumran Text,* 156–57) and therefore it may well be original. At least, it represents another text type (cf. Lemke, *HTR* 58 [1965] 357). The MT of 2 Samuel may have lost the relevant portion of text due to haplogr (so Ulrich).

20 4QSam^a must have had a longer text; at least we have the addition [מתכסים] בשקים וארנא דש חטים "[covering themselves] with sackcloth. Araunah was threshing wheat"; see Ulrich, *Qumran Text,* 157–58. Also 1 Chr 21:20–21 contains an expanded version but in a somewhat corrupt form; it refers to Araunah threshing the wheat, and adds the appearance of the angel and the fright of Araunah's sons. McCarter (507) has contended that MT is derived from a longer primitive text, and is the result of a homoioteleuton. On the other hand, the longer text may contain a reduplication which was subsequently altered, thus producing the Chronicler's version and the 4QSam^a reading.

22 This verse as well as vv 23–24 give an insight into the existing conventions in business dealings which involved purchase (see also the more complicated parallel in Gen 23:3–16).

23 MT ארונה המלך, if original, can be treated in two ways; either המלך "the king" is a description of Araunah (as if he were a Jebusite king of Jerusalem) or it can be taken as a vocative referring to David ("All this, *O king*, has Araunah given to the king"), in which case it is rather verbose. McCarter (508) has very plausibly suggested that the primitive reading was הכל נתתי לאדני המלך) "I give it all to my lord, the king," and that the corruption came about when אדני "my lord" was misread as ארונה "Araunah."

24 David is said to have bought the threshing floor and the oxen for fifty shekels of silver. However, the Chronicler (1 Chr 21:25) states that David paid six hundred shekels of *gold* for the site alone. Rashi has argued that the "fifty shekels" was the price paid for *each* of the twelve tribes (see J. M. Myers, *1 Chronicles* [AB 12. Garden City, NY: Doubleday, 1965] 149).

The conversation between David and Araunah is reminiscent of Abraham's bargaining with the Hittites (Gen 23:3–16).

25 According to the present narrative the building of the altar and the sacrifices were, in a sense, an expression of David's gratitude to Yahweh for halting the plague (v 16) as well as a way of forestalling its possible repetition.

It is not impossible that the *lack* of the altar may have been regarded as the ultimate cause of the plague (cf. v 1 and 1 Chr 21:28–29).

The Chronicler (1 Chr 22:1; 2 Chr 3:1) identifies this site with the temple hill. The fact that this identification is not explicitly suggested in 2 Sam 24 is noteworthy but the reasons for this are not clear.

Explanation

In this chapter David is portrayed as a man who is capable of making mistakes and who sins greatly (v 10) yet, at the same time, he is concerned for the welfare of his people (v 17) and knows how to repent. Consequently, Yahweh's favor remains with David, and is not permanently taken away as it was removed from Saul and his house. Thus this chapter is a practical illustration of the outworking of the everlasting covenant given to David and his heirs (see 7:15–16; 23:5). Herein lies the significance of this chapter for all later generations in that it offers a model whereby deliverance may become a possibility, even a reality through the mercy of God.

At least at a later time, this narrative was understood also as an etiology for the choice of the temple site (1 Chr 22:1; 2 Chr 3:1); so both the site and the altar served, in a sense, as a permanent sign of Yahweh's covenant love and mercy.

Index of Authors Cited

Index of Principal Subjects

Index of Biblical Texts

A. The Old Testament

B. The New Testament

Index of Key Hebrew Words